D0349631

MONEY AND BANKING

MONEY AND BANKING

by

CHARLES L. PRATHER, Ph.D.
Professor of Banking and Finance
University of Texas

THIRD EDITION

1947

RICHARD D. IRWIN · INC.

CHICAGO, ILLINOIS

THIRD EDITION
First Printing, August 1946
Second Printing, November 1946
Third Printing, February 1947
Fourth Printing, August 1947

PRINTED IN THE UNITED STATES OF AMERICA BY
THE INLAND PRESS, INC., CHICAGO, ILLINOIS

PREFACE

THIS book has been written to set forth the elementary principles of money and banking, with emphasis on present-day problems. Changes during the war have made it desirable, if not imperative, to bring the subject matter up to date. There has been some rearrangement of material and some changes in the approach to monetary and banking problems. The three major divisions remain substantially the same, with greater emphasis on monetary problems in the light of the international situation and the growing role of governments in the monetary and banking fields.

The first division, on money and credit, consists of thirteen chapters, entitled: "Nature and Functions of Money," "Qualities of a Good Monetary System," "Introduction to the Theory of the Value of Money," "The Gold Standard and the Commodity Theory of Money," "The Gold Standard in the United States since 1930," "Silver and the Standard Problem," "Silver—A Subsidiary Metal," "A Managed Paper Money Standard," "Paper Currency," "Deposit Currency," "Clearing and Collection of Checks," "International Monetary Principles," and "International Monetary and Banking Organizations."

The second division of the book deals with commercial banking: institutions, organizations, functions, operations, problems, and reform from the viewpoint of the individual banker as well as from the standpoint of the banking system. In line with the current trend, the government's role in banking has been treated in regard to its relationship to banking policies and problems. The chapter titles in this division are: "Credit and Credit Instruments," "Functions and Management of Banks," "Commercial Banking before the Civil War," "Commercial Banking since the Civil War," "The Bank Statement and Changes in Earnings," "Deposit Functions of Commercial Banks," "Bank Reserves and Deposit Insurance," "Lending and Investing Functions of Commercial Banks," "Commercial Bank Portfolio Problems," "Foreign Exchange Markets," "Foreign Trade Finance," "Government Supervision and Ownership of Banks," "The Organization of the Federal Reserve System," "Operations of the Federal Reserve Banks," "Credit Policy of the Federal Reserve System," and "Monetary Policy and Economic Stabilization."

The last part of the book is devoted to specialized financial institutions and foreign banking systems. The chapters in this division include: "Consumer Financing Institutions," "Savings Banks," "Trust Banking," "Investment Houses and Allied Institutions," "Federal Urban Mortgage Banking," "Agricultural Credit Institutions," and two chapters on "Foreign Banking Systems."

This revised edition is written for students who are beginning their study of money and banking. For this reason many difficult and controversial topics have been surveyed, with the purpose of giving students information and familiarity with the subject matter in the field. The Table of Contents is in fairly complete form in order that it may serve as an outline for study and teaching. The questions and problems at the end of each chapter include those dealing directly with the material covered in the chapter and also quotations, and thought-provoking types of questions designed to stimulate discussion among students and to serve as an application of the principles in the text. A number of statistical problems have been included in order to familiarize students with government publications and other sources of information in the field of money and banking.

The author's indebtednesses are many. He wishes to make a blanket acknowledgment to government and banking officials who generously met his requests for documents and other information. He offers his sincere thanks for the many constructive criticisms, to the teachers of money and banking who used the earlier editions of this book whether made directly to him or through the publishers. He desires to repeat his indebtedness to the following, who aided him in the preparation of the first and second editions: Professor James W. Bell of Northwestern University; Professor S. E. Thomas of the Charleston State Teachers College; Dr. John K. Langum of the University of Minnesota; and Mr. W. W. Wiard, Mr. Burton Furman, Dean C. L. Raper, and Professors T. C. Bolton, S. P. Toadvine, L. W. Adams, and H. T. Viets, all of Syracuse University.

In addition to those mentioned in the preface of the first and second editions, the author wishes to note a special indebtedness to Richard A. Graves of the University of Minnesota, for reading and criticizing the present manuscript before it went to press. As in the earlier editions, the author depended greatly upon his wife, Katherine F. Prather, for checking references, verifying statistics, typing the manuscript, and reading proof.

C. L. P.

TABLE OF CONTENTS

CHAPTER I

NATURE AND FUNCTIONS OF MONEY

Significance of Money and Credit

The Place of Money.—Money, the medium of exchange and standard of value, is the central problem around which all other economic problems tend to cluster. Modern wars and postwar developments are certain to cause serious disturbances in the field of finance because of their effects on the supply of money and credit, the volume of goods, and the general price level. Governments and banks are the chief sources of money substitutes (credits). So it was appropriate that "Money and Banking" was the subject of one of the two most important international economic conferences held during World War II. Just why money and money substitutes (credits) are so important is suggested by the paragraphs that follow.

Money and Credit in Production.—From the viewpoint of economics, production is the creation of economic value, the correct purpose being to provide man with the necessities, conveniences, and luxuries of life. In modern industrial society, money is used as the device for measuring the expenses and returns from business. Production is planned and carried on with the view of making a money profit. Considered from a social viewpoint, the use of money and credit permits a degree of specialization, division of labor, and co-operation not possible in any other type of economy except the most autocratic, in which all phases of production would be specified by the government.

The seemingly disjointed, unrelated, and individualistic economic activities of specialists are made effective through the market place. There is undirected co-operation among those who work upon a good in the different stages of production, from the raw material to the finished product. The need for co-ordination increases with the increase in quantity and variety of products, the number of specialists, the increase in size of the market, and the increase in the number of steps and time involved between the original producer and the ultimate consumer. The producer, keeping in mind not only his own plans but also those of his competitors, must estimate the quantity and quality of goods consumers will demand. Specialization and division of labor increase "the productivity of labor on the technical side," but the money exchange economy "tremendously increases the problems of finance and management."[1] The present structure and productive efficiency of American business bear witness to the ability of financiers and entrepreneurs to solve these problems.

Money and Credit in Consumption.—In economics, consumption is the use of goods and services to satisfy human wants. It results in the destruction or diminution of the utilities embodied in goods. Throughout, money takes a leading role. The consumption problem of the individual is to budget his liquid money income in order to care for his immediate and future needs to the best advantage. In making decisions, his choice is determined primarily by the size of his money income and the quantity and quality of goods that can be bought with it. Although the obtaining of money income is the prime motivator of economic effort, the price at which this money income can be converted into goods and services is of equal importance.

The use of money permits the consumer to shift purchases from one commodity to a second, to buy certain goods today or to postpone consumption, to buy in one community or a second, or to buy from one merchant or another. The consumer's time and place options are important to buyers and sellers. Much of modern advertising is explainable only in terms of this liquid purchasing power, which is always limited in amount and shiftable from goods to goods, from the present to the future, and from market to market. At no time in history has the volume of liquid assets been as great as at the close of World War II. This was due to the wartime record-breaking national incomes and the curtailment of production of civilian goods.

Money and Distribution.—In economics the word "distribution" is used in a technical sense to mean the apportionment of the national income among the four factors of production: wages to labor, interest to capital, rent to land, and profits to the entrepreneur.[2] In a modern

---

[1] Hansen, A. H., *Business Cycle Theory*, pp. 120-21.

[2] The economists and sociologists stress personal distribution, the distribution of income or wealth of society among families and individuals; and the teachers of commerce and transportation stress the distribution of commodities, or the moving of goods from place to place.

society the total national income and the shares allotted to the factors of production are computed in terms of money. Wages are the prices paid to laborers for their services, interest is the price paid to the capitalist for the use of capital, rent is the price paid to landowners for the use of land, and profits are the money returns to the entrepreneur for assumption of risks. Thus wages, interest, rent, and profits are all expressed in terms of money. Theoretically, each factor of production tends to share in the national income according to its contribution. Like all value concepts, the contribution of each agency is more easily appraised when expressed in terms of money.

Money and Prices.—In modern society goods are usually exchanged for money and not for other goods. The amount of money for which a unit of a given good is exchanged is the price of that good. The concept of price is closely associated with the more general concept of exchange value. By the latter is meant the ability of one good to command a second good in exchange. But instead of measuring the value of one good in terms of a second, it is customary to compare prices, that is, the exchange value of the two goods expressed in terms of money. If the price of one good in a particular market is one dollar and the price of a second is two dollars, the conclusion is that the second is twice as valuable as the first.

Value is the central theme in the treatises on economic principles, but prices are of major interest to businessmen. The use of money as a measure of value permits the substitution of a simple, easy understood price system for an unwieldy, disjointed exchange-value ratio system. Prices, the functional guides to economic activity, are determined by custom, public authority, and the varying degree of competition in the market. Normally, the last is the most important, for it involves all the problems of demand and supply.

As war measures, the Price Control Act of January, 1942, and the Inflation Control Act of October, 1942, provided for broad and generally adequate government control over prices of commodities, residential rents, wages, and salaries. With a postwar increase in supply of foods, automobiles, washing machines, and similar items, justification for price control and rationing of goods disappears. Then prices may serve as a guide to economic activity.

Barter, the First Type of Exchange

In the early days, before the development of specialization, division of labor, and world markets, trade took the form of barter. By "barter" is meant the direct exchanging of one commodity for another.[3] In this system grain, for instance, is traded directly for other types of foods or other articles and no third commodity is used as a medium of exchange and/or as a standard of value.[4]

The barter system of exchange is simple and economical, being the most natural and direct way of carrying on trade. This is illustrated by the activities of children. At first they are inclined to take things by force, but later they learn to exchange gifts. During this period bartering is thought of in terms of giving one thing for a second. Finally, when children use the word "trade" to cover their exchanges, they have reached the last stage in the development of pure barter. At first a child's sense of value is purely subjective, and, from the viewpoint of his parents, he makes ridiculous exchanges. As he becomes older he is influenced by the wants of his companions. At this stage marbles and other seasonal toys make up his barter stock. He has learned to exchange things which he has for things which he wants, without the use of a third commodity as a medium of exchange or as a standard of value.

With the increase of desires brought on by widening horizons, the difficulties of bartering become more numerous. The child finds it more difficult to discover someone who has what he wants and who, at the same time, wants what he has to trade. When children become more discriminating, their valuations become more accurate and more widely separated. Their trading is impeded by higgling over values.

Children in their barter activities experience most of the disadvantages of the barter system. These disadvantages include lack of double coincidence of wants and the difficulty in agreeing upon exchange values. In primitive exchange, as in the case of children's barter, a great deal of time is wasted in looking for one who has

---

[3] For illustrations of modern barter, see Anderson, B. M., *The Value of Money*, pp. 196-200.

[4] Many so-called "barter transactions" involve the use of money as a standard of value. This is true of most of the exchanges at country stores, trading-in of automobiles, furniture, etc. Such transactions are not pure barter but may be called "money barter" or money transactions.

what is wanted and who wants what is offered in exchange. Even though two traders may desire what the other has to barter, there may be no exchanging because of disagreement as to values. In a barter system vague ideas of value prevail, so that in the course of trade development it becomes necessary to find a medium of exchange and a standard of value.

Commodity Currency, the First Type of Money

In a system where barter dominated, the manner of overcoming many of the obstacles to exchange is easy to imagine. Three, four, or more exchanges may have been entered into in order to get the commodity desired. In order to balance values of goods where commodities could not be divided, a third commodity, or promise to pay, may have been used to make up the difference in value.[5] If this third commodity was in general demand, it was easier for the recipient to satisfy other wants. When traders could not agree upon values of goods in terms of each other, they may have used a third commodity as a standard of value. Without doubt they were familiar with barter transactions in which a third, generally traded, commodity was exchanged for the two commodities over whose values they were in disagreement.

When the dominant type of exchange is one in which a third commodity serves as a go-between or a standard of value, or both, it is called a "money system."[6] Commodity currency is merely a good which is used as a medium of exchange and a standard of value. In the cruder stages of economic development, little difference existed between barter and money exchanges. The commodity used as money was often more desired for its own utility than as a medium of exchange. As a matter of fact, most kinds of money have emerged from commodities that have high utility in nonmonetary uses. Articles that have been favored include: those that are used for ornament and display, such as beads, gold, and silver; consumable necessities, such as salt, all types of grains, cattle, and skins; capital

[5] For an interesting discussion of the various types of commodities used as money, see DuPuy, W. A., "The Geography of Money," *National Geographic Magazine*, Vol. LII, No. 6 (December, 1927), pp. 744-68. There are thirty-one different illustrations.

[6] For short descriptions of our colonial experiences with barter, see Dewey, D. R., *Financial History of the United States* (11th ed.), pp. 18-21.

goods, such as knives, nails, copper pots, and weapons; and tokens, such as pieces of leather and fur.[7]

Coins, the First Type of Modern Money

Fairly early in the history of exchange, metals were used as a medium of exchange. They were first used in bullion form, and each exchange transaction in which they entered involved weighing and testing for quality.[8] Later, goldsmiths, bankers, and rulers aided trade by marking the weight and quality of pieces of metals passing through their hands. This process permitted ready identification, made weighing and testing for fineness unnecessary, and increased the acceptability of the pieces of metal. Modern coinage developed from this system of marking metals.

Coinage is the process of identifying by marking or stamping a piece of metal which is intended to be used as money. The product, a coin, is a definite weight of metal of definite fineness, and the weight and the quality are certified by the stamp of a king, a government, a goldsmith, a banker, or a trusted individual. Gradually governments assumed all rights to stamp and mark all pieces of metals to be used as money. During the Middle Ages kings and petty rulers used this monopoly for private gain; but today profit from coinage, which is called "seigniorage," is a minor factor in determining coinage policies.

During the middle of the nineteenth century there were in circulation in the United States several types of private gold coins which bore the names of the makers and were of the same weight and fineness as federal coins. Since these coins were not imitations of federal coins, they were not counterfeits; but the danger in their circulation was the possibility of four dollars' worth of gold being stamped as five dollars. Actually the private "five dollar" gold pieces in circulation from 1830 to 1860 ranged in value from $4.36 to $5.00. These gold coins were popular on the Pacific Coast and in other sections of the United States. Although legislators recognized the opportunity for public exploitation in their coinage and circulation, it was not until 1864 that Congress made illegal the private minting of gold.

---

[7] Burns, A. R., *Money and Monetary Policy in Early Times*, pp. 1-36; Angell, Norman, *Story of Money*, chaps. iii and iv.

[8] Burns, *op. cit.*, pp. 37-74.

Government coins are classified according to the metals from which they are made: iron, bronze, copper, nickel, silver, and gold. An even more important classification is one made according to their value relationships, that is, as standard coins and subsidiary coins. A standard coin is one made from a standard metal, and its money value is the same as its bullion value. Before 1934 the federal government permitted individuals to bring gold to the mint and have it minted freely into gold coins under the rules and regulations of the mint. The privilege of taking standard metals to the mint freely or without limit as to amount is called "free coinage." The word "free" as used here is one of the most misunderstood words in economics. It means unlimited coinage and not necessarily coinage without the payment of a fee. There was unlimited or free coinage of gold in the United States from 1792 to 1934. During the first eighty years of our national life, free coinage of silver was permitted. This applied to fractional silver coins from 1792 to 1853 and to the standard silver dollar from 1792 to 1873. At the present time, there is no free coinage in the United States.

A subsidiary or token coin is one that has less value as bullion than as a coin. It may be made from the standard metal or from a cheaper metal. Free coinage of subsidiary coins is never permitted. Responsibility for manufacturing a sufficient supply of subsidiary coins rests with the government. These coins are minted only on government order and not by individual order, as in the case of free coinage. Subsidiary or token coins are a form of credit money "printed" upon metal, the values of which are kept equal to the standard by limiting their supply and redeeming them in standard money. In the United States bronze, copper, and nickel coins have been subsidiary coins since their origin; silver dollars have been subsidiary coins since 1873; and all the other silver coins have been subsidiary since 1853.

Paper Money, the Second Type of Modern Money

Coin money was a satisfactory medium of exchange until payments became large and trade spread beyond local communities. Paper money and bills of exchange came into wide use to meet these new demands for money, but coins were not driven out of use. Coins continued to circulate side by side with paper money, being used in the exchanges for which they were first created, that is, in local transactions where small payments are involved.[9]

Paper money, engraved or printed, is a widely accepted medium of exchange which may be issued by individuals, banks, governments, and any other institution in which the public has confidence. At present, paper money is put into circulation by both banks and governments. The present world trend in monetary legislation is to place more and more responsibility on the central banks for issuance of proper amounts of this type of medium of exchange.

The origin of paper money in Western civilization is generally traced to the activity of British goldsmiths. They accepted gold for safekeeping and gave receipts for the deposits which merchants found convenient to pass back and forth in payment of obligations. As long as the goldsmiths' notes were backed 100 per cent in specie, which was held in trust for the noteholder and was turned over to him on demand, they were representative money. This type of promise to pay is similar to a warehouse receipt. There are two important types of representative money in the United States—gold and silver certificates.

Gold certificates, backed by 100 per cent reserve, are promises of the government to pay gold. Two types of gold certificates have been issued: those put out before 1934, which were designed for circulation because paper money was more convenient than gold coins; and those issued since 1934, which are designed only for reserves of the twelve Federal Reserve banks. The latter do not circulate; that is, they are not used by the general public as a means of payment. There are less than $50,000,000 of the first type of gold certificates still in circulation, and these are being withdrawn. In 1933, before the policy of retirement was adopted, slightly more than $1,000,000,000 of these gold certificates were in circulation. Under provisions of the Gold Reserve Act of 1934 the second type of gold certificate was issued to the Federal Reserve banks in exchange for their gold.

Silver certificates are promises of the government to pay silver on demand. Since the bullion value of a silver dollar is less than its exchange value as a coin, the value of a silver certificate and a silver dollar depends in part upon the credit of the United States government. Silver certificates are used in place of coins or bullion,

---

[9] For a history of early paper money experiments, see Angell, *op. cit.*, chap. x.

which they represent, because the public finds paper money in denominations of $1.00 and higher to be more convenient than bullion or coins. Legally, silver certificates are representative money; but, as long as the market value of silver is less than its coined value ($1.29 per ounce), they are in fact credit money.

No advantages other than convenience and reduction of abrasion of coins result from the use of representative paper money. Goldsmiths and early 100 per cent Reserve bankers were justified in charging depositors interest or fees for the safekeeping of their money and other valuables. But early bankers soon learned that all promises to pay would not be presented for redemption each day. This situation made it possible for bankers to issue notes in excess of their reserves, and thus credit money appeared. Credit money, the value of which is partly dependent upon the credit of the issuing agency, is a promise to pay. It may be only partially covered by a specie reserve which is kept on hand to redeem it. Less emphasis is now placed upon the specie backing and more upon the debtors' willingness and ability to pay in any form of legal tender money.

In the United States all paper money is issued under the auspices of the federal government. Federal Reserve notes, the most important type of money used by the general public, are "promises to pay" of the United States government; but they are issued by banks and so are technically bank credit money. They are issued by Federal Reserve banks and must have at least 100 per cent backing, of which 25 per cent must be gold certificates. There is one type of government credit money, United States notes, or greenbacks; but the government has assumed responsibility for two types of obsolete, though not extinct, forms of bank paper money—the Federal Reserve bank note and the national bank note. These two currencies are classified for administrative purposes as treasury currency (see Chap. IX). United States notes are backed by approximately 40 per cent gold and the credit of the United States government.

With the assumption of responsibility by governments for coinage, a new concept of money appeared. This concept, known as the State Theory of Money, has become increasingly more important because of the wide use of paper money. The proponents of this theory claim that governmental sanction is the only requisite of money. The acceptance of this theory would mean the abolition of representative and credit paper money as described above. All currency would be fiat money, that is, money created by fiat or law. There would be no legal gold or silver reserve requirements, and currency would be permanently irredeemable in so far as precious metals are concerned.

Deposit Currency, a Form of Credit Exchange

Between 85 and 90 per cent of the money value of all transactions in the United States are made by personal checks and bank drafts. The use of these two credit instruments dominates large exchanges and the transfer of funds between communities. The steady increase in the practice of making payments by personal checks and bank drafts is closely associated with the growth of commercial banking.

One of the chief functions of modern banks is the keeping of checking accounts. Depositors merely accept memoranda in banks' ledgers or account books in lieu of money. These bookkeeping entries are bank promises to pay money, bank credits, which are drawn on by individuals and banks. If the order is in the form of a personal check, the drawer is an individual; if in the form of a bank draft, the drawer is a bank.

The recipients of checks (payees) may cash them, but most firms and individuals prefer to deposit them with their banks. Later the deposits thus created are drawn upon by depositors to pay obligations. The result is a change of ownership of deposits, that is, rights to money.

Since bank credit in the form of deposits is used as a means of payment, some writers classify it as "money"; however, it seems more appropriate to use the term "deposit currency," since it is a more inclusive one, emphasizing current means of payment. The credit instruments—checks and bank drafts—used to transfer title are not generally acceptable, are never legal tender, are not considered to be money by the general public, and cannot be a standard of value. Although there is some justification for calling deposits "money," in this book the term "deposit currency" is used.

Our present institution of exchange is called a "credit system" because of the wide use of checks and bank drafts as means of payment. The advantages to the individual of paying obligations with a "stroke of the pen" are apparent. However, it is the social significance of the use of this means of payment that explains why the subjects "banking" and "money" are linked in this book.

The conclusion that our present institution of exchange is a credit system does not mean that the other types of exchange have disappeared. Barter is current, as illustrated by experiences of American soldiers in European and other countries, where they found cigarettes to be one of the most widely accepted means of payment. In the United States paper money and coins are in circulation in greater volume than at any other time in history. Although we have gone through three stages of exchange (barter, money, and credit) in our economic development, it must be recognized that during any one of these stages the other two were present. In what sense, then, may one speak of the evolution of exchange? In the sense that, while all means of exchange are in use at all stages of economic development, they are used in varying degrees and with changing emphasis at different stages.

Two Primary Functions of Circulating Media

Modern money is defined in a technical sense as "something specifically designed by the government to perform the money function." The two primary functions of money, broadly speaking, are to serve as a medium of exchange and to act as a standard of value. These two functions, as well as all secondary ones, are interdependent.

Medium of Exchange.—The expression "medium of exchange" may be illustrated as follows:

Goods and Services→Money→Goods and Services

Thus, money is the means by which goods and services are exchanged indirectly for goods and services. Sales are made for money, and money is used to purchase goods. Two transactions are necessary instead of one, as in the case of barter. The second exchange may be delayed, transferred to a second market, or used to purchase any one of a large number of goods. This option to chose the time, the place, and the article is a valuable privilege resulting from the use of money as a medium of exchange. In addition, the medium of exchange function includes the loan medium, the store of value, and the reserve functions which are considered below as secondary functions of money.

A Standard of Value.—"Value" is the ability of one good to command others in exchange for itself. Without a common denominator, the value of a commodity is found by comparing it to all the others that appear in the market. A list of ten articles exchangeable against each other would involve forty-five different comparisons. The first article would have to be measured against the other nine, the second against the next eight, and so on throughout the list. Even in a simple economic regime it would be impossible for anyone to keep these exchange ratios in mind. By expressing value in terms of a standard, the problem is greatly simplified, for under this system only ten prices must be kept in mind. Saying that money is a standard of value means that money is the common denominator for expressing exchange ratios.

The reader must not assume that the material of which money is composed needs to be used both as the standard and as the medium of exchange. From 1920 to 1933 little gold was in circulation in the United States, but gold was the standard of value throughout this period. Before the Revolutionary War the money in circulation was chiefly Spanish coins, but in many colonies the money of account was the same as that in England.

In considering the two primary functions of money, it should not be concluded that the standard of value functions resulted from the use of a commodity as a medium of exchange. During ancient times the value of armors and gifts offered in exchange for other commodities were valued in terms of oxen, sheep, reindeer, skins, wheat, or some other commodity that was the chief form of wealth in the community. The barter unit of value often remained as the standard even after coined money appeared. Sometimes the new coins were made equal in value to the thing that had been the barter unit of account. When gold coins were first created, the gold content was made equal to the value of an ox. The word "pecuniary" is derived from the Latin word *pecus,* meaning "cattle," which was used not as a medium of exchange but as a standard of value.[10]

At the present time money is much more frequently used as a measure of value than as a medium of exchange, because values are often measured many times before exchange takes place; the standard

---

[10] "In spite of their [cattle] capacity to become current in the most literal sense, they were probably much more used as a unit of value than as a medium of exchange. . . . (Burns, *op. cit.,* p. 10).

function is present during money barter, that is, where eggs are traded for groceries, old cars are traded in, bills and commissions are traded out at stores; and the standard is used to measure value even though there is no trade. An additional reason why the standard of value function is so important is the fact that money is used as a standard of deferred payments.

Secondary Functions of Money

Standard of Deferred Payment.—Money serves as a standard of deferred payments when obligations to make future payments are expressed in terms of it. By using money as the standard of deferred payment the debtor contracts to give to his creditor a given sum of money. This promise may arise from the purchase of a house, a commodity, some type of credit instrument, or anything that may be bought or sold in a modern economy. Where payments are deferred, the transactions require a common denominator in which to express obligations; otherwise debt contracts would call for the repayment in kind. Normally creditors prefer to receive money, rather than goods, in order to avoid the same difficulties as those existing in a barter economy. Fluctuations in the value of money make the use of money as a standard of deferred payments very significant. When the value of money is increasing, debtors are forced to repay, in addition to interest, more in goods-equivalent than they borrowed. When the value of money is decreasing, creditors are forced to take less in goods-equivalent than they lent.

Loan Medium.—An individual may buy a house directly from the builder, pay 20 per cent cash, and give a promise to pay in annual installments for the remainder. Money is used as a medium of exchange and a standard of deferred payment but not as a loan medium. However, if the buyer borrows enough from his bank to pay the contractor in full, money is used as a loan medium. The bank exchanges money for a promise to pay money at some future date.

Money may be the loan medium but not necessarily the standard of deferred payments. For example, one American corporation issues bonds that call for the repayment of a sum of money equal to the purchasing power of the money borrowed. The sum of money to be repaid is not fixed in terms of dollars but in terms of purchasing power.[11] If the general price level is 10 per cent higher at the maturity of the loan than when funds were borrowed, the holder of a $1,000 bond will receive $1,100. But if the price level has decreased 10 per cent during this period, he will receive only $900. In St. Paul, Minnesota, the number of dollars in wages paid to city employees is adjusted to changes in the purchasing power of the dollar.[12] In both of these cases the loan or salary medium is money, but the standard for the contracts is the purchasing power of the dollar as measured by index numbers.

Store of Value.—Money is also used as a store of value. In early times people found it desirable to conceal their wealth from robbers and tax collectors. This was done by converting their goods into jewels and money. Money was well suited for hoarding because it represented value in generally acceptable form and had certain physical characteristics that made it a good store of value. Money was almost the only store of value of an exchangeable character until the creation of negotiable instruments. With the development of government and law, every man has been given some guarantee in his rights to property. Now money is less used as a store of value. Since money hoards bring in no income, the modern saver normally finds it wise to keep his store of value in the form of money as small as possible. At the present time considerable currency and an even larger amount of bank deposits are being kept as stores of value.

Reserve.—Closely related to the use of money as a store of value is its use as a reserve. Banks and business concerns have many money claims against them. In commercial banking, for example, the flow of funds into the banks tends to offset the outward movement, but the amount of payments and receipts rarely coincide. In

---

[11] A description of the Rand Kardex Co., Inc., "7 per cent 30 year stabilized debenture bonds" is found in the *Stabilization Hearings before the Committee on Banking and Currency*, House of Representatives (H.R. 7895), Part I, pp. 58-61. The index number used is the U.S. Government Bureau of Labor Statistics Index Number of Wholesale Commodity Prices. Interest, as well as principal payments, is adjusted to compensate owners for changes in the value of money. This debt contract standard is called "tabular standard."

[12] Probst, J. B., *Standardizing Salaries* (pamphlet; June, 1922). The cost-of-living index published by the U.S. Government Bureau of Labor Statistics is the guide to salary adjustments to offset losses due to changes in cost of living. The adjusted percentage is applied only to lower-paid employees. In October, 1936, General Electric Company announced that it was adopting a similar plan, which applies to all employees. During 1940 the extra cost in terms of money was estimated to have been $3,500,000 over 1939. This plan was abandoned in April, 1941.

order to take care of unlooked-for contingencies, it has been found necessary to keep a cash reserve. Money and money substitutes are used for this purpose, and usually money substitutes are preferred to money itself. Business corporations keep most of their cash reserve on deposit at banks, and even banks are keeping most of their reserves as deposits in central banks.

Legal Qualities of Money

The use of money in all its primary and secondary capacities has been strengthened by legal tender and other laws. "Legal tender" is money which the law requires creditors to accept when tendered in payment of money obligations. In disputed cases over money values, some method must be provided to settle definitely when a debt is paid. When cases come before the court, they usually involve amounts rather than questions of legal tender. Offering of legal tender money, even though refused, does not discharge the debtor's obligation; but, if the court decides that the amount offered was the proper sum and that it was legal tender, then the amount must be paid, but no interest can be charged from the time the tender was first made. In the Thomas Amendment to the Agricultural Adjustment Act, May, 1933, and Public Resolution No. 10, July, 1933, Congress made all types of money legal tender.[13]

Before 1930, money in the United States was classified as full legal tender, limited legal tender, and "optional" money. Gold, gold certificates, and silver dollars were full legal tender. United States notes were legal tender for everything except import duties and interest on the public debt; subsidiary silver coins were legal tender for amounts not exceeding ten dollars in one payment; and pennies and nickels were legal tender for amounts not exceeding twenty-five cents in one payment. Federal Reserve notes, Federal Reserve bank notes, national bank notes, and silver certificates were optional money without legal tender qualities.[14]

Often confused with "legal tender" is "lawful money," the as-

[13] United States Code, title 31, sec. 821, defines legal tender as follows: "All coins and currencies of the United States shall be legal tender for all debts, public and private, public charges, taxes, duties, and dues. . . ."

[14] For a description of the old legal tender qualities of United States money, see *Monetary Units and Coinage Systems of the Principal Countries of the World* (compiled in Office of Director of the Mint, 1929), pp. 11-12.

sumption being that what is "legal" is also "lawful." However, lawful money means the type or types of money which may be used lawfully for certain purposes; for example, by Federal Reserve banks as reserves against deposits. The importance of this distinction is apparent when one recognizes that Federal Reserve notes, which are "promises to pay" of Federal Reserve banks, are not lawful money for use as reserves against deposits in Federal Reserve banks even though they are legal tender.[15]

In the past, governments have increased the acceptability of certain types of money by making them government tender in payment of taxes or other obligations due the government. In 1913 the Federal Reserve Act provided that Federal Reserve notes shall be receivable "for all taxes, customs, and other public dues." Federal Reserve bank notes and national bank notes were made government tender "at par in all parts of the United States in payment of taxes, excises, public lands, and other dues to the United States, except duties on imports . . . ."[16]

The acceptability of nonlegal tender money has also been enhanced by making such money receivable in payment for obligations of the government including salaries and debts due to individuals, corporations, and associations within the country. However, exceptions may be made, as in the case of the United States notes which were not "receivable" in payment of interest on the public debt or in redemption of the national currency.

QUESTIONS AND PROBLEMS

1. What is the significance of the use of money in (*a*) production, (*b*) consumption, and (*c*) distribution?
2. What relationship, if any, is there between the use of money and the following slogans: "Patronize home industry," "Buy American," "Say it with flowers," and "Buy now and end the depression"? Discuss.
3. What is meant by "prices, the functional guide to economic activity"?
4. What are the disadvantages of barter and how have they been solved?

---

[15] On June 12, 1945, gold certificates alone were made lawful for reserves against notes and deposits in the Federal Reserve banks.

[16] *United States Code* (1940 ed.), title 12, sec. 109, p. 771. National bank notes were made receivable in payment of duties on imports under section 648 of the Tariff Act approved June 17, 1930.

5. Define: (*a*) coin, (*b*) standard coin, (*c*) subsidiary or token coin, and (*d*) free coinage.

6. "There have been great and elaborate civilizations . . . . that knew no such thing as coined money. . . . . The civilizations of those who erected the Pyramids and sculptured the Sphinx, who built the Temples of Karnac, Babylon and Ninevah were such practically moneyless civilizations, moneyless that is in so far as the daily lives of the mass of people was concerned" (Angell, *The Story of Money*, p. 18). What was the legal and economic status of the masses in these civilizations? Did they use credit instruments or other substitutes for coined money?

7. "Is the substance of which money is made important? No. It is legal status given it by government stamp that makes it acceptable by all as money, whether it be made of metal (punch press money), or of paper (printing press money)" (Coughlin, Rev. Charles E., *Money: Questions and Answers*, p. 29). Do you agree with Father Coughlin's answer? Why or why not?

8. Does one who possesses money own wealth? No. The possession of money is the evidence that the holder is *owed* wealth by the community" (*ibid.*, p. 28). Do you agree? Give reasons for your answer.

9. "Throughout history there has been a persistent effort to reduce the cost, to the issuer at least, of the material from which money is made. The final stage is that in which the issuer not only pays practically nothing for the money material but does not assume even a future obligation in the matter" (Graham and Whittlesey, *Golden Avalanche*, p. 221). Do you agree? Why?

10. Distinguish between representative paper money and credit paper money. What are the advantages and disadvantages of each?

11. Why are bank notes classified as money while bank deposits are not?

12. Explain what is meant by the "evolution of exchange."

13. What are the functions of money? Explain.

14. Is there any relationship between the commercial geography of nations and their money? Use for reference DuPuy, "The Geography of Money," *National Geographic Magazine*, Vol. LII, No. 6 (December, 1927), pp. 744-68.

15. Assume that all Federal Reserve notes would bear interest at the rate of 2 per cent payable January 1 of each year. What would be the effect upon their circulation? Explain.

16. "In many and important respects economic organization appears to be the product of money, and it is, therefore, inadmissible to ascribe the origin of money to its special suitability for our existing scheme of things" (Helfferich, *Money*, p. 3). Are you in sympathy with this rejection of the "rational theory of the origin of money"?

17. Jones is paying his divorced wife $40 per month alimony. In 1932 he made a payment using the maximum amount of small-value coins and silver dollars allowed by the legal tender laws. Compute number and value of the various coins used. Make a calculation for a payment following the passage of the 1933 legal tender law.
18. Distinguish between "legal tender" and "lawful" money.
19. "Therefore, it seems that the correct definition of money is that it is anything which a . . . . national government declares to be receivable in payment of taxes which it levies" (Jerome, E. C., *Governments and Money*, p. 44). Analyze this definition.
20. Examine carefully all types of money which you have. Write a brief description of each one. Hand in.

REFERENCES

See end of Chapter II

Chapter II

QUALITIES OF A GOOD MONETARY SYSTEM

Emphasis on the System, Not on One Type of Money

In constructing a monetary system, the needs of all economic classes must be considered in regard to the sizes, forms, and denominations of money. Emphasis must be placed upon the system and not upon one type of money within the system. A country may have an excellent standard and excellent paper money but lack a satisfactory subsidiary coinage system. Furthermore, the dependence on deposit currency in the United States is so great that a breakdown in the banking system impairs even the strongest type of monetary standard. In other words, the interdependence among currency, standard money, and banking is so great that it is meaningless to speak or write of one type of money—gold, for example—as possessing the ideal qualities of money without at the same time recognizing the part taken by others. The basic problem today is not to select one commodity that possesses all the characteristics of good money but to create a monetary system which will have all these qualities.

Suitable Denominations to Care for Large and Small Value Transactions

An economic group needs money which may be used in all sorts of amounts. In some exchanges small values are involved, while in others there is a demand for large sums. There must be a series of related units or values, that is, a denomination system.

Primary Unit.—In the United States the basic or primary unit is the dollar. At the present time the dollar is defined as 15 5/21 grains of standard gold, 9/10 fine. The gold dollar is not coined and exists only in bullion form. It has, however, many substitutes in the form of paper money, metallic coins, and credit instruments.

Secondary Units.—The secondary denominations are multiple or fractional parts of the dollar. Currency units designed for circulation vary in values from 1 cent to $10,000. Gold certificates are made in denominations of $100,000, but they are used only for central bank reserves. The banking system makes possible much larger units, for single checks of millions of dollars may be and have been written.

One-half Cent Coins.—One criticism of our denomination system is the lack of small coins.[1] The 1 cent piece has from two to ten times the value of most of the smallest coins in European countries. It has been urged that persons of small incomes could be more economical in their expenditures if the ½ cent were added to our present list of coins. An acute need for less than 1 cent pieces has resulted from the passage of many state retail sales tax laws. Some states have met the need for small coins by issuance of tokens that may be used for tax payments. Among the most famous of these mill pieces are the "milk cap" paper tokens of the state of Missouri.[2]

Money of Account.—The United States money of account system is more complete than the monetary system because it includes the mill. The mill is a unit of accounting having the value of 1/10 cent. It is the unit in which most state and local governments express the tax rate on general or real property. The people in the United States are fortunate in having the decimal system. If English, rather than Spanish coins, had been the chief circulating money during the colonial period, the English system, with all its disadvantages, might have been inherited. In the English system 4 farthings equal 1 penny, 12 pence equal 1 shilling, 20 shillings equal 1 pound, and 21 shillings equal 1 guinea. Although these units provide for the varying values which are being exchanged, the work of recording, adding, multiplying, and comparing values is much more difficult than with our decimal system.

Conclusion.—When monetary demands fell upon one commodity, it was imperative that this commodity should have the quality of divisibility in order to permit either division into small pieces or reunification without loss in value. This quality is possessed by all metals and explains in part why bronze, copper, zinc, iron, platinum, aluminum, nickel, silver, and gold have been used for money. The use of credit and paper money has lessened the importance of this physical characteristic of metallic money, for paper money

[1] One-half cent coins were struck under provisions of the coinage act of 1792. They were discontinued in 1857. See *United States Coinage Laws, 1792-1894*, p. 95.

[2] In 1935 it was rumored that the Treasury planned to coin under provisions of a proposed law a 1 mill and a ½ cent piece. The papers reported that the President had suggested a ½ cent piece with a hole in it and a square 1 mill piece.

may be printed in any denomination and checks may be written for any amount. Experience in the United States indicates that the most economical and convenient results in exchanging exist when payments of less than $1.00 are made with coins and amounts above $1.00 are made with paper money and checks. Checks should not be used for small amounts in local exchanging, for the work of clearing and posting a check for $1.00 is the same as for a check for $100.

Convenient Shapes and Sizes

Not only is convenience in values necessary in a good monetary system but also convenience with reference to physical shape and size of the various units. Money is continuously moving from place to place to effect sales and purchases. It is kept on hand as a store of ready purchasing power. It is held by banks and business firms as "till money" and for reserve purposes. It must have considerable value in small bulk in order to reduce the burden of transporting and the space necessary for storing.[3]

Practically all our modern coins are circular disks of uniform size for each denomination. This makes the coins easy to handle, to stack, and to store. They must not be too large or too small. The silver dollar, sometimes called a "cartwheel," is so large that many people refuse to accept it. The gold dollar and even the $2.50 gold pieces proved too small for convenient handling. The Gold Reserve Act of 1934 discontinued all gold coinage and directed the Treasury to melt down all gold coins into gold bars.[4] Monetary gold is now used only for reserve and export purposes, and bars are more convenient for these purposes than coins. Even before the passage of the Gold Reserve Act of 1934, most of the monetary gold was in bar form. The favorite size of bar for export purposes is 400 ounces, but bars as small as 5 ounces are made for domestic purposes.

This need for convenience in size is recognized for paper money as well as for coins and gold bars. The paper currency as issued

---

[3] Burns, A. R., *Money and Monetary Policy in Early Times*, pp. 54-74.

[4] Gold Reserve Act of 1934, sec. 5 (*Federal Reserve Bulletin*, February, 1934, p. 65). There is before Congress a bill that provides for the minting of a gold coin equal to thirty-five times the weight of the gold dollar. The Engle Bill provides for gold coins of $10, $20, and $50 in value.

after 1929 is 6 5/16 by 2 11/16 inches. This is the same size as the standard bank checks. It fits into a business envelope without folding and is very easy to handle in packages. The old size, 7 7/16 by 3 1/8 inches, had been in use since 1862 but had little in the way of convenience to warrant its continuance.

Durable in Order to Reduce Costs of Replacement

For obvious reasons, money should possess the quality of indestructibility. If money deteriorated quickly, it could not be used as a medium of exchange, as a store of value, or for reserve purposes. Unless a commodity is durable, it has very little value as money. Silver money is the preferred medium of exchange in tropical countries, because paper money may be destroyed by insects.

Coins Are Durable.—Coins were originally manufactured from pure metals; but, since gold and silver are soft, the coins were subject to a large amount of abrasion. This was corrected by adding an alloy to give them hardness. Now our silver coins contain 90 per cent pure metal and 10 per cent alloy. The old 5 cent piece consisted of 75 per cent copper and 25 per cent nickel; and the new 5 cent piece consists of an alloy of copper, silver, and manganese.[5] The pre–World War II 1 cent piece consisted of 95 per cent copper and 5 per cent tin and zinc, and the new 1 cent piece consists of 95 per cent copper and 5 per cent zinc.[6]

The early coins bore a design on only one side, which made it possible to clip or file off a part of the metal. This weakness was corrected by stamping a design on both sides. Still the edges could be cut away. In order to prevent this clipping, coins were milled, that is, coined with a furrowed edge. All United States coins except our 1 cent and 5 cent pieces have these edges. A slight rim is raised around the edge of all coins so that the weight does not rest on the whole surface of the coin. This process reduces the abrasion and

[5] The 5 cent pieces are issued under authority of the Second War Powers Act approved March 27, 1942. The composition is an alloy of 56 per cent copper, 35 per cent silver, and 9 per cent manganese. No nickels of the old type have been coined since 1942. *Annual Report of the Director of the Mint for the Fiscal Year Ended June 30, 1944* (Washington, D.C.: Government Printing Office, 1945), p. 2.

[6] Production of zinc-coated steel 1 cent coins, originated in 1942 as part of the program to save critical metals, was discontinued on December 31, 1943. Production of the new coin began January 1, 1944. The availability of salvaged fired brass cartridge cases resulted in this change. *(Ibid.)*

adds not only to the life of the coin but to its cognoscibility, for the design is not easily worn.

Paper Money Lacks Durability.—The government's main problem is to make a form of paper money that possesses durability. All the paper currency in circulation must be replaced on an average of once every year, but $1.00 bills must be replaced on the average of once every six months. The hard day-to-day wear works havoc with these bills, and it would be far more economical to substitute a smaller-size silver dollar for the $1.00 bills. When in office, Secretary of the Treasury Mellon and his assistants made a vain attempt to popularize the silver dollar, and his administration led to the printing of the small-size paper money now current in the United States. The amount of paper in each new bill is about two-thirds of that found in the old bills. A great deal of folding is avoided; and if this could be eliminated entirely, the life of each paper unit, it is estimated, would be increased ten times.[7]

Easy Recognition to Increase Acceptability

Money will be more acceptable and, therefore, a better medium of exchange if it is easily recognized. If bullion were still used as money, it would be necessary to weigh and test the purity of the metal each time it was used in exchange. In order to save time and trouble, coinage developed. Much thought is given to designing coins so as to make them difficult to imitate and easy to recognize. The United States formerly coined a 3 cent nickel piece that was about the size of a dime, but there were so many mistakes made in the use of the two that the 3 cent piece was discontinued.

The technique in the manufacture of coins has now reached such a high standard that the problem of cognoscibility has shifted chiefly to the necessity of manufacturing paper money that cannot be imitated by counterfeiters. Fraudulent currency must be kept at a minimum in order to prevent loss to the public. Existence of even a small percentage of counterfeit bills may lead to a decrease in confidence in all paper money and, therefore, a loss in its acceptability.

Paper currency is protected from counterfeiting by a secret process in the manufacture of the paper, secret designs, secret pat-

[7] The new paper currency has a much higher folding endurance than the old (*Annual Report of the Treasury of the United States on the State of the Finances for Fiscal Year Ended June 30, 1929*, p. 332).

terns, and special texture of paper. In spite of these safeguards, frequent imitation of the official currency appears. Possible profits for the counterfeiters are greater in this field than in that of coined money. The equipment necessary for printing is less expensive than for coinage, raw materials cost less, and the denomination of a paper unit may be much greater. As a result, secret-service men are kept busy running down paper money counterfeiters, and bank clerks are constantly on the alert for the appearance of the counterfeits.

Counterfeiters were given greater opportunity to carry on their work before 1929 because of the large size of the design of the bills and the greater variety of types. The new paper currency, which was first issued in that year, makes irregularities easier to detect.[8] Previously there were thirty-nine various models of paper money with portraits of "obscure statesmen, bankers, and hump-backed buffaloes." The new currency contains portraits of eleven statesmen. These statesmen are ranked according to their popularity and placed upon each denomination of paper money according to its popularity, as indicated by the number of units in circulation.[9] (See Table 1.)

TABLE 1

PAPER CURRENCY: TYPES OF IDENTIFICATION

PORTRAIT			
$ 1	Washington	$ 100	Franklin
2	Jefferson	500	McKinley
5	Lincoln	1,000	Cleveland
10	Hamilton	5,000	Madison
20	Jackson	10,000	Chase
50	Grant		

SEALS AND BACKS

The backs of the new currency are printed uniformly in green; the faces in black; and the Treasury seals and the serial numbers in the following colors:*

United States notes	Red
Silver certificates	Blue
Federal Reserve notes	Green

* The new gold certificates have yellow backs and denominations up to $100,000, but they are not designed for circulation. The obsolete but not extinct national bank notes and Federal Reserve bank notes (national currency) have brown seals. Yellow-seal dollars were printed for use as "spearhead currency" in military operations in Europe. For economic and political reasons the yellow-seal dollars were not used in Germany and liberated countries, and later the supply on hand was given to soldiers on their way home in exchange for European currencies. Brown-seal dollars, marked "Hawaii," were used in the Central Pacific area. Originally these currencies were legal tender only in the area for which they were created; but later they were recognized as being legal tender in the United States.

[8] *Ibid.*, pp. 42-45, 324-34.

[9] *Ibid., 1928*, p. 58.

Uniformity in Value to Prevent Operation of Gresham's Law

The needs for different denominations and different kinds of money will be met only by a monetary system in which all forms of money have equitable value. One hundred pennies, ten dimes, one paper dollar, and one gold dollar must all have the same purchasing power. If one form is more valuable than the others, it will be hoarded and will disappear from circulation. For example, during the Civil War, paper money issues drove all types of coins out of circulation. Many serious retail problems arose because of the absence of small coins. Many small tokens were issued by individuals, but they were not a satisfactory substitute for government money. Finally the government recognized the seriousness of the situation and authorized the issuance of fractional paper money. This money first took the form of postage currency, issued by the post offices. Later, fractional paper money was issued by the Treasury. The small units of paper money were derisively called "shinplasters."[10]

The tendency for the less valuable money to drive out of circulation the more valuable needs further explanation. Sir Thomas Gresham explained this monetary principle to Queen Elizabeth in 1560. She replaced the coins issued during her father's, sister's and brother's reigns with more valuable coins, and she was greatly surprised to find that the poorer coins were seemingly preferred to her more valuable ones, for only the poorer coins remained in circulation. It seems a strange contradiction that, while in most lines the best articles capture the market, in the case of money alone the poor is preferred to the good as a medium of exchange. The reasons for this situation are obvious after one reviews his own experience and considers what is meant by the demand for money.

Assume that a person possesses a new one dollar bill and one old one. In exchanging, most persons will use the old one and keep the new one. The same tendency is noticed in spending coins: the worn ones are used for spending first, while the new ones are held back from active circulation. If this situation exists when there is no difference in value, it is evident that it would be far more pronounced when two moneys differ in value. The debtor decides which of the forms of legal tender money he will use, and self-

[10] Carothers, Neil, *Fractional Money*, pp. 170-85.

interest results in the use of the cheaper form. If the cheaper money exists in sufficient quantity, it will entirely displace the more valuable money. The better coins will be melted down and used in the arts or will be exported. Since there are no legal tender laws in international trade, only weight and fineness of coins count. If money is to be melted down or hoarded, or if payments are to be made abroad, it is but natural that the best coins or forms of money be used for these purposes.

Gresham's law, named for Sir Thomas Gresham, was first formulated with reference to heavy and light coins of the same kind.[11] It was later applied to the two standard coins of bimetallism. Later it was used to explain the disappearance of metallic money when paper money was overissued.

Stability in Value

If the qualities already considered were the only requisites, the present monetary system of the United States would be nearly perfect. However, another quality necessary for a good monetary system is stability in value. The growth of credit and the increasing complexity of our present economic system makes this, according to many writers, the most important quality of good money.

Meaning of the Value of Money.—By the "value of money" is meant its purchasing power, that is, the amount of goods and services that may be exchanged for money. When all prices on the average are going up, the value of money is going down. When all prices on the average are going down, the value of money is going up. Stability in value of money is synonymous with stability in the general price level.

Measuring Changes in the Value of Money.—In order to have a true picture of changes in the value of money, the prices of all things which are bought and sold should be considered. Such a comparison is possible to a remarkably accurate degree because of the construction of index numbers.[12] A commodity price index number is a device for determining the average change in the prices of a number

[11] McLeod first named this principle Gresham's Law (*Elements of Economics*, pp. 270-72).

[12] See Mitchell, W. C., *The Making and Using of Index Numbers*, Bull. No. 173 of U.S. Department of Labor, Bureau of Labor Statistics (1915); No. 284 (1921 rev.); No. 656, Part I (1938).

of commodities. By various mathematical devices one number is selected to represent the group of prices studied. The purpose of the index number is to make it possible to compare prices at different times. Over a period of time some prices do not change, others rise, and others fall. For example, between October and November, 1929, the general price level decreased 0.3 per cent; but there was no change in the prices of 416 commodities, while the prices of 137 commodities decreased and those of 260 increased.[13] Only by finding some type of mean or average can a student follow general price movements from week to week or month to month.

Fortunately, newspapers, trade associations, research foundations, business and financial publications, banks, governments, and others have not only recognized the need for special and general index numbers but are constructing them. Thousands of statisticians and their assistants are giving all their working time to this task. As a result, index numbers of almost every type are now available. Interest in the question is suggested by the following names of price index numbers: United States Department of Labor (Bureau of Labor Statistics), United States Department of Agriculture, National Fertilizer Association, Moody's Annalist, Dun and Bradstreet, Federal Reserve Bank of New York, and Harvard University of Business Research.[14]

Some index numbers are constructed to show daily changes in prices and others cover a weekly period, but the most common time period is a month. At one extreme are found index numbers based upon only a few staple wholesale commodity prices, and at the other extreme are index numbers which are based upon commodity and noncommodity prices. The last type is known as a "composite index number," and its most famous exponent is Dr. Carl Snyder. His index is based upon the component groups which are weighted according to importance. The groups include prices of industrial products, prices of farm products at the farm, retail food prices, rents, miscellaneous costs of living, transportation costs, realty prices, security prices, equipment and machinery prices, hardware prices, automobile prices, and wages.

---

[13] U.S. Department of Labor, Bureau of Labor Statistics, *Wholesale Prices*, November, 1939, pp. 2-3.

[14] For a list of index numbers, see Fisher, Irving, *The Making of Index Numbers*, pp. 432-38.

CHART I

WHOLESALE PRICES

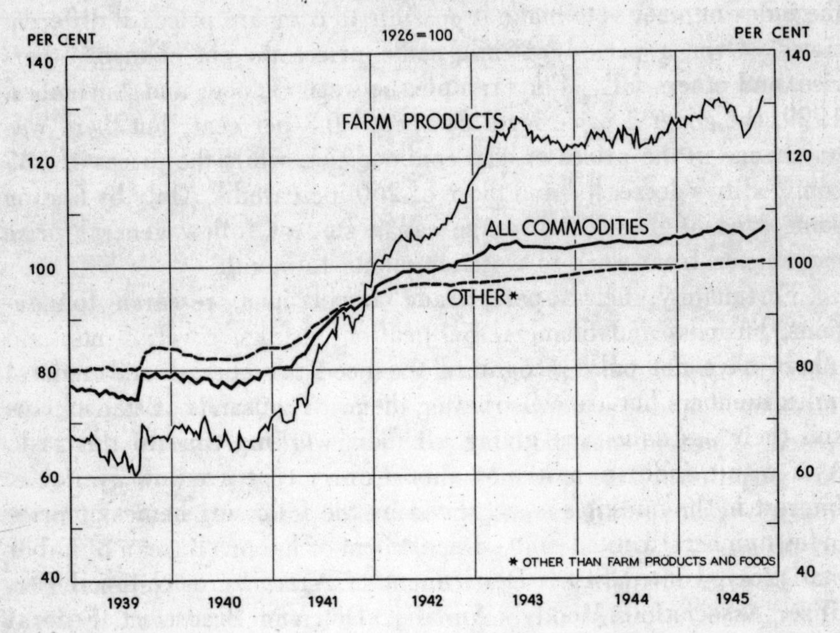

This chart, showing changes in wholesale prices of all commodities, is further subdivided into prices of "farm products" and "other." "Other" includes those other than farm products and foods. It emphasizes the volatile nature of prices of farm products.

Source: U.S. Department of Labor, Bureau of Labor Statistics

Certain index numbers are constructed for special purposes, and constant danger exists that they will be used for purposes for which they are not intended. For example, the use of a wholesale commodity index number based upon a few staple commodities is valuable for forecasting but inadequate as a measure of changes in cost of living. Therefore, it is a poor index to use in computing real wages.

Some Technical Problems Involved in Making an Index Number. —To the popular mind the word "average," or "mean," suggests merely an arithmetical average. But the number selected to represent the group may be the mode or most popular one. It may be the median, or the one that is in the middle of the group. All the num-

TABLE 2

ARITHMETIC AVERAGE INDEX NUMBER

Commodity	Base Year (1936)		Current Year	
	Price	Index Number or Price Relative	Price	Index Number or Price Relative
Sugar	$0.10 lb.	100	$0.05 lb.	50
Wheat	0.50 bu.	100	0.75 lb.	150
Cotton	0.14 lb.	100	0.07 lb.	50
Hogs	0.12 lb.	100	0.06 lb.	50
		4)400		4)300
		100		75

bers may be added and the total used to show changes up or down. Geometric and harmonic means of price relatives may be computed. The four most popular methods used for computing averages are variations of the arithmetic mean, the median, and the geometric mean of price relatives, and the unweighted or weighted aggregates of prices.

If price changes of some commodities are of more significance than others, as, for example, wheat and cotton compared to pocket knives and fountain pens, the important ones may be counted a number of times, that is, weighted to indicate relative importance. The Bureau of Labor Statistics index number of wholesale commodity prices is weighted by using "averages of the data for 1929 and 1931, except for farm products, for which the quantities used are averages of the data for the three years 1929, 1930, and 1931."[15]

Expressed as Percentages.—Prices are quoted in terms of all sorts of denominations: coal per ton, hogs per hundredweight or pounds, potatoes per bushel, etc. Such quotations are not comparable with one another, and in constructing index numbers they must be reduced to a common basis. Price index numbers are usually expressed as relatives or percentages, although Dun and Bradstreet's is a notable exception. The prices of all commodities are expressed as 1 or 100 per cent. If, during the following period, the price of sugar falls from 10 cents to 5 cents per pound, the new relative number for sugar is 50. If the price of wheat increases

[15] Cutts, J. M., and Dennis, S. J., *Revised Method of Calculation of the Wholesale Price Index of the United States*, U.S. Department of Labor, Bureau of Labor Statistics, Serial No. R. 666. Reprinted from the *Journal of American Statistical Association*, December, 1937, p. 665.

from 50 cents to 75 cents per bushel, the new relative number for wheat is 150, and so on for other commodities. An average of the relatives is secured which shows the price level with reference to the base year. If it has dropped from 100 to 75, the value of money—purchasing power—has increased relative to the base year. Then, 75 cents will buy in general what formerly $1.00 would purchase. Thus the change in the value of money is the reciprocal of the change in general prices. Some index numbers have the averages of prices for a number of years as the base prices, but the principle of an average for one year as the price-base line is more popular. For greater accuracy the base period is adjusted frequently. The 1926 base year is now most commonly used; but it is already out of date, and some statisticians have recognized this situation by shifting the base periods for their numbers.

Effects of Changes in the Value of Money

If, owing to mystic rays, the length of our yardstick and everything else in the universe were to shrink 10 per cent, nobody would be the wiser. On the other hand, if some geological formations, plants, animals, and human beings were reduced 5 per cent, others 10 per cent, others 25 per cent, and so on, the average being 10 per cent, the results would be tragic. So it is with changes in the value of money. If all prices and money contracts changed equally, a rise of 10 per cent in the value of money would not be significant. It is because prices do not change equally that a change in the general price level is so disturbing and of such wide importance. Every individual is interested in prices from two distinct and conflicting points of view: as the buyer of services and commodities, on the one hand, and as the receiver of income, on the other.

Falling Prices.—The broad statement that creditors, laborers, salaried classes, pensioners, and landlords gain from falling prices is based upon the assumption that they continue to receive for a time the same money income. After the fall in prices, $1.00 will buy more goods and services. Therefore, the real income of creditors, laborers, salaried classes, pensioners, and landlords has increased—provided, of course, that they have the same number of dollars to spend. If there is a rapid change in prices, many in the foregoing groups will not gain, because the advantage from the increase in purchasing power of money is more than offset by a decrease in the number of dollars received. This is particularly true of the laboring class, which "gains in real income in the upswing of the price cycle, and loses in the downswing."[16]

When prices are falling rapidly, day laborers bear the major part of the burden resulting from business and other adjustments. A sharp decline in prices causes a decrease in production and leads to a business depression. In many fields, services of labor are not wanted and unemployment results. Many who keep their jobs are forced to take cuts in wages. The ten to fourteen million who were unemployed during 1932-33 is an illustration of the injury suffered by laborers and salaried men during a period of falling prices.

TABLE 3
EFFECT OF PRICE CHANGES ON ECONOMIC CLASSES

Falling Prices		Rising Prices	
Gain	Lose	Gain	Lose
Creditors Laborers Salaried classes Pensioners Landlords	Debtors Businessmen Stockholders	Debtors Businessmen Stockholders	Creditors Laborers Salaried classes Pensioners Landlords

Debtors, businessmen, and stockholders are generally considered to be losers from a fall in general prices. Economic literature is full of discussions of the effects of falling prices upon debtors, who, in terms of purchasing power, repay more than they have borrowed, after prices have fallen. Interest burdens are greater because of the lag in the adjustment of the real rate of interest to the money rate of interest. If the decline in prices is rapid and there is a serious depression, many debtors find it impossible to repay funds borrowed and to meet interest, taxes, and other fixed charges. As a result, there are many bankruptcy and other settlements, resulting in the loss of all the property of debtors.

Businessmen and stockholders are managers and risk takers. They are in a vulnerable position during falling prices because they are usually debtors and are bound by wage, interest, and other contracts covering short or long periods. Goods in process of manu-

[16] Garver, F. B., and Hansen, A. H., *Principles of Economics* (rev. ed.), p. 327.

facture or distribution are purchased during preceding months at high prices. During falling prices the margin between cost and selling prices decreases and profits change to losses. Even where per unit costs may be contracted almost as rapidly as prices decrease, losses still occur because of the decline in the volume of business. Profits from partnerships and dividends on common stock are reduced or omitted, and businessmen and stockholders who were enjoying prosperity during high prices suddenly become poor.

Rising Prices.—Periods of rising prices are generally considered as being good times, particularly for businessmen, stockholders, and debtors. When prices are rising, costs of production are lagging behind, and profits increase. The wage rate tends to increase but not so rapidly as wholesale prices; rent is being paid according to a contract drawn for a year or longer; and the interest rate on long-term promises to pay is fixed at the time the loan is made. Costs increase with higher commodity prices; but, because of the lag in adjustment, businessmen have larger profits. In addition, many firms profit because of the increase in money value of inventories and other assets. But, normally, the greatest increase in profits is due to the expansion in volume of sales. This last source of profit is particularly important in industry, where most goods are produced under conditions in which the per unit costs decrease with the expansion of total output.

Debtors are in a favored position because they are able to pay their debts with smaller amounts of goods and services. For example, an Illinois farmer may give a bank a mortgage for $10,000 when corn is selling for 50 cents per bushel. His debt corresponds to 20,000 bushels of corn. If this debt matures when corn is selling for $1.00 per bushel, his debt in terms of his chief product has been reduced to 10,000 bushels of corn; and, other things being equal, it is just twice as easy to pay the mortgage. But many debtors do not gain from higher prices, because their incomes do not increase in proportion to the change in prices. For example, many urban homeowners are pensioners, fixed salaried employees, and wage earners who have no commodities to sell. Unless their money incomes increase, they receive no debt relief from higher prices.

Rising prices are not necessarily the solution for the debt problem, for they stimulate speculation, and the volume of debts increases during such periods. Although many debtors take advantage of the better times to pay off their obligations, a much larger number do the contrary. As a result, when most boom periods end, the people of the country are more deeply in debt than they were during the preceding period of low prices.

When prices are rising, creditors tend to lose, because the real interest rate lags behind the price change. If the rate continues at 3 per cent per year, this income will buy fewer goods. This loss in income may be small compared to the loss in principal during a period of falling prices and accompanying business failures. It is this situation that explains the large number of bank failures during depressions.

When prices rise, the purchasing power of fixed income, wages, and salaries decreases. Although the wage rate tends to lag behind the rise (or fall) in prices, this is not the most important thing to consider in discussing the position of a laborer. If he receives $1.00 per hour for working but eight hours a week, he is not nearly so well off as a second worker who receives 50 cents per hour but works forty hours per week. During slowly rising prices production increases and the laboring classes share in prosperity because of increase in number of hours of work, overtime pay, and the larger number employed. The increase in total number of wage dollars offsets many-fold the loss in purchasing power of one dollar, due to the rise in prices.

The conclusion to be reached from the above discussion is that changes in the purchasing power of a unit of money are of no advantage if the decrease in the number of dollars to be spent more than offsets the change in purchasing power. Between the two types of price changes, up and down, rising prices tend to be the most beneficial because of the effects on production. Thus, if production is stimulated up to a point where all available capital, land, and labor resources are in use, society benefits. However, a rise in prices beyond that point leads only to competition among businessmen for already employed resources.

Stable General Prices Are Best.—The ideal is to have the general price level stabilized at a high level of employment, subject to the qualification that over a long period of time prices should be permitted to fall if justified by a decrease in cost of production. In this way advantages resulting from technical improvements may be passed along to the general public in the form of lower prices.

While the effects of changes in the value of money on distribution of wealth and income have been properly stressed in economic literature, the total welfare may not be affected, because losses of one group will be offset by gains of the other group. But when a prolonged period of monetary instability undermines business confidence, lessens the volume of credit used in production, causes debtors to repudiate contracts, promotes strikes and other labor disturbances, leads to fluctuating international exchange rates, and causes harmful trade restriction policies, the whole system of contract, on which modern business is built, is threatened.

The foregoing conclusion that major price changes due to changes in the volume of money and credit should be eliminated has the same meaning as a statement that there should be no inflation or deflation of general prices. By "deflation" is meant a major contraction or decrease in general prices that is due to or conditioned by a decrease in the supply or turnover of money and credit. By "inflation" is meant a major expansion or increase in general prices that is due to or conditioned by an increase in the supply or turnover of money and credit. It does not mean merely creating new "printing press" money, leaving the gold standard, devaluing the gold dollar, permitting free coinage of silver, or any other development which may increase the supply of money and credit. While such changes are inflationary in nature, no inflation exists until there is a general increase in the price of things, for such changes in the supply of money and credit may be offset by a number of other factors. Many alarming monetary changes may have no general effect on prices.

QUESTIONS AND PROBLEMS

1. Make a list of all the qualities of a good monetary system. Should there be added: "The costs of materials used should represent only a small part of the wealth of the community"? Why?
2. What relationship, if any, was there among (*a*) the 1935 proposal to issue a 1 mill and ½ cent pieces, (*b*) state sales taxes, and (*c*) the opposition of "liberal" senators to the two proposed new coins?
3. Identify: (*a*) primary monetary unit, (*b*) secondary monetary units, and (*c*) money of account.
4. What steps have been taken to make United States money "easy to handle, to stack, and to store"?

5. What justification is there for the United States Treasury "Know Your Money" campaign? Have you co-operated to the extent that you can give the names of the statesmen whose portraits appear on the five lowest denominations?
6. In financial military literature there appeared brown-seal dollars and yellow-seal dollars. Identify each.
7. Is Gresham's law in operation at all times or only during periods of financial disturbances? Why?
8. What is meant by "the value of money"?
9. How are changes in the value of money measured? Explain.
10. Define an index number.
11. "But the original purpose of index numbers—to measure the purchasing power of money—will remain a principal, if not the principal, use of index numbers" (Fisher, *Making of Index Numbers*, p. 369). Do you agree? What are other uses of price index numbers?
12. Why is the following advice important: "Know your index numbers"?
13. "The fall in the general level of commodity prices clearly can have no effect on the physical equipment of the world. . . . . Whence, then, arises the disturbance that impedes the smooth course of exchange of the commodities the world produces?" Sources and reference: Strakosch, Sir Henry, "The Economic Consequences of Changes in the Value of Gold," *Selected Documents Submitted to the Gold Delegation of the Financial Committee*, (Geneva: League of Nations, 1930), pp. 20-37. Discuss.
14. Do you agree with the following? Why? "That the interests which would suffer most from serious inflation are: (*a*) Our working people whose wages would rise less rapidly than their costs of living; (*b*) The beneficiaries of life-insurance policies; (*c*) Our bank depositors; (*d*) Hospitals; (*e*) Colleges; and (*f*) Other great scientific and public welfare institutions, most of whose endowment funds are invested in bonds and mortgages." Statement of the Executive Committee of the Economists' National Committee on Monetary Policy, November 24, 1933.
15. Comment on each of the following: (*a*) a five dollar bill with the portrait of Washington on its face, (*b*) a mill equals one-hundredth of a cent, and (*c*) farmers do not gain from inflation because their costs increase in proportion to their money income.
16. What types of price movements are shown by Chart I? Note significance of each. Is there any relationship between your answer to this question and your answer to (*c*) of Question 15?
17. Which do you think is the more serious aspect of price fluctuations: the effects upon distribution or the effects upon the creation of wealth?
18. Define carefully what is meant by "inflation" and "deflation"; also, "inflationary" and "deflationary."

REFERENCES

Annual Report of the Director of the Mint for the Fiscal Year Ended June 30, 1944. Washington, D.C.: U.S. Government Printing Office, 1945.

Annual Reports of the Secretary of the Treasury on the State of the Finances for Fiscal Years, 1928 and *1929.* Washington, D.C.: U.S. Government Printing Office.

Burns, A. R. *Money and Monetary Policy in Early Times.* New York: Alfred A. Knopf, Inc., 1927.

Carothers, Neil. *Fractional Money.* New York: John Wiley & Sons, Inc., 1930.

Coughlin, Rev. C. E. *Money: Questions and Answers.* Royal Oak, Mich.: National Union for Social Justice, 1936.

Dewey, D. R. *Financial History of the United States,* pp. 18-24; 28-30., 11th ed. New York: Longmans, Green & Co., 1931.

DePuy, W. A. "The Geography of Money," *National Geographic Magazine,* Vol. LII, No. 6 (December, 1927), pp. 744-68.

Kinley, David. *Money,* chaps. i-v. New York: Macmillan Co., 1904.

Layton, W. T., and Crowther, G. *An Introduction to the Theory of Prices,* chaps. i and ii. 2d ed. London: Macmillan Co., Ltd., 1935.

McLeod, H. D. *The Elements of Economics,* Vol. I, pp. 270-72. New York: D. Appleton & Co., 1881.

Mills, F. C. *Statistical Methods,* chaps. vi and ix. Revised. New York: Henry Holt & Co., Inc., 1938.

Mitchell, W. C. *The Making and Using of Index Numbers.* Bull. No. 173 of U.S. Department of Labor, Bureau of Labor Statistics (1915); No. 284 (1921 rev.); No. 656, Part I (1938).

Monetary Units and Coinage Systems of the Principal Countries of the World. Washington, D.C.: Compiled in Office of Director of Mint, 1929.

Money and Banking, 1935/1936, Vols. I and II. Geneva: League of Nations, 1936.

United States Coinage Laws, 1792-1894. Washington, D.C.: U.S. Government Printing Office, 1894.

Young, J. P., *European Currency and Finance,* pp. 189-204; 396-404. Commission of Gold and Silver Inquiry, U.S. Senate. Washington, D.C.: U.S. Government Printing Office, 1924.

Chapter III

INTRODUCTION TO THE THEORY OF THE VALUE OF MONEY

The Problem of Monetary Science

Changes in the Value of Money.—A study of money is of almost universal interest because extreme changes in its value disrupt the current social and economic system more than any other type of national or international emergency, with the exception of wars. In the preceding chapter the value of money was identified as its purchasing power, that is, the amount of goods and services for which it may be exchanged. It was noted that, if the value of money is increasing, the general price level is decreasing; and if the value of money is decreasing, the general price level is increasing. Thus, an explanation of why the value of money changes is also an explanation of why general prices change. Since businessmen are greatly interested in prices, most of the literature on the value of money is written in terms of price changes rather than in terms of changes in the value of money; but students must realize that they are but different aspects of the same problem.

TABLE 4

Price and Value of Money Changes

Year	Prices	Value of Money	Year	Prices	Value of Money
1913	69.8	143.3	1940	78.6	127.7
1920	154.4	64.8	1941	87.3	114.0
1926 (base)	100.0	100.0	1942	98.8	101.2
1929	95.3	104.9	1943	103.1	96.9
1932	64.8	154.3	1944	104.0	96.0
1937	86.3	115.9	1945	105.6	94.7
1939	77.1	129.7			

Source: Bureau of Labor Statistics, Index Number of Wholesale Commodity Prices. (1945 estimated.)

Actual changes in general prices and the value or purchasing power of money are roughly illustrated by changes in general price index numbers and their reciprocals. Since Table 4 is based on wholesale commodity index numbers only and not on all things for which money is spent, it merely suggests some price changes and value of money changes that have occurred since 1913 in the United States. The fact to keep in mind is that, as general prices change, the value of money varies inversely.

Special versus General Causes of Price Changes.—Changes in general prices rarely receive more than academic interest unless the rate of change is rapid and extreme enough to attract the attention of the public. When there is an increase in the price of wheat from 50 cents to $1.00 per bushel, most individuals immediately conclude that there has been a sudden decrease in the supply of wheat or a sudden increase in the demand, or both. When the value of a dollar increases from a purchasing power of from three to six dozen eggs, ten to twelve loaves of bread, ten to twenty-five pounds of cotton, fifteen to thirty-seven pounds of brown sugar, seven to eleven quarts of fluid milk, etc., the public seldom asks if there has been a sudden decrease in the supply of money, a sudden increase in the demand for money, or both.

Changes in the general price level are usually attributed to what appear to be immediate causes. Rising prices are ascribed to the actions of the party in power, to strikes and other labor union activities, to the monopolists, to the speculators, to the capitalists, and to unfavorable weather. Likewise, falling prices are ascribed to the activities of the party in power, to reduction in hours of labor, to unemployment, to the "money trust," to speculators, to businessmen's strikes, to consumers' strikes, to oversaving, and to favorable weather. Although these lists of stated reasons for rising and falling prices are not complete, they give an idea of the confusion that still exists even though the general principles that govern changes in general prices or purchasing power of money are more widely understood today than in the past.

If the stabilization of the value of money is to be brought about, knowledge of the basic causes of its fluctuations must be generally understood. If "concentrated attention is paid to the problem, there is good reason to hope that it will not ultimately prove to be beyond the wits of mankind to devise means of taming and controlling the monetary system, the most wonderful of all his social inventions."[1]

---

[1] Layton, W. T., and Crowther, G., *An Introduction to the Study of Prices* (2d ed.), p. 222.

During a Given Period of Time in the Markets, the Flow of Money Payments Equals the Money Value of the Flow of Things

The value of money, like the value of any other commodity, is determined by the supply and the demand. Such an approach to the explanation of the value of money does not mean that the supply and demand factors are identical with those employed in the explanation of the value of other goods, but merely that two sets of value-determining factors must be recognized. During a given time period there is a flow of money against a flow of things (goods, services, and securities) in the market places. A stream of money includes coins, paper money, checks, and other money substitutes. The stream of things for which money is spent includes goods, services, and securities.[2] Within a given time period the value of the two flows will be the same, because the dollar value of money given for things must equal the money value of things given for money.

Money is different from things for which it is exchanged because it is designed for continued use in the markets. The same coins will be offered repeatedly for things and will continually be changing owners. Thus a dime which is used ten times during a given period has the same effect as one dollar used but once. During a given period of time the supply of money is the product of two factors—the number of monetary units (including money substitutes) times the velocity at which money circulates.

The physical flow of things varies during a given time period. Services of teachers, doctors, barbers, and others appear once, to be replaced by new services on the following days; goods are soon withdrawn from the markets to be consumed by individuals; and new securities are purchased by investors to be held for income or appreciation in value. In addition to the number of units, the turnover of things in the market is a factor to be reckoned with in explaining the total volume of transactions; for example, a bushel of wheat that appears ten times in the market has the same effect as ten bushels that appear but once.

The relationship noted between the flow of money and the flow of things may be presented in an algebraic equation. There are a

[2] Marget, A. W., *The Theory of Prices*, Vol. I, p. 576, *passim*. Also see chap. xvii.

number of so-called "equations of exchange" in use today, but the most famous is that of Dr. Irving Fisher,[3] who states it thus:

$$MV + M'V' = PT.$$

In this equation all the symbols on the left side of the equation represent flow of money, and the symbols on the right side of the equation represent the money value of the total transactions. The definitions of these symbols are as follows:

M = Money in circulation (coin and paper money except that in bank reserves and in the Treasury)
V = Velocity of circulation (found by dividing the total volume of money payments in a period by the number of units in circulation)
M' = Bank demand deposits. (Bank deposits with other banks are excluded so as not to count redeposited funds twice)
V' = Velocity of circulation of deposits (found by dividing "bank debits to individual accounts" in a given period by the average number of dollars of individual deposits during that period)
P = General price level
T = Volume of total transactions

Such an equation of exchange tells nothing about the causal relationship between changes in the money factors, volume of transactions, and prices. If desired, both sides of the equation may be divided by T and the equation would appear as

$$\frac{MV + M'V'}{T} = P.$$

The equation may also be written as

$$PT = MV + M'V' \quad \text{or} \quad P = \frac{MV + M'V'}{T}$$

Different definitions may be given to symbols in the equation without destroying its value as a simple approach to the problem of explaining the value of money. The term $M'V'$ may be dropped and MV used to stand for all money factors. Other symbols may be added to represent special divisions of the money side or the goods side of the equation.[4]

The equation of exchange in its "Fisherine" or other forms is "nothing more or less than shorthand expressions designed to indicate the nature of the variables whose operations can be shown to

[3] Fisher, Irving, and Brown, H. G., *The Purchasing Power of Money*, chap. 8.

[4] Marget, *op. cit.*, pp. 570-72, *passim.*

influence prices."[5] It is a simple algebraic formula representing the statement which appears at the beginning of this section: "During a given period of time in the markets, the flow of money payments equals the money value of the flow of things."

The Flow of Money Payments

The equation of exchange may be broken down into two divisions: the factors that make up the flow of money payments and the factors that make up the flow of things. In terms of the equation, the first problem is one of explaining how changes in the symbols M, M', V, and V' tend to affect P; and the second problem is one of explaining how changes in T tend to affect P. The flow of money payments, which is considered in this section, involves (1) the quantity of the circulating media (M and M') and (2) the velocity of the circulating media (V and V').

The Quantity of the Circulating Media.—In Chapter I it was noted that there are three important means of payment: standard money, paper money and coins, and deposit currency. The supply of money is the total stock of money in a country. One part is held by individuals, business firms, and public corporations as cash balances ready for spending; the second part is "kept as currency and banking reserves held against forms of money substitutes which, in turn, make up part of the total of cash balances."[6] The existing stock of gold money is used for reserves and for settlement of unfavorable balances in international trade and finance. It is almost wholly removed from actual contact with the exchange of things in the market places. It influences prices indirectly through its effects upon the supply of currency and credit.

The supply of currency affecting the price level is properly thought of as the hand-to-hand money used by the public for spending or held at a particular time as a cash balance for spending purposes. It includes all coins and paper money outside of banks, Federal Reserve banks, and the United States Treasury; that is, money in circulation minus the amount held by banks.[7] Actually, at any one

[5] *Ibid.* p. 81. Italics in the original are omitted.

[6] *Ibid.* p. 462.

[7] See current issues of the *Federal Reserve Bulletin* for statistics of "Money in Circulation," and "Deposits and Currency and Adjusted Deposits of All Banks and Currency outside of Banks."

time, there will be but a small percentage of money in circulation, that is, "on the wing" or moving from hand to hand.

Most of this money will be in the pocketbooks of individuals, in money safes, in cash registers of business firms, and in other places where it is kept as a cash balance. The total number of times that the average monetary unit changes hands during a year may be sixty, and the total amount of time involved in transfers of money for things may not be more than one hour. During the remainder of the year the average unit is held for spending as a cash balance. The total M will be represented by the total average cash balance held during the year by the public in the form of coins and paper money.

The supply of deposit currency affecting the price level is defined as total demand deposits minus those redeposited with other banks.[8] At any particular time, title to only a small part of deposits will be changing hands in payment for things. The total M' will be represented by the total average cash balance held during the year by the public in the form of demand deposits. Time deposits are excluded because they are normally transferred into hand-to-hand money or deposit currency before they are spent.

The absolute amount of an individual's cash balance will depend in part upon the size and nature of his income, both actual and anticipated. If it is small and is received weekly, it will be spent more or less regularly throughout the week. If it is large and received monthly or quarterly, the absolute size of the cash balance will tend to be much larger and will be spread over a longer period of time. It will be greater in commercial and industrial sections, where there is greater dependence on markets, than in agricultural sections, where more of the needs of the people are provided without the use of money. It will be small when purchases are made on credit and large when cash payments are made. Every family will keep available some cash and/or money on deposit with banks to purchase food, clothing, shelter, and services demanded from day to day. In addition, many individuals keep funds for investments, emergencies, and unusual expenditures of other types.

[8] The item "demand deposits adjusted" that appears as a memorandum item in the tables in the *Federal Reserve Bulletin* showing assets and liabilities of banks shows the aggregate net balances in the checking accounts of individuals, partnerships, corporations, and state and local governments, after allowing for checks outstanding against these deposits. It excludes interbank and United States government deposits. In a general way it represents the cash resources of the community placed on deposit with banks.

A person who has an income of $2,000 per year does not have $2,000 in money and credit at a given time. If he keeps an average of $150 in his pocketbook and at his bank, this constitutes his average cash balance or his supply of money and credit. If the bank finds it necessary to hold a reserve of $30 against his deposit, the total stock of money and credit involved is $180, not $2,000. Likewise the cash balance of a business firm is not its total receipts in money but the average amount of funds kept as hand-to-hand money and deposit currency. During a year the average amount of money and credit in businessmen's cash balances, as compared to the total volume of trade and income of the country, is extremely small; and the total volume of money and credit of the nation relative to the total volume of money payments for goods, services, and securities is likewise small.

Quantity Theory of Money.—The supply of the circulating media consists of the total amount of funds kept as cash balances by the public in the form of money and deposit currency. How do changes in the supply of hand-to-hand money and deposit currency tend to affect general prices? Economists differ in the amount of emphasis they place upon the effects of changes in the supply of money and bank credit upon changes in the value of money or the price level. At one extreme are the rigid quantitative theorists who assume that a definite relationship exists between changes in the quantity of money and bank deposits, on the one hand, and changes in prices and the volume of transactions, on the other. They take the position that the value of money depends upon its supply.

When the supply of money and bank credit is relatively plentiful, its value will be low, because many units will be needed to make purchases. When the supply of money is relatively scarce, its value will be high, because fewer units will be needed to make purchases. If there are ten million units of money to be exchanged against a million units of goods and services, the average price per unit will be ten; but if there are only one million units of money to be exchanged against a million units of goods and services, the average price per unit will be one. John Stuart Mill said of this: "That an increase of the quantity of money raise prices and a diminution lowers them is the most elementary proposition in the theory of currency."[9]

[9] Mill, J. S., *Principles of Political Economy* (Ashley's ed.), p. 495.

But such an "elementary proposition" is naturally subject to qualification in order to make it fit modern circumstances. The effects of an increase in the supply of the circulating media may be more than offset by an increase in the supply of goods. Prices will tend to fall when there is an increase in the supply of circulating media which is accompanied by an even greater increase in the supply of goods. The available supply of money and bank credit is used over and over again during a given time period. A change in this turnover will cause a similar change in prices, provided, of course, that the other factors remain the same.

Similarly, an increase in the supply of money and deposit currency may have little or no effect on prices if there is a decrease in the turnover of money. On the other hand, during certain periods there may be an increase in prices and an increase in the volume of business which is financed entirely by an increase in the turnover of money and deposit currency. This change in velocity of money tends to be one of the most important factors operating during the short-term swing in business that is known as the "trade, or business, cycle."

In order to meet these criticisms of the quantity theory, writers have usually stated that changes in the supply of money and credit will cause similar and proportionate changes in prices if other things remain the same. Of course, other things never remain the same, but the assumption is similar to that made by other social scientists. The economists are trying to do in the theoretical field what the physicists and chemists are able to do in part in their laboratories, that is, to eliminate all the disturbing factors while studying the nature of just one factor. Certainly in studying the effects of changes in the supply of money and credit, it is necessary to take into account such factors as changes in the volume of transactions and changes in the velocity of money and deposit currency. These elements are so important that some writers have questioned the "quantity theory" in its entirety. However, as stated by Dr. E. W. Kemmerer,[10] "the differences between the supporters of the quantity theory and its opponents" amounts to "differences in the relative importance attributed to certain factors entering into the determination of the general price level." The quantity theory is merely a doctrine em-

[10] Kemmerer, E. W., *Money and Credit Instruments in Their Relations to General Prices*, p. 2.

phasizing the importance of money among the factors which affect prices.

Unfortunately, many beginning students and others forget the fact that a change in the quantity of money and credit will affect prices only if other things remain the same. The best illustration of this fact may be found in the manipulation of the price of gold during 1933 and the first month of 1934. To summarize, the quantity theory of money is that a change in the supply of money and deposit currency, other things remaining the same, will be accompanied by a similar and proportionate change in the price level. The value of money changes inversely and is the reciprocal of the change in the quantity of money, provided other things remain the same. These changes may be illustrated as follows:

Supply of Money and Deposit Currency	Prices	Purchasing Power, or Value of a Dollar
A. Increase 25%	Increase 25%	Decrease 20%
B. Decrease 25%	Decrease 25%	Increase 33⅓%

Velocity of the Circulating Media.—The remaining factors on the money side of the equation which affect prices are the velocity of money and the velocity of bank deposits. As previously stated, during a given period of time, money and demand deposits appear on the average many times in payment for things purchased. The more often a unit of money or credit is presented in payment for things, the greater is the turnover, velocity, or efficiency of this unit. It is obvious that a $1.00 bill moving rapidly from hand to hand will do as much exchanging as a $20.00 bill which moves twenty times less rapidly. This has been recognized for many years and is illustrated by the old English axiom: "A nimble six-pence will do the work of a lazy crown."

The average velocity of money is found by taking the total number of hand-to-hand dollar transactions completed with the use of money and dividing it by the average number of dollars in circulation or held as cash balances by the general public. Pocket money leaves no record of the number of times it is used in exchanging, but this is not true of deposit currency. Checks are charged against individual accounts at the banks, and photographic or written copies are kept as part of the permanent ledger record. The velocity of deposit currency for a year is found by dividing the total debits, or charges to individual accounts, by the average demand deposit for that period.[11] The assumption may be made that changes in the velocity of pocket money will be approximately the same as changes in the velocity of deposit currency. This does not mean that the two will circulate at the same rate, but merely that the changes in velocity are assumed to be the same.

In analyzing the reasons for changes in the velocity of the circulating media, it is necessary to examine what individuals do "to retard or advance the rate at which they spend their cash balances," velocity being "the simple resultant of the decisions which the individuals in charge of the administration of cash balances make with respect to the size of the cash balance that they choose to keep relative to outlay."[12]

The amount of money kept as cash balances relative to outlay or expenditure within a given time is subject to wide fluctuations; and this is particularly true of the cash balances of businessmen. Relative cash balances increase during depressions and falling price periods and decrease during booms and rising price periods. During depressions businessmen make commitments cautiously, thereby conserving their supply of ready purchasing power. They postpone buying of goods as long as possible in order to profit from lower prices. As machinery, plants, and other capital assets are not replaced immediately, the durable goods industries operate at only a fraction of their capacities. The opposite situation exists during boom periods. Consumers purchase about the same volume of goods during good years as during bad years, but during the latter periods many purchases may be postponed until the economic skies brighten. As a result, the production curve of the durable goods industries is subject to much wider fluctuation than that of light manufacturing industries.

---

[11] Because of their importance as barometers of changes in business, several series of bank debits are now being gathered and published by the Board of Governors of the Federal Reserve System in the *Federal Reserve Bulletin.* These series, covering 334 reporting centers, include debits to total deposit accounts, except interbank accounts; and debits to demand deposit accounts, except interbank and government. By dividing these debit figures by the average demand deposits, the Board computes and publishes the annual rate of turnover of total deposits, except interbank for New York City and 333 other reporting centers; and the annual rate of turnover of demand deposits, except interbank and government for New York City and 100 leading cities. See current issues of *Federal Reserve Bulletin* and Board of Governors of the Federal Reserve System, *Banking and Monetary Statistics,* pp. 230-33.

[12] Marget, *op. cit.,* p. 419, *passim.* Italics in the original are omitted.

If people thought in terms of an increase in the value of money or a fall in general prices, they would act and reason as follows: "There is an expected rise in the value of money of which we will take advantage by disposing of our holdings of goods and securities and by increasing our supply of money." If the supply of the circulating media remains the same, this movement away from goods and securities will increase the demand for the circulating media and decrease its velocity. If other factors remain the same, the value

CHART II

Rate of Turnover of Deposits at Commercial Banks

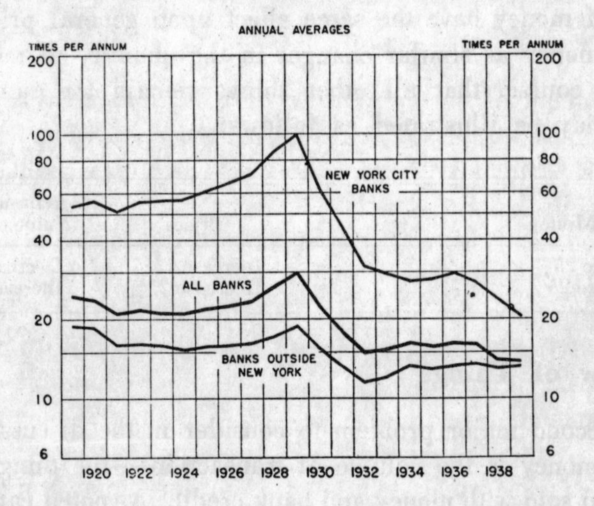

Plotted on ratio scale. Based on ratio of estimated debits excluding interbank deposits and items in process of collection.

Source: *Federal Reserve Bulletin,* January, 1940, p. 7.

of money will increase (the general price level will fall), and their expectations will be realized.

The same results follow whether people are guided by price changes or changes in the value of money. They expect a fall in prices of goods and securities and therefore sell them and transfer their stores of wealth to currency and deposits in banks. Then, instead of spending their cash balances at the normal rate, they hold them, with the effect that the velocity of the circulating media decreases and the price level tends to decrease. The use of money for hoarding is included in the cash balance; otherwise one must conclude that hoarded money is never spent.

Changes in velocity of circulation of demand deposits have played an important role in recent American monetary history. From 1929 to 1933 deposits decreased over 20 per cent, and their velocity decreased by 45 per cent (see Chart II). The recovery during 1933 was financed entirely by an increase in velocity.[13] Since 1934 the increase in production and prices has been financed by an increase in deposits. On the other hand, there has been a decline in velocity, and the expansion in prices and production has not been in proportion to the increase in volume of money and credit. Changes in the velocity of money have the same effect upon general prices or the value of money as similar changes in the quantity of money, provided, of course, that all other things remain the same. These changes may be illustrated as follows:

Velocity of Money	Prices	Purchasing Power, or Value of a Dollar
A. Increase 25%	Increase 25%	Decrease 20%
B. Decrease 25%	Decrease 25%	Increase 33⅓%

The Flow of Things

The second major problem to consider in the discussion of the value of money is the volume of transactions—the things that are bought and sold with money and bank credit. As noted earlier in the discussion, within a given period of time the dollar value of these transactions is equal to the money and bank credit dollars given in payment for them. The question to be answered here is how changes in the volume of transactions (T) will tend to affect changes in the price level.[14]

Since the total volume of transactions is used in the equation of exchange as one of the two factors explaining the total value of things for which money and credit are spent (PT), it logically follows that the prices of all things should be used as a guide to changes in the purchasing power of money. To use other price index numbers, for example, index numbers for consumers' goods, would leave

[13] *Federal Reserve Bulletin*, October, 1933, p. 595.

[14] See Marget, *op. cit.*, p. 484, *passim.*

the door open to erroneous conclusions because of the increase in prices of things not included in the construction of the index numbers. The use of a wholesale commodity price index number during the late nineteen twenties as a guide to changes in purchasing power showed a decline in the general commodity price level, while the prices of services and securities were increasing.

If there are objections to the combination of the prices of such different things as commodities and securities, separate index numbers may be constructed, using different symbols for each of the major types of price groups. The plurality of prices may be shown by letting PT appear as $Pg\ Tg$, $Ps\ Ts$, and $Psec\ Tsec$, representing, respectively, the money values of goods, services, and securities.

Within a given period of time the demand for money or the volume of business transactions changes for one or both of two reasons: (1) changes in the volume of goods, services, and securities to be exchanged and (2) changes in the frequency or velocity of circulation of goods, etc. Changes in velocity or turnover are of minor importance compared to changes in the actual volume of things. A change in output of goods is the most important factor causing changes in goods transactions. Changes in frequency of transactions are of most importance when the purchase and sale of securities, real estate, and other goods of a more permanent nature are considered. The number of times that services and goods change hands is small compared to the number of times that securities may appear upon the market. Whether due to a change in the volume of things or merely to a change in the number of transactions, an increase or decrease in the volume of transactions means an increase or decrease in the demand for the circulating media (money and deposit currency).

An increase in the demand for the circulating media will tend to increase its value. If the supply of circulating media and its velocity remain fixed, an increase in the volume of transactions will mean that each monetary unit will be exchanged for a larger volume of things (commodities, services, and securities). In other words, the general price level will fall, and the purchasing power of money will increase by the reciprocal of this change.

A decrease in the demand for the circulating media as represented by a decrease in the volume of transactions tends to decrease the value of money. If the supply of circulating media and its velocity remain fixed, a decrease in the volume of transactions will mean that each monetary unit will be exchanged for a smaller volume of things. In other words, the general price level will increase and the purchasing power of money will decrease by the reciprocal of this change. These changes may be illustrated as follows:

Volume of Transactions	Prices	Purchasing Power or Value of a Dollar
A. Increase 25%	Decrease 20%	Increase 25%
B. Decrease 25%	Increase 33⅓%	Decrease 25%

Summary of the Theory of the Value of Money

During a given time period there is a flow of money against a flow of things (goods, services, and securities) in the market places. The stream of money payments includes those made with coins, paper money, and deposit currency. If the flow of money payments increases, owing to an increase in the volume or an increase in turnover relative to the flow of things actually sold, prices of things increase and the value of money decreases. In terms of symbols in the equation, if there is an increase in M, M', V, and V' relative to changes in T, then P will increase. If the flow of money actually spent decreases, owing to a decrease in volume or a decrease in turnover relative to the flow of things sold, prices of things decrease and the value of money increases. In terms of the equation, if there is a decrease in M, M', V, and V' relative to changes in T, then P will decrease.

Underlying the changes in the money factors are all phases of economic life which influence the size of cash balances held by individuals and others for spending during a given time period. An increase in total amount of funds held, with no changes in spending habits, will tend to cause prices to increase, because the increase in the money income of an individual will be spent for things. If there is no increase in spending to accompany the increase in the amount of the circulating media, the relative size of cash balances will increase, the velocity of the circulating media will decline, and there will be no increase in prices.

In addition, it must be appreciated that the symbol T includes a multitude of transactions of all types during a specified time period.

Instead of there being one price level, there are many price levels to be considered in breaking down the total transactions; these include those for goods, for services, and for securities. Each of these may in turn be subdivided. If the assumed increase in the absolute size of cash balances for a period of time is spent for things, the effects will vary depending upon whether the outlays are for goods, services, or securities. Similarly, the volume of things and the prices (actual and expected) will have a considerable effect upon the outlays for them by consumers, traders, and others. Because of the large number of variables involved, the effects of a change in one of the factors in the equation of exchange is not always predictable without knowledge of how the others are changing. All of the factors influencing the supply and demand for money and money substitutes must be recognized in explaining changes in the value of money.

War Changes

Following the brief summary of the theory of the value of money, let us consider some of the significant changes that occurred during World War II. According to the Treasury's circulation statement, the amount of money in circulation increased from $11,000,000,000 at the end of 1941 to $27,000,000,000 on August 31, 1945. Total demand deposits in all banks increased from $44,000,000,000 to $85,000,000,000, and "adjusted demand deposits" increased from $39,000,000,000 to $64,000,000,000. All currency statistics suggest that inflationary changes took place in M and M' during the war years.

Business index numbers suggest the extent to which the total physical volume of transactions increased during the war period.[15] This expansion occurred not only in war goods but also slightly in civilian goods. In the latter field most of the expansion was primarily in nondurable goods, because production of durable consumers' goods (household appliances, homes, and automobiles) declined sharply. Since most of the war increase in production was purchased by the government and withdrawn from the civilian markets (except government sale of surplus goods), there was no flow

[15] See *Federal Reserve Bulletin* for business index numbers showing changes in volume of production, employment, income payments, department store sales, and others.

of goods to offset the expanded supply of money and deposit currency. This created what economists call an "inflationary gap."

To aid in financing the war and to shorten this gap, consumers were urged to invest in government bonds. Repayment of mortgages and other forms of debt retirement were urged. Thus saving was encouraged, while transactions in nonwar goods and services were discouraged by rationing, priorities, allocations, requisitioning of plants and property, control over manpower, and other types of restrictive measures.

Deflationary changes in V and V' took place. Individual holdings of money increased; and, although this does not necessarily mean a decline in V, there are a number of reasons that suggest that velocity declined. Among these reasons are an increase in large denomination units of currency in circulation, rationing and other restrictions on purchase of consumer goods, and collection of federal income taxes at the source. These factors also affected V'. The annual rate of turnover of demand deposits, except interbank and government, in 100 leading cities declined from 19.4 in 1941 to 15.3 in August, 1945.

The increase in the supply of funds in excess of goods, services, and securities in the market has no inflationary effect on prices as long as the increase is held as an idle cash balance. With removal of war restrictions on spending, this situation may change. If the conclusion is that prices are going to rise, the general public will be more reluctant to hold money and more desirous to acquire goods before the value of money declines further.

One must not conclude from the changes noted above that there has been no change in prices. The Bureau of Labor Statistics index number of wholesale prices showed an increase of 12 points (93.6 in December, 1941, and 105.6 in August, 1945). Other price index numbers tend to confirm the conclusion that price changes were moderate, but price statistics do not tell the whole story. Reduction in quality of goods and services and black market operations are not adequately reflected in the price index numbers.

As noted in Chapter I, money is the center around which all other economic problems tend to cluster. Change in the value of money or general prices is one of the most important of these economic problems. The theory of the value of money offers no solution to this problem; it merely explains why the value of money changes.

Although it states that an increase in the supply of money and deposit currency tends to increase prices, it does not explain why the supply of money and bank credit increases. Furthermore, the theory of the

CHART III

CONSUMERS' PRICE INDEX IN TWO WORLD WARS*
(For Moderate Income Families in Large Cities)

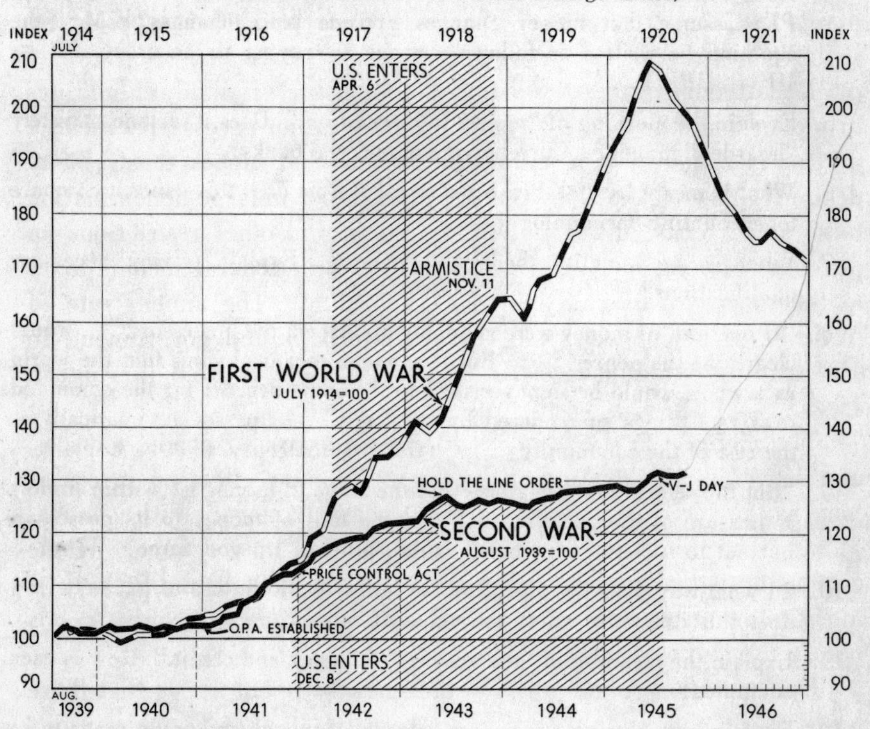

Source: U.S. Department of Labor, Bureau of Labor Statistics.

value of money should not be confused with the objectives of monetary policy. These objectives may be to keep the value of money equal to gold, to stabilize prices, to secure and maintain full employment, or to bring about a redistribution of wealth and income.

QUESTIONS AND PROBLEMS

1. Are economists justified in assuming "that other things remain the same" in developing economic theories? If not, are geographers who measure heights of land formation from sea level, physicists who assume that

certain things happen in a vacuum, and other scientists who base judgments upon assumptions also unjustified? Why?

2. Explain why the value of money varies inversely with the general level of prices.
3. Explain: "During a given period of time in the markets, a flow of money payments equals the value of the flow of things."
4. Does Fisher's statement of the equation of exchange ($MV + M'V' = PT$) assume that money changes precede price changes? May the equation be written as follows without destroying its accuracy, $PT = MV + M'V'$?
5. Explain the meaning of "money in circulation." Does it include privately "hoarded" money? Currency in commercial banks?
6. What is meant by "total cash balances"? How does this concept compare to accounting terminology?
7. What is the quantity theory of money? Explain, giving necessary qualifications.
8. "If one unit of money were suddenly abolished, the possessor . . . . would clearly be the poorer. . . . . But it is by no means obvious that the world as a whole would be impoverished in the same degree: for the command over real things surrendered by the loser . . . . passes automatically to the rest of the community . . . ." (Robertson, *Money*, p. 30). Explain.
9. "But the central fact remains—that the value of money is (within limits) a measure of the usefulness of any one unit of money to its possessor, but not to society as a whole" (*ibid.*, p. 31). Do you agree? Why?
10. In what way does the use of money differ from the use of goods? How does this difference affect the value of money?
11. Explain the meaning of "the velocity of money and credit." How is each computed?
12. Explain how, during a year, the velocity of money and credit tends to be affected by an increase in the size of your cash balance relative to your expenditures and outlays.
13. "In the United States, the velocity of circulation of demand deposits in the last quarter of 1935 was still only half as great as in 1929, while, in the United Kingdom, the rate of turnover of current accounts [demand deposits] was only about 30% less than at the beginning of 1930" (League of Nations, *Money and Banking, 1935/36*, Vol. I, p. 38). Account for these differences in velocity? Are these differences significant?
14. What is meant by the "plurality of prices"? Has this concept destroyed the meaning of PT? Explain.
15. Explain the differences among (*a*) volume of transactions, (*b*) volume of things, and (*c*) velocity of circulation of goods.

16. Explain how changes in each of the following tend to affect general prices: (*a*) increase in the circulating media, (*b*) decrease in the velocity of money and credit, and (*c*) increase in the volume of transactions.
17. May there be a general increase in the value of all commodities? In the prices of all commodities? Explain.
18. How did each of the factors in the equation of exchange change during World War II? Explain.
19. What is meant by an "inflationary gap"?
20. Variations in the value of money may originate in M, M', V, V', or T, but most frequently they result from concomitant changes in all five. Discuss.
21. The fruits of our postwar prosperity "can be divided three ways: To owners of industry in the form of profits, to labor in the form of wages, to consumers in the form of low prices of goods" (Sullivan, Mark, "Low Prices Deemed Essential if Depression Is to Be Avoided," *New York Herald Tribune* (September 30, 1945, sec. 11, p. 2). Discuss.
22. Distinguish between the theory of the value of money and objectives of monetary policy. Illustrate.

REFERENCES

Anderson, B. M. *The Value of Money*, Part II. New York: Macmillan Co., 1922.

Angell, J. W. *The Behavior of Money*. New York: McGraw-Hill Book Co., Inc., 1936.

Board of Governors of the Federal Reserve System. *Banking and Monetary Statistics*, pp. 230-54. Washington, D.C.: Board of Governors of the Federal Reserve System, 1943.

Chandler, L. V. *An Introduction to Monetary Theory*, chap. iv. New York: Harpers & Bro., 1940.

Currie, L. B. *The Supply and Control of Money in the United States*. Cambridge: Harvard University Press, 1934.

Fisher, Irving. *Stabilizing the Dollar*. New York: Macmillan Co., 1920.

Gayer, A. D. (editor) *The Lessons of Monetary Experience*. Farrar & Rinehart, Inc., 1937.

Halm, G. N. *Monetary Theory*, chaps. ii, vi, vii, and viii. Philadelphia: Blakiston Co., 1942.

Hansen, A. H. *Economc Stabilization in an Unbalanced World*, chaps. xviii and xx. New York: Harcourt, Brace & Co., 1932.

Keynes, J. M. *A Treatise on Money*, Vol. I, Book II, London: Macmillan Co., Ltd., 1930.

Keynes, J. M. *Monetary Reform,* chaps. i and iii. New York: Harcourt, Brace & Co., 1924.

King, W. I. *The Causes of Economic Fluctuation.* New York: Ronald Press, 1939.

Layton, W. T., and Crowther, G. *An Introduction to the Theory of Prices,* 2d ed. London: Macmillan Co., Ltd., 1935.

Marget, A. W. *The Theory of Prices: A Re-examination of the Central Problems of Monetary Theory,* Vol. I. New York: Prentice-Hall, Inc., 1938.

Saulnier, R. J. *Contemporary Monetary Theory.* New York: Columbia University Press, 1938.

Warren, G. F., and Pearson, F. A. *Gold and Prices.* New York: John Wiley & Sons, Inc., 1935.

Chapter IV

THE GOLD STANDARD AND THE COMMODITY THEORY OF MONEY

The Meaning of the Standard of Value

The standard of value is that which is established by custom or authority as a rule for measuring exchange power of goods and services. Money appears in many forms, but one type is usually referred to as the "standard unit," and the thing that fixes the value of this standard unit is called the "monetary standard." The standard of value is merely a means to an end, a tool to be used in measuring value relationships at a particular time and also over a period of time. The value of the standard is important at a particular time because of its influence on the value of cash balances and debt contracts. Over a period of time, changes in the value of the standard, both actual and expected, are even more important because of their effects upon production, employment, and size and distribution of future income.

The main test of a standard is constancy. Custom, science, and governments have stabilized most of the units which are used to measure time, length, weight, etc. Most standards are artificial, but there are several exceptions. For example, nature has given man the year and the day, both natural units of time. Standardization of measuring units has permitted the standardization of machinery and manufacturing for international markets. In brief, modern production is possible because of standards of weights and measures.

But goods that are produced are not directly exchanged for other goods, and the vehicle by which exchanging takes place is money. If money is changing in value it adds to the hazards of trade. This change in value of money, as already noted, is one of the most disturbing factors in modern business. A standard of value that is free from expansion and contraction in value is just as essential to modern business as a constant system of weights and measures. Such a monetary standard would eliminate much of the instability of trade and employment and much of the fluctuation in the value of debts.

A relatively stable standard of value is no panacea for all industrial problems. It gives no assurance of full employment, and the price paid for premature stabilization might even mean stagnation. If there existed a monetary standard free from contraction and expansion in value, there would still be dislocations in trade, production, and employment because of changes in methods of production, changes in demand, mistakes in estimations of future markets, unwise use of credit, labor disputes, and changes in tax policies; but these changes are generally considered unimportant compared to general changes in industry caused by changes in the value of money. Few monetary problems have given rise to more controversy than the question of the standard of value. Throughout most of the nineteenth century the debate was over the relative merits of bimetallism and the gold standard (see Chap. VI). The current discussion is over the relative merits of at least a partially automatic gold standard and a managed paper money standard (see Chap. VIII).

What Is a Commodity Standard?

A country has a commodity standard if the value of its money is kept equal to that of some valuable good. For example, the gold standard is one in which the value of money is kept equal to gold. Theoretically, any single commercial staple, such as iron, steel, wheat, or copper, may be used. The primary requisite is that the commodity selected as the standard must have a stable value. It is unnecessary for everyone to have a use for the commodity, but its form should be such that promises to deliver may be accepted upon demand. These promises serve as media of exchange, and redemption of them is necessary even though there is no desire on the part of the owner to hold the thing which is promised. Millions of Americans used gold certificates for decades without seeing the gold they represented; likewise, certificates representing wheat, cotton, or iron might serve as well if one of these were the established standard.

The world has used many kinds of metals as standards of value because these commodities have been the best suited for coining and as media of exchange. They are divisible without loss and are homogeneous, durable, easy to recognize, capable of being impressed, portable, and valuable. Within recent times, being on a commodity standard has meant either gold or silver, or both; but gold has gradually been established as the ruling or standard commodity.

Reasons for Adoption of the Gold Standard

There are a number of reasons why gold became the standard of value for all leading Western nations during the nineteenth century. Bimetallism, operated on a national basis, proved unworkable in practice (see Chap. VI). The growth of international trade strengthened the desire of all commercial and industrial nations to be on a gold basis. England adopted the gold standard after the close of the Napoleonic Wars, and her commercial and industrial prosperity were the envy of the Western world. Her leadership in commerce, finance, and industry influenced all nations, and the ambitious ones naturally followed her example and adopted the gold standard. Finally the development of subsidiary coinage, paper money, and deposit currency permitted specialization in the monetary system. No longer was it necessary for the money commodity to serve as both the medium of exchange and the standard of value.

Since subsidiary coins, paper money, and deposit currency came to serve as the domestic media of exchange, gold was freed to serve as international money. Its great value in small bulk, its stability in value as compared to other commodities, and its prestige as a precious metal, all made gold an ideal international commodity standard of value and international medium of exchange. This conclusion does not mean that international conditions were ideal under the gold standard but merely that gold has been the best commodity standard with which the world has had any experience.

When most of the countries of the world are on a gold standard, the advantages of belonging to this group are increased. Considered from an international viewpoint, the main advantage of adherence to the gold standard is that it gives the world a uniform basis, after allowance for obstacles to trade, for comparing commodity and security prices. Since the moneys of all countries are kept equal to gold, they must be equal to each other. This uniform basis greatly facilitates foreign trade and international investment, which have never been so great as during the present century. Gold does give the world an international medium of exchange though not an international stable standard of value. The value of gold is subject to the same fluctuations in foreign as in domestic markets. Obviously, it cannot be a stable standard of value in one market and an unstable standard of value in another.

Characteristics of the Gold Standard

Types of Gold Standards.—The gold standard exists wherever the unit of value consists of a fixed quantity of gold.[1] There are three types of gold standards: the gold coin standard, the gold bullion standard, and the gold exchange standard. The three types often overlap and usually vary as to details, but each does have certain specific characteristics.

Countries on the gold coin standard provide for free coinage of gold, circulation of gold coins, unlimited legal tender for gold coins, redemption of paper money in gold coins, and freedom to melt gold coins. Countries on the gold bullion standard provide for purchase and sale of gold bullion by the government or central bank at fixed prices while countries on the gold exchange standard provide for purchase and sale of gold exchange by the government or central bank at fixed prices. All gold standard countries have a free market for gold which includes freedom to hoard, to export, or to import gold.

The Standard Monetary Unit.—In adopting a gold standard, countries customarily define the value of their standard monetary unit in terms of a fixed quantity of gold. But situations may exist in which countries are on a gold basis without having their monetary unit defined in that way. For example, a country may specify that its standard unit is a silver coin. If free coinage is not allowed and the value of the unit is kept equal to a fixed quantity of gold through foreign exchange operations, the country has a gold standard.

At one time the standard unit was nothing but a weight denomination of gold or silver. Illustrations of names of units which originated from weight units are the English pound and the Hebrew shekel. When governments inflated their currencies by debasing coins, that is, reducing fineness and weight, the pound and other weight-names as applied to money units lost all their original significance. The standard monetary unit in all gold standard countries, however, is a weight and not a value unit.

---

[1] Dr. Kemmerer's definition is as follows: "The gold standard, I would say, is a monetary system in which the unit of value, be it the dollar, the franc, the pound, or something else, in which prices and wages are customarily expressed, and in which debts are usually contracted, consists of the value of a fixed quantity of gold in an essentially free gold market" (Kemmerer, E. W., *The Gold Standard—Its Nature and Future*, p. 5).

The size or weight of the unit is significant, because it determines the number of dollars, francs, etc., that may be made from an ounce of gold and, therefore, the exchange ratio with all other countries on the gold standard. A country that selects as the size of its monetary unit one weighing 1/70 of an ounce of fine gold establishes an exchange ratio of 2 to 1 with a second country with a monetary unit weighing 1/35 of an ounce of fine gold. Since the exchange ratio influences the relative purchasing power of one currency in terms of all others in international trade, the selection of the size of a country's monetary unit is of great importance to all countries on the gold standard and to all others planning to adopt it.

For about one hundred years the United States gold dollar contained 23.22 grains of fine gold, and for this reason only $20.67 was coined from one ounce of fine gold. The new gold dollar contains only 13.714 grains of fine gold, which is 1/35 of a fine ounce, troy weight, of gold. In other words, one ounce of fine gold is $35.00 of standard money. In arriving at the present weight of the dollar, the President of the United States fixed the mint price of gold at $35.00 per ounce, and from this was calculated the weight of the dollar, that is, 480 grains divided by 35 equals 13.714 grains. But the theoretical gold dollar is only 9/10 fine, and so a dollar is defined as 15.238, or 15 5/21 grains of standard gold, 9/10 fine.

Keeping the Value of Gold Equal to a Fixed Amount of Money.—Parity in value is obtained between the value of gold and a fixed amount of money by free coinage of gold and by governmental purchase of gold and gold exchange at a fixed price. If the price of gold or gold exchange declines, owners will refuse to sell at the market price. Instead they will take the gold to the mint and have it minted into gold coins (assuming that there is free coinage) or will sell it to the government at the mint price. Similarly, the gold exchange draft will be sold to the government agency responsible for the operation of the gold exchange standard. Thus the value of gold and the value of gold exchange will be kept equal to a fixed amount of money.

Keeping the Value of the Circulating Media at Parity with the Gold Unit.—Parity in value is obtained between the circulating media and the gold unit by redemption of all types of the circulating media directly or indirectly in gold. If paper money and other types of the circulating media fall in value relative to gold, the public will demand gold coins,[2] gold bullion, or gold exchange. This privilege of redeeming the circulating media in gold provides the public with a means of testing the quality of their money at any time. If it is as good as gold, as the issuing agencies claim, then gold may be obtained in exchange for it.

In gold bullion standard countries, parity between gold and the circulating media is obtained by redeeming paper money in gold bullion, which in practice means the sale of gold at a fixed price. Since gold money is now used almost exclusively for reserve purposes and as a medium for the payment of international obligations, gold bars are more convenient than gold coins. The effects of freely selling gold bullion at a fixed price to the public will be practically the same as a policy of redeeming currencies in gold coin.

Since no gold coins are in circulation, one advantage of the gold bullion standard is the resulting economy in the use of gold. When Great Britain was operating on this type of gold standard (1925-31), an individual was required to present currency equivalent to 400 ounces of gold in order to get gold bullion. This provision eliminated most of the domestic demand for gold other than for reserve and arts purposes. On the other hand, the "gold bullion standard is a rich man's standard, operating above, and out of reach of, the man of small means. It would be responsive only to the behavior of the rich man, the banks, other business enterprises, and the government."[3] If the gold standard is thought of as an automatic brake in the hands of the public on banks and governments, there should be "no discrimination against any individual, particularly the man with small capital, and it is most important that he be able to exercise his preferences and thereby to register his doubts because these are part of the machinery of automatic braking which the gold coin standard provides."[4]

In gold exchange standard countries, redemption of paper money is in the form of exchange equal to gold in value, which in practice means the sale of gold drafts at a fixed price. Sight or demand drafts

---

[2] If gold coins are thought of as part of the circulating media, parity between them and gold is maintained by accepting gold coins at face value if within the legal tolerance of the mint; otherwise at weight value. Legal tolerance in weight for United States gold coins was 1/1,000 variation from the standard.

[3] Spahr, W. E., *The Case for the Gold Standard,* p. 28.

[4] *Ibid.,* p. 29.

are drawn upon a bank located in a foreign country on the gold standard, and if gold is wanted it is obtained abroad. This system places the country one step away from gold, but it is effective in keeping the value of the circulating media equal to gold. Between 1925 and 1931 over two-thirds of the countries were relying upon this method in whole or in part to remain on the gold standard. The chief disadvantage of this practice is that it places the future of the standard in the hands of the country in which it keeps its reserves. Its chief advantage is that it is the most economical type of gold standard to operate.

Free Gold Market Is Essential.—The keeping of the value of money equal to a definite quantity of gold is meaningless if the value of gold is manipulated as desired by governments that control the bulk of the world's gold supply. This situation is possible when governments hoard gold, preventing it from being used by the general public as a store of value in the industrial or commercial markets except as specified by those responsible for the gold hoards, and in international trade except under licenses issued by governments.

When countries are operating on a gold standard, in order to achieve parity between gold and the circulating media, there will be the utmost freedom with reference to the buying and selling of gold at home or abroad, with the governments and central banks holding the reservoir of gold that may be tapped at will by the general public without penalty or payment of excessive fees. As a consequence, the value of currency of any one gold standard country will not only be equal to gold in value but will be stable in value in terms of the currencies of all other gold standard countries.

Functions of Gold.—It is apparent from the preceding discussion that the quantity of gold held as reserves will set a limit to the volume of all forms of means of payment that may be issued. Whether desirable or not it would tend to act as a brake on the expansion of deposit currency and other means of payment. The adoption by all countries of the gold standard would tend to make all currencies interchangeable, one for the other, at the same value. A decrease in the value of gold in one country by 10 per cent would cause this country to be a good market in which to sell, a poor one in which to buy, thus tending to cause it to lose gold to pay for its unfavorable balance of trade until equilibrium would be re-established between its price structure and that of other gold standard countries. This readjustment would be aided by capital movements and other changes in the balance of payment items. Since these problems are discussed in detail in a later chapter, it is sufficient to note here that gold does give all gold standard countries a common monetary standard on which to carry on international trade, travel, and investment.

The Recent Gold Situation.—At the outbreak of World War II the United States was the only country that maintained a money value equivalent to that of a fixed weight of gold. Although the United States possessed about two-thirds of the monetary gold stock of the world, it did not make all forms of money redeemable in gold. It permitted neither a free domestic gold market nor the hoarding of gold. Furthermore, even the export of gold was subject to special rulings of government officials. The United States government did purchase gold at the price of $35 per fine ounce (or the foreign money equivalent in value) in unlimited quantities.

During the war the United States bought gold from its allies and sold it to those countries with which it had an unfavorable balance of trade. As a result of large imports of goods, particularly from Latin-American countries, the gold stock of the United States declined from over $22,785,000,000 in December, 1941, to $20,088,000,000 in August, 1945. Although gold has ceased being an international monetary standard, it is still being used for reserve purposes and is still the world's most generally acceptable commodity. However, all the automatic characteristics of the international gold standard have disappeared.

The Commodity Theory of the Value of Money

The commodity theorists explain the value of money in terms of a specific quantity of the commodity of which it is composed. By analyzing the factors which determine the demand for and the supply of this commodity, they provide an explanation for changes in the value of money or general prices. The commodity theory of the value of money is similar to the one discussed in Chapter III in so far as both are stated in terms of supply and demand. The chief difference between the two theories is one of emphasis. In the quantity theory supply and demand for all types of money are considered, while in the commodity theory emphasis is on the supply of and the demand for the commodity out of which the standard money is made. The existence of other types of money is recognized only in so far as it affects the supply and the demand for the standard commodity.

Factors Controlling Gold Supply.—Gold is a durable good, and a large percentage of the supply that has been mined throughout the ages is still in existence. Since the average annual output of newly mined gold is only 3 or 4 per cent of the existing gold stock,[5] an increase of even 100 per cent in annual output would have little effect upon its value. On the other hand, if the world's annual output of wheat were increased by 100 per cent, there would be a very noticeable and immediate effect upon its value.

When a country is on a gold standard, gold mining is carried on under fixed price conditions. In 1837 the statutory price of pure gold was fixed at $20.67 per ounce troy weight, and that remained the legal government price until 1933, when it was changed to $35.00. With an increase in general prices, most producers are faced with an increase in the costs of production. With the exception of gold mining, an increase in production costs may be offset in whole or in part by an increase in the price of the product. Because of the fixed price of gold, the gold mining industry tends to be depressed when the general price level is rising. Furthermore, gold mining, like all extractive industries, operates under the law of increasing costs. New mines may be opened, cheaper ores may be exploited, deeper shafts may be dug, but with each intensive or extensive development unit costs increase. This increase in unit costs intensifies the depressing effect of increasing general prices upon the gold mining industry.

When the price level is declining, gold production tends to increase even though other industries may be curtailing production. With the price of gold fixed and the costs of production decreasing, it becomes profitable to reopen abandoned gold mines and to extract gold from cheaper ores. Profit beckons, and the sourdoughs head for the hills. The conclusion to be drawn from an analysis of the factors controlling the gold supply is that the conditions under which

---

[5] For current estimates of world production of gold, see current issues of the *Federal Reserve Bulletin.* Unfortunately, these estimates do not include production in the Union of Socialist Soviet Republics. For other statistics, see the tables entitled "Production of Gold and Silver since the Discovery of America," "World's Industrial Consumption of Gold and Silver during the Calendar Years, 1942 and 1943," and others in the "Addenda" to the *Annual Report of the Director of the Mint for the Fiscal Year Ended June 30, 1944,* pp. 93-102.

gold is produced tend to bring about stabilization in the value of gold.

Factors Controlling Gold Demand.—There are two important monetary demands for gold: as reserves for bank credit and currency and as means of payment in settling international obligations when these obligations may be more cheaply settled with gold than with credit. There are also two nonmonetary demands for gold: the commercial or industrial demand and the hoarding or store-of-value demand.

The amount of the world's demand for gold for monetary purposes depends upon the world's demand for means of payment, for which gold serves directly or indirectly as a reserve, and the amount of gold that is used as a means of payment. Thus an increase or decrease in the volume of transactions and an increase or decrease in the size of the cash balances will tend to increase or decrease the monetary demand for gold. The amount of gold demanded as a means of payment depends in part on the form of currency in use. This demand is largest when gold coins are used and smallest when deposit currency is involved.

Over a long period of time there has been a world-wide tendency for the monetary demand for gold to decline relative to the demand for total means of payment. A number of developments have permitted the more economical use of gold, including the use of paper money and token coins as pocket money, the development of commercial banking which brought with it the spread in the use of checks and bank drafts as means of payment, the use of central bank credit for reserve purposes, the restrictions placed on the use and ownership of gold, and the establishment of judicial procedure and legal codes that encourage the investment in things other than gold as stores of value. Any development that would destroy confidence in paper money and token coins, in commercial and central banks, or in the government would tend to increase the demand for gold.

Although the proportion of gold to the total circulating media is less today than in the past, it does not mean that the volume of gold used for money is less. First, it must be recognized that the increase in money value of transactions may be greater than the increase in supply of gold, either because there is an increase in the volume of things exchanged or because there has been an increase in the price level at which exchanging takes place. Secondly, it must be realized that increases in gold holding of governments and central banks may be sufficiently large to offset economies in the use of gold in other parts of the economy. Much of the current production of gold as well as most of the existing gold stock is now being used for monetary purposes.

Now the question may be asked: Does the monetary demand for gold tend to stabilize its value or is it subject to seasonal, cyclical, unusual, or trend demands? When countries were operating on the gold coin standard, there was a small Christmas demand for coins to be used for gifts; otherwise there was no seasonal demand for the circulating media that could not be met by an expansion of the volume of paper money and token coins without imposing a strain on the monetary gold supply.

The cyclical demands for gold varied, depending on the variation in the swing of the business cycle. During the upward swing the demand for new circulating media usually took the form of deposit currency and pocket money. The demand for new gold reserves depended on the rigidity of the proportion between these expanding means of payment and gold reserves. If the banks followed a policy of permitting the reserve ratio to fall, the need for new gold reserves were minor; but if governments required central banks to maintain a minimum gold reserve ratio at all times, the monetary demand for gold would be increased. Since this might be in excess of new gold production, this new gold could be obtained only by bidding for it in foreign markets by offering a higher interest rate for funds.

During the downswing in the business cycle the money value of transactions declines, thus decreasing the demand for the circulating media. But this decrease may be offset by an increase in the demand for the circulating media to be used as cash balances. If, added to this factor, there is a desire to hoard or keep gold or a type of paper money that requires large gold reserves, the increase in demand for gold will be great. Therefore the monetary demand for gold may vary widely during the business cycle, depending upon the amplitude of the business changes, the presence or lack of confidence in paper money and the banking system, and the reserve policy followed by the central banks.

In addition to the seasonal and cyclical demands for gold, there may be those that accompany extraordinary events, such as wars, famines, or radical changes in the monetary or banking structure. Thus abandonment of the gold standard during wars, for example, and the adoption of the paper standard may lead to a decrease in the monetary demand for gold. On the other hand, a world adoption of the gold standard may lead to a "scramble for gold" that will considerably increase its value (for example, from 1870 to 1878).

The final type of change in the monetary demand for gold is that due to an increase in the volume of transactions over a long period of time. Throughout the world, since the Middle Ages, there has been an increasing volume of things produced and sold in the market places. This has given rise to a steady yearly demand for an increase in the supply of the circulating media. The ideal would be to have the supply of gold increase yearly at a rate just equal to new monetary and nonmonetary demands. This ideal is rarely achieved, and as a result there have been long periods of rising and falling prices.

One may conclude that the monetary demands for gold are very important in determining its value. Since these demands are subject to considerable variation, the value of gold is likewise subject to considerable variation. Futhermore, it may be that if gold were not used as money it would have greater stability in value than it has when so used. Finally, if the value of money is kept stable, the value of gold will be stable. This does not mean that the value of gold has no influence on the value of money or that if gold were demonetized its value would be at the present high level.

The Nonmonetary Demands for Gold.—The commercial or industrial demand for gold include those for making plates, for gilding books and other articles, for manufacturing processes, for dental and surgical purposes, for architectural effects in churches and other buildings, and, most important, for jewelry. Any increase or decrease in the commercial demand for gold tends to have a corresponding effect on its value. To what extent does this change in the nonmonetary demand tend to stabilize the value of gold? During rising and high prices the value of gold is low and nonmonetary demands increase, thereby reducing the relative supply of gold money and tending to check the upward price trend. During periods of falling prices just the opposite conditions exist. Purchases of luxuries, including gold articles, decrease, freeing gold for monetary purposes. If the depression is severe, there may be a movement of old gold from the arts to the monetary field. For example, during 1943 the reclaimed gold in the United States was valued at $10,521,000, as compared to a commercial demand for $96,864,353. During the last seventy-five years about 25 per cent of the world's supply of newly mined gold has been used in the arts, but the annual consumption varied from 10 to over 50 per cent.

The second nonmonetary demand for gold is for hoarding in the Orient, particularly in India, but technically most of the gold is hoarded only in the sense of being held in the form of ornaments. Because of inadequate or unsound banking facilities, together with religious and social customs, about 14 per cent of the world's output has been taken by India since the discovery of America.[6] Because orthodox Mohammedans are prohibited from receiving interest, they buy ornaments as investments. The Hindu laws of inheritance make women ineligible for receiving any share in immovable and real property, and so considerable capital is invested in ornaments for their inheritance. During the prosperous years following World War I, the annual demand for gold in India increased, having been about $110,000,000 annually, or more than 25 per cent of the annual output for this period. This investment demand for gold is affected by business conditions. As a result of the depression beginning in 1929 and the increase in the world price of gold following England's departure from the gold standard, the annual amount taken by India not only decreased, but much of the so-called "hoarded" gold was attracted out of hoards. It flowed out of the country in large amounts, although at a decreasing annual rate, until the outbreak of World War II. Although the Oriental demand for gold is now but a small part of the total, it tends to be greatest when the value of gold is lowest and to be smallest when the value of gold is highest. To this extent it does help to stabilize the value of gold.

The Value of the Standard Determines the Price Trends

Gold and the Supply of Money and Credit.—Although gold is rarely used in domestic exchange, it serves as a reserve for paper money and bank credit. The strict commodity theorists assume that there will be a direct relationship between the supply of gold, paper

---

[6] During this same period it was estimated that America and Europe consumed 30 per cent of the gold output for nonmonetary purposes. When it is recognized that India contains 20 per cent of the world's population, the hoarding demand for gold of 14 per cent of the world's output is not excessive (Pananditar, S. G., *Banking in India*, pp. 331-33).

money, and bank credit; but such a conclusion is justified only in part, and then only over long periods of time.

When new gold enters the monetary and banking system, it normally becomes the basis for new paper money or bank credit. The increase in new paper money or credit may be delayed for years, depending upon, in a general way, the condition of business but, more particularly, upon the stage of the trade cycle at the time of the new gold influx. If business is active and expanding and if a demand for new credit and currency exists, new gold will be used immediately as reserves (assuming that there is no surplus of reserves already available for currency and credit expansion). If business is inactive and contracting and there is a decrease in demand for credit and currency, the immediate effects of new gold reserves will be limited and of minor importance.

The way in which gold affects the reserves of banks may be illustrated as follows: The Homestake Mining Company sells $1,000,-000 worth of gold to the United States government and receives a check from the United States Treasury. The company deposits the check with the Chase National Bank in New York, which deposits it with the Federal Reserve Bank of New York. The company's deposits are increased by $1,000,000, and the deposit reserve account of the Chase bank is increased by $1,000,000. The government pays the check from its account with the Federal Reserve Bank of New York, which is replenished by depositing $1,000,000 in gold certificates. The gold will be kept in trust as reserve for the new gold certificates. The effect of the new gold has been to increase deposits, to increase the reserve account of the Chase National Bank, and to increase the gold reserves of the Federal Reserve Bank of New York.

The Homestake Mining Company buys supplies and equipment and pays salaries, etc., by writing checks on its deposit account at the Chase National Bank. The recipients of these checks deposit them in other banks, which in turn send them to their Federal Reserve banks and receive credit for them in their reserve accounts. As the checks are paid out of the account of the Chase National Bank, many banks participate in the increase in reserve, due to the original sale of gold to the government.

The future effects of the new reserves upon the volume of credit and currency depend upon the demands for credit and currency. If new currency is requested for payrolls, it is sent by the Federal Reserve bank and the reserve account of the requesting bank is debited. If businessmen borrow new credits, their deposit accounts will be credited; and, when these deposits are used for business payments, the reserves of the lending banks will be redistributed as noted above in the case of the Chase National Bank. The general effect will be an expansion of bank credit reserves throughout the banking system.

CHART IV

WHOLESALE PRICES: ALL COMMODITIES, YEARLY AVERAGE*
(1926 = 100)

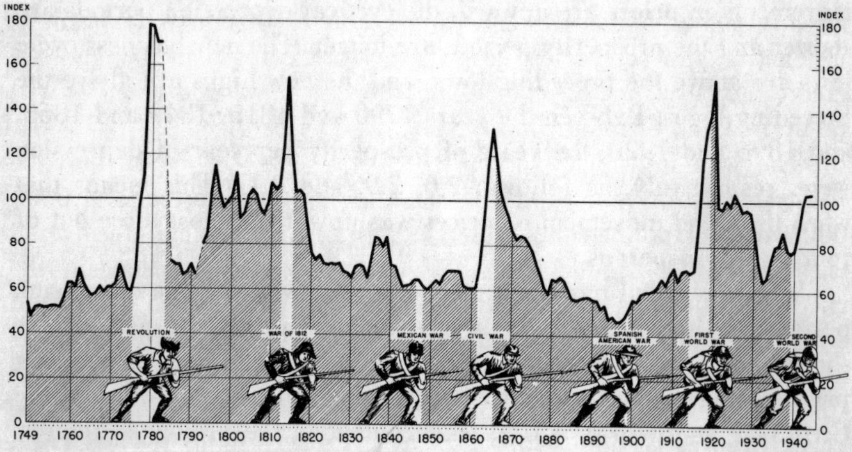

The influence of major wars upon long-run price movements is clearly shown.
The long-run price movements are 1749-1815; 1815-50; 1850-65; 1865-97; 1897-1920; and 1920-date.

* *Source:* U.S. Department of Labor, Bureau of Labor Statistics, prices in primary markets.

Because of large reserves, money tends to become cheap in the money market. Gradually interest rates are reduced throughout the country, and businessmen are encouraged to borrow and spend for raw materials, machinery, labor, etc. A whole series of results follows, one being a tendency for prices to rise, owing to an increase in the demand for things.

Gold and the Price Level.—A steady stream of gold coming into the money and banking structure creates a tendency for prices to rise gradually. However, the increase in the volume of transactions will tend to offset the increase in the flow of money against things, and so the long-run effect on prices will depend upon the relative increase in gold compared to the monetary and nonmonetary demand for gold. In the United States there have been several periods during which the trend of prices has been rising or falling. These periods include: (1) 1790 to 1815, rising prices; (2) 1815 to 1849, falling prices; (3) 1849 to 1865, rising prices; (4) 1865 to 1896, falling prices; (5) 1896 to 1920, rising prices; and (6) 1920 to date, falling prices.[7] These periods have superimposed on them the cyclical and unusual movements already described.

The most significant characteristic to note is that, when the trend movements in prices are upward, the cyclical depression periods are shorter and the prosperity periods are longer. The new business cycle lows are above the preceding lows, and the new highs are above the preceding highs. Between the years 1790 and 1815, 1849 and 1865, and 1896 and 1920, the years of prosperity per year of depression were, respectively, as follows: 2.6, 2.9, and 3.1.[8] This means that when the trend movement of prices was upward, almost three out of four were prosperous.

When the trend movement of prices is downward, the depression periods are longer and more severe, and the prosperity periods are shorter and less prosperous than during the long-run periods of rising prices. The two most gloomy of these long-run periods followed the Civil War and World War I, which included the prolonged depressions of the seventies and the thirties. Between the years 1815 and 1849 and 1865 and 1896, the years of prosperity per year of depression were, respectively, 0.8 and 0.9.[9] This means that, when the trend movement of prices was downward, less than one out of two years was prosperous.

The long-run movements in prices have been explained in terms of a relative scarcity or a relative surplus of gold. For example, the compound rate of increase in the world's annual stock of gold money was 1.9 per cent from 1873 to 1896, which is an annual deviation of minus 1.1 per cent from the estimated ideal of 3 per cent. The average annual rate of decline in wholesale commodity prices expressed in terms of gold was minus 1.65 per cent.

---

[7] On the basis of the old gold dollar.

[8] Mitchell, W. C., and Thorp, W. L., *Business Annals*, p. 66, Table 8.

[9] *Ibid.*

The increase in volume of gold may be greater than the increase in volume of trade, thus resulting in an upward movement of prices, as illustrated in all gold standard countries during the period from 1896 to 1914. The compound rate of increase in the world's per annum stock of gold money was at the rate of 3.5 per cent for this eighteen-year period, which is an annual deviation of plus 0.8 per cent from the estimated ideal.[10] The average annual rate of change in wholesale commodity prices was plus 2.55 per cent.

Monetary Reform with Particular Reference to Gold

The conclusion that changes in the value of the standard (gold) have been a factor in influencing the supply of money and credit and, therefore, the general price level has led to numerous proposals for reform of the monetary system by stabilizing the value of the standard. All the reformers accept the quantity theory of money in a rigid or modified form and propose to secure stabilization by controlling the supply of standard money. Two of these plans which pertain to gold are: (1) the Lehfeldt Plan and (2) the Compensated Dollar Plan. Other plans for monetary reform are discussed more conveniently elsewhere.

The Lehfeldt Plan.—This plan is named for former Professor Lehfeldt of Johannesburg, South Africa, who proposed to stabilize the value of gold by controlling the production of gold. If the annual demand for gold is increasing faster than gold production, governments should encourage greater production by subsidizing the mining of gold. If the annual supply of new gold is increasing faster than the demand for it, production should be decreased by limiting the output of gold mines. In order to function successfully, an international syndicate, composed of the chief producers of gold, would have to be organized so as to control output. If the plan could not be made to function under private ownership of gold mines, then control could be attained by government ownership. The weaknesses of the plan are: (1) difficulties associated with organization of producers, (2) difficulties in securing international agreements among govern-

[10] The ideal of normal production for this period was assumed to be 2.7 per cent of the existing gold stock, which is in keeping with the tendency for the yearly percentage of the new gold necessary to stabilize prices to taper down, owing to greater dependence upon other types of media of exchange (see Edie, L. D., *Money, Bank Credit and Prices*, p. 253).

ments necessary for subsidizing the industry according to the plan, and (3) technical difficulties of securing an increase in output during periods when more gold is necessary to stabilize general prices.

Compensated Dollar Plan.—A much easier way to adjust the supply of standard monetary units is to decrease the weight of the gold monetary unit when there is a relative scarcity of gold and to increase the weight when there is a relative surplus of gold. This plan would automatically provide for subsidization of gold production by increasing the price when too little gold is being produced and discouraging gold production by decreasing the price when too much gold is being produced. The effects of changes in the weight of the dollar upon (1) the price of gold, (2) number of gold dollars, and (3) the assumed price level are illustrated as follows:

Monetary Stock (in Ounces)	Weight of Dollar (in Grains)	Price per Oz. of Gold	Number of Dollars	Price Level (Assumed)
200,000,000	24	$20	4,000,000,000	100
200,000,000	16	30	6,000,000,000	150
200,000,000	20	24	4,800,000,000	120

If the Compensated Dollar Plan were inaugurated when no depression or unemployment exists, only minor monthly adjustment in weight of the dollar would be necessary. Dr. Irving Fisher proposes that such changes should be limited to 1 per cent per month until stabilization has been achieved. In order to discourage speculation in gold, a seigniorage charge of 1 per cent per month is proposed. No gold coins would be issued, and the effects in changes of the weight of the standard dollar would be reflected in the volume of gold certificates or gold credits held by the Federal Reserve banks.

All losses or gains from the operation of the Compensated Dollar Plan would be assumed by the United States Treasury. Changes made in the standard unit would take place after the index number of prices used as a guide had changed; consequently, no forecasting in anticipation of future developments would be necessary. Such a system would function best if adopted by all countries. If adopted by a single country, it would cause fluctuations in the foreign exchange rates, lead to speculative and undesirable international gold movements, and probably create more problems than it would solve. It would neither correct the short-term cyclical fluctuations in prices nor prevent the serious price changes due to wars.

Does the Gold Standard Have a Future?

With the end of World War II and the emphasis on international co-operation, may not the countries of the world re-adopt the gold standard? The answer is an important one to the United States, because the permanent demonetization of gold would cause heavy losses as a result of our ownership of over 60 per cent of the world's monetary gold stock. The answer is also of great importance to the British Empire and Russia, because most of the current gold produced is from mines located within their boundaries. If gold were demanded only as a commodity, it would affect not only the value of the present stocks in the British Empire and in Russia but also the future value of the output of their mines.

Considered from a broader viewpoint, the future of the gold standard depends upon recognition of the fact that it has given the world a common basis for financing international trade, investments, and travel, with all the economic advantages resulting from this system. Historically, all communities have adopted some generally acceptable commodity as a medium of exchange and a standard of value. If one is to expect the continuance of international trade and finance under the most satisfactory conditions, there must be some type of international standard. To date, no country has permanently refused to accept gold in payment for goods, services, and investments. Gold's acceptability, its great value in small bulk, and its relative stability in value seemingly assure its place in the future international monetary system. On the other hand, may not the advantages of an international standard be secured through some type of international organization without the use of gold as the standard?

Considered from a domestic viewpoint, the chief argument in favor of the gold standard is its relative stability in value. In preceding pages the economic forces which tend to stabilize the value of gold have been considered; but, owing to the development of paper money and deposit currency and the rapid changes in their volume, fluctuations in the value of money do take place. However, historical experiences justify the conclusion that these fluctuations are less when a country is on the gold standard than when a country is off the gold standard.

In every country in the world the quantity of gold money is but a small percentage of the total volume of currency and bank credit commonly used as media of exchange. The purpose of the gold standard is to limit fluctuations in the value of money; but, to an increasing degree, the volume of credit and currency now affects and perhaps even fixes the value of gold. In other words, the tail now wags the dog. This situation demands that more attention be given to conditions which determine the supply of and the demand for money and bank credit, but it does not mean that the "baby must be thrown out with the bath water."

To the man in the street, and nearly everyone is a man in the street when the standard of value is considered, the standard problem is bewildering. In spite of his bewilderment, he usually has definite opinions on this subject. This lack of understanding, on one hand, and strong prejudices, on the other, make any type of scientific monetary system impracticable. Businessmen want a foolproof and knaveproof standard without knowing exactly what one is. In the United States they may be thinking of it in terms of gold; and in England they may be thinking of it in terms of a "managed paper money standard."

QUESTIONS AND PROBLEMS

1. What is meant by a "standard of value"? What is its most desirable characteristic? Why?
2. What is a commodity standard? Illustrate.
3. Give and explain the reasons for adoption of the gold standard.
4. What are the three types of gold standard? Give their characteristics.
5. If a country adopts a gold standard, why is the weight of the monetary unit selected of importance to other countries?
6. How may a country operating on a gold standard keep (*a*) the value of gold equal to a fixed amount of money, (*b*) the value of money equal to a fixed amount of gold?
7. What is meant by a "free gold market"? Why is it essential to the proper functioning of a gold standard?
8. What is the present gold standard situation in the United States?
9. Discuss the "commodity theory of money."
10. Explain why gold tends to be more stable in value than other commodities.
11. To what extent has the "hoarding instinct" been a factor in determining

the international distribution of gold? The value of gold? Has hoarding ceased since nations stopped coining gold? Explain.

12. Is it more accurate to call the demand for gold in India an "investment" demand or a "hoarding" demand? Why?
13. Why did gold mine stock prices soar (1929-33) while other stock prices fell to rock bottom?
14. How do changes in the monetary gold supply affect (*a*) supply of money and credit, (*b*) the price level, (*c*) trend changes in prices?
15. "The use of the metal [gold] was unsatisfactory in the 19th century and is as completely out of date as bows and arrows." Comment.
16. What is the Lehfeldt Plan? What difficulties would be encountered in putting it into operation?
17. Assuming that a nation adopts the Compensated Dollar Plan, how may changes in the weight of the gold dollar affect the international distribution of the gold supply and thereby defeat the purposes of the plan?
18. How would the permanent demonetization of gold affect (*a*) the United States, (*b*) the United Kingdom, and (*c*) Russia?
19. "The contention that gold cannot meet all the burdens which may be thrown upon it. . . . could be applied to all our economic instrumentalities that have value. The basic requisite of value is scarcity—therefore there is not enough of anything that has value. . . . . All who have a 'right' to use the elevators in a building could not use them at once in case of a panic. Therefore fire escapes are provided, and these are precisely what any good monetary standard requires no matter how nearly perfect it may be—fire escapes to meet panic conditions. Our monetary fire escapes have not been good, nor have they been adequate. There is still room for improvement, and it is to this point that more careful attention should be directed" (Spahr, W. E., *The Case of the Gold Standard*, p. 5). Discuss.
20. Compare the statement in Question 19 to the following: "A return to international bimetallism would see the end of the gold era of the world, and it would depart unmourned. It had brought endless trouble with it and at last broke down ingloriously. . . . . People are still living who were born before the American dollar was fixed at 23.22 grains of fine gold and millions have never realized that within the past decade it has been reduced to 13.71 grains. The successive devaluations of the franc, the lira and the yen brought confusion to the international exchanges, dishonest profits to arbitrage operators and disturbance to both national and international price levels. Such perils must never be allowed to assail the world again" (Mitchell, H., *The Place of Silver in Monetary Reconstruction*, pp. 17-18).

REFERENCES

See end of Chapter V

CHAPTER V

THE GOLD STANDARD IN THE UNITED STATES SINCE 1930

Introduction

In the preceding chapter it was noted that the United States was keeping the value equivalent of its monetary unit equal to a fixed weight of gold. Although the United States does purchase gold at $35 per fine ounce, it has abandoned the other features of the gold standard. The movement away from the gold coin standard, which existed in 1932, is described in this chapter. These changes were preceded by an international collapse of the gold standard, which meant that countries discontinued keeping the value of their currencies equal to a fixed amount of gold. The chief reason for the abandonment of the gold standard was the rapid increase in the value of gold, owing to a world-wide decline in the volume of credit and a tendency to hoard currency and gold. As a result, all countries on the gold standard were faced with a severe and rapid downward trend in prices. This deflationary movement of prices increased debt burdens, discouraged production, increased unemployment, and brought many countries face to face with the gravest peacetime problems with which they had ever been confronted.

Countries such as Argentina, Brazil, and Australia, which exported chiefly raw materials and had large debts abroad, were the first to leave the gold standard. A decrease in the supply of new loans from abroad, high foreign debt services, and a rapid decline in world prices placed such a strain upon their limited gold supply that a breakdown in the gold standard within their borders was inevitable.[1] The collapse of the gold standard in a number of countries producing raw materials in 1930 was followed by a similar suspension in a number of industrial countries in 1931. Of the latter group, the most important country to leave the gold basis was Great Britain.[2]

---

[1] Smith, Lawrence, "Suspension of Gold Standard in Raw Material Exporting Countries," *American Economic Review,* Vol. XXIV (September, 1934), pp. 430-49.

[2] For descriptions of the attempts made through international co-operation to keep European countries on the gold standard, see *Annual Report of the Federal Reserve Board,* 1931, pp. 10-14; "Second Annual Report of the Bank for International Settlements," *Federal Reserve Bulletin,* June, 1932, pp. 366-75.

The 1930-36 collapse of the gold standard was unusual for various reasons: (1) It was the first time in its history that a general breakdown of the gold standard occurred while countries were not engaged in war. (2) Suspension of the gold standard was due to a fall in the general price level. Previously, countries suspended gold payments because of a rise in general prices. (3) At no time in its history has there been such general opposition to its readoption. Monetary reformers have a greater following today than at any period in the past, based upon a popular view that the automatic gold standard has certain inherent defects.

Events Leading up to the Collapse of the Banking System

From 1930 to 1933 the United States was served by the strongest monetary system in the world; but, because of bank failures and a decrease in the volume of deposit currency, it was under a great strain until relief was provided following the national banking holiday and the passage of the Bank Emergency Act of 1933. For three and a half years there was an almost unbroken recession in industrial and other forms of business activity caused or accompanied by precipitous declines in prices of securities, real estate, and commodities. Much forced selling of these at progressively lower prices took place. Bank suspensions added to the chaos by tying up liquid purchasing power which otherwise would have been available for spending.

In 1932, 1933, and 1934 wide publicity was given in the press to the hearings being held before the Senate Committee on Banking and Currency. This committee was investigating banks, stock markets, and other financial institutions. Its revelations in 1932 and 1933 of unsound banking practices in certain high places merely added to the growing lack of confidence in banks.[3]

In 1932 numerous steps were taken by Congress to increase the supply of currency. The requirement that only gold and commercial paper could be used as collateral for Federal Reserve notes was liberalized to include government bonds, which freed gold for reserve purposes. A rider to the Home Loan Bank Bill permitted national banks to issue for a three-year period their notes backed

[3] See summary statement of these findings in Committee on Banking and Currency, "Stock Exchange Practices," *Senate Report No. 1455,* 73d Cong., 2d Sess.

by United States government obligations that bore not more than 3⅜ per cent interest. This permitted a potential expansion by $900,000,000.

New lending agencies were created, including the Reconstruction Finance Corporation, the Home Loan Bank System, twelve regional agricultural corporations, and certain loan offices set up by the Secretary of Agriculture. Certain other lending agencies were strengthened with the use of government funds. The federal land banks were refinanced with new capital provided by the government. Conditions under which Federal Reserve bank funds could be borrowed were liberalized. The Reconstruction Finance Corporation made loans to banks, insurance companies, railroads, and to municipalities and other local governments, to aid them in financing their ever increasing relief burdens.

Charges and countercharges conspicuous in the political campaign of 1932 added to the general feeling of unrest and insecurity. The publication in December, 1932, of the list of borrowers from the Reconstruction Finance Corporation caused many depositors to lose confidence in banks included on the list. Credit flowed from weak to strong banks and to the government-operated postal savings system.

In his Des Moines, Iowa, speech of October 4, 1932, President Herbert Hoover made the alarming statement: "The Secretary of Treasury informed me that unless we could put into effect a remedy, we could not hold to the gold standard but two weeks longer because of inability to meet the demands of foreigners and our own citizens for gold." The period referred to was early in 1932, just before the passage of the Glass-Steagall Bill, which permitted government bonds to be used along with gold and commercial paper as collateral for Federal Reserve notes. Because of the lack of commercial paper in the portfolios of Federal Reserve banks, gold was being used in excess of the legal minimum requirements of 40 per cent. While this statement dealt with an event already past, the mere suggestion that the gold standard was in danger brought indignant protest from Senator Glass, the press, and others.

From 1931 to the week prior to the national banking holiday in March, 1933, the external drain of gold (demands for export) was over $1,000,000,000, or roughly 20 per cent of the record-breaking figure reached in the spring of 1931. Of this loss of gold, $726,000,000 was withdrawn in the six weeks following England's departure from the gold standard.

In addition, there was considerable pressure upon the gold reserve because of internal or domestic drain. This was the result of the hoarding of currency and gold. By the middle of 1932 the hoarding of currency at home was estimated to be as high as $1,600,-000,000. In 1933 this hoarding increased, with the withdrawals from the Federal Reserve banks being particularly large during the week preceding Black Friday, March 3. In less than a month, approximately $1,750,000,000 of gold and other forms of currency were paid out, and an additional $300,000,000 in gold was ear-marked for foreign bank accounts.[4]

On March 3 the Federal Reserve bank's reserve ratio fell below the legal requirements, and that night the Federal Reserve Board suspended all Federal Reserve banks' reserve requirements. The pressure to which the Federal Reserve banks would have been subjected on March 4 is impossible to imagine. On this day a one-day banking holiday was declared in New York, Illinois, and in twenty-three states where banks had not previously been closed. The problem of a banking moratorium was a national one calling for drastic action by the national government rather than piecemeal action by civil authorities in forty-eight states.

Suspension of the Gold Standard in the United States

National Banking Holiday Proclamation.—The day following his inauguration, President Franklin D. Roosevelt issued his national banking holiday proclamation, which was to remain in effect until Congress met in a special session on March 9.[5] All banking activities were suspended except those authorized by the Secretary of the Treasury with the approval of the President. In order to protect our gold supply, an embargo was placed upon all gold exports. In order to impound the domestic gold supply,

---

[4] Federal Reserve Board, *Annual Report*, 1933, p. 8.

[5] This proclamation is printed in the *Federal Reserve Bulletin*, March, 1933, pp. 113-14. Supplementary regulations of the Secretary of the Treasury, executive orders, the proclamation of March 9, the President's radio address on March 12, and the Emergency Banking Act of 1933 are found in this same issue of the *Federal Reserve Bulletin*.

which the government wanted in the hands of the Federal Reserve banks, where it could be used for reserve purposes, individual hoarders were ordered to surrender their holding of gold and gold certificates to their banks. The banks were prohibited from paying out gold and gold certificates.

Emergency Banking Act.—When Congress met on March 9 it passed the Emergency Banking Act. This law confirmed all of the emergency steps taken by the President,[6] made provisions for continuance of these policies, and inaugurated plans for reopening the banks. The act empowered the President to investigate, regulate, or prohibit transactions in gold or foreign exchange, thus inaugurating a system of exchange control which was in effect until 1934.

Special attention was given to the banking situation. No banks could be reopened without the consent of the Secretary of the Treasury; the Comptroller of Currency was directed to appoint conservators for unsound national banks; and the Reconstruction Finance Corporation was authorized to buy, with the approval of the Secretary of the Treasury, preferred stock and "capital notes" of banks. The act further liberalized the conditions under which member banks and others could borrow temporarily from the Federal Reserve banks. The banking holiday was extended for the remainder of the week, while provisions were being made to issue licenses for the opening of the sound banks on Monday, Tuesday, and Wednesday of the following week. The act authorized an emergency currency in the form of Federal Reserve bank notes which could be backed by government bonds or any type of commercial paper (in the latter case, up to but 90 per cent of the estimated value).

Departure from Gold.—Following the national banking moratorium, there was a return flow of currency, gold, and other types of paper money to the banks.[7] Pressure upon the reserves of the country was removed, and public confidence in the reopened banks was restored. The future of the dollar in international markets seemed assured, and it remained at or near par in the exchange

---

[6] *Ibid.*, p. 115.

[7] Currency other than gold was also returned to the banks. Between March 4 and May 10 this movement was very rapid, aggregating $1,595,000,000. Almost one-half was gold coins and gold certificates. *Federal Reserve Bulletin*, May, 1933, p. 265.

markets of the world. The gold holdings of the United States were over $4,000,000,000, or 40 per cent of the world's monetary supply. These reserves were more than ample to care for any emergency which might arise, particularly since the supply of Federal Reserve bank notes which required no minimum gold coverage could be issued to care for all conceivable domestic demands for currency. No foreign nation or group of nations was in a position to demand any important part of the gold supply of the United States.

During 1933 the antihoarding of gold campaign was continued, and about $1,000,000,000 were surrendered to the government. Under rulings of the Treasury all gold was nationalized, and future gold imports, as well as the product of American gold mines, had to be sold to the government. The Secretary of the Treasury issued licenses to manufacturers of fabricated gold articles, to dentists, and to others who were using gold legitimately in their businesses or professions; but the hoarding of gold was illegal.[8]

Nationalization of gold could not be politically supported at home if foreigners were allowed to withdraw gold without restrictions. Fairness to domestic holders of gold demanded that everyone be placed in the same position relative to gold withdrawals. So, along with the prohibitions placed upon domestic uses of gold, the President forbade all exports,[9] earmarkings for exports, or transfer abroad in any manner of gold coin and gold bullion. Since an absolute veto of all requests for permission to export gold would be unfair to many central banks and others, the Secretary of the Treasury was given authority to specify conditions under which export licenses could be obtained.[10] Until the middle of April, 1933, the Secretary was fairly generous in his gold export policy, and licenses were obtained without much difficulty. On April 19, however, a Treasury announcement was made that

---

[8] Regulations of April 5, 1933, permitted limited gold holdings when required for legitimate and customary use in industry and professions; when held in trust for foreign governments and banks; when the gold was in the form of certain rare and unusual coins of special value to collectors; and when the treasury licensed the holdings of gold coins for other proper transactions. *Federal Reserve Bulletin,* April, 1933, pp. 213-14.

[9] This is no longer true because certain foreign governments may obtain gold freely from the United States. Warburg, J. P., *Money Muddle,* p. 92.

[10] See *Federal Reserve Bulletin,* March, 1933, p. 125.

gold export licenses for all ordinary purposes would be suspended.[11]

This new gold embargo was especially important, because it made an immediate return to the gold standard improbable. For the first time the President and the Secretary of the Treasury publicly admitted that the United States was not on a gold basis. After these announcements, newspaper headlines, and administrative and other comments, little doubt remained as to the immediate future of the gold dollar. It was neither coming back as soon as was expected nor would it return in its old form. The gold discount of the dollar increased immediately and gradually rose on inflationary news to about 30 per cent by the middle of July.

Beginning of a New Currency Era.—The executive proclamation of March 6 and the Emergency Banking Act marked the beginning of a new currency era in the United States. But few realized at this time that the United States was entering a period of currency experimentation involving manipulation of the value of gold, reflation of the credit structure by government-borrowing from banks, and the purchase of hoards of the "political metal," silver. The basic theory underlying the gold and reflation of bank credit policies was the quantity theory of money, which held that prices could be raised to, and then stabilized at, any desired level by merely increasing and controlling the supply of money and credit.

Temporary Rejection of International Stabilization

Before April, 1933, the country had every reason to expect an early return to the gold standard. But the powerful inflationary groups in Congress began to show their hands. Fiat paper money, free coinage of silver, devaluation of the gold dollar, and bank credit inflation received support from important congressional and administrative leaders.

When the second gold embargo was announced (April 19), a number of foreign political leaders were on their way to Washington to hold previously arranged conferences with the President. The purpose of these visits was to discuss many of the topics which

[11] This executive order of the Secretary of the Treasury is printed, together with its supplementary regulations, in the *Federal Reserve Bulletin*, May, 1933, pp. 266-69.

were to appear before the London Monetary and Economic Conference. Representatives of Great Britain and France were on ships bound for the United States when the new gold embargo regulations went into effect. They were greatly disturbed by the proposed inflationary policy of the United States, for it was certain to add more uncertainties to international monetary and economic relationships, the elimination of which, ironically enough, had been the reason for calling the conference. The embargo was a serious shock to all foreign exchange markets and was the subject of much criticism from all countries. In spite of the embargo, the President proceeded with his conferences, which were followed by joint statements to the press.[12] In general, the statements favored higher commodity prices, elimination of artificial exchange and trade barriers, and the re-establishment of the international gold standard.

On June 12, 1933, delegates from sixty-six different nations met in London.[13] More preparatory work had been done in order to present and clarify issues than had been the case in any other conference of its kind. A group of experts prepared an agenda, or program of work, to be brought up at the meeting. In spite of the excellent preparatory work, however, the conference accomplished little of significance. Even before the conference had met, the United States had shifted from emphasis on an international to emphasis on a national monetary policy. This move, coming so soon after Great Britain left the gold standard, marked the end of the international gold standard, at least temporarily.

Controlled Inflation[14]

In May, 1933, considerable light was thrown upon the future credit and money policy of the United States government by the President in a radio address to the American people. He stated:

[12] The American-British statement was released on April 26; the American-French statement, two days later; and the American-Italian, on May 6. These joint statements were reprinted as Appendix B in Pasvolsky, Leo, *Current Monetary Issues.*

[13] See *ibid.*, chaps. ii, iii, and iv. For an interesting nontechnical discussion of the conference and preliminaries, see Lindley, E. K., *The Roosevelt Revolution*, pp. 180-218.

[14] See Kemmerer, E. W., "Controlled Inflation," *American Economic Review*, Supplement, Vol. XXIV, No. 1 (1934), pp. 90-100, for discussion of principles involved in controlled inflation.

"The Administration has the definite objective of raising commodity prices to such an extent that those who have borrowed money will, on the average, be able to repay that money in the same kind of dollar which they borrowed. . . . We do not seek to let them get such a cheap dollar that, in effect, they will be able to pay back a great deal less than they borrowed."

Thomas Inflation Law.—In this same talk the President referred to certain powers which were then in the process of being granted to him. They appeared as Title III of the Agricultural Adjustment Act of May 12, 1933. The President was not forced to use the discretionary powers granted, which was probably the most important provision in the act. Practically every type of inflationary device was involved, including fiat paper money issues, debasement of the gold dollar, free coinage of silver, and bank credit inflation. This law is popularly known as the Thomas Inflation Law. It may be summarized as follows:[15]

1. The President may direct the Secretary of the Treasury and the Federal Reserve Board to permit the Federal Reserve banks to purchase and hold $3,000,000,000 additional United States government obligations without penalties for deficiency in reserves. (Later the Reserve banks purchased $600,000,000 of government securities.)
2. If Reserve banks refuse to act, then the Secretary of the Treasury may be directed to issue United States notes or greenbacks up to $3,000,000,000 which may be used to purchase maturing obligations or bonds of the United States government. The Secretary was also directed to retire notes so issued at the rate of 4 per cent each year. All coins and currencies of the United States that had been issued or may be issued are to be given the full legal tender quality. (Repealed June 12, 1945, without being used.)
3. The President may, by proclamation, provide for bimetallism at a fixed mint ratio, that is, allow the free coinage of gold and silver. (This provision was used in part in December, 1933.)
4. The President may reduce the gold content of the standard gold dollar by not more than 50 per cent. (This power was used in part in 1934.)
5. The President was authorized to accept silver at a price of 50 cents per ounce up to $200,000,000 from foreign governments in payment of debts past due or to become due during a period of six months following the date of the act. The silver accepted was to be placed in

[15] See *Federal Reserve Bulletin*, May, 1933, pp. 317-18.

circulation by using silver certificates. (This provision was unimportant.)

6. The Federal Reserve Board, during the emergency, may change the reserve requirements to be maintained against demand and time deposits. (In 1935 this provision was made permanent.)

The Gold Purchase Plan in Operation.—On October 22, 1933, in a radio address, the President restated his price program and announced his new plan to secure it. This plan was based on the commodity theory of money. It reflected the theories of the late Professor Warren, who considered the postwar scarcity of gold to be the chief cause of the depression.[16] The failure of gold production to keep pace with gold demand raised the value of gold and produced a sharp fall in prices in all gold standard countries. This relationship between changes in gold supply and prices has been recognized by numerous writers, but few go to the extent that Professor Warren did in giving it the chief role in explaining the depression.

In order to restore prices to an equitable basis, presumably that of 1926, he advocated a reduction in the weight of the gold dollar. Since any reduction in the weight of the gold dollar means a reciprocal increase in the mint price of gold, Warren's theory is that with each rise in the price of gold there would be a corresponding rise in general prices. After obtaining the desired price level, the second part of the Warren program is to stabilize the value of the dollar by putting into operation the Compensated or Commodity Dollar Plan.[17] The business slump which came in September and October seemingly called for some stimulating action.

On October 25, three days after the gold purchase plan was initiated, the Reconstruction Finance Corporation announced that it would purchase all domestic gold offered at $31.36 per ounce.[18] Four days later government purchases were extended to foreign markets through the facilities of the Federal Reserve Bank of New York. The policy used in both domestic and foreign purchases was to offer a price above the market price and then raise it, at first daily and

---

[16] See Warren, G. F., and Pearson, F. A., *Gold and Prices*, pp. 107-16, and Warren, G. F., "Some Statistics on the Gold Situation," *American Economic Review*, Supplement, Vol. XXIV, No. 1 (1934), pp. 111-29.

[17] Warren and Pearson, *op. cit.*, pp. 292-96; 452-57.

[18] *Federal Reserve Bulletin*, November, 1933, pp. 669-70.

then at irregular intervals. As a result of progressive increases, the price was $35.00 per ounce on February 1, 1934.

While these changes were taking place, the general price level was not moving in the pattern that was expected by the administration. The Bureau of Labor Statistics index number of wholesale commodity prices remained at 71 (1926 = 100) for the last four months of 1933. It did increase one point during January, 1934.

The plan aroused a storm of protest from the very first. It was not understood by businessmen, and the resulting uncertainty was enough to prevent its successful operation, assuming that it was scientifically correct in the beginning. The chief lesson to be learned from the experiment is that no plan, even though it may be correct considered from a laboratory viewpoint, will succeed without general public understanding and confidence. The gold purchase plan was unorthodox and unsuited to an economy dependent on paper money and deposit currency.

Just because the mint price of gold is increased and more paper money (gold certificates) is printed and deposited with the Federal Reserve banks, it does not follow that the supply of pocket money or deposit currency will increase. Even if the supply of the circulating media did increase, the price level or volume of transactions or both will not increase if businessmen and others hold more funds and spend relatively less. A decrease in velocity of money and credit may even cause a decline in general prices. The main result of the gold purchasing policy was to prepare the country for the devaluation or debasement of the gold dollar which became effective on January 31, 1934.

Gold Reserve Act of 1934[19]

Numerous important changes were made in the monetary system of the United States by the Gold Reserve Act of 1934, which was approved by the President on January 30. The stated purposes of this act are: (1) to protect the currency system of the United States, (2) to withdraw gold from circulation, (3) to provide for the better use of the monetary gold stock, and (4) to stabilize the value of money. Virtually all the powers necessary to operate on a managed

---

[19] *Federal Reserve Bulletin*, February, 1934, pp. 63-67.

gold currency plan are present. The principal provisions of the act are as follows:

1. The upper limit for the weight of the gold dollar was fixed at 60 per cent of the dollar's former weight, but the lower limit, 50 per cent of the dollar's former weight, was not disturbed. (This means that the President was permitted to change the price from $20.67 to any price between $34.45 and $41.34 per fine ounce.)
2. Title of all gold owned by the Federal Reserve banks was transferred to the United States government. The Reserve banks received in exchange gold certificates equal to the old statutory price of the gold, that is, at the rate of $20.67 per fine ounce. Since no monetary gold was legally outside of the Treasury and Reserve banks, the effect was to give the government control over the entire stock of gold reserves of the country.
3. Complete control over all gold transactions was delegated to the Secretary of the Treasury. With the approval of the President, he may issue regulations covering the conditions under which gold may be acquired, earmarked, imported, exported, held, melted, and used for nonmonetary as well as monetary purposes.
4. The Secretary of the Treasury was given the right to purchase and sell gold and, therefore, all the authority which was necessary to place the United States upon an international gold bullion standard. However, the sale of any gold which is required to be maintained as a reserve for currency issued can be made only "to the extent necessary to maintain such currency at a parity with the gold dollar."
5. The act provided that any increase or decrease "in the value of gold held by the United States" as a result of the alterations in the weight of the gold dollar shall be received, or covered, by the government. This part of the act allocates to the government all profits from devaluation of the dollar and all losses which would result from an increase in weight which might occur if the dollar were revalued upward.
6. In event of reduction in the weight of the gold dollar, $2,000,000,000 of the profits derived from this step are to be used to finance a stabilization fund. The primary purpose of this fund is to stabilize the foreign exchange value of the dollar.
7. The act prohibited coinage of gold into American coins, and demonetized those outstanding. In the future, United States monetary gold is to appear only in bar form.
8. Reserve requirements of Federal Reserve banks were changed to the general effect that the words "gold certificate" were substituted for the word "gold" wherever it appeared in the Federal Reserve Act in connection with reserve requirements, redemption funds, etc.

Devaluation of the Gold Dollar

Under this act the President issued a proclamation fixing the weight of the gold dollar at 15 5/21 grains, 9/10 fine. This new weight is 59.06 per cent of the former weight of 25.8 grains, 9/10 fine. By making this reduction in weight, the President did not give up the power to devalue the dollar as much as 50 per cent of its former weight, as was first authorized in the Thomas Inflation Act, and this part of the law was not repealed until June, 1945. The effect of devaluation on the number of gold dollars was immediately apparent in the United States Treasury Daily Statement of February 1, which included "increment resulting from reduction in the weight of the gold dollar, $2,805,512,060.87." After February 1, 1934, additional profits of over $10,000,000 were reported as a result of subsequent surrender of hoarded gold.

The proclamation became effective immediately; and beginning February 1, 1934, the Secretary of the Treasury began buying gold at $35 per fine ounce less the usual mint fees and a handling charge of 1/4 of 1 per cent. Although the Treasury adopted a policy of freely purchasing gold, which is one of the essentials of the gold bullion standard, it did not freely authorize the sale of gold bullion, which is the second essential of the gold bullion standard. The mints were authorized to sell gold to those persons who held licenses to acquire it for use in the arts, professions, or industries where it is customarily used. The sales price was $35 plus a handling charge of 1/4 of 1 per cent.

The primary purpose of the devaluation of the dollar was to raise the general price level to a satisfactory level. As a result of the new policy of counting one ounce of gold $35.00 instead of $20.67, the number of gold dollars held by the government increased from $4,033,000,000 to $6,841,000,000. Devaluation or debasement was a device used by kings and emperors in ancient and medieval times to increase their revenues. By reducing the weight or fineness of coins coming into the Treasury and replacing them with debased coins of the same nominal value, more coins and, therefore, more revenue were secured from the same quantity of metal. Although the primary purpose of devaluation in 1934 in the United States was not to secure profits, nevertheless that has been one argument used to support this move.

Devaluation was supported by the argument that it increases the export trade of the United States. The cheapening of the dollar in foreign exchange markets acts as a bounty on exports so long as there is no proportionate increase in American prices and wages. It also tends to act as a deterrent to imports, thereby aiding sellers and hurting buyers in domestic markets. It increases the cost (in terms of dollars) of traveling and living abroad, thereby encouraging Americans to live and spend at home.

These so-called advantages of devaluation may be offset by similar policies of foreign governments. The chief dangers are that there will be international competition in devaluation, retaliatory tariffs, extension of the quota system, exchange regulations, and destruction of all international trade. If a country cannot sell in the United States, it can buy there only so long as it has gold and credits. Furthermore, the advantages resulting from cheapening the international value of the dollar can be but temporary. Finally, the devaluationists are considering only the interests of a minority of the American people, that is, the producers of export commodities. The gains of this group are offset by higher prices paid by importers of raw materials, foods, and other articles not produced at home. These higher prices are passed along to consumers, who may be forced to adopt a lower standard of living.

The Gold Clause Decisions

Legal tests of the gold policy of the United States were inevitable. Several cases arose, and sample ones were carried to the United States Supreme Court. The fundamental question in them all was: Does the government have the right to violate a contract?

One provision of the Thomas Inflation Act was the legal tender clause, which read: "that notes and all other coins and currencies heretofore and hereafter coined or issued by or under the authority of the United States shall be legal tender for all debts public and private." Was this clause retroactive? Did it apply only to future debts drawn in terms of dollars? Could creditors draw contracts in terms of gold dollars and defeat legal tender laws in that way? Did this law permit governments and corporations to pay with paper money contracts specifying that the obligations were payable in gold dollars containing 25.8 grains of gold, 9/10 fine?

To eliminate doubts and confusion, on June 5 the President signed a clarifying resolution previously approved by both houses of Congress. The resolution stated in effect that any obligation, previously or subsequently incurred, purporting to give the obligee a right to require payment in gold or a particular kind of coin or currency was against public policy, and that such obligation could be discharged by payment of any legal tender money. All debts, including those which contained the gold clause, could be settled with legal tender money. The practical effects of this legislation were (1) to remove all the peculiar restrictions as to legal tender qualities previously existing between the various circulating media in the United States; and (2) to place all obligations, past and future, upon the same footing. But was this law constitutional?

On February 18, 1935, the United States Supreme Court gave a five-to-four decision which upheld the gold policy of the administration. In cases which involved privately issued bonds, the court held that these were not contracts for payment in gold coin as a commodity, or in bullion, but were contracts for the payment of money.[20]

In a second case, the question of the right of the United States to repudiate its own gold bond contract was involved.[21] The court stated that Congress was without power to reduce expenditures by abrogating contractual obligations of the United States. However, the court added that the plaintiff had not suffered any damages and therefore had no right to demand payment on the basis of $1.69 in present currency for each old gold dollar. In making this decision, the court accepted a new definition of stability, that is, one in terms of purchasing power. Most of the gold bonds containing the gold clause were issued when the value of money was lower than it was in 1935. To repay the same number of dollars, plus an amount to offset the effects of devaluation, would be "an unjustified enrichment." The purchasing power of 59 cent gold dollars was higher than that of those borrowed by the government when the bonds were issued.

The case involving gold certificates was similarly disposed of. The court ruled that the plaintiff, who claimed that he should receive $170,634.07 for $106,300 in gold certificates surrendered to the

---

[20] Norman *vs.* Baltimore and Ohio Railroad Co., 293 U.S. 546 (1935); United States *vs.* the Bankers Trust Co., 293 U.S. 548 (1935).

[21] Perry *vs.* United States, 294 U.S. 330 (1935).

government, had showed no damage and hence could not sue in the Court of Claims.[22]

Based upon economic reasoning, the Supreme Court's decisions were wise. When cases are taken to the Court of Claims, the plaintiffs must show that they have suffered from loss of purchasing power in terms of goods and services and not gold. This decision is in keeping with the generally more intelligent attitude taken toward money and monetary reform. Stability in terms of purchasing power of money is more important than stability in terms of gold. In the summer of 1935 Congress followed up the decision of the Supreme Court by making provisions for (1) retiring, dollar for dollar, the gold-clause securities of the government and (2) making coins and currency redeemable in money which could be legally acquired under the law.

In addition, Congress withdrew the privilege of suing the United States after January 1, 1936, for claims arising out of the gold-clause securities, requisitions of coins, currency, gold, or silver, and others "involving the effect or validity of any change in the metallic content of the dollar, or other regulation of the value of money."

Stabilization Fund

The Stabilization Fund authorized in the Gold Reserve Act of 1934 was created, and $2,000,000,000 was placed under the direct control of the Secretary of the Treasury, who could use the fund to buy gold, foreign exchange, government securities, and other credit instruments which might be deemed necessary to secure international stabilization of the dollar. When the fund was set up $200,000,000 were deposited with the Reserve banks, and the remainder, $1,800,000,000, was credited to the Stabilization Fund on the books of the Treasury.

In general, the activities of the fund have been limited in nature, because the dollar, after devaluation, was undervalued in terms of foreign currencies and has needed no special support. There has been little need to insulate the money market from the deflationary effects of exodus of capital, because most of the new capital movements have been toward the United States. To the extent that gold credits are being kept idle, there will be a decrease in the danger

[22] Nortz *vs.* United States, 294 U.S. 317 (1935).

of inflation. But the fund has not been able to impound new inflows of gold; and, as a result, in 1936 the United States Treasury set up temporarily an "inactive account" to absorb new gold credits to prevent further increases in the volume of member bank reserves.

The British government was the first major one to establish an exchange or stabilization fund.[23] This fund is being financed with government credit and being managed jointly by a committee of the government and the Bank of England. Like other stabilization funds, it is operated in secrecy, and its long-run purpose has been to stabilize the exchange rates and to stabilize domestic credit and price conditions. At first the fund was used to keep the pound cheap in terms of foreign monetary units because of the resulting export trade advantages. This aim was realized until the United States and, later, France and other members of the gold bloc left the gold standard. From 1933 to 1939, the fund was used to stabilize the foreign value of the pound in so far as external conditions would permit, but its chief activity was to help stabilize domestic credit conditions.

The Exchange Equalization Account of Great Britain has been operated to prevent influx or efflux of funds from disturbing the exchange markets, money markets, and the domestic price level. When the value of sterling exchange is rising because of an inward movement of short-term capital or because of other reasons, the managers sell treasury bills to the commercial banks and use the funds to purchase foreign exchange and gold. Thus the effects of the influx of funds is offset by the Equalization Fund's holdings of foreign bank balances, acceptances, and gold. Later, if there is a shift of funds away from the London money market, the depressing effects may be offset by releases of foreign funds and sales of gold held by the Equalization Fund. From 1936 to 1939 it was operated in close agreement with the American and French funds; but during the war it was used as a device to help finance the war.

Tripartite Agreements

The Tripartite Agreement of October, 1936, introduced a four-year period of exchange stability by linking the dollar, the sterling,

[23] For discussion of the history and operation of exchange funds, see Hall, N. F., *The Exchange Equalization Account.*

and the franc areas. In the autumn of 1936, the gold bloc countries (France, the Netherlands, Belgium, Switzerland, and Poland) departed from their policy of keeping the value of their currencies tied to the old gold units and devalued their currencies. With the unpegging of the French franc, the Tripartite Agreement between France, the United Kingdom, and the United States was announced. Later Belgium, the Netherlands, Switzerland, and the Bank for International Settlements joined this accord. Each agreed to sell gold to any equalization fund or central bank willing to sell it at prices not to be changed without twenty-four hours' notice. This step introduced an element of exchange stability by tying all the currencies temporarily to gold and by permitting nonspeculative day-to-day exchange operations in terms of gold. Countries not accepting the accord have benefited from its international stability by keeping the value of their currencies equal to the value of the dollar, the pound sterling, etc., because things equal to the same thing must be equal to each other.

Following this agreement there was a tendency to lessen exchange control throughout the world, but this development was short-lived because of the economic recession of 1937 and the outbreak of the war in 1939. Although the Tripartite Agreements were in effect during the war, they were of minor importance because of war restrictions on exchange movements and the operations of Lend-Lease.

The Cross of Gold

In 1933 the gold problem facing the world was one of scarcity, but in less than a decade it had changed to one of surplus. Because of the increase in gold production, because of recovery from hoards and the arts, and because of revaluation, the world's monetary gold stock in terms of dollars has increased from $12,500,000,000 to over $33,000,000,000. The United States is particularly concerned with the increase, because three-fourths of the new gold dollars have been added to the stock of the United States, thereby multiplying the dollar gold supply more than fivefold and increasing its holdings from 40 per cent to about 60 per cent of the world's total monetary gold stock.

Sources of the Increase.—As already noted, $2,800,000,000 were added to the dollar gold stock of the United States by devaluation at the end of January, 1934, when the mint price of gold was changed from $20.67 per fine ounce to $35.00 per fine ounce. About $200,000,000 was acquired at home and abroad under the gold-buying program in effect from October, 1933, to the end of January, 1934. All the remainder of the increase has been acquired since January, 1934, at a price of $35.00 per fine ounce, minus a handling charge of 1/4 of 1 per cent. Of the gold acquired since January, 1934, less than $2,000,000,000 was obtained under circumstances accruing directly to the benefits of the American people.

The amount of gold purchased during 1939 and 1940 provided the democracies with what was later obtained through Lend-Lease. Support for this part of the program may be justified from the viewpoint of the United States, on the basis that gold will be more valuable than future receipts from Lend-Lease. The disadvantage of this program was that, encouraging the gold-mining industry to operate, labor and other productive resources were used that might have been used in winning the war. Since 1941 the allies of the United States have secured their supplies in the United States through Lend-Lease. Gold imports declined and gold exports increased. As a result, the gold stock of the United States declined from $22,800,000,000 to $20,000,000,000 in 1945.

About $11,000,000,000 of the present gold stock has been acquired from abroad, which is a small amount compared to the cost of the war and less than one-half of what was given away under Lend-Lease. But, looking to the future, if other countries do not adopt the gold standard, are the purchases of gold to be continued for years to come with great profit to foreign miners and other owners of gold?

What Has Been the Effect of Devaluation?—Since the price of any gold sold in international markets tends to be the same after allowances are made for artificial and natural barriers to trade, the price of gold which enters international markets will tend to be the same the world over, that is, the equivalent of about $35 per fine ounce.

Although it may not be concluded that gold is coming to the United States because the price of $35 per fine ounce is above the world price, it must not be assumed that devaluation has nothing to do with the present gold problem of the United States. Not only has the 1933 gold supply been increased by $2,800,000,000 in terms of dollars, due to the devaluation of the gold stock, but each ounce that has been added since magnifies the problem by roughly 69 per cent more than would have been true at the old gold price. Without devaluation, the present United States gold stock would have a manageable monetary value of a little more than $12,000,000,000, as compared to $20,000,000,000. In addition, it appears most unlikely that the present gold stock would have been so large, because gold production profits would have been less, and there would have been less new gold produced. Because of devaluation and no corresponding increase in commodity and security prices, the price and value of gold are greater today than they have ever been in the past.

The natural assumption to draw from the fact of an increase in gold reserves to five times the 1929 level would be that there has been inflation in the United States; but this conclusion is untrue. To date, the chief effects of the gold inflow have been to permit an increase in the volume of currency in circulation, to support an increase in the volume of deposit currency, and to expand the volume of member bank reserves. Considered from a national viewpoint, it is more than probable that the New Deal gold policy has created more problems than it has solved, as well as having cost the nation billions of dollars in payment for an asset which has an uncertain future value. But considered from the viewpoint of individuals who received bank deposits in exchange for goods and services sent abroad, there was an increase in production, employment, wages, and profits.

Proposed Solutions of the Gold Problem

The avalanche of gold has been the subject of discussion by economists, federal officials, congressmen, and others. Numerous proposals have been made to eliminate or lessen the dangers of inflation due to the present gold stock of the United States. Included in the proposals are: (1) abandonment of the gold standard, (2) decrease in the price of gold, (3) sterilization of gold and increase in member bank reserve requirements, and (4) return to the "full" or gold coin standard.

Abandonment of the Gold Standard.—Among those who favor abandonment of the gold standard in the United States are those who recommend only a temporary abandonment until other nations are willing and able to return to the international gold standard and those who favor permanent abandonment. This latter group would make gold subsidiary to a managed currency unit. Assuming successful management, this system would give each country a nominally independent and stable currency divorced from gold but would sacrifice the advantages of belonging to an international monetary system. To offset this loss an international stabilization fund would be created. Its function would be to keep exchange rates stable, and in its operation gold would move in international exchange primarily as a commodity, at prices which would be changed from time to time. The monetary use of gold would include its use in making payments into the international monetary fund to settle current trade balances.

Those in favor of abandonment of the gold standard have many arguments in favor of this move, but one of the most significant is that the development of money is away from gold. "The key to the evolution of money lies . . . . in the element of cost. Throughout history there has been a persistent effort to reduce the cost, to the issuer at least, of the material from which money is made. The final stage is that in which the issuer not only pays practically nothing for the money material but does not assume even a future obligation in the matter."[24] If this is true, the chief regret is that Congress did not make this discovery before 1934, because abandonment of the gold standard now would mean a potential loss of most of the $24,000,000,000 invested in gold and silver. While from a national viewpoint the gold and silver has already been paid for in terms of goods and services, a real loss would result in the sense that these "tokens" could not be spent for goods and services. This is true of any kind of money which has lost its purchasing power.

Decrease in the Price of Gold.—Many proposals have been made which would have as their effect a reduction in the mint price of gold. Some favor a return to the old mint price of $20.67, which would mean that the Treasury would have to absorb the loss as provided in the Gold Reserve Act of 1934; but it appears unlikely that Congress will vote for such a change. Another proposal is that a seigniorage charge of 41 per cent on the new gold presented to the Treasury be levied. This would have the effect of lowering the

---

[24] Graham, F. D., and Whittlesey, C. R., *Golden Avalanche*, p. 221.

mint buying price but would have no effect upon the present stock in the United States. In order to remove this difficulty, it has been proposed that a bonus equal to the seigniorage charge be given in order to encourage the buying of gold from the United States. If inaugurated at the present time, these plans would have little effect on the world-wide distribution of gold abroad, because they would not reach the underlying causes that explain why gold has been coming to the United States.

Sterilization of Gold and Increase in Reserve Requirements of Member Banks.—Both of these devices of control have been used since 1934 and are discussed later. The first consists of buying gold as required by law and then borrowing an equal amount of bank credit, which is kept idle in an inactive account. When in operation, it increases the federal debt, which is already at a dangerously high level. It is no cure for the gold problem but merely a device to lessen the inflationary effects of its presence. Member banks' legal reserve requirements have been increased, but this is another device similar to that above, with the burden of keeping funds idle falling upon the affected banks and their customers.

Return to the "Full" Gold Standard.—Another proposal to be considered here is that the United States should make provisions for the free coinage of gold, circulation of gold certificates, and the adoption of a policy of freely paying out on demand gold coins and gold bullion to all who request it. In brief, the program calls for a sale of any part of the present gold stock to anyone who wants to buy it. Such a plan could do little or no harm and might be the means of bringing about a partial redistribution of gold at home and abroad. At present there is a tendency for Americans and foreigners to hoard American paper currency. This tendency suggests a demand for hoarding which could be met with the surplus of gold in the United States, with the advantage of removing at least a part of the dangers of inflation, without loss to the United States government.

In conclusion, the opinion of L. J. A. Trip, a former president of the Bank for International Settlements and former head of one of the most important central banks of Europe may be of value. He assumed that the present monetary policy of the United States would be maintained.

> The importance of this both to the world and to the country itself [the United States] can hardly be overestimated. There is no denying that the world price of gold is founded on this policy. If the present fixed relation between the dollar and gold were abandoned, a general monetary dislocation would, in my opinion, set in, which would involve very detrimental consequences for economic and financial conditions in the world including America herself . . . . . If experience, especially that of the last few years, has placed one fact beyond doubt, it is this, that we cannot dispense with gold as an international means of payment.[25]

Although made in 1939, this statement is just as appropriate today as it was at that time.

Conclusion

At the present time the United States does not have a full or complete gold standard. Neither is there an international gold standard in the world, in the sense that most countries directly or indirectly adhere to the practice of keeping the value of their standard monetary units equivalent to a fixed weight of gold.

Because of the artificiality of the market for gold, conditions governing the price level in the United States are more important in determining the value of gold than the value of gold is in determining the price level. Normally, changes in gold reserves are a factor in determining changes in the supply of money; but now, at home and abroad, expansion and contraction in the volume of money are only slightly related, if at all, to changes in the total volume of gold reserves.

The United States now has a managed paper standard based on gold. It is important to recognize this hybrid characteristic of the present standard situation and either abolish gold and concentrate on improving management or else strengthen the gold standard on an international basis. At the present time the United States is in a key position, and any action which it takes on the re-establishment of a full gold standard will have great influence on the rest of the world.

QUESTIONS AND PROBLEMS

1. Why was the world-wide departure from the gold standard during the early thirties unusual? Explain.

---

[25] Trip, L. J. A., "Annual Report to the General Meeting of the Shareholders of the Netherlands Bank, June, 1939," *Federal Reserve Bulletin*, December, 1939, p. 1071.

2. Describe the events leading up to the national banking holiday.
3. Identify "internal and external drain of gold."
4. Which of the characteristics of the gold coin standard were suspended by the national banking holiday proclamation of March 6, 1933?
5. In one sense, we did not abandon the gold standard on April 19, 1933, "because the legal gold content of the dollar was unchanged and because the Government and the banks retained all gold as the basis for currency" (Roosevelt, Franklin D., *On Our Way*, p. 61). Discuss.
6. What is the Warren gold price theory? Explain.
7. Give the provisions of the Thomas Inflation Act. Which one is the most important? Why?
8. "Devaluation of currency on the part of a government is equivalent to the repudiation of a part of its debt" (Lichenstein, Walter, *Banking*, Sec. 2 [October, 1936], p. 3). Is this true? Explain.
9. Outline the Gold Reserve Act of 1934.
10. How may the gold clause decisions be justified? Discuss.
11. "Why should the foreigner, but not our citizens, be able to get our gold? The answer is—and it should be obvious—that our government cannot control the foreigner as it does our citizens. It can compel our citizens to take something less desirable than gold, but if it deals with the foreigners—buys his goods or services—he can demand the gold or refuse to accept our domestic currency except at a discount" (Spahr, W. E., *The Case for the Gold Standard*, p. 9). Discuss.
12. Comment on the following: If the United States leaves the gold standard, the loss in value of its gold will be chiefly a bookkeeping loss.
13. During the period between the wars much attention was given to the two gold problems, namely, international gold scarcity and the maldistribution of gold (see *Interim Report of the Gold Delegation of the Financial Committee, 1930*, League of Nations, pp. 11-20). Have these problems been solved since 1930? See "International Financial Statistics," *Federal Reserve Bulletin* for current statistics.
14. Dr. W. R. Burgess: "To my mind, the primary purpose of the Stabilization Fund is to provide a good vault for locking up that gold and keeping it out of use" ("Credit Control," *Proceedings of the Institute of Public Affairs*, University of Virginia, July 6-11, 1936). Is this statement in keeping with the purposes of Congress when it provided for devaluation of the dollar? Do events since 1934 justify the management policy of the Stabilization Fund as suggested by the above quotation? Why?
15. Identify Tripartite Agreements. Are these agreements still in effect?
16. Explain why the gold stock of the United States declined during World War II.

17. "The gold standard was better adopted to the prevention of inflation than the prevention of deflation." Explain. (See Hardy, C. O., *The Postwar Role of Gold*, p. 8).
18. Operation of the gold stabilization fund in secrecy has been criticized because "one of the valuable barometers of the international financial weather" is lost. Explain. (See Lyon, W. A., "Bankers Urge Open Dealing in Currencies," *New York Herald-Tribune*, October 25, 1936, Sec. IV, p. 1.)
19. Compare the present gold situation in the United States to the situation in 1896, when Mr. W. J. Bryan made his "Cross of Gold" speech.
20. Describe the present monetary standard of the United States.

REFERENCES

Brown, Jr., W. A. "Comments on Gold and the Monetary System," *American Economic Review*, Vol. XXX, No. 5 (February, 1941), pp. 38-51.

Brown, Jr., W. A. *The International Gold Standard Reinterpreted, 1914-1934.* New York: National Bureau of Economic Research, Inc., 1940. 2 vols.

Chandler, L. V. *An Introduction to Monetary Theory*, chap. v. New York: Harper & Bros., 1940.

Federal Reserve Bulletins. Washington: Board of Governors of the Federal Reserve System.

Gilbert, M. *Currency Depreciation and Monetary Policy*, pp. 104-50. Philadelphia: University of Pennsylvania Press, 1939.

Graham, F. D., and Whittlesey, C. R. *Golden Avalanche.* Princeton, N.J.: Princeton University Press, 1939.

Gregory, T. E. *The Gold Standard and Its Future.* New York: E. P. Dutton & Co., 1932.

Halm, G. N. *Monetary Theory*, chap. xii. Philadelphia: Blakiston Co., 1942.

Hardy, C. O. *Is There Enough Gold?* Washington: Brookings Institution. 1936.

Hardy, C. O. *The Postwar Role of Gold.* New York: Monetary Standards Inquiry, 1944.

Hardy, C. O. "The Price Level and the Gold Problem: Retrospect and Prospect," *American Economic Review*, Vol. XXX, No. 5 (February, 1941), pp. 18-29.

Hawtrey, R. G. *The Gold Standard in Theory and Practice.* 4th ed. New York: Longmans, Green & Co., 1939.

Heilperin, M. A. *International Monetary Economics*, chaps. i-iv. New York: Longmans, Green & Co., 1939.

International Gold Problem. Collected papers covering studies of members of the Royal Institute of International Affairs. London: Oxford University Press, 1931.

Kemmerer, E. W. *The Gold Standard—Its Nature and Future.* New York: Economists' National Committee on Monetary Policy, 1940.

Langum, J. K. "Treasury Gold Policy and Member Bank Reserve Balances, 1934-1939," *Financial and Investment Review,* Vol. VII, No. 12. School of Business Administration, University of Minnesota.

Layton, W. T., and Crowther, G. *An Introduction to the Theory of Prices,* chaps. iii-xii. London: MacMillan Co. Ltd., 1935.

League of Nations. *First Interim Report of the Gold Delegation of the Financial Committee* (1930); *Second Interim Report of the Gold Delegation of the Financial Committee* (1931); *Selected Documents on the Distribution of Gold Submitted to the Gold Delegation* (1931). Geneva.

Machlup, Fritz. "Eight Questions on Gold: A Review," *American Economic Review,* Vol. XXX, No. 5 (February, 1941), pp. 30-37.

Mahr, Alexander, *Monetary Stability.* Public Policy Pamphlet, No. 9. Chicago: University of Chicago Press, 1933.

National Industrial Conference Board. *The New Monetary System of the United States,* chaps. i and ii. New York: National Industrial Conference Board, Inc., 1934.

Neisser, H. P. "The Price Level and the Gold Problem," *American Economic Review,* Vol. XXX, No. 5 (February, 1941), pp. 1-17.

Palyi, Melchior. *Monetary Chaos and Gold.* Public Policy Pamphlet, No. 11. Chicago: University of Chicago Press, 1935.

Pasvolsky, Leo. *Current Monetary Issues.* Washington: Brookings Institution, 1933.

Spahr, W. E. *The Case for the Gold Standard.* New York: Economists' National Committee on Monetary Policy, 1940.

Spahr, W. E. *Alternative in Postwar International Monetary Standards.* New York: The Monetary Standards Inquiry, 1944.

Warren, G. F., and Pearson, F. A. *Gold and Prices,* chaps. i, v, and xxvi. New York: John Wiley & Sons, Inc., 1935.

CHAPTER VI

SILVER AND THE STANDARD PROBLEM

Introduction

The same principles which govern the gold standard also apply to the silver standard. For example, a country on the silver coin standard is one which has as its unit of value a fixed weight of silver. It provides for free coinage of silver, makes silver coins full legal tender, and requires redemption of paper money in silver coins. Finally, it permits the operation of a free silver market, both domestic and foreign, which includes freedom to hoard and to export and to import silver.

Silver and gold have many of the same characteristics. Both are precious metals whose values are stated in terms of ounces (troy) and not pounds or tons. Both are generally acceptable for hoarding purposes. Both are widely used in the arts, and both are used as money. The dominance of gold as the standard metal has been of recent origin even in Western countries. It was only during the few years just prior to the Great Depression that the East and West were united in adherence to the gold standard.[1] As noted in the preceding chapter, this universal reign of gold as a monetary standard was of short duration.

Now memories of the Great Depression and its accompanying deflation in prices, rightly or wrongly associated with gold scarcity in individual countries, are the chief obstacles to the readoption of the international gold standard. Memories of the monetary chaos that existed after World War I are the chief obstacles to the adoption of managed paper money standards. If emphasis is to be placed on national rather than on international affairs, it is technically possible for the countries of Europe to operate on paper money standards, the Americas on a gold standard, and the Far and Near East on a silver standard. Such a program would be a step backward and undesirable in an atomic age and inconsistent with the present emphasis on the creation of some type of international monetary system.

[1] Brown, W. A., *The International Gold Standard Reinterpreted, 1914-1934*, Vol. II, p. 773.

What Is Bimetallism?

Legal bimetallism exists when provisions are made for the use of two metals, at a fixed weight proportionate to each other, called the "mint ratio," to form at the same time the standard of value. Any two metals may be the ones chosen, but the world's experience has been with gold and silver. There must be an open mint ready to coin or purchase at fixed prices any quantity of gold and/or silver that may be brought to it. In addition, debtors must be given the right to discharge their obligations by using standard coins made from either of the two metals. In other words, (1) provisions must be made for the free coinage of gold and silver, and (2) standard coins made from the metals must have unlimited legal tender.

Like other standards, to function successfully, the bimetallic standard should be adopted on a world-wide basis. Experiences of the world have been primarily with national bimetallism, and these have been the basis for the conclusion that this standard is unworkable in practice. Most Western nations have had a legal bimetallic system; but because of the differences in mint ratios, the metal overvalued at the mint tended to become the *de facto* (in fact) monetary standard of the country. During the eighteenth and part of the nineteenth centuries, Spain had a 16 to 1 ratio, France and the members of the Latin Monetary Union had a 15½ to 1 ratio, and the United States a 15 to 1 ratio (later 16 to 1). If all the countries on the bimetallic standard had had the same mint ratio, the record of this standard would have been much better. This will be apparent after a discussion of the compensatory principle of bimetallism.

The Effects of Gresham's Law

There is a natural tendency for individuals to use the cheaper metal (i.e., cheaper in terms of money value) within an area covered by a legal tender law. This means that the cheaper money will be used as hand-to-hand money to redeem paper money and to serve the other domestic demands for money. Likewise, there is a natural tendency to hoard the more valuable money and to use it in all international transactions that are not covered by legal tender laws. While this tendency of cheaper money to drive the dearer out of circulation is operating at all times in a free economy, one standard metal will not displace the other entirely if the supply of the cheaper money is not sufficiently great to displace the dearer from use as a standard.

When countries have operated on a legal bimetallic standard, their experiences have justified the conclusion that legally the standard of value may be gold and silver, but in practice it usually is gold or silver. In other words, the standard tends to be monometallic rather than bimetallic. In order that bimetallism be effective, the

ILLUSTRATION I

EFFECTS OF DIFFERENCES IN MINT AND MARKET RATIOS

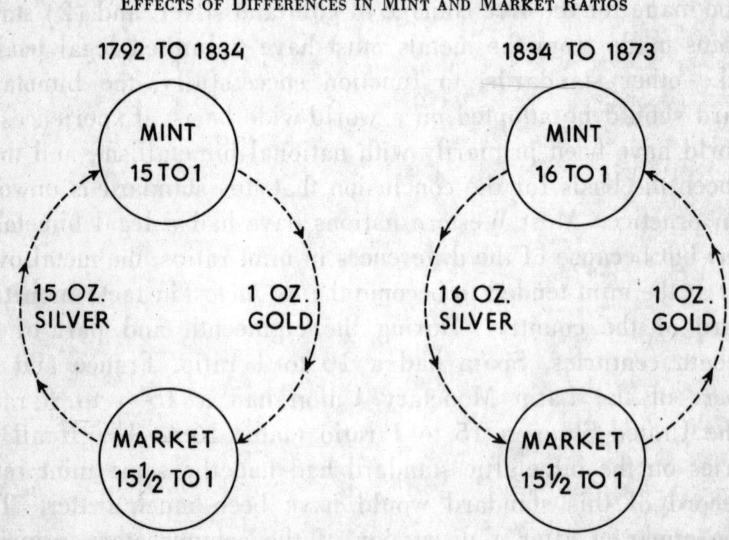

value of gold and silver in world markets must be in the same ratio as that fixed by law in the country on the bimetallic standard. The mint ratio is a weight ratio, and the assumption is that it will also be the value ratio.

In Illustration I, these assumptions are made: (1) the mint ratio is 15 to 1, as was the case between 1792 and 1834; (2) the mint ratio is 16 to 1, as was the case between 1834 and 1873; and (3) the market ratio is $15\frac{1}{2}$ to 1 in both instances, which was about the average commercial ratio for the period from 1792 to 1873.[2] As

[2] *Annual Report of the Director of the Mint for the Fiscal Year Ended June 30, 1941*, p. 91.

indicated by Illustration I, silver would flow to the mint during the first period, and gold coins and gold bullion would flow to the market. Soon the mint would be exhausted of gold, and only silver would be left to serve as the domestic metallic reserve of the country. This situation would continue until the market ratio changed to correspond to the mint ratio, or until Congress changed the mint ratio as it did in 1834.

The situation following the change of mint ratio to 16 to 1 is shown in Illustration I. Now the mint would lose silver, and gold would flow to the mint until the mint would be exhausted of silver; and gold would be left to serve as the domestic metallic reserve of the country. Prices would be quoted in terms of the dollar, which would be in fact a gold standard dollar. The double standard would have disappeared, and the nation would have a *de facto* gold standard.

The Compensatory Principle of Bimetallism

The bimetallists realize the theoretical possibilities of shifts in the market ratio which would cause the metal overvalued at the mint to drive the other metal out of circulation. But they argue that the workings of the compensatory principle of bimetallism would prevent the disappearance from circulation of one or the other metal. The compensatory principle of bimetallism is that one standard metal would not become the single standard, because the other standard metal, which would leave the monetary system for the commercial market, would so flood this market that the surplus would cause the value to decrease, and it would automatically return as a monetary metal. The effects would be to bring the market ratios in line with the mint ratios, that is, 15 to 1 before 1834 and 16 to 1 after 1834. Thus the dual character of bimetallism would be retained. Before rejecting this principle, as based on the experiences in the United States, it should be noted that France was operating successfully on a bimetallic standard with a mint ratio of 15½ to 1 during most of this period.

The operation of the bimetallic standard tends (1) to compensate the cheaper monetary standard metal for its loss in value in the commercial market by having the work of the standard transferred to it; and (2) to decrease the value of the dearer metal by transferring it from the monetary to the commercial market, where the added supply would tend to decrease its value. Of course, this is only a statement of tendencies and no assurance that the shift in values would be enough to justify the expectation that the weight ratio of the mint would be at the same time the commercial ratio of the two metals.

Only the shifting of gold or silver in large amounts can effectively lower their prices.[3] Likewise, the monetary demand for silver or gold must be large enough to have the desired value-raising effect in order to bring the market ratio in line with the mint ratio. Therefore, an important additional inference from the compensatory principle is that the more widely bimetallism is adopted, the greater is the possibility of its success. The ideal condition would be one in which all countries would operate on a bimetallic standard with the same mint ratio.

An Illustration of National Bimetallism

The conclusion that when one country adopts a legal bimetallic standard it in reality adopts a gold *or* silver standard, not a gold *and* silver standard, is illustrated by the early history of this standard in the United States. The Coinage Act of 1792 contained the two essential provisions for a bimetallic standard: (1) free or unlimited coinage of gold and silver at a fixed mint ratio, and (2) full legal tender for coins made from the two metals. There were three periods in the history of the bimetallic standard in the United States: (1) from 1792 to 1834, when the mint ratio of 15-1 overvalued silver; (2) from 1834 to 1862, when the mint ratio of approximately 16-1 overvalued gold; and (3) from 1862 to 1873, when issues of irredeemable government paper money forced both legal standard metals out of use as standard money.

Overvalued Silver—1792-1834.—Our first mint ratio, 15 to 1, overvalued silver and undervalued gold. Soon after the Coinage Act of 1792 was passed, the market ratio of silver to gold was 15½ to 1.

[3] Professor L. A. Froman questions this effect. "Purely on the basis of the effect of an increased supply, this would seem to be the case, but there is a great deal of evidence to support the conclusion that countries possess an almost unlimited capacity to absorb supplies of the various metals without materially affecting their market or mint prices. Consider the cases of the United States since 1920 and France since 1928. Both of these countries have absorbed very large amounts of gold without causing the price of gold to go down in terms of the price of silver" ("Bimetallism Reconsidered," *American Economic Review,* Vol. XXVI, No. 1 [March, 1936], p. 59).

While the mint was offering only 15 ounces of silver, or its equivalent, for gold, buyers in the arts market and international bankers were giving the equivalent of 15½ ounces. In terms of American money this half-ounce of silver represented about 65 cents. As a result, little gold was taken to the mint. Down to 1800 less than $700,000 of gold were minted, and during the next thirty-five years the total amount coined was less than $15,000,000. The gold coins which were minted did not stay in circulation, because their value as money was less than their bullion value.

By 1834 the market premium on gold amounted to as much as 90 cents per fine ounce. In other words, the equivalent of $100.00 in gold bullion would buy $104.50 in silver. Under these conditions it was only natural that gold bullion was sold in the market and was not taken to the mint. By 1818 gold had completely disappeared from circulation.[4] The American Silver dollar likewise failed to circulate during this period, but for a very different reason.

The new American silver dollars were coined for the first time in 1794. They passed for the same value as the Spanish dollars, or pieces of eight, which were slightly heavier and more valuable. Yankee traders and bullion dealers soon took advantage of this situation. The West Indian natives preferred the new shiny American dollars to the heavier Spanish coins. Traders gathered the Spanish dollars and took them to the United States mint to be melted down and made into new American dollars. Coinage was unlimited and gratuitous, and a profit of about 1 per cent resulted. About $1,500,000 were manufactured at the expense of the government, with little or no effect upon our circulating medium, because the American dollars disappeared from the domestic market as fast as they were struck.

President Thomas Jefferson saw no reason for operating the mint for the profit of bullion traders, and so on May 1, 1806, he ordered the suspension of the coinage of silver dollars, a ban which remained in effect until 1834. This did not mean the legal abandonment of the bimetallic standard, for the free coinage of fractional silver pieces was allowed. The silver one-half dollar was the most popular American coin, and it was coined in large amounts.

Overvalued Gold—1834-62.—As early as 1818, Congress con-

[4] There was no gold coinage during the years 1816 and 1817 (*United States Coinage Laws, 1792-1894* [Washington, D.C.: U.S. Government Printing Office], p. 95).

sidered changing the legal ratio, but action was not taken until 1834. Representative C. B. White of New York recommended the adoption of a silver standard, but later in the same session he completely changed his position and reported a bill favoring gold over silver (16 to 1 ratio). Senator Thomas Benton was in favor of a ratio that would place this country in a position to compete with Spain for gold from Mexico, Central America, and South America. The Spanish ratio was 16 to 1; and, as a result, the exportable gold flowed to Spain, while their surplus silver came to the United States, where the ratio was 15 to 1. Spain was on a *de facto* gold standard, and the United States was on a *de facto* silver standard.

Senator John C. Calhoun from South Carolina felt that gold should be the preferred metal but that silver should also be retained. The result of this powerful congressional support was the Gold Bill of 1834, so called because it aimed to increase the number of gold coins and to keep them in circulation. The method was simple—a reduction of the fine gold content of the gold dollar from 24.75 grains to 23.20 grains. The effect of this shift was to increase the mint price of gold by almost $1.25 per fine ounce. Silver coins were not altered, and so the mint ratio was changed from 15 to 1 to slightly more than 16 to 1.

In 1837 another act was passed that provided for the readjustment of the amount of alloy in coins, making them 9/10 fine. The weight of the gold coin remained the same, but the fine gold content was increased 0.02 grains—from 23.2 to 23.22 grains. Since the pure silver in the silver dollar was not changed, this made the new ratio slightly less than 16 to 1, where it remained until the gold dollar was devalued in 1934. Unfortunately for the success of bimetallism, this ratio overvalued gold at the mint. Silver, now the undervalued metal, was driven out of circulation.

The amount of gold coined increased during this period immediately following the change in mint ratio, but the greatest flow of the yellow metal to the mint began after the discovery of gold in California in 1848. At a mint ratio of 16 to 1, silver owners could dispose of their silver bullion at the United States mint only at a loss, it being necessary to give one-half ounce more silver to obtain the money equivalent of an ounce of gold than was necessary in the commercial market or in France, where the 15½ to 1 ratio prevailed.

Since the standard silver dollar had not been coined in any important amount, no hardship resulted because of the change in mint ratio in so far as this coin was concerned, but the gradual disappearance of the silver one-half dollar and other fractional silver coins resulted in real hardship. In 1853 the government solved this problem by abolishing the free coinage of silver for all coins from the 3 cent piece to the 50 cent piece. These coins were made light weight to prevent their being melted down and sold as bullion. They were token coins, manufactured from silver bullion bought by the government and sold in convenient quantities to banks and the public. No action was taken on the silver dollar, and that section in the law authorizing the free coinage of silver bullion into standard silver dollars remained. Hence legal bimetallism was retained until after the passage of the Coinage Act of 1873.

Paper Money Drove All Coins Out of Circulation.—Throughout the early history of coinage in the United States, the federal government issued coins which were forced to compete with state bank notes issued in small denominations. Banks found it profitable to issue notes in denominations as small as 6 1/4 cents because they were less likely to come back for redemption. All that were lost or destroyed meant 100 per cent profit to the issuing bank. There was a scarcity of specie, and so small notes were justified on this basis. However, the very existence of small-denomination notes explains in part the scarcity of specie. This operation of Gresham's law was not appreciated, and so banks usually received wide support for their small-note issues.

Several state governments recognized by legislation the advantages of having only bank paper notes with denominations of $5.00 or more, but the beneficial effects of these laws were largely nullified by circulation of small notes which originated in other states. Steps were taken by states to keep these foreign notes out of circulation within their borders; but opposition was great, evasion easy, and in practice most of such acts became dead letters. The subsidiary silver coinage act of 1853 did much to rectify the unsatisfactory small-change currency situation, but this law was in effect for less than ten years before the outbreak of the Civil War. During this war issuance of United States notes, greenbacks, placed so great a strain upon the metallic currency system that all types of coined money were driven out of circulation.

"Crime of 1873."—Between 1920 and 1928 most European coun-

tries faced the problem of reorganizing their subsidiary coinage systems, as well as that of returning to the gold standard. Where inflation was extreme, most silver and other token coins had been driven out of circulation by cheap, excessive issues of irredeemable paper money. Similarly, when the United States was on the paper standard during the sixties and seventies of the last century, the federal government faced this same problem. In 1869 two Treasury employees undertook a revision and codification of the scattered coinage laws. This reorganization bill was brought before Congress in 1869 but was not passed until 1873. This law was a general revision of all laws which affected coinage and mints in the United States. No change was made in gold coinage other than some technical changes which dealt with variations in weight and allowance for wear. Silver coins were made legal tender to $5.00, and certain minor technical allowances were made for variation in their weight. The minor coins were made legal tender for 25 cents in one payment.

The part of the act which later made it of immense political importance was the discontinuance of the provisions for the free coinage of the practically unknown silver dollar. During the three years that the bill was before Congress, no congressman or senator questioned the wisdom of this policy. The committees in charge of the bill wished to do something for the silver mining industry; so they created a subsidiary trade dollar containing 420 grains of silver. Silver producers gave little thought to the domestic market for silver coins, but they welcomed the help of the United States in manufacturing silver coins which would add to the use of American silver in the Orient. American traders were anxious to hold or to regain their commercial markets in that part of the world, and it was assumed that the trade dollar would be of some help. Although the trade dollar was not intended for circulation in the United States, it was given legal tender up to $5.00.

Two additional blunders were made by Congress: (1) the act did not require the redemption of all forms of money in gold, thereby failing to recognize gold as the only standard, and (2) the way was left open for the most acrimonious monetary controversy in our history, by merely omitting the silver dollar from the list of coins and by not taking more positive action in abolishing bimetallism.

Two developments which began in 1874 made the act of 1873 of political significance. One was the discovery of rich silver mines in Nevada, and the other was the fall in the market price of silver below the old mint price. The new silver interests soon discovered that if the silver dollar had not been dropped they could have taken their silver bullion to the mint and disposed of it at the mint price of $1.29+ per fine ounce.[5] The drive for the restoration of the bimetallic standard and the return of the standard silver dollar began. Although the silverites have secured many concessions from Congress, including the return of the standard silver dollar, they have not secured a law permitting the free coinage of silver and the return of a bimetallic standard.

Limping Standard.—In 1878 Congress passed the Bland-Allison Act followed twelve years later by the Sherman Silver Purchase Act. Details of these acts are found in the next chapter, but they are introduced at this time because they provided for the return of the standard silver dollar, and we are concerned with the effects of these laws on the standard.

From an administrative viewpoint the Bland-Allison Act provided for the return of the standard silver dollar in the same way as the return of the other silver coins was provided for in 1853. Silver bullion was to be purchased by the government, minted into token coins, and then sold to banks and the public. However, there were three ways in which the return of the silver dollar was handled differently from the return of the half dollar and other silver coins. (1) The weight of the silver dollar was not reduced, as was true of the other silver token coins; and, in order to distinguish it from the "trade" dollar, the nomenclature "standard silver dollar" was retained. (2) The government was required to purchase from two to four million dollars worth of silver per month and to coin it into standard silver dollars. This is contrary to subsidiary coinage principles, because all token coins should be manufactured and issued according to the need for small-change currency. (3) The standard silver dollar was given the unlimited legal tender quality, while the other silver coins had but limited legal tender.

The new silver dollar injected into the currency system remained unwanted except in the West and among certain groups in the South. The public preference for paper money in denominations of $1.00

[5] In the commercial market the average ratio of silver to gold annually since 1687 appears on page 91 of the *Annual Report of the Director of the Mint for the Fiscal Year Ended June 30, 1944.* It fluctuated between 14 and 16 to 1 from 1687 to 1874. During 1940, 1941, and 1942 the ratio was over 99 to 1.

and above was recognized, and silver certificates were issued to replace the silver dollars. Thus the Treasury went through the procedure of buying silver bullion, coining it into unwanted silver dollars, printing silver certificates, passing the silver certificates on to banks and the general public, and retaining the unwanted silver dollars as a reserve for the silver certificates.

The Sherman Silver Purchase Act of 1890 added to the increasing strain and complexity of the monetary system in two ways: (1) Congress required the monthly purchase of silver to be increased to 4,500,000 ounces per month, which doubled the quantity of silver bullion purchased, and (2) Congress required that the silver purchased be paid for with Treasury or "Sherman" notes. Now the Treasury went through the procedure of buying silver bullion, paying for it with paper money called "Treasury notes," coining silver into silver dollars, issuing silver certificates to retire the Treasury notes, and retaining the silver dollars as a reserve.

Under the gold standard, all forms of money are redeemable directly or indirectly in gold, but Congress failed in 1878 and again in 1890 to make provisions for redeeming silver dollars and silver certificates in gold. Even the Treasury notes of 1890 were redeemable in either gold or silver at the option of the Treasury. The country was practically on a gold standard, but the uncertainty of the status of the silver dollar caused this period to be referred to as one in which we had a "limping" or "peg-leg" standard. This condition was corrected in part in 1900, when the Treasury was given the task of keeping all types of money equal to gold in value. By implication this made silver dollars, silver certificates, and the Treasury notes of 1890 redeemable in gold. This act is known as the Gold Standard Act of 1900. It is unfortunate that the name "standard silver dollar" was retained, because it has given a connotation to this token or subsidiary coin not possessed in fact.

International Bimetallism

Latin Monetary Union.—The only experience the world has had with international bimetallism was that provided by the Latin Monetary Union. This experiment involved only a few countries and was of short duration. In 1865 agreements were made by France, Italy, Belgium, and Switzerland to adopt the same standard unit (worth

19.3 cents); to allow the free coinage of gold and silver at the same mint ratio (15½ to 1); to issue coins of uniform size, weight, and fineness (the coins might differ in design); and to accept one another's coins.[6]

In financing the costs of its reorganization as a kingdom, Italy issued large quantities of irredeemable paper money. The paper money issues drove specie out of circulation in Italy, sending it to other members of the Latin Monetary Union.[7] By terms of the bimetallic agreement, these countries were legally bound to accept them; and, as a result, the supply of coins in these countries became excessive. In 1867, at an international monetary convention, a vote was taken upon the question of standards. Although Great Britain was the only country on the gold standard at that time, most of the delegates voted in favor of the gold standard. France hoped that most of the other nations would join the Latin Monetary Union or agree upon some international bimetallic system. Greece did join, but her currency structure was in such a plight that her addition was harmful rather than beneficial to the union.[8]

The Franco-Prussian War hastened the end of the Latin Monetary Union. France was decisively defeated and was forced to pay an indemnity of five billion gold francs. German troops were to occupy France until it was paid. In order that the country might be freed from the presence of the Germans, the French people made pathetic sacrifices to pay this indemnity. To the surprise of the world, France succeeded in paying it in full within three years, and Germany took this opportunity to adopt the gold standard.

France and other members of the Latin Monetary Union, fearing a flood of silver no longer wanted by Germany, higher prices, and erratic exchange rates, abolished the free coinage of silver. England had adopted the gold standard following the Napoleonic Wars; and the United States, with the exception of the paper money period of the Civil War, had been on the *de facto* gold standard since 1834. In 1872 Sweden, Norway, and Denmark adopted the gold standard. By the end of the century, most of the Western countries of the world had the value of their money tied to gold. The shift from bimetallism

---

[6] The Treaty of 1865 made provisions for the Latin Monetary Union. It is published as Appendix I in Willis, H. P., *A History of the Latin Monetary Union.*

[7] Willis, *ibid.*, pp. 61-70.

[8] *Ibid.*, pp. 78-81.

to gold not only decreased the international attractiveness of bimetallism but also made adherence to it difficult, if not impossible. The increase in demand for gold for monetary purposes increased its value. As the value of gold in terms of silver rose, the price of silver in terms of gold declined. Under such conditions, if the free coinage of silver had been continued by only a few countries, their mints would have been flooded with silver.

Although the Latin Monetary Union failed to maintain a bimetallic system, its members continued to maintain uniformity in the standard unit and in silver coins until World War I. Furthermore, the Latin Monetary Union gave recognition to the basic principles of international bimetallism. These included a fixed universal legal or mint ratio of silver to gold with free coinage of both metals, unlimited legal tender for both gold and silver coins, and redemption of paper money in the standard metals. In a global bimetallic system it may not be necessary to have uniformity in size, weight, and fineness of coins; but such a practice would expedite their circulation.

Global Bimetallic Standard.—Assuming that all governments were to agree to adopt an international bimetallic monetary standard, the first question to be answered would be, what is to be the legal or mint ratio? This ratio should be approximately the same as the market ratio in order to avoid confusion in the market and to prevent a breakdown in the bimetallic standard. If a wide divergence from the market ratio existed, it would result in a scarcity in the commercial market of the metal which is overvalued at the mint and a surplus in the commercial market of the metal which is undervalued. But, given a bimetallic mint ratio near the market ratio, there would be little danger of a breakdown in the standard, owing to the operation of Gresham's law.

Because of the number and variety of vested interests involved in the markets for gold and silver, it would be difficult to secure international agreement on the legal or mint ratio. Countries in which gold or silver is produced would want a ratio which would favor their product. Silver interests might seek a mint ratio of 16 to 1 instead of perhaps 50 to 1. In terms of the present price of $35.00 per ounce for gold, this would mean 1/16 of $35.00, or $2.19, as the mint price per ounce of silver instead of 1/50 of $35.00, or 70 cents, per ounce of silver.

If free coinage of both gold and silver were permitted, would the influx of new money resulting from monetization of silver cause inflation? The answer would depend upon the reaction of the general public throughout the world to their government's new hard money. Since all types of the circulating media would be redeemable in the new coins, the result might be that as the volume of new coins in circulation increased the volume of paper money in circulation would decline. If, added to this factor, there were an increase in the average size of cash balances held by individuals, because of a hoarding or store-of-value demand, the result might be the lowering rather than the raising of general prices. On the other hand, if the general public should prefer to use paper money as hand-to-hand money, coins would become redundant and would remain in the vaults of the governments and central banks.

At present the world is using silver in large quantities in subsidiary coins. If the bimetallic standard were adopted, these coins would have to be retired and replaced with new ones of standard fineness. To expedite the operation of the new standard and to facilitate the circulation of coins, it would be desirable to follow the leadership of the Latin Monetary Union and have all coins uniform as to weight and size as well as fineness.

Arguments in Favor of Bimetallism

Bimetallic Standard Is More Stable in Value than Gold.—Those in favor of bimetallism start with the same premise as those in favor of the gold standard. It is necessary to have some widely acceptable commodity to serve as the standard of value in order to maintain confidence in the media of exchange and to prevent inflation brought on by an overissuance of irredeemable paper money. They favor the use of two commodities as the standard, because they claim that it will give the world a more stable standard than either gold or silver alone. Since the quantity of value to be influenced would be greater, an increase in the supply of gold or silver would be less disturbing than if reliance were placed upon one metal.

Jevons illustrates this argument in favor of bimetallism by assuming that there are two reservoirs of water, one representing gold and the other silver.[9] When the two are disconnected, both are sub-

[9] Jevons, W. S., *Money and the Mechanism of Exchange*, p. 138.

ject to considerable fluctuation, owing to changes in supply and demand in either one. But if the two reservoirs are connected, any disturbing element in one is distributed over the entire area. The average effect is less than if the entire disturbance were confined to one reservoir.

In addition, gold and silver are produced under different economic conditions, production of gold being more stimulated by depressions than silver, because the output of silver depends to a large degree upon the demands for copper and other metals. It is a joint product of mines, and therefore its production is greatly influenced by economic demands for other metals. The assumption is that the value of gold and silver will vary, but in opposite directions. The effect on the value of money is to replace a series of major fluctuations in prices with a large number of minor ones. Professor Fisher's illustration is that of "arm-in-arm drunken men." If two intoxicated men of the same approximate size and weight locked arms and were inclined to fall in opposite directions at the same time, the linking together would bring stability.

The value of gold and silver do vary, but not always in opposite directions. For example, the value of both gold and silver was falling from 1896 to 1914; and, if the value of money had been tied to gold and silver, general prices would have increased even faster than they actually did. During the period 1921-29 the value of gold was unusually stable, while silver was subject to fluctuation. Unquestionably during this and the preceding period bimetallism would have been more harmful than helpful. On the other hand, if both gold and silver had been used as a standard from 1873 to 1897, it might have been of considerable aid in stabilizing international prices. But in recent years, as already noted in preceding chapters, the supply of deposit currency and hand-to-hand money have been much more important factors than the volume of standard money in determining the actual price level.

Scarcity of Gold.—Another argument in favor of international bimetallism is a scarcity in the supply of gold. During the late twenties there was much anxiety over the dwindling supply of new gold, but since that time the situation has changed markedly. Since 1929 the monetary gold stock, estimated in dollars, has more than tripled. This has been due to revaluation, to increase in gold production, and to dehoarding in India.

Unless it is assumed that most of the paper money in circulation is to be replaced by hard money, there is little to be found in the scarcity-of-gold argument to support international bimetallism. Even if the government made available large quantities of coined money in the form of gold, it is doubtful if any large amount would be demanded in the United States to replace paper money. However, this situation might be different in other countries which have been plagued with inflated issues of paper money issues. One may conclude that in the near future the large stores of silver will not be needed to buttress an international gold standard except in a subsidiary capacity.

QUESTIONS AND PROBLEMS

1. Define or explain: (*a*) bimetallism, (*b*) mint or legal ratio, (*c*) mint price, (*d*) undervalued at the mint, and (*e*) overvalued at the mint.
2. Define and illustrate "compensatory principle of bimetallism."
3. Compare experiences of the United States with gold coinage before and after 1834.
4. Why was the mint ratio changed in 1834? (References: Dewey, *Financial History of the United States* [11th ed.], pp. 210-12; Carothers, *Fractional Money*, chap. viii.)
5. Why do political movements in favor of bimetallism gain the support of inflationists?
6. Even before 1834 there were few silver dollars in circulation. Why?
7. Did the Act of 1853 abolish "free coinage" of silver? Explain.
8. Who called the Coinage Act of 1873 the "Crime of 1873"? Why?
9. What effects did the Bland-Allison Act and the Sherman Purchase Act of 1890 have on the standard? Explain.
10. In the middle of the seventies of the last century "silver" congressmen were asking for a recoinage of the "dollar of our daddy." Was this a legitimate description of the silver dollar? Why?
11. Identify "the Gold Standard Act of 1900."
12. Distinguish carefully between "national bimetallism" and "international bimetallism." Illustrate.
13. Describe the Latin Monetary Union.
14. Give the arguments in favor of the international bimetallic standard.
15. Bimetallism "combines the worst features of both the gold and paper standards while it is actually in operation, and tends in practice to

become gold or silver monometallism" (Gayer, A. D., *Monetary Policy and Economic Stabilization,* p. 183). Discuss.

16. Coinage of "gold and silver at a fixed ratio causes movements of prices to be governed chiefly by the production of gold and silver alternately" (Marshall, *Money, Credit and Commerce,* p. 64). Explain. (Italics omitted.)

17. The principal currency in France was silver in 1849 but was almost wholly gold in 1860. "France absorbed the cheapened metal in vast quantities and emitted the dearer metal, which must have had the effect of preventing gold from falling and silver from rising so much in value as they would otherwise have done." What principles are illustrated? Explain. (Jevons, *Money and the Mechanism of Exchange,* p. 139.)

18. At one time the English pound was equal in value to a pound of silver, troy weight. If the English pound were still of the same weight, what would be its value today? Compare to the value of the present English monetary unit.

19. "The first objection that is always advanced is that bimetallism has failed in the past and therefore must fail again in the future. This is not so. What those who argue along that line really mean, and they are correct, is that attempts by a single country to maintain a bimetallic standard have failed and always will fail." Do you agree? (Mitchell, *The Place of Silver in Monetary Reconstruction,* p. 12.)

20. A universal bimetallic standard "would allow the devastated and impoverished nations of Europe and Asia to restore their domestic currencies, get rid of their worthless paper and mint silver coins that would possess unlimited legal tender." Do the people of the world want this standard? (*Ibid.* p. 6.)

REFERENCES

See end of Chapter VII

Chapter VII

SILVER—A SUBSIDIARY METAL

Introduction

In the preceding chapter the use of silver as a standard of value, either alone or jointly with gold, was considered. In 1834, in the United States, silver ceased being a standard metal because it was undervalued at the mint. Legally the United States abandoned the bimetallic standard in 1873 by discontinuing the free coinage of silver.

Silver is still used as money in the United States, both in the form of subsidiary coins and as reserves against silver certificates. Subsidiary silver coins are a characteristic of all monetary systems, but the silver certificate is a peculiarity of the United States monetary system.

At the present time the volume of silver money, in the form of bullion and coin, is in excess of the total amount of money which was in circulation prior to World War I. About one-third of this silver is in the form of subsidiary or token coins. Therefore, if Congress permitted the Treasury to adhere to the subsidiary coinage principles discussed below, less than one-third of the present stock of monetary silver would be sufficient for the United States, leaving about $2,000-000,000 unaccounted for on the basis of monetary need. The $2,000,000,000 question is: "How did this huge surplus stock of silver become a part of the monetary system?"

Subsidiary Coinage

Fractional Silver Coins.—Subsidiary or token coins are credit money printed or stamped on metal. As indicated in the Chapter VI, prior to 1853 silver coins with values of less than one dollar were not token coins but fractional parts of the standard. The free coinage privilege applied to both gold and silver. Hence silver dimes, quarters, and half dollars were not subsidiary to standard money but were legally a fractional part of it.

Subsidiary Silver Coinage Act.—The legal status of fractional silver coins was changed by the Subsidiary Silver Coinage Act of

1853. In order to understand the need for this law, it is necessary to review the effects upon silver coinage of the Gold Bill of 1834. This bill changed the mint ratio to approximately 16 to 1; it overvalued gold at the mint, and it undervalued silver. Full-weight silver coins were worth more as bullion than as coins. The circulating supply of American silver coins, which had never been sufficient, decreased. The distress became acute after the discovery of gold in California, which was followed by an increase in the flow of gold to the mint, higher general prices, including the price of silver, and the melting-down of most of the remainder of the worn as well as the full-weight silver coins.

In order to keep the fractional coins in circulation, three steps were taken. The act of 1853 provided for the reduction of fine silver content by about 7 per cent, and this decrease in weight eliminated the profit from melting them. This change made silver coinage profitable, but the government pre-empted the privilege by providing that all small silver pieces were to be coined only from bullion bought by the government.

Minor Coins.—The Subsidiary Coinage Act of 1853 was not the first experience that the United States has had with money manufactured under conditions of limited coinage. Since 1792 copper 1 cent and ½ cent pieces had been manufactured on this basis, but their coinage was discontinued in 1857. Then the government experimented with a 1 cent nickel piece (1857-64), but it was discontinued in favor of a bronze cent. Two bronze coins were authorized in 1864: a 2 cent piece, which was discontinued in 1873, and a 1 cent piece, which is still a part of the currency system. A 3 cent piece was authorized in 1865 and discontinued in 1890, and a 5 cent piece composed of 75 per cent copper and 25 per cent nickel was added in 1866.

During World War II, warring countries drew heavily upon their circulating media to meet the armament needs for critical metals. Copper, silver, and nickel coins were replaced with paper money or coins made from noncritical materials, which varied from country to country. Germany and Japan exploited not only their own monetary systems but also those of the countries which they conquered. As discussed in Chapter II, a zinc-coated 1 cent coin was minted in the United States, but it was abandoned at the end of 1943, when salvaged, fired, brass cartridge cases became available for use in making a new copper coin which is practically the same as the pre-war coin, except that no tin is used as an alloy. The government ceased using nickel in the manufacture of coins in 1942, the composition of the new 5 cent piece being an alloy of copper, silver, and manganese. Thus experimentation continues, but throughout history the basic token currency principles have been recognized in so far as minor coins are concerned.

Foreign Coins.—Not only did the United States government experiment with minor and silver coins, but it was forced by the needs of the country to allow foreign coins to be used in domestic transactions. In February, 1793, the legal tender quality was given to certain designated foreign coins. The legal tender status was to hold for but three years after the active opening of the United States mint. An exception was made in favor of Spanish milled dollars, which were to be the only foreign coins to possess the legal tender quality thereafter. A presidential proclamation was issued in July, 1791, announcing that coinage of silver had begun.

Three years thereafter foreign coins were to lose their legal tender quality in the United States, but, when the date arrived, the status of our currency was such as to warrant an extension by Congress for another three years, and this was renewed at various times until 1857. By this time the United States was well on the way toward developing a satisfactory token coinage system, but, as noted in the preceding chapter, this development was interrupted by the Civil War and the currency chaos which resulted from ill-conceived methods of financing it. As a result of the Coinage Act of 1873, the United States was soon on the way toward re-establishing a sound token money system, a development which was confused by return of the so-called standard silver dollars. Before discussing this movement, it is well to summarize the subsidiary or token money principles, thereby providing a background on which to appraise the history of silver or token money in the United States since 1878.

Subsidiary Coinage Principles.—There are four subsidiary or token coinage principles: (1) Coinage must be limited, that is, manufactured from bullion purchased by the government. (2) Coins must have a bullion or metal content value low enough so that they will not be melted down and sold as bullion and high enough to make it unprofitable for counterfeiters to imitate them. (3) The supply should be limited to the amount necessary to meet the small-change demand for currency. In order to prevent any quantity from remaining in circulation after the coins have become redundant, the government must make provisions for repurchasing them in reasonable quantities at the request of the general public. (4) Token coins should have limited legal tender in order that debtors may have some legal means whereby they may discharge their small debts.

The history of United States currency contains many illustrations of the importance of these principles. Reference has already been made to experiences with the silver coins issued under the free coinage acts of 1792, 1834, and 1837. During the Civil War greenbacks drove all types of coins out of circulation. Trade and commerce were so handicapped by the scarcity of small change that merchants, railroads, hotels, and other business firms issued their own coins and paper money in denominations of less than one dollar.

Private issuance of fractional paper money and tokens was forbidden by Congress on July 17, 1862, and on that same day the post office department was directed to issue special postage stamps which could be used for money. The department had difficulty in providing a satisfactory quantity of this so-called "postage currency"; consequently, nine months later, Congress made provisions for fractional paper money in the form of promissory notes. These fractional notes ("shinplasters") were about one-third the size of the greenbacks, and their legal status was the same. Under these two laws about $35,000,000 in postage currency and fractional greenbacks were issued. Large quantities were destroyed, for small denomination money of all types receives hard wear.

For a short period during World War I, the price of silver was high enough to justify the melting of subsidiary coins into bullion. When the price of silver rose above $1.29 an ounce, it became profitable to melt down silver dollars; but fractional coins contain 7 per cent less silver, and therefore the melting of fractional silver coins did not become profitable until silver sold for $1.38 per ounce. In November, 1919, the market price of silver reached $1.38. A bill was introduced in Congress to reduce the silver content of subsidiary coins, but no action was taken, and none was necessary, because of the decline in the price of silver.

Token coins must have legal tender, but there is no uniformity of opinion as to the importance of the legal tender quality, nor is there any uniformity as to the legal tender status of subsidiary coins throughout the world. From 1873 to 1933 subsidiary silver coins were legal tender to the amount of $10 in one payment, and minor coins, that is, nickel and copper coins, were legal tender to the amount of 25 cents in one payment. Standard silver dollars have always had unlimited legal tender quality, which, since 1933, all types of money in the United States have been granted.

There are two weaknesses in the present unlimited legal tender status of subsidiary coins; the first is chiefly theoretical, but the second is of practical importance and warrants correction. First, the dangers of standard money being driven out of circulation are increased, because there is no limit to the extent that subsidiary coins may be used in debt payments. Formerly there was a check upon the use of these coins for debt payments, which insured at least some demand for other types of money. Second, debtors may use small denomination coins without limit as "spite money." Since creditors are never popular with debtors, the latter are in a position to take advantage of this new law to make their creditors uncomfortable. Certainly creditors deserve protection as well as do debtors, and no creditor should be subjected to the inconvenience of having an excessive quantity of small coins forced upon him.

Steps must be taken to prevent subsidiary coins from becoming redundant. Individuals and banks should have the right to exchange their surplus coins for other types of money. As long as the government agrees to accept subsidiary coins as unlimited government tender, this method may be used. Such coins should not be permitted to have less value than standard money, for one of two things would result: (1) either the coins would lose their circulation, which seems unlikely as long as they are legal tender, or (2) they would drive out the standard money, which likewise is improbable, as long as the amount is carefully limited. As an extra precaution against poor management in limiting the quantity of subsidiary coins, most governments make direct provisions for their redemption in reasonable amounts in standard money or other money which may be lawfully held. The laws of the United States require the Treasury to redeem subsidiary coins in lawful money when the coins are presented in quantities of $20 or more. By forcing the use of silver dollars and silver certificates on the general public, this principle of limiting the quantity of a subsidiary metal to trade needs is being violated. This will be apparent after reading the remainder of this chapter.

The First Silver Movement

Actually silver has been a subsidiary coinage metal since 1834, and gold has been the standard metal. Congress recognized this situation in 1873, and, although gold had been the standard and silver had been subsidiary to it, no serious objections to this situation were raised for forty years. Then, for reasons discussed in the preceding chapter, the "doing something for silver" political campaign began. Although the silver mining industry is unimportant, it has been ably represented in the Senate by men coming from the sparsely settled states, where most of the domestic silver is produced. This group has provided the foundation on which was built a strong political silver bloc. Its greatest strength, however, came from the believers in inflation, and so the political successes of the silverites have varied inversely with general business conditions. The silverites and their supporters have never been able to achieve bimetallism, but they have been successful in securing direct subsidies for silver.

Bland-Allison Act.—The act of February 28, 1878, popularly known as the Bland-Allison Act, required the government to purchase not less than two or more than four million dollars worth of silver bullion each month at the market price and to coin it into standard silver dollars. The amount to be purchased was to equal the expected output of American mines. The Secretary of the Treasury refused to purchase much more than the minimum amount of silver, $24,000-000, each year, and the total quantity of money added by the act aggregated 378,000,000 silver dollars, or about fifty times the amount coined from 1792 to 1873. The holders of silver dollars were given the privilege of depositing them at the Treasury in sums of not less than $10, in exchange for silver certificates. The Sherman Act, which practically forced the Treasury to double its purchases of silver bullion, was passed in 1890.

Sherman Act.—The act of July 14, 1890, popularly known as the Sherman Act, provided that the Secretary of the Treasury should purchase silver bullion to the aggregate amount of 4,500,000 ounces per month. Payment was to be made in Treasury notes. These notes were redeemable on demand in gold or silver and had full legal tender for all debts, public and private, except where otherwise expressly stipulated in the contract. The purchasing clause of the Sherman Act was in force until repealed by the act of November 1,

1893. During this period $156,000,000 in Treasury notes were issued in exchange for 169,000,000 ounces of fine silver.

Sections 5 and 8 of the Sherman Act provided for the cancellation and retirement of Treasury notes. When the silver bullion was coined, silver certificates were exchanged for the Treasury notes. Over 187,000,000 standard silver dollars were added to those already in existence in the United States by this act.

The effect of the increasing quantity of silver in the monetary stock of the country was to lessen confidence in the ability of the United States to remain on the gold standard. A number of domestic and foreign factors account for the panic of 1893, but the silver issue played an important part. In 1893 India went off the silver standard. On November 1, 1893, a special session of Congress repealed the silver purchase clause of the Sherman Act. From 1893 to 1897 the United States government had great difficulty in keeping the United States on the gold standard. Not until the end of the campaign of 1896 was there a return of general confidence in the United States' monetary system and with it a decrease in the pressure upon the country's gold reserves.

Although the silver senators finally consented to the repeal of the purchase clause in the act of 1890, they secured the insertion of a statement that it was the policy of the United States to work for a return of a bimetallic standard if a workable one could be devised. Although the party favoring free coinage of silver was defeated in the elections of 1896 and 1900, the silverites were able to keep the way open for a return to bimetallism. The gold dollar was declared to be the standard unit, but reference was still made to the standard silver dollar. Although the Treasury was given responsibility for keeping all United States currency equal to gold in value, the law did not specifically provide for redemption of the silver dollar in gold and thereby recognize this coin as token money, which it had been since 1873.

Pittman Act of 1918

The legislation affecting silver since 1873 has had as one of its aims the increase in the price of this metal. The one exception to this statement was the act of April 23, 1918,[1] which resulted from just the

[1] Silver transactions under the act of April 23, 1918, are described in the *Annual Report of the Secretary of the Treasury on the State of Finances of the Fiscal Year Ended June 30, 1928*, pp. 71-75.

opposite situation—the high price of silver. During World War I, when silver went above $1.30 per ounce, it threatened not only the existence of our standard silver dollars but also our fractional coins.

In 1918 inflation was greater in European countries than in the United States, and most of the belligerent Continental countries lost their subsidiary coins. They were forced to adopt the same makeshift fractional paper systems as were used in this country during the Civil War. The United Kingdom met the problem by lowering the fine silver content of its silver coins, and later thirty-two other countries used this method to keep their "small change" from being melted down and sold as bullion.

In 1918 the United States missed a golden opportunity to simplify its currency structure by selling at a profit its dead silver hoard, most of which had been lying idle in the Treasury since the end of the last century. Great Britain was confronted with an extraordinary demand for silver in India. The latter country was a great user of subsidiary silver coins, because paper money was unpopular, banks were undeveloped, and the hoarding or investment demand for silver had increased tremendously because of the "war prosperity."

Under the provisions of the Bland-Allison and Sherman acts, the United States Treasury purchased 460,000,000 fine ounces of silver. This metal was coined into standard silver dollars, but they did not circulate. Their place was taken by silver certificates, which in practice were redeemable in gold. The silver dollars were not used, because nobody wanted them, and in 1918 the high price of silver made it profitable to sell them as bullion.

Because even a 30 per cent reserve in gold is preferable to a 100 per cent reserve in silver, which nobody wants, thoughtful students welcomed the opportunity to dispose of our dead silver hoard. In what is popularly known as the Pittman Act, Congress authorized the retirement of 350,000,000 silver certificates and the melting-down of a similar quantity of silver dollars. In pursuance of this act, the Treasury sold slightly over 200,000,000 fine ounces of silver to Great Britain. The melting of the necessary quantity of dollars (259, 121,554) was completed in May, 1919. The sales price was $1.00 per ounce plus a charge to cover cost of melting, recoining, and other items. In addition, 11,101,168 standard silver dollars were melted and used for subsidiary coins.

Most silver certificates circulated in the form of $1.00 and $2.00

denominations. Trade need for the retired certificates was met by issues of Federal Reserve bank notes. These had no gold reserves and so were far more economical than the money which they replaced. All the government's gains from the Pittman Act were eliminated by a provision that as soon as the emergency was over the Treasury must buy silver to replace the dollars which were melted. Purchases were to be made from American producers at $1.00 per ounce. Purchases began in 1920 and continued through 1923. Federal Reserve bank notes were retired when new silver was purchased, and new silver certificates were issued.

Doing Something for Silver

During 1932 the average gold price of silver was 28.2 cents per ounce. This meant that the ratio of silver to gold was about 80 to 1, then an all-time record. Although the fall in price of silver was not out of line with the decrease in price of other metals, a "doing something for silver" movement began in Congress. This meant securing governmental purchases that would increase the price of silver. In order to get political support, the silverites used many arguments, including the following: (1) the inflationary argument, (2) the increasing foreign trade argument, and (3) the stimulating industry argument.

Inflationary Argument.—The silverites' chief arguments have been those of the inflationists: financially distressed farmers, debtors, and businessmen must be given economic relief by raising prices; scarcity of money in general, and of gold in particular, is the reason for low prices; and in order to raise prices it is necessary to increase the supply of money. The conclusion of the silverites is that the best way to raise prices is to use more silver for reserves and for circulation.

If more money is needed it can be provided without buying silver and then issuing silver certificates. Operations under the Pittman Act of 1918 demonstrate how easy it is to replace one type of paper money with a second and then to function more efficiently without being burdened with handling, guarding, and accounting for tons of silver.

When the argument for the use of silver as a reserve is advanced, it should be noted that it has yet to be demonstrated that the silver reserves have added one iota to the acceptability of the silver certificates. Furthermore, it cannot be demonstrated that the purchase of silver inaugurated by the New Deal contributed in any way to the increase in general prices. Finally, $2,000,000,000 in silver has been added to our monetary system without increasing the total stock of money, because the silver certificates have merely replaced other more economical types of paper money.

Increasing Foreign Trade Argument.—The second argument used by those in favor of raising the price of silver is that it would increase foreign trade by increasing the purchasing power of Asiatic countries. The contention is that if the price of silver were doubled Chinese merchants would be able to buy just twice as much American goods as before.

The reasoning that a higher price for silver would help China assumes that the purchasing power of Chinese merchants depends upon the value of silver; but the purchasing power of a country depends upon its income. For example, in 1932 the purchasing power of the American dollar was 40 per cent higher than it was in 1929, but the income of the nation had decreased by an even larger percentage. The effect of a higher price of silver would be to raise the value of Chinese money, which means a fall in general prices and all the disadvantages which accompany this change. China does not pay for goods purchased abroad with silver, because normally China imports silver. Confronted with dissension at home and on the verge of war, China took a pessimistic view toward the silverites' foreign trade argument. The beneficiaries from a higher price for silver are countries that mine it, and they profit according to the economic importance of this industry. Therefore, Mexico, and not China, would gain from a higher silver price.

Stimulating Industry Argument.—This argument is as follows: Higher prices for silver would reopen silver mines, give employment to labor, and create a new demand for goods. This new demand for goods would bring prosperity to industries directly affected, and in time to all industries. This same argument has been used by farmers, building trades, and all industries seeking government aid. It has a special appeal to the group favored but is opposed by those who must pay for the initial prosperity.

Is the silver industry important enough to stimulate general prosperity? In the seven silver states, only 1½ per cent of the population depends directly upon silver production, and these states are among those most sparsely populated. The value of the 1934 silver output even at the artifically high price was less than $15,000,000. Even in the mining industry silver is unimportant, for it is a by-product of the output of other metals. The ore is usually complex, containing lead, copper, or zinc. Thus the production of silver depends in large part upon the demand for these metals; and since 1934 it has been the increase in demand for them which primarily accounts for the increase in production of silver in the United States. Although the 1944 domestic price of silver was approximately 50 per cent above the average price for 1934, the total silver output of domestic mines was worth less than $27,000,000. If Congress is sincere in its desire to stimulate industry, it will look elsewhere for one of importance to subsidize.

New Deal Silver Policy

The administrative and legislative phases of the New Deal policy will be discussed historically under five subtopics, namely, (1) Thomas Inflation Act, (2) international silver agreements, (3) presidential proclamation of 1933, (4) Silver Purchase Act of 1934, and (5) international opposition to the silver policy.

Thomas Inflation Act.—Title III of the Agricultural Adjustment Act approved in May, 1933, provided: that all silver coins and silver certificates would be full legal tender; that the President could place the United States upon a bimetallic standard, which included the right to select a new mint ratio; and that the President was authorized to receive silver in payment of war debts. The maximum price authorized was 50 cents per ounce, when the world price was 35 cents per ounce. The amount to be accepted was limited to $200,000,000, which sum was approximately equal to the obligations due or coming due during the six months that this provision was in effect.

With the exception of Finland, no country made full use of the easy "silver way" of meeting the 1933 inter-Allied debt payments; but several countries did make partial or token payments in silver. Under this act the United States received $11,135,000 in silver, and an equal number of silver certificates were issued. Countries making token payments were Czechoslovakia, $179,505.25; Finland (full, not token), $148,315.44; Great Britain, $10,000,518.42; Italy,

$1,000,020.76; Lithuania, $9,990.35; and Rumania, $29,061.46. Eleven other countries made no payments.

International Silver Agreements.—Senator Pittman, the leader of the silver bloc and one of the United States representatives to the World Economic Conference,[2] held in London in 1933, succeeded in getting the conference to approve of a resolution that requested: (1) that an agreement be sought between countries producing and those using or holding silver, with the purpose of lessening the fluctuations in price; (2) that other nations not parties to the agreements should co-operate by refraining from measures which would severely affect the silver market; (3) that all the sixty-six states represented at the conference should refrain from new legislative measures leading to further debasement of silver coinage below a fineness of 80 per cent; (4) that all the sixty-six nations represented should substitute silver coins for low-price paper currency, in so far as the budgetary and local conditions of each country would permit.

The supplementary agreements under provision 1 were signed July 22, 1933, by representatives of Australia, Canada, China, India, Mexico, Peru, Spain, and the United States. Under this eight-nation agreement the Indian government agreed to limit its sales of silver to 140,000,000 ounces for a four-year period, Spain agreed to limit her sales to 20,000,000 ounces for a similar period, and China agreed not to sell silver resulting from demonetized coins for four years. Australia, Canada, Peru, Mexico, and the United States governments agreed not to sell any silver during this period and to purchase an amount equal to what India was allowed to sell in the world's markets, that is, 35,000,000 ounces yearly. The 35,000,000 ounces were distributed in such a way that the United States government's annual share was 24,421,000 ounces, an amount approximately equal to the annual output of the United States mines. Furthermore, if any one nation refused to ratify the agreement, it would still be in effect if the remaining nations purchased 35,000,000 ounces.[3]

Presidential Proclamation of 1933 and Purchase of the Current Product of Domestic Mines.—The eight-nation agreement was not submitted to the Senate for ratification, and instead the President made use of the free coinage provision found in the Thomas Inflation

[2] Westerfield, R. B., *Our Silver Debacle*, pp. 43-49.

[3] Carothers, Neil, and Bradford, F. A., "Legal Aspects of Silver Policies of the United States in Recent Years," *Money and the Law*, p. 46.

Law. On December 21, 1933, a presidential proclamation was issued which authorized the Director of the Mint to accept all newly mined domestic silver for a period of four years at a mint price of $1.2929 per fine ounce, minus a seigniorage charge of 50 per cent. Inasmuch as only newly mined silver of the United States was affected, free coinage was not allowed. Twice during April, 1935, the seigniorage charge was reduced, thereby increasing the price received by domestic silver producers. The net price received by them was first 64.64 cents, then 71.11 cents, and then 77.57 cents per fine ounce. This juggling of the domestic price of silver, plus the effects of the foreign silver buying policy, led to speculative excesses in the silver market. The price reached 81 cents per fine ounce before the collapse came. Nevertheless, the domestic producers were assured of a price of 77.57 cents until December 31, 1937, provided, of course, that the seigniorage charge remained the same.

At the end of 1937 the President provided for the continuance of the domestic silver buying policy by executive order at a price of 64.64 cents, and this remained undisturbed until 1939. In this year the President asked for continuance of the laws providing for the Stabilization Fund and renewal of his power to change the weight of the gold dollar. As a result of vote trading and retrading, these laws were renewed; but there was placed on the statute books a law that required the government to buy all the domestically mined silver at a price of 71.11 cents per fine ounce (raised to 90.5 cents in 1946).

Silver Purchase Act of 1934.—During the nineteenth century, when silver held equal rank with gold in bimetallism, it was properly held as reserves. At the end of that century silver made up 25 per cent of the total metallic reserve of eighteen foreign banks of issue. Most of this silver was a legacy from bimetallism, and during the next thirty years many of these banks liquidated all or part of their silver holdings.[4] As gold reserves increased, the percentage of reserves represented by silver became smaller, until the average for the five-year period, 1925-29 inclusive, was but 7 per cent.[5] In 1933, at the world Economic Conference in London, one of the proposals of Senator Pittman was that central banks should be allowed to use

[4] In 1932 the Indian and Spanish governments had large sums which they wanted to sell. Only the United States had a policy of holding on to the useless monetary hoard that it had accumulated during the last century.

[5] Bratter, H. M., *The Monetary Use of Silver in 1933*, p. 11.

silver as reserves until it was equal to one-fourth of their metallic reserves. This proposal was rejected by foreign countries, but in June, 1934, Congress accepted it as the policy of the United States.

On June 19, 1934, the President approved an act of Congress called the Silver Purchase Act of 1934.[6] Section 2 of the act is as follows: "It is hereby declared to be the policy of the United States that the proportion of silver to gold in the monetary stocks of the United States should be increased, with the ultimate objective of having and maintaining one fourth of the monetary value of such stocks in silver." This act, unless repealed, definitely places the United States government in the international silver market for many years to come.

In August, 1934, the President issued a proclamation directing that all silver be turned into the Treasury within 90 days. Over 113,000,000 ounces were surrendered, at a cost of $56,500,000.[7] This step cleared the domestic market of silver and forced domestic users to buy in foreign markets or else match the Treasury's price for the current output of domestic mines. The price paid for silver in foreign markets depends on market conditions, and, since 1934, it has varied from a high of 90.5 cents to a low of 35 cents per ounce. During World War II, the Office of Price Administration fixed the ceiling price for foreign silver at 45 cents per ounce. After V-J Day it was raised to 71.11 cents, and in July, 1946, by congressional action, to 90.5 cents per fine ounce.

The Secretary of the Treasury pays for the silver purchased with credits resulting from the issuance of new silver certificates. He may issue silver certificates in amounts equal to the coinage value of silver, which means that, if he buys 100 ounces of silver, he may issue $129 in silver certificates.

International Opposition to the Silver Policy.—The heaviest blow given to the future market for silver resulted from the departure of China from the silver standard. China, normally an annual buyer of 92,000,000 ounces, became a seller of 275,000,000 ounces annually. The increase in 1934 and 1935 of the world price of silver made it profitable for the Chinese to export silver. This movement continued, even though the Chinese government placed a tax on silver exports.

---

[6] For a copy of the act see *Federal Reserve Bulletin*, July, 1934, pp. 436-38.

[7] The average price paid was $50.01 cents. By waiting to nationalize the domestic supply, the President increased the cost of this silver by $5,500,000.

The loss of money and reserves for paper currency caused a crisis in China—almost unheard-of bank failures and a deflation in general prices similar to that which the United States experienced from 1930 to 1933, when the value of gold was appreciating.

China protested to the United States government against the silver purchasing policy, pointing out that it was counter to the stabilization principle involved in the Eight-Nation Silver Control Agreement. Almost doubling the price of silver in less than one year was not the Chinese idea of stabilization, but all her appeals to the United States government for relief from her financial difficulties met with evasive or unsatisfactory answers. Realizing the futility of trying to sway the silver policy of a stubborn administration, it began a series of steps that finally resulted in the establishment of a paper money managed currency system in November, 1935. The immediate, and probably the long-run, effect has been to release a large supply of monetary silver for use elsewhere. In addition, Hong Kong also abandoned the silver standard, and Mexico, Costa Rica, Guatemala, Ecuador, Colombia, Peru, and Iran were forced to replace their subsidiary coins with paper currency or lighter-weight silver coins. Thus more silver was freed for export to the United States, and the world markets for monetary silver were further reduced.

Is the Silver Program Justified?

The silver policy was condemned from its inauguration by American economists, and today its failure should be apparent even to the layman. The plan has been in operation more than twelve years, and the world's price of silver is still far below the goal of $1.29.[8] Although tons of silver have been purchased by the United States government, owing to the increase in gold stock, the one-to-three ratio between silver and gold is no nearer attainment than when the plan was inauguated. As administered, the silver purchase program has created chaos among the nations formerly dependent upon silver as their standard metal, and, by making the melting-down of silver coins profitable, it has further decreased the monetary demand for silver.

---

[8] In July, 1946, the silver bloc in the United States Senate secured the passage of a compromise bill that fixed the Treasury's buying and selling price of silver at 90.5 cents per fine ounce.

On July 12, 1943, the President signed the Green Bill,[9] which permitted the sale of Treasury silver to both war and civilian industries at 71.11 cents per ounce. Although the Treasury, the War Production Board, and the Navy wanted this silver to be sold to war industries at 50 cents per ounce, so as to encourage its use as a substitute for scarce materials, the silver bloc held up passage until its terms were accepted. Similar legislative tactics were used in 1946 to block continuance of the selling policy authorized by the Green Bill until both the purchase and selling price had been increased to 90.5 cents per fine ounce.

All types of silver coins are token or credit money, and their status as an integral part of our monetary system depends upon parity with the gold dollar. The bullion content of a silver dollar is worth only a part of its token value. For example, when the world's price of silver was 70 cents per ounce, the bullion value of the silver dollar was about 54 cents. In order to be effective, reserves must be used, and, as long as silver is not in demand for this purpose, it is ineffective. Judging from the experience of the United States and other countries, silver is a dead and useless reserve.

The full effects of the various plans to do something for silver will not be apparent for many years, but, if the lessons of history are properly interpreted, the United States at some future time will be in the same position as that in which India and Spain found themselves in recent years. The United States will be holding large quantities of "dead silver." The only way whereby it may be made to work effectively as a reserve is by adopting a silver, bimetallic, or symmetallic standard. If other countries adopt similar standards, which seems highly improbable, the result may be beneficial.

QUESTIONS AND PROBLEMS

1. Identify: (*a*) fractional coins, (*b*) token coins, (*c*) "standard silver dollar," (*d*) trade dollar," (*e*) minor coins, and (*f*) legal tender coins.

[9] Silver has been loaned to industry for use in defense plants as follows: slightly less than 700,000,000 fine ounces for the fiscal year ended June 30, 1943, and slightly less than 900,000,000 ounces for the next fiscal year. This silver is to be returned to the Treasury. For the latter period, over 200,000,000 ounces were lend-leased, and over 40,000,000 ounces were sold under the Green Act (*Public Law 137*, 78th Cong., approved July 12, 1943). See *Annual Report of the Director of the Mint for the Fiscal Year Ended June 30, 1944,* pp. 2-3.

The amount of silver released in 1945 was reported to have been about three times the amount released in 1944 (1944, 46,200,000 ounces). See *New York Herald Tribune,* January 20, 1946, Sec. IV, p. 5.

2. How was silver coinage affected by: (*a*) the Gold Bill of 1834 and (*b*) the Act of 1853?

3. During World War II, what changes were made in minor coins in the United States and in other warring countries?

4. Give the four subsidiary coinage principles? To what extent is the Treasury following each of them?

5. Identify: (*a*) fractional paper money, (*b*) "shinplasters," and (*c*) postage currency. Explain their existence.

6. What would be the effect upon circulation of silver dollars, quarters, and dimes, if the price of silver were 40 cents per ounce; $1.35 per ounce; $1.40 per ounce? Why?

7. If silver should rise 20 per cent in value, would the silver dollar increase in value? Explain.

8. "Silver," according to former Senator Gore, "has all the attributes of money—except value." Discuss.

9. "The political successes of the silverites have varied inversely with general business conditions." Discuss.

10. Outline the New Deal silver policy from 1933 to date.

11. This Santa Claus silver policy of ours is "good for foreign trade. It would be good for foreign trade if we give away at regular intervals $1 billion, first come first served." See *Report No. 1332* of Senator Townsend to accompany S. 785, 76th Cong., 3d sess. Discuss.

12. Mr. Eccles stated: "The only use we have for silver is to make more excess reserves which are already excessive, and more bank deposits, which also are already excessive" (*ibid.*). Discuss.

13. "What we have done . . . . is to buy the metal in huge amounts and write its value up to $1.29 an ounce as a basis of currency issue. As far as I can see, it would have been just as sound economically to have used discarded paving blocks. . . . . Using them as a basis of currency issue would not have subjected foreign silver-using countries to severe pressure, as our silver policy has done" (Robey, "Fiscal Policy and Credit Control," *Proceedings of the Academy of Political Science*, Vol. XVII [May, 1936], p. 13). Discuss.

14. "It has been demonstrated that rising prices for silver do not increase China's trade or her importations of metal." (Source and reference: Roberts, G. B., "The Silver Purchase Program and Its Consequences," *Proceedings of the Academy of Political Science*, Vol. XVII [May, 1936], pp. 18-25.)

15. Silver has been called a "political metal." One of the best illustrations of its political role occurred during the last part of June and the first part of July, 1939, when the President asked for renewal of the Stabili-

zation Fund and his powers to reduce the weight of the gold dollar. Check in the *New York Times, United States News,* and other papers on this episode.

16. "The volume of money is not the cardinal factor which determines the volume of business. The vital matter is—the size of people's incomes, in other words, the size of the national income" (Towers, G. F., "Address at the First Annual Meeting of Shareholders of the Bank of Canada, February 25, 1936"). Discuss.
17. The "seigniorage profits from subsidiary coinage, universally regarded as net gains and so reported officially, are in a sense illusory and imaginary." Explain. (Carothers, *Fractional Money*, pp. 300-302.)
18. Compare the Pittman Act of 1918 to the Green Act of 1943.
19. Explain carefully what is meant by saying that silver is a "dead reserve." Under what circumstances may this statement cease being true? Explain.
20. How would you answer the "2 billion dollar" question? See page 121 of this chapter.

REFERENCES

Annual Report of the Director of the Mint for the Fiscal Year Ended June 30, 1944. Washington, D.C.: U.S. Government Printing Office, 1945.

Annual Report of the Secretary of the Treasury on the State of the Finances, for Fiscal Year Ended June 30, 1944. Washington, D.C.: U.S. Government Printing Office, 1945.

Blackett, B. P. *Planned Money,* chap. vi. New York: D. Appleton & Co., 1933.

Bratter, H. M. *Should We Turn to Silver?* Public Policy Pamphlet No. 6. Chicago: University of Chicago Press, 1933.

Bratter, H. M. "The Monetary Use of Silver in 1933," *Trade Promotion Services,* No. 149. Washington, D.C.: Department of Commerce, 1933.

Carothers, Neil. *Fractional Money,* chaps. viii, xvi, and xxi. New York: John Wiley & Sons, Inc., 1930.

Carothers, Neil, and Bradford, F. A. "Legal Aspects of Silver Policies of the United States in Recent Years," *Money and the Law,* pp. 43-53. Supplement of the *New York University Law Quarterly Review,* 1945.

Dewey, D. R. *Financial History of the United States,* chaps. xvii and xix. 11th ed. New York: Longmans, Green & Co., 1931.

Froman, L. A. "Bimetallism, Reconsidered in the Light of Recent Developments," *American Economic Review,* Vol. XXVI, No. 1 (March, 1936), pp. 53-61.

Hirst, F. W. *Money, Gold, Silver and Paper*, chaps. iv, ix, and xv. New York: Charles Scribners' Sons, 1934.

International Monetary Conferences Held in Brussels, 1892. Washington, D.C.: U.S. Government Printing Office, 1893.

International Monetary Conference Held in Paris, 1878. Washington, D.C.: U.S. Government Printing Office, 1879.

Jevons, W. S. *Money and the Mechanism of Exchange.* New York: D. Appleton & Co., 1921.

Kreps, T. J. "The Price of Silver and Chinese Purchasing Power," *Quarterly Journal of Economics*, Vol. XLVIII (February and May, 1934), pp. 245-87; 568-71.

Laughlin, J. L. *History of Bimetallism in the United States*, chaps. i-iv, vii, xiii, and xiv. 2d ed. New York: D. Appleton & Co., 1894.

Leavens, D. A. *Far Eastern Post War Monetary Standards.* New York: The Monetary Standards Inquiry, 1943.

Leavens, D. A. *Silver Money*, chaps. iii, vi, and xxiv–xxxi. Bloomington, Ind.: Principia Press, Inc., 1939.

Mitchell, H. *The Place of Silver in Monetary Reconstruction.* New York: The Monetary Standards Inquiry, 1944.

Report of the Monetary Commission of 1876. Washington, D.C.: U.S. Government Printing Office, 1877.

Westerfield, R. B. *Our Silver Debacle.* New York: Ronald Press Co., 1936.

Willis, H. P. *A History of the Latin Monetary Union.* Chicago: University of Chicago Press, 1901.

Chapter VIII

A MANAGED PAPER MONEY STANDARD

Introduction

The question of a monetary standard has been prominent in discussions of plans for the postwar period. Opinions on the subject, as expressed by official spokesmen, vary within each country as well as among the different countries. Usually the current views of the experts as well as of the public are greatly influenced by the experiences of their countries. In money matters memories are long, and that is particularly true when economic relations have been fundamentally affected. In Great Britain the deflation following the return to the old gold unit (1925-31) is being used as the chief argument against the readoption of the gold standard, and as a result this country is the chief exponent of the managed paper money standard.

On the other hand, there is a strong sentiment in certain countries for the gold standard, because of past experiences with paper money. The monetary policy of France has been considerably influenced by her experiences with the inflationary disasters associated with John Law's note issue bank of 1716 and the issue of "assignats" of the Revolution. In the United States irredeemable paper money was issued by the colonies, by the Continental Congress during the Revolutionary War, by the states from 1775 to 1789, by state-chartered banks prior to 1863, and by the federal government (greenbacks) during the Civil War. From 1924 to 1940, the German government's monetary policy was greatly influenced by the inflation that occurred from 1919 to 1924.

Can Paper Money Be the Standard of Value?

Many writers deny that irredeemable or fiat paper money can ever be a standard of value. They claim that the value of irredeemable paper money depends upon the value of the standard, the discount or depreciation varying with the prospects of future redemption in the standard. In the case of fiat money, which contains no promise to pay, the same argument is used—that is, that the value fluctuates according to the prospects of redemption at some future time in a standard metal.

After a country leaves the gold standard, prices may be quoted in terms of gold; however, this period is short, and it may not exist at all. In the United States from March, 1933, to February, 1934, prices, incomes, and credit instruments were quoted or computed in terms of irredeemable paper money. Silver coins, minor coins, and bank deposits were equal to paper dollars, and gold itself was quoted in terms of paper money. Instead of saying that paper money was worth 75 cents, gold was usually said to be at a premium. The process of price-making did not resolve itself into a comparison between the value of goods and the value of gold bullion. Gold moved in trade as a commodity, and money value was not a question of gold value.

At the present time in the world, the exchange values of things are expressed in terms of each country's own paper money unit. Within a country, the circulating media and deposit currency are equal in value to its paper standard unit, increasing in value as it increases and decreasing as it decreases. However, this does not presuppose that just because of the existence of a paper money standard that one is justified in writing about it as a managed paper currency standard.

The basis for the argument that paper money cannot be the standard of value is that the thing that serves as the standard must have intrinsic or substance value. But no commodity has intrinsic or substance value. Value in exchange depends upon human desire plus a scarcity in supply. Without the first, goods would have no utility; without the second, goods would be free goods. As long as there is a money demand for and a limited supply of paper money, it will have value just as truly as gold coins or any other type of money. It may be desirable, although it is not required, for money to have a use value other than for monetary purposes in order to serve as a medium of exchange and a standard of value.

A country has a paper standard if the value of its circulating media and deposit currency is kept equal in value to a paper monetary unit. For example, the value of all means of payment in Great Britain is kept equal to the value of the Bank of England note, which is issued in denominations of the pound sterling and the 10 shilling note. Prices are quoted in terms of the pound sterling, and debt contracts are in terms of this unit. Token coins are kept equal to it in value, and Bank of England notes are held by banks as reserves against deposit liabilities. Being legal tender, the Bank of England notes are assured of a place in the circulating media, but even without this quality they would circulate as money because of habit and the demand for some type of hand-to-hand money of these denominations. In the domestic economy the paper pound sterling serves in all the monetary capacities in which gold formerly served.

Characteristics of the Paper Standard

Types of Paper Money Standards.—The chief feature of the paper standard is the lack of convertibility of money into a standard metal. If one accepts the lack of convertibility as the chief test of a paper money system, three types may be recognized: (1) irredeemable credit money, (2) pure fiat money, and (3) a type of irredeemable paper money, the value of which is kept equal to gold by management rather than by conversion or redemption in gold.

During periods of great stress, governments or banks may not be able to redeem their promises to pay in specie on demand. With the exception of 1930-32, such periods in the past have been during wars, when governments were forced to increase their revenues and were dilatory in increasing taxes and in making use of other noninflationary sources of revenue. Usually laws were passed that released the bank of issue from its contract to redeem its promises to pay in gold, thereby making it possible not only for the volume of hand-to-hand money to expand without limit but also for expansion of cash reserve credit on which deposit currency is based. This irredeemable paper money is usually made legal tender by decree or fiat of the government. Although irredeemable paper money usually has some specie backing, this specie is not used to maintain its value at par with the old metallic unit. The value of irredeemable credit money may be influenced by the credit position of the issuing agent and the amount of specie reserve which may be used at some future time to redeem it. It is still a promise to pay specie or its equivalent on demand.

Pure fiat paper money is utopian money created by fiat or law to serve not only as the medium of exchange but also as the standard of value; therefore it has no specie backing and contains no promise of redemption. Its value is not kept equal to gold, silver, or any other commodity or group of commodities but depends upon its usefulness as money and its scarcity. Management is presupposed. Pure fiat money is not influenced by the credit position of the issuer or by hope of redemption in specie. It is not a promise to pay but merely a piece of paper or a coin printed or stamped by a government or agency stating that it is, for example, one dollar.

The last type of irredeemable paper money was considered in Chapter V. It combines certain of the characteristics of the gold standard and of managed currency. The value of currency is kept equal to gold, and in this respect it resembles the gold standard. But the currency is not redeemable in gold for which there is no free market, and the value of currency is regulated by management. This standard is called the "managed gold" standard in recognition of the dual characteristics of this monetary system.

Most of the world's experiences with paper money standards have been with those of the first type. The second is the utopian standard, which may result from the evolution of money. The last type is a compromise between the advocates of the automatic gold standard, on one side, and the advocates of the fiat money standard, on the other.

Arguments in Favor of the Paper Standard

The arguments in favor of the paper standard include those based on economy or cheapness as compared to the use of gold; historical arguments which point to the evolution of exchanges away from the use of a commodity medium of exchange to one which has only token value; and the argument that the paper standard gives freedom of action to a government in developing a national monetary system. Since the standard money is printed, any amount necessary may be made available to redeem other means of payment. If the public desires to exchange deposit currency for paper money, the latter will be forthcoming—that is, if the supply of paper is not exhausted or the printing presses do not break down. So at no time may the value of other types of means of payment be less than the value of the standard because of nonredeemability. In this respect the paper standard differs fundamentally from the gold standard. It is this power of a monetary authority to regulate the quantity of the standard money at will which constitutes at the same time the chief weakness and the chief strength of the paper standard. The importance of this statement is apparent after noting the effects of a small loss (or gain) of gold from a nation's reserve stock when a country is operating on an automatic gold standard.

ILLUSTRATION II

INVERTED PYRAMID OF CREDIT

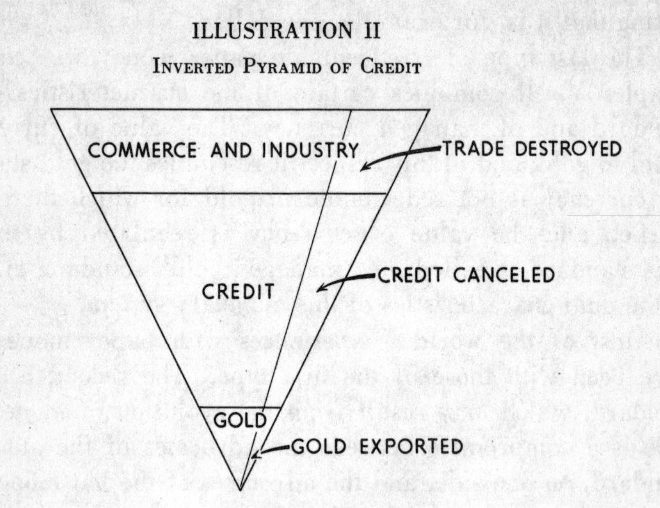

In Illustration II, it is assumed that a small quantity of gold is exported. In a country operating on a small gold reserve, which was typical of Great Britain in the past, the effects of this loss are suggested by that part of the inverted pyramid on the right marked "credit canceled" and "trade destroyed." Thus the loss of a relatively small amount of gold would tend to mean a 20- or 30-fold contraction in the volume of bank credit.

If a country is operating on a paper standard, it is in a position to expand the volume of legal tender money, replacing the loss of gold and preventing the contraction of credit and trade. On the other hand, if gold is imported the monetary authority is under no obligation to buy it; but, if he does, he can contract the volume of legal tender so as to prevent the gold from increasing the reserves on which an inflationary expansion of credit can be based. It is this desire to insulate national monetary systems against the effects of imports or exports of claims to money as well as to gold that has given rise to exchange control. (See Chapter XIII.)

Goal of Monetary Management

Any monetary system should facilitate optimum production and equitable distribution of income and wealth. Much confusion results from the fact that there is disagreement as to the immediate means by which these goals may be achieved. However, a part of this confusion is more apparent than real, because different situations call for different policies. For example, a policy of price stabilization during a period of economic depression and stagnation might be achieved at the risk of economic paralysis. At such a time a policy of price inflation may be desirable to the extent that it would be helpful in securing something approaching full employment.

Attention has been directed by monetary reformers to each of the monetary factors in the equation of exchange. There is one proposal to keep the total quantity of money and deposit currency constant in terms of normal increase in productive factors, population, or current output. If this yearly rate is 3 per cent, then the supply of the total quantity of money and deposit currency would be increased at that rate. A similar policy could be followed with reference to population, current output, or increase in productive factors, or any combination of the three, with appropriate weights applied to each. Other guides to policies could be added. Adherents to this method claim that seasonal and cyclical changes in the demand for money and deposit currency could be cared for by changes in the velocity of money and deposit currency (V and V'). This system would differ from others in that action on the part of the monetary management agency would be arbitrary and not optional, as is true at the present time.

A second proposal for monetary policy is to hold constant the aggregate quantity of money and deposit currency. With the increase in production, trade, and other factors, there would be no increase in the supply of money. This would give rise to a long-run downward swing in prices and would be of doubtful value in an expanding economy. The success of such an economy would depend on the ability of entrepreneurs to lower per unit costs by new techniques in production, such as inventions and other labor-saving devices.

A third proposal is to stabilize the total of money expenditures ($MV + M'V'$) for goods, services, and securities. Because of the inclusion of velocity of money and credit among the things to be stabilized, this proposal has more to recommend it than those applying only to the quantity of money. But, as noted in Chapter III, the reasons for changing the size of cash balances held by individuals vary from time to time. It is the variation in demand which could make the control of the velocity of money and deposit currency difficult, if not impossible.

Other proposals for monetary management pertain more to the goods side of the equation of exchange (*PT*). The advantages of having stable prices and stable exchange rates (prices of foreign money) are treated elsewhere. If price stability is adopted as the goal of monetary policy, the following questions must be answered: What prices should be stabilized—general, cost-of-living, retail, wholesale? What margin of price fluctuation should be permitted before corrective action is taken by the monetary authority? The stabilization of exchange rates, as a goal of monetary action, was one of the advantages resulting from the international gold standard. The International Monetary Fund has for one of its goals the attainment of stable exchange rates through international currency management.

The most popular proposal for monetary management is the stabilization of production and employment at the high level achieved during World War II. Those who advance this proposal claim that depressions are due to deficiencies in purchasing power and cannot be prevented unless the government adopts a corrective monetary and fiscal policy, thereby achieving full employment and stability in effective purchasing power.

A modification of this proposal is based on the theory that governmental deficit spending is necessary at all times in order to compensate for long-run structural changes in the economy. Because of the tendency for the absolute volume of savings to increase more rapidly than the opportunities for profitable investment, some purchasing power will be withheld from the markets. National income will tend to decline until there is equilibrium between savings and investments. When this is achieved, national income will be at a lower level, and there will be idle labor and other productive resources. The conclusion is that fiscal policy must be introduced at all times in order to provide enough purchasing power to maintain full employment.

Although the foregoing methods of achieving the goals of monetary management have been briefly stated, they suggest the complexity of the problems involved. Most of them are discussed in more detail in other parts of this textbook. However, it should be kept in mind that: these problems are not peculiar to the paper money standard, one method does not preclude the others, circumstances abroad may justify a policy indefensible in the United States, and a policy which was justifiable in 1936 may not be justifiable in 1946.

Past Experiences with Government Paper Money in the United States

New government paper money issues may be used directly by governments to retire debts, to pay employees, and to purchase services and goods necessary to operate the government; or the government notes may be deposited with banks and the resulting bank credit used to retire debts, to pay employees, and to purchase services and goods necessary to operate the government. Under modern circumstances, the Federal Reserve banks would probably be made responsible for distribution of new government paper money issues in the United States. There would be no good accomplished by such a move, however, because these banks are already issuing a satisfactory type of money which is fully guaranteed by the federal government.

The money-creating problem in the United States is no longer one which involves the creation of hand-to-hand money but a question of who shall control the issuance of bank credit in the form of demand deposits—the most important means of payment. Before the development of deposit currency—and commercial banking, which it presupposes—the United States did have difficulty with government paper money issues. The government issues are discussed under three headings: (1) the Continental currency, (2) Civil War greenbacks, and (3) Confederate currency.

Continental Currency.—One of the main tasks of the Second Continental Congress was to provide means for financing the Revolutionary War. The new government's credit was too poor to permit borrowing, the colonists were opposed to heavy taxes, and so paper money was issued. Notes equivalent to two million Spanish milled dollars were authorized on May 10, 1775. As usual, the process was repeated many times during the next few years, and over $240,000-

000 were issued. Coins were driven out of circulation and the notes became the circulating money of the people.[1]

The notes purported to be credit money—a promise of the Continental Congress to pay coin. There were no coins for this purpose, and from the first the notes were irredeemable and fiat money. Depreciation was rapid, and in 1780 in certain eastern cities flour was $150 a barrel, butter and coffee $12 a pound, and other prices in proportion. The people who accepted and held the notes suffered heavy losses, and many were financially ruined. The losses were unevenly distributed and were far greater than would have been the case had a direct tax been levied to carry on the war.

Opposition to the acceptance of the bills developed even within the ranks of the Continental troops, and by 1781 they ceased to circulate as money. They were bought up by speculators at rates of from 400 to 1, to 1,000 to 1. Ten years later about $6,000,000 were turned in, to be redeemed at a rate of 100 to 1. The inference is that the others had been destroyed. Thus ended the most disgraceful paper money period in our national history. During this period and later, things that were considered valueless were referred to derisively as "not worth a Continental."

The task of keeping the Continental notes at par was made doubly difficult by the issuance of fiat money by the different states. With the outbreak of the war, the restraining influence of the English government, which had only partially succeeded in checking the paper money issues of the colonists, was removed. In the aggregate, state paper money issues exceeded the issues of Continental currency. Stringent measures were enacted to keep the state notes and those of the Continental Congress at par. Committees were at work as early as 1776 prosecuting persons who discriminated against paper money. Confiscation of goods, flogging, and declaring offenders to be enemies of their country were common penalties.

States met in conventions to fix prices of goods, and speculation in commodities was made a severe offense. Arrangements to pay rents and other obligations in produce were looked upon with suspicion. In 1780 the army was at the point of revolt, and Washington could not move his troops to Yorktown until hard money was borrowed from France for their back pay. The loans from the French government in the form of hard money saved the day. Certain cities

[1] Dewey, D. R., *Financial History of the United States* (11th ed.), pp. 36-44.

were on the verge of famine in the midst of plenty, and the starvation at Valley Forge of the Continental troops was due to a scarcity of good money. The British army in Philadelphia was able to care for all its needs, paying for its supplies with hard money.

Legal tender quality, fixed prices, and severe penalties, including death, are not sufficient to keep an excess of fiat money at par. Economic laws are stronger than political, and, when an attempt is made to substitute the latter for the former, only temporary success may be expected. At best, governments can but set the stage on which economic forces play. If the governments had provided for limitation of supply and convertibility in specie, there would have been no trouble with the government issues. After the war, seven states issued paper money which rapidly depreciated, with the same results to production, trade, and unfair redistribution of wealth that accompanied preceding governmental paper money issues.

Greenback Issues.—The new federal Constitution forbade any state to "coin money, emit bills of credit; make anything but gold and silver coin a tender in payment of debts." Since the powers of the federal government were delegated powers, and, since there was no specific power granted to issue paper money, the Fathers of the Constitution assumed that there would be no government credit paper money issues in the United States after the adoption of the Constitution. However, on February 24, 1815, Congress authorized the issue of Treasury notes which were noninterest-bearing in denominations as low as $3.00. They lacked any legal tender quality; but they, as well as the War of 1812 issues of interest-bearing Treasury notes, were receivable in payment of custom duties and taxes. During and following the war, the notes were rapidly funded in long-term bonds. It is not unlikely, if the war had continued, that legal tender notes would have been issued.[2] During the Civil War, Congress provided for three issues of United States notes (greenbacks). Almost all of the $450,000,000 authorized by Congress were issued by the Treasury. In July, 1864, these notes had depreciated to such an extent that $100 in greenbacks were worth but $35 in gold, and in out-of-the-way places the depreciation was even greater. In California the people refused to accept United States notes, but greenbacks gave the remainder of the country a pure fiat money system for sixteen years—1862-78.

[2] Dewey, *ibid.*, pp. 135-38.

The existence of $346,000,000 in United States notes (greenbacks) at the present time illustrates how difficult it is for governments to liquidate paper money after it has been placed in circulation. The Lincoln administration issued paper currency with the understanding that it would be retired immediately after the close of the emergency. In 1865, after the close of the Civil War, the Secretary of the Treasury recommended that a policy of contracting the currency should immediately be adopted. An act to carry out this policy was passed, but it had been in force only twenty-one months when it was repealed.

More than one congressman objected to retiring the noninterest-bearing debt and replacing it with bonds. During the next ten years, the monetary conservatives were not only forced to give up their plan to retire the greenbacks, but they also had difficulty in preventing the authorization of additional issues of government paper money. In 1875 Congress passed the Resumption Act, which provided for the redemption in specie of all the greenbacks presented to the Treasury on and after January 1, 1879. In addition, the act provided that the total circulation was to be reduced to $300,000,000.

The panic of 1873 was followed by more than five years of bad business, low prices, and heavy debt burdens. The West had borrowed large sums in order to pay for the cost of developing its agricultural resources, and the South was forced to borrow heavily in order to reconstruct the sections devastated by the war. Circulation of national bank notes was carefully limited, state bank notes had been taxed out of existence, and the Confederate currency had disappeared. Because greenbacks were only slightly below par and could be used to meet debt contracts, political leaders considered them to be the solution to the monetary problems and, therefore, wanted more of them in order to stimulate business and raise prices.

Extreme inflationists met in Indianapolis in 1876 and organized the Greenback Party. They advocated government fiat money, opposed the Resumption of Specie Payment Act of 1875, and condemned the sale of gold bonds to foreigners. This party received its largest number of votes in the congressional election of 1878, when it chose fifteen members of the House. Although the inflationists were unable to secure more greenback issues, they did secure a compromise (May, 1878)—that the volume of greenbacks would be permitted to remain at the figure in circulation ($346,681,016).

The premium on gold which existed during the irredeemable greenback period disappeared on December 17, 1878, and the shift from an inconvertible to a convertible basis was made on January 1, 1879, with no internal or external drain on gold.

During the period 1890-96, considerable difficulty in maintaining the gold standard resulted from the existence of the greenbacks, silver certificates, and Treasury notes of 1890. Responsibility for maintaining convertibility in gold rested with the Treasury Department, which had a policy of keeping at least $100,000,000 in gold in the Treasury. There were over $346,000,000 in greenbacks, over $153,000,000 in Treasury notes of 1890, and $380,000,000 in silver certificates for which the Treasury was responsible. In addition, there were $66,000,000 in minor and subsidiary coins and $175,000,000 in national bank notes in circulation. However, there was an adequate supply of gold coins and gold certificates in the country outside of the Treasury, the total having been more than $500,000,000.

During the nineties, the problem was to keep a greater part of this gold in the Treasury, where it could be used in case of need for redemption of paper money. Unfortunately, the law requiring that greenbacks were to be reissued after they were redeemed permitted the "endless chain" demand for gold. The crisis of 1893 was accompanied by an increased demand for gold, and Treasury reserves shrank below the $100,000,000 level. The gold standard was carried through 1895 by obtaining gold from banks in exchange for greenbacks and Treasury notes and by borrowing from international bankers. However, by January, 1896, the reserves fell below $50,000,000.

The 1895 borrowing from international bankers was greatly criticized (a syndicate, headed by Morgan and Belmont lent $62,500,000 to the government at 104½ and later resold the bonds to the public at 118). In 1896 the Treasury offered the public a $100,000,000 issue of bonds, which was heavily oversubscribed. Reserves were still under pressure until the tide turned late in 1896, when there was a large import of gold from abroad. Following the campaign of 1896, gold came out of domestic hoards, and the gold standard was no longer under pressure. Four years later provisions were made for strengthening the gold standard.

The Gold Standard Act of 1900 provided that: (1) all forms of money were to be maintained at parity with gold; (2) a gold reserve of $150,000,000 was to be set apart from the general Treasury balance, and this reserve could never be drawn upon to cover general expenses, as happened in 1893; (3) if the reserves fell below $150,-000,000, redeemed United States notes could be withheld from circulation; (4) gold reserves could be replenished by bond sales; (5) new bonds would be issued to replace those coming due, in order to have collateral available for national bank notes; and (6) the Treasury notes of 1890 were to be replaced by silver dollars and silver certificates.

From 1878 to 1933 the greenbacks or United States notes were redeemable in standard money and properly considered as credit money. In 1914 it was expected that the Federal Reserve banks' excess profits, collected by the government as a franchise tax, would be used to increase the $150,000,000 in gold reserves behind the greenbacks. It was planned that when the reserves reached 100 per cent, that is $346,000,000, the greenbacks were to be withdrawn. Before this amount had accumulated the United States was in World War I, and since then the proceeds from the franchise tax have been used to retire government securities[3] and to build up the surplus accounts of the Federal Reserve banks.

The present supply of government notes (greenbacks), which represents an insignificant part of the monetary system of the United States, is adequately secured by a gold reserve of about 40 per cent and the credit of the United States. The profits resulting from devaluation of the gold, originally held as backing for these notes, plus $80,000,000 more from the remaining unassigned gold profits would be sufficient to retire them. They should be eliminated, because their existence is a continuous invitation to the inflationists to vote an increase in supply. The Thomas Inflation Act provided for $3,000,-000,000 in greenbacks, and this part of the act was not repealed until June, 1945.

Confederate Currency.—The government of the Confederate States of America financed a considerable part of its war with the northern states by issues of paper money in the form of Confederate Treasury notes. In addition, throughout the South paper money

[3] This so-called franchise tax was discontinued in 1935, and now all excess earnings of the Federal Reserve banks other than dividends are placed in the banks' surplus accounts.

issues of banks, states, and cities were in circulation. Because of the scarcity of small coins, fractional paper money (called "shin-plasters") was issued by individuals, corporations, and cities. At one time the total volume of paper currency in the South was about $1,000,000,000. This currency was irredeemable, although there was a considerable supply of gold and silver coins in hoarding in the South.

After the war, the fate of the different types of southern currency varied. The Confederate currency and many state and city issues were worthless. However, some of the other governments did fund their currency obligations, and most of the banks were able to retire their promises to pay. The experiences of the South with inflation and other monetary disturbances were even more severe than those of the North during the same period.

The Fear of Irredeemable Paper Money

These past experiences of the United States and the more recent experiences of European countries with irredeemable paper money have caused many people to distrust any type of irredeemable currency system. The chief fear is that the volume of paper money will be overissued and inflation, with all its harmful results, will follow. The function of gold in a monetary system based upon it is to limit the supply of paper money. When gold payments are suspended, governments must artificially restrict the supply of paper money; it is argued that they usually fail in this public trust.[4]

When a country is on a paper standard, pressure to increase the amount usually comes from two sources: (1) debtors, speculators, and others who benefit from rising prices, and (2) politicians and others who think that they have found in government issues a burdenless substitute for unpopular taxes and interest-bearing bonds. When a government once starts new issues of paper money, resulting conditions seemingly justify second, third, and additional issues.

The psychological effects of additional issues of printing-press money cause speculators and others to purchase goods, land, and securities in anticipation of higher prices. This new demand for things forces prices up to a higher level. Thus prices rise in anticipa-

[4] For a discussion of paper money inflation, see Spahr, W. E., "Currency Inflation," *American Economic Review*, Vol. XXIV, No. 2 (1934), pp. 208-24.

tion of the increase in the supply of paper money, and there are many complaints about the high cost of living and the scarcity of money. There is a demand for more currency in order to meet the higher cost of goods. If a second issue of money follows, a third will be anticipated by speculators. Any attempt to stop the inflationary movement causes panic. If new money is not forthcoming, speculators unload their holdings of goods, land, and securities; prices tumble, business collapses, and unemployment follows. Those in charge of the financial program are blamed for the collapse, and no politician wants to take responsibility for this chaos. To continue the monetary program is but to postpone the day of reckoning, but most politicians prefer to take this easier course, and the ultimate collapse is much greater because of the postponement.

If governments use the new issues to finance governmental expenditures, there is an additional reason for successive issues.[5] Higher prices increase the cost of governmental services, and, in order to secure the same purchasing power from an issue of paper money, it is necessary to increase the amount. If prices double, the new issue must be twice the original in order to have the same purchasing power. Usually governments lose real revenue in the form of taxes during periods of new paper money issues. The cost of governmental operations go up; budgets are out of balance; and money income may increase, but not as rapidly as expenses. Taxes are levied for the budget period, but they do not yield the purchasing power expected at the time of the levy, and so an unbalanced budget is but another reason for a new paper money issue. This ultimate effect of such a method of financing is to destroy the value of the monetary unit.

Overissuance of Bank Paper Money

During World War I, the most common practice among belligerent nations was for their governments to permit their central banks to suspend specie payment. Other restrictions on circulation were either repealed or liberalized. Then the government proceeded to use the bank's note issue facilities as freely as if the bank were an agency of the government, a role which, as a matter of fact, most of

[5] The inflationary effect of borrowing deposit currency from commercial banks is discussed in Chap. X.

them were forced to assume. Wherever the central bank was entirely dominated by the government it became an engine of inflation.

The procedure used in increasing note issues was to take bonds or government obligations to the central bank and receive bank notes in payment. If the bank was running short of paper money, new notes were printed and government bonds were used as security. The first borrowing transaction may be repeated, for each time a government loan is made the security for another batch of paper is given to the bank in the form of government bonds. This process may be repeated almost without limit as long as notes are secured only by general assets or a specific pledge of government bonds. Between 1921 and 1923 Germany experienced to the extreme limit the evil effects of uncontrolled bank currency inflation. Italy, Belgium, and France escaped the same fate only by the most heroic efforts. Needless to say, the earnings of central banks increased rapidly, but governments were in a position to demand and collect a large share of these earnings.

Expansion of currency through use of bank notes is more effective than through the use of government fiat money, because bank note issues may be increased without attracting much attention. On the other hand, a bill authorizing the government to issue paper money is debated on the floors of Congress and is certain to attract national and international attention. The flight of capital, hoarding, and other evidences of a loss of confidence in the monetary structure are certain to have harmful effects upon public and private credits. In terms of the equation of exchange, the major effects will be upon the velocity of money.

Central banks may double their circulation with little or no loss of public confidence, because issues may be increased enormously without attracting particular attention. Furthermore, the public will not hesitate to accept notes which have been in circulation for many years and with which it is familiar. Perhaps the greatest advantage of leaving paper currency expansion to banks is the fact that it is easier for the central bank to follow a liquidation policy when conditions no longer justify the existence of all or part of the emergency currency. This is the main argument in favor of irredeemable paper money issues by banks in preference to similar issues by governments.

Although all the arguments are in favor of issuance of emergency paper money by banks, after World War I a paper money nightmare occurred in Germany, where the extreme rise in prices was due to bank currency inflation. At the end of the war, note issues had increased more than eleven-fold—from 2,000,000,000 to 22,000,000,-000 marks. The increase in deposits and investments of the Reichsbank paralleled this movement, and the assets of the large private commercial banks reflected the inflationary effects of government borrowing. On the average, their cash items — bills (including treasury bills) and demand deposits—were inflated about fivefold. In spite of these figures, the inflation was fairly well controlled, and the rise in prices was only slightly more than doubled (+ 117 per cent).[6]

After the war the government still depended upon the Reichsbank for funds, and the printing of paper money continued. With each increase in volume the purchasing power fell, and in order to get the same results an ever increasing volume had to be printed and borrowed. During 1919 and 1920 foreign puchases of marks contributed to the relatively small decrease in the value of the mark as compared to the increase in the volume of currency; but by the end of 1920 the wholesale price index was at 1,500 per cent and by December, 1921, at 3,500 per cent.

Bad as the price situation was, inflation did not proceed at a runaway rate until 1922 and 1923. By the end of 1922 the index number reached 147,479, and by October, 1923, it had soared to 709,483,656,000. During this phase of the depreciation of the mark, it was no longer used as a store of value or a standard of deferred payments, and it was rapidly losing its function as a medium of exchange. The rate of decline in value was much faster than the increase in volume. In 1924 Germany practically repudiated all her paper money by providing for redemption at a ratio of 1 trillion to 1.

Many lessons may be drawn from Germany's experiences. Giving a monopoly of the note issue privilege to the central bank is no protection against inflation if the gold standard is suspended and control of the bank falls into the hands of the government, and if the government has an unbalanced budget and uses the bank to finance its fiscal needs. Another lesson to be learned is that the virus of

---

[6] Young, J. P., *European Currency and Finance*, Commission of Gold and Silver Inquiry, U.S. Senate, Part I, pp. 396-403.

inflation works slowly in its early stages but very rapidly during the latter part of the inflationary spiral.

The amount of currency deterioration that took place during World War II is more difficult to estimate because of the development of price and exchange control systems. Thus, price changes in the United States, the United Kingdom, Canada, and Germany, for example, were much smaller from 1940 to 1945 than during 1914 to 1919. On the other hand, in the Balkan countries, the Near East, and the Orient, price changes were much greater. Even before the end of hostilities, wholesale commodity prices had increased over 500,000 per cent in Greece, over 200 per cent in India, over 360 per cent in Turkey, and over 10,000 per cent in China.[7]

If the rate of increase in the volume of currency is used as a measure of the extent to which currencies have deteriorated in the countries that have had a fairly successful price control system, the record of Great Britain was better during World War II than during World War I, but the records of the United States and Germany were worse. However, the increase in industrial production in the United States did much to offset the inflationary increase in the quantity of currency. Furthermore, it should not be forgotten that approximately two-thirds of the Allied financial costs of World War II were borne by the United States.

As already noted, most of the postwar currency difficulties followed World War I. During the early twenties, there was a complete collapse of currency in Austria, Germany, Hungary, Poland, and Russia. The deterioration of currency was more prolonged but less extreme in Belgium, France, and Italy. Several developments sug-

---

[7] As previously noted, China was forced to leave the silver standard at the end of 1935 as a result of the "doing something for silver" program of the United States. The Chinese dollar was pegged at about 30 cents, in terms of the United States dollar. This system worked effectively until the beginning of the undeclared war with Japan in 1937. As a result of conquest of Chinese territory, the government lost most of its revenue from customs duties, salt taxes, and taxes on manufacturing and trade. Because of this loss of revenue, the increase in governmental war expenditures, and the lack of a market for the sale of its bonds to private investors, the government had to sell bonds to banks. The four government banks of issue (the Central Bank of China was given a monopoly of note issue in 1942) purchased government bonds printed for this purpose. As this method of financing was used repeatedly, the volume of currency expanded and prices increased 10,000 to 15,000 per cent. These price changes were not uniform among commodities and varied among geographical regions. Certain merchants, manufacturers, landowners (who fixed rent in terms of rice and other products), and speculators profited, while the masses suffered. This confirms the old statement that the evils of war and inflation are twins.

gest that similar catastrophes may be avoided after World War II. Reasons for optimism include: (1) an awareness in governmental circles of the seriousness of inflation; (2) actions already taken by certain governments to reduce the quantity of money outstanding; and (3) plans for multilateral action on currency rehabilitation and foreign exchange problems.[8]

QUESTIONS AND PROBLEMS

1. Give illustrations of the effects of monetary experiences on present monetary policy.
2. Can paper money be a standard of value? Explain.
3. Identify: (*a*) irredeemable paper money, (*b*) pure fiat or utopian money, and (*c*) managed paper money based on gold.
4. Give the arguments in favor of the paper standard.
5. What is the chief weakness and chief strength of the paper standard? Explain.
6. " 'So this is the basis of your civilization,' mused the Martian, gazing at the squat (gold) bars which made a pile 60 feet long, 40 feet wide and 22 feet high. ' . . . . Well, Gentlemen, we shall take this stuff away as a gift for the Martian museum. . . . the loss of this metal may induce you to solve your problems more intelligently' " (Thompson, C. P., "The Gold Bug," *This Week*, July 12, 1936, p. 6). What would be your solution?
7. Explain the inverted pyramid of credit and why the loss or gain of gold reserves is so important when on the gold standard.
8. "Any monetary system should facilitate optimum production and equitable distribution of income and wealth." Discuss.
9. Discuss the proposals (*a*) to keep the volume of the circulating media stable in terms of changes in demand over a long period of time, and (*b*) to hold the aggregate quantity of the circulating media constant.
10. Was the issue of Continental paper money necessary? Was its repudiation inevitable? (see Dewey, *Financial History of the United States*, pp. 41-43; Sumner, *Financier and Finances of the Revolution*, Vol. I, chap. iv; McLaughlin, *Confederation and Constitution*, chaps. iv and ix).
11. In 1789 what justification was there for the assumption that governments in the United States were not authorized to issue paper money? Why were the "Fathers of the Constitution" prejudiced against government paper money issues?

[8] Attention is invited to the currency plans put into effect in Belgium and Luxembourg immediately following their liberation in 1944: the exchange of old bank notes in Greece on November 11, 1944, at a rate of 50,000,000,000 old drachma for one new one; the work of United Nations Relief and Rehabilitation Administration; the organization of the International Monetary Fund; and the International Bank for Reconstruction and Development.

12. In 1870 the gold dollar was worth $1.21; the silver dollar was worth $1.23; the United States note (greenback) was worth $1.00. Which one was the standard money? Explain.
13. What is the chief difficulty in administrating a "controlled inflation" program? Explain.
14. Note advantages and disadvantages of new issues of government paper money as compared to new issues of bank paper money.
15. Note the relationship between government budgetary deficits and expansion in bank note issues during wars. May there be a similar relationship between government budgetary deficits and expansion of deposit currency?
16. "What is raised by printing note is just as much taken from the public as is a beer-duty or an income-tax. What a Government spends the public pays for" (Keynes, *Monetary Reform*, pp. 68-69). How does John Public pay for paper money?
17. "The truth is that all money is fiat money. The word fiat means 'let it be made' " (Coughlin, Rev. Charles E., *Money: Questions and Answers*, p. 164). Is this true?
18. "How ancient, how virile, is the repugnance to paper money is illustrated in the still remembered attempt of Kei Khatu, the thirteenth century overlord of Persia, to introduce paper money. . . . . A royal edict was issued, forbidding the circulation of the precious metals as currency. So violent was the public reaction, however, that the minister who proposed the idea was torn to pieces by a mob, the throne itself was threatened, and the edict, after three days, was repealed. For over six hundred years, ... no Persian government, ... dared to emit paper money . . . . the misery in which Iran finds itself today is a direct product of the attempt to create and manage a paper currency" (Groseclose, Elgin, *Near Eastern Postwar Monetary Standards*, p. 4). Compare to the quotation in Question 19.
19. "I contend that the use of gold (as money) is an absurdity. I think it is a relic of barbarism; it is a superstition. It is not essential at all. All that gold does is to restrict the volume of currency . . . . " (Source: *Minutes of Evidence* taken before the Committee on Finance and Industry, Vol. I, p. 357). Discuss.
20. "Monetary authorities can play an important constructive role in the postwar economy by contributing to economic stability. To do this they must be prepared to view economic problems in a broad way and to fit their policies not only to changing conditions but also the other economic and fiscal policies of the government" (Source and reference: Goldenweiser, E. A., in *Jobs, Production, and Living Standards*, p. 15). What specific things may the monetary authorities do?

REFERENCES

See end of Chapter IX

Chapter IX

PAPER CURRENCY

Classes of Paper Currency

Normally, the role of paper money is to act as a substitute for the standard in the form of credit or representative money, and it is this function of paper money in the monetary system which is being considered in this chapter. In the United States there are seven types of paper money: (1) gold certificates, (2) silver certificates, (3) Treasury notes of 1890, (4) national bank notes, (5) Federal Reserve bank notes, (6) Federal Reserve notes, and (7) United States notes. This situation contrasts markedly with conditions abroad, where there usually exists but one type of money—notes issued by the central bank. However, the actual situation is less confusing than suggested, because the Treasury notes of 1890, the national bank notes, Federal Reserve bank notes, and gold certificates denominated for circulation are being retired. Although they still appear in the Treasury's statement as "money in circulation," some of these forms are now in the category of "collectors' money."

The paper money of the United States is often classified as "representative paper money" and as "credit money." Gold and silver certificates and the Treasury notes of 1890 are classified as representative money, and the remaining types are classified as credit money. A final classification of United States currency is "gold currency," "Federal Reserve notes," and "Treasury currency." The advantage of this classification is that it draws attention to the true status of certain types of currency. Gold currency includes gold bullion, gold coins, and gold certificates; the Federal Reserve note is currency issued by the Federal Reserve banks; and all the other types are treasury currency.

Representative Paper Money Adds Little of Value to a Monetary System

This form of paper money is peculiar to the United States, and its existence is explained by the fact that American people normally prefer paper money in large denominations to gold coins and silver dollars. The gold coins were too small, and the silver dollar was and is too big; hence the preference for gold certificates and silver certificates. The Treasury notes of 1890 are a different type of currency, the origin of which is traced to the Sherman Act of 1890.

Gold Certificates.—The gold certificates (yellowbacks) were first provided for by the law of March 3, 1863. At first they were issued in denominations of $20 and over and were most widely used by commercial banks as reserves. After their denominations were lowered to $10 (March, 1907), they became a more common type of hand-to-hand money. During World War I they were impounded by the Federal Reserve banks as a war measure, but after 1921 they were put into circulation. During the following decade they made up approximately one-fourth of the total amount of money in circulation.

Since gold certificates were supported by an equal amount of gold, they were a very expensive type of hand-to-hand paper money. However, their circulation was justified, since it provided a harmless way in which to use part of the large gold imports of that period and thereby to some extent lessened the dangers of inflation. By substituting Federal Reserve notes for the gold certificates in case of need, the Federal Reserve banks could strengthen their reserve positions. Since the volume of paper money tends to flow through the Federal Reserve banks twice yearly, the mechanics of this plan were simple, merely holding back gold certificates as they came in and paying out Federal Reserve notes. This plan worked with some success during 1930-33, but it was not entirely successful, owing to some hoarding of gold certificates in preference to other types of paper money (an illustration of Gresham's law as applied to different types of paper money).

Since 1933, as noted in Chapter V, the status of the gold certificate has changed materially. In 1933 all the old gold certificates were called in, and it became illegal to hold them. They are being retired as fast as they reach the banks and the United States Treasury. The new gold certificates provided for in the Gold Reserve Act of 1934 are to be used for reserve purposes by the twelve Federal Reserve banks. They are redeemable in gold only when, in the judgment of the Secretary of the Treasury, redemption is necessary to secure gold to settle international balances or "to maintain the equal purchasing power of every kind of currency in the United States."

The existence of the gold certificates now adds nothing of value to the currency system of the United States. The justification for their existence ended with the termination of gold coin circulation, which they were created to replace, unit for unit. Unless there is to be more tinkering with the weight of the gold dollar and the mint price of gold, all the gold bars now earmarked as reserves for gold certificates should be given to the Federal Reserve banks in exchange for their gold certificates and their gold credits with the Treasury. But if the government should decide to return to a full gold standard, then gold certificates of the old type should be reissued, and free coinage of gold should be permitted.

Silver Certificates.—This form of representative paper money was first authorized in the Bland-Allison Act of 1878. The silver dollars and silver bullion supporting them as reserves are only token coins and token money. Their money value depends, in part, upon the legal provisions appearing first in the Gold Standard Act of 1900 and later in the Gold Reserve Act of 1934, which imposed upon the Secretary of the Treasury the duty of maintaining at par with gold all the money issued or coined for the United States.

Treasury Notes of 1890.—This type of representative paper money was first issued in 1890 to pay for silver which was purchased under provisions of the Sherman Silver Purchase Act. Only $1,000,-000 of the original $153,500,000 is outstanding. These notes are backed unit for unit in silver and are being replaced by silver certificates when they are retired. They are of minor importance at the present time, and probably the government would be justified in demonetizing them after making public announcement of its intention.

Credit Paper Money Is the Most Important Type of Circulating Money

Credit paper money has all the advantages of convenience possessed by representative paper money. In addition, it is more economical than representative money, requiring only a small fractional reserve instead of unit-for-unit backing. Normally, a nation has in circulation paper credit money considerably in excess of its holdings of the standard metal.

Paper money permits governments and banks to get resources with which to carry on their activities. The banks of issue give their noninterest-bearing promises to pay in the form of bank currency in return for the interest-bearing promises to pay of their customers. Banks must redeem their promises to pay on demand, but as long as there is no doubt as to their ability to pay, they are seldom asked to do so. As long as these notes remain in the hands of the public, they represent a noninterest-bearing loan to the bank of issue.

In the early history of commercial banking, particularly in communities which had no funds to leave as deposits with banks, profits from note issues made it possible for banks to open. In the United States during the formative period, the right to carry on banking was considered synonymous with the privilege of issuing bank paper money. In England before 1825 and in the United States before the Civil War, all commercial banks were institutions of note issue. However, almost from the beginning there has been a mingling of public and private finance in the development of note issue banking. In 1696 the Bank of England and in 1863 the national banks in the United States were given charters requiring purchase of government bonds with the banks' capital, but in return they were authorized to issue bank notes. Today, as never before, the bank note issue privilege is limited to government-owned or controlled central banks of issue, which are functioning as public or quasi-public institutions, with profit making as a secondary consideration.

Since the note issue privilege is valuable, there are many objections to "the surrender of the government's right to print and issue paper money" to banks, but the government usually makes provisions to share in or to take all note issue profits. This is done in many ways, including limitation of dividends to be paid to shareholders, franchise or other taxes, owning banks of issue, borrowing at favorable rates, or by some other means. For example, in Canada the government owns the central bank of issue; recently the Bank of England was nationalized, but prior to that time all profits of the note issue department belonged to the government; and in France the government borrowed without cost, secured other free services, and participated in excess earnings by taxation of the Bank of France. In the United States (1) national banks paid taxes on their circulation and purchased government bonds as collateral backing for notes at par or at a premium which yielded about one-half the current rate of interest; (2) Federal Reserve banks not only gave many free services to the government but also paid a franchise tax of $150,000,-

000 out of excess earnings. In addition, the surplus of any Federal Reserve bank (since 1935 the recipient of net earnings except dividends of 6 per cent) belongs to the government in case of liquidation.

During emergencies, governments or governmental agencies, such as government-owned or government-dominated central banks, have made use of their powers to issue paper money in order to finance their fiscal needs. Usually the revenue secured in this way is not enough to offset the losses in real income (because of inflation) derived from financing in other ways, namely, by borrowing and by taxing. Under modern economy, the amount of governmental revenue which could be raised by paper money issues would be so small that any attempt to finance seriously in this way would mean death for the monetary system. During the fiscal year 1939 federal tax collections were $6,100,000,000, or as much as all types of paper money then in circulation in the United States. Even this amount failed by $3,600,000,000 to balance the budget. During World War II our federal government provided for expenditures equal to over four times the amount of money in circulation, that is, $110,000,000,000 as compared to $25,000,000,000. These figures suggest how unimportant paper money issues are as a device for financing expenditures over a period of time.

Finally, the use of credit paper money makes it possible for a nation's monetary system to have the important quality of elasticity. This characteristic is treated below under the general heading of the qualities of a good note issue system.

Qualities of a Good Note Issue System

The best results in note circulation are obtained by making provisions for easy and prompt redemption of notes in standard money and by making provisions for safety of bank notes. A good note issue system has three qualities—safety, parity, and elasticity.[1]

Safety.—Safety or security of bank notes may be obtained in a number of ways. It may be done by limiting issues to one bank or group of banks; by placing a maximum limit on circulation; by requiring specific security for notes which are limited in quantity; and by numerous technical devices such as limiting territory in which notes may circulate and allowing only large denomination notes to be

[1] See Taylor, F. M., *Some Chapters on Money*, chap. viii.

issued. The most common method now used to obtain safety is to require that specific pledges of assets be held in trust as security for notes. The preferred types of security are gold, government bonds, and commercial paper, but general assets of the bank may be used.

The safest type of security is gold, but notes permanently backed 100 per cent in this way are called representative and not credit money. Bonds are objected to because the quantity of bonds varies according to the fiscal needs of the governments and not according to trade needs. Commercial paper is considered to be an ideal type of security, because the volume tends to change with seasonal and cyclical changes in business; but at present the quantity is insufficient.

Land and commodities have been used as a basis for paper money issues, and there is a popular fallacy that they make good backing for bank notes; but the history of land-secured and commodity-secured currency has been one of overissue and ultimate loss to the noteholders. They are not safeguards against overissue, because no provisions are made for redemption of the notes on demand. Each increase in the volume of notes tends to raise the prices of land and commodities and therefore the monetary value of the backing of notes. A second issue of notes is followed with the same effects upon prices of land and commodities. This new rise in land and commodity prices seemingly justifies a third issue of notes, and so on indefinitely, until the value of paper money is practically nothing. If the backing of notes is to be effective it must be used, and land and commodities are not physically well suited for conversion purposes.[2]

At the present time all types of paper money in the United States are either issued by or guaranteed by the federal government.

Parity.—Paper money must be at par with the standard money. Notes must not be at a discount in any community or territory within the area served by them as money. Before the Civil War, notes of many of the best banks circulated in distant places at discount, and note brokers found it profitable to buy up these notes and then to

[2] These objections would be met in the commodity reserve plan by redeeming paper money in commodities. In this plan the central bank would be required to hold, in place of a monetary gold reserve, "goods in designated units of a composite of important, storable, staple, primary commodities, weighted according to their significance in our economy and exchangeable at *fixed prices*, both ways, against monetary certificates" (Graham, F. A., "The Primary Function of Money and Their Consumption in Monetary Policy," *American Economic Review*, Supplement, Part 2, Vol. XXX No. 1 [March, 1940], pp. 1-16). Italics are added. The chief objection to this plan is the difficulty in administering the plan. See Westerfield, R. B., and Opie, R., "Discussions," *ibid*, pp. 39-41.

present them for redemption at the bank of issue. This system placed the burden of redemption upon the noteholders rather than upon the banks, where it properly belongs. Rather than bear this burden, noteholders passed in local trade the notes issued by banks in distant places. When specie was desired, local notes, which were at par, were used. Thus, according to Gresham's law, cheap notes drove the good notes out of circulation. As a result, certain banks did not have their fair share of notes in circulation. For example, this was true of banks located in the financial centers of the country, for there was a tendency for large quantities of rural bank notes to drift to cities in payment of goods. This situation explains the development of the Suffolk Banking System.

Provisions must be made for easy and prompt redemption. The ideal plan is to provide for local redemption agencies to be scattered throughout the country. Under our present banking system, notes must be accepted at par by national and Federal Reserve banks. This protects the public but not the converting bank. However, the converting bank is adequately cared for by two provisions of the law. All issuing banks must keep a redemption fund equal to 5 per cent of their circulation in Washington. This fund is used to redeem bank notes, and all costs of maintaining it are charged against issuing banks. In addition, the issuing banks are required to redeem their notes at par over their own counters. A final step to insure the parity of bank notes in the United States was taken in 1933, when all types were given the full legal tender quality in payment of all debts, both public and private. At the present time it is the policy of the Federal Reserve banks to pay costs of shipping currency of all types.

A special problem arises when a bank is in the process of liquidation. The period between the dates when a bank fails and when all of its note liabilities are paid may be months and even years. During this period notes may be passed at a discount, even though ultimate payment in full is certain. In order to prevent this temporary loss to noteholders, three devices may be used. (1) Banks may be compelled to contribute to a safety fund, from which notes may be redeemed. This system was used in New York State (1830-60) and was later adopted in Canada (1890). (2) Provisions may be made for payment of interest on bank notes from the date of failure until the notes are paid. If this method were adopted, notes would be held as an investment by those familiar with their true status. (3) Provisions may be made for immediate redemption by the government, which would act as a guarantor of the notes. Notes would be redeemed by the government with its own funds, but later the government would sell bonds and other property of the bank in order to reimburse itself. Many states used this method before 1860, and it was the policy adopted by the federal government. Now the Federal Reserve banks must keep government bonds, gold certificates, and/or commercial paper with Federal Reserve agents, as collateral for their notes. Because of other protective features, such a practice appears unnecessary.

Elasticity.—By elasticity is meant the ability of the volume of currency to expand or contract as the need arises. Fluctuations in the demand for currency and credit may be due to: (1) gradual increase in production as population and volume of trade increase; (2) extraordinary conditions, such as hoarding during financial panics and bank failures; (3) cyclical fluctuations in business; (4) seasonal demands for harvesting purposes, Christmas shopping, and seasonal payrolls; and (5) minor changes due to week-end payrolls and household purchases calling for more currency on Thursday, Friday, and Saturday, and less on Monday, Tuesday, and Wednesday. Some of these changes in business seem to demand changes in one type of currency or credit, and others seem to demand other types of currency or credit.

As noted in Chapter IV, the long-run or trend demand for money can best be provided for by changes in the supply of standard money with corresponding changes in the volume of credit and currency. The supply of standard metal is incapable of being increased rapidly, and, at best, gold mining can be adjusted to care for only the long-run fluctuations in the needs of business. This long-run type of expansion is of the chewing-gum variety, with little need for contraction. Since elasticity involves the ability to expand and contract, the currency problems of elasticity are those associated with the seasonal and cyclical changes in business, hoarding and dehoarding of currency, and weekly and holiday demands for ready spending.

The seasonal changes in demand for currency are closely associated with the seasonal changes in retail trade and in payrolls. Many department stores do as high as 50 per cent of their business during the last quarter of the year. Purchase of Christmas gifts and larger amounts of food and increased spending for travel and recreation tend to increase the demand for currency. Payrolls likewise increase. The figures for currency withdrawals from the Treasury and Federal Reserve banks often increase from $300,000,000 to $500,000,000 to care for these seasonal demands. Within three weeks following Christmas, most of this currency returns to the Reserve banks, where it technically becomes money out of circulation. A seasonal decline to one of the lowest amounts in circulation is reached during the summer months.

When reserves are low, banks rarely keep surplus till money on hand; therefore, when member banks start preparing for the week-end currency demands for household expenditures and payrolls, there is an increase in the amount of money demanded from the Federal Reserve banks and their branches. These demands are largest on Thursday, Friday, and Saturday, when more currency is withdrawn. This weekly demand from Federal Reserve banks is most noticeable in the cities where the Reserve banks or their branches are located. Currency in other communities is returned less promptly and the flow of currency to and from their institutions is smaller.

During World War II family income increased to a new record high. As a result, there has been a noticeable increase in the amount of currency in circulation. Other factors which have been at work for some time are: (1) more domestic hoarding of currency, as indicated by the increase in the volume of large denomination notes in circulation; (2) foreign hoarding of American currency, as indicated by pre-war shipments abroad; (3) greater use of currency in consumer purchases and decrease in the relative number and use of checking accounts, probably because of bank service charges; and (4) sales taxes, "which appear to have increased the use of coins."[3]

Bank credit money issued by central banks best meets the requirements of elasticity, because these institutions are expected to keep part of their resources unused in order to be able to provide this highly desirable element in the banking system. Only minor costs are involved in keeping a supply of paper money ready for seasonal or emergency demands for currency, and additional amounts may be printed in anticipation of future needs. The criticism may be made that idle bank note currency means idle reserves, but this criticism

[3] See *Federal Reserve Bulletin,* May, 1939, p. 355.

would be more applicable if directed at the minimum legal requirements, since they have the effect of keeping reserves idle even during emergencies.

The development of deposit banking decreased the cyclical and most other fluctuating demands for hand-to-hand currency, but it greatly increased the emergency demands for currency. Most of the money not in cash balances of individuals or corporations is normally deposited with banks. But if there is loss of confidence in banks, there will be a decline in the normal flow to banks, and many depositors will demand that their claims be paid in cash. Since deposits are normally many times the total amount of money in circulation, the need for great emergency elasticity is apparent. Ideal emergency elasticity would permit depositors, should they so desire, to exchange en masse their deposits for pocket money. Small withdrawals of currency will effect the reserve deposit accounts of member banks, and, if new funds are not available, there will tend to be a general tightening of credit, higher interest rates, decline in business, and deflation.

Types of Obsolete and Extinct Bank Paper Credit Money

While the Fathers of the Constitution thought they had eliminated all government paper money issues, they had not anticipated the extent to which the state and federal government could create banks having the privilege of note issue. Not only did the state and federal governments authorize the establishment of banks of issue, but they often participated in the financing of these institutions.

Banks of the United States.—During the two periods 1791-1811 and 1816-36, there were in operation federal incorporated banks of the United States, partly government owned, with the privilege of note issue. Each institution operated branches which were located in various parts of the country. Their notes were generally acceptable, well secured, and circulated at par. The volume of these notes fluctuated in different sections with trade and business needs. These banks gave the country an excellent note issue system.

The United States banks exerted a wholesome restraint on state bank note circulation by forcing the state institutions to redeem their notes. This procedure compelled the state banks to limit circulation and keep their notes at par. Total circulation of the two United States banks was not large, being limited to the capital stock of the banks, that is, $10,000,000 and $35,000,000, respectively. Both of these banks were chartered for but twenty years and were not rechartered because of political reasons.

State Bank Notes.—Thousands of banks were chartered by states between 1781 and 1860, and millions of dollars of bank paper money were issued by them.[4] Some excellent note issue systems were developed, but in general the currency situation was unsatisfactory. The main criticisms of the state bank note circulation were (1) lack of uniformity (too many types of notes), (2) lack of general security and safety, (3) lack of general parity, and (4) lack of adequate provisions for redemption. After 1866 a tax of 10 per cent was placed on state bank notes by the federal government, and, as a result, all were withdrawn from circulation.

National Bank Notes.—These notes came into being as a result of the Civil War. They were issued by banks incorporated under the National Banking Act (1863).[5] The federal government financed its military campaigns by a combination of taxes, bond flotations, and issues of United States notes or greenbacks. The interest rate on government bonds was high, and the market for them was narrow. All national banks were forced to buy bonds. This requirement was not burdensome to banks, because they not only received a substantial rate of interest on these bonds but could also use them as backing for currency note issues. Banks were in a position that permitted them to invest their money and at the same time use it for other banking purposes.

Banks incorporated under state laws were issuing their notes under similar or even more liberal state laws. The new National Banking System was not popular with banks, until in 1866 the state banks were forced to give up their note issues because of a 10 per cent federal tax on their circulation.

The national bank note system was a great improvement over the preceding lack of system. The notes were safe because they were guaranteed by the credit of the federal government. For seventy years thousands of banks of varying degrees of soundness issued them by the hundreds of millions of dollars, without a single loss to

[4] For descriptions of note issues by state banks, see Dewey, D. R., "State Banking before the Civil War," *National Monetary Commission*, pp. 53-112.

[5] "History and Development of the National Bank Note," *Seventy-third Annual Report of the Comptroller of the Currency*, pp. 817-42.

noteholders. The name of the issuing bank had little significance to the public, because the holders looked to the government for protection. But the national bank notes were not a satisfactory form of currency, since their volume was not responsive to the fluctuating demands of business. These notes lacked the essential characteristic of elasticity, and this currency situation was made more serious by the absence of a central banking system.

The Aldrich-Vreeland Act of 1908 made provisions for emergency issues of national bank notes amounting to $500,000,000. Notes could be issued by individual banks or a group of banks, and commercial paper and assets other than federal government bonds could be used as security. This act was but a stopgap to tide the country through an emergency which arose before the organization of the Federal Reserve System. In modified form the currency provisions of the Aldrich-Vreeland Act were used extensively during the first part of World War I.

In 1913 the Federal Reserve Act provided for the retirement of the national bank notes, but war financing prevented their withdrawal.[6] Bonds issued during and following this war could not be used as security for national bank notes, and so the eligible bonds outstanding were limited to less than $900,000,000. In 1925 alone, over $100,000,000 of them came due and were retired.

In 1932 there were outstanding over $675,000,000 of bonds which were eligible for backing of national bank notes. In this same year a rider was attached to the Home Loan Bank Bill permitting all government bonds bearing 3⅜ per cent interest or less to be used for backing of national bank notes for a three-year period. Previous to this law the limiting factor on circulation was the volume of eligible bonds; but following this law it was the aggregate capital stock of all national banks, or about $1,600,000,000.[7] All banks did not use this new privilege, and many used it only in part; the total increase in circulation was about $300,000,000. The temporary feature of the measure, which expired in 1935, made full use of the note issue privilege unattractive to bankers.

In 1935 the Secretary of the Treasury issued a call for all the 2 per cent bonds which were outstanding, and part of the profits which resulted from devaluation of the dollar was used to purchase them.

---

[6] Sec. 18, *Federal Reserve Act.*

[7] *Federal Reserve Bulletin,* August, 1932, pp. 478-80.

The banks, which were using the bonds as backing for their issues, left the funds resulting from these purchases with the government, in order to cover their financial responsibility for their outstanding bank notes. Since that time the national bank notes have been in the process of being retired, but at the end of ten years there were still $120,000,000 outstanding, and many of these notes will always remain in the hands of collectors.

Federal Reserve Bank Notes.—The Federal Reserve Act of 1913 made provisions for two new types of currency—Federal Reserve bank notes and Federal Reserve notes.[8] When the authors of the Federal Reserve Act arranged for the retirement of national bank notes, they were desirous of preventing sudden changes in the volume of currency and losses to national banks because of their holdings of 2 per cent government bonds. These low-yielding bonds owed much of their market value to the fact that they could be deposited to secure national bank notes. The Reserve banks could be required to purchase these bonds by the Federal Reserve Board. To prevent a too sudden contraction of currency, bonds could be used to back new Federal Reserve bank notes.[9] Otherwise, the 2 per cent bonds could be exchanged for 3 per cent gold notes or 3 per cent gold bonds. The pre-war (World War I) gold imports and Federal Reserve note issues made Federal Reserve bank note issues unnecessary. Some were retired during 1916, followed by an increase beginning June, 1917. However, the volume remained unimportant until after the passage of the Pittman Act in April, 1918. Refinancing of 2 per cent bonds was discontinued soon after our entry into World War I, and matters other than the retirement of national bank notes occupied the attention of the Federal Reserve authorities.

The Pittman Act provided for the melting-down of not more than $350,000,000 in silver dollars and its sale to Great Britain for export to India. This withdrawal of silver necessitated the retirement of silver certificates, which circulated primarily in the form of small denominations—$1.00, $2.00, and $5.00. Consequently, a famine of small bills threatened. This emergency could have been met by permitting Federal Reserve notes to be issued in denominations of less than $5.00, but instead authorization was given for new issues of

---

[8] Sec. 16, *Federal Reserve Act.*

[9] Sec. 18, *Federal Reserve Act.*

Federal Reserve bank notes in these small denominations, secured by one-year gold notes and certificates of indebtedness. Thus began the second chapter in the history of the Federal Reserve bank note. In January, 1920, about $270,500,000 of these were in circulation. Later, when new silver was coined and new certificates issued, the Federal Reserve bank notes were retired. In May, 1924, the Federal Reserve banks discharged their liability for the Federal Reserve bank notes still outstanding by turning over to the Treasury an equal amount of lawful money. At the end of 1933 there were less than $3,000,000 still outstanding.

The third chapter in the history of the Federal Reserve bank note began during the national banking holiday of March, 1933. The government desired to issue a type of currency, if necessary, which would not place any additional strain on the banking reserves of the country. So Congress, in the Bank Emergency Act, provided for the issuance of Federal Reserve bank notes secured by commercial paper or any type of federal government security. When the President proclaimed the end of the emergency, the notes were to be issued only against certain United States government bonds. Under the misleading label "national currency," $912,000,000 of these notes were printed. The post-banking-holiday demand for currency was not so great as expected, so less than $265,000,000 were issued, and most of these were secured by government bonds. Soon thereafter these notes were retired, and the Federal Reserve banks discharged their liabilities for those outstanding in the spring of 1935 by depositing funds with the Treasury.

The policy of retiring those government bonds which were eligible as backing for the national bank notes also retired the "regular" backing for Federal Reserve bank notes. It was assumed that, as a result, both the Federal Reserve bank notes and the national bank notes would be retired and not reissued.

The fourth chapter in the history of the Federal Reserve bank note started in December, 1942. Since the President had not terminated the emergency proclaimed in 1933, the provisions for new issues of Federal Reserve bank notes, stipulated in the Bank Emergency Act of 1933, were used as the legal basis for issuing $660,000,000 of them. Since these notes were already printed, the justification for using them was conservation of labor and material during the war period.

The Federal Reserve banks, on receipt of the notes, gave the government deposit credit for them, thereby eliminating their liability for the Federal Reserve bank notes. Hence, even before these notes were issued to the public by the Federal Reserve banks, they ceased being bank paper money and became Treasury currency. The issuance of these notes by the government was criticized both in and out of Congress.[10] On June 12, 1945, an act of Congress which repealed all power and authority with respect to the issuance of Federal Reserve bank notes was signed by the President.[11] At the time of the enactment of this law there were $545,000,000 in circulation. Since that time the amount outstanding has decreased, but it will be years before all will be retired. So ends the history of the Federal Reserve bank note, which has had the most checkered legislative career of any type of currency in United States history.

Federal Reserve Notes Are the Only Type of Bank Credit Money in the United States

The most important type of circulating paper money in the United States is the Federal Reserve note. It is a direct obligation of the United States government, but it is put out through banking channels and, therefore, has all the characteristics of a bank note currency. The condition of its issuance meets with the scientific tests of a good bank note system. In addition to possessing the qualities of the other two types of bank paper money, it is elastic, that is, the volume in circulation increases or decreases with trade needs. The flow of currency from the Board of Governors of the Federal Reserve System to the public is illustrated by Chart V.

The demand for currency originates with businessmen and consumers who need currency for payrolls or retail trade purposes. The demand for currency is made effective by use of existing deposits with banks, by borrowing, or by the sale of securities. The 6,400 member banks use similar methods to secure currency from the twelve Federal Reserve banks. The Federal Reserve banks secure the notes from their Federal Reserve agents, who receive and hold 100 per cent collateral in the form of gold certificates, government

[10] See Spahr, W. E., *Open Letter to Congress*, January 20, 1943, published by Office of Economists' National Committee on Monetary Policy.

[11] See Sec. 3 of *Public Law 84*, 79th Cong.

CHART V

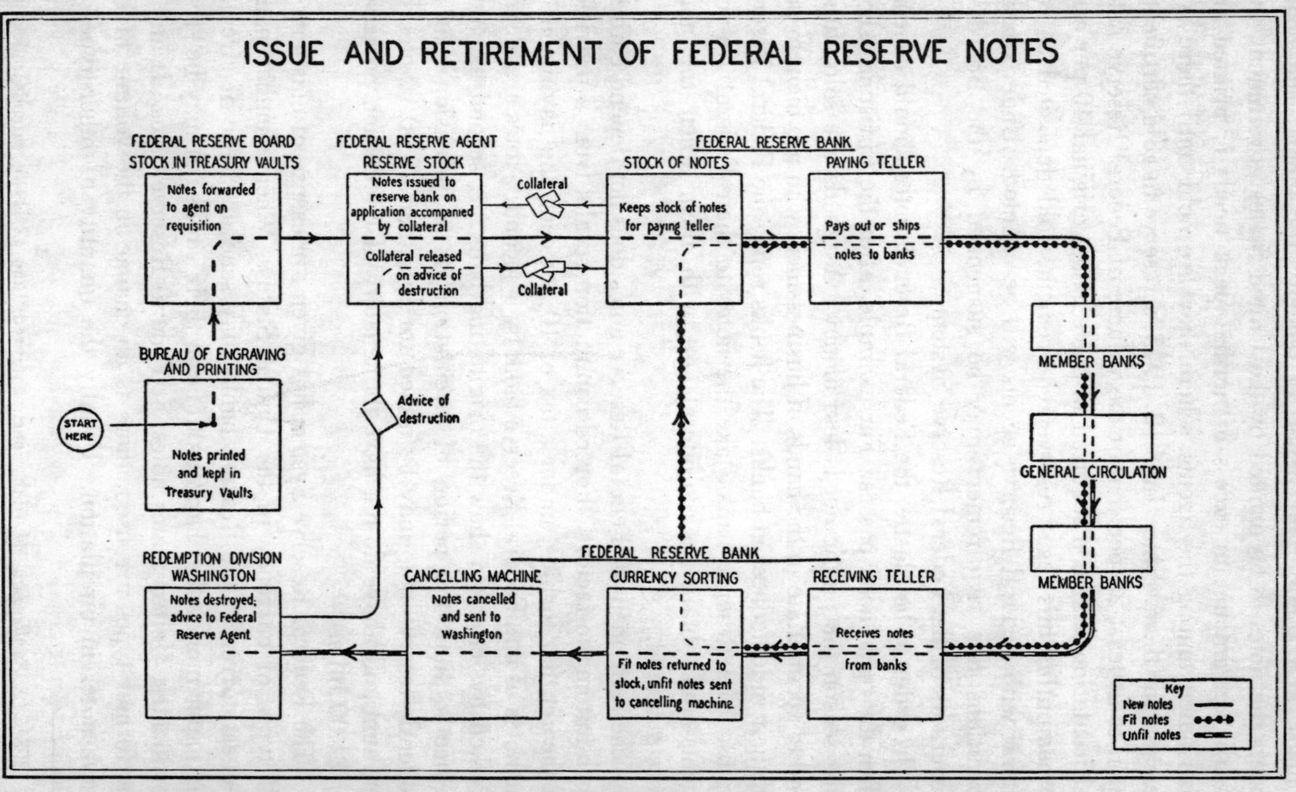

Source: Federal Reserve Bank of New York, *The Federal Reserve System Today*, p. 27.

bonds,[12] and commercial paper as security for them. The board orders the notes to be printed by the United States government, and usually an amount in excess of normal peak needs is printed and distributed among the agents, where they are held until there is a demand for them. Since June 12, 1945, a reserve in gold certificates equal to at least 25 per cent of the volume of Federal Reserve notes in circulation has been required in place of the original 40 per cent. In computing this legal reserve requirement, gold deposited as collateral with Federal Reserve agents will be counted. Under certain conditions this requirement may be suspended by the Board of Governors of the Federal Reserve System.

In order to be elastic, the Federal Reserve notes should contract when the trade need passes. For example, after the Christmas shopping season the public needs less money. As goods are sold, funds tend to accumulate in the hands of businessmen, who use them to pay off their indebtedness at banks. The banks repay the Federal Reserve banks. The Reserve banks take the notes to their Federal Reserve agents and obtain the collateral left with them when the notes were obtained.

The retirement of Federal Reserve notes does not depend entirely upon automatic factors. Forced contraction results from a provision of the act that forbids, under a tax of 10 per cent, the paying-out of the notes of one Federal Reserve bank by a second. Notes are clearly marked by letters to show the originating bank. A second technical device to limit the period of circulation is the provision that no Federal Reserve note may be issued for less than $5.00. Notes for this sum and above do not have the tenacity of circulation possessed by $1.00 bills.

The Federal Reserve System has given a measure of elasticity to all types of currency in the United States. When member banks request currency, the Reserve banks may send any type of circulating paper money that happens to be in their vaults. It may be silver certificates, United States notes, or Federal Reserve notes. If any of the former types are used, there is no change in the volume of Reserve notes in circulation. Usually the quantity of other types of

---

[12] Sec. 2, *Public Law 84*, 79th Cong., approved June 12, 1945, extends indefinitely the authority to use direct obligations of the federal government as collateral against Federal Reserve notes. The Federal Reserve agents' division of the Federal Reserve bank's organization is a bank note issue department within each Federal Reserve bank.

money in the vaults of the Federal Reserve banks is less than the amount necessary to care for seasonal or other fluctuating demands. As a result, the volume of Reserve notes in circulation shows some congruence with elastic demand. As may be expected, the greatest similarity is found when changes in the total amount of money in circulation are compared to weekly, seasonal, cyclical, and emergency demands for money.

Two Principles of Bank Note Issue

The Banking Principle.—The development of commercial banking was at first closely associated with and dependent upon the note issue privilege. The original theory governing note issues contended that if bankers were left free to use their own judgment notes would not be issued in excess. Notes would be issued only in connection with regular lending and investment operations of the bank. To be sure, the supply of hand-to-hand money would increase, but only in response to an increase in the demand. Just as soon as the need which called the new currency into existence had passed, currency would be returned to the bank of issue.

Theorists held that no guarantee other than the ordinary law of contract was necessary, because all redundant notes would be returned promptly for redemption. Therefore overissue would be impossible, provided the notes were always convertible into standard money. The only security necessary for notes would be general assets of the banks, which must include some specie in order to maintain the liquidity of the banks of issue. Lacking legal tender quality, note issues of each bank would be forced to circulate on their merits. This banking principle of note issue works best when notes are issued by a few banks, preferably central banks. Facilities for the prompt redemption of notes in standard money must be provided for at the expense of the issuing banks. The management of circulation must be fairly conservative, and reserves must be adequate at all times.

The banking principle was experimented with during the early monetary history of England and the United States. The results were unsatisfactory, because the note issue privilege was given to hundreds of banks of varying integrity and responsibility. Inability of the general public to distinguish between good and bad notes led to governmental intervention, first by the separate states and then by the federal government. So a century ago emphasis was placed on required reserves, collateral requirements, and other types of positive protection; and this emphasis is being continued today, even though the basic reasons for it have disappeared.

The Currency Principle.—The critics of the banking principle urged that bank notes be considered in the same category as other types of hand-to-hand money or currency. For centuries coins were minted and issued by or under conditions specified by governments. If the government finds it necessary to regulate one type of money, should not the same policy be applied to a second type? Hence the name "currency principle." The chief disadvantage of the use of the currency principle is the resulting inelasticity of note issues, and the chief advantage is the resulting safety of note issues. However, the price paid for safety may be a currency system which contains too little emergency or other types of elasticity.

The rigid collateral and reserve requirements provided by law for the Federal Reserve notes caused considerable difficulty during the period from 1931 to 1933. Instead of courageously abolishing the 40 per cent legal minimum reserve and 100 per cent commercial paper and gold collateral requirement, redress was taken to the discarded bond-secured note issue system. In 1932 the Glass-Steagall law was passed to permit the temporary use of government bonds as backing for Federal Reserve notes, thereby freeing gold for use as reserves. Provisions were also made for the issuance of additional amounts of national bank notes and Federal Reserve bank notes. If the Federal Reserve banks had been issuing notes based on the banking principle, these changes would have been unnecessary, and it is even possible that the national banking moratorium could have been avoided.

Statistics of United States Currency

Gold Currency.—Table 5 gives statistics of United States currency for selected years. The increase in gold currency in the United States has been due to devaluation of the gold dollar, gold imports, and increase in gold production. This gold is held by the government as reserve against gold certificates ($18,107,000,000) and against United States notes and Treasury notes of 1890 ($156,039,431). In addition, $1,800,000,000 is held for the account of the Stabilization Fund; and the $144,000,757 is shown as the balance of the increment resulting from the reduction in weight of the gold dollar. Since July 31, 1945, this last item is not shown in the circulation statement.

Gold certificates are now held as cash reserves by the twelve Federal Reserve banks. There are in circulation a small quantity of these certificates which were issued prior to 1933. They are being retired and cancelled when received. Now Federal Reserve banks are required to hold a minimum legal reserve of 25 per cent against their circulating notes and deposits in the form of gold certificates.

TABLE 5

STATISTICS OF UNITED STATES CURRENCY
(In Millions of Dollars)

Type of Currency	June 30, 1933		June 30, 1939		June 30, 1945	
	Amount	Circulation†	Amount	Circulation†	Amount	Circulation†
Gold coin and bullion	$ 4,318	$ 321	$16,110‡	$ 0	$20,213‡	$ 0
Gold certificates	(1,231)*	265	(13,595)*	72	(18,107)*	52
Silver dollars and bullion	549	28	1,777	42	2,014	125
Silver certificates	(480)*	361	(1,702)*	1,453	(1,816)*	1,652
Treasury notes of 1890	(1)*	1	(1)*	1	(1)*	1
Subsidiary silver coins	299	257	380	361	825	788
Minor coins	127	113	161	155	304	292
United States notes	346	269	346	266	347	323
Federal Reserve notes	3,337	3,061	4,764	4,483	23,651	22,867
Federal Reserve bank notes	141	125	26	25	534	527
National bank notes	971	920	189	186	121	120
Total	$10,078	$5,721	$23,753	$7,044	$48,010	$26,747

* These amounts are not included in the total, since the gold and silver held as security against gold and silver certificates and Treasury notes of 1890 are included under gold and silver dollars and gold and silver bullion, respectively.

† "Money in circulation" includes all money outside of the United States Treasury and Federal Reserve banks.

‡ Since February, 1933, this figure does not include gold other than in the Treasury. Before February, 1934, gold dollars contained 25.8 grains of standard gold 9/10 fine; since February, 1934, they have contained 15 5/21 grains of standard gold 9/10 fine.

Source: "Circulation Statements of United States Treasury."

Gold currency is not permitted to circulate in the United States, and what justification once existed for printing gold certificates has disappeared. In order to simplify the currency system of the United States, Congress should repeal the laws that provide for their issuance and permit the gold they represent to be used directly by the

Federal Reserve banks as reserves. If the United States is to adopt a gold standard, these central banks should be permitted to use freely this gold in bullion or gold coin form to redeem their promises to pay.

Federal Reserve Notes.—Among the different types of currency in circulation, the most important is the Federal Reserve note. Since this currency is issued under conditions which permit it to expand readily to meet new needs for currency, it has had the greatest increase during the war years. The 1945 legislative changes, which permit government obligations to be used indefinitely as collateral backing and require a gold certificate minimum reserve of but 25 per cent, will add to the elasticity of this type of currency. Although these changes may be labelled inflationary, the important thing to remember is that an increase in volume of money tends to follow an increase in the volume of deposit currency. This will be discussed more fully in the next chapter.

Treasury Currency.—All the remaining types of currency are now classified as Treasury currency. There are two classes—those that are being retired and cancelled by the government and those that are being issued by the government. In the first group are the Treasury notes of 1890, the national bank notes, the Federal Reserve bank notes, and the gold certificates issued prior to 1933. In volume the silver certificate is the most important type of Treasury currency. Its existence is due to the various political movements which have as their purpose an increase in the price of silver. It is an expensive type of money, which has no place in either a gold standard or a paper money standard system. The tenacity in circulation of this certificate is due chiefly to the fact that it is issued in small denominations. The volume outstanding is determined more by politics than by economic needs.

Unlike the silver certificate and silver dollars, the quantity of subsidiary silver and minor coins is determined by economic needs, particularly those of the retail trade fields, where goods and services are sold for small amounts.

The United States notes, or greenbacks, of the Civil War period now represent but a small part of the total amount of money in the United States. In the interest of economy and simplification of the currency system, Congress should provide for their retirement and cancellation. Although Congress did repeal that part of the Thomas

Inflation Act which permitted new United States notes to be issued, it did not make provisions for retiring and cancelling those outstanding.

Perhaps Congress should provide by statute for measures which will expedite the retirement of obsolete but not extinct types of paper money, including the Treasury notes of 1890, the national bank notes, the Federal Reserve bank notes, and gold certificates issued prior to 1933. A date might be fixed after which all types of obsolete currency would cease being money and after which they would be deleted from the circulation statements of the United States Treasury.

QUESTIONS AND PROBLEMS

1. Identify by name each of the seven types of paper money in circulation in the United States.
2. What are the advantages of grouping all types of pocket money as "treasury," "gold," and "Federal Reserve"?
3. Explain why provisions were made originally for gold and silver certificates? Do these same reasons explain why these two types of money are still being printed?
4. Explain why the note issue privilege was so prized by chartered banks during the formative period of banking. Compare the present period, in which commercial banks do not have this privilege.
5. Compare the bank note issue systems before the Civil War to the system existing after the Civil War and at the present time.
6. Income from government paper money issues represents "small change" to modern governments. Explain.
7. Identify the three qualities of a good note issue system.
8. Describe extinct types of currency in the United States. Obsolete types of currency.
9. "This is in no sense a provision for an elastic currency . . . . (Federal Reserve Bill). It provides an expansive currency, but not an elastic one. It provides a currency which may be increased, always increased, but not a currency for which the bill contains any provision compelling reduction . . . . " (Root, Elihu, *Congressional Record*, December 13, 1913). Quoted by Jerome, *Government and Money*, p. 207. Discuss.
10. Outline the procedure for issuance and retirement of Federal Reserve notes. Use Chart V.
11. Distinguish between the "banking" and "currency" principles of note issue. Which one has dominated the history of note issue for the last 100 years?

12. Account for the changes in volume of the different types of money as shown by Table V.
13. For whom is most of the gold in the United States held in trust? How is it being used to support the currency and credit structure? Explain.
14. Comment on the following suggestions: "The United States should use its present idle gold 'to build new houses for the under-privileged'"; or "to finance the establishment of the gold standard in foreign countries." How much gold is available for these purposes? If more is desired how would the government secure it?
15. Keynes writes (*Monetary Reform*, p. 200) that the tendency today "is to watch and to control the creation of credit and to let the creation of currency follow suit, rather than, as formerly, to watch and control the creation of currency and to let the creation of credit follow suit." Do you agree? Do the silverites agree? Why?
16. All types of money in the United States are redeemable in money "which may be legally held." Does this mean that the United States is on a gold standard? Silver standard? What does it mean?
17. During the war large denomination currency accounted for much of the increase in the total volume of currency? Why? For statistics, see current issues of the *Federal Reserve Bulletin.*
18. How has the Federal Reserve System given a measure of elasticity to all types of currency in the United States?
19. If the United States were to readopt the full gold standard, what changes would be made in the treatment of gold and gold certificates?
20. If the United States were to adopt a paper standard, what would be the proper place for the silver certificate? Are they justified at the present time? Explain their existence in the present-day currency system.

REFERENCES

Breckenridge, S. P. *Legal Tender.* Chicago: University of Chicago Press, 1903.

Comptroller of Currency. *Annual Reports.* Washington, D.C.: U.S. Government Printing Office.

Director of the Mint. *Annual Report.* Washington, D.C.: U.S. Government Printing Office.

Edie, L. D. *Dollars*, chaps. xi and xii. New Haven: Yale University Press, 1934.

Federal Reserve Board—Board of Governors of the Federal Reserve System. *Annual Reports.* Washington, D.C.: U.S. Government Printing Office.

Fisher, Irving. *Stabilizing the Dollar.* New York: Macmillan Co., 1920.

Gayer, A. D. *Monetary Policy and Economic Stabilization,* chaps. vii and viii. New York: Macmillan Co., 1935.

Graham, F. D. *Exchange, Prices and Production in Hyper-Inflation. Germany 1920-1923,* Parts I and II. Princeton: Princeton University Press, 1930.

Groseclose, E. *Near Eastern Postwar Monetary Standards.* New York: Monetary Standards Inquiry, 1943.

Hepburn, A. B. *A History of Currency in the United States,* chaps. vii-xiii. New ed. New York: Macmillan Co., 1924.

Jerome, E. C. *Governments and Money,* chaps. iii and v. Boston: Little, Brown & Co., 1935.

Jevons. W. S. *Money and the Mechanism of Exchange.* New York: D. Appleton Co., 1921.

Kemmerer, E. W. *Money,* chaps x-xiii. New York: Macmillan Co., 1935.

Keynes, J. M. *A Treatise on Money,* Vol. I, chaps. i and ii. London: Macmillan Co., Ltd., 1930.

Leavens, D. H. *Far Eastern Postwar Monetary Standards.* New York: Monetary Standards Inquiry, 1943.

Lester, R. A. *Monetary Experiments.* Princeton: Princeton University Press, 1939. See chapters dealing with Revolutionary Continentals and Civil War greenbacks.

Mitchell, W. C. *A History of the Greenbacks.* Chicago: University of Chicago Press, 1903.

Money and Banking, 1942-1944. League of Nations, Economics and Finance (Geneva, League of Nations). New York: International Documents Service, Columbia University Press, 1945.

Phillips, C. A. *Readings in Money and Banking,* chaps. iv and v. New York: Macmillan Co., 1921.

Secretary of the Treasury. *Annual Reports.* Washington, D.C.: U.S. Government Printing Office.

Spahr, W. E. *Alternatives in Postwar International Monetary Standards.* New York: Monetary Standards Inquiry, 1944.

Taylor, F. M. *Chapters on Money,* chap. viii. Ann Arbor Press, 1906.

Walker, F. A. *Money,* Parts II and III. New York: Henry Holt & Co., 1878.

White, A. D. *Paper Money Inflation in France.* New York: The Society for Political Education, 1882.

White, Horace. *Money and Banking.* Book II, chaps. i and v. 5th ed. Boston: Ginn & Co., 1914.

Young, J. P. *European Currency and Finance,* Part I. Commission of Gold and Silver Inquiry, United States Senate, Washington, D.C.: U.S. Government Printing Office, 1924.

CHAPTER X

DEPOSIT CURRENCY

Introduction

In 1945 the volume of the circulating media (total demand deposits adjusted and currency outside banks) was over $100,000,000,000, of which one-fourth was in the form of hand-to-hand currency. Because of this overwhelming importance of deposit currency, it is apparent that consideration must be given to the management of deposit currency if the objectives of monetary control are to be achieved. This does not mean that the volume of gold currency and cash held by banks, but not included in the above statistics, is of secondary importance. They are used for reserves, and changes in their volume tend to affect the volume of deposit currency. Hence, instead of decreasing the importance of money, the development of deposit currency has in one way greatly increased its importance.

Meaning and Development of Deposit Currency

About 95 per cent of the wholesale and 65 per cent of the retail transactions in the United States are paid for with personal checks and other credit instruments. A check is an order written by the drawer, ordering the drawee (bank) to pay a definite sum of money to himself or to some designated person (payee). The bank is expected to honor it if it is covered by a deposit and is properly drawn and presented. Checks are transferable, but they rarely change ownership more than once or twice. Usually they arc deposited, and then the payee draws his own checks in payment of his obligations; or they may be converted into money. Thus the banks serve as collectors and paymasters for their depositors; between 50 and 75 per cent of their operating expenses are traced to cost of services given to depositors.

Blank checks are printed by banks and given to their customers. They are usually fastened into convenient book form, but valid checks may be written or typed on any form of paper. The blank checks have printed on them the name of the city and state, year, name of the bank, clearinghouse number, convenient spacing for the date, number of the check, amount, name of the payee, and the signature. The check is the credit instrument used in transferring title to deposits; but the thing transferred is bank credit, a promise to pay of a bank. Hence the name "deposit currency" is used as the title of this chapter.

The existence of deposits is as old as banking, but the wide practice of transferring title to these deposits by orders written by individuals is a fairly recent development. It resulted logically from the practice of banks using bank drafts to transfer funds between domestic centers and between foreign countries.

Fairly early in the history of exchange, funds were transferred by written orders drawn by one individual on an agent near the center where payment was to be made. These bills of exchange were used by private bankers, merchants, and agents of the Catholic Church.[1] The use of bills of exchange made it possible to transfer funds within and between communities without the dangers of confiscation by robber barons and others. The popularity of the bills of exchange was due partly to the practice of discounting them, a means used to circumvent the church usury laws, which prevented the taking of all interest for loans. But the legitimate use of bills of exchange increased with the growth of trade in medieval and early modern times. About 1722 a private banking firm in London, Messrs. Child & Co., "began to supply their customers with printed cheque forms which they might complete as drafts for any amount and payable to any of their creditors."[2] These personal checks became very popular and marked the beginning of the present modern deposit currency system.

In what is now the United States, instruments similar to checks were used in connection with some of the embryo banks that were established during the colonial period. Our chartered commercial banking system originated during the post-Revolutionary War period, and with it came deposit currency. At first, checks were used only in making large business payments in cities. They were used by deposit customers of the First and Second United States banks and by the deposit customers of the early state banks. By 1850 their importance as a means of payment about equaled that of bank notes.

---

[1] Jevons, W. S., *Money and the Mechanism of Exchange*, pp. 293-97.

[2] Evitt, H. E., *Practical Banking*, p. 5.

During the decade following the Civil War, the development of deposit currency was accelerated by restricting the privilege of note issues to banks that had charters granted by the federal government (so-called "national banks"). The amount of paper money that each national bank could issue was limited to its capitalization, and state chartered banks were denied this privilege altogether. Thereafter, in order to carry on a profitable banking business, it was necessary for banks to develop deposit banking as distinguished from note issue banking.

By 1875 the volume of payments completed with the use of checks and similar instruments was approaching the present dominant percentage. The development of the local clearinghouse system facilitated this movement, and, since 1915, the Federal Reserve par collection system has made the check a national instrument of exchange. In 1929 the use of deposit currency reached its peak, when debits to individual deposit accounts in principal cities were $982,500,000,000. In 1944 the number of checks handled by the Federal Reserve banks alone was 1,700,000,000, an increase of more than 50 per cent over the last pre-war year,[3] and more were cleared or collected on the banks' own books, through local clearinghouses and through non-Federal Reserve channels. Current reports of debits against individual accounts, which are chiefly personal checks, are made by the Board of Governors of the Federal Reserve System in its monthly *Federal Reserve Bulletin.*

Differences between Deposit Currency and Bank Notes

Deposit currency differs from bank notes in the following ways: (1) degree of government protection, (2) personal relationship between the bank and its creditors, (3) acceptability as a means of payment, (4) physical form, and (5) the amount of time it remains outstanding before it is redeemed or cancelled.

When governments began to regulate banks, it was but natural that the note issue function should have been the first to receive attention. Today most countries have given the legal tender quality to bank note issues, which is not true of deposit currency, and checks may therefore be refused in trade.

---

[3] *Federal Reserve Bulletin,* August, 1945, p. 730.

Many years ago Professor C. F. Dunbar gave another reason for the special protection of noteholders, that is, the failure on the part of legislators generally "to perceive the similarity of the two kinds of liability, and the claim of equal consideration which can be made, with some show of reason, on behalf of depositors."[4] This criticism of legislators is still true. Perhaps there is no better demonstration of this fact than the rejection of an amendment to the Banking Bill of 1935, which would have permitted the issuance of Federal Reserve notes on a more liberal basis, and the passage of other provisions of the same bill, permitting greater expansion of deposit currency.[5]

Many noteholders are unaware of the fact that they are creditors of banks, but this is not true of depositors. Noteholders seldom pay attention to the type of money they have, and the name of the bank whose promise to pay they hold is seldom noticed. The holder of notes may be unfamiliar with the bank and even the town in which it is located, and this was particularly true when thousands of national banks had the circulation privilege. The relationship between banks and their noteholders is impersonal; the relationship between banks and depositors is very personal. Depositors are supplied with bank statements, are regularly in contact with their banks, and are in a position to keep themselves informed about their banks' conditions. The close relationship between banks and their depositors is evidenced by the fact that every depositor regards the institution in which he keeps his account as "my bank."

Checks are personal credit instruments, and their acceptability is closely related to the credit rating of the individual. They are not accepted among strangers but are confined to business circles where there is some knowledge of the drawers and endorsers. On the other hand, the acceptability of bank notes is at least national in extent. Now bank notes are usually issued by central banks which are either owned by governments or carefully supervised and regulated by them. To an increasing extent, bank notes are being issued under conditions that link their credit standing to that of their national

[4] Dunbar, C. F., *The Theory and History of Banking*, p. 63.

[5] J. H. Williams sums up this situation as follows: "It is rather absurd to have passed the other amendment admitting government securities and all other sound bank assets to eligibility for member bank borrowing of reserves, where they can serve as a basis for manifold expansion of deposits, and to have rejected the amendment broadening the collateral for [Federal Reserve] notes" ("Banking Act of 1935," *American Economic Review*, Supplement, Vol. XXVI, No. 1 [March, 1936], p. 97).

government. Unlike bank checks, the acceptability of bank notes is divorced from the credit standing of the one who presents it and, to some extent, even from the credit standing of the issuing bank.

Deposits and bank notes are both credit agreements or contracts, but their physical forms are different. Bank notes are engraved on durable pieces of paper, while bank deposits are bookkeeping accounts which may be transferred by the order of the owner to others by means of bank checks. Obviously, notes are expected to remain in circulation for a long period, while checks are not expected to be exchange more than once or twice before they are returned to the banks for cancellation. They are not for use as pocket money or continuing currency. However, this does not mean that after a deposit is drawn upon it is destroyed when the check is collected. The check is an instrument for transferring title to a new owner either in the same or in a different bank.

In the United States checks are tested as soon as they are presented for payment, but banks are seldom requested to convert their notes into standard money or other forms which may be lawfully held. The "homing" power of bank notes is small compared to that of checks. This is true for a number of reasons, among them the ever-present question as to the credit standing of the drawer and sometimes that of the bank. In addition, a check is customarily drawn for the exact amount of payment involved, which is usually some odd figure rather than the convenient denominations of bank notes; this makes it inconvenient for further use. A check is usually made out to a specific person, who must endorse it before it can be legally transferred. In order to limit his contingent liability to as short a period as is possible, the holder of a check usually presents it for payment immediately after endorsement.

Legal practice now demands that checks be presented for payment within a reasonable period. This varies according to a number of factors, but the courts realize that a successful deposit currency system rests upon prompt presentation and payment of checks. The longer a check remains in circulation, the greater becomes the danger of fraud and forgery. Furthermore, a check may be good at the time it is written, but it may be invalidated by the removal of the deposit, the failure of the bank, or the refusal of the bank to honor it.[6] Difficulties may be avoided by prompt presentation, di-

[6] Most banks will not honor checks that are more than thirty days old.

rectly or indirectly, to the drawer's bank for payment. If the check is not presented within a reasonable period, the drawer is discharged from the liability of loss caused by the delay.

Advantages of Deposit Currency

Economy of Reserves.—The use of deposit currency has many social as well as other advantages, which account for its popularity as a means of payment in the United States. From the viewpoint of the community, it is the most economical way in which to use its surplus funds. It permits use of pooled resources and the multiplication of the total means of payment. If one assumes that there are no banking facilities, the aggregate amount of money held as cash balances would be greater than if these cash balances were held by banks. Banks mobilize idle cash balances which would otherwise be kept in the pocketbooks of the owners. Then, by making them available to merchants and others, the banks increase the efficiency or velocity of money.

The deposit banking system permits the substitution of claims to money (checks) for money as media of exchange and permits the original supply of money to perform many times the amount of work which could have been done by the supply of hand-to-hand currency. As noted earlier, checks are usually deposited with banks, and the amount of cash actually paid out is small. In the case of individual banks, claims to money presented by other banks will be matched by claims against them at clearinghouses and the Federal Reserve banks. Balances are usually settled through the facilities of the Federal Reserve System without the use of cash. Although some cash will be withdrawn by customers of individual banks, this outward flow will usually be offset by new deposits of money. So the actual cash which the bank finds it necessary to keep for cashing checks is exceedingly small compared to the amount of money represented by the checks which have been used as a means of payment during a year.[7]

Accounting Advantage.—When a check is presented, the bank

[7] In the United States, there may be greater expansion of deposit currency based on gold than expansion of paper money because of the use of Federal Reserve bank deposit credit as reserves for member bank credit. Thus a dollar in gold certificates supports four dollars in member banks' reserve accounts, and these four dollars support twenty dollars in deposit currency. In the case of the use of Federal Reserve notes, the maximum expansion is from one to four.

pays the sum designated to the holder. The check is cancelled and later returned to the drawer, and it serves as a receipt. This permanent evidence of payment is valuable in case a dispute should arise later. If cash is used and the payee should die, the payer has no protection unless he has a written receipt or had made the payment in the presence of witnesses, because the oral testimony of the payer is not sufficient in most legal jurisdictions. When checks are used they may be submitted as evidence, and an excellent practice is to write upon the face of the check the purpose for which it was drawn. Naturally, this adds to its value as evidence of payment.

In business considerable collecting is done by agencies, and when checks are used there is more assurance that the funds will reach creditors. If the check is drawn to the order of the creditor, there is no need to investigate the authority of the collector, for there is direct evidence of payment, and funds are easy to trace. Use of machines to photograph checks and bank statements have added to the value of checks as a record of payment of obligations. Cancelled checks are an aid to businessmen and individuals in keeping accounting records of expenditures and in making out income tax statements.

Checks Are Safe.—When payments are made by mail, checks are safer than currency, for there is no danger of loss by theft. If currency is stolen, it is difficult to recover, because it passes into the hands of innocent persons. Most checks cannot be negotiated unless they are endorsed. A thief may forge the signature of the payee, but if a bank cashes the check it must take the responsibility for the loss. Checks that are burned, destroyed, or lost may be replaced with little difficulty. Currency, under the same conditions, is usually not recovered. The practice of carrying large sums of currency or of keeping money in one's house encourages robbery. The habit of using deposit currency is an excellent protection against unauthorized appropriations of funds.

Checks have the advantage of giving temporary protection to drawers if errors have been made. Immediately after a transaction, the purchaser may discover that there has been a mistake in quantity or quality. If payment has been made with currency, he may have difficulty in getting back his money. If a check has been used in payment, he may call his bank and request it not to honor the check when it is presented. Similar precautions should be taken if a check is lost or stolen. In all cases where stop payment is to be made, immediate action is necessary.

Checks Are Convenient.—Checks may be for odd amounts, an advantage which decreases the demand for small change. When payments are made by mail, there is no difficulty in sending a check for $4.48. If currency is used, it is necessary to send four one-dollar bills and the remainder in coins. The advantage of drawing a check for the entire amount is apparent. Checks may also be drawn for large amounts, and this advantage over paper money is obvious. Checks may be written at a moment's notice, thereby making prompt payments possible during emergencies or upon unexpected occasions. Thus deposit currency is very adaptable to individual circumstances.

There Are Limitations on the Use of Deposit Currency

There are several reasons why checks will not entirely replace paper money and small coins: (1) they are not generally acceptable; (2) they are impractical in personal payments of small sums; (3) checking accounts are expensive; and (4) checks may be altered or forged.

The acceptability of a check depends on knowledge of the credit standing of the drawer, the bank on which it is drawn, the endorser, and the person presenting the check for payment. Checks are obviously impractical for payment of such items as postage stamps, streetcar tickets, and small retail purchases, except where charge accounts are used. The cost of handling, posting, and collecting a check for $1.00 is as great as it is for $100, and since service charges have been adopted these costs have been passed along to bank customers. Checks are often carelessly drawn and easily altered, and therefore great care should be exercised in writing them. Credit money may be counterfeited, but this danger is small compared to the danger of forging checks.

A Good Deposit Currency System Has Three Qualities

The three qualities of a good deposit currency are the same as those found in a good note issue system: (1) parity, (2) security, and (3) elasticity.

Parity.—All checks should be paid at par at all times by the banks on which they are drawn. This means that when a check for $100 is presented by mail to a bank on which it is drawn, the bank should not deduct 25 cents and mail the payee a draft for $99.75. This is discussed in detail in the next chapter.

Security.—In a sound deposit currency system, the security behind the deposits must be adequate, because depositors will not knowingly keep their funds in a bank which is unsound. In a sound banking system the security behind deposits is adequate, consisting of cash in vault, reserve deposits in other banks, commercial paper, government bonds, and other assets of the banks. The record of bank failures in the United States from 1920 to 1934 was so disheartening that special steps were taken by the federal government to protect and reassure depositors.

In March, 1933, after the banking holiday, weak banks were kept closed or allowed to operate only under restrictions. Later they were liquidated or refinanced, primarily with government funds. In June provisions were made for insurance of deposits by the Federal Deposit Insurance Corporation, and the plan now in force gives 100 per cent coverage to depositors for all amounts up to $5,000. About 98 per cent of the commercial banks in the country participate in the plan. The percentage of deposits insured is less because of the limitation on the amount of coverage to $5,000, irrespective of the size of the account. The main protection of depositors, however, will always be the assets in the portfolios of banks, and their value depends primarily upon the foresight and judgment of bankers. Deposit insurance cannot replace sound banking practices.

Elasticity.—In the ideal system the volume of deposit currency in use increases with each increase in demand and decreases when the demand has passed. One of the chief criticisms of deposit currency is that it overexpands during periods of rising prices and business booms and overcontracts during periods of falling prices and business depressions. When prices are falling bankers refuse to make loans and carefully husband their resources. With each fall in prices they tighten their loan and investment policies, the result being to drive prices down through forced sales of commodities and securities. Each fall in security or commodity prices impairs loan margins, resulting in more calls for repayments of loans and further liquidation of loans. Each wave of liquidation forces prices down and sets off a second wave of liquidation. Thus the vicious spiral of deflation continues until broken by the suspension of the gold standard, a favorable crop, or some other fortuitous event.

An excellent illustration of the relationship between falling prices and a decrease in the volume of deposit currency is provided by the experiences of the United States during the period 1930-33. The volume of demand deposits decreased by about $8,000,000,000, or one-third of the amount in existence in 1930. Naturally this decrease in the volume of bank credit was preceded, accompanied, or followed by a record fall in prices of securities, real estate, and commodities.

During periods of rising prices and business booms bankers lend or invest freely. The volume of deposits in use increases. Further credit expansion takes place with each increase in prices or extension of business. Thus expansion of credit continues to feed the inflammatory movement of prices and business. This vicious upward cycle continues, and sooner or later a collapse takes place, to be followed by a depression. Thus commercial bankers are "the stokers of the business cycle," supplying excessive fuel during boom periods and insufficient quantities during depression periods. The fault lies with the banking system, and not with individual bankers. The heart of the problem is found in the ability of the commercial banking system as a whole to create deposits by making new investments and new loans. This will be made clearer by a discussion of origin of deposits.

Deposits Are the Result of Three Types of Transactions

These transactions are (1) exchanging metallic and paper money for the right to draw upon the bank; (2) leaving of checks, notes, drafts, and coupons to be collected by the bank, with the understanding that the proceeds are to be credited to the account of the customer; and (3) borrowing at banks, the proceeds of the loans being credited to the deposit account of the borrower. Considered from the viewpoint of the individual bank, the second type is the most important, for it has been estimated that in some sections 98 per cent of bank deposits are made in the form of checks.[8] But considered from the viewpoint of the banking system as a whole, the third type is the most important.

Exchanging Metallic and Paper Money for Deposit Claims.—

[8] Kniffen, W. K., *The Practical Work of a Bank*, p. 16.

From the viewpoint of the banking system, the imports of gold and the printing and coining of new money may be of great significance. In 1940 the volume of bank deposits, including interbank deposits at all banks in the United States, was at a new record high, having been about $6,000,000,000 above the peak of 1929. While the increase was general throughout the banking system, the greatest increase was in banks in New York City and in other financial centers.

This increase in deposits was due in part to the increase of deposits created by shipments of gold and silver to the United States. When gold was sent to the United States by foreign central banks, foreign commercial banks, and other domestic concerns, the gold had to be surrendered by the owners to the United States government. A Treasury check drawn on a Federal Reserve bank was given in payment. Assume that the owner of the gold was a dealer in New York and that he deposited the Treasury draft with his bank. The bank presented it to its Federal Reserve bank for payment, which gave the member bank a deposit reserve credit on its books. The liability of the Federal Reserve bank was offset by debiting the government Treasury account. The government replenished its deposits by printing gold certificates and depositing them in the Federal Reserve banks. Thus gold imports increased the volume of deposits in the banking system, member banks' reserve with the Federal Reserve banks, gold certificates held by the Federal Reserve banks, and the volume of gold in the government vaults.

The effects would have been similar if silver had been purchased by the Treasury; Treasury checks would have been given in payment, and silver certificates would have been printed and deposited with the Federal Reserve banks to replenish the government's checking account.

Leaving Claims to Money to Be Collected.—Considered from the viewpoint of an individual bank, the most important sources of new deposits are checks, matured notes, and other claims to money which are turned in by depositors at their banks to be collected and then credited to their deposit accounts. As noted in the foregoing, even funds resulting from gold imports are evidenced by government checks drawn on Federal Reserve banks. These deposits, whether from currency receipts or credit instruments, are called "primary deposits" because they give the depository bank new funds with which to operate. This is true even though the check may be drawn upon a deposit created by the lending operations of a second bank.

Lending of Bank Credit.—When a borrower sells securities, discounts promissory notes or other paper, or borrows on his own promise to pay, he usually receives deposit credit in the bank's books. The bank in making a loan has a surplus of reserve credit, due, let us assume, to a deposit of a Treasury check given in payment for gold. Since borrowers usually withdraw all or most of these credits soon after receiving them, by writing checks in favor of others, the temporary increase in the bank's total deposits, owing to its so-called "derivative deposits" (derived from lending and investing), is of small importance. If the checks are followed, it immediately becomes apparent that, when they are left with other banks, they become primary deposits in so far as the receiving banks are concerned. If these banks lend their new funds, the process is repeated, until the total expansion is many times the original cash deposit. Just how far the banking system may expand bank deposits depends on a number of factors, including (1) the effective demands of borrowers for funds, that is, credit extensions of the type which banks would be justified in granting, and (2) the amount of reserves which banks are required to keep against deposits.

Why Government Borrowing from Commercial Banks Is Inflationary

The best illustration of the interrelationship between the increase in loans and the increase in deposits is provided by the sale of government securities to banks during World War II. From the end of 1941 to June 30, 1945 (six weeks prior to V-J Day), total investments in government obligations of all commercial banks increased from over $21,000,000,000 to over $84,000,000,000, while total deposits increased from over $71,000,000,000 to over $136,000,000,000; that is, commercial banks' investments in government obligations increased by over $62,000,000,000, while total bank deposits increased by over $65,000,000,000.[9]

[9] The banking system lost gold, but this deflationary development was offset by increases in volume of Federal Reserve bank credit, temporarily exempting banks from the necessity of keeping reserves against Treasury balances arising solely as a result of subscriptions for government securities (*Public Law 37*, 78th Cong.); and reduction in reserve requirements of member banks located in central reserve cities (New York and Chicago).

Although the banks' deposit figures were already inflated in 1941 because of budgetary deficit financing, they increased almost 100 per cent because of war financing. In order to obtain funds, the government gave the banks interest-bearing promises to pay, and the banks gave the government deposit credit subject to check. Thus the assets of the banks were increased, and the banks' liabilities in the form of government deposits were similarly increased.

The government used the newly created deposits for war and other governmental expenditures. The checks thus drawn were spent by the recipients, gradually coming back through business channels to the banks on which they were drawn. In this way title to the newly created deposits in banks was transferred from the government to the recipients of the Treasury checks. After eight years of peacetime and four years of war financing of the governmental deficit by borrowing from banks, the volume of bank credit was at the highest level in the history of the United States.

However, it must not be assumed that all governmental borrowing leads to an increase in bank credit in the form of deposit-account promises to pay. If individuals, insurance companies, savings banks, and others purchase government bonds with spendable funds already existing in the form of currency or checking accounts, no new means of payment are created. For example, if individual bank accounts are used, the government receives checks which are charged against individual accounts and credited to the government account without any effect upon total deposits.

When the Treasury disburses the funds derived from its sales of securities, those receiving the checks deposit them with their own banks. The banks in turn deposit them with their Reserve banks, and the total deposits and total reserves are restored to their former levels. But, if individuals borrowed from banks to buy government bonds, as happened during World War I, the effects would be the same as if the government borrowed directly from the banks.[10] The advantage of this method of financing, over the method used in World War II, is that bankers were in a position to bring pressure on individuals to reduce their debts, as postwar financial and economic conditions

[10] During World War II bank loans were made to individuals and others for purchase of government bonds, but only for a short time and in anticipation of income. The amount involved was small compared to the total funds obtained by direct sale of government obligations to banks.

seemed to justify. With the government as the chief debtor of banks, this freedom of action is lacking.

Certain economists and statesmen are in favor of reducing the volume of deposit currency by increasing taxes, selling government bonds to noncommercial bank buyers, and using the funds to retire part of the government debt held by commercial banks. The procedure may be illustrated by assuming that an individual pays an income tax of $1,000 by writing a check on his bank; the check is used by the government to retire a $1,000 bond held by the bank. When all the bookkeeping transactions are completed, the taxpayer will have lost a checking account of $1,000, and the banking system will have been relieved of this deposit liability and will have lost an asset in the form of a government bond. If an individual purchased a government bond from a bank with savings, the effect on the volume of deposit currency would be the same, but the government's obligation would be to the individual and not to the bank. Although these descriptions of the procedures have been simplified, they illustrate how the volume of deposit currency may be reduced by the adoption of a policy of curtailing the volume of government securities held by commercial banks. Of course, such contraction of bank credit could be offset by banks if they invested their funds in other types of securities or lent them to businessmen and others. This policy would depend upon a business demand for funds, which in turn would depend upon business conditions.

The traditional method of monetary control is to manipulate the supply of reserve money in order to bring about the desired changes in the volume of the means of payment. Experience suggests that a decrease in the supply of reserves usually results in a decrease in the supply of the circulating media; but an increase in the supply of reserves is less of a factor in explaining an increase in the supply of circulating media. It is for this reason that financial and monetary policies which would have a direct effect on the supply of deposit currency have been recommended in recent years. One of these is that fiscal policy should be used as a monetary device, and another is the "100 per cent reserve plan." Both are discussed in later chapters.

QUESTIONS AND PROBLEMS

1. Explain what is meant by "deposit currency." How important is it in the United States? Will it displace hand-to-hand money entirely? Why?

2. Enumerate and explain the differences between deposit currency and bank notes. Make a list of the characteristics which the two have in common. Explain.
3. Deposits are due to three types of transactions. Discuss.
4. If you went to a commercial bank in your community and were shown the bank's deposits, what would you see? Explain.
5. "Owners of deposits do not spend them as freely as currency" (Carothers, Neil, "No More Inflation," *This Week*. March 31, 1935, p. 9). What is the significance of his statement when one considers deposit currency inflation versus money inflation?
6. "A single transaction accomplished with deposit currency effectively divorces it from all connection with its origin. . . . " (Robinson, G. B., *Monetary Mischief*, p. 9). Is this statement significant? Why?
7. "Who does originate [create] our money? Private corporations, commonly called banks, now originate practically *all* our money" (Coughlin, Rev. Charles E., *Money: Questions and Answers*, p. 30). Is this true? Explain.
8. "The sale of bonds for war financing has in the first instance given rise to an increase in Government deposits. Then, as expenditures have been made, the bulk of these deposits has shifted to the accounts of individuals and business enterprises" (source: *Annual Report of the Federal Deposit Insurance Corporation for the Year Ended December 31, 1944*, p. 42). Explain.
9. In fact "not only have we lately resorted to printing-press money, but we have had a vast volume of it in use ever since the offering of the First Liberty Loan in 1917" (Robinson, *op. cit.*, p. 129). Does this question apply to the period from 1940 to 1945? What are the differences and of what significance are they?
10. Compare the ways in which the greatest amount of new bank credit was created in the following periods: (*a*) 1917-20; (*b*) 1922-29; (*c*) 1933-40; and (*d*) 1941-45.
11. "To say the inflation threatens is alarming. But to say that bank deposits are rapidly increasing is not alarming at all. Most people fear the first statement and applaud the second, yet these words mean exactly the same thing" (Peterson, Elmore, *Banking*, Sec. 2 [October, 1936], p. 1). What does Dean Peterson mean?
12. "We advocate a sound currency to be preserved at all hazard. The first requisite to a sound and stable currency is a balanced budget" (Republican National Platform, 1936). Explain.
13. Professor Viner writes: "Of all the possible sources of credit deflation during the depression, the most formidable, when it occurs, is a mass movement of depositors to convert their bank deposits into legal tender

money or into gold" (*American Economic Review, Supplement,* Vol. XXVI, No. 1 [March, 1936], p. 110). Explain.

14. A government's debt-retiring policy may be used to help prevent inflation. Explain the monetary phases of this statement.
15. What is meant by changes in velocity or turnover of bank deposits? Why is it significant when applied to present conditions in the United States?
16. Compare the qualities of a good note issue system to those of a good deposit currency system. Does the United States have both at the present time?
17. May the "banking principle of note issue" and the "currency principle of note issue" be applied to deposit banking? Explain. Use Chapter IX of this text as a reference.
18. "While monetary expansion in the war period has been at least equal to and probably in excess of all of these needs [cash balances for trade, taxes, future capital expenditures], this has been the inevitable result of providing all the financing needed for effective prosecution of the war at a low and stable level of interest rates" (*source and reference:* "Wartime Monetary Expansion and Postwar Needs," *Federal Reserve Bulletin,* November, 1945, p. 1092). Discuss.
19. Do commercial banks create money or are they simply intermediaries between creditors and debtors?
20. Are checks being used in greater volume as a means of payment now than a year ago? Has the velocity or turnover increased or decreased? Use table "Bank Debits and Deposit Turnover" in the current issue of the *Federal Reserve Bulletin* to answer these questions.

REFERENCES

Agger, E. E. *Organized Banking,* chaps. ii, iv, and v. New York: Henry Holt & Co., 1918.

Goodbar, J. E. *Managing the Peoples Money,* chaps. i and ii. New Haven: Yale University Press, 1935.

Halm, G. N. *Monetary Theory,* chap. iv. Philadelphia: Blakiston Co., 1942.

Hansen, A. H. *Full Recovery or Stagnation?* chap. ix. New York: W. W. Norton & Co., Inc., 1938.

Harr, Luther, and Harris, W. C. *Banking Theory and Practice,* chaps. viii, ix, and x. 2d ed. New York: McGraw-Hill Book Co., Inc., 1936.

Harris, S. E. "A One per Cent War?" *American Economic Review,* Vol. XXXV (September, 1945), pp. 667-71.

Keynes, J. M. *A Treatise on Money*, Vol. I, chap. ii. New York: Harcourt, Brace & Co., 1930.

Phillips, C. A. *Bank Credit*, chap. iii. New York: Macmillan Co., 1920.

Phillips, C. A., McManus, T. F., and Nelson, R. W. *Banking and the Business Cycle*, chaps. v and viii. New York: Macmillan Co., 1937.

Warburg, J. P. *The Money Muddle*, chaps. iv-vii. New York: Alfred A. Knopf, Inc., 1934.

"Wartime Monetary Expansion and Postwar Needs," *Federal Reserve Bulletin*, pp. 1091-99. Washington, D.C.: Board of Governors of the Federal Reserve System, November, 1945.

Whittlesey, C. R. *Bank Liquidity and the War.* New York: National Bureau of Economic Research, 1945.

Whittlesey, C. R. *Banking and the New Deal.* Public Policy Pamphlet No. 16. Chicago: University of Chicago Press, 1935.

CHAPTER XI

CLEARING AND COLLECTION OF CHECKS

Domestic Exchange

In the preceding chapter the national use of deposit currency was discussed. Transfer of the right to deposits in payment for things is customarily made by personal checks and bank drafts, which are identical, except that in the latter case the drawer is a bank. The use of deposit currency as the chief means of payment throughout the United States was made possible by the clearing and collection work of commercial banks and the Federal Reserve System.

Prior to the organization of the Federal Reserve System, it was as common a practice for banks to buy and sell rights to deposits in banks in different cities in the United States (domestic exchange) as it was to buy and sell rights to deposits between foreign countries and the United States (foreign exchange). A bank could build up its balance in a New York bank by shipping currency, but, rather than go to this expense, it was more economical to find a bank having a claim on a New York City bank that it was willing to sell. The bank might even have paid a premium for the claim, provided this premium was less than the total cost of expressing currency, loss of interest while in transit, insurance, packing, and other charges.

It was desirable for out-of-town banks to have funds in New York, in order to earn interest in the call market, to invest in the capital market, and to help customers in financing commercial and other obligations coming due in that center. Because customers' demands tended to be seasonal, the price for New York exchange was at a premium during certain times of the year and at par or at a discount during the remainder of the time. To a lesser degree, all large centers were subject to similar demands for exchange from the banks and businessmen in the regions which they served.

To cover the cost of keeping balances in larger centers, it was customary for banks to make exchange charges. These took the form of either selling their drafts at a premium or remitting for checks presented by mail at a discount. Thus a merchant in Troy, New York, having a $100.00 trade bill payable in New York City could obtain a draft from his bank by paying the bank $100.10, the 10 cents being an exchange charge. If he preferred to pay with his personal check in order to avoid the 10 cent charge or because it was more convenient to do so, he drew a check for but $100.00. When the check was presented by the creditor in New York City through banking channels to the Troy bank, the latter drew a draft for $99.90 and sent it to the bank that presented the check for payment. The merchant's deposit account was debited for $100.00, and the 10 cents was retained by the Troy bank as an exchange charge. This exchange charge was either absorbed by the New York City bank or passed along to its depositor. In either case the Troy bank received 10 cents on the transaction, but in one case the burden fell on its depositor and in the other on the New York bank or its depositor.

As the volume of out-of-town checks increased, the burden of exchange charges increased, and, as a result, arrangements were developed whereby they could be avoided in whole or in part. Since banks are required by common law to pay checks drawn on the accounts of their depositors at par, when presented to them over the counter, agreements were made among banks (called correspondents) to collect checks for one another on banks in their communities. If there had been but a few banks, this system would have worked smoothly; but, since there were thousands of banks in the United States, much time was lost in trying to route each check so that it would go to a correspondent who had a correspondent in the community of the bank on which it was drawn. Although exchange charges, correspondent banking, and indirect routing of checks have not been eliminated, they have been greatly reduced because of the development of the Federal Reserve clearing and collection system. This system has made it possible for many of the principles and practices developed by local clearinghouses to be used on a national scale.

Clearinghouses Clear Local Checks

Since a check is an order upon the drawer's bank to pay a certain sum of money to the payee, it must be presented to the bank on which it is drawn. Without the aid of banks, a department store would be forced to collect these funds by sending messengers, armed guards, and perhaps armored cars to all the banks on which checks were written. Banks perform this valuable service for their customers. The depositor lists his checks on a deposit slip and leaves it and the checks with his bank.[1]

A bank receives three classes of checks, namely, those drawn upon itself, those drawn upon out-of-town banks, and those drawn upon local banks. A bank sends the checks drawn upon itself to its own bookkeeping department, where they are credited to and charged against the accounts of its depositors. The checks drawn upon out-of-town banks are sent to the transit division of the bank, where they are sorted and mailed to correspondent banks or to the Federal Reserve bank. These collection procedures involving out-of-town banks are described in another part of this chapter. The checks drawn on local banks are sent to the clearinghouse division of the bank, where they are arranged and prepared for the local clearinghouse.

All local checks are endorsed with a clearinghouse stamp. They are sorted and placed in pigeonholes according to the names and numbers of the clearinghouse members. The value of the checks drawn upon each of the several banks is computed, and all these totals are then added in order to secure the sum due from the clearinghouse. The clearinghouse meeting hour is fixed by mutual agreement, usually at 10 o'clock in the morning or later, in order to permit deposit items appearing in the morning mail to be included in the daily clearings. The clearinghouse settlement sheet is completed just before the clerk goes to the clearinghouse. The characteristics of the clearing process are: (1) it is simple, (2) little currency is involved, and (3) cost of operation is small.

Clearing Process Is Simple.—The mechanical work of clearing checks is in charge of the clearinghouse manager. As soon as the clerks arrive, they give the manager a statement of the amount of items listed as "On Clearinghouse." The amount includes all items which each bank has decided shall be cleared. The list commonly includes not only checks but drafts and notes. In a large association, each bank has a cage or desk in the exchange room, arranged in the sequence of the members' numbers. The settling clerk takes his place behind his desk, and the messenger from his bank passes around the batches of checks to the proper banks. In a smaller clearinghouse,

[1] American Bankers Association, Bank Management Commission, *City Clearinghouse Associations*, pp. 9-12. The Federal Reserve authorities define a check as a draft or order upon a bank or banking house, purporting to be drawn upon a deposit of funds, for the payment at all events of a certain sum of money to the order of a certain person therein named, or to him or his order, or to bearer, and payable on demand.

the manager sits at the head of a table, and the clerks place themselves around it. Each clerk enters on his clearing sheet, opposite the presenting bank's name and in the column headed "From Clearinghouse," the amount due to that bank. This column is then added, and the difference between "On Clearinghouse" and "From Clearing-

ILLUSTRATION III

ILLUSTRATION OF CLEARING PROCESS
(In Thousands of Dollars)

DUE FROM CLEARINGHOUSE

Bank A		Bank B		Bank C		Bank D	
B	26	A	21	A	28	A	25
C	34	C	29	B	19	B	30
D	15	D	29	D	31	C	13
Total	75	Total	79	Total	78	Total	68

DUE TO CLEARINGHOUSE

Bank A		Bank B		Bank C		Bank D	
B	21	A	26	A	34	A	15
C	28	C	19	B	29	B	29
D	25	D	30	D	13	C	31
Total	74	Total	75	Total	76	Total	75

CREDIT OR DEBIT

Bank A	Bank B	Bank C	Bank D
+1	+4	+2	−7

Total due from clearinghouse	$300,000
Total due to clearinghouse	300,000
Total credits	7,000
Total debits	7,000

house" is found. If the first is greater than the second, the bank has a credit balance of "Due from Clearinghouse"; otherwise, he has a "Due to Clearinghouse" debit.

When the manager of the clearinghouse enters the clearinghouse room, he receives a statement from each clerk of the amount "On Clearinghouse," and the totals are posted on his settling sheet. As soon as the total "From Clearinghouse" of each bank is found, it is entered in the correct place on his record. The net credit or net debit of each bank is then entered, and the clearings are proved by adding and comparing the totals of the debits and credits. If totals balance, the clerks are dismissed. If the totals do not balance, the clerks must remain until the mistake is found.[2] The clearing operations are shown by Illustration III. The clearing process is proved by (1) comparing total of "Due to Clearinghouse" items to "Due from Clearinghouse" items, and (2) by comparing totals of credits and debits.

Just as soon as the clearing is over, the messengers and clerks hurry back to their banks, carrying with them the checks and other items drawn against their banks, where they are charged against the accounts of each depositor. If a check, note, or draft has been missent, an account overdrawn, or any other mistake made, it is adjusted at a second clearing held at a later time during the same day. All dishonored checks and missent items are sent back to the banks which presented them at the first clearing.

If there are only two banks in a community, the clearing arrangement is similar to that described above. No clearinghouse is necessary, for the clerk of one bank will go to the other bank for one-half of the year, and during the remainder of the year the reverse will be true. The balance will be settled by New York draft, by currency, or by using the facilities of the Federal Reserve System.

Settling Balances Usually Involves No Currency.—Only balances are settled, and they represent a small percentage of the total volume of items which are cleared. The task of settling is given to the manager, who uses the method previously agreed on by the members. There are four possible procedures in settling: (1) Some associations permit the manager to draw checks in favor of the creditor banks upon the debtor banks. He starts drawing checks on the largest debtor in favor of the smallest creditor, until all creditors are paid. The checks are settled in currency or by New York draft. (2) The manager of the clearinghouse may receive the cash and take the responsibility for settling. (3) In other associations all members keep a balance with the clearinghouse manager, who uses it to settle, crediting or debiting the accounts of banks according to the day's settlement sheet record. (4) The most modern procedure is for the clearinghouse manager to make a certified copy of the net position of each bank and send it to the Federal Reserve bank. The Federal Reserve

---

[2] Clerks are fined for making mistakes in amounts which vary from 10 cents for the first offense up to $25. The fines are usually paid by the bank, which keeps a record of the clerk's mistakes. The proceeds from fines are used to defray the expenses of the clearinghouse association.

bank credits or debits the deposit account of each bank according to this record. Since all Federal Reserve member banks must keep a reserve deposit with their Reserve bank, and since many nonmember banks keep clearing balances, it is economical to use this last procedure in settling.

Cost of Operations Is Small.—The clearing principle is hundreds of years old, but the first clearinghouse in the United States was not established until 1853. There may or may not be a clearinghouse building, although the term "clearinghouse" is commonly used to describe the place where the clearing is done. In many communities the place of the clearing is rotated among the members. A centrally located office may be rented when a number of nonclearing functions are to be performed. In Boston all the clearing functions for the clearinghouse are performed by the Federal Reserve Bank of Boston. The New York Clearinghouse owns its building, but hundreds of clearinghouses have little or no property other than the necessary office equipment, books, and stationery. Fees vary with the size of banks, volume of clearings, and amount of trade association activities, or nonclearing functions.

Control of the clearinghouse is placed in the hands of an executive committee. Officers—president, vice-president, secretary, treasurer, and manager—are elected or appointed. The president, vice-president, and members of the executive committee are usually keymen in the banking community where the clearinghouse is located. With, perhaps, the exception of the manager, they serve without pay.

Membership in clearinghouse associations is voluntary, but, in order to make the rules effective, the constituent banks' boards of directors agree, by resolution, to abide by its rules. Rules of the association provide that any penalty inflicted on a member bank becomes an enforceable claim against the bank.

Clearinghouses Have Nonclearing Functions

A simple type of organization is necessary to handle the work of the clearinghouse when only clearing functions are performed,[3] but numerous nonclearing activities are now carried on by most clearinghouses. Some of the regional clearinghouses use the association

---

[3] American Bankers Association, Bank Management Commission, *City Clearinghouse Associations*, pp. 14-19.

for nonclearing activities only.[4] The nonclearing functions include (1) operation of credit bureaus, (2) examinations of members, (3) issuance of clearinghouse certificates, (4) regulation of banking routine, (5) fixing interest payments, service charges, fees, and rental charges for safe deposit boxes, and (6) maintenance of better public relations.

Credit Bureau.[5]—Numerous clearinghouse associations have set up credit bureaus in order to check on duplicate borrowing. To this bureau all banks in the association report all loans over $500, with the names of the borrowers, but without the amounts borrowed. The information is recorded on cards, and, if the same person is borrowing from two or more banks, this information is reported to the lending banks. The latter may take such steps as conditions appear to justify. Surveys have revealed that a surprisingly large number of borrowers were borrowing from two or more banks and that often the creditor banks were unaware of the multiple borrowing. When large sums are involved, multiple borrowing is necessary because of (1) the legal limitation of loans to one name, (2) the large number of small banks, and (3) the absence of a nation-wide branch banking system.

In England and Canada there is little or no multiple borrowing, because in these countries all the banking needs of any business firm are cared for by a single bank. Branches are scattered throughout the country to care for banking needs in distant places. If the head office of a firm is moved to another center or if a new office is opened, there is almost certain to be a branch office in that city to carry the account. For this reason many old business houses have done their banking business with one bank for generations. The one-bank policy is so strongly intrenched in the Canadian and English bank systems that a borrower may find it difficult to shift from one bank to a second. He must give a satisfactory explanation of where he formerly did his banking and why he is changing.

Mutual credit bureaus are helping to solve the problem of multiple borrowing; that is, they are preventing borrowers from going from bank to bank and obtaining from each of several banks all the

[4] American Bankers Association, Bank Management Commission, *Regional Clearinghouse Associations;* and Kniffen, W. R., *Better Banking,* pp. 335-44.

[5] American Bankers Association, Bank Management Commission, *City Clearinghouse Associations,* pp. 20-31.

credit that their statements would justify any one bank in advancing. Where credit bureaus have been in operation for a few years, the percentage of duplication has decreased; this is a fair indication that a considerable volume of multiple borrowing was not justified.

Activities of the credit bureaus of clearinghouses are not confined to checking upon multiple borrowing. Credit bureaus have been instrumental in building up improved credit policies of banks within their associations. They have succeeded in reducing the ratio of unsecured to secured loans, and they have directed attention to the large amount of borrowing from banks by nondepositors.

ILLUSTRATION IV

CLEARINGHOUSE CERTIFICATE

CERTIFICATE OF SYRACUSE CLEARING HOUSE ASSOCIATION

MEMBERS

FIRST TRUST AND DEPOSIT COMPANY THE SYRACUSE TRUST COMPANY THE MERCHANTS NATIONAL BANK AND TRUST COMPANY OF SYRACUSE

THE SALT SPRINGS NATIONAL BANK OF SYRACUSE LINCOLN NATIONAL BANK AND TRUST COMPANY OF SYRACUSE

No. 33 SYRACUSE, N. Y., MARCH 10, 1933

FIVE 5 DOLLARS

SAMPLE

Securities having been deposited with the Committee on Clearing House Certificates of the Syracue Clearing House Association, this Certificate will be accepted by the member banks of said Association for the sum named.

MANAGER PRESIDENT

Examinations.—A second continuing service of a clearinghouse is the clearinghouse examination. The movement started in Chicago in 1906. Since that time numerous clearinghouses have conducted periodic examinations of all their members. Until recent years, examinations were conducted in only thirty-five clearinghouse cities, but the number of such examinations has increased manyfold with the growth of regional and county clearing associations. Results from examinations by clearinghouse examiners have been most satisfactory when they have been made independently of public examinations.

The idea of clearinghouse examinations resulted from the threat of bank failures in Chicago in 1906. If they had been permitted to occur, the effects on banking would have been serious. Sound banks are almost forced to make large financial sacrifices in helping threatened banks or in liquidating those that have failed. Since part of the burden of a bank failure falls upon all the local banks, the stronger banks have taken the position that, for their own protection, they must take measures to prevent these failures. If an unsound situation is discovered soon enough, it may be possible to correct the condition before there are serious consequences. Now, in working out local difficulties, the clearinghouse has the assistance of the Federal Deposit Insurance Corporation, the Comptroller of Currency, the Reconstruction Finance Corporation, the Federal Reserve System, and state banking officials, depending, of course, on the bank or banks involved.

Clearinghouse Certificates. — During many panics preceding March, 1933, the emergency demands for currency were met in part by issuing clearinghouse certificates. These certificates were demand promises to pay which were signed by the officers of the clearinghouse and in some cases by the president and cashier of each member bank of the clearinghouse. They were issued in convenient denominations, that is, $1.00, $2.00, $5.00, and $10.00, and were used locally as currency. Following the March, 1933, panic and the national banking holiday, many clearinghouse certificates were printed. Few were circulated, however, because bank notes issued by Reserve banks were sufficient for all needs. Before the existence of the Federal Reserve System, clearinghouse certificates were used during many financial panics, having been a useful, although a not too satisfactory, type of emergency currency.

Regulation of Banking Routine.—Many types of routine banking problems are subject to mutual action through clearinghouse associations. Among these activities are the establishment of (1) hours for banking, (2) hours for clearing, (3) special and other holidays, (4) method of analyzing checking accounts, and (5) the basis for computing interest payments.

Regulation of Interest Payments and Fees.—Many years before the Board of Governors of the Federal Reserve System and the board of directors of the Federal Deposit Insurance Corporation fixed the maximum interest payments on deposits, clearinghouse associations were performing this function. Even though the Board and the Federal Deposit Insurance Corporation now fix the maximum interest payment on time deposits, a clearinghouse association may fix, and most have fixed, a lower rate, which applies to all their members.

Many types of service charges are still regulated by clearinghouse associations. They include (1) rental schedules for safe deposit boxes, (2) fees for travelers' checks, letters of credit, drafts, and cashier checks, (3) collection charges for checks, coupons, etc., (4) charges for trust services, and (5) service charges made against checking accounts.

Public Relations. — Finally clearinghouse associations have adopted policies governing the relationship of local banks to the public. They have adopted rules controlling methods and extent of advertising. In some communities they have eliminated the buying of business by offering gifts, donations, and prizes. Mutual resistance has been made against "drive" committees and other pressure salesmen, and maximum donations have been fixed by the clearinghouse rules. Considerable educational work has been done by clearinghouse groups. This includes sponsoring thrift clubs and distributing histories of the local community, home modernization plans, income tax instructions, household budgets, and other educational materials to school children and the public.

Out-of-Town Checks May Be Collected through Correspondent Banks

Banking co-operation is not confined to the clearinghouse association movement, for banking needs of business firms are both national and international in scope. Checks, drafts, matured notes, coupons, and other credit instruments payable in other communities are left by depositors with their banks for collection. In collecting, the simplest method is to send the checks directly to the banks on which they are drawn; for example, by an Austin bank directly to one in Houston. The Houston bank would be forced to remit through the mail the amount involved by drawing a draft on a bank acceptable to the Austin bank or, under unusual circumstances, by shipment of currency. The time involved would include not only the time necessary to present the original check but also the time necessary for the return of the draft (or currency) sent in payment and the collection of this draft.

A more serious objection to direct collection of checks than the time element is the continuance of the practice of many banks of not remitting at par for checks drawn on them when presented for payment by mail. In 1946 there were still about 2,200 banks that were on the Federal Reserve System's nonpar list.[6] Most of these banks are small and located in rural areas in the South and West. While they represent about 18 per cent of the total number of banks, they hold only 2 per cent of the total commercial bank deposits.

Many sellers of goods refuse to accept checks drawn upon banks which make exchange charges on checks, for the obvious reason that they are not being paid in full for goods sold. Wholesalers, manufacturers, and others located in New York, Chicago, St. Louis, and other large cities stamp bills to their customers thus: "This bill payable only in New York [Chicago, etc.] funds." Buyers are thus forced to purchase bank drafts from their local banks, and these drafts are used in place of the checks of individual firms. The buyers of goods usually pay their local banks several dollars a month for the drafts, the usual charge being $1.00 for $1,000.00 of domestic exchange. By using this plan of settlement, the seller of goods bears the burden of collection only, while the cost of exchange falls on the buyer. At the present time, if all checks were subject to both collection and exchange charges, the annual burden upon American businessmen would be millions of dollars.

Receipts from exchange charges make up an important part of the revenue of rural banks, and many of them claim that they are in no financial position to surrender them. The monthly receipts from exchange charges vary from $125 to $500 per bank. Collecting banks, in order to avoid exchange charges, still enter into reciprocal correspondent agreements with banks in different sections of the country. They agree not only to remit at par for their own checks but also to collect at par checks drawn upon banks in their vicinity. The natural desire to avoid exchange charges still leads to circuitous routing of checks, lengthening of time of collection, and multiplication of the number of times checks are handled; but the volume of checks involved is relatively smaller than the volume so handled prior to 1914.

Banks in metropolitan centers still act as par collecting agents for other banks. Some of the larger banks have thousands of accounts of banks, and interbank deposits are the largest in history. Past experience with the practice of these banks of absorbing exchange

[6] On August 10, 1945, the Nebraska legislature passed an act providing for the collection at par of checks drawn on banks and trust companies organized under the laws of the state, except those checks sent as special collection items. This is similar to a law passed in 1943 in Iowa, requiring its bank to remit at par.

charges warrants the conclusion that this may be used as a device to obtain balances in the same way as payment of interest on demand deposits.[7] Under present rulings of the Board of Governors of the Federal Reserve System, if exchange charges are made, the correspondent banks may not absorb them. Being a compensation for keeping a balance with another bank, the Board ruled it illegal under Section 19 of the Federal Reserve Act, which prohibits the payment of interest on demand deposits.

There is nothing in the Federal Reserve Act that prevents member banks from making reasonable charges for collecting and remitting for checks, provided that such charges are not made against the Federal Reserve banks.[8] Under present regulations of the Board, the Federal Reserve banks are not permitted to receive checks or bank drafts for collection that cannot be collected at par in funds acceptable to the Federal Reserve banks. This regulation makes it necessary for the banks that are not remitting at par to collect their checks through correspondent banks.

Prior to 1939, many member banks and nonmember clearing banks were not making full use of the collection facilities of the Federal Reserve System. This was because their correspondent banks were handling the sorting, listing, and other details of the clearing and collecting operations, which Federal Reserve regulations required the member banks and nonmember clearing banks to do. As a result of the revised rulings of the Board, this situation has been changed since 1939, and today much of this work is done by the Federal Reserve banks. Now about 90 per cent or more of all out-of-town checks are collected through the Federal Reserve collection system. The cost of handling these checks is borne by the Federal Reserve banks and does not represent any expense to the member banks or their customers. In addition to the savings of exchange charges, other advantages include the reduction in number of times which checks are

[7] See *Federal Reserve Bulletin*, September, 1943, pp. 817-18; February, 1944, pp. 126-32; March, 1944, p. 237; and April, 1944, p. 339.

[8] Section 13 of the Federal Reserve Act as amended reads as follows: "Provided, further, That nothing in this or any other section of this act shall be construed as prohibiting a member or nonmember bank from making reasonable charges, to be determined and regulated by the Board of Governors of the Federal Reserve System, but in no case to exceed 10 cents per $100 or fraction thereof, based on the total of checks and drafts presented at any one time, for collection or payment of checks and drafts and remission therefor by exchange or otherwise; but no such charge shall be made against the Federal Reserve banks."

handled, in time of collection, and in amount and distance of currency shipments, if any.

Provisions for Federal Reserve Collection

Statutory.—Section 16 of the Federal Reserve Act authorizes the Board of Governors of the Federal Reserve System to require each Federal Reserve bank to act as a clearinghouse for its member banks; and Section 13 as amended authorizes each Federal Reserve bank to perform for any nonmember bank similar functions, provided the nonmember bank keeps a bank balance with its Federal Reserve bank sufficient to offset the items in transit held for its account. Under these two provisions of the act, the Board of Governors has arranged to have each Federal Reserve bank exercise the functions of a clearinghouse and to collect checks for such of its member banks and nonmember clearing banks as desire to use its privileges.

In addition, two national settlement funds are being operated: the Interdistrict Settlement Fund and the Federal Reserve Agents Fund. It is through the Interdistrict Settlement Fund that interdistrict settlements of checks, Federal Reserve drafts, telegraphic transfers, and other interdistrict items are settled without the physical movement of gold or currency, the title only being transferred. It is through the Federal Reserve Agents Fund that interdistrict clearings of Federal Reserve notes are settled without the movement of gold.

Checks.—The general rules under which the Federal Reserve banks clear and collect checks are outlined in Regulation J, which was revised in 1939 to supersede the series of 1930.[9] Two general changes in the new rulings aim to make the Federal Reserve banks' collection services more attractive to member banks and nonmember clearing banks: (1) The amount of work required in preparing the checks for deposit with Federal Reserve banks has been reduced; and (2) member banks receive reserve credit within three days or less for all checks deposited, even though the total collection time of transcontinental checks may be two or more weeks. Most checks are credited to the reserve account of the depositing bank immediately, or within one or two days, and so items involving distant places will be most affected by the new rulings.

Noncash Items.—Federal Reserve banks are permitted to collect

---

[9] *Federal Reserve Bulletin,* September, 1939, pp. 719-21.

noncash items for member banks, nonmember clearing banks, and other Federal Reserve banks. These items include maturing notes, trade acceptances, bankers' acceptances, drafts, orders on savings deposits with passbooks attached, maturing bonds and coupons (other than obligations of the United States and its agencies, which are redeemed as cash items by Federal Reserve banks as fiscal agents), municipal warrants, and certain other items payable in the continental United States.[10] The Federal Reserve banks act only as agents for the banks from which they receive noncash items, and the latter must compensate them for any loss or expenses sustained. The procedures involved in collections vary according to circumstances, but in general they are the same as those for checks, which are discussed below under the headings of intradistrict collection of checks and interdistrict collection of checks.

Intradistrict Collection of Checks by Reserve Banks

Although many banks, particularly the small ones, still use in whole or in part the collection services offered by correspondent banks, the bulk (at least 90 per cent) of collection of out-of-town items is made directly through the district Federal Reserve bank.[11] Furthermore, many of the checks which are sent to city correspondents are collected by them through their Reserve banks. As a result, most out-of-town items go through the hands of a Federal Reserve bank.[12] The normal procedure for intradistrict collection of checks is shown by Table 6.

Credit within Three Days.[13]—For all cash items received, the sending bank is given immediate or deferred credit by Federal Reserve banks. Items credited immediately are collected on the day they arrive. Since the transit department of Reserve banks operate

[10] "Regulation G" (effective February 1, 1940), *Federal Reserve Bulletin*, January, 1940, pp. 15-16. Checks and bank drafts drawn on nonmember banks which cannot be collected at par in funds acceptable to Federal Reserve banks are still barred by this regulation.

[11] Federal Reserve Bank of Richmond, *The Collection of Checks by Reserve Banks*, Letter No. 5, April, 1922.

[12] For a treatment of the history of the Federal Reserve System's clearing and collection system, see Preston, H. H., "The Federal Reserve Bank's System of Par Collections," *Journal of Political Economy*, Vol. XXVIII, pp. 565-90.

[13] "Revision of Regulation J," *Federal Reserve Bulletin*, September, 1939, pp. 719-21.

twenty-four hours each day, immediate credit items include checks drawn upon banks in a wide geographical area in the vicinity of Reserve banks and their branches. The deferred credit items are credited to the deposit account of the sending bank according to a time schedule, which before September 1, 1939, was based upon the actual time required to collect the checks. On September 1, 1939, the Federal Reserve banks adopted a new plan for giving member banks credit within three days or less for all checks deposited with them for collection. Three days or less is sufficient time to collect checks

TABLE 6

INTRADISTRICT COLLECTION OF CHECKS

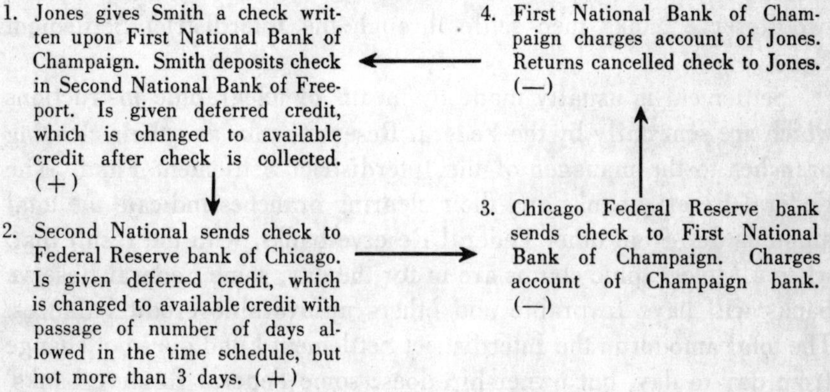

1. Jones gives Smith a check written upon First National Bank of Champaign. Smith deposits check in Second National Bank of Freeport. Is given deferred credit, which is changed to available credit after check is collected. (+)
2. Second National sends check to Federal Reserve bank of Chicago. Is given deferred credit, which is changed to available credit with passage of number of days allowed in the time schedule, but not more than 3 days. (+)
3. Chicago Federal Reserve bank sends check to First National Bank of Champaign. Charges account of Champaign bank. (—)
4. First National Bank of Champaign charges account of Jones. Returns cancelled check to Jones. (—)

within most of the eastern Federal Reserve districts but not all interdistrict checks. This new practice of giving member banks credit for all checks within three days or less has increased the "float" (uncollected items minus deferred availability items) counted as member bank reserves by several hundred million dollars.

Intradistrict Settlements Are Simple.—Since all member banks and nonmember clearing banks within a district keep balances with their district reserve banks, the mechanism for settling intradistrict items consists of crediting and debiting the accounts of the banks involved in the transaction. Sometimes, in order to reduce the time of collection to a minimum, the collecting bank is permitted to send checks directly to the drawer's bank. An "advice" is sent to the Reserve bank, notifying it of the transaction. The Reserve bank then settles in the customary way by making the necessary changes in its books.

Interdistrict Collection of Checks

Many businessmen receive checks drawn upon banks located in other Federal Reserve districts. The local banks still send these checks to their Federal Reserve banks. The Reserve banks give deferred credit as noted above, changing it to available credit according to the number of days allowed in the time schedule, with a maximum of three days. But from here on the collection differs from that already described and proceeds as follows: The first Reserve bank sends the check to the Federal Reserve bank of the district in which the drawer's bank is located. This Reserve bank charges the deposit account of the drawer's bank, sending the check to the latter, which charges the account of the drawer and later gives him the cancelled check. The two Reserve banks then settle through the Interdistrict Settlement Fund.

Settlement is usually made by means of telegraphic instructions which are sent daily by the Federal Reserve banks and their clearing branches to the manager of the Interdistrict Settlement Fund. The Federal Reserve banks and their clearing branches indicate the total amounts due from other Federal Reserve banks, with the result that, when all telegraphic claims are in for the day, some Federal Reserve banks will have favorable and others unfavorable credit balances. The total amount in the Interdistrict Settlement Fund does not change from day to day, but ownership does; some Federal Reserve banks' balances are credited, while others are debited.

The manager of the Interdistrict Settlement Fund credits the account of the sending Reserve bank and charges the accounts of the other Reserve banks.[14] At the end of the day all interdistrict obligations are settled by changing the total of the balance held by each Reserve bank. In the evening the manager of the Interdistrict Settlement Fund notifies the Reserve banks of changes, and the latter make the necessary adjustments on their books.

The Interdistrict Settlement Fund was set up in 1915 by the old Federal Reserve Board. Each Federal Reserve bank is required to keep a minimum balance of $1,000,000 in the fund, but the average amount kept is much larger. These funds are held in the United

---

[14] The deposits in the fund were originally in the form of gold, hence the name Gold Settlement Fund. Since the passage of the Gold Reserve Act of 1934, this is no longer true.

States Treasury in Washington and count as part of the Reserve banks' legal reserves. Checks and other items collected through the fund are not sent to Washington. A chart showing the normal procedure in interdistrict collection of checks appears as Table 7.

TABLE 7

INTERDISTRICT COLLECTION OF CHECKS

1. Jones gives Smith a check written upon First National Bank of Atlanta. Smith deposits check in First Trust in Syracuse. Receives deferred credit, which is changed to available credit after check is collected. (+)

2. First Trust sends check to Federal Reserve bank of New York. Is given deferred credit which is changed to available credit according to number of days allowed in time schedule, but not more than 3 days. (+)

3. New York Federal Reserve bank sends check to Atlanta Federal Reserve bank. Notifies Interdistrict Settlement Fund. (+)

Interdistrict Settlement Fund in Washington credits the account of New York Federal Reserve and charges account of Atlanta Federal Reserve bank. (+) (—)

4. Atlanta Federal Reserve bank charges the account of the First National of Atlanta. (—) Sends check to First National of Atlanta.

5. First National Bank of Atlanta charges account of Jones. (—) Later, it gives cancelled check to Jones.

6. Jones receives cancelled check, which he gave to Smith in Syracuse.

Numerous steps have been taken to speed up the collection process described in Table 7. Some branches of Federal Reserve banks are classified as clearing branches, and items sent to them are settled directly through the Interdistrict Settlement Fund. Sometimes one Reserve bank is given permission to send checks directly to a member bank located in a second district. An advice explaining the transaction is sent to the second Reserve bank. This step shortens the journey of the check but otherwise does not change collection procedure. Member or clearing nonmember banks may send checks directly to a second Federal Reserve bank, merely advising its own Reserve Bank of the transaction. This system provides a great saving in the expense and time of transferring funds between Federal Reserve districts.

Telegraphic Transfers Speed Exchange of Titles to Funds

Telegraphic transfers are orders sent by telegraph to a bank or some other agency, instructing it to transfer deposits from one account to another or to pay money to persons who will call for it. Telegraph companies have offices in most cities and towns in the United States, and for many years they have been selling telegraphic transfers to all types of customers. The amount involved in individual orders is usually small. The wire facilities of telegraph companies are used by banks to transfer title of funds kept on deposit with their correspondent banks.

The twelve Federal Reserve banks offer similar transfer services to their member banks. A member bank may, without cost, make telegraphic transfer in round numbers ($100 or more) through its Federal Reserve bank to another Federal Reserve bank for the credit of a second member bank. For example, if Chicago Bank A wants to send $1,000,000 to Bank B in New York, it will notify its Reserve bank to charge its account and transfer the sum to the Reserve bank of New York for the credit of Bank B. The transfer takes but a few minutes. The New York bank will then use the balance as advised by a second wire sent directly to it. These transfers are made by code in order to lessen the dangers of fraudulent transfers and payment of funds to the wrong party. Funds which otherwise would be idle are put to work immediately.

Transfers in odd or even amounts are also made by the Federal Reserve banks over commercial wires for the account of banks, individuals, firms, or corporations. They make no charge other than the cost of the necessary telegram. Thus, by merely paying for the commercial wire, a member bank may make specific and immediate transfers of funds for its customers to distant places within the United States. In 1930 the number of transfers by Federal Reserve banks and their branches was 1,868,000, and the value of these transfers was $198,800,000,000. During the year 1944 the number of transfers was 906,000, with a value of $215,000,000,000.

Federal Reserve Exchange Drafts

For many years money orders and drafts have been sold by express companies, post offices, and banks. They may be collected by messengers, but usually they are sent by mail. They are orders to pay money to designated parties on demand or after the elapse of a specific length of time.

Title to deposits with Federal Reserve banks may be transferred by messengers, but usually they are sent by mail. It is slower than a wire, but it permits the sending bank to keep funds in its own possession while the item is in transit. Any member bank may make

TABLE 8

VOLUME OF PRINCIPAL CLEARING OPERATIONS OF FEDERAL RESERVE BANKS
(Number in Thousands—Amounts in Thousands of Dollars)

Operation	Number of Pieces Handled*		Amounts Handled	
	1943	1944	1943	1944
Checks handled:				
U.S. government checks	266,686	426,460	113,791,554	127,931,710
All others	1,246,384	1,288,465	509,640,311	532,755,045
Collection items handled:				
U.S. government coupons paid†	16,527	17,054	1,481,520	1,840,647
All others	5,072	4,622	7,882,053	7,962,994
Issues, redemptions, and exchanges:				
U.S. government obligations‡	270,608	357,782	211,749,395	264,138,176
Transfer of funds	865	906	203,510,209	215,006,532

* Two or more checks, coupons, etc., handled as a single item, are counted as one piece.

† Includes coupons from obligations guaranteed by the United States.

‡ Exclusive of war savings stamps received for redemption.

Source: Thirty-first Annual Report of the Board of Governors of the Federal Reserve System, Covering Operations for the Year 1944, p. 29.

arrangements with its Federal Reserve bank to draw drafts against it. Such drafts are known as Federal Reserve exchange drafts. They will be accepted by any Federal Reserve bank or branch. After a draft has been paid, it is settled through the Interdistrict Settlement Fund. In using a draft, the issuing bank notifies its Federal Reserve bank on a special form prepared for this purpose. The Reserve bank immediately charges the account of the bank for the amount sent. Wire transfers and drafts are settled daily through the Interdistrict Settlement Fund.

Summary

Each Federal Reserve bank acts as a regional clearinghouse for its par clearing banks, and the Interdistrict Settlement Fund serves in a similar capacity for the United States. Currency movements for settling balances within the United States have been almost eliminated, and practically all their costs are borne by the Federal Reserve banks. The Federal Reserve System's collection system has made the check a national as well as a local means of payment. The elimination of exchange charges on millions of items and the reduction in collection time have saved business houses millions of dollars annually. The volume of clearing and collecting work done by the Federal Reserve banks is suggested by Table 8.

Unfortunately, there are over 2,200 banks in the United States that still deny their customers the advantage of having their checks paid at par in distant places when presented for payment by mail. These banks are small, and, although they represent 18 per cent of the total number of commercial banks, their deposits amount to less than 2 per cent of the total net deposits of all commercial banks. The problems created by nonpar banks are serious in the Minneapolis and Atlanta Federal Reserve districts, not only because of their effects upon the acceptability of the checks of their customers and the unfair burden upon those who receive them, but also because of the competitive advantage the nonpar paying banks have over member banks and nonmember par clearing banks.

The correct practice for all banks to follow is to place the burden for handling checking accounts upon their own customers in the form of service and collection charges. Since most of the nonpar banks are insuring their deposits with the Federal Deposit Insurance Corporation, this corporation should take steps to force all insured nonpar paying banks to meet their check obligations at par.

QUESTIONS AND PROBLEMS

1. Compare methods of settling for domestic and foreign purchases as they existed before the Federal Reserve System was organized.
2. Explain why New York exchange formerly sold at a premium in Chicago during certain seasons of the year.
3. Distinguish between clearance and collection operations. What are the advantages of clearance?

4. What items are cleared through a clearinghouse? How are balances settled? Why must the total credits and debits balance?
5. Were clearinghouse certificates issued during the February-March panic in 1933? Are these certificates script money?
6. How do clearinghouse credit bureaus and other types of credit associations strengthen the credit system?
7. Distinguish between exchange charges and collection charges. Compare to service charges on deposit accounts.
8. What is meant by interdistrict collection of checks? Intradistrict collection of checks? Which one is the more complicated? Why? Describe each.
9. The settlement of balances among Federal Reserve banks are collected through the Interdistrict Settlement Fund in such a way as to minimize currency shipments. Explain and compare to the settling procedure of the local clearinghouse.
10. "The general principle of wire transfer is . . . . similar to the principle of check collection through the Reserve System" (Burgess, *The Reserve Banks and the Money Market* [rev. ed.], p. 103). Explain.
11. How would the development of branch banking on a wide scale affect the clearing and collection of checks?
12. Explain why the local clearinghouse has had a more extensive development in the United States than in foreign countries.
13. What is the correspondent bank system for collecting credit instruments between cities in the same country; and cities in different countries?
14. Are the volumes of bank clearings through the local clearinghouse an index of local business? Why? Can you think of a better local index of business? May bank debits be used as a barometer of business?
15. "A check on a Sag Harbor, New York, bank was deposited in a Hoboken bank. The check was then sent to New York City, a distance of 3 miles, then to Boston—200 miles, then to Tonawanda—405 miles, to Albany—210 miles, to Port Jefferson—105 miles, to Far Rockaway—45 miles, to another bank in New York City—20 miles, to Riverhead—75 miles, to Long Island City—70 miles, and then to Sag Harbor—90 miles, a total distance of 1,223 miles" (Vest, G. B., "The Par Collection System of the Federal Reserve Banks," *Federal Reserve Bulletin*, February, 1940, p. 90). If direct collection through the Federal Reserve System were used today, how long would it take to collect this check?
16. "It has been a matter of primary concern with all banks to see that checks are presented for payment at the earliest possible time. . . . . However, the complexities of our banking system—par and nonpar banks, states divided by Federal Reserve District lines, special collection

arrangements, etc.—have presented barriers to the complete solution of the transit routing problems" (Bank Management Commission, American Bankers Association, *Check Routing Symbol*). Discuss.

17. "The public wants sound banking institutions, and, therefore, expects a bank to be adequately compensated in order that it may at all times maintain its soundness, assuring the safety of its depositors' funds and its stockholders' investment. Legitimate charges for services are fundamental to such a program" (Bank Management Commission, American Bankers Association, *Service Charge Survey*), p. 4. Do you agree? Explain.

18. Do you agree with banks that advertise the following advantages of a checking account? (*a*) The bank is your financial accountant and prepares periodic statements showing the funds paid out and money received, as well as the condition of your account. (*b*) The bank acts as your agent and collects the money represented by the checks deposited. (*c*) The bank invests or loans your money so that the interest earned may pay for all or a part of the checking service you use.

19. Following the September, 1943, rulings of the Board that the absorption of charges (exchange) were interest payments and therefore illegal, the House of Representatives passed a bill to provide that the absorption of exchange and collection charges by member banks shall not be deemed to be payment of interest. In the Senate, an amendment to the pending Federal Crop Insurance bill, containing the same provision, was defeated 45 to 25. The Board of Governors of the Federal Reserve System and the Federal Deposit Insurance Corporation were in disagreement on this proposed law. Aside from legal issues, why? See *Thirty-first Annual Report of the Board of Governors of the Federal Reserve System, Covering Operations for the Year 1944*, pp. 15-23; and *Annual Report of the Federal Deposit Insurance Corporation for the Year Ended December 31, 1944*, pp. 72-95.

REFERENCES

American Bankers Association, Bank Management Commission. *Pay-as-You-Go Checking Accounts and Remittance Check Service.* (Booklet.)

American Bankers Association, Bank Management Commission. *Proceedings, Annual Clearinghouse Round Table Conference,* Bulletin No. 72, October, 1937; and No. 76, November, 1938.

American Bankers Association, Bank Management Commission. *Service Charge Survey, 1938,* Bulletin No. 77, January, 1939. New York: American Bankers Association.

American Bankers Association, Bank Management Commission. *City Clearinghouse Associations.*

American Bankers Association, Bank Management Commission. *Regional Clearinghouse Associations.*

Bolles, A. S. *Practical Banking,* pp. 217-78. 2d ed. New York: Homans Publishing Co., 1884.

Burgess, W. R. *The Reserve Banks and the Money Market,* chap. v. Revised ed. New York: Harper & Bros., 1936.

Cannon, J. G. *Clearing-Houses.* New York: D. Appleton & Co., 1908.

Dunbar, C. F. *The Theory and History of Banking,* chap. iv. 4th ed. New York: G. P. Putnam's Sons, 1922.

Harr, Luther, and Harris, W. C. *Banking Theory and Practice,* chap. xvi. 2d ed. New York: McGraw-Hill Book Co., Inc., 1936.

Rodkey, R. G. *The Banking Process,* chap. v. New York: Macmillan Co., 1928.

Spahr, W. E. *The Clearing and Collection of Checks.* New York: Bankers Publishing Co., 1926.

Vest, G. B. "The Par Collection System of the Federal Reserve Banks," *Federal Reserve Bulletin,* February, 1940, pp. 89-96.

Willis, H. P., and Steiner, W. H. *Federal Reserve Banking Practice,* chap. xx. New York: D. Appleton & Co., 1926.

Chapter XII
INTERNATIONAL MONETARY PRINCIPLES

International Exchange Is Similar to Domestic

Within the United States, an economy has been developed wherein dollars are interchangeable one with another, and the dollar means the same in New York as in Texas. Thus trade between communities is not handicapped by the thought that, when a trade bill is paid in New York and funds are remitted to Austin, the seller will collect but 75 per cent of its value in dollars. Furthermore, there are no regulations which prevent him from withdrawing his funds from New York or from disposing of them as he desires. Most of the goods that are sold in other communities are paid for with deposit currency, that is, checks or drafts drawn on bank balances or deposits in banks.

Correspondent relationships between banks and the clearing and collecting work of the Federal Reserve System make it simple for Mr. White in New York to meet his obligations within the United States without shipments of currency. He writes a check upon his bank and mails it to his creditors. If Mr. White does not have a checking account, he may buy a bank draft, a postal money order, an express money order, or, if time is limited, a telegraphic transfer.

Similar facilities are available for settling foreign obligations. Practically all foreign payments are made with credit instruments. For example, when an American importer buys goods from a British exporter, he meets his obligation, not with a personal check, as is customary in domestic trade, but with a sight draft or cable transfer purchased from his bank. Mr. White's bank, or one of its correspondent banks, keeps a balance with one in London in order to be in a position to help customers who need foreign funds. As a result, the payment abroad is made by a transfer of part of the American bank's deposits in London to the British exporter. The American bank is compensated for its loss of funds abroad by an increase of funds in New York, plus its profit from the transaction.

When cotton is sold by American exporters, the results are similar to those which take place in domestic trade. American exporters receive drafts drawn on English banks. These claims to deposits in

English banks are sold to or left with American banks for collection in the same way that personal checks are left with local banks. Cotton exporters gain funds in the United States, and American banks gain funds abroad. Their foreign balances are increased in the same manner that the deposits with Federal Reserve banks and domestic correspondents are increased in domestic exchange when banks collect checks drawn upon banks located in distant communities. Foreign exchange banks are at the same time buyers and sellers of claims to foreign money. When they sell claims to their deposits abroad, they immediately purchase claims in the exchange market to replenish the balances sold. By matching purchases with sales, risk is reduced to a minimum.

In foreign exchange, credits and debits are offset on the books of international bankers in the same manner as they are by the Federal Reserve banks and correspondent banks in domestic exchange. The world lacks an Interdistrict Settlement Fund, but in future years central banks may use the International Monetary Fund as a world clearinghouse. During the last hundred years the large private banks located in London have served as a world clearing center in much the same way as banks in New York City have served the United States as a national clearing center.[1] Relative to the total volume of payments, little currency or gold moves in domestic exchange; and, relative to the total volume of international payments, little currency or gold moves in foreign exchange.

Before World War II international transactions, whether they were in payment for goods, services, or investments, had two things in common with similar domestic transactions: (1) they were negotiated between individuals, partnerships, and corporations, and (2) they were reckoned in terms of money and settled primarily with bank deposits. But during World War II governments dominated not only their domestic economies but also international trade. Owing to Lend-Lease, most of the exports from the United States moved abroad without regard to the ability of the recipients to pay either in goods or in services. In the aggregate, payments for these exports, including goods and services made available to the United States Military

[1]"It is found to be advantageous to deposit money in London, or to obtain credit and make bills payable there, rather than elsewhere. By such a concentration of banking operations, London tends to become the seat of a *world-wide* Clearing House" (Jevons, *Money and the Mechanism of Exchange,* p. 189; in addition, see pp. 297-302).

Forces abroad under mutual agreement pacts, were very large; but relative to the amount of goods and services provided by the United States to foreign governments, they were small. Instead of bank credit, government credit dominated these bookkeeping transactions.

The end of the war has eliminated the need for most Lend-Lease transactions, and the resumption of private financing of foreign trade should follow. The strengthening of the Export-Import Bank and the organization of the International Monetary Fund and the International Bank for Reconstruction and Development have as their primary purpose the development of a framework within which trade activities among private financial and commercial institutions in different countries may be carried on with a minimum of governmental interference. To be sure, foreign governments will continue to buy goods in the United States, but these purchases will be of minor importance compared to those made during World War II.

Technical Differences between Foreign and Domestic Exchange

The similarities between fundamental principles of foreign and domestic exchanges are obscured by certain technical differences. In foreign exchange, transactions are generally in terms of foreign currencies. Buyers of goods from foreign countries must not only consider the price quoted in terms of foreign money but must also convert this quotation into dollars. For example, how much will a consignment of British goods cost an American importer if the total cost is £5,000 sterling? The answer is found by checking upon the rate (price) of the English monetary unit and multiplying by 5,000.

The rate of exchange is subject to considerable day-to-day fluctuation, and this so-called "risk of exchange" is a hazard not found in domestic transactions. It is greatly increased when countries are not on a gold standard, and one of the primary reasons for the organization of the International Monetary Fund is to eliminate or reduce this risk. Distances are usually greater in foreign than in domestic trade, and the time periods involved are usually longer; therefore the financing of these transactions tends to be more hazardous and calls for more elaborate financing techniques while goods are in transit. As a result, bills of exchange and cable or telegraphic transfers tend to be more important in foreign than in domestic trade. In addition, more formal documents are used in financing foreign trade than in financing domestic trade. Other conditions which add to the hazards of foreign trade financing are the different systems of measurements of length, weight, and quantities, different legal systems, and, finally different languages.

Because of these special risks and the long-time period involved in foreign trade, buyers prefer not to make cash payments before they receive title to the goods purchased, and sellers prefer not to sell without receiving payment in some type of credit instrument which can be sold immediately for cash. As a result of centuries of experience, the bill of exchange and the accompanying documents have been developed. Such a bill is merely an order by the seller (drawer) on the buyer or the buyer's bank (drawee) to pay to a specified party (the drawer or usually the drawer's bank or order) a definite sum of money at some time in the future. It may be payable at sight or after a given number of days following presentation and acceptance by the drawee. Irrespective of whether a "sight" or "time" bill of exchange is used, banking services are utilized in collecting and making payments. Even personal checks are sometimes used in foreign trade financing. But in foreign exchange, emphasis is placed on cable transfers, bank drafts, and other bills of exchange.

Exchange Rates and Gold Movements

When countries are on the gold standard, the sight rates of exchange fluctuate around the mint par of exchange and within the gold points. The mint par of exchange is found by comparing the amount of fine gold in the two standard monetary units of two countries. In 1930 the dollar contained 23.22 grains of pure gold, and the pound sterling contained 113.0015 grains. When one compares these two units, it is obvious that the pound contained as much gold as was found in $4.8665. This figure was the mint par of exchange between the dollar and the pound. The mint par of exchange remains fixed only so long as the weight and fine gold contents of the standard gold units are not changed. When the United States government decreased the weight of fine gold in the standard dollar to 13.71 grains, the mint pars of exchange between this and other countries were changed; but as long as other countries are off the gold standard, this change is of no practical importance.

When countries are on the gold standard, the extreme fluctuations of sight and demand rates are fixed by the gold export and gold import points.[2] The gold export point is found by adding the cost of exporting gold to the mint par of exchange. The gold import point is found by subtracting the cost of importing gold from the mint par of exchange. The cost of moving gold from one country to a second includes the costs of preparing for shipment, shipping, insuring, mint charges, and loss of interest on the sum while in transit. If the price of sight exchange rises above the mint par, plus the cost of shipping, it is more economical for international bankers to ship gold than it is to build up balances by purchases of exchange. As soon as gold is shipped, bankers may and customarily do sell more exchange. This increase in supply, on one hand, and decrease in demand, on the other, automatically keeps the exchange rate at or below the gold export point. When the rate of sight exchange is below the gold import point, international bankers find it profitable to import gold. As a result, the supply of bills offered is decreased, and the price tends to rise. This movement has a tendency to keep the exchange rate at or above the gold import point.

The export and import points are not fixed, and they are, in fact, zones rather than points. As the cost of moving gold increases, there will be an increase in the maximum fluctuations of exchange; as the cost of moving gold decreases, there will be a decrease in the maximum fluctuations of exchange. It may be profitable to move $10,000,000 in gold but not profitable to move $300,000. Bankers, in moving gold, sometimes anticipate changes in exchange rates rather than follow them, as the foregoing theory assumes. Bankers differ in their calculation of the profitable exporting and importing point for gold. Central banks have at times arranged for gold shipments without allowing for the chief cost involved—loss of interest while in transit. Finally, the theory assumes that countries are on the gold standard and that there are no artificial restraints on international gold movements. Sometimes the rate of exchange may justify gold exports, but, if bankers cannot secure gold for export, there will be no corrective foreign exchange gold movement to keep the fluctuations in the price of bills of exchange within these zones. At the present time gold is not allowed to perform its important international function of keeping exchanges at or near their par values.

[2] See Heilperin, M. A., *International Montary Economics*, p. 121, *passim.*

Gold Movements and Interest Rates

When countries are on the gold standard, if the sight rate of exchange reaches a premium large enough to pay the cost of exporting gold, gold will leave the country. This loss of gold will usually be reflected in the gold reserves of the central banks, which in turn affects the supply of credit and currency available for use in the money markets within the country. A reduction in the supply of money and credit is inclined to be followed by higher interest rates in the money market. If these interest rates are above those in other international markets, there will be a tendency for short-term funds to flow in from other countries. The central bank may even bid for gold reserves held abroad by raising its discount interest rate. As a result, the outward movement of gold will tend to be checked, and may even be reversed. The opposite of these developments are prone to take place in the countries receiving the gold (increase in reserves, increase in supply of money and credit, and a decrease in interest rates), and equilibrium will be re-established.

When the discount on the sight rate of exchange is sufficient to cover the cost of gold shipment, then gold will have a tendency to flow to this country. The gold imports will increase the reserves of the banks of the importing country, money rates will decline, and other foreign money markets will be more attractive, particularly those in countries which are losing gold reserves. Thus, when countries are on a gold standard, international specie movements will be relatively small and will tend to maintain equilibrium in the international money market.

Between World War I and World War II, the importance of international foreign exchange disturbances caused by short-term and long-term capital changes increased because of the growth of international investments. In placing or withdrawing funds abroad, particularly short-term funds, safety has often been a more important factor than yield. Shifts of short-term funds from money market to money market in search of safety was the chief immediate cause of the international breakdown in the gold standard during 1931. One of the principal reasons for the creation of government-owned and operated exchange funds was the protection of the countries' domestic economies from the bad effects of the influx or efflux or "hot money." For the most part, the exchange funds provide a system whereby the impact of short-term money movements on the money market is minimized, the shock being absorbed by the exchange funds.

The effects of gold imports and exports upon domestic economy are not automatic but depend upon the behavior of the aggregate of individuals who control the community's power of investing and spending. Their behavior may modify the velocity of the circulation of money and credit so as to offset the effects of import or export of gold. On the other hand, their behavior may intensify these effects. Central banks may intervene to offset the loss of gold by increasing the volume of reserve credit or may neutralize the effects of gold imports by decreasing the volume of reserve credit. Thus, when a country has a large supply of gold, it may insulate itself against many of the depressing effects which normally accompany the loss of gold. On the other hand, many of the inflationary effects of gold imports may be offset by central bank and government control over bank reserves.

Gold Movements and Price Levels

When countries are on the gold standard, a third automatic factor which tends to bring about equilibrium between countries is the effect of gold movements on money incomes and on price levels. Loss of gold will tend to lead to restrictive credit policies, a decrease in the supply of money and credit, a decline in money incomes, and a lower domestic price level. An increase in the supply of gold may increase the supply of money and credit, increase money incomes, and bring about a higher price level. The home market will be a more favorable one for domestic producers to sell in and a less favorable one for foreign buyers to buy in. International buyers and sellers of goods will take advantage of this situation, and the country with the lower price level will tend to have a more favorable balance of trade. Gold will have a tendency to flow from the country with the higher price level to the country with the lower price level, and, as a result, the difference in these levels will tend to disappear. Therefore, the international price level will be in equilibrium for all countries that are on the gold standard and are trading freely with each other.[3]

Before World War I, among the most common and most serious

[3] League of Nations, *Second Interim Report of the Gold Delegation of the Financial Committee* (1931), p. 11.

artificial factors interfering with the equilibrium of prices were tariff barriers, bounties on exports, and "dumping." In the United States, customs duties, which make up the tariff, are levied only on imports; but some foreign countries levy duties also on exports. These duties (taxes) are a fixed percentage of the price of the imported goods (*ad valorem*)—so many cents per yard, per gallon, etc. (specific); or a combination of so much per unit and a percentage of value. Other things being equal, the effect of an import duty is to increase the price of the goods in the protected country and to decrease it in the unprotected country. If international trade is carried on over tariff walls, allowance must be made for this artificial barrier to foreign trade and to the tendency for gold movements to bring about equilibrium in international prices. The system of free movements of gold was overthrown by World War I and only partly restored during the 1920's. Between 1931 and 1945 it was abandoned by all countries.

The Purchasing Power Par of Exchange[4]

When countries are on the gold standard, there is no wide fluctuation in exchange rates; bills rise and fall in price, depending upon supply and demand, but the fluctuations are confined to the limits set by the gold points. The norm around which rates fluctuate is the mint par of exchange. When countries leave the gold standard, gold movements are no longer effective. Exchange continues to mean an exchange of rights to bank deposits located in different international financial centers. But the mint par of exchange is replaced by the purchasing power parity norm.

The formula for determining the purchasing power parity between two countries is as follows:

$$\frac{\text{Index number—Country A}}{\text{Index number—Country B}} \times \text{Old mint par of exchange.}$$

For example, if the United States index of wholesale prices is at 120 and that of Great Britain at 160, the purchasing power parity is computed as follows:

---

[4] Graham, F. D., "Recent Movements in International Price Level and the Doctrine of Purchasing Power Parity," *American Statistical Association Journal*, Supplement, Vol. XXX (March, 1935), pp. 159-66; U.S. Tariff Commission, *Depreciated Exchange and International Trade.*

$$\frac{120}{160} \times \$4.86 = \$3.645.$$

If the purchasing power parity is $3.645 and the exchange rate in the market is $3.50, that is, below the purchasing power parity, it is obviously to the advantage of international buyers to purchase goods in England, because the equivalent of $3.50 will buy $3.645 in goods in that country. The increase in purchases abroad will tend to bring the actual exchange rate and the purchasing power parity together. The adjustment is a three-way process: (1) Buying abroad will make it necessary for merchants to go into the exchange market and purchase exchange; other things being equal, the rate of exchange will increase. (2) Buying goods abroad increases prices in that market. (3) A decrease in purchase of goods in the United States lowers prices of goods in the domestic market. The first movement tends to increase the exchange rate, and the last two movements tend to lower the purchasing power parity. For example, should prices go up two points in England and down two in the United States, the new purchasing power parity would be

$$\frac{118}{162} \times \$4.86 = \$3.54.$$

Assuming also that in the meantime the exchange rate would increase 4 points, to $3.54, the exchange rate and the purchasing power parity would thus be brought together.

If the exchange rate is above the purchasing power parity, just the opposite of these movements will take place. That is, goods will be purchased in the United States, the rate of dollar exchange will rise, domestic prices will increase, and foreign prices will decrease. In studying the purchasing power parity, the most satisfactory results are secured when only prices of goods bought and sold in international markets are considered. International arbitragers in wheat, cotton, and other commodities are on the alert for opportunities to make profits. Their operations bring about the adjustments described above. When sheltered goods are considered, differences in purchasing power of money in two markets may be great. Further deviations result from domestic price control and other restrictions placed on the markets. In a free economy, adjustments which tend to take place are those which involve individual prices rather than the general price level, as when on the gold standard.

What Are the Foreign Trade Advantages of Being off the Gold Standard?

This question has been asked many times since 1931 and will be treated first under the assumption that most other countries remain on the gold standard. The primary argument in favor of such a step is the fact that depreciated currency will stimulate the export of goods. In 1932 an English merchant selling goods to buyers in the United States was in a position to offer over £1,000 worth of goods at a price of $3,600 (exchange rate $3.60). In 1931, before England left the gold standard, a similar shipment of goods would have cost $4,850 (exchange rate $4.85), assuming, of course, that other things had remained the same. In both cases the exporter would have received the same amount of English money, that is, £1,000; but the change in price to American buyers would have been $1,250. This situation would have given the British exporter a decided advantage over American sellers, which could have been met only by cutting prices. In calculating the possible profits of English exporters, recognition must be given to the following facts: (1) Their costs of raw materials from abroad would have increased in terms of the depreciated unit, and (2) their domestic costs would have increased because of a greater demand for goods. Finally, it should be recognized that the exchange rate would have been increased by the greater demand for English currency with which to pay for goods purchased.

Depreciated currency gives a country temporary advantages in the export market, but these are soon lost in the natural course of events, even though other countries remain on the gold standard.[5] But other countries have not remained on the gold standard, and the temporary advantages held by those first to leave gold disappeared quickly. When all countries are off the gold standard, the country with the greatest amount of depreciation has the export advantage, and for this reason there is danger of a vicious cycle of more and more depreciation. However, there are recognizable benefits in not being on a gold standard, which were considered in Chapter VIII, entitled "A Managed Paper Money Standard."

---

[5] For an appraisal of the effects of devaluation of the gold dollar on foreign trade, consult Silverstein, N. L., "Effects of the American Devaluation on Prices and Export Trade," *American Economic Review*, Vol. XXVII, No. 2 (June, 1937), pp. 279-93.

The Balance of International Payments

Credit instruments in terms of moneys of foreign countries are used to purchase foreign goods, services, and securities. The total money value of these items represents the demand of businessmen and others for foreign exchange. Sales of goods, services, and securities to foreigners give Americans claims or rights to foreign funds. These claims (bills of exchange) are sold to banks, which send them abroad to be collected; after collection, the funds are deposited with foreign correspondent banks. These deposits are the basis for sale of foreign drafts to be used by Americans to pay for foreign goods, services, and securities. Similarly, foreign bankers keep deposits with American banks to finance the needs of their customers for dollar exchange.

The totals of purchases and sales of goods, services, and securities are computed by the Bureau of Foreign and Domestic Commerce from all sources available and are published in a statement called *Balance of International Payments of the United States*. All items representing cash claims against foreigners are classified as "credits," while those transactions which cause funds to be sent abroad are classified as "debits." The word "balance" is correctly used, because, regardless of the length of time, the totals of credits and debits always balance. The claims that Americans may hold against foreigners as a result of sales of merchandise may exceed similar claims of foreigners against residents of the United States, thus giving the United States a favorable balance of trade; but the credits are adjusted in numerous ways; for example, by importing foreign evidences of indebtedness (foreign lending by Americans), by gold imports, by tourist expenditures abroad, and by shipping services.

The methods of international settlement are numerous, but, in the aggregate, all receipts and payments must balance. Because of the fluctuations in value of foreign currencies, it is impossible to gather information on some transactions (for example, operations of the Stabilization Fund, mailing currency in letters by immigrants, and unreported exports) and to evaluate with exactness others; therefore, the balance of payment statement contains an item representing credits or debits unaccounted for. The Bureau of Foreign and Domestic Commerce defines the balance of international payments statement as "an itemized account of the commercial and financial transactions conducted, within a stated period of time, by all people of that nation with the people of all other nations."[6]

The concept of balance of payment may be visualized by studying Chart VI, which shows for 1934, 1935, 1936, 1937, and 1938 the

CHART VI

BALANCE OF INTERNATIONAL PAYMENTS, 1934-38

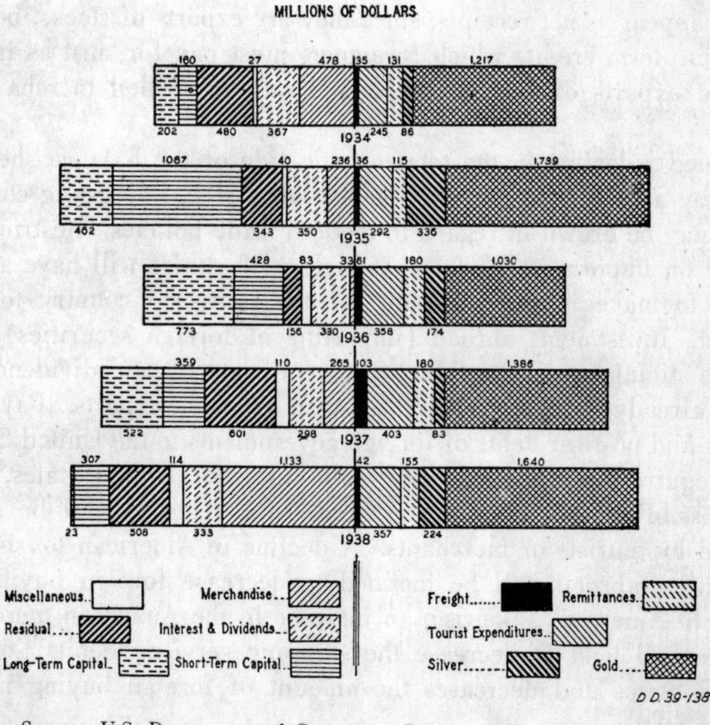

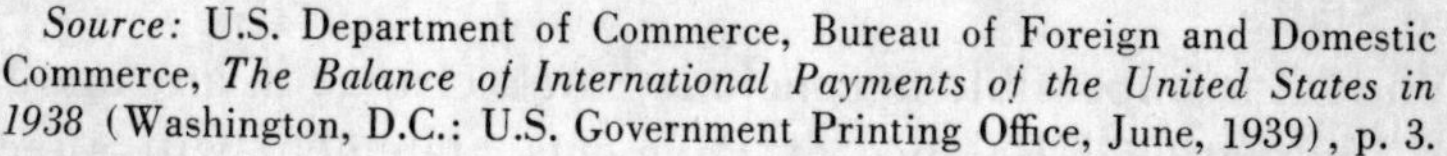
Source: U.S. Department of Commerce, Bureau of Foreign and Domestic Commerce, *The Balance of International Payments of the United States in 1938* (Washington, D.C.: U.S. Government Printing Office, June, 1939), p. 3.

net receipts and the net payments to the left and right of a dividing line that appears in the center. If the chart is correctly drawn, the size of the bar on the left, showing the total net receipts, will be

[6] This definition appears in the yearly bulletins of the U.S. Department of Commerce, Bureau of Foreign and Domestic Commerce, *Balance of International Payments of the United States.*

exactly the same as the size of the bar on the right, showing total net payments for 1934 or for any other one year. Likewise the total of the net receipts will equal exactly the total of the net payments for the five-year period. Imports of gold and silver are correctly classified as debit transactions, because they represent items requiring payments by Americans to foreign countries, just as in the case of imports of tin, rubber, or other commodities. The extent to which gold and silver have dominated net payments since 1933 is apparent. Short-term and long-term foreign capital investments in the United States appear as net receipts, since they are exports of stocks, bonds, and short-term credits which foreigners must pay for, just as in the case of exports of wheat, cotton, and other so-called merchandise items.

Since a decline in the total on one side of the balance sheet is offset by a decline in the total on the other side, interesting conclusions may be drawn in regard to modern trade policies. Restrictions placed on imports in the form of high tariff duties will have a tendency to make it more difficult for the protected country to sell abroad. Investments abroad (importing of foreign securities) will tend to stimulate exports; but payments of interest and dividends on funds already invested abroad will tend to lessen exports. Payment of war and postwar debts of foreign governments to the United States may require the collection of fewer taxes in the United States, with the possibility that part of the funds thus released will be spent abroad by tourists or merchants. A decline in American tourist expenditures abroad will be inclined to decrease foreign buying of goods in America. Likewise, an increase in the American merchant marine will tend to decrease the shipping service "debits" of the United States and decreases the amount of foreign buying in the United States.

While it is impossible to conclude how a change in any one factor in the International Balance of Payments Statement will affect the total, certain policies may be definitely classified as "promotive," while others may be described as "detractive." During the decade preceding World War II, governments adopted, to an increasing extent, the detractive types of policies, with the result that the total credits and debits for most countries decreased. Since international trade, investments, selling of securities, etc., means more efficient use of the factors of production, shrinking of the total in countries' balances of payments means a world-wide decline in real income and lower standards of living.

Equilibrium Theory of the Exchange Rate

During World War II exchange rates were pegged by government action, and the items within the balance of payments were brought under rigid control. In so far as most of the world was concerned, free trade and free exchange markets disappeared. One of three policies may be adopted by countries in their change from war to peace: (1) Countries may continue to control and restrict the demand for foreign exchange and maintain the exchange rates at the present levels; (2) they may remove the controls and permit exchange rates to seek their own levels; or (3) they may adopt a combination of the above by maintaining control over certain items in the balance of payments, such as investments, and permit exchange rates to fluctuate within certain limits above or below those now in existence.

Eventually the international goal should be to eliminate all types of government control and establish equilibrating mechanisms such as existed under the international gold standard. Although the credit and debit items in the balance of payments are always equal, this situation does not mean that underlying conditions are satisfactory. The large influx of gold during the 1930's suggests that the United States was importing too few goods, services, and securities to offset export of these items. Normally, if all countries had been on a gold standard, equilibrium would have resulted from an increase in interest rates and a decline in prices in foreign countries, which would have increased short-term investments and purchases of goods in them. At the same time lower interest rates and higher prices in the United States would have resulted in fewer short-term investments and fewer purchases in the United States. A minor factor, bringing into equilibrium the balance of payments without gold movements, would be the minor fluctuations of the rate of exchange within limits set by gold import and export points. Thus the high dollar rate in foreign countries and the low foreign rates in the United States would have encouraged American purchases and investments abroad and would have discouraged similar foreign transactions in the United States.

When countries depart from the international gold standard,

fluctuations in the exchange rate cease being a minor factor in a free economy in bringing about equilibrium in the balance of payments and become the major one. Where a drop in the rate of exchange or price of the pound sterling to the gold import point would have had only a minor influence on the international credits and debits of that country, a decline of 25 per cent would tend to increase sharply the export or credit items and decrease sharply the import or debit items. Thus an equilibrium rate of exchange would be established without gold movements being involved, and this rate, as already noted, would correspond roughly to the purchasing power parity of the two units involved.

It is apparent that if there is direct control over the items in the balance of payments and over the exchange markets, no equilibrium rate may be obtained, and gold movements such as those which took place during the 1930's may continue indefinitely. But, if all controls are removed, rates of exchange may fluctuate widely, with a depressing effect on international trade. If depreciation is expected, it would be to the advantage of exporters to delay exports and of importers to hasten imports. Thus speculation in commodities would tend to replace normal trade. Because of the fear of inflation, "flights of capital" would be encouraged. Countries most in need of capital because of war damage would probably be the most affected by the loss of capital, for the fear of inflation would tend to be greater here than in other countries.

QUESTIONS AND PROBLEMS

1. Before World War II, in what two ways were international and domestic transactions similar? What changes took place during World War II?
2. What are the technical differences between domestic and foreign exchange?
3. Identify: "risk of exchange," "bill of exchange," "rate of exchange."
4. "What then is foreign exchange? Foreign exchange is direct barter of monies used in different countries. E.g., Exchanging dollars directly for pounds, francs, marks, yens, etc." (Coughlin, Rev. Charles E., *Money: Questions and Answers.* p. 154). Is this a good definition of foreign exchange? Can you do better? Try it.
5. The general principle of foreign exchange is, "that bills of exchange drawn on any particular place constitute a new kind of article, subject

to the laws of supply and demand" (Jevons, *Money and the Mechanism of Exchange*, p. 296). Explain.

6. "Foreign exchange transactions are but transfers of book-credit that appear on banks' books as deposits, even though gold is used." Explain.
7. Identify: "mint par of exchange" and "gold points."
8. What relationship exists between gold movements and interest rates?
9. What is meant by purchasing power parity?
10. Does the purchasing power parity theory apply to exchange between countries on a gold standard as well as to countries on paper standards?
11. Jevons writes: "Thus the cost of transmitting specie is the limit to the premium on bills." Why? Is it also the limit on the discount on bills? What bills? (Sight, time, or cable?) (*Money and the Mechanism of Exchange*, p. 297).
12. The "financial question of the day was: whether we should carry on the [Civil] War on specie currency, low prices, and small imports, or on paper issues, high prices, and heavy imports" (Sumner, W. G., *A History of American Currency*, p. 193). Pick out the exchange fallacy in the foregoing statement.
13. "Many of the advantages which theoretically should have resulted from international depreciation of currency have not materialized because of the steps taken by countries to protect their domestic markets from foreign competition." Explain.
14. "Most of the advantages of being off the gold standard are illusory and those that are not illusory are temporary." Explain.
15. Explain the existence of a "free exchange market" and a "restricted" or "official exchange market" in London. Are the prices for dollar exchange the same? Explain.
16. Discuss, "Currency devaluation is a wholesale erection of trade barriers. Import and export duties, quotas, and barter arrangements are kindred weapons of a retail sort" (Burgess, W. R., *Banking*, January, 1939, p. 92).
17. What is the Equilibrium Theory of the Exchange Rate?
18. "The greatest single contribution that the United States can make to world stability is to maintain the integrity of the American dollar. This can be done only by the maintenance of the fixed value of the dollar in terms of gold and the attainment as soon as practicable of a sound national budget and other sound internal policies. The adoption of a trade policy greatly reducing restrictions on United States imports would also contribute to world stability" (*Bretton Woods Proposals*, Report of the Committee on International Monetary Matters of the New York Bankers Association, p. 20). Do you agree? Why?

REFERENCES

Bloomfield, A. I. *The British Balance-of-Payments Problem.* Princeton: International Finance Section, Princeton University, 1945.

Brown, W. A., Jr. *The International Gold Standard: Reinterpreted 1914-1934.* 2 vols. New York: National Bureau of Economic Research, Inc., 1940.

Cassel, Gustav. *Money and Foreign Exchange after 1914*, pp. 137-86. New York: Macmillan Co., 1938.

Einzig, Paul, *International Gold Movements.* 2d ed. London: Macmillan & Co., Ltd., 1931.

Ellsworth, P. T. *International Economics,* Part I; Part II, chap. xi. New York: Macmillan Co., 1938.

Graham, F. D. "Recent Movements in International Price Level and the Doctrine of Purchasing Power Parity," *American Statistical Association Journal,* Supplement, Vol. XXX (March, 1935).

Haberler, G. "The Choice of Exchange Rates after the War," *American Economic Review,* Vol. XXXV (June, 1945), pp. 308-18.

Hall, N. F. *The Exchange Equalization Account.* London: Macmillan & Co., Ltd., 1935.

Harris, S. E. *Exchange Depreciation.* Cambridge: Harvard University Press, 1936.

Hayek, F. A. *Monetary Nationalism and International Stability.* New York: Longmans, Green & Co., 1939.

Heilperin, M. A. *International Monetary Economics,* chaps. iv-x. New York: Longmans, Green & Co., 1939.

League of Nations. *Second Interim Report of the Gold Delegation of the Financial Committee.* 1931.

McKinley, G. W. "The Residual Item in the Balance of International Payments," *American Economic Review,* Vol. XXXI, No. 2 (June, 1941), pp. 308-16.

Nurkse, R. *Conditions of International Monetary Equilibrium.* Princeton: International Finance Section, Princeton University, 1945.

Pumphrey, L. M. "The Exchange Equalization Account of Great Britain, 1932-1939: Exchange Operations," *American Economic Review,* Vol. XXXII (December, 1942), pp. 803-16.

Silverstein, N. L. "Effects of the American Revaluation on Prices and Export Trade," *American Economic Review.* Vol. XXVII, No. 2 (June, 1937).

Taylor, A. E. *The Need for a "Settler" of Balances in International Payments.* New York: The Monetary Standards Inquiry, 1943.

United States Department of Commerce, Bureau of Foreign and Domestic Commerce. *The Balance of International Payments of the United States.* Annual Reports.

United States Tariff Commission. *Depreciated Exchange and International Trade.* Washington, D.C.: U.S. Government Printing Office, 1922.

Wright, L. *The History and Mechanism of the Exchange Equalization Account.* New York: Macmillan Co., 1939.

Whittlesey, C. R. *International Monetary Issues.* New York: McGraw-Hill Book Co., Inc., 1937.

Young, J. P. *Inter-war Currency Lessons.* New York: Monetary Standards Inquiry, 1944.

Chapter XIII

INTERNATIONAL MONETARY AND BANKING ORGANIZATIONS

Introduction

Although the basic documents and principles involved in the financing of foreign trade have not changed during the years since 1930, the conditions under which foreign trade is carried on have undergone decided changes. The automatic gold standard that gave the chief commercial nations of the world a common standard of value and relatively stable exchange rates has disappeared.

The attempts to restore the international gold standard after World War I met with but temporary success. Nations failed to appreciate that it was necessary, first of all, to set their own financial houses in order before currency values could be stabilized. Without domestic stability, foreign stability in the value of money could not be maintained. Attempts to stabilize were delayed; and, as a result, the economic chaos was greater following the war than during the war itself. Individual nations took action in fixing their currency units without much, if any, consideration as to the effects on other nations. Thus by undervaluing the franc in 1926 (formal stabilization was in 1928) and the dollar in 1934, the French and the United States governments attracted gold from other countries, thereby adding to their domestic and foreign exchange problems.

In its broadest sense, "exchange control" means any measure used by a government or governmental agency to influence foreign exchange rates. The history of central banking provides many illustrations of the use of the discount policy, open market operations, and other devices to influence the money market and foreign exchange rates. However, these devices were used to affect the exchange markets indirectly, through their effects on the demand for and the supply of money. For example, it was stated that the Bank of England could pull gold out of the ground by raising its discount rate.

Although the Federal Reserve banks had sufficient authority to deal actively in the foreign exchange markets, their role has usually been a passive one, limited to the purchase and sale of bills of exchange under certain conditions. This position of the Federal Reserve banks was probably justified by the special hazards of holding foreign bills during periods of extreme fluctuations in the exchange rates. For example, the losses of the Bank of France were so great in 1931 that a governmental payment, under a preceding guarantee, had to be made to maintain its solvency.

Since the abandonment of the international gold standard, governments have taken the leading role in controlling the foreign exchange markets. By the middle of the 1930's foreign exchange markets were subject to two types of control—indirect control, which affected the market as a whole, and direct control, which affected specific transactions in the markets. The first type aimed to preserve free exchange markets within a framework dominated by such governmental agencies as the American Exchange Stabilization Fund and the older British Equalization Fund.

The Tripartite Agreement of September, 1936, which was discussed in Chapter V, aimed to stabilize exchange rates by multilateral actions among the adherents to the declarations. In addition to calling for consultative action on exchange policy, the declarations also called for an expansion of international trade and the future abolition of the trade quota system and exchange control. The Tripartite Agreement proved insufficient for the needs of the participating countries before World War II, and it was even less adequate during the war. So the indirect type of control over foreign exchange markets and foreign trade was abandoned in favor of the direct type.

Direct Foreign Exchange Control

The extreme form of exchange control consists of state control over the exchange markets and complete, or almost complete, suppression of free dealings in exchanges. This form of control was initiated in Germany in 1931, was introduced in most warring countries at the outbreak of World War II, and is the type which has usually been introduced in order to support a foreign exchange value of a currency at a level above its purchasing power. Such a policy tends to discourage exports and to promote imports. In order to pay for imports, a country must have foreign exchange. Under Lend-Lease this was provided with United States government credit; but in transactions among other nations purchases could be made only with bank credit, which was usually blocked until after the war, or with proceeds from foreign sales of securities or other assets.

Controlling Demand.—If goods are imported by individuals, usually under authority of a government license, foreign exchange must be obtained through or from a foreign exchange control agency. The selling price is fixed by the control agency and may vary according to the type of transaction that is being financed; that is, a rate of 40 cents may be applied to commercial transactions and a rate of 25 cents for tourist expenditures.

The control authority must decide upon the apportionment of the supply of foreign exchange for commodity imports, debt service, tourist expenditures, and other items. The next type of decision involves the distribution of the funds among different countries. This power involves all types of international favoritism, often in violation of existing most-favored-nation clauses in existing treaties. For example, applicants for exchange who want to buy goods from X country may be refused, while applicants who want to buy from merchants in Y country will be sold exchange.

Further complications arise because of the question of the distribution of available exchange among different commodities. These decisions make it possible to favor certain industries at the expense of others, to favor industry at the expense of agriculture, and to bring about a redistribution of national income among the domestic classes. For example, manufacturers of chemicals may be permitted to buy abroad, while manufacturers of cloth may be forced into bankruptcy because they cannot secure raw materials from abroad. Finally, the exchange authority must allot exchange among competing business firms, a source of one of the most vicious types of abuses in exchange regulation. For example, Firm A is permitted to buy exchange and therefore raw materials abroad, but Firm B is denied foreign exchange and is forced to get along with inferior domestic substitutes, or change the nature of or liquidate its business.

Thus arbitrary administrative decisions are substituted for the old system of free exchange, in which price served as the mechanism of allotment. In the free system of exchange, if the total demand for foreign exchange for all purposes is greater than the total supply, its price rises until supply and demand are balanced; therefore, there is no problem of discriminating among buyers in different fields and among individuals in the same field. "The less urgent needs are excluded by price, and there is no direct interference in the process of production and trade. Vested interests do not grow up which are dependent on the continuance of an artificial system of control and allocation and which accordingly resist any attempt to change that system."[1]

Controlling Supply.—The control agency not only controls the use of foreign exchange but also the supply. Exports are the most important source of supply, and the owners of the resulting bills of exchange are required to sell all or part of them to the exchange authorities at a rate fixed by the control agency. Exchange is then available to finance governmental payments abroad and to sell to importers and to others. If the plan in operation permits the exporter to retain a part of his foreign exchange funds, he may use them to buy goods abroad, or he may sell them to an importer at a negotiated price, usually above the official buying price. Such private transactions are carefully watched in order to prevent transfers of funds abroad, where they would be used to buy back debts at bargain prices, to invest, to build up bank balances, or for other purposes not in keeping with the governments' official economic policy.

In addition to the seizure of bills of exchange resulting from exports, foreign exchange holdings of the exchange authorities may be increased by requiring all persons to report and to surrender title to all bank balances abroad, all foreign securities, and other assets, including in certain countries even real estate. In this way the United Kingdom and France were able to accumulate an important foreign exchange "war chest."

The export of the national hand-to-hand currency of exchange-control countries is permitted in small amounts, and its import is forbidden or limited. Thus soldiers going from the United States to Great Britain could take any amount of United States currency, but they were limited as to the amount of Bank of England notes they could bring into Great Britain. Before the war tourist expenditures of nationals and of other residents abroad were limited and carefully watched for evidence of hidden assets. American tourists within exchange-control countries were permitted to declare, retain, and take out American currency in their possession, but not in excess of the amount declared; and all that was spent within the country was usually acquired as a source of foreign exchange.

[1] League of Nations, Committee composed of members of the Economic and Financial Committee, *Report on Exchange Control* (1938), p. 39.

During the war, foreign countries preferred that United States troops use only indigenous currency in order to keep United States dollars out of the black market. Furthermore, by supplying the United States Army with funds for troop pay and other purposes, they received United States government credit and hence claims to foreign exchange in the United States. Although yellow-seal dollars and Hawaiian-stamped dollars received much publicity because of their novelty, only a relatively small amount of them was used in foreign areas. The types of currency printed prior to liberation for the use of the military forces are being treated as types of indigenous currency. Thus the French, Belgian, Netherlands, and other governments are receiving Lend-Lease credits for the amounts borrowed for the use of the United States Army. The present policy is to hold the German government responsible for redemption of the Allied Military Mark, for which it will be given credit when occupation, reparations, and other charges are made against it.

Controlling Investment Transfers.—In the balance of international payments statements, the second most important group of items are short-term and long-term capital and interest and dividend payments. As short-term capital movements are the most dynamic among all items in the balance of payments, exchange control was first introduced in many countries in order to prevent these short-term debt transfers from causing exchange disturbances. Governments commonly decreed that nationals must pay their interest and principal charges into a fund at the central bank. These payments were made in domestic currency calculated at the debtor country's official exchange rate. The coupons of foreign bondholders were then presented to the central bank for payment.

In the case of Germany, bank balances and acceptance credit outstanding when exchange control was introduced were regulated under standstill agreements signed by debtor and creditor institutions. Under the auspices of the central bank, arrangements were made for payment of interest, commissions, and some repayment of principal. As in the case of long-term debts, the conditions under which these funds could be utilized varied greatly; but usually these "blocked accounts" were used for tourists' requirements and purchase of goods within the country where they were held. The use of exchange control reduced the dangers of a drain of foreign funds and a flight of domestic capital to other monetary centers.

No international banker will place funds in an exchange-control country where he knows restrictions will be placed on their withdrawal. Before capital movements may be expected, confidence in the future of exchange-control countries must be re-established. Experience suggests that this may not be expected so long as these countries follow any policy of exchange control which prevents the creditor from receiving in free exchange interest, dividends, and instalment or other payments on principal. Therefore, exchange control tends to restrict international lending and to shrink the total volume of transactions involved in the balance of international payments statement. This situation may be corrected in part in the long-term credit field by the guaranteeing of credits by the International Bank for Reconstruction and Development.

In recovering funds abroad, American banks have been forced to take losses other than those due to interest concessions made by private agreements. "Blocked funds" held by central banks have been sold at a heavy discount to those who wanted to travel or to buy goods in the country where the blocked currency could be spent. In addition, the foreign bonds held in the United States were usually sold at a discount, which made their repatriation very profitable. Although these purchases were usually forbidden, many illicit transfers were made, and the debts of many exchange-control nationals (private and public corporations and others) were reduced at a cost of but a fraction of their original value.

Exchange-control authorities were charged with practices which drove prices of their nations' bonds to low levels in foreign markets so that they could be repurchased at heavy losses to American bondholders; but their answer was that illicit purchases prevented even greater losses by creating a demand without which the bond prices might have been lower. Exchange control has been particularly harmful to American creditors, because the United States normally has a favorable balance of trade with the most important exchange-control countries. This means that the demand for blocked currency is not great enough, relative to the supply, to permit its sale at or near the official exchange rate. This situation may call for a fundamental change in the United States foreign trade policy from one in which exports exceed imports ($10,000,000,000 in 1944) to one in which imports are more important.

While the United States and other countries with relatively free exchange have suffered from exchange-control practices of foreign countries, evidence supports the conclusion that exchange-control countries are the chief losers. As noted, they tend to suffer from loss of the use of foreign capital, and, in addition, both imports and exports tend to decrease, while production tends to decline. "In consequence the total national income in a country resorting to exchange-control is likely to be lower than it would have been had it allowed its currency to fall to an equilibrium level."[2]

Methods of Trade Control

Parallel to restrictions placed on the foreign exchange markets were restrictions placed on foreign trade. Some of these were introduced by countries in order to protect domestic industry from foreign competition resulting from international depreciation of currency. Thus certain countries adopted a sliding duty system, the duties increasing or decreasing in percentages equal to the changes in value of the monetary unit of the country in which the goods originated.

An even more rigid control of imports was obtained by the quota system. Four different quota systems were used: (1) Some countries merely indicated the number or value of goods which could be imported, without any attempt to prorate the volume among the importers at home or exporters abroad. This system favored exporters in neighboring countries because of the nearness to the market and was soon abandoned. (2) Some countries decided upon the number of units of certain foreign goods they would import during a year and then prorated this quantity among the nations from whom they had bought in the past. Thus, irrespective of the price advantage which a foreign country may have had, owing to depreciated currency, only a given number of units originating therein could be imported. (3) Even more rigid control resulted after the adoption of the policy of issuing import licenses covering in each case specific importation of goods. (4) Finally, control was developed on a bilateral basis in which imports were regulated by agreements either with the governments of the exporting countries or directly with the exporters. The last two systems avoided much of the undesirable scramble for trade which had developed among the exporters in different countries and those in the same country.

[2] *Ibid.*, p. 49.

The increase in import duties and the quota system both contributed to the decline in international trade. Both tended to bring on retaliation from other countries, and many charges of unfair administration were made.

Some of the steps taken by exchange-control governments increased the volume of foreign trade. One of the most important promotive steps taken was that resulting from "clearing agreements," or "barter transactions." In brief, trade agreements covering general or specific imports and exports were entered into between two countries whereby, for example, so many bushels of wheat would be received in exchange for so many tractors and automobiles. Buyers in each country paid for the goods purchased by remitting to their central bank or some other governmental agency. From the funds received, each control agency paid exporters in their own country for the goods shipped to the other country. Thus goods were purchased and sold without the use of foreign exchange, settlement having been made by domestic drafts upon or paid to the control agency. Final settlement of any balance between the two countries was made according to arrangements between the two exchange authorities.

Many countries which lacked foreign exchange were able to increase their volume of foreign business by use of these clearing agreements. For example, manufacturing countries were able to secure an outlet for their finished products, while agricultural nations were able to secure a market for their goods. Naturally such clearing agreements led to the development of international trade along bilateral lines between the two parties involved.

A major problem inherent in clearing agreements was that of arriving at the correct exchange rate to be used. Trade was often carried on at artificially high prices, because high prices paid for agricultural products were offset by high prices received for industrial goods. This tying-together of the economies of two countries at an artificially high price level tended to deprive them of freedom of action in dealing with other countries operating at the international price level. This was particularly true of the smaller of the two countries because of the relatively greater importance of its trade with the larger country, and therefore its economy suffered a greater shock when other markets had to be found.

Thus in many ways foreign trade, foreign investments, and even foreign travel have been placed in a strait jacket by devious devices. Under such conditions normal functioning of exchange markets is impossible. It is generally realized that the losses from international depreciation of currency offset the temporary export advantages resulting from depreciation. The ability to undersell competitors is nullified by preferential tariffs, increases in import duties, series of quotas, and exchange regulations. The effect is a decrease, rather than an increase, in international trade. In addition, depreciated currency forces consumers and other buyers to pay more for imported goods. These increased costs alone tend to offset all theoretical advantages from any increase in export trade. It is an extremely shortsighted policy for a nation as well as an individual to sell cheap and buy dear, which, in brief, is the policy followed by a country which has depreciated its currency more than other countries. Finally, it must be recognized that creditor countries which have depreciated their currencies have automatically reduced foreign indebtedness to them by the percentage of the depreciation, provided other things remain the same.

Preliminary Postwar International Monetary Planning

In approaching the postwar exchange problem, it is apparent that, if the financing of international trade, investments, and travel is to be carried on with the minimum of financial risks, fairly stable rates of exchange and free exchange markets are requisites. An international arrangement should be created whereby rights to foreign currencies may be bought and sold freely at prices that are fairly stable. This would relieve merchants, bankers, and others from the fear that their receipts would be reduced by depreciation of currency in terms of their own or that their receipts would be blocked and would have to be spent according to the dictates of a foreign government. By their nature these problems are international in character and require international co-operation for their solution.

The policy of the United States has been to secure the elimination of discriminatory and restrictive exchange practices and to secure international co-operation in the maintenance of stable exchange rates. The United States Treasury, through its Stabilization Fund, has made bilateral agreements with a number of countries to help maintain exchange stability. These agreements provide for purchase of the other country's currency (under repurchase agreements and at the same rate of exchange) in order to stabilize the dollar rate of exchange. These agreements, as well as those of the multilateral tripartite declaration of September, 1936, provide for consultation on economic problems and provide that the exchange rate would not be changed without prior consultation with the Treasury.

Even during the war plans were drawn for postwar stabilization of currency. In 1941 Mr. H. D. White presented to the Secretary of the Treasury a memorandum of a plan for the International Stabilization Fund and a Bank for Reconstruction and Development. Lord Keynes proposed an International Clearing Union, and Canada and other countries submitted similar plans. However, most of the debates were over the merits of the White and Keynes plans, which ultimately were submitted to the Ministers of Finance of the United Nations. After many discussions among the technical representatives of thirty nations, a joint statement was issued in April, 1944, recommending an International Monetary Fund.

In July, 1944, at Bretton Woods, New Hampshire, representatives of forty-four nations met and approved the Articles of Agreements for the International Monetary Fund and the International Bank for Reconstruction and Development. Although the actions of the representatives were not binding on their respective governments, thirty-five nations had approved by the end of 1945.[3] Denmark, which was not represented at the Bretton Woods Conference, was the forty-fifth nation to be included in the plan. Now that the agreements are in force, each approving nation appoints a governor of the Fund and a governor of the Bank. Since the United States had the largest quota (Fund) and the largest subscription (Bank), it had the responsibility of calling the first meeting of each of the boards. This meeting was held in March, 1946, in Savannah, Georgia. Although Russia had not approved of the agreements, it, as well as other nations who were not members, had observers at the Confer-

[3] The United States was the first country to take action on the agreements. *Public Law 171*, 79th Cong., or the Bretton Woods Agreement Act, was approved by the President on July 31, 1945. The governments of Russia, Australia, New Zealand, Venezuela, Haiti, El Salvador, Nicaragua, Panama, and Liberia failed to approve of the Agreement. During the course of the first meetings of the Boards of Governors (started March 8, 1946, at Wilmington Island near Savannah, Georgia) El Salvador, Nicaragua, Panama, and Denmark were admitted to membership; Washington, D.C., was selected as the site of the Fund and Bank; and directors were selected, salaries determined, and other matters pertaining to organization were settled. See *Federal Reserve Bulletin*, April, 1946, pp. 361-72.

ence. The member nations voted to give the ten nonjoiners until the end of 1946 to become charter members. Mr. Camille Gutt of Belgium was elected "managing director" of the Fund and Mr. Eugene Meyer of the United States was elected president of the bank.

International Monetary Fund

Purposes.—The purposes of the International Monetary Fund are: (1) to promote international monetary co-operation through a permanent institution which provides the machinery for consultation and collaboration on international monetary problems; (2) to facilitate the expansion and balanced growth of international trade, thereby contributing to high levels of employment and real income; (3) to promote exchange stability and avoid competitive exchange depreciation; (4) to assist in the establishment of a multilateral system of payments in respect to current transactions, thereby eliminating foreign exchange restrictions that hamper the growth of trade; (5) to provide members with resources with which to correct temporary maladjustments in their balances of payments; and (6) to shorten the duration and to lessen the disequilibrium in the international balance of payments.[4]

Quotas.—The Fund is to be financed by participating countries, with each country's quota fixed according to the relative importance of its pre-war national income and international trade. Of the $8,800,000,000 total, the five major powers' contributions are as follows: United States, $2,750,000,000;[5] United Kingdom, $1,300,000,000; Russia, $1,200,000,000; China, $550,000,000; and France, $450,000,000. Although the contributions are measured in dollars, they will be made in gold and the currencies of the participating countries. The part of a nation's quota that will be payable in gold will equal one-fourth of its total gold holdings, or 10 per cent of its gold holdings and dollar balances, whichever is the smaller.[6]

---

[4] *Articles of Agreement of the International Monetary Fund,* Art. 1.

[5] The Bretton Woods Agreement Act directs the Secretary of the Treasury to use $1,800,000,000 of the Stabilization Fund and to borrow $950,000,000 under the Second Liberty Bond Act to pay the United States quota. See Sec. 7 of *Public Law 171,* 79th Cong.

[6] Holdings of gold and dollar balances will be measured as of the date on which the Fund notifies members that it will begin exchange operations. It is estimated that total gold subscriptions will be $1,643,000,000, of which two-fifths will be subscribed by the United States.

Management.—The Fund will be managed by a Board of Governors (one from each member nation) and twelve or more executive directors.[7] Five directors would be appointed by the five members having the largest quotas and seven selected by the other members. Policies will be carried out by a Managing Director and his staff. Voting power of member countries depends in part on the size of their quotas, each member having 250 votes plus an additional vote for each $100,000 of its quota. The United States would have about 28 per cent of the total of 99,000 votes, the United Kingdom about 13.5 per cent, Russia, 12.5 per cent, China, 5.8 per cent, France, 4.8 per cent, and India, 4 per cent. Decisions do not always depend upon a majority; for example, a change in quotas requires a four-fifths vote, and this would give the United States a veto power.[8] It also provided that, in important questions relating to loans, a country's voting power increases on a sliding scale as the loans of its currency increase, with a corresponding decrease in the voting power of borrowing countries. If the dollar is borrowed freely from the Fund, the maximum vote of the United States may reach 35 per cent of the total.[9]

Exchange Rates.—The first function of the Fund will be to fix the rates of exchange of each member nation, with the latter's co-operation, in terms of gold or the United States dollar of the present weight and fineness. After the par value of a member's currency has been established, the Fund will provide a margin above and below which gold may not be bought and sold. Exchange transactions between currencies will also be subject to limitations, for example, the range for sight or spot exchange being 1 per cent above or below par.

The Fund does not place the members on the gold standard as it

[7] See Article XII for provisions for Organization and Management of the Fund. The Bretton Woods Agreements Act (*Public Law 171*, 79th Cong.) provides that the United States representatives be appointed by the President with the advice and consent of the Senate. These include a governor and alternate of the Fund, who shall also serve as governor and alternate of the Bank, and an alternate for each of the executive directors.

[8] Unless Congress by law authorizes such action, the President or any other person or agency representing the United States shall not propose or consent to any change in the quota of the United States (Sec. 5[a], *Public Law 171*, 79th Cong.).

[9] In order to co-ordinate the policies and operations of the representatives of the United States on the Fund and the Bank with all the agencies of the United States government on lending and other matters, the Bretton Woods Agreements Act provides for the establishment of a National Advisory Council on International Monetary and Financial Problems, consisting of the Secretary of the Treasury as chairman, the Secretary of State, the Secretary of Commerce, the chairman of the Board of Governors of the Federal Reserve System, and the chairman of the Board of Directors of the Export-Import Bank in Washington.

existed before 1930. It is recognized that changes in rates may be necessary, and the procedure whereby they may be made is provided. No change may be made except on a member's own proposal, and members agree not to propose any change except to correct a fundamental disequilibrium in the balance of payments. Member countries, after consultation with the Fund but without the latter's concurrence, may increase or decrease the par value of their currencies by 10 per cent from those initially established.[10] A proposed change of more than 10 per cent must either be concurred in or objected to by the Fund within 72 hours after a member makes the request. Since other countries must be protected from the ruinous effects of competitive depreciation of exchanges, concurrence will follow only if there is a fundamental reason for the change. If such a change is made without the Fund's concurrence, it has authority to declare the country ineligible to use the Fund's resources and to force it to withdraw from membership. There is a special arrangement that permits the Fund to make a uniform proportionate change in the par value of all currency. This change must have the approval of each country which has a quota equal to more than one-tenth of the total, that is, the United States, the United Kingdom, and Russia. Since this change would mean a change in the value of domestic currency in terms of gold, it may be refused by a country provided it notifies the Fund within 72 hours.[11]

Exchange Control.—Members agree not to engage in discriminatory currency arrangements or multiple currency practices without the approval of the Fund. Only with the approval of the Fund may members impose restrictions on the use of exchange in making payments for transfers for current transactions, including those due for trade, services, short-term banking and credit activities, interest on loans and net income of other investments, amortization of loans or depreciation of direct investments, and moderate remittances for family living expenses. On the other hand, current transactions do not include payments for the purpose of transferring capital. Neither do member countries agree to remove trade control practices which

[10] The provisions pertaining to "Par value of currencies" and changes thereof are contained in Article IV of Articles of Agreement of the International Monetary Fund.

[11] Congress, in the Bretton Woods Agreement Act, prohibited, without its authorization, the President or any other person or agency acting for the United States to propose or agree to any change in the par value of the United States dollar or any general change in the par value of currencies.

may be used along with control of capital movements to influence balances of payment items. Furthermore, any member, after consultation with the Fund, may impose temporary restrictions on operations in any scarce currency."[12] Starting three years after the Fund begins operations, the Fund must issue annual reports on the restrictions still in force. After five years any member still imposing such restrictions must consult with the Fund and the latter may then take action to force withdrawal of the restrictions.

Transactions.—The ordinary transactions in exchanges will continue to be effected through private agencies. Only when there is a shortage of foreign currencies will the market come to the central authorities for help, and then the latter will apply to the Fund. Transactions with the Fund are through each member's central bank, treasury, or similar agency and the Fund deals only with or through the same agencies.

The Fund may be compared to a pool of dollars, pounds, francs, etc., contributed by all members to finance certain current needs.[13] Thus France may add French francs and withdraw dollars with which to buy goods in the United States. Similarly other countries may add their currencies to the pool and withdraw dollars for making purchases in the United States; and the United States may add dollars to the pool and withdraw francs to buy goods in France.

If and when a member country applies for a certain type of foreign exchange, usually it will be provided by the Fund if the latter has not given notice that its holding of this currency has become scarce or if the transaction would not increase the amount of the applicant's currency in the Fund by more than 25 per cent of its total quota during the preceding 12 months[14] or by more than 200 per cent of its total quota.

[12] The United States representatives in the Fund are forbidden by Congress to vote in favor of a declaration that the United States dollar is a scarce currency without the prior approval of the Advisory Council on International Monetary and Financial Problems.

[13] The Bretton Woods Agreement Act authorized the Secretary of the Treasury to borrow a total of $4,125,000,000 to finance the Fund and the Bank. Since this sum is in addition to the $1,800,000,000 in the Stabilization Fund that is to be used to pay the United States subscription, the amount already authorized by Congress is $5,925,000,000. Without the approval of Congress, neither the President nor any other person or agency may subscribe to additional shares of stock of the Bank, make any loan to the Fund or the Bank, or vote for an increase of the capital stock of the Bank (Sec. 5 [c], [e], *Public Law 171*, 79th Cong.).

[14] This rule applies only if the applicant's currency in the Fund is above 75 per cent or if the transaction would bring it above 75 per cent of its quota.

In addition to the restrictions on borrowing, there is a requirement that qualified members whose currencies in the Fund are equal to or above 75 per cent of their quotas must make an annual cleanup in whole or in part of their borrowings by repurchasing with gold or foreign exchange part of their currencies in the Fund. Their ability to repurchase is measured by their monetary reserve positions at the end of the year. If reserves have remained the same, they must repurchase one-half of their borrowings; and, if reserves have changed, they are obligated to make an additional adjustment for this change by an amount equal to one-half the increase or one-half the decrease (plus or minus). If these adjustments reduce the monetary reserves of a member country below a certain level, they do not apply.

It may be that a country's reserve position has been improved by transactions in a member's currency (or gold), through a third country. In this case it is under obligation to use these assets to repurchase its own currency from the Fund. Thus, if France gains dollar credits by sales to Argentina, it is under obligation to use these assets to repurchase francs in the Fund. The purpose of this provision is to keep the Fund supplied with the currency (or gold) in wide demand by the members. Another provision that would tend to increase the gold assets is the requirement that members acquire currency with gold payments through the Fund if there are no disadvantages in doing so.

Charges.—The charges made against members are arranged so as to discourage the continuous use of the Fund as a source of foreign exchange. The rates charged members increase with the time and with the amount borrowed. Thus, for an amount not more than 25 per cent in excess of a quota, there is: no charge for three months, one-half per cent per annum for the next nine months, and thereafter an increase in the charge of one-half of 1 per cent for each subsequent year.[15] All charges, including interest, service charges of three-fourths of 1 per cent,[16] and a handling charge for gold, are payable in gold and are based on the par value of the exchange.

Conclusions.—Because of its nature, the Fund has been subject to careful analysis both at home and abroad. In general, there is no

[15] Goldenweiser, E A., and Bourneuf, Alice, "Bretton Woods Agreements," *Federal Reserve Bulletin*, September, 1944, p. 858.

[16] This may be lowered to ½ or increased to 1 per cent by the Fund.

quarrel with its aims, but there have been doubts expressed as to its successful operation. The Fund is an international settlement fund with assets varying as to content from day-to-day and from hour-to-hour. By operating through central banks or governmental agencies, it would balance the international exchange markets in much the same way as the Interdistrict Settlement Fund balances payments between Federal Reserve districts in the United States. In order to assist in this balancing of payments, a provision is added that each country may have an unfavorable balance equal to twice its quota. It is this lending aspect of the Fund that has been most criticized in the United States.

In the United States bankers claim that the United States quota of $2,750,000,000 will be withdrawn and will be replaced by paper currencies of questionable value. In foreign countries bankers claim that because of our high protective tariff we would not buy sufficient goods and services abroad and that, therefore, there would not be sufficient demand for their (foreign) currencies.

On the other hand, it is not the purpose of the Fund to adjust permanent disequilibrium in foreign trade. Countries in need of foreign capital, other than that needed to offset temporary disequilibria in current transactions, are supposed to obtain it from other sources, including private banks, governmental institutions such as the Export-Import Bank in Washington, and the International Bank for Reconstruction and Development.

True, over a period of years, the chief reason for the failure of the Fund might be the failure of countries with scarce currencies to lower their tariff barriers and to increase their foreign investments so as to increase the imports of goods from abroad. For example, before the dollars in the Fund become scarce, it is hoped that they will be replenished by purchases of foreign goods and services in sufficient quantity to offset the increase in other currencies in the Fund. In the long run, the United States must buy from foreign countries as much as it sells to them; and, with continued expansion of foreign loans, the volume of imports should exceed the volume of exports. Thus the United States would gradually assume the position occupied by the United Kingdom during much of the period since the Industrial Revolution, that is, of being able to live in part on its foreign investments.

International Bank for Reconstruction and Development

Organization.—The organization of the Bank is similar to that of the Fund, except that the Bank will have, in addition to the Board of Governors and twelve executive directors, an Advisory Council and Loan Committees.[17] The executive directors would select a president as head of the operating staff of the Bank, with the principal office located in the United States. Each member country would have 250 votes, plus one vote for each additional $100,000 of its capital subscription.[18] Members of the Bank would be members of the Fund, or vice versa, with those accepting membership before the end of 1945 being original members. New members may be accepted on conditions and terms the Bank may provide.

Capitalization.—The Bank is to have an authorized capital of $10,000,000,000, of which the 44 nations represented at Bretton Woods would subscribe 91 per cent. The Bank began formal operations in June, 1946. Calls for 10 per cent of the subscribed capital have been announced with 2 per cent payable in gold or the United States dollar and 8 per cent in the member countries' own currencies. At present the Bank has 38 members and a subscribed capital of $7,670,000,000 of which $3,175,000,000 is subscribed by the United States. Russia, with an authorized capital of $1,200,000,000, is the chief nonparticipating country.

Functions.—The primary function of the Bank is to stimulate long-term international lending for the benefit of member countries. The Bank may use an amount equal to one-fifth of its subscribed capital and additional borrowed funds to lend directly, either alone or in participation with other lenders. The Bank may stimulate private lending, in addition to participation, by guaranteeing loans in whole or in part. The total of these guarantees, plus direct loans, is limited to the Bank's unimpaired subscribed capital, surplus, and reserves.

Conditions under which the Bank may guarantee or make loans are limited as to procedures, in order not to infringe on the sovereignty of the nations involved. Loans will be made by the Bank to governments of member countries to finance specific projects such as

---

[17] See *Articles of Agreement of the International Bank for Reconstruction and Development,* Art. V.

[18] *Ibid.,* Art. 1.

repairing devastated areas, buying rolling stock for railroads, acquiring equipment for government-owned communications, and other projects that have been approved by the loan committees and that give reasonable evidence of being credit-worthy ventures. A private firm may borrow for similar purposes, provided its government, central bank, or some other governmental agency guarantees the repayment of the principal and the payment of interest and other charges on the loan. This means that the loans will be based directly or indirectly on the credit of the government in whose territory the project being financed is located.

The Bank imposes no conditions that the proceeds of a loan be spent in the territory of any particular member country; it will, however, endeavor to provide a country with the currency desired for expenditures in countries other than its own. As in the case of the Fund, each country will deal with the Bank only through its treasury, central bank, stabilization fund, or similar fiscal agency, and the Bank will deal with members only through the same agencies.

The United States must approve of any loan made by the Bank when the dollars paid in as part of its capital subscription are lent (and the same applies to all member countries). This gives the United States the right to pass upon the projects being financed with the dollars contributed to the Bank. Unless an agreement is made to the contrary, the principal and debt services will be repaid in dollars or gold. Approval must be given when the Bank desires to borrow in the capital markets of member countries or to denominate debts in their monetary units. If the Bank's debts are to be denominated in a foreign currency—for example, the pound sterling—the approval of that country would be necessary.

The Bank is to assist private financing by guaranteeing private loans subject to the approval of the country in whose market the funds lent originate. The Bank will be compensated for guaranteeing loans at rates of between 1 and 1½ per cent per annum for the first ten years.[19] These earnings are to be set aside as a special reserve fund to cover losses in case of defaults by borrowers. Since these loans either are made directly to governments or are guaranteed by governments, losses should be small.

Depositories.—In addition to the main office in the United States,

---

[19] This corresponds to the spread between what the Bank must pay for borrowed funds and what it receives when it relends them.

the Bank will have regional offices, the location of which will be determined by the board of directors. The central banks of member countries will be used as depositories for the currencies of these countries. For example, the Bank of France will be the depository for the French franc, the Central Bank of Canada for the Canadian dollar, and the Central Bank of China for the Chinese dollar. However, a member country may designate some other agency as the depository for its currency. Gold and other assets will be kept in depositories designated by the five members having the largest subscriptions.[20] Currency holdings may be in forms other than paper money, that is, notes or obligations of the government, of the central bank, or some other designated depository agency, provided that these obligations are nonnegotiable, noninterest bearing, and payable on demand to the International Bank for Reconstruction and Development.

Conclusion.—Although bankers have been critical of the Fund, they have generally approved of the Bank. They would favor the surrender of certain functions of the Fund to the Bank, including the responsibility for arranging and negotiating agreements among members with respect to removal of exchange control and stabilization of currencies. They would broaden the lending powers of the Bank so as to permit the making of loans for currency stabilization purposes.[21] In order to have an agency that would make loans prior to the organization of the Bank, the bankers recommended an increase in the capital of the Export-Import Bank in Washington.

Export-Import Bank

The Export-Import Bank in Washington was established in February, 1934, to assist exporters in dealing with Soviet Russia. A second one was created a month later to handle transactions with Cuba and other countries, except Russia. In 1936 the second bank was liquidated and its assets transferred to the first Export-Import Bank. Since 1936 the assets and resources of the bank have been increased by Congress, the last of these changes having been made in

[20] Initially at least one-half of the gold will be held in the country that has the principal office (United States). Congress authorized the Federal Reserve banks to act as fiscal agents for both the Bank and the Fund.

[21] American Bankers Association, *Practical International Financial Organization through Amendments to Bretton Woods Proposals*, pp. 22-25.

1945.[22] The bank is an agency of the United States, owned and financed by the government. As now organized, it has an authorized capital of $1,000,000,000. In addition, it may use its net earning and raise additional capital by sale of notes, debentures, bonds, and other obligations to the United States Treasury in amounts not to exceed at any one time two and one-half times the authorized capital—that is, $2,500,000,000.

The management of the bank is vested in a board of directors consisting of the administrator of the Foreign Economic Administration as chairman, the Secretary of State, and three persons appointed by the President of the United States by and with the consent of the Senate.[23] The term of office for appointee members is five years, and the annual salary is $12,000 (unless an appointive member is an officer of the bank and elects to take the salary of such officer). In addition, there is an ex officio advisory board consisting of the chairman, the Secretary of State, the Secretary of the Treasury, the Secretary of Commerce, and the chairman of the Board of Governors of the Federal Reserve System.[24]

The purpose of the bank is to "make loans, to discount, rediscount, or guarantee notes, drafts, bills of exchange, and other evidences of debt, or participate in the same, for the purpose of aiding in the financing and facilitating of exports and imports and the exchange of commodities between the United States and any foreign country or agencies or nationals thereof."[25] In carrying out its functions the bank is directed by Congress to supplement and encourage private capital, and not to compete with it, and to make loans for specific purposes that offer reasonable assurance of repayment. The bank is forbidden to have outstanding at any one time loans and guarantees in excess of three and one-half times its authorized capital, but the amount of business handled may exceed this figure because of

---

[22] See "Export-Import Act of 1945," *Public Law 173*, 79th Cong., which was signed by the President on July 31, 1945.

[23] If the Secretary of State deems advisable, he may designate a member of the Department of State who has been appointed by and with the advice and consent of the Senate to act for him as a director. If the Office of Foreign Economic Administration ceases to exist, the vacancy on the Board will be filled by the appointment of a fourth director.

[24] The membership of this Advisory Council is the same as the National Advisory Council on International Monetary and Financial Problems, with the exception that the Secretary of the Treasury is the chairman of the latter.

[25] Sec. 2 (*a*), *Public Law 173*, 79th Cong.

participation in lending by private banks and the sale of paper from its portfolio without endorsement or guarantee.[26]

The bank is prepared to aid in financing both imports and exports of products and the purchase of engineering and other technical services in the United States. Most experience has been with the financing of exports, for which the bank offers (1) credits for the benefit of individual exporters in the United States and (2) a line of credit to a foreign government, foreign bank, or foreign firm to facilitate the purchase of specific goods (material and equipment) and services in the United States.

When the Export-Import Bank operates in the short-term and intermediate credit fields, it will not be in competition with the International Bank for Reconstruction and Development; but, when long-term loans are made to foreign governments and to private foreign companies, its activities will be co-ordinated with the International Bank through the National Advisory Council on International Monetary and Financial Problems.

Bank for International Settlements

Between the World War I and World War II, improvements in means of transportation for ideas, as well as for goods, made the countries of the world more interdependent. A major economic disturbance in one country was certain to cause repercussions in others. International disturbances are felt first in the exchange and money markets, for there is "nothing as timid as a million dollars." Modern exchange facilities make it possible to transfer huge sums at a moment's notice from one financial market to another, and these transfers leave serious situations in their wake. Before 1914 these problems were handled in a fairly satisfactory manner by the Bank of England and other financial institutions in the London money market. Since 1914 London's dominant position in international finance has been weakened by the growth of money markets in other financial centers, particularly in New York and Paris. Even before World War II it was realized that, if international monetary problems were to be handled in a satisfactory way, there had to be cooperation among these three and other financial centers.

[26] Taylor, W. C., "General Policy Statement of the Export-Import Bank in Washington," *Federal Reserve Bulletin*, October, 1945, pp. 1000-1005.

International co-operation existed on a wide scale during World War I but disappeared temporarily soon after hostilities ceased. The rehabilitation needs of European countries were great, and capital was necessary in order to rescue central Europe from complete economic, political, and moral collapse. Loans were made under the supervision of the League of Nations, and the United States government assisted by making many rehabilitation loans. Practically all the post-World War I funded government debts to the United States (except Great Britain's) were those involving postwar loans to former Allies and enemy governments alike, involving both new and old governments. In addition, American bankers extended short-term credit and raised capital funds by selling foreign bonds to American investors.

As a result of these credit extensions and war debts, the United States had a large financial stake in Europe. It is not surprising, therefore, to find the United States playing a leading role in the work of the Dawes Commission of 1924, the Young Commission of 1929, and the organization of the Bank for International Settlements in 1929 and 1930.

Functions and Organization.—On May 20, 1930, "a bank for central banks" was opened at Basle, Switzerland. Its chief functions were (1) to promote co-operation among central banks, (2) to provide additional facilities for international financial operations, and (3) to act as trustee or agent in regard to international financial settlements (reparations).[27] The co-operation among central banks was to be obtained, in part, by bringing together governors of the central banks of seven leading countries of the world, namely, Belgium, England, France, Germany, Italy, Japan, and the United States. They were made ex officio directors of the Bank for International Settlements. Each of these directors was permitted to appoint a second director to represent industry and commerce. As long as reparations payments were handled by the Bank for International Settlements, Germany and France were each allowed one additional director. These sixteen directors were permitted to select nine more from other countries, thus making twenty-five.

The authorized capital of the Bank for International Settlements

[27] Jackson E. Reynolds, president of the First National Bank of New York, and Melvin A. Traylor, president of the First National Bank of Chicago, were active members of the Organization Committee that produced the charter of the Bank for International Settlements.

was 500,000,000 Swiss francs, divided into 200,000 shares. Each of the founders was allotted 8 per cent of the stock. Private interests in Japan and the United States purchased the allotment of these countries. Some of the central banks retained their shares, but others sold them to private investors. The remainder was distributed to other countries, thereby bringing the total number of central banks co-operating up to twenty-six, not including Japan and the United States. Private stockholders received dividends but did not have the right to vote. The shares could be sold, but the officers of the Bank for International Settlements could refuse to authorize transfer of shares from one country to another.

The Federal Reserve Bank of New York was not permitted officially to participate in the bank, but private banking groups here and in Japan did select representatives. Mr. Gates McGarrah, Federal Reserve agent of the Federal Reserve Bank of New York, and Mr. Leon Fraser were designated as the American directors. They were elected by the board of directors as the first president and vice-president of the Bank for International Settlements. When Mr. McGarrah resigned he was succeeded by Mr. Fraser as president. Thus during the first five years the Bank was under American leadership.

Powers and Restrictions.—The specific authorized operations of the Bank included the right to:

1. Buy and sell gold and gold bullion for its own account, or for the account of central banks;
2. Make secured advances to or borrow from central banks;
3. Deal in bills of exchange, Treasury bills, and other short-term securities for its own account or the account of central banks;
4. Accept deposits of various kinds from central banks and make similar deposits with central banks;
5. Act as agent or correspondent for central banks and arrange for the latter to act in similar capacity for it;
6. Carry on credit operations for banks and others, in any market, provided that the central bank in the country where the money market is located does not object;
7. Enter into special agreements with central banks to facilitate the settlement of international transactions among them. This power permits the Bank for International Settlements to operate an international gold settlement fund similar to that of the Federal Reserve System, if and when central banks decide to use it for this purpose.

The Bank for International Settlements has been denied certain rights and privileges usually granted central banks. Among other things, it may not (1) issue notes payable at sight to bearer, (2) accept bills of exchange, and (3) make advances to governments.[28]

History.—The history of the Bank for International Settlements may be divided into four parts: the organization period, the period of the international collapse of the gold standard, the period of economic nationalism, and the World War II period. During the first thirteen months of its existence, it carried on its customary functions of holding central bank reserves, of aiding in stabilizing currencies, of receiving and distributing intergovernmental payments, and of expanding its business relationships.[29] Its primary function of acting as trustee and reparation agent in the collection of German reparations was ended by the Hoover International Debt Moratorium (June 20, 1931). The Bank's revenue was not seriously affected by this change, the loss in commissions having been $183,000. A more serious blow was dealt the Bank when one country after another left the gold standard.

During the spring and summer of 1931, the officers of the Bank for International Settlements were very busy making loans to help the Bank of Spain, the Bank of Portugal, the National Bank of Yugoslavia, the National Bank of Hungary, the National Bank of Austria, the Reichsbank, and the Bank of Danzig. Syndicates of central banks and the Bank for International Settlements were formed to help the Reichsbank, the Hungarian National Bank, the Central Bank of Austria, and the Bank of England. When England left the gold standard in September, 1931, the Bank for International Settlements ceased making international loans to keep currencies tied to gold.

The nationalistic monetary policies and continued shrinkage of international trade which followed the widespread departure from the gold standard decreased any immediate prospect of the Bank's organizing and operating an effective international clearinghouse for transfer of credit. During the trying months of the economic crisis, the Bank served as a rallying place for the officials of the central banks of the world. It served then "as a common center of contact,

[28] See Dulles, Eleanor L., "The Bank for International Settlements in Recent Years," *American Economic Review*, Vol. XXVIII, No. 2 (June, 1938), pp. 299-304.

[29] "Second Annual Report of the Bank for International Settlements," *Federal Reserve Bulletin*, June, 1932, p. 366.

counsel, and collaboration." Until 1939 the Bank worked for stable exchanges and for better international monetary, credit, and trade conditions.

During World War II the Bank continued to operate, but on a reduced scale. In the discussions leading up to the Bretton Woods Agreements, official spokesmen gave little consideration to the Bank for International Settlements. The reasons are obvious. Germany, Japan, and Italy, three of the seven original members of the plan, were waging a savage war to conquer the world. France and Belgium, two of the other founders, had been conquered by Germany. Most of the other countries of Europe that had been participating in the Bank were either under German control (the Netherlands, Denmark, and Norway, for example) or in sympathy with Germany's war aims (Spain, for example).

In thinking and planning for the future, it is not surprising that the other two "charter members" of the Bank for International Settlements, the United States and Great Britain, should not consider the Bank seriously as the agency to bring about postwar stabilization of currency. The gods of war, by placing the Bank for International Settlements under the influence of the Axis, relegated the Bank to a secondary position, the future of which "as a going concern" has not been decided at this time.

QUESTIONS AND PROBLEMS

1. What is meant by "exchange control"? Distinguish between "direct" and "indirect" controls in so far as specific transactions are involved.
2. What are the specific administrative problems confronting exchange-control authorities when the available foreign exchange is sold?
3. Explain how the control agency replenishes its day-to-day supply of foreign exchange.
4. What is the significance of the following to exchange-control authorities: "Nothing is more timid than a million dollars in a foreign money market."
5. In what ways do control of foreign exchange and foreign trade affect the American foreign investments and foreign trade?
6. "It is apparent that if the financing of international trade, investments and travel is to be carried on with the minimum of financial risks, fairly stable rates of exchange and free exchange markets are requisites." Explain.
7. Distinguish between the International Monetary Fund and the Interna-

tional Bank for Reconstruction and Development. How is each managed and financed?

8. "The Fund does not place the members on the gold standard as it existed before 1930." Explain.

9. What is meant by member borrowings from the Fund? What provisions in the Articles of Agreement would tend to limit indebtedness of each member?

10. What is the chief criticism of the Fund in the United States? In certain foreign countries? Explain.

11. "It [the Fund] is a plan which recognizes and makes use of the value of gold, but which does not in any sense restore a gold standard" (Ayres, L. P., *The International Monetary Fund,* p. 10). Explain

12. "Fixed rates in the foreign exchanges are eminently desirable. A temperature of 98.6 in the human body is eminently desirable, but a rigging of the thermometer so that it will always record 98.6 regardless of the fluctuations in the temperature of a sick patient is a rather futile performance" (Anderson, B. M., *Postwar Stabilization of Foreign Exchange; The Keynes-Morgenthau Plan Condemned; Outline of a Fundamental Solution,* p. 10). Are the two comparable? Explain.

13. What is meant by the statement that the loans made by the International Bank are "based directly or indirectly on the credit of the government in whose territory the project being financed is located"?

14. Since members borrow from the Fund, in what ways will the Bank's loans be a better credit risk than those made by the Fund? Explain.

15. What are the functions of the Export-Import Bank? Does it duplicate the work of the International Bank? Explain.

16. One alternative to the Fund is the "key currency" approach that would stabilize the dollar-pound rate. Is this an alternative or an essential for the success of the Fund? (See Beckhart, B. H., *The Bretton Woods Proposals versus Alternatives,*" reprinted from the *Commercial and Financial Chronicle,* January 18, 1945, by Economists' National Committee on Monetary Policy. Also see "The United Kingdom and Postwar International Trade," "Anglo-American Trade and Financial Negotiations" and "British White Paper Published in Connection with Anglo-American Financial Agreement" in *Federal Reserve Bulletin,* January, 1946, pp. 1-27).

17. If the financial burden of postwar financial reconstruction falls upon the American taxpayer, what economic advantages may he expect in return?

18. Explain why the Bank for International Settlements was not selected as the postwar international bank to bring about stabilization of currency and to promote postwar lending for reconstruction and development.

REFERENCES*

American Bankers Association. *Practical International Organization through Amendments to Bretton Woods Proposals.* New York: American Bankers Association, 1945.

Anderson, B. M. *Postwar Stabilization of Foreign Exchange; The Keynes-Morgenthau Plan Condemned; Outline of a Fundamental Solution.* New York: Economists National Committee on Monetary Policy, 1943.

Ayers, L. P. *The International Monetary Fund.* New York: Economists National Committee on Monetary Policy, 1944.

Bernstein, E. M. "A Practical International Monetary Policy," *American Economic Review,* Vol. XXIV (December, 1944), pp. 771-84.

"Bretton Woods Agreements Act," *Federal Reserve Bulletin,* August, 1945, pp. 764-67.

de Vegh, I. "Peace Aims, Capital Requirements and International Lending," *American Economic Review,* Vol. XXXV, No. 2 (May, 1945), pp. 253-61.

Draper, E. G., and Gardner, W. R. "Goods and Dollars in World Trade," *Federal Reserve Bulletin,* November, 1944, pp. 1049-53.

Einzig, P. *Currency after the War: The British and American Plans.* Forest Hills, New York: Transatlantic Arts, 1945.

Ellis, H. S. *Bilateralism and the Future of International Trade.* Princeton: International Finance Section, Princeton University, 1944.

"Export-Import Bank Act," *Federal Reserve Bulletin,* August, 1945, pp. 764-67.

Fellner, W. "The Commercial Policy Implications of the Fund and Bank" *American Economic Review,* Vol. XXXV, No. 2 (May, 1945), pp. 262-71.

Gardner, W. R. "The Future International Position of the United States as Affected by the Fund and the Bank," *American Economic Review,* Vol. XXXV, No. 2 (May, 1945), pp. 272-88.

Goldenweiser, E. A., and Bourneuf, Alice. "Bretton Woods Agreements," *Federal Reserve Bulletin,* September, 1944, pp. 850-70.

Heuser, H. *Control of International Trade.* Philadelphia: The Blakiston Co., 1939.

League of Nations. *Enquiry into Clearing Agreements.* Geneva: agent, Columbia University Press, 1935.

League of Nations. *Report on Exchange Control.* Submitted by a committee composed of members of the Economic and Financial Committee. Geneva: agent, Columbia University Press, 1938.

* For additional reference on postwar currency plans presented in chronological order, see Turnbull, L. S., *Post War Currency Plans* (Princeton; International Finance Section, Princeton University, June, 1944).

Money and Postwar World: The Story of the United Nations Monetary and Financial Conference. New York: United Nations Information Office, 1945.

Morgan, C. *Bretton Woods: Clues to a Monetary Mystery.* Boston: World Peace Foundation, 1945.

Official Text of Final Act of United Nations Monetary and Financial Conference, Held at Bretton Woods, N. H., July 1 to 22, 1944. Reprinted from the *Commercial and Financial Chronicle,* July 27, 1944.

Report of the Committee on International Monetary Matters by New York State Bankers Association. *Bretton Woods Proposals.* New York: New York State Bankers Association, 1945.

Smithies, Arthur. "The International Bank for Reconstruction and Development," *American Economic Review,* Vol. XXXIV (December, 1944), pp. 785-97.

Szymczak, M. S. "Monetary and Credit Agreements Entered into at Bretton Woods," *Federal Reserve Bulletin,* April, 1945, pp. 306-12.

Viner, J. T., and others. *The United States in a Multi-National Economy.* Studies in American Foreign Relations. New York: Council of Foreign Relations, 1945.

Chapter XIV

CREDIT AND CREDIT INSTRUMENTS

Credit, Credit Instruments, and Credit System

Introduction.—In the preceding chapters, credit instruments used as means of payment were considered. These include: (1) printed legal tender, noninterest-bearing promises to pay of governments and banks used as hand-to-hand money; and (2) bookkeeping, nonlegal tender, noninterest-bearing promises to pay of commercial banks transferred from one name to another, on order, in the form of a personal check or a bank draft. In this chapter a more general treatment of all types of credit and credit instruments is presented. There are two reasons for introducing this treatment at the present time: (1) credit instruments are the tangible things that commercial banks and other financial institutions buy and sell; and (2) certain legal principles are introduced which are basic for an understanding of the way that financial institutions operate.

Credit.—The word "credit" has many meanings, but in economics it usually refers to the ability to obtain something of value in the present in return for a promise to pay for it at some future time. The thing received may be goods, securities, services, or money. The thing which is promised to be paid in the future may take the form of goods, securities, services, or money. In any credit transaction, there are two parties involved: the creditor, who surrenders the thing borrowed, and the debtor, who assumes the obligation to pay. Usually ownership as well as possession is transferred. Otherwise the renting of houses, where possession alone is transferred, would have to be considered a credit transaction.

Credit transactions differ from money transactions in that they leave something to be done before the transactions are completed. This is true even though payment may be made with a check, because this transaction is not completed until the check is "collected." Although such a transaction is usually regarded as a "cash transaction," a deferred payment is involved, and this time element is the distinguishing characteristic of a credit transaction. In banking and allied fields, with the exception of the stock market, where stocks are borrowed daily, a credit transaction usually involves a promise to pay a definite sum of money. These are the largest and most important of all credit transactions.

Credit Instruments.—If the obligation of the debtor and the rights of the creditor are written, the paper is called a credit instrument. Certain types of credit contracts must be in writing if they are to be enforceable by law; but there are others, based on oral agreements alone, that are legally binding on both parties. In the latter case, there is no credit instrument although the value of the thing borrowed may be large, as is true when brokers on organized exchanges deal with one another. Credit instruments vary according to purposes, customs, and the statutes of the states in which they originate. In some fields of credit, considerable uniformity in credit instruments has resulted from the adoption by states of uniform laws, the influence of federal legislation, and the decisions of the courts.

Credit System.—The term "credit system" is used to include credit, credit instruments, credit agencies, and laws and customs pertaining to the granting of credit and to the collecting of obligations. The credit system is growing in complexity and size because of the trend in production which is placing more and more emphasis upon indirect rather than direct production of consumer goods. Accompanying this more complicated and indirect system of production is an increase in the proportion of fixed capital to total wealth.

Under a simpler social order, wealth was chiefly in the form of personal ornaments, clothing, rude shelters, stores of food, and implements. But even in ancient society there is evidence that credit instruments were in use, as promissory notes baked in clay have been discovered. However, credit instruments then represented only a small fraction of the total wealth, while today about one-half of the wealth of the United States, entirely aside from the federal government debt, is represented by these documents. A highly specialized and complex financial structure and extremely complicated legal machinery have been developed to handle this tremendous volume of credit instruments.

The basis for the development of a credit system is a high sense of business morality, which gives creditors, who give up present wealth or rights to wealth, assurance of repayment in the future. The growth of the credit system has been aided by custom and law. Owners of surplus funds are more willing to lend them when they know that they have a legal right of action against debtors if the latter default on their obligations. While credit instruments do represent a legal right of action against debtors, the future of the credit system depends primarily upon the debtors' willingness and ability to repay and wise management on the part of those on whom the responsibility for grants of credit rests. In general, the credit system has had its greatest development in those nations where customs and laws exact the highest moral and business standards not only from debtors but also from creditors. The shyster lawyer, the fraudulent stock salesman, and the Shylock small-loan dealer are as harmful to the credit system as the dead beat, the forger, and similar characters. This situation is fully appreciated by legitimate dealers in credit, and they have been the leaders in promoting blue-sky, antifraud, and small-loan laws.

Advantages and Disadvantages of Credit

Advantages.—Credit has been described by Daniel Webster in the following glowing terms: "Credit is the vital air of the system of modern commerce. It has done more, a thousand times more, to enrich nations than all the mines in the world." However, credit is not wealth, nor does it create wealth, since no more goods, no more capital, and no more wealth exist after credit is granted than before. Credit is the agency of transfer. Total wealth, total income, and total well-being are increased by credit only to the degree by which land, labor, and other goods may be utilized more efficiently and pleasurably.

Credit enriches consumption by permitting consumers to possess homes, cars, electrical equipment and appliances, and other types of durable consumer goods in the present in return for promises to pay in the future. Credit enables individuals to purchase goods and services to meet the emergency financial needs that accompany births, sickness, and death. Credit is also used in the retail field because it is convenient for both sellers and buyers to charge things purchased.

Credit aids in production by contributing to a general increase in size and efficiency of production units. Credit may be said to have made possible our modern productive system, because few businessmen possess the necessary funds with which to purchase land, build a plant, equip it with modern machinery, buy raw materials, and pay labor. An honest and capable businessman may obtain these factors of production on a large scale if he has credit. Inactive businessmen, small savers, widows, and orphans lend him funds with which to carry on his business activities. Thus credit makes it possible to shift capital into the hands of those who are able and willing to use it. Most credit is used for productive purposes, thus making more goods available for exchange. More goods make possible more credit, and the cycle continues unless there is a breakdown in confidence.

Credit serves as an aid in making payments, by serving as a substitute for money. By stimulating exchange it contributes to the general efficiency of production, making possible specialization, division of labor, and production for the market. This advantage of credit has been considered first under the heading of credit money and later under the title of deposit currency.

Disadvantages.—Much has been written about the advantages of credit but little about the disadvantages. The justification of credit depends upon how wisely it is used. Possession of credit—that is, the ability to borrow—may prove to be a curse as well as a blessing. The debtor mortgages his future income. The pleasure of having consumption goods ahead of income may be offset by the burden of forced savings and loss of consumption in the future. The expected profits from increased production may not materialize, thus leaving the proprietors with large obligations. Governments that borrow may be forced to decrease future activities, because a large part of their revenues must be used to pay interest and repay loans. From 1930 to 1933 this situation was serious for state and local governments, because relief demands on their budgets were large, and, as a result, defaults on their interest and principal payments were common. In case of the federal government the situation was different, because it was in a position to resort to measures that monetized its credit on a scale sufficiently large to meet the emergency.

From 1922 to 1929, during one of the "new eras" of economic advancement, long-term credit increased three times as fast as our wealth and income, and speculation went to extremes in all fields. Real estate debts increased threefold in seven years. The debts of industrial corporations increased twofold. The only exceptions to the general plunging into debt during this period were the farmers, the railroads, and the federal government.[1]

---

[1] Clark Evans, *The Internal Debts of the United States*, pp. 3-23.

Along with the excess in the use of credit went waste and extravagance, and, according to many, this was the chief cause of the great depression. However, another group of economists holds that there need not have been a major depression, even though the reckless lending of the twenties (earlier for farmers and railroads) was certain to cause losses. These economists base their conclusion on the quantity theory of money, involving a central bank policy of credit expansion which would have kept the supply of bank credit from decreasing seriously in volume. Without presenting any statement as to how the depression started, the fact remains that once "business has turned downward, ... there is little room for doubt that debt difficulties were among the chief influences which made the situation grow cumulatively worse."[2]

Under a simpler money and credit economy, such a world-wide breakdown in the economic structure in a time of plenty would not have been possible. Unless sparingly used and carefully managed, credit is the greatest threat to our present system of private property. If businessmen, bankers, and others cannot handle the savings of society in such a way as to strengthen our productive machinery, some other form of organization will take the place of private initiative and private enterprise.

Those who extol the virtues of credit sometimes forget that every credit obligation is also a debt obligation. The more freely credit is used, the deeper becomes the indebtedness of the members of society. The two problems, credit and debts, should not be studied separately, for they are parts of the same problem. The development of credit with all its advantages must be weighed carefully against the disadvantages of debts, which is another way of regarding the same problem.

There Are Three C's of Credit

Since payment for value received in the present is to be made in the future, the creditor must have confidence in the willingness and ability of the debtor to pay. In the case of individuals or corporations, this faith is based upon the character, the capacity, and the capital of the borrower. These three C's of credit are the most widely used

[2] The Twentieth Century Fund, *Debts and Recovery*, p. 8.

bases on which to form a judgment of the merits of an applicant for credit.

Character.—The first C, character, refers primarily to one's determination to pay. It is reflected by a person's past business record, such as bankruptcies and reputation for honest dealing. It involves one's personal habits and activities, such as social affiliations, associates, gambling tendencies, style of living, and political and social ambitions. Character must be possessed by all borrowers, and this holds true for nations as well as for individuals.

Capacity.—The second C, capacity, refers primarily to one's ability to use wisely and well the control over wealth that has been granted him. This depends in part upon one's age, business experience, education, common sense, and shrewdness. In granting credit to corporations and other large borrowers of funds, special attention is given to credit ratios. These include the ratio of current assets to current liabilities, merchandise to receivables, net worth to fixed or noncurrent assets, sales to receivables, and sales to fixed or noncurrent assets.[3] Although many credit men take the position that these ratios do not show the ability of the applicants, others regard them as excellent indices of the ability of the management. If they are constructed for a period of years, the resulting comparative ratios give an excellent statistical picture of the history of the corporation. There are, however, other important factors, such as the geographical location of the business, nature of the enterprise, and general economic conditions.

Capital.—The third C, capital, is usually considered by the uninitiated as the most desirable and practically the only one needed in order to obtain credit. This belief is common, in spite of the numerous testimonies of lenders to the contrary, as well as the innumerable experiences of men who possessed only character and ability but who have obtained fame and fortune. Too often those who applied for credit have lacked not only capital but also those other characteristics necessary for credit. However, the reader should not draw the conclusion that capital is not a desirable basis for credit. Perhaps a perfect credit applicant would be given 40 per cent for character, 30 per cent for capacity, and 30 per cent for capital.

The basic requirement in business, in so far as credit worthiness

---

[3] For a discussion of these ratios, see Bliss, J. H., *Financial and Operating Ratios in Management.*

is concerned, is good management. Good management is based primarily on the character and capacity of the individuals responsible for the formulation and execution of policies. There are various ways of classifying the causes of business failures—those due primarily to poor management and those in which the quality of management plays little or no part.[4] Studies of the causes of failures suggest that inexperience and incompetence, lack of capital, extravagance, neglect, and fraud are the chief causes of business failures. All these reasons, even the lack of capital, suggest the importance of character and capacity in management. When one considers the more specific causes of failures for small business concerns, two are of primary importance: too large an investment in merchandise or inventory and too liberal grants of credit to customers. The two chief causes of failures of large business concerns are overexpansion of plant and too many fixed or long-term debts.

Credit and Credit Instruments Are Classified in Many Ways

Public and Private.—Students of public finance and investments emphasize the nature of the recipients of credit. There are, under this classification, two chief types of credit—public and private. Public credit includes all grants of credit to governments: federal, state, local, and foreign. This credit is usually unsecured, in that it has no liens specifically pledged as backing for the obligations. Because of the government's powers of taxation, this type of credit usually has the highest credit rating in the market.

Private credit involves all grants of credit to individuals, partnerships, and private corporations. It may or may not be secured by specific pledges of assets as backing for the obligations. The credit ratings of private credit instruments vary widely, depending upon the nature of the business of the borrower, the financial structure of the corporation if incorporated, the phase of the business cycle, and the financial hazards of the money and capital markets.

Secured and Unsecured.—A second classification of credit is according to the presence or absence of a special lien on property or a property right pledged as security. Only when credit rests upon some specifically segregated thing, legally set aside to guarantee payment of an obligation, is it classified as being secured. The thing pledged

[4] See Prochnow, H. V., and Foulke, R. A., *Practical Bank Credit*, pp. 563-81.

may be real property (land and improvements attached to land); tangible personal property (merchandise, machinery, raw materials, household property, automobiles, etc.); and intangible personal property (stocks, bonds, royalties, and patent rights).

The term "unsecured loan" is misleading, because in practice such loans are adequately protected by the general assets of the borrower. Technically, it is a loan for which the borrower has not pledged an asset; but usually the credit rating of the individual or firm that borrows in this way is better than the credit ratings of those who are required to pledge specific assets as security.

Use Classification.—Credit and credit instruments are sometimes classified according to the use made of the borrowed funds. The four major subdivisions of this type of classification are: investment, speculative, commercial, and consumption. This classification, with certain subdivisions, is particularly important, because many financial institutions are specialists in granting one or more of these types of credit.

Investment credit is that which is used to secure durable or fixed forms of capital goods, such as buildings, farms, factories, mines, railroads, and stores. It is usually borrowed for long periods of time and is repaid out of accumulated earnings for the business during the life of the capital goods. For example, a farmer mortgages his farm in order to build a new barn, rather than wait until he has saved enough to construct it. The expected savings from better storage of farm implements, machinery, grain, and forage crops help to pay for the barn while he is using it. In addition, he is able to engage in more profitable farming by increasing his output of, let us assume, dairy products. The savings, made possible through better storage and the new income from expansion of farm operations, may be used to amortize the mortgage.

Speculative credit is, in some respects, very similar to investment credit. It includes uses of credit in enterprises where the risk of loss is great. One common way of distinguishing between the two is the intention of the borrower. If risk is consciously assumed, the credit is called speculative; but, if the intention of the borrower is to avoid all substantial risks, the transaction is classified as an investment.

Usually speculators buy and sell because they expect changes in prices. They seek to gain profits from differences in prices at different times rather than to secure income from their investments. Most margin buyers of securities and commodities are speculators. The mere fact that they are buying more in the present than they can pay for is sufficient evidence that they are expecting a rise in prices. Practically all short sellers are speculating for a fall in prices. The obtaining of funds for speculative purposes usually involves short-term credit transactions.

Commercial credit is used to finance trade and commerce. For example, a retailer borrows from a bank in order to pay for goods which are to be sold during the Christmas shopping season. The transaction financed is the movement of goods from the hands of the manufacturers or wholesalers to consumers. The resale of the goods provides the means with which commercial credit is repaid. For this reason it is granted for but a short period of time.

Consumption credit is used to finance the utilization of consumer goods. Borrowers use this type of credit as a means of securing goods to satisfy personal wants. Funds may be borrowed to pay for a birth or a funeral and every intervening want. Consumption credit does not normally increase the borrower's income, and therefore liquidation of the debt involves a curtailment of future spending.

Time Classification.—One of the simplest ways of classifying credit and credit instruments is according to the time period involved in the credit contract. If the credit period is less than a year, it is called "short-term"; if more than five years, it is called "long-term"; and if it is more than one year and less than five years, it is called "intermediate" credit.

Long-term credit instruments are also known as investment credit instruments; but the funds may be used by governments for financing wars, relief, or other consumption purposes. When borrowed by individuals or corporations, the funds are usually used to buy land, construct buildings, and purchase machinery. The documents evidencing investment credit transactions are more complicated and formal than those used for short-term credit purposes. Since credit is extended for long periods of time, the need for greater legal protection against loss is apparent.

Short-term credit instruments are sometimes called commercial credit instruments. They are used when funds are transferred from creditor to debtor for a short period of time. Usually, these credit instruments result from the transfer of title to goods in exchange. The goods may be used for consumption or in one of the processes in production and distribution. A manufacturer may borrow funds to purchase raw materials, or he may merely order the goods and promise to pay the seller sometime in the future. Similar procedures may be used by merchants in securing possession of goods to sell. Short-term credit may be used to finance commerce, speculation, and short-term investment needs.

Intermediate credit instruments are those which fall in time between short-term and long-term, arising from transactions which call for the use of funds from one to five years. They may appear in all fields of production and consumption, being common in livestock raising and marketing; curing, storing, and marketing of tobacco; instalment plan purchasing of farm machinery, more expensive home equipment, home repairing, automobiles, and trucks. Intermediate credit instruments appear as part of a serial bond issue of local governments, as Treasury notes of the federal government, and as capital loans made by the Federal Reserve and other banks.

There Are Four Classes of Long-Term Credit Instruments

Stock Certificates.—Stock certificates should not be considered as credit instruments if one accepts the legal definition. The holder is not a creditor but one of the owners in the enterprise. He receives a share in the earnings, which is called a dividend. Dividends are paid only when earned and voted by the board of directors. The economic justification for classifying stock certificates as credit instruments is the status of the majority of stockholders. For all practical purposes, they are not partners in the enterprise, because management is in the hands of a small group of insiders. Most stockholders have little to say about the policies of their company, and, if they vote at all, it is by proxy. In deciding to buy stock, investors are guided by investment rather than by managerial motives.

There are many ways of classifying shares of stock, but the two most general classes are "preferred" and "common." Preferred stockholders have prior claims on earnings and, in the event of liquidation, upon assets. In return for this preferred position, this class of stockholders usually accepts a limited rate of return and surrenders its right to vote. The preferred stock may be cumulative or noncumulative, participating or nonparticipating. If it is 6 per cent cumulative participating stock, it means that, if dividends are only 3 per cent one year because of low earnings, an equal amount becomes an obligation due preferred stockholders, which must be paid for before dividends are paid to common stockholders. If earnings are above 6 per cent, the participating preferred stockholders may share, depending of course upon the participation clause, in the excess earnings on the same basis, or some other basis, as common stockholders.

The common stock certificates of a corporation represents the claims of stockholders after creditors and preferred stockholders have received interest and dividends. They may have a definite face or par value, or they may be issued without par value. They have a residual claim to earnings and assets. Common stock prices fluctuate widely with business changes.

TABLE 9

FINANCING ON EQUITY AND LEVERAGE

	Capital	4%	6%	8%	10%
Bonds (5%)	$100,000	$ 5,000	$ 5,000	$ 5,000	$ 5,000
Preferred stock (7%)	100,000	7,000	7,000	7,000	7,000
Common stock	100,000	....	6,000	12,000	18,000
Total	$300,000	$12,000	$18,000	$24,000	$30,000

In addition to the risks assignable to the nature of the business, there is an added risk, owing to the financial structure of the corporation. Two financial terms are involved—"trading on equity" and "leverage." If one assumes that a corporation has outstanding $100,000 in 5 per cent bonds, $100,000 in 7 per cent preferred stock, and $100,000 in common stock, changes in rates earned by capital will have the effects upon the amount assigned to each $100,000, as shown in Table 9. When earnings of the corporation were 4 per cent, no income was available for the common stockholders, but, when the rate of earnings had increased to 6 per cent, the percentage assignable to common stockholders was 6 per cent. If one assumes that the preferred stock is noncumulative and nonparticipating, every increase in the earnings of 1 per cent will increase the earnings assignable to common stockholders by 3 per cent. This method of financing with senior securities, bonds, and preferred stock is called "trading on equity." Any increase in earnings is passed through the senior securities and pyramided into a wide fluctuation of earnings assignable to common stock. In financial circles "this resultant intensified swing in common stock" is called "leverage."

The danger in the use of trading or financing on equity is that the corporation will overborrow during good times and have too large a fixed debt to be serviced when returns on capital are very low. One of the primary reasons for the failure of railroads and other large corporations has been too much financing on equity. That corporate managers now appreciate this danger is suggested by certain recent changes in corporate financing. One development is that bond issues are being avoided entirely by an increasing number of corporations, and some corporations have been purchasing large amounts of their bonds, in the open market, for retirement. Furthermore, there is a tendency to shorten the duration of debts, to set aside larger sinking funds, and to insert call clauses in bonds.

Stock Rights.—A stock right is the privilege given to stockholders to subscribe to new stocks. The stockholder receives a warrant which he may use or sell to an investor. The rights are prorated; for example, assume that a corporation has 10,000,000 shares of stock outstanding and 1,000,000 new shares to be sold, then each old stockholder will receive the right to purchase one share of new for each ten shares of the old stock. Roughly, the value of rights is the difference between the issue price of the new stock and the prospective market price.

Bonds.—A bond is an evidence of debt. As the term is used in finance, it means any formal written agreement signed and sealed, specifying the obligation of the maker to pay interest on stipulated dates and to pay the principal at the end of a given period of time. Now, a bond is usually thought of as the promise to pay of a corporation or government, running for five years or more. Corporate bonds are classified in many ways, the most common being as debenture bonds, mortgage bonds, and collateral trust bonds.

Debenture bonds are unsecured promises to pay, "dignified by a formal debenture, the interposition of a trustee, and marked by the participation of many creditors . . . . "[5] The debenture agreement,

[5] Livermore, S., *Investment Principles and Analysis*, p. 24.

which is held by a trustee, describes the rights and remedies of holders of bonds for broken promises given by the debtor. In general, limitations are placed upon (1) the issuance of new bonds, (2) dividend payments when working capital is depleted, (3) procedure to be followed by trustees when agreements are violated, and (4) the use of funds raised by the bond sale. As in all types of bond issues, many creditors are participating in advances of funds to but one corporate debtor. Like all general credit obligations, stress is placed upon the willingness and ability of the debtor to pay on demand. This type of bond is increasing in popularity among corporations operating in industries which are expanding, because when they need more capital they are usually able to secure it on the most favorable terms.

Mortgage bonds differ from debenture bonds in that they are promises to pay secured by special liens upon tangible property. The mortgage is held and supervised by a trustee, who acts for the holders of the bonds. The original type of mortgage bonds (with rigid provisions for foreclosure in case of failure to pay interest and taxes, to maintain insurance, and to meet instalment principal payments) has been modified by law and court actions. For these reasons the indenture agreements now used in this type of financing, as well as debenture bonds, are of increasing importance. Mortgage bonds are the most common type still outstanding in the railroad and public utility fields.

The collateral trust bond is similar to the mortgage bond, but it is secured by pledges of other securities, which are held by a trustee. As in the case of mortgage bonds, there is a supplementary agreement obliging the debtor to pay if the pledged property is insufficient. Collateral trust bonds are most often issued by holding companies and investment trusts which have chiefly stocks and bonds to offer as security for public borrowing.

Many minor classes of bonds have appeared as corporation finance has become more complex. Mortgage bonds may belong to an open end or to a closed end issue. If open end, additional bonds may be issued under certain specified conditions under the mortgage deed of trust or agreement. If closed end, no new bonds of the same lien as those already outstanding may be issued. Bonds may be issued with or without convertible features. If convertible, the holder can, under certain conditions, exchange them for shares of stock. The bonds may be callable or noncallable. If callable, the debtor company may call them under certain stipulated conditions. Bonds may be registered both as to principal and as to interest, or they may be registered as to principal only. If bonds are not registered as to principal, they are payable to bearer. If bonds are not registered as to interest, coupons are usually attached which are payable to bearer.

Bonds are also classified according to the provisions made for repayment of the principal. If a certain quantity of the total borrowed is repayable annually or at definite periods, the bonds are called serials. Serial bond issues are common among public issues, particularly those of local governments. If all the bonds are due on a particular date, they are called term bonds. The term bonds are paid either out of a sinking fund that has been built up over the life of the bond issue for this purpose or with proceeds of a new security sale. If the bonds are put out for a definite period, for example, twenty years, but are callable after a fixed period, say ten years, they are known as callable term bonds. This type is common among the federal issues. Perpetual bonds, with no maturity date, are common among government issues in foreign countries. Bonds are usually in $1,000 and $5,000 denominations. The federal government and certain private corporations have, however, experimented successfully with smaller denominations.

Long-Term Notes.—Long-term notes usually contain a promise to pay in five years or longer. They may be secured or unsecured. The legal agreement is less formal than that found in a bond. Practically the only distinction between a short-term and a long-term note is one of time. Mortgages are a class of long-term notes which differ from mortgage bonds in that they are obligations for smaller amounts and are usually held by one creditor or a small group of creditors. In recent years banks have been supplying corporations with funds in exchange for serial notes, with the first coming due in two years and the others annually, and with the longest-term note coming due in eight or ten years.

There Are Three Classes of Short-Term Credit Instruments

These instruments are classified as open book accounts, promises to pay, and bills of exchange or orders to pay.

Open Book Accounts.—In the strict sense of the term, a book account is not a credit instrument, but it is an important instrumentality of credit. It is used by bankers, retailers, wholesalers, and others in granting or receiving credit. Banks receive credit from depositors, indicating their obligations in individual pass books and by a book entry on the ledgers of the banks. Proceeds of bank loans to customers are usually placed to the credit of the borrower in this form. Department stores and other mercantile institutions cater to on-account customers, and, where best collection practices exist, bills are presented at the end of each month. In turn, merchants buy from wholesalers, jobbers, and manufacturers on account.

The bill for the goods may contain a provision authorizing the buyer to discount the amount by 2 per cent if he pays cash within ten days; if payment is not made during the first ten days, the total amount is due at the end of a specified period, for example, within thirty days. This discount of 2 per cent for the twenty days between the end of the discount period and the due date is equal to an annual interest rate of 36 per cent. To take advantage of this high discount, most merchants without cash borrow from their banks under terms of a previously arranged line of credit.

In case a firm does not have adequate bank credit, one of the first outside indications of a strained position is its failure to take its cash discounts. The reason for failure to do so is usually a lack of current funds, which in turn is due to a poor collection policy, to a too large inventory, or both. Help may be secured from a finance or discount company or some other lending institution which is willing to make a loan based upon a pledge of accounts receivable or merchandise. The high discount or interest charged may be more than offset by the cash discount offered by the seller. In rare cases, failure to take a cash discount may be due to the ignorance of the merchant as to the advantages of the cash discount system, which would not be a good credit recommendation.

There are many objections to the open book account system, such as: many accounts are never paid, many orders are cancelled just before delivery date, a great deal of credit is tied up in a non-negotiable form, and collection of past due accounts is difficult and expensive. Attempts have been made to substitute trade acceptances and promissory notes for book credit, but these attempts have been successful in only a few major industries.

Promissory Notes.—A promissory note is an unconditional promise in writing by one person to another, signed by the maker, agreeing to pay on demand or at a fixed or determined future time a certain sum of money to the order of a specified person or bearer. The person making the promise is called the maker, the one to whom the promise is made is called the payee. The maker and the payee may be the same person or firm. For example, when firms finance in the open market through commercial paper dealers, their notes are made payable to themselves and are then endorsed by them "in blank" on the back. It is single name paper and may be negotiated by delivery.

Promissory notes may be single name or double name, interest-bearing or noninterest-bearing, payable upon demand or at the end of a specified period, and unsecured or secured by the pledge of some specified collateral. The promissory note is the credit instrument used in borrowing from banks. In the retail trade it is used when goods having great value are sold on a credit basis.

Bills of Exchange.—A bill of exchange is a third form of credit instrument, being defined in the Negotiable Instrument Law as "an unconditional order in writing addressed by one person to another, signed by the person giving it, requiring the person to whom it is addressed to pay on demand or at a fixed or determinable future time a sum certain in money to order or to bearer." The one who originates the draft or bill is known as the drawer and is usually the seller of goods. The person to whom the draft or bill is addressed is the drawee, and in trade he is usually the buyer of the goods. The drawee is ordered to pay to the bearer or his order the sum of money involved. The bearer is the agent of the drawer or the agent of the bank to whom the draft is sold.

Bills or drafts may be payable on sight or after a definite period of time. They are called sight or demand and time bills. They are also classified according to place, party, and purpose. Some writers classify all bills drawn and payable within a state as inland bills[6] and all others as foreign bills; but in this text all bills drawn and payable in the United States, except as noted to the contrary, are classified as "domestic," and all others are classified as "foreign" bills. A bill drawn upon a concern other than a bank is called a trade bill, and one drawn on a bank by a bank is called a bank bill

---

[6] According to the Negotiable Instrument Law, an "inland bill" is one that is payable in the state where it is drawn, and, unless the contrary appears on the face, holders may treat it as an inland bill. Foreign bills include all others, whether payable in a second state or in a foreign country.

or bank draft. But, if it is drawn on a bank by an individual, it is called a personal check or a commercial bill. Bills and drafts are used to finance commerce and short-term investments, the former being known as commercial bills and the latter as finance bills.

Because of the longer time period and therefore greater risk, time bills are usually sent to the drawees for acceptance. The drawer wants written assurance that the bill will be paid when it comes due, and usually the title to the goods being financed is held until the buyer or his bank accepts the bill. Accepting consists of writing or stamping on the face of the draft the word "accepted," followed by

ILLUSTRATION V

TRADE ACCEPTANCE

ACCEPTED
DATE Jan 17-1936
PAYABLE AT Security Bank
Name of Bank
Hamburg, Ohio
Location of Bank
E F Doolittle Inc
Signature of Acceptor
BY

Lincoln National Bank and Trust Company
OF SYRACUSE 50-46

Jan 10th 1936 $250.00

Thirty days After date Pay to the Order of OURSELVES

Two Hundred & fifty Dollars

THE TRANSACTION WHICH GIVES RISE TO THIS INSTRUMENT IS THE PURCHASE OF GOODS BY THE ACCEPTOR FROM THE DRAWER. THE DRAWEE MAY ACCEPT THIS BILL PAYABLE AT ANY BANK, TRUST COMPANY OR BANKER'S OFFICE IN THE UNITED STATES WHICH HE MAY DESIGNATE.

To E. F. Doolittle Inc
Schenectady NY

I. F. Smith & Co. Inc

Due Feb 9 1936 By E. G. Tilley Pres.

COL 11

Note that the trade acceptance has been drawn on and accepted by E. F. Doolittle, Inc., which makes this company the drawee and acceptor. I. F. Smith & Co., Inc., is the drawer. The place of payment is the Security Bank, Hamburg, Ohio.

the date of acceptance, and the signature of the drawee. It corresponds to an endorsement on a promissory note. When the time period expires, the drawee pays the amount stated in the draft. If the draft or bill is accepted by a bank, it is called a bankers' acceptance; but, if it is accepted by a concern other than a bank, it is called a trade acceptance.[7]

[7] The term "trade acceptance" does not appear in the Federal Reserve Act or in the Negotiable Instrument Law. It is applied in banking and business circles to a time bill on which appears the legend, "The transactions which give rise to this instrument is the purchase of goods by the acceptor from the drawer" (see Illustration V). The use of this statement was suggested by the Federal Reserve Board as a result of certain court decisions, including that of Lane Co. *v.* Crum, 291 SW 1084 (Texas, 1927), throwing doubt on the negotiability of trade acceptances containing the statement "the obligation of the acceptor hereof arises out of the purchase of goods from the drawer, maturity being in conformity with the original terms of the purchase." The statement that appears in Illustration V has been held by the courts not to impair negotiability.

Negotiability, Endorsement, and Presentment

The wide use of credit instruments has resulted in legal rules covering their purchase and sale and the rights of owners. One of the most important legal features which pertains to them is the quality of negotiability. Ordinary transfers of wealth or property rights pass by assignment, because most types of property possess the legal qualities of saleability and transferability. The buyer (assignee) is subject to all the defenses that may exist between original parties. Any defect in the title is passed along from the assignor to the assignee. For example, if a man purchases a stolen car, the original owner may reclaim it by proving that he is the legal owner. The assignee may sue the assignor, if he can find him, but he has no adequate defense against the legal owner. Most forms of credit instruments have the legal qualities of saleability and transferability, but in addition they may also possess the legal quality of negotiability.

Negotiability.—The legal title of negotiable instruments is transferred by endorsement and delivery, or by delivery only. The transferee obtains a good title provided that he is a purchaser for value and has no notice or knowledge of the infirmity or defect of the instrument. This is true even though the title of the transferer is defective, which is very different from the ordinary contract, wherein the assignee is subject to all the defects and defenses that may exist between the original parties. The presence of the quality of negotiability explains why bankers and others purchase billions of dollars worth of negotiable instruments annually without being forced to assume risks that would have prevented the organization of financial markets as we know them today. In contrast, every buyer of real estate must make or have a title search made, which normally costs from $25 to $75, before he completes his plans for assuming ownership and the financial obligations involved in the transfer of the title to real property to his name.

All credit instruments do not possess the quality of negotiability, because they do not meet the legal conditions provided for in the Uniform Negotiable Instrument Law, which has been adopted by all the states. In order to be negotiable, the instrument must (1) be in writing and signed by the maker or drawer, (2) contain an unconditional promise or order to pay a certain sum in money, (3) be payable on demand or at a fixed or determinable future time,

(4) be payable to order or to bearer, and (5) name the drawee, if addressed to him, or otherwise indicate him with reasonable certainty. The chief classes of negotiable credit instruments are promissory notes and bills of exchange, which includes the check. Nonnegotiable credit instruments are contracts which pass by assignment, involving all the defects and defenses that may exist between the original parties.

Endorsements.—In order to avoid delays and losses, the legal procedure covering the handling of negotiable instruments must be observed, including endorsements, when required, and proper presentation. Endorsement is necessary whenever a credit instrument is an order or promise to pay to a specified party. Endorsements may be special, in blank, restrictive, qualified, or conditional. The first type—special—specifies to whom or to whose order the instrument is to be paid. For example, Jones receives a check from Smith endorsed as follows: "Pay to John Jones or order," signed "Henry Smith." Jones' endorsement is necessary for further negotiability. An endorsement in blank specifies no endorsee, being in the foregoing case simply "Henry Smith." When Henry Smith restricts his endorsement to some special purpose, such as "for deposit to the account of," "for collection only," or "pay to John Jones only," further negotiation of the instrument is limited, and the endorsement is restrictive.

A qualified endorsement may be made by adding to the endorsement the words "without recourse." The holder who signs an obligation in this way refuses to assume any financial responsibility for the check. This type of endorsement may impair the acceptability but not the negotiability of the check. Conditional endorsement makes payment of the credit instrument conditional on some happening. Thus a father may endorse a check "Payable to my son, John Smith, when he finishes college," signed "Henry Smith."

Presentment.—The act of handing to the maker or drawee a matured note, draft, or bill of exchange is known as presentment. The word also applies to the act of handing to a drawee a time bill of exchange for acceptance. Presentment must be made at the place and time specified in the credit instrument. If payment or acceptance is refused, the instrument has been dishonored. If the obligation involves a party in a second state or foreign country, it must be protested in order to hold endorsers responsible in event of nonpayment. Inland bills, that is, within states, may be protested. The protest consists of a formal statement sent to endorsers and to the maker or drawer that a demand for payment or acceptance has been made and that the credit instrument has been dishonored. It is signed by a notary public. The purpose of protest is to hold liable all primary and secondary parties. Notice of dishonor may be waived by makers, drawers, and endorsers. The costs of protesting are added to the amount of the credit instrument which has been dishonored.

Conclusion.—The extent to which credit has been used in the United States is sufficient evidence of the importance of this system of transfer of goods and services. Practically every adult in any one month uses some type of credit instrument. Primary responsibility for the correct use of credit remains in the hands of the bankers, but the responsibility is shared by every user or grantor of credit. On the economic side, the growth of credit is due (1) to the change in the nature of modern production, which calls for the accumulation of large savings in order to finance public and private buildings, railroads, manufacturing plants, machinery, and equipment; (2) to more stable and democratic governments, which permit them to borrow and to tax in order to finance routine and socialized activities; (3) to the existence of a productive system that makes it possible to accumulate a surplus which may be invested in capital goods; and (4) to the development of financial institutions which specialize in the business of accumulating, handling, and investing the savings of society.

QUESTIONS AND PROBLEMS

1. Identify: (*a*) credit, (*b*) credit instruments, and (*c*) credit system.
2. Discuss the "advantages and disadvantages of credit."
3. Show why all "three C's of credit" must be present in most credit transactions.
4. What are the two chief causes of failures for (*a*) small companies and (*b*) large companies?
5. Usury was formerly considered as the taking of interest on loans of money or goods (*Leviticus*, XXV, *37*). Now it means the taking of a rate of interest for money above that allowed by law. Give reasons for this change.
6. What is the distinction between an equity and a debt? What justification is there for treating a stock certificate as a credit instrument?

7. What are the chief classes of short-term and long-term credit instruments?
8. What is meant by "accepting" a draft? Compare to an endorsement on a promissory note. What is the significance of the date which is placed on the draft at the time of acceptance? Explain.
9. Show why common stock prices fluctuate more widely than prices of (*a*) bonds, (*b*) preferred stocks, and (*c*) short-term notes.
10. Explain carefully the conditions necessary to render a credit instrument negotiable. May a credit instrument be transferable without being negotiable? Illustrate.
11. Assume that you have received in change a five dollar bill which is later identified by a friend as a Federal Reserve note that he has lost. What are your rights to the note?
12. Assume that you have rented an apartment and purchased the furniture from the former occupant and later received a notice that an instalment payment on the furniture is due to a furniture store. Are you liable?
13. "If we add up the wealth of all individuals in the country we would find that something, like half, measured in money terms, was in the form of debt" (Clark, *Internal Debts of the United States*, p. 399). What does this mean?
14. The wisdom of the practice of meeting long-term maturities with the issuance of other long-term obligations (refunding) in the railroad field is seriously questioned. What alternative is there? Explain.
15. Assume that you have checks and want to endorse them in order to accomplish the purposes listed. Write out your endorsements: (*a*) To make the check negotiable without further endorsements. (*b*) To limit your financial responsibility. (*c*) To prevent anyone except your bank from collecting. (*d*) To make it necessary for the party to whom you give the check to endorse it, thereby making it easier to trace payments.
16. During the period of 1927-29 banks were charged with overemphasizing the importance of collateral in making loans. Do you think this criticism is justified? Was capacity, as evidenced by individual earning power, neglected? Were similar mistakes made in 1918-20? What is the situation at the present time?
17. Classify the following credit instruments into two or more groups: (*a*) three-year United States Treasury note; (*b*) demand promissory note given by a stock exchange broker to a New York bank; (*c*) 90-day endorsed bill or acceptance; (*d*) 1949-53 Treasury bonds; (*e*) Great Northern Railway Company 30-year 3½ per cent general mortgage bond; (*f*) Boston Metropolitan District 1 to 25 years 2¼ per cent serial bond issue; (*g*) federal intermediate credit bank 1 to 9 months' debenture; (*h*) bank draft drawn by Lincoln National Bank on Chase National Bank of New York; (*i*) personal check which has been written by M. C.

Jones on his bank; and (*j*) stock certificate of National City Bank of New York.

18. Look up money rates and bond yields on classes of paper which appear below. Use current issue of *Federal Reserve Bulletin.* (*a*) Prime commercial paper 4 to 6 months; (*b*) prime bankers' acceptances 90 days; (*c*) rates charged customers by banks in principal cities; (*d*) stock exchange call loans; (*e*) United States Treasury bonds; (*f*) high-grade municipal bonds; (*g*) corporate industrial bonds; (*h*) railroad bonds; (*i*) corporate bonds with Aaa rating, and (*j*) corporate bonds with Baa rating.

REFERENCES

Bliss, J. H. *Financial and Operating Ratios in Management.* New York: Ronald Press Co., 1923.

Brady, J. E. (ed.) *Uniform Negotiable Instruments Act.* Cambridge, Mass: Brady Publishing Co., 1932.

Bretton, W. E. *Bills and Notes.* St. Paul: West Publishing Co., 1945.

Foulke, R. A. *The Commercial Paper Market,* chaps. i-iii. New York: Bankers Publishing Co., 1931.

Guthman, H. G. *The Analysis of Financial Statements.* 3d ed. New York: Prentice-Hall Inc., 1942.

Husband, W. H., and Dockeray, J. C. *Modern Corporation Finance.* Chicago: Richard D. Irwin, Inc., 1942.

Masson, R. L., and Stratton, S. S. *Financial Instruments and Institutions.* New York: McGraw-Hill Book Co., Inc., 1938.

Prendergast, W. A., and Steiner, W. H. *Credit and Its Uses,* chaps. i and iii. New York: D. Appleton-Century Co., Inc., 1931.

Prochnow, H. V., and Foulke, R. A. *Practical Bank Credit,* chaps. iii, vii-xiii, and xxii. New York: Prentice-Hall, Inc., 1940.

Wall, Alexander. *Basic Financial Statement Analysis.* New York: Harper & Bros., 1942.

Willis, H. P., and Bogen, J. L. *Investment Banking,* chap. xiii. Revised ed. New York: Harper & Bros., 1936.

8 *Corpus Juris: Bills and Notes.* Brooklyn: American Law Book Co., 1938.

10 *Corpus Juris Secundum: Bills and Notes.* Brooklyn: American Law Book Co., 1938.

11 *Corpus Juris Secundum: Bills and Notes.* Brooklyn: American Law Book Co., 1938.

CHAPTER XV

FUNCTIONS AND MANAGEMENT OF BANKS

Bankers Were Money Changers

The same economic functions that explain the development of money also explain the development of banking. The growth of trade and the development of large-scale production have made banking an essential part of our present-day economy. The first function of bankers was to serve as money changers.[1] This business was made necessary by the lack of uniformity of currency within nations as well as among nations. During medieval times many types of money were in use, because thousands of feudal lords, small and large, used their minting prerogative. Progressive debasement of coins added to the confusion, and so most currencies were useless except in local exchanges. The early bankers gave local coins for foreign ones and new coins for old, a procedure which has its present counterpart in the foreign exchange market, but only on a relatively small scale, because of the development and use of credit instruments.

Early European bankers were the fiscal agents for their governments and the official coin inspectors, functions now largely performed by central banks. (However, the latter function has been enlarged to include the handling of all coins, paper currency, and government checks.) Early bankers kept their own funds and those of merchants in strong vaults, a service still performed by banks that carry on a safe deposit business. Early bankers arranged for the transfer of deposits among merchants in the same locality and between communities, this being the forerunner of the present transfer service involved in the collection and payment of checks, bank drafts, and other obligations.

The word "banking" is often used in its broadest meaning to include all business activities primarily involved in the issue, ex-

[1] "The term bank is supposed to be derived from *banco,* the Italian word for bench, the Lombard Jews in Italy having benches in the market-place where they exchanged money and bills. When a banker failed, his bench was broken by the people and he was called a 'bankrupt'." Actually the term probably originated in financing the city of Venice in 1171, when each citizen was forced to buy stock. This joint stock fund, *monte,* was managed by commissioners appointed to receive revenues, pay interest, and handle transfers of stock. Since northern Italy was controlled by Germans, the word *Banck,* which the Italians changed to *banco,* as well as *monte* was used (see Bolles, A. S., *Practical Banking,* pp. 3-5).

change, lending, or custody of money and credit. The word "bank" was generally reserved for institutions of deposit, loan and discount, and note issue. In more recent years, stress has been placed on the acceptance of deposits as the chief criterion of a bank. Such institutions of deposit include national banks, state commercial banks, mutual savings banks, trust companies, Morris Plan or industrial banks, and the Federal Reserve banks. However, there is a tendency to broaden the meaning of the word "bank"; and now there are many financial institutions, not primarily institutions of deposit, to which the word is legally applied. They include federal land banks, federal intermediate credit banks, banks for co-operatives, joint stock land banks (in process of liquidation), and federal home loan banks. Other institutions engaged in some phase of banking other than the holding of deposits are classified as financial institutions unless the word "bank" is preceded by such qualifying words as "investment," "agricultural," or "trust."

The growth in complexity of the present economic system, on one hand, and the division of labor, on the other, have been accompanied by similar changes in the organization and development of banking. Many institutions have greatly enlarged their functions and activities. This movement is known as the integration of banking. It is best illustrated by the so-called department store of finance, which may be a national bank, a trust company, or a state commercial bank. (See Illustration VI.) All major banking functions are concentrated in one building and under one corporate head. There may be included savings, commercial, trust, title insurance, and safe deposit departments or divisions.

The second type of banking development is specialization, that is, the creation of special types of institutions catering to but one class of borrowers or dealing in but one type of credit. There are about fifty types of lending agencies in the United States, which may be classified roughly as (1) commercial, (2) trust, (3) savings, (4) home mortgage, (5) investment, (6) agriculture, and (7) personal or household finance companies.

Bankers Now Deal in Credit

Gradually banking has shifted from a business dealing in money to a business dealing in credit. This movement has paralleled the

ILLUSTRATION VI

CUTAWAY VIEW OF A BANK

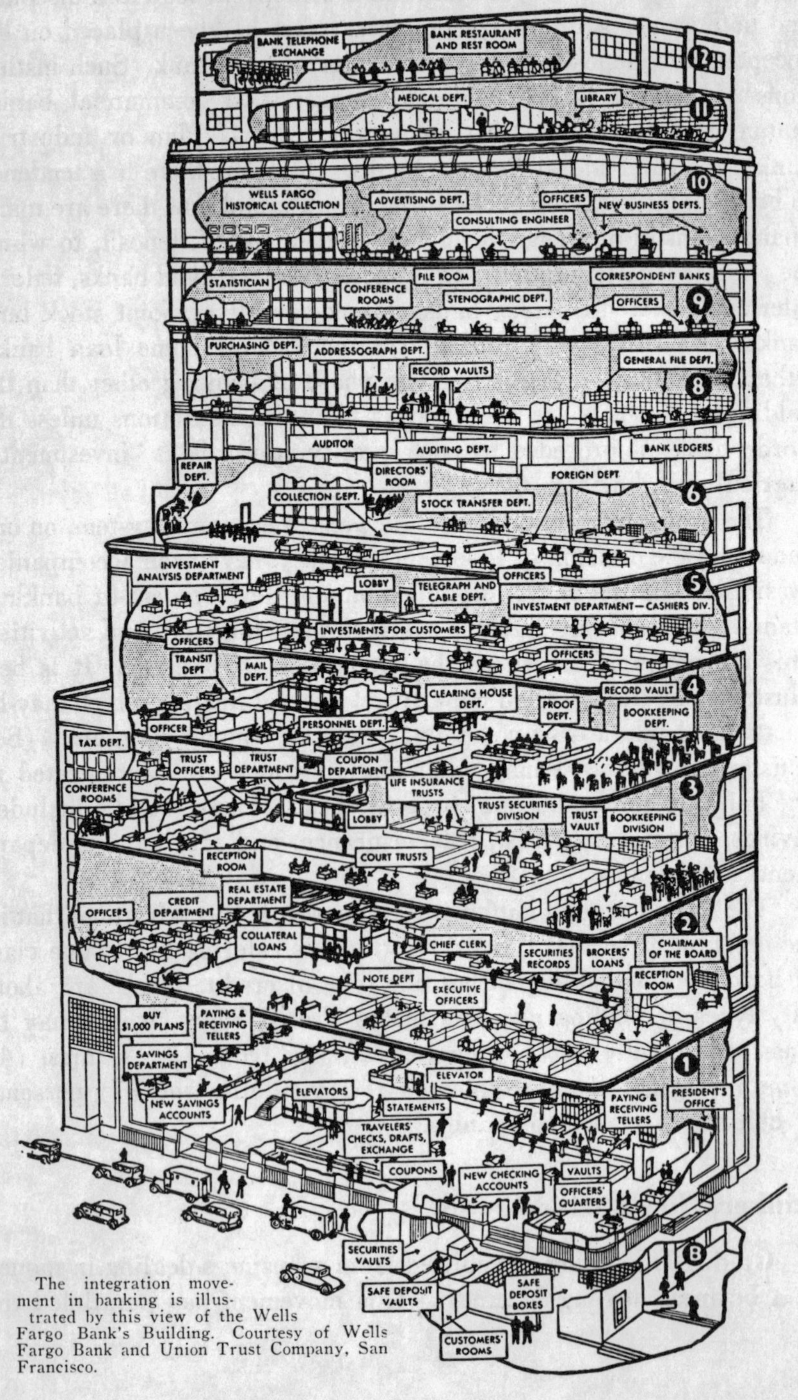

The integration movement in banking is illustrated by this view of the Wells Fargo Bank's Building. Courtesy of Wells Fargo Bank and Union Trust Company, San Francisco.

shift from a money economy to a credit economy. Formerly, emphasis was placed upon money transactions, but now credit transactions are dominant. Deposits are received in the form of checks, loans take the form of ledger balances, investments are made with the use of credit instruments, settlement is made in distant places by use of bills of exchange, legal reserves are in the form of deposits, and most of the assets of the banks are in the form of credit instruments. The pocket money handled by a bank during a typical business day will be considerably less, relative to total amount of business done, than the money handled by firms that operate in certain retail fields, groceries, 5 and 10 cent stores, and service lines.

Two types of capital are necessary in a modern capitalistic economy—"free" ("circulating," "working") and "permanent" ("fixed," "investment"). Circulating capital is the amount necessary to provide for the orderly marketing and continuous flow of goods from producers to consumers. This form of capital is used in financing the carrying of goods from season to season and from market to market; and in financing the change of raw materials into finished products and their ultimate sale to consumers. This capital is thought of as "free" in the sense that the specific funds involved are tied up only temporarily in agriculture, industry, or trade. A specific amount of funds involved in the financing of the wheat harvest, the sale of flour on a sixty-day grant of credit, and an outlay of capital to carry the purchase of goods through the normal Christmas shopping season would be illustrations of the use of circulating capital. In addition to circulating or working capital, agriculture, industry, and trade need capital which is tied up for long periods of time in farm improvements, industrial plants, machinery, warehouses, retail store buildings, and other forms of fixed physical equipment. This long-term capital is known as fixed or permanent capital.

Commercial banks and facilitating institutions are specialists in supplying agriculture, industry, and trade with working capital. In the ordinary course of events, working or circulating capital will be free, so that it will be returned to the banks. This permits commercial banks to adjust their lending policies according to the needs of their customers. Investment institutions are specialists in supplying farmers, industrialists, merchants, railroads, homeowners, and others with fixed capital. Since the proportion of the world's wealth in the form of real estate (land and buildings) has increased, the demand for fixed capital has also increased. The distinction between commercial and investment banking institutions is functional rather than institutional, and, as will be demonstrated later, many institutions carry on both types of banking.

Banks Make Savings More Efficient

Banks Stimulate Savings.—In order to supply the needs of those who are engaged in the creation of fixed capital goods, surplus goods must be available in the community, a fact that is obscured by the existence of money and credit. The individual who sets aside part of his income instead of using all of it for consumption is foregoing his rights to goods in the market place. His "claim checks" on the community's store of goods may be transferred to a neighbor, who uses them to pay men constructing some capital improvement. The workmen, while producing capital goods, are able to secure the consumer goods necessary for their existence.

Modern commercial banks may be instrumental in forcing the members in a community to save by expanding the volume of bank notes and deposit currency. If bank currency is expanded and used to finance production of public and private improvements, capital equipment is increased. The flow of money into the markets, relative to the supply of things, will be increased, and prices will tend to rise. All those who have fixed money incomes will be able to consume less, because their claim checks will buy a smaller proportion of the supply of things. Thus savings result just as truly as if individuals had voluntarily postponed using their claim checks.

A great deal of capital would lie idle if it were necessary for all savers to lend to neighbors and others who wanted funds. The greater part of the transactions involving lenders and borrowers are executed by specialists, that is, by banks and other financial institutions that gather the idle funds of society and make them available to borrowers in the same community, in other communities, in the same country, or in foreign countries. Modern commercial banks are so efficient that they make cash balances in the form of checking accounts available for use in business and at the same time give the depositors most of the advantages of holding currency. Banks create no new wealth, but, as accumulators of savings and idle funds and as lenders and investors of these funds, they do make the existing supply of capital, land,

and labor more efficient, which has the same effect as increasing wealth.

Provide Mobility of Credit.—One of the requisites of a good banking system is its ability to provide mobility of capital, that is, its ability to move credits from place to place according to the varying requirements of business. The banking system of the United States is basically local in nature. Most of the units are local in organization and management and are not national or even regional in scope of operations. Foreign banking systems differ markedly in this respect; they are dominated by a few large banks with many branch offices scattered throughout the territory served. The nearest counterpart of this type of bank organization in the United States is in the investment banking field. Most of the large bond or investment houses have or have had branch offices scattered throughout the United States. In addition, large commission houses or brokerage firms have branch offices in the leading cities of the country.

In the United States some mobility of credit is provided by facilitating organizations which take credit instruments of local origin and sell them in the money market. In this group are included the acceptance dealers, bill brokers, commercial paper houses, cattle loan associations, and a few mortgage dealers and brokers. It is primarily because of the local nature of financial institutions in the United States that more central banking systems have been created here than in any other country. There are six central banking systems, including one for commercial banks, one for homeowners, and four for agricultural borrowers. Although these institutions do provide for greater mobility of funds, as is evidenced by greater uniformity of interest rates throughout the United States since their establishment, the results have not been as satisfactory as many had anticipated.

The present localized nature of banking units also explains in part why so many government agencies have been created to help special groups and local interests. Many borrowers would not find it necessary to turn to the government for aid if metropolitan banks were permitted to open branch offices in their midst. Many businessmen, farmers, and others must go without funds or apply to the government for help because existing local facilities are inadequate for their needs. Since governmental agencies are securing funds from metropolitan banks at very low interest rates and lending them to borrowers, why should not these banks be allowed to lend directly to distant borrowers through local branch offices?

Provide Elastic Credit System.—In addition to geographical mobility of credit, the banking system provides for an elastic credit system, that is, one that is capable of expanding and contracting in volume as the credit needs of business expand and contract. With perfect elasticity, two undesirable developments would be avoided—an expansion which outruns the need and a contraction which causes businessmen to liquidate assets and to postpone or curtail production.

The amount of credit necessary is determined primarily by the volume of trade and the efficiency or turnover in the volume of bank credit. The determination of the exact amount of credit necessary for business is complex and difficult to ascertain, but among the objectives sought are: the maintenance of full employment, a stable price level, and low interest rates. Among the indices of an overexpansion of credit are inflated commodity, security, and real estate prices; speculative excesses in many markets, accompanied by a tendency to hold things from the market until further advances in prices; dispersion in price changes, causing losses to groups not favored by rising prices; and, in general, the boom phenomena which are followed by panic, liquidation of assets, unemployment, falling prices, etc. Among the indices of an overcontraction of credit are deflated commodity, security, and real estate prices; liquidation and forced selling of assets to repay loans which have been called or have not been renewed; curtailment of production because of uncertainty in the markets; increases in unemployment; decreased buying because further declines are expected; hoarding of currency because of the fear of bank failures, etc. While it cannot be said that overexpansion and overcontraction of bank credit cause the business cycle, it can be said that they at least accompany and intensify the boom and depression phases of the business cycle.

Banking Is Vested with Public Interest

Bankers are merchants of credit through whose organizations the long-term and current needs of commerce, industry, agriculture, and governments are provided. The successful operation of financial institutions is imperative for the proper functioning of the present economic system. The credit activities of banks are essential to the maintenance of a steady flow of goods and services through the "channels of production and distribution, from the farm, the forest, and the mine to the ultimate consumer."[2] Bankers differ from capitalists in being largely dependent upon other peoples' money, and, as such, they must give consideration to those who have intrusted them with funds as well as to the interests of those who have invested their funds in the banking business.

A safe and successful financial institution is one that will be in a position to meet its own obligations and aid those who are using its facilities to do the same. A safe and successful bank is one which meets the tests set by creditors, borrowers, stockholders, and the government. At first thought it may appear that the interests of these groups are in conflict. Stockholders are interested in high profits, which motive may cause the management to speculate with the bank's funds. In the long run, such a policy is certain to bring losses, which may not be large enough to make the bank insolvent, but which may prevent dividends on stocks from being paid for many years. Borrowers want a permanent place where they can secure funds in case of need, and they have a right to expect that all their reasonable requests for loans will be granted. If a bank is too free in its loan policies, this source of new loans may be destroyed by the bank's failure, and depositors as well as borrowers and owners will suffer.

The government is primarily interested in the welfare of the community. If loans are made too freely, many speculative projects are embarked upon, with resulting loss of capital, unemployment, and many social and economic disturbances. If too strict a loan policy is adopted, the business of the country may be retarded because of lack of capital. A decrease in production lowers the total income of the country and therefore lessens the general prosperity of the people. The government expects banks to consider questions of general public interest as well as those of creditors, borrowers, and stockholders. For this reason banks have long been considered to be vested with public interest and classified as quasi-public institutions as well as profit-seeking organizations. Finally, it should be kept in mind that commercial banks provide the nation with its most important means of payment—deposit currency—which plays such a dominant part in a modern credit system.

---

[2] Board of Governors of the Federal Reserve System, *Problems of Banking and Bank Supervision*, p. 1.

Financial Institutions May Be Corporations, Associations, or Partnerships

Financial institutions secure their bank charters from either state or federal governments. Charters are but certificates of association or incorporation that authorize banks to carry on the business described in the certificates. Banks and specialized financial institutions incorporated under federal laws usually have the word "national" or "federal" in their titles. The use of these words in the titles of federal chartered institutions should not be interpreted as meaning that the banks operate over a national area or that they are owned by the federal government. Most of the national banks are locally owned, managed, and operated. Among the local, specialized, financial institutions with federal charters are the federal savings and loan associations, the federal credit unions, the federal farm loan associations, and the federal production credit associations. Since 1862 the federal government has showed little restraint in authorizing specialized financial institutions, duplicating those first authorized by state laws.

All banks organized under state laws are known as state banking institutions. Duplicating in part the financial institutions authorized by national laws, they include state commercial banks, trust companies with commercial banking powers, state building and loan associations, and state-chartered credit unions. Although mutual savings banks are all state chartered, the federal government permits national banks to compete with them for savings deposits. Similar competition exists in the trust banking field, which, before 1914, was the exclusive domain of state-chartered institutions. Many problems have resulted from this dual chartering of banks and financial institutions, not the least of which has been "competition in laxity" in passing regulatory laws and in supervision.

Only when very broad regional or national interests are involved has the federal government obtained a near monopoly of the granting of bank charters. This situation is illustrated by the existence of the twelve Federal Reserve banks, the twelve federal land banks, the twelve intermediate credit banks, the twelve federal production credit corporations, the twelve federal banks for co-operatives, and the twelve federal home loan banks. The state-chartered institutions are far more numerous than national or federal banks, but, in the aggregate, the latter are larger and more important. Private banks do not have a charter, but usually their banking activities are limited by state and national laws. At the present time private banking is important only in two states—New York and Pennsylvania.

The procedure followed in the organization of new banks varies according to general banking laws of forty-eight states and the federal government, but there is a tendency for administrators, legislators, and judges to be influenced by others, and, as a result, the forty-nine commercial banking codes are more alike in fundamentals than different. In the organization of a national bank, the organizers must write to the Comptroller of the Currency, sending name of the proposed bank, which must contain the word "national," and the name of the city in which the bank is to be located—e.g., the Lincoln National Bank and Trust Company of Syracuse. If the Comptroller of the Currency approves of the proposed name, he sends the organizers blank forms which must be filled in and signed as required by law and by the regulations of the Comptroller. This application to organize must give the title, location, capital, and surplus of the proposed bank; the proposed costs of building, fixtures, and equipment, or annual rental if building is not purchased; and the signature of five or more applicants, their proposed interest in the bank, and information about their banking and business experiences. This application must be endorsed by three prominent local government officials.

The Comptroller directs a national examiner to examine and report on the personnel (organizers and proposed officers), the community's present and expected future need for the proposed bank, the existing local banking situation, and the prospects for success of the new bank if efficiently managed. While in the community, the examiner may call public meetings and personally interview individuals to hear the arguments in favor of and those opposed to the proposed bank. Unless the examiner's report is favorable, there is little prospect that the charter will be granted. In the meantime, additional information is obtained about the local banking situation from the Federal Reserve bank of that district, from the state banking department, and from the Federal Deposit Insurance Corporation.

After approval of the application for a charter by the Comptroller of the Currency, all necessary blanks for completing the formation of the bank are mailed to one of the members of the organization committee. Subscriptions are then taken for the stock, which is usually sold above par to create a paid-in surplus of at least 20 per cent. Articles of association and an organization certificate are then drawn up in duplicates and signed by preferably the same persons who signed the application to organize the national bank.

The articles of association become the charter of the bank after the Comptroller issues a certificate of authority to the organizers to commence business. One-half of the capital must be paid for before the issuance of this certificate, and the remainder must be paid in within six months from the date of the issuance of the certificate of authority. The organization certificate contains the name, residence, net worth, and number of shares of each shareholder. Pending the first annual election, a temporary board of directors is agreed upon by stockholders, and that board takes responsibility for selecting the president, vice-president, cashier, and other officers of the bank.

National Bank Management

Banks are managed by boards of directors or similar groups of men who are responsible to the owners, creditors, and the government for the well-being of their institutions. Directors of privately owned banks are elected by stockholders, but all or part of the directors of government banks are selected by the government. Self-perpetuating boards of trustees control mutual savings banks. Management of commercial banks, with emphasis on national banks, is discussed in the remainder of this section, while managements of other banks are discussed in the text where their organizations and activities are described.

Directors.—Formerly national banks were required to have a board of directors of not less than five members, but no maximum was set. The Banking Act of 1933 limited the number to twenty-five. The directors are elected by stockholders for a term of one year, and they are eligible for re-election. Voting is cumulative, that is, each shareholder has the same number of votes as he has shares for as many persons as there are directors to be elected; he may give one candidate as many votes as the number of shares he owns times the number of directors to be elected, or he may divide his votes among two or more candidates. Thus Mr. Jones, owning five shares in a bank that is electing twenty directors, may give one hundred votes to one candidate, fifty votes to two candidates, or five votes to twenty candidates. The new plan of voting will make it easier for the minority interest in banks to secure representation on the board of directors.

In order to insure a personal and direct interest in his bank, a director is required by law to own a large block of stock. When a bank's capital is not more than $25,000, a director must own $1,000 par value of stock in his own right; when the bank's capital is more than $25,000, but does not exceed $50,000, the amount required is $1,500; and in all other cases the amount is at least $2,500. Each director must be a citizen of the United States and a resident of the state, territory, or district in which the bank is located, or reside within fifty miles of the bank, regardless of state lines. Furthermore, at least three-fourths of the directors must have so resided at least a year before election.

In addition to these legal qualifications, a director should be an able executive in his own business and thus be in a position to give valuable advice to the management of the bank. He must help in formation of major bank policies and give advice as to the wisdom of granting specific loans. A director's standing in the community should be such that his name will add to the prestige of the bank, and he should be in a position to bring new business to the bank, not only at the time of election but in later years as well. Directors usually represent the leading business interests in the community.

The boards of directors have legislative power over banks. They formulate major policies and select officers to execute them. They supervise these officers, review their acts, audit their accounts, enact bylaws, and otherwise control the banks' operations. In large banks committees of directors are formed which meet regularly; in some banks the discount committee meets daily.

There are two types of directors. One type regards his position as one of trust; he holds himself as a custodian of the bank's assets and feels that he is responsible to the depositors and the stockholders for his stewardship. The second type of director regards the bank as a medium to foster personal gains; he believes the assets of the bank to be a source of personal loans. This type of director is a menace to his bank.

Directors seldom receive salaries unless they are serving in an official capacity, but they are compensated by fees and the indirect advantages attached to the position. Directors are liable for neglect of duty and lack of diligence in administering their banks. Even though thousands of banks have failed during the last twenty-five years, only a few directors and officers have been prosecuted for fraud. Directors are liable for breach of statutory or charter provisions which result in losses, and they may be sued severally as private individuals by shareholders to recover damages. In addition

CHART VII
BANK MANAGEMENT—ORGANIZATION CHART

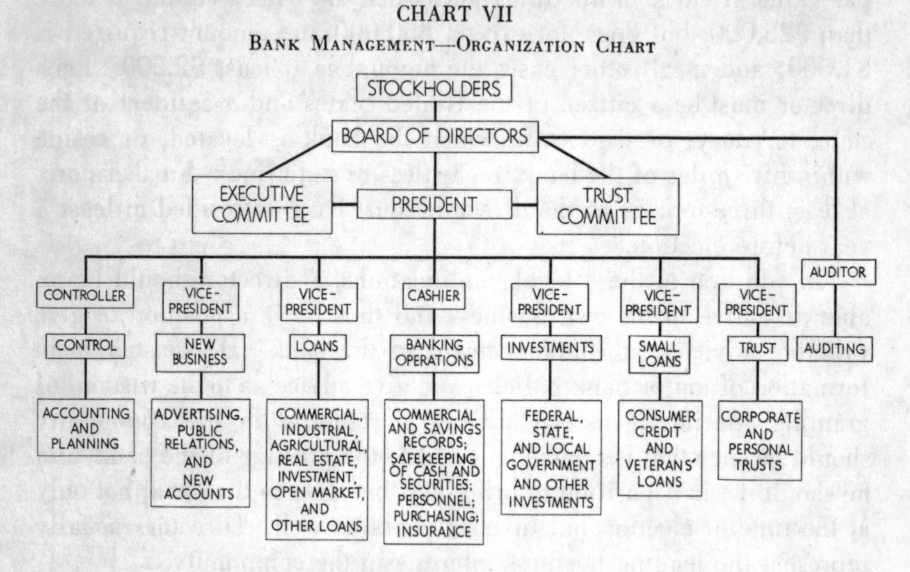

This chart is based on the organization of a medium-size commercial bank and is presented to show the channels of administrative responsibilities of the chief officers. The number of departments will vary according to the volume of business of the bank. There may be added foreign exchange, bond, real estate, savings, branch management, legal, and other departments as needed. In small banks all the activities of the bank may be in the banking operations department.

they are under a common-law obligation to shareholders, depositors, and borrowers to exercise at least ordinary care and prudence in the administration and supervision of the bank's affairs. Without knowledge on the part of the general public, many directors have made large contributions to their banks in times of stress.

Officers.—Officers are selected by boards of directors to manage their banks. An officer's relationship to the board is that of an employee to an employer. The chief officers are known as president, vice-presidents, and cashiers, or by some similar titles. Usually the chief officers are members of the board of directors and are large stockholders. They may be, and often are, in a position to dominate the bank's policies as well as its administration.

The president is selected by the directors from their own number for one year. He is usually re-elected from year to year. He may be a trained banker developed by years of experience in banks or a businessman who has been active in the bank's affairs. In a city bank he gives all his time to its affairs, but in rural communities he may leave the operation of the bank to the cashier and only devote a small part of his time to the bank's business.

His duties vary with the size of the bank, with its location, and with other factors. He may be merely a figurehead, or he may be the chief administrative officer. When he is the active head he has all the authority that law and custom confer on the office. In small banks he is usually the chairman of the board, but the volume of business of large metropolitan banks is so great that the chairman of the board of directors is not only a separate officer but one who gives all his time to the bank's affairs.

The chief duty of the president is to lend the bank's funds. Unfortunately, this work is often subject to little supervision by the board of directors. Small loans may be made safely in this way, but the opening of major lines of credit to prospective borrowers should be carefully examined by the discount committee of the bank. Most banks have credit officers who assist in this work. This division or department analyzes financial statements, checks the character of the applicant, and in numerous other ways collects information as to the customer's credit standing; but the responsibility for judicious lending rests with the chief executive officers in charge and the board of directors.

Most banks have one or more vice-presidents, whose duties vary with the size of the bank. In small banks the vice-president merely substitutes for the president when the latter is not present; but in the large institutions he is a full-time employee. Most banks have numerous vice-presidents, who are placed in charge of branches, departments, and other special divisions of the banks. The tendency for banks to have a large number of vice-presidents has resulted from the development of department store banking and bank mergers. Many officers in the formerly separate institutions are provided with positions and titles in this way. A large bank has, in addition to the chairman of the board of directors, the president and vice-presidents, officers known as executive managers, and assistants, or junior vice-presidents.

The cashier is secretary, treasurer, and chief clerk combined. In a large bank he has charge of the internal operations of the institution. In a small bank he is the active operating officer performing, in addition to his ordinary routine functions, the work of the president. He sometimes has the rank of vice-president and may have one or more assistant cashiers to help him in the performance of his many duties. As secretary, he makes out the bank's reports, keeps a record of the directors' meetings, signs certificates of stock, takes charge of the stock ledger and dividend books, and has charge of the bank's correspondence. As treasurer, he is responsible for all the assets of the bank and signs cashier's checks, bank drafts, and vouchers. As cashier, he has charge of the transactions when his bank sells securities, borrows money, or rediscounts papers; he endorses notes and drafts before they are sent to other banks for collection. As chief clerk, he must know the status of his bank at all times. He has general supervision over the internal affairs of the bank, the condition of depositors' accounts, and the payment of expenses. He passes upon new accounts and is primarily responsible for all the actual transactions after lines of policy have been determined by the president and the board of directors. He is a trained banker and usually has had experience in most of the different bank departments.

The national banking law gives the board of directors the power to appoint other officers in addition to the president, vice-president, and cashier. Titles and duties are not uniform, but next in rank are the tellers. They are in charge of all the incoming and outgoing funds. In large banks they have many assistants, but in small banks all the work is done by one or two persons. Other junior officers are the note teller, mail teller, discount clerk, and chief clerk.

Stockholders.—Stockholders are the owners of the banks, but they are not legally responsible for the banks' obligations in excess of their investment. Until 1937 they were liable for an additional sum equal to the par value of their stock.[3] All stockholders are

---

[3] Banking Act of 1935, Sec. 304. Sec. 22 of the Banking Act of 1933, as amended, is amended by adding at the end thereof the following sentences: "Such additional liability shall cease on July 1, 1937, with respect to all shares issued by any association which shall be transacting the business of banking on July 1, 1937: *Provided*, That not less than 6 months prior to such date, such association shall have caused notice of such prospective termination of liability to be published . . ." in a local newspaper.

morally responsible for the general well-being of their bank. They select the board of directors, which in turn selects the officers. They may aid their bank by taking a direct interest in its affairs and by bringing new customers to the bank. A stockholder should be in the position of an educated voter, eager to exercise his voting franchise in the interest of good banking.

Many years ago Walter Bagehot wrote that "the main source of profitableness of established banking is the smallness of the requisite capital. Being only wanted as a 'moral influence' it need not be more than is necessary to secure that influence."[4] One of the weaknesses of American banking has been the ease with which small, under-capitalized banks have been organized. Until recently, some states had no minimum capital requirements, and in others they were as low as $5,000 and $10,000. From 1900 to 1933 even national banks could be organized in communities with populations of 3,000 or less with $25,000 capitalization. In Canada no commercial bank may be organized with a subscribed capital of less than $500,000. In the United States minimum capital requirements for new national banks in communities of 6,000 or less is $50,000; in communities of from 6,000 to 50,000, $100,000; in communities of 50,000 and above, $200,000. The $200,000 requirement may be waived by the Comptroller of the Currency for banks located in the outlying districts of a city where a state law permits state banks to be organized with a smaller amount of capital.

Until 1933 there was only one class of bank stock—common—but the Bank Emergency Act changed this situation.[5] Now any national bank may, with the approval of the Comptroller and a majority of the stockholders, "issue preferred stock of one or more classes, in such amount and with such par value as shall be approved by said comptroller. . . . " The preferred stockholders are entitled to cumulative dividends at a rate not to exceed 6 per cent per annum. They have the same voting rights and other privileges of common stockholders and have preference to earnings and also to capital in case of liquidation.[6]

---

[4] Bagehot, Walter, *Lombard Street*, p. 245.

[5] Secs. 301-4 of this act (approved March 9, 1933) were amended on March 24 and June 15, 1933.

[6] No dividends are permitted on common stock until cumulative dividends on preferred stocks are paid in full (Sec. 302, Emergency Banking Act of 1933).

Preferred stock was authorized to facilitate the reorganization of insolvent banks. Restoring many banks of the country to a sound basis involved a decrease of deposit liabilities, the banks' chief debts. This objective could be obtained if depositors were willing to accept preferred stock of their bank, or that of a new bank, in exchange for deposits. Because of their preferred position, any recovery in the value of assets of the bank would at once accrue to their benefit, thus giving them an opportunity to recoup their losses. The Bank Emergency Act permitted bankers to use a reorganization plan similar to that used in the reorganization of nonbanking corporations It is a common practice in railroad, industrial, and other reorganizations for the bondholders to agree to a scaling-down in their claims and to accept preferred stock of the reorganized company in lieu thereof.

A Single Banking System Is Being Developed

Statistics reveal that the number of bank failures was much greater among nonmember than among member banks of the Federal Reserve System. The assumption is that member banks are more effectively supervised and regulated, and the suggested solution is that commercial banks should be forced to be members of the system. All such moves have been defeated in Congress. However, many of the desired results are being accomplished through the Federal Deposit Insurance Corporation. This corporation has always taken the position that, in order to protect itself, only sound banks may continue to participate in the federal deposit insurance system. The corporation is engaged, therefore, in a program that has as its chief purpose the elimination of all weak banks and the improvement of banking practices.

The changes affecting the capital account have been referred to, but most banking difficulties are traced to losses suffered as the result of loan and investment policies. While large losses sustained by depositors suggest the need for a larger "proprietor" account, they also indicate the necessity for sounder investments and safer loans and discounts. Although students recognize that free banking often results in unsound banking, no government has repealed its free banking laws.

Since 1933 more limitations have been placed upon the granting of state bank charters and the licensing of branches than during the entire preceding period under free banking laws. The present practice is to require the approval of newly created state banking boards as well as the approval of the superintendent of banking. In addition, the approval of the facilitating agencies (Federal Deposit Insurance Corporation and the Federal Reserve System) may be required before a charter or a license to open a branch office is granted. No longer does the formal meeting of the requirements of a free banking law insure the organizers that their application for a new charter will be granted.

Most of the difficulties of banks are traceable to their loans and investments, and for this reason consideration should be given to the argument that best results can be obtained through improved bank management. This situation has been recognized by the federal government, and steps have been taken which should result in better types of stockholders, directors, and officers. Repeal of the double liability clause should make bank stock more attractive to conservative investors, who make good stockholders and directors. Since bank directors must own stock of their banks, they will tend to have greater interest in them. Cutting down on the number of directors from, in some cases, eighty to a maximum of twenty-five should increase the individual responsibility of each director.

Cumulative voting makes it possible for the minority interests to be represented on a board of directors. New laws covering borrowing by bank officers should serve as a salutary check upon speculation by those who occupy positions of trust in banks. Wholesome results should follow from the power of the Board of Governors of the Federal Reserve System to remove an officer or a director who is using his position of trust for selfish purposes. Although this power may never be used, its existence serves as a healthy reminder that a bank must be considered first of all as a quasi-public institution and second as a private business.

QUESTIONS AND PROBLEMS

1. Show why bankers cannot properly be called "money changers."
2. Explain "Banks make savings more efficient."
3. What is a "safe and sound" bank? Do interests of borrowers, depositors, and owners (stockholders) clash? Why?
4. Distinguish between "mobility of credit" and "elastic credit system." What are the effects of the presence or lack of each on interest rates?

5. Distinguish between a "capitalist" and a "banker." Why is banking "vested with public interest"?
6. What are the seven chief functional classes of banking institutions in the United States? In what other ways may banks be classified?
7. From what sources do financial institutions obtain their authority to operate? Show how one can identify by their titles banks incorporated under federal law.
8. Distinguish between integration and specialization in banking.
9. Draw an organization chart of a local bank. Compare it to Chart VII and account for the chief differences.
10. What are the principal duties of (*a*) stockholders, (*b*) directors, and (*c*) president of a bank? Do depositors share in the responsibility of their banks? Explain.
11. What is meant by "double liability"? What is its present status? Give arguments in favor of and opposed to its elimination.
12. Explain carefully how cumulative voting for bank directors may operate. How may this system of voting affect representation of minority interests on the board of directors? What other steps have been taken to improve the quality of directors of banks?
13. Use Illustration VI to answer the questions that follow:
    a. Account for the location of the safe deposit boxes and vault on the basement floor and the nonbanking facilities on the tenth, eleventh, and twelfth floors.
    b. Which departments are located on the first floor? Why?
    c. Assume that you want to do the following: (1) cash a check; (2) make a savings deposit; (3) draw up a will; (4) purchase a federal government bond; and (5) send a cable to London. Where would you go in each case?
14. "A private bank [in the colonial period] was an emission of notes by private persons, to supply a supposed deficiency of the medium of exchange" (White, H., *Money and Banking* [5th ed.], p. 232). Compare to the modern idea of a bank.
15. In Scotland banks have boards of ordinary directors and boards of "extraordinary directors." The first type manage their banks, but the office of the latter "is an honorary one, and the connection between its holder and the Bank conferring the distinction is more nominal than real" (Mackenzie, *The Banking Systems of Great Britain, France, Germany, and the United States of America*, p. 80). Do you recommend this system to the banks in the United States? Why?
16. The management of the Northern Bank of Ireland is "in the hands of four managing directors who devote their whole time to the bank's service . . . ." (*ibid.*, p. 97). May not "professional directors" be

provided, advantageously, for American banks? Are there any on a bank's board of directors?

17. "The bigger bank may be able to stand a shock that the small bank may not. . . . . The larger bank may become so large as to get out of touch with its customer's personality and become more or less remote from the actual individual" (MacMillan, Lord, *Minutes of Evidence*, Vol. I, p. 164). Comment on the foregoing quotation.

18. In what respect is "a single banking system being developed"?

REFERENCES

Anderson, T. J. *Federal and States Control of Banking.* New York: Bankers Publishing Co., 1934.

Beaty, J. Y. *How to Understand Banks*, chaps. i-iv. Chicago: Business Publications, Inc., 1935.

Bradford, F. A. *The Legal Status of Branch Banking in the United States.* New York: American Economists Council for the Study of Branch Banking, 1940.

Chapman, J. M., and Westerfield, R. B. *Branch Banking: Its Historical and Theoretical Position in America and Abroad.* New York: Harper & Bros., 1942.

Comptroller of the Currency. *Annual Reports.* Washington, D.C.: U.S. Government Printing Office.

Cory, H. A. "Administering Bank Personnel," *Bankers Magazine*, March, 1940.

Ebersole, J. F. *Bank Management: A Case Book*, secs. 19 and 21. 2d ed. New York: McGraw-Hill Book Co., Inc., 1935.

Harr, Luther, and Harris, W. C. *Banking Theory and Practice*, chaps. i-iv. 2d ed. New York: McGraw-Hill Book Co., Inc., 1936.

Hazelwood, C. B. *The Bank and Its Directors.* New York: Ronald Press Co., 1929.

Instructions of the Comptroller of Currency Relative to the Organization and Powers of National Banks, chaps. i, ii, iv, v, vi, and viii. Washington, D.C.: U.S. Government Printing Office, 1930.

Kniffen, W. H. *Better Banking*, chaps. i-iv. New York: McGraw-Hill Book Co., Inc., 1934.

Members of the Staff, Board of Governors of the Federal Reserve System, *Banking Studies*, pp. 87-109. Washington, D.C.: Board of Governors of the Federal Reserve System, 1941.

Ostrolenk, B. *The Economics of Branch Banking.* New York: Harper & Bros., 1930.

Patten, C. B. *The Methods and Machinery of Practical Banking.* 7th ed. New York: Bradford Rhodes & Co., 1896.

Popple, C. S. *Development of Two Bank Groups in the Central Northwest: A Study in Bank Policy Organization.* Cambridge: Harvard University Press, 1944.

Rodkey, R. G. *Sound Policies for Bank Management: A Discussion for Bank Officers and Directors.* New York: Ronald Press Co., 1944.

Stronck, H. N. *Bank Administration*, chaps. iv-ix. Chicago: Rand, McNally & Co., 1929.

Trant, J. B. *Bank Administration.* New York: McGraw-Hill Book Co., Inc., 1931.

Willis, H. P., and Edwards, G. W. *Business and Banking*, chap. v. Revised. New York: Harper & Bros., 1925.

Woolley, E. S. *Bank Management Control.* New York: George S. May Co., 1940.

Chapter XVI

COMMERCIAL BANKING BEFORE THE CIVIL WAR

American Banking Was First Organized on Sound Principles

Chartered Banking from 1781 to 1800.—When the Declaration of Independence was signed, there was not a single incorporated bank in the United States. At that time this situation was not extraordinary, because the century of commercial banking was still around the corner. To be sure, the "Old Lady of Threadneedle Street" (Bank of England) had been in existence since 1694, but banking was still in its pioneer stage. Merchant princes, private bankers, pawnbrokers, and goldsmiths dominated the poorly developed financial machinery of the period.

In the United States the incorporation of the Bank of North America (1781) marked the beginning of twenty years of sound banking. New banks were located in cities where there was a legitimate demand for such financial institutions. Passage of a special chartering act was necessary before a bank could be incorporated, and successful applicants for charters were usually men of financial responsibility. Most of the early banks were partially private and partially state-owned institutions, having been regarded as the agents of the state as well as having been recognized as private corporations. When considered from a functional viewpoint, these early banks were primarily commercial in nature. Most of the loans made by them were to finance commerce, were secured by the commodity being financed, were for short-term periods of time, and were liquidated from the proceeds of the commercial transactions.

All early American banks differed widely as to details, but they had many qualities in common. The chief business of the banks consisted of exchanging their noninterest-bearing notes, payable on demand, for the interest-bearing promises to pay of merchants, farmers, private corporations, partnerships, and public corporations. These early banks lent their credit in the form of paper money rather than in the form of deposit currency, as is true today. All early chartered banks in the United States were banks of issue.[1] The powers of the

[1] Bagehot justifies the use of the note issue privilege as follows: "No nation as yet has arrived at a great system of deposit banking without going first through the preliminary stage of note issue. . . ." (Bagehot, Walter, *Lombard Street*, pp. 89-90).

banks were drawn in the most general banking terms, which permitted them to accept deposits and to buy and sell foreign and domestic exchange, federal government bonds, and gold and silver bullion.

Before the end of the eighteenth century, only a few were organized in communities other than the commercial centers of the country. Although the merchants were the bankers of the frontier, the demands for paper money were so insistent that soon banks were formed for no other purpose than to capitalize on this need. What the frontiersman needed was more capital goods with which to develop mineral resources, exploit the forest, establish foundries and mills, and build factories, barns, and homes.

The expanding demand for capital goods had its counterpart in the demand for credit, which could not be met with the limited resources of the merchants. It is this pressing demand for credit which explains the development of frontier banking throughout the early history of the United States and also the breakdown in the traditional type of banking as first developed here. Instead of being based on commercial transactions, bank credit in certain areas was based on agricultural, industrial, and similar long-term demands for credit.

From the beginning of chartered banking, there appeared in charters the "thou shalt not" type of restrictions, which have continued to be an important part of American banking legislation. Most of the early banks were not allowed to own real estate except that which was taken in on bad loans and that which comprised the business site of the bank itself. Most of the banks were not allowed to deal in commodities except when necessary to protect the bank against losses due to bad loans. This restriction set them apart from the merchant bankers, who combined merchandising and banking. In some bank charters no limit was placed upon the volume of notes that could be issued; in others it was placed at two, three, or four times the capital stock. Generally, the actual volume of notes issued was considerably less than the legal limit.

When new banks were organized their capital stock was sold on the instalment plan, and the banks were allowed to open before all of it was paid. Most of the first instalment was paid for with government bonds, and, as a result, most of the banks were started with only a small amount of specie. In many cases the funds used to pay second, third, and fourth instalments were obtained by loans made by the bank and secured by the bank stock. Obviously, most of the banks were financing themselves and had little solid capital for backing. When one recognizes the small amount of capital paid for with specie, the record of some of these institutions is remarkable.

The First Chartered Banks.—In 1781 Robert Morris secured permission from Congress to incorporate the Bank of North America, which was established in Philadelphia. Of the bank's capital stock of $400,000, the government subscribed for $250,000, part of which was paid for with silver obtained from France. As a result, this bank was one of the few early banks that started on a specie basis. It was incorporated during the Revolutionary War, but too late to render much war service. The government did borrow about $1,250,000 from the bank, which was later repaid partly with cash and partly with that part of the bank's own stock which was owned by the government. Although the bank was founded largely with government funds, it was under private management. In 1782, because of grave doubts as to the constitutional powers of the Congress to charter a bank under the Articles of Confederation, the bank's managers asked for and obtained charters from the states of Pennsylvania, New York, Massachusetts, and Delaware. Most of its business was carried on under the charter of the state of Pennsylvania, until some eighty years later, when it received another federal charter under the National Banking Act of 1863.

The Bank of New York was formed by Hamilton and others in 1784, but the officers were unable to secure a charter from the state legislature for seven years; however, the bank was operated in the meantime without a charter. When the charter was granted, among the provisions was one that the "debts of the bank, 'over and above the monies then actually deposited in the bank,' should not exceed three times the amount of the capital actually paid in."[2] The public had not forgotten its experience with the excessive issues of paper money by the states and the Continental Congress. Since banks were still considered to be institutions created for the primary purpose of issuing paper money, they were naturally regarded with suspicion.

On February 7, 1784, a bank was chartered in Massachusetts, known as the Bank of Massachusetts. Before it began operations, $253,500 of its $300,000 capitalization was collected in specie.

[2] White, Horace, *Money and Banking* (5th ed.), p. 249.

Thus there were three banks in operation before the adoption of the new Federal Constitution. Actually, this is an understatement of the situation, because there were also individuals and partnerships who were accepting deposits, buying and selling foreign and domestic exchange, and making loans.

In 1790 the legislature of the state of Maryland chartered the Bank of Maryland, and the next year the Providence Bank was chartered in Rhode Island. Other charters were granted in rapid order by other states, and soon there was at least one bank in each of the original thirteen states.[3] Each of them had a large capitalization, the average being $1,000,000 per bank. Many of these institutions supplied their state governments with the same services which were being given by the Bank of the United States to the federal government. Many of these early banks are still in existence, and there are now more than two hundred banks in the United States which are over a century old.

The First and Second Banks of the United States

Introduction.—The most famous of the early banks are the two which were operated under federal charters, the first and second banks of the United States. Before considering these two institutions, it is desirable to keep in mind that the United States of 1790 was very different from the United States of today. When the first Bank of the United States was formed, the population of this country was about 4,000,000. Most of the people lived along the Atlantic seaboard, although the westward movement "over the mountains" was beginning. Only 3.3 per cent of the people lived in towns of 8,000 or more. The largest city was New York, with a population of 49,000. The second, third, and fourth ranking cities were Philadelphia, 28,550; Boston, 18,320; and Baltimore, 13,500. The two chief industries were farming and commerce. Shipbuilding and fishing were important in New England, but manufacturing and mining were of little importance.

First Bank of the United States, 1791-1811.[4]—In December, 1790, the Secretary of the Treasury, Alexander Hamilton, recom-

[3] Other banks organized were: Bank of Pennsylvania (1793), Nantucket Bank (1795), Merrimac Bank of Newburyport (1796), Hartford Bank (1792), Bank of Alexandria (1792), Union Bank of Boston (1793), and the Bank of Baltimore (1795).

[4] See Holdsworth, J. T., and Dewey, D. R., *The First and Second Banks of the United States*, National Monetary Commission, 61st Cong., 2d sess., Senate Document No. 571, pp. 1-144; Conant, C. A., *A History of Modern Banks of Issue*, pp. 286-94.

mended to Congress the establishment of a Bank of the United States. Although Hamilton stressed the need for an institution that would act as the fiscal agent for the federal government in raising, collecting, safekeeping, and disbursing government funds, he also emphasized the importance of having a uniform note issue system and the need for a national source of credit where merchants could discount their bills of exchange, obtain advances, make deposits, and secure domestic and foreign exchange services.

Although it was assumed that the federal government could not issue paper money, Hamilton saw no reason why it should not be a partner in a bank that did, provided the bank was operated on a business rather than a political basis. Hamilton stated that, on account of the scarcity of specie and the local nature of state banks, there was a need for currency that would have uniform value and be acceptable in all parts of the country. State governments were forbidden by the Constitution to issue paper money, and the federal government was not given this specific power. The paper issues of previous years were disappearing, and there was a possibility that state governments would freely charter banks that would issue a large quantity of unregulated currency.

After a bitter controversy, a bank act was passed by Congress in 1791 which included Hamilton's major recommendations. Washington's cabinet of four members was equally divided on the merits of the chartering bill, but Washington finally signed it, and it became a law early in 1791. The charter of the bank ran for twenty years, and during that period no other banking institution was sanctioned by Congress. The bank had a nominal capital of $10,000,000. Of this amount, $8,000,000 was opened to public subscription, and the other $2,000,000 was subscribed to by the federal government. Since the government had no funds, it borrowed its subscription from the bank. Since the bank had no money to lend, a series of bookkeeping transactions followed, which resulted in the government receiving shares of stock and the bank receiving a promissory note of the government. The government paid 6 per cent on its note, but the bank paid 8⅜ per cent dividends on the government-owned stock. During the next eleven years the shares held by the government were sold at a profit of $671,860. The last sale was made in 1802 to the investment banker, Sir Francis Baring, at a large premium, and he retailed the stock to English investors at an additional markup in price.

It was argued that the scarcity of specie in the United States made it impossible to start a large national bank on a specie basis, and so Hamilton recommended that government securities be used. His recommendation was accepted, and it was provided that private subscribers could pay for their stock three-fourths in federal government bonds and one-fourth in specie. The subscriptions were due in four instalments, but the bank was allowed to open after the first one was paid. Many of the second, third, and fourth instalments were paid with proceeds of funds borrowed from the bank, and it has been estimated that no more than $500,000, or 5 per cent, of the bank's capital was paid for with specie.

TABLE 10

STATEMENT OF THE FIRST BANK OF THE UNITED STATES, JANUARY, 1811

Resources (in Millions)		Liabilities (in Millions)	
Loans and discounts	$14.6	Capital	$10.0
United States 6 per cent and other United States stock	2.8	Surplus	0.5
Due from other banks	0.9	Circulation	5.0
Real estate	0.5	Individual deposits	5.9
Notes of other banks	0.4	United States government deposits	1.9
Specie	5.0	Due to other banks	0.6
		Unpaid drafts outstanding	0.2
Total	$24.2	Total	$24.2

Source: Annual Report of the Comptroller of the Currency, 1916, Vol. II, Table 93, p. 912.

The first Bank of the United States was governed by a board of twenty-five directors, all of whom had to be citizens of the United States. Foreign shareholders were not allowed to vote by proxy, and this restriction guaranteed American control of the bank, even though, as later happened, 18,000 of the 25,000 shares were held abroad. The Secretary of the Treasury was given the power to call for reports and to inspect the affairs of the bank. Only two reports were submitted to Congress (see Table 10), and it is not known whether the Secretary of the Treasury ever used his right of inspection. Practically all the documents pertaining to the bank were destroyed when the British troops burned the Capitol during the War of 1812.

The liabilities of the bank, except to depositors, could not exceed the amount of the bank's capital stock. This restriction limited the note issues to $10,000,000, but at no time, according to available reports, did the amount in circulation reach as much as 52 per cent of this figure. The bank notes were not legal tender, but as long as they were redeemed in gold and silver they were receivable for all payments due the United States government. The bank was allowed to sell, but not to buy, government bonds. It was allowed to deal in bills of exchange and gold and silver bullion and to make loans. It could sell real estate and goods that had been taken to protect the bank from losses due to bad loans. The chief office was in Philadelphia, and there were seven branch offices.

Judging from available reports, the relationship between the bank and the government was very satisfactory. The bank transacted most of the fiscal business of the government and lent money to the Treasury in anticipation of tax revenues. It acted as the custodian of public funds and transmitted them from place to place through its branch banking system.

The life of the first Bank of the United States as a federal institution ended on March 4, 1811. A rechartering bill, which had the support of Secretary of the Treasury Gallatin and powerful leaders in Congress, did not pass. The old bugaboo of nonconstitutionality, politics, opposition of more than eighty state-chartered banks, fear of a money trust, and foreign ownership of stock have all been given as reasons for the non-rechartering of the bank. When the bank's assets were liquidated, a bonus of $34 on each share was paid to the shareholders. The good-will and assets of the main office and some of the branches were purchased by individuals, who operated them as banks. Since this country was on the eve of the second war with Great Britain, the loss of the fiscal services that the bank had given the government was particularly serious. Although the government did use the services of private bankers and state-chartered banks, results were none too satisfactory. Among the private bankers or capitalists who helped finance the War of 1812 were Stephen Girard, who acquired most of the assets of the main office of the Bank of the United States, David Parish, and John Jacob Astor.

Second Bank of the United States, 1816-36.—The charter of the second bank was similar to the first, but there were a number of differences which show the development of banking principles during the intervening period.[5] All deposits as well as notes were to be redeemed in specie. While it was the prevailing conception that notes should be redeemed in legal tender money (gold and silver), little consideration had been given to deposits. As a result, even when banks were operating on a specie basis, depositors were often paid in bank notes which were at a discount. In 1790 deposits were not important, but in 1816 this situation had changed, particularly in the cities.

No note was to be issued of a smaller denomination than $5.00, and post notes were limited to denominations of $100.00 or more and to maturity of not more than sixty days. Post notes—time promises to pay—were a means of borrowing from the public with or without interest. They were widely used at this time, but often they were issued in such small denominations that the recipients mistook them for demand notes.

The bank's capital was three and one-half times that of the first bank, but the government subscribed to the same percentage of stock (20 per cent), or $7,000,000. The government was permitted to pay for its stock in specie or in its own promise to pay, bearing 5 per cent interest. The second method was used, and this note was not fully paid until 1831. In addition to securing this valuable subscription privilege from the bank, the government received a franchise tax of $1,500,000 for granting the twenty-year charter. The government secured the right to appoint one-fifth of the twenty-five directors, and Congress reserved the right to examine the bank or inspect the books through special committees appointed by either House.

The bank was to provide means for transporting public funds to all places in the United States without cost to the government. As part compensation for the many services given the government, provisions were made for keeping the surplus funds of the Treasury with the bank. The bank was forbidden to purchase public bonds, but it could lend $500,000 to the United States without further authorization from Congress.

Branch banking was permitted, and by the end of 1817 branch offices had been established in New York, Boston, New Orleans, Pittsburgh, Baltimore, Washington, Richmond, Portsmouth (N.H.),

---

[5] For reprints of statements of resources and liabilities of the second Bank of the United States, see *Annual Report of the Comptroller of the Currency*, 1916, Vol. II, Table 94, p. 912.

Providence, Norfolk, Fayetteville (N.C.), Charleston, Savannah, Louisville (Ky.), Lexington, Cincinnati, Chillicothe (Ohio), and Middletown (Ohio). Later branches were opened at Natchez, Utica, Burlington, Buffalo, St. Louis, Portland (Me.), Nashville, Mobile, and Hartford.

These branches gave geographical, industrial, and seasonal diversification to the bank's assets. Risks as a result of unfavorable factors in a particular section were thereby decreased. If there was a strong demand in the cotton marketing section in November, funds could be transferred rapidly to the New Orleans or Charleston branches from the parent office or from other branches. Seasonal surplus funds of one section could thereby be transferred and used in meeting the peak demand from other sections, and, as a result, an equalization of money rates would follow. Money was transferred economically for the government and for private customers. The bank funds, being under centralized control, were economically used.

One of the first tasks of the bank was to secure a resumption of specie payments. With the co-operation of the large state banks, this task was finally accomplished. The bank was able to exercise considerable control over the volume of notes issued by state banks by sending them back for redemption. Notes were payable on demand in specie, and those banks which could not meet their obligations were forced to close. Those banks that survived followed conservative note issue policies. Thus inflation of state bank notes was checked, and the country throughout the East and part of the South and West had an excellent paper money system. In the process, the bank won the bitter opposition of many local banks. Legal attacks were made on the bank, and Maryland attempted to tax the Baltimore branch out of existence. The Supreme Court upheld the constitutionality of the chartering act (1819) and also stated that without the consent of Congress a state could not interfere by taxation or otherwise with the operation of a bank chartered by Congress (1824).[6]

The second Bank of the United States played a major role in the industrial and commercial development of the nation. It was during this period that the small community bank began to thrive in the frontier states in the Mississippi Valley. This continuous increase in the number of banks made the task of regulation of bank note issue a

[6] See McCullock *v.* Maryland, Wheat 316; and Osborne *v.* United States, 9 Wheat 738.

difficult one. Many friends of state banks were opposed to the idea of a central bank with a monopoly of banking privileges under federal law, and in addition there was a general distrust of all banks.[7] When a rechartering bill was passed by both Houses of Congress, it was vetoed by President Jackson, and so the bank's federal charter expired in 1836.[8]

The second Bank of the United States was reorganized under a charter granted by the state of Pennsylvania. After five years it was closed because of financial difficulties due primarily to poor management. This final closing of the Bank of the United States of Pennsylvania in 1841 brought to an end the only chartered bank which was organized to become a national institution, and this event, together with the failure of President Tyler to sign a bill providing for a third Bank of the United States, gave rise to events which have handicapped United States banking down to the present time.

As the result of a depression, the Democratic party lost the presidential election of 1840. Harrison and Tyler were successful candidates of the Whig party, which was in favor of a third Bank of the United States. Congress passed a bill creating such an institution, but the death of Harrison elevated Tyler to the presidency, and he vetoed the bill. Tyler was a Democrat and was placed on the national ticket merely to secure the votes of discontented members of his party. After he became President, he acted like a Democrat on all important measures, and the Whigs' victory was a hollow one.

If the third Bank of the United States had been chartered, the whole history of United States banking would have been changed. The chartering period (20 years) would have carried the central banking system down to the Civil War, and then, faced with unusual war needs, the Republican party would unquestionably have rechartered it. If such circumstances had prevailed, United States banking developments would have been along more orthodox lines, including nation-wide branch banking. In time the position of this bank would have been similar to that of the Bank of England.

---

[7] It was contended that states as well as the national government did not have the legal right to charter banks issuing paper money, and it was not until 1837 that the power of states to do so was confirmed by the Supreme Court.

[8] See Marquis James, *Andrew Jackson, Portrait of a President*, chaps. xiii, xvi, and xvii, for description of Jackson's fight against the bank.

There Were Many Banking Experiments

Sound banking practices and sound banking systems were developed earlier in the older and commercial sections than in the newer and agricultural parts of the country. Banking standards reflected the growth in commerce, the industrialization of business, and the greater stability of conditions which accompanied the increase in population. The frontier banks prospered immensely during periods of land booms, because real estate mortgages made up an important part of their loans and investments. There were many interesting banking experiments before the Civil War, some of which had a great effect upon present-day banking, but others were only of temporary interest.

State Ownership of Bank Stock.—In nearly all states, the government subscribed for a portion of the stock of new banks. In the East, where banking needed little encouragement, the chief desire was to participate in the large profits which the banks were expected to earn. In 1816 practically all the older states, with two or three exceptions, owned bank stock. In most cases the expectation of profits was justified. A second reason for purchase of stock was to give the states, through ownership, participation in the management of the banks. Stock purchases placed the states in the position of favored customers when they desired to borrow. The state governments could and did demand free fiscal services from the banks.

In the South and West the chief reason for government banking was the scarcity of private capital. In the Southwest planters were expanding their plantations, and most of their assets were invested in slaves and land. The money interests of the country would not lend on such security, and the planters had great difficulty in securing private credit. Numerous government banks were established to meet their needs. The states had no money for this purpose, but they were able to borrow it. Similar conditions existed in the West. The extent to which certain states had gone into debt up to 1838 for this purpose is shown in Table 11.

State-owned Banks.—In 1837 the federal government had a surplus revenue, part of which was distributed among the states. Thirteen of the states, of which ten were in the South, invested part of their shares of this windfall in banks. Many of the states engaged directly in banking on their own financial responsibility, but few of these experiments were successful. The state banks of Illinois (1821 and 1835), Bank of the Commonwealth of Kentucky (1820), Bank of the State of Alabama (1823), Union Bank of Mississippi (1838), Union Bank of Florida (1833), Tennessee (1820), and Louisiana (3 banks, 1832) are illustrations of unsuccessful classes. When government banks were administered by bankers, they were fairly successful. This was true of the Bank of Indiana, the Bank of South Carolina, the Bank of Missouri, and the Farmer's Bank of Delaware. Usually when banks were successful they had difficulty in securing rechartering bills, probably because creditors are never popular with debtors. In 1857 the State Bank of Indiana was replaced by a private

TABLE 11

CAUSES OF STATE DEBTS UP TO 1838

States	For Banks	All Others	Total
Alabama	$ 7,800,000	$ 3,000,000	$10,800,000
Arkansas	3,000,000	....	3,000,000
Illinois	3,100,000	8,500,000	11,600,000
Indiana	1,390,000	10,500,000	11,890,000
Kentucky	2,000,000	5,379,000	7,379,000
Louisiana	22,950,000	335,000	23,285,000
Mississippi	7,000,000	....	7,000,000
Missouri	2,500,000	....	2,500,000
Tennessee	3,000,000	4,148,166	7,148,166
Total	$52,740,000	$31,862,166	$84,602,166

Source: Bogart, E. L., *An Economic History of the United States* (4th ed.), p. 206.

bank, because of a provision in the New Constitution that "the State shall not be a stock-holder in any bank at the expiration of the present bank charter."

Suffolk Banking System.—The development of a strong banking system under leadership of bankers is illustrated by the Suffolk Banking System in the New England states, 1825-66. Previous to 1825 the cost of redeeming country bank notes in Boston was borne by the holders of the notes. As a result, these notes circulated at less than par, for the holders did not want to bear the cost of having them sent back to the issuing banks for redemption.

The Suffolk Bank managers developed the plan to force the issuing banks to bear the cost of redeeming their own notes and to eliminate the discount on them. The Suffolk Bank in Boston agreed to redeem all country banks' notes at par, if the banks kept deposits with it for this purpose. In other words, a regional par clearing and collecting system for notes was offered to all New England banks.

Originally many interior banks refused to join the Suffolk Banking System, but after other Boston banks agreed to participate, the interior banks were forced to join the system. The forcing process used was simple. The Suffolk Bank (later other Boston banks cooperated) collected all the available notes of interior banks not in the system and promptly sent them to the issuing banks for redemption. If the notes were reissued, the process was promptly repeated. At times, the Suffolk Bank would gather a large sum of notes and give the issuing banks their choice of paying in specie or joining the system. Since specie payment would have meant bankruptcy to many of them, they joined the system. By 1825 virtually all New England banks were in the system, and from then on until the Civil War the notes of New England banks circulated at par throughout that section. Moreover, they were in considerable demand in other parts of this country and in Canada. During the fifties about $300,000,000 of New England bank notes were redeemed annually.

The Suffolk system of note redemption continued in revised form until the notes were taxed out of existence by the federal government in 1866, and national bank note currency replaced state bank notes. The principles involved were later used by the national government in providing for central redemption of national bank notes in Washington, D.C. A sectional par clearing system for checks was developed along the same lines by the Federal Reserve Bank of Boston in 1914.

Safety Fund System.—Prior to 1828 bank notes were issued by New York banks, secured by the general assets of the banks. Usually special bank charters were for a limited period, and by 1828 about three-fourths of those in existence in New York states were about to expire. In that year Mr. Joshua Forman of Syracuse suggested a safety fund insurance system in order to protect bank creditors from loss in case of bank failure. This system is of special interest because it is the grandfather of the present Federal Deposit Insurance Corporation.

Under the Safety Fund System each new or rechartered bank was required to pay an annual amount equal to ½ of 1 per cent of its capital stock, until 3 per cent had been paid into a guarantee or safety fund to be used in paying off liabilities of insolvent banks. Although the state was managing the fund, it did not guarantee that all an insolvent bank's liabilities would be covered. The system was severely tested during the panic of 1837 and would probably have covered all losses if the contributions had been based upon the notes and deposits instead of upon the capital stock of each bank. In 1845 the Safety Fund System was amended, insuring only banks' liabilities in the form of notes. The number of banks operating under special charter gradually decreased, and the relative importance of their notes declined. The new banks were joining the free banking system, to which the Safety Fund System did not apply. The New York Free Banking Act of 1838 should be considered as a protest against monopoly in banking rather than as a criticism of the Safety Fund System.

Free Banking System.—A number of famous banks had grown and prospered under special charters, and others equally famous were developed under government monopoly and government ownership. In 1850, in spite of these developments, most of the states were committed to a policy of free banking under general banking laws.

Until 1838 one could not obtain a charter to start a bank without a special act of the state legislature, and even the purchase of new bank stock was subject to government supervision. Prior to 1804 there were only six banks in New York State, and they made common cause against all applicants for bank charters. Care was taken to prevent securing of bank charters by subterfuge, as happened in the case of the Manhattan Water Company.[9] By lavish expenditures of funds, however, bank charters could be secured, in spite of the opposition of bankers. The new bank charters invariably went to friends of the political party in power. By 1828 forty-three bank charters had been granted, and forty banks were in existence, three having failed. White summed up the situation as follows: "In short, politics, monopoly, and bribery constitute the key to banking in the early history of the state."[10]

[9] The history of the Manhattan Water Company charter is one of the best illustrations of the use of subterfuge in securing a bank charter. During the 1790's, the city of New York suffered from an epidemic of typhoid fever, attributed to impure water. Burr, an anti-Federalist and later a Democrat, and his friends secured a charter from the Federalist-controlled legislature, permitting them to operate a water company. A clause in the charter authorized them to use the company's surplus in any manner not in conflict with the state and federal laws. One-half of the company's funds were used for a water company and the other half for a bank. The first function was given up in 1840. The bank, under the name "President and Directors of the Manhattan Company," is still in existence. See Ninety-third Annual Report of the Superintendent of Banks, State of New York, Part I, *Report on State Banks, Trust Companies, Industrial Banks and Private Bankers*, Legislative Doc. (1944), No. 21, p. 311.

[10] White, *op. cit.*, p. 303.

Numerous protests were made against the monopolistic nature of banking and other abuses, including the failure to honor their circulating notes. It was not until the depression, following the panic of 1837, that the reformers were able to gain control of the state government and pass their banking reform bills. The most significant provision in the Free Banking Act was that which permitted any person or group of persons to organize a bank by complying with the conditions set forth in a general bank incorporation law. Second in importance to elimination of the special charter system were the provisions regulating the conditions of note issue.

Banks organized under the free banking law were required to deposit collateral with the state treasury or banking department in amounts equal to the volume of notes issued. If a bank failed, the collateral was sold, and the proceeds were used to pay its noteholders. At first mortgages and bonds were used as collateral, but later higher standards were set, and, as a result, a sound note issue system was developed. The democratic nature of the free banking system and the possibilities of abundant paper money appealed to the public. Within a short time sixteen states had adopted similar laws, and during the Civil War the free banking and bond-secured note issue principles were adopted by the national government. State banks discontinued issuing notes in 1866 and national banks in 1935. The present delegation of bank note issuing power to the Federal Reserve System has removed this problem from the noncentral banking field.

The United States is still committed to a free banking policy (granting charters to practically all qualified applicants under general statutory laws), because no government has repealed its general banking incorporation law. It has been only within the period since World War I that the wisdom of the practice of giving charters to all applicants has been seriously questioned. The criticism of free banking is that it has sometimes resulted in unsound banking. Too many banks have been formed, resulting in cutthroat competition; too many of the banks were undercapitalized, that is, financial interest of proprietors was not great enough; and too many unqualified persons were permitted to go into banking, resulting in poor management. The combination of a large number of small, undercapitalized, poorly managed banks has resulted in too many bank failures. The special charter banking system was "reeking with political favoritism and bribery," but its successor, the free banking system, was even less successful in securing one of the requisites of a good banking system, that is, correlation between commercial banking needs and commercial banking facilities. The corollary of these developments has been the increase in bank regulation to protect depositors from the financial pitfalls created by free banking.

Wildcat Banking.—With the growth of democracy and the westward movement, there was a change in attitude toward banks and banking. New banks were chartered as private business enterprises, with little or no consideration for the needs of commerce. Banking was still thought of as the right to issue bank notes, promoters were greedy for the profits which could be made from banking, and the general public was hungry for paper money. In the West, free banking degenerated into "wildcat" banking, so called because banking offices were located in the wilderness, where wildcats were the chief inhabitants. This location of a bank, in an inaccessible place, was an advantage to the banker, because few noteholders would ever find the bank and demand redemption of its notes. For more than fifty years the country suffered from bank paper money issues which, on the average, became worthless every twenty years. During this wildcat period the average bank capitalization was further reduced; and in most states, prior to 1837, there were no penalties for failure to redeem notes, and many people even considered it improper to ask a bank to redeem its promises to pay in specie.

All geographical sections were affected by the speculative boom that preceded the panic of 1837, and many new banks were established in the East as well as in the South and West. The transfer of government deposits from the second Bank of the United States to state banks greatly stimulated their expansion. During the thirties, before the panic started, the number of banks increased about threefold, note issues increased in proportion, and loans increased about fourfold. When the collapse came, the banks suspended specie payments, and during the next four years over one-third of them failed. The misery and hardships resulting from bank failures were so great that some states outlawed banks.[11] The 1933 condemnation of banking and bankers was mild compared to that of this period. One

[11] The state constitutions of Iowa and Texas prohibited the incorporation of banks, but the former operated a state bank. Indiana and Iowa also operated state banks and forbade the organization of private banks. By 1860, most of these states had adopted free banking laws.

aftermath was the development of state regulation and supervision of banks by banking codes and state banking departments.

Louisiana Banking Act of 1842.—Between 1837 and 1860, most states enacted laws requiring banks to keep reserves against deposits as well as against notes, because deposit liabilities had become equal to bank note liabilities in importance. During the panic of 1857 the record of the banks in Louisiana was outstanding because of the passage of and adherence to the Louisiana Banking Law of 1842. This act made no provision for increasing the number of banks and required all banks to keep a minimum reserve in specie equal to one-third of their notes and deposits, plus collateral backing in short-term paper equal to the remainder. It provided for quarterly examinations by state officials, monthly publication of bank statements, and weekly settlement of interbank balances. It forced contraction of bank notes in circulation by prohibiting banks from paying out notes other than their own. These provisions, plus the favorable trade position of New Orleans, made it possible for the banks in Louisiana to operate on a specie basis until the Civil War.

Independent Treasury System

During President Jackson's quarrel with the second Bank of the United States, he directed his Secretary of the Treasury to withdraw the deposits of the government and place them in state-chartered banks. Jackson's purpose in giving this order was to lessen the shock upon credit and currency which was expected to result from the liquidation of the second Bank of the United States with the lapse of its federal charter. When the secretary refused, Jackson removed him and appointed another. When this secretary likewise failed to withdraw the government's deposits, he was replaced by a third man, who gradually withdrew them and placed them in state banks. The panic of 1837 caused all the banks to suspend specie payments and compelled many of them to close their doors. Many depositors, including the government, lost large sums of money. These disastrous experiences with state banks led to the establishment of the independent treasury system.[12]

---

[12] The following comment of Bagehot was doubtless based in part upon the experiences of the United States. "In the infancy of Banking it is probably much better that a government should as a rule keep its own money" (Bagehot, *op cit.*, p. 103).

The independent treasury system was first started in 1840, but the Democrats were defeated, and the Whig party abolished the system and tried to start a third Bank of the United States. President Tyler prevented them from doing this by vetoing a chartering bill, and when the Democrats came into power four years later they re-established the independent treasury system. According to this plan of handling government funds, subtreasuries were established in different cities in the United States. They collected all the government's revenues in specie and made all its disbursements. This flow of specie to and from the government's subtreasuries was disturbing to banks and business. In earlier years, when the government's revenues and disbursements were small, the system worked very well; but, during the Civil War, the hard money policy and system of exclusive treasury depositories for government funds had to be modified.

Early Private Banking in the United States

To assume that the history of banking can be outlined without some consideration of nonchartered banks is to ignore the role of banking houses, which have often been dominant in the banking affairs of the nation. In most countries and communities, banking is much older than chartered banks. During the early history of the United States, conditions were very favorable to the development of private banking. Where chartered banking is inadequate or unreliable or handicapped by governmental regulations, where currency is in a state of confusion, and where business is expanding rapidly, there is a place for the private banker, the broker, the speculator, and the promoter.

While one important group of private bankers traces its origin to the financing of international trade and international lending, another group is indigenous in origin. It was natural for the frontier merchant to carry on limited deposit banking, to extend credit, and to participate in the financing of local ventures such as turnpikes, railroads, and canals. Too often the frontier chartered banks were formed solely for the purpose of issuing paper money, and the more modern type of banking was left to the merchants and private bankers.

The private domestic bankers (1) accepted deposits; (2) dealt in domestic exchange; (3) issued paper money in convenient denominations, which circulated as money even though it was sometimes disguised as a bill of exchange; (4) bought bank notes of chartered banks at a discount and presented them to the issuing banks for payment; (5) sold gold and silver at a premium during periods of banks' suspensions of specie payments, a common occurrence during the first half of the nineteenth century; and (6) acted as loan brokers for merchants and others who, in those days, for some unexplained reason, did not borrow from chartered banks.

During the eighteenth and first half of the nineteenth centuries, most of the American securities sold in London were exported by American merchant bankers. In 1811 Stephen Girard acquired most of the assets and good-will of the first Bank of the United States and created the first important private bank in this country. Later other merchants gave up their mercantile business and specialized in the buying and selling of foreign exchange and securities. In addition, most of the international bankers accepted deposits and made short-term loans, competing actively with the chartered banks. They issued bills of exchange or drafts in convenient denominations, which were used for money. These drafts, called "shopnotes," could always be redeemed in goods at the store or warehouse of the issuing merchant. Naturally there were abuses inherent in this system, and, as a result, it is not surprising that all early note issue chartered banks were prohibited from trading in commodities. These merchant bankers sold bills of exchange and travelers' letters of credit on their London banks and agents. They replaced their bank balances by purchasing exporters' bills of exchange drawn on London banks and sold securities of American governments and corporations to London bankers.

Many of the twentieth-century private banking houses trace their origin to this early period in American private banking. Joseph Drexel, an immigrant portrait painter who "made money buying and selling 'wild-cat' currency issued by state banks, became a broker dealing in gold from California and gradually built up a successful banking business inherited by the sons."[13] George Peabody, a Yankee dry-goods trader, organized a London company which specialized in foreign exchange and buying and selling of American securities. It later became Morgan, Greenfell, and Company. Kuhn, Loeb, and Company, Brown Brothers, J. and W. Seligman and Company, Lazard Freres, J. P. Morgan and Company, and others also had their origin in the mercantile business. In June, 1854, the "American *Bankers'*

[13] Corey, Lewis, *The House of Morgan*, pp. 116-17.

Magazine listed 240 private bankers, exchange dealers, and brokers in New York City, and 369 private bankers in the principal towns and cities in the United States outside of New York. There were 20 private bankers in Philadelphia, 10 in Boston, 23 in Cincinnati, 15 in St. Louis, 11 in Chicago, 16 in New Orleans, and 16 in San Francisco."[14]

The organization of the National Banking System during and following the Civil War had a tremendous effect upon the business of the private bankers. The act provided for a safe and uniform currency system, which destroyed the opportunity for profits resulting from the previous disorganized bank paper money system; it reduced the bankers' profits from domestic exchange transactions, which became much simpler and less speculative; and it gave a monopoly of note issue for almost fifty years to national chartered banks under conditions so attractive that many private bankers found it profitable to incorporate and carry on banking under its provisions.[15]

Jay Cooke, able financier of the Civil War, was responsible for the organization of three national banks, including the First National Bank of Philadelphia, which received Charter No. 1, on July 11, 1863.[16] Members of the sales organization that Cooke built up to sell government bonds were instrumental in organizing many national banks, particularly in the West, which was more friendly than the East toward the new system.

Private banking continued after the Civil War, but along more specialized lines. Private bankers continued to dominate investment banking and the foreign exchange business and to compete with chartered banks for deposits. Other private bankers were specialists organized as security brokerage firms, commercial paper dealers, mortgage concerns, and acceptance dealers.

The main contribution to banking during the period before the Civil War was the development and testing of banking principles. Many of these principles were incorporated in the National Banking Act of 1863. Since the Civil War, most of the states have remodeled their laws to conform to those passed by the national government. No fundamental changes were made in reorganization of the Banking System until 1913, when the Federal Reserve Act was passed.

---

[14] Larson, H. M., *Jay Cooke, Private Banker*, pp. 52-53.

[15] *Ibid.*, p. 145.

[16] *Ibid.*, p. 139.

QUESTIONS AND PROBLEMS

1. Early American chartered banks were created to serve as fiscal agents for the government and to function as commercial banks. Explain.
2. What is meant by the statement that all the early chartered banks were "banks of issue"? Why not "banks of deposit"?
3. How did the frontier demands for credit affect the traditional policy of expansion of bank credit based on commercial and other short-term assets?
4. Identify: (*a*) Bank of North America, (*b*) Bank of New York, and (*c*) Bank of Massachusetts.
5. In what ways did the charter of the second Bank of the United States differ from that of the first Bank of the United States? What developments explain the need for these differences?
6. The first mistake of a monetary nature was made "when Congress refused to renew the charter of the first Bank of the United States in 1811" (Jerome, *Governments and Money*, p. 172). Was this a serious monetary mistake? Explain.
7. Were note issues of the two United States banks based upon the banking or currency principle of note issue? Explain.
8. What principle of note issue was developed and used by each of the following banking systems: (*a*) Suffolk, (*b*) Guaranty, and (*c*) free banking? Why was protection to noteholders stressed?
9. "The redemption Bureau at Washington is the old Suffolk Bank System revised and improved?" (Patten, C. B., *The Methods and Machinery of Practical Banking*, p. 202). Explain.
10. "The legislature of Massachusetts testified its approval of the [Suffolk] system by passing a law prohibiting banks from paying out any notes but their own. . . . " (White, *Money and Banking* [5th ed.], p. 302). Explain. (Note similar provision in the Louisiana Banking Act of 1842.)
11. Many early bankers issued notes far beyond their ability to redeem them. They "hoped that the notes would fly so far that they would never find their way home." Why? Was "home" made as accessible as possible? Why were many of the banks called "wildcat" banks?
12. One reason Boston banks established and supported the Suffolk System was because of the effect of the operation of Gresham's law on the circulation of their notes. Explain.
13. The "small man with big votes" feared the two United States banks, 1791-1811 and 1816-36. Explain.
14. Who decides whether the proceeds of a loan are to be taken in the

form of deposits or bank notes? Why were bank notes preferred before 1850?

15. About 1800 what change took place in the attitude toward banks? How did it affect the development of banking?
16. "The principal drawback about 'free banking' is that it is sometimes not safe banking" (Burgess, W. R. *The Reserve Banks and the Money Market* [2d ed.], p. 24). Discuss. Is free banking superior to special charter or limited banking? Why? Account for the origin of free banking in the United States.
17. The "best way to diffuse banking in a community is to allow the banker to issue bank-notes of small amount that can supersede the metal currency. This amounts to a subsidy to each banker to enable him to keep open a bank till depositors choose to come to it" (Bagehot, Walter, *Lombard Street*, p. 84). Was this method used in the United States? Was it successful?
18. Explain why private banking was so lucrative before the Civil War. What changes resulted from the passage of the National Banking Act? Explain.
19. Calculate the percentage of notes of the first Bank of the United States in circulation in January, 1811, to the total liabilities. Use Table 10.
20. Were note liabilities larger than deposits in the first Bank of the United States?

REFERENCES

Bolles, A. S. *Practical Banking.* 2d ed. New York: Homans Publishing Co., 1884.

Catteral, R. C. H. *The Second Bank of the United States.* Chicago: University of Chicago Press, 1903.

Collins, A. W. *Rural Banking Reform,* chaps. i-iv. New York: Macmillan Co., 1931.

Conant, C. A. *A History of Modern Banks of Issue.* 5th ed. New York: G. P. Putnam's Sons, 1915.

Corey, Lewis. *The House of Morgan.* New York: G. H. Watt, 1930.

Dewey, D. R. *Financial History of the United States.* 11th ed. New York: Longmans, Green & Co., 1931.

Hepburn, A. B. *A History of Currency in the United States.* New ed. Select. New York: Macmillan Co., 1924.

Hoggson, N. F. *Banking through the Ages.* New York: Dodd, Mead & Co., 1926.

James, M. *Andrew Jackson, Portrait of a President,* chaps. xi, xiii, xvi, and xviii. Indianapolis: Bobbs-Merrill Co., 1937.

Larson, H. M. *Jay Cooke, Private Banker.* Cambridge: Harvard University Press, 1936.

Members of the Staff, Board of Governors of the Federal Reserve System, *Banking Studies,* pp. 5-15; 39-43; and 65-73. Washington, D.C.: Board of Governors of the Federal Reserve System, 1941.

Patten, C. B. *The Methods and Machinery of Practical Banking.* 7th ed. New York: Bradford Rhodes & Co., 1896.

Sumner, W. G. *The Financiers and Finance of the American Revolution.* New York: Dodd, Mead & Co., 1891.

White, Horace. *Money and Banking,* chaps. iv-xiii. 5th ed. Boston: Ginn & Co., 1914.

See the following volumes in the *Report of the National Monetary Commission.* Washington, D.C.: U.S. Government Printing Office: (*a*) Chaddock, R. E. "The Safety Fund System in New York, 1829-1866" (1910); (*b*) Dewey, D. R. "State Banking before the Civil War" (1910); (*c*) Holdsworth, J. T., and Dewey, D. R. "The First and Second Banks of the United States" (1910); (*d*) Kinley, David. "The Independent Treasury of the United States and Its Relations to the Banks of the Country" (1910).

Chapter XVII

COMMERCIAL BANKING SINCE THE CIVIL WAR

The National Banking Act Was a War Measure

In 1863 Congress passed a law which is now known as the National Banking Act. It was revised in 1864 and amended as to details by more than sixty different acts. There was a general revision in 1913. Originally, it was a war measure with the three following purposes: (1) the setting-up of a banking machinery which would be a help in financing the war, (2) the organization of a sound and conservative banking system, and (3) the creation of a safe and uniform note issue system.

To Aid in Financing the War.—The Lincoln administration took over a Treasury that was practically bare of funds and a federal indebtedness of $100,000,000. After the outbreak of the war, increase in taxation was delayed; funds had to be borrowed, and the government turned to the banks for them.

In the fall of 1861 the banks had recovered from the shocks accompanying the election of a Republican president, the secession of seven southern states, and the cancellation by southern debtors of their obligations to northern creditors. The banks agreed to assist in the $150,000,000 bond issue which the government proposed to float, and, subsequently, they purchased most of the bonds. The Treasury insisted on being paid in specie, over the protest of the banks, which wanted to hold funds until they were used to make government purchases. The gold and coin received by the Treasury was paid out promptly, going back to the reserves of the banks; but the Treasury's hard money policy decreased the willingness of the chartered banks to co-operate in future bond issues. A panic at the end of 1861 caused the banks to suspend specie payment.

Secretary S. P. Chase's policy was to finance the war by borrowing, and his proposal for a new national banking system was colored by this fact. Secretary Chase was very distrustful of the state banks, because they were increasing their circulations where state laws permitted, were not redeeming their notes in specie but were selling the latter privately at a premium, and were not co-operating with the

Treasury to the extent that the secretary thought they should. In the meantime, a private banker, Jay Cooke, had assumed the job of merchandising government securities directly to the public, and he was responsible for carrying the issue of the new banking system directly to the people.

The unpopularity of the state banks was capitalized on in a political way, and the new National Banking Act was passed in 1863. The law contained many defects but was revised the next year under the able leadership of Hugh McCulloch, the first Comptroller of the Currency. The new commercial banks were required to invest a considerable portion of their assets in government bonds, thereby providing the government with a new market for its securities, if and when, new national banks were organized.

To Organize a Sound and Conservative Banking System:—The act permitted groups to organize new banks under the same type of free banking act which had become common throughout the nation. In general, the standard of banking practices which had to be maintained were higher than those required by most state free banking laws. National banks were required to keep minimum reserves against deposits and notes (later the note reserve requirement was dropped) and to build up their surplus account to 20 per cent of their capital. The shareholders were required to pay in one-half of their capital subscription before the bank could open and the remainder before the end of the next six months. Until 1935 they were subject to double liability on their shares. National banks were permitted to receive and hold deposits of the federal government, were limited to 7 per cent interest charges, and were prohibited from making real estate loans.

The National Banking Act did provide for better unit banks but not for a better banking system. It was a compromise between the school wanting a third Bank of the United States, similar to the first and second, and that in favor of free banking under state laws. The new national banks were fundamentally the same as the privately owned local banks operating under the free banking laws of the states. No central bank was created to guide and strengthen them until fifty years later, when the Federal Reserve System was provided for. The National Banking Act of 1863 created a special bureau in the Department of the Treasury to supervise national banks. This bureau was placed under the control of the Comptroller of the Currency, who was to be appointed by the President, with the consent of the Senate, for a term of five years.

The most important of the Comptroller's duties with reference to national banks are: (1) to supervise the organization, chartering, and regulation of national banks, (2) to bring suits for deliberate violation of the law, (3) to maintain a banking information service, (4) to examine national banks, (5) to permit mergers involving national banks, (6) to permit the establishment of branches, (7) to make annual reports to Congress on the condition of national banks, (8) to make legislative recommendations, and (9) to make detailed decisions which involve administrative interpretation of the law. Before their retirement in 1935, the Comptroller had jurisdiction over the issuance, redemption, and retirement of national bank notes. He is an ex officio member of the board of directors of the Federal Deposit Insurance Corporation and was formerly a member of the Federal Reserve Board. Finally, he is superintendent of all banks located within the District of Columbia, as well as of all national banks in the United States.

To Create a Sound and Uniform Note Issue System.—Like the Peel Act in England in 1844, the chief contribution of the National Banking Act was not in the field of banking but in the field of currency. In 1860 there were 1,600 different types of state banks' notes in circulation. They varied in value from worthless to those which were as "good as gold." In order to make a place for the greenbacks, a small tax was levied on state bank notes; and after it was certain that the new national banks could issue notes in volume large enough to prevent contraction of the currency, this tax was made prohibitive (10 per cent) in 1866.

National Banking System's Success Was Due to Bank Note Issue Monopoly

The tax on state bank notes had far-reaching effect. It guaranteed the success of the National Banking System and provided the nation with a safe and uniform bank currency. At first the new National Bank Act was unpopular, only 134 national banks having been established during 1863, of which only 23 were rechartered state banks. There were 40 national banks formed during 1864, of which one-third were reorganized state banks. In 1865 the situation changed because of the prohibitive 10 per cent tax on state bank note issues (effective in 1866), and by the end of this year there were over 1,600 national banks in existence.

The provision for national bank notes was the heart of the National Banking Act and the one from which ultimately most of the benefits of the act flowed. The notes of the new national banks were backed by federal government bonds, which were deposited with the government and held in trust for the depository banks. Each bank was required to invest in government bonds equal to at least one-third of its capital stock and in no case less than $30,000. If a bank desired, it could invest much more in government bonds, but the amount of its note issue was limited to its capital. Originally, the aggregate note issues of all banks were limited to $300,000,000, allocated among the states—one-half according to population and the other half according to the capital of the banks.[1]

The compulsory purchase of government bonds was no hardship on the banks, because they could deposit them with the Treasury, receiving new national bank notes in exchange. While receiving interest on the bonds pledged as backing for the notes, the banks also received interest on the promissory notes secured from borrowers when the banks lent the national bank currency. Thus they were in the unique position of having their capital invested and also having funds to be used for banking purposes. Since state banks were operating under equally liberal state note issue laws, the latter were lukewarm toward the National Banking System until after their note issuing privilege was made unprofitable. Owing to the slowness in organizing the National Banking System, it was not of much help in financing the war.[2]

The disappearance of the state bank notes gave the new national banks a monoply of circulation from 1866 to 1914. The two advantages of the new currency were safety and uniformity. Adequate security was provided by government bonds deposited with the federal government, by the 5 per cent redemption fund in Washington, and by making the notes first liens on the assets of the issuing banks. Parity was maintained by requiring the issuing banks to redeem

[1] Provision for a maximum volume was modified later and finally repealed in 1875.

[2] That the old banks were slow in joining the new National Banking System is shown by the fact that the Bank of North America (1781) holds Charter No. 602, and the Bank of Massachusetts (1784) holds Charter No. 794.

their notes in Washington and at their own offices and by requiring other national banks to take them from the public. All the notes were printed and engraved by the federal government, and all were issued under the same conditions, thus insuring uniformity.

The chief beneficiaries from the new national bank note issues were the people of the South and West, who had been plagued with "red dogs," "stumptails," and "shinplasters." In the East, the national bank notes largely replaced other fairly satisfactory note issue systems. National bank notes were safe and uniform in value, but they lacked elasticity, one of the characteristics of a good note issue system. Beginning in 1914, their circulation was supplemented by notes issued by Federal Reserve banks. Since 1935 Federal Reserve banks have had a monopoly of bank note issue in the United States, which is the logical solution for the problem. However, because of the increased importance of deposit currency, the problem of bank note issue is of secondary importance.

Development of Deposit Banking Was an Aid to Banks

In 1862, prior to the passage of the National Banking Act, there were 1,492 state banks, but by 1866 the number had decreased to 247. This number included some of the most powerful and the most conservative of the original state-chartered banks. In New York the clearinghouse association showed its disapproval of the new national banks by not admitting the First National Bank of New York for many years, although this bank took over the private banking house of Jay Cooke and Company of New York, which had the best possible connections of the period.

Growth of Deposit Banking.—The chief reason for the original shift to incorporation under national law was the desire for the then valuable note issue privilege. In any pioneer community where transportation facilities are poor and daily or weekly contacts with banks are impossible, banks find a demand for currency rather than for deposit credit. By 1840 the checking account system had developed to such a degree in metropolitan centers that it rivaled or exceeded note issue in importance. The increase in regulation of state bank note issues that followed disastrous failures in the period from 1837 to 1841 hastened this movement, but the most rapid shift from note issue to deposit banking followed the Civil War.

This shift to deposit banking meant that banks were lending their credit in the form of promises to pay deposits on demand instead of lending their credit in the form of bank notes. National banks were interested in this type of lending because there was no legal limit to the deposit-capital ratio, while note issue was limited to the capital of the issuing bank. Today deposit-capital ratios of more then fifteen to one are not uncommon. After 1866, bankers discovered, as English bankers had during the second quarter of the nineteenth century, that deposit banking may be just as profitable as note issue banking. Both state and national banks, by emphasizing the advantages of checking accounts, encouraged depositors to allow funds to be used by the banks pending withdrawals.

New Types of Banking Services.—The development of deposit currency lessened the importance of the note issue privilege and eliminated the near monopoly of commercial banking which national banks enjoyed during the first decade of their history. In the settlement of the West, one of the first business enterprises to be established in a new town was a bank. Although the note issue privilege was desired, there were other factors which often led the sponsors to favor a state-chartered institution. In the West and South the minimum capital requirements for a state-chartered bank were less than for a federal chartered bank. Formerly, in ten states there were no minimum capital requirements, and in others it was as low as $5,000. In addition, the states required less rigid or no examinations and fewer restrictions on lending and investment policies. State charters gave banks much broader banking privileges than national charters; and it was customary for many state banks to combine the banking business with the farm mortgage, fire insurance, life insurance, and real estate businesses. Savings, safe deposit, and trust banking were later added. By 1900 the banking picture as shown by statistics of chartered banks appears as indicated in Table 12. This expansion in number and variety of banks and banking services multiplied the problems, which still remain paramount, of banking legislation and banking supervision.

Growth of Correspondent Banking.—An unexpected effect of the passage of the National Banking Act as amended was the strengthening of the correspondent system of banking in the United States. The legal requirements of the act as amended required banks located in New York and, after 1887, in Chicago and St. Louis to hold all their required reserves against deposits in their own vaults in the form of lawful money (all kinds except national bank notes). Other banks, however, were permitted to carry part of their required reserves with these banks as "bankers' balances" or deposits. As early as 1870, about two-fifths of the banking reserves of the country were in the form of bankers' balances, and a large percentage was kept with the nine "superbanks" in New York. From that date to 1914, these large New York banks, with thousands of correspondents, were the chief factors in determining national credit policies.

TABLE 12

BANKING STATISTICS, 1900 AND 1910

(Dollar Amounts in Millions)

Year and Class of Banks	Number	Capital Accounts	Deposits	Note Liabilities	Loans and Discounts	Investments
1900						
National...	3,871	$1,020	$2,602	$284	$2,710	$ 776
State......	4,369	367	1,267	....	1,039	190
Trust......	290	275	1,028	....	728	326
Total..	8,530	$1,662	$4,897	$284	$4,477	$1,292
1910						
National...	7,145	$1,851	$5,287	$676	$5,456	$1,612
State......	12,166	689	2,728	....	2,407	304
Trust......	1,091	866	3,073	....	2,257	1,542
Total..	20,402	$3,406	$11,088	$676	$10,120	$3,458

Source: U. S. Comptroller of Currency, *Annual Reports.* Does not include private banks. Reports of state-chartered institutions are admittedly incomplete but are the only ones available.

Later Legislative Changes Aided National Banks

Act of March 14, 1900.—The act of March 14, 1900, which is popularly known as the Gold Standard Act, gave the National Banking System a new lease on life, particularly in small communities. It provided for the issuance of national bank notes up to 100 per cent of the par value of the bonds (previously only 90 per cent); and it refunded part of the existing debt in 2 per cent, thirty-four year bonds, in order to assure the banks of a supply of government securities which could be used to back their notes. At the same time it fixed a circulation tax of 0.5 per cent on all notes backed by these bonds but did not change the existing tax of 1 per cent on notes supported by bonds that carried a higher yield.

The act also reduced the minimum capital requirements from $50,000 to $25,000 in towns with a population of 3,000 or less. (Thirty-three years later Congress decided that this had been a mistake, because it restored the old $50,000 minimum for banks located in these communities.) From 1900 to 1905 the number of national banks increased about 50 per cent, and by 1910 they had almost doubled in number. Most of these new banks were small and operated in rural communities, where the note issue privilege was more highly valued than in cities. However, during the same decade, the number of state banks and trust companies had almost tripled. (See Table 12.)

Intensive Development in Banking.—One of the most striking developments in banking from 1900 to 1913 was the growth in size and number of loan and trust companies, a type of banking that is almost entirely confined to metropolitan areas. These institutions had their origin and greatest development in the United States. A modern trust company contains trust, savings, bond, and commercial banking departments, thereby earning the title "department store of finance." (See Illustration VI in Chapter XV.) This represents the intensive development of banking rather than the extensive one illustrated by the growth in the number of state and national banks. Another phase of the intensive development in commercial banking was the merger movement that paralleled the trust movement in the industrial fields. In New York, Boston, and other centers there was a tendency to pile "banking assets a mile high." In the South and West chain and branch banking were developed (extensive development).

More Liberal Laws for National Banks.—In 1913 national banks were threatening to withdraw from the National Banking System because they wished to carry on savings, trust, and other noncommercial banking activities in order to compete more successfully with the state-chartered institutions. Under such conditions it is not surprising that many concessions were made to this group. In the Federal Reserve Act, the national banks were authorized to accept savings deposits, to undertake a limited mortgage banking business, to perform trust functions under rules and regulation of the Federal Reserve Board, to grant acceptance credit, and to carry on foreign finance business. The Federal Reserve Act was signed by President

Wilson in 1913, and the twelve Federal Reserve banks were opened in November, 1914. All national banks were required to be member banks. The war and postwar boom greatly increased the number of banks in the United States, until a peak was reached in 1921. These changes for selected years are shown in Table 13.

TABLE 13

BANKING STATISTICS—1915, 1920, 1930

(Dollar Accounts in Millions)

Year* and Class of Bank	Number	Deposits†	Loans and Investments	Loans	Investments
1915					
National	7,597	$ 6,609	$ 8,688	$ 6,663	$ 2,025
State member	17	68	76	57	19
Mutual	639	3,951	4,040	2,170	1,870
Others	18,352	8,502	8,662	6,763	1,899
Total	26,605	$19,131	$21,466	$15,653	$ 5,813
1920					
National	8,024	$14,316	$17,547	$13,499	$ 4,048
State member	1,374	7,600	8,012	6,035	1,977
Mutual	631	5,187	5,308	2,591	2,716
Others	19,800	10,618	10,817	8,714	2,104
Total	29,829	$37,721	$41,684	$30,839	$10,845
1930					
National	7,247	$20,556	$21,749	$14,874	$ 6,875
State member	1,068	13,134	13,906	10,340	3,567
Mutual	606	9,197	9,747	6,009	3,739
Others	14,931	12,067	12,706	9,415	3,290
Total	23,852	$54,954	$58,109	$40,638	$17,471

* Reports for June 30 or nearest reporting date.
† Deposits exclusive of interbank deposits.
Source: Nineteenth Annual Report of the Federal Reserve Board, 1932, pp. 117-21.

The Federal Reserve Act Provided for an Improved Banking System

Although the Federal Reserve System is discussed in other parts of this volume, the major contributions to the banking system are summarized here as follows:

1. Creation of twelve regional banks, called Federal Reserve banks
2. Creation of a Federal Reserve Board (now Board of Governors) to supervise the general functioning of the Federal Reserve System

3. Creation of a new elastic currency, the Federal Reserve note
4. Centralization of gold reserves in the hands of twelve Federal Reserve banks
5. Provision of sources of new credit for commercial banks
6. Creation of new machinery for transferring funds between cities within the United States
7. Provisions of new fiscal agents for the federal government

War Adjunct of the Treasury.—Fortunately, the Federal Reserve System was well established before the United States entered World War I in 1917, and for three years thereafter it operated as an adjunct of the Treasury. It oiled the wheels of credit inflation by rediscounting bank customers' notes backed by Liberty and Victory bonds, by lending to member banks on their notes backed by government bonds, and by buying federal securities in the open market. It met the increased currency needs by expanding the volume of Federal Reserve notes, and it offset the effects of the decrease in volume of silver certificates, as provided for in the Pittman Act of 1918, by increasing the volume of Federal Reserve bank notes. During the deflation of 1920-22, the Federal Reserve System aided the banking system by expanding the volume of currency and credit, thereby preventing a financial panic which would have intensified the hardships of the business recession.

Unsolved Banking Problems.—The Federal Reserve Act left unsolved many problems which had faced the people of the United States since before the Civil War. There remained the problem of weak, poorly managed, small local banks.[3] Bank failures were not eliminated, and banking codes and government regulation were as fruitless in protecting the creditors of banks as they had been before 1914. Branch banking was still restricted or prohibited. Every community thought it necessary to have its own locally owned and locally operated bank; as a result, there were "too many banks and not enough bankers." There was a tendency to lower banking standards, and apparently too much reliance was being placed upon mere mem-

[3] Professor Jacob Viner gives as the cause of the "peculiar weakness of the American banking system. . . . . the fact that of all the modern national banking systems it alone has adhered predominantly to the eighteenth-century model of individual small-scale units, as distinguished from large-scale banking institutions with many branches" ("Recent Legislation and the Banking Situation," the *American Economic Review,* Supplement, Vol. XXVI [March, 1936], p. 107).

bership in the Federal Reserve System.[4] The popular expression which indicates this attitude was "members of the Federal Reserve System cannot fail." Even the belief that money panics were impossible under the Federal Reserve System proved to be false in February and the first three days of March, 1933.

From 1913 to 1933, the congressional and administrative tendency to cater to national and other member banks had considerable influence on American banking. In 1917 state member banks were exempt from examination by the Comptroller of the Currency and were also exempt from compliance with certain national laws that they objected to because compliance would have meant loss of their competitive advantage over national banks. The act of 1918 strengthened the right of national banks to engage in the trust business. The McFadden Act of 1927 was passed to "put new life into the national banking system" and, according to one banker, probably caused more bank failures than any federal act passed since 1863. It enlarged the power of national banks to make real estate loans, recognized their right to purchase investment securities, modified the limitations on the amount of loans to one name, permitted reduction in the par value of bank stock to less than $100, simplified procedure for consolidation of state with national banks, permitted national banks to establish branches within the corporate or city limits where they were located, and forbade state member banks to establish new ones outside the corporate limits. The purposes of these laws were to bring more banks under federal supervision and to enlarge the activities of national banks by permitting them to perform banking services formerly experimented with and developed by state-chartered banks. However, all this "competition in laxity" was not beneficial, as will be shown later.

The Federal Reserve System Did Not Eliminate Failures

The most important banking phenomenon between 1921 and 1934 was the large number of bank failures. Before 1930 failures were generally in the agricultural sections of the country, the mortality

[4] Professor J. H. Williams sums up this situation as follows: "Nevertheless, many of our people undoubtedly regarded the Reserve Act of 1913 as a complete and final answer to our banking troubles. In their view, it was to mark the end of banking crises and bank failures in this country" ("The Banking Act of 1935," the *American Economic Review*, Supplement, Vol. XXVI [March, 1936], p. 105).

rate having been particularly high among small banks located in communities with populations of less than 1,000. Between 1930 and 1934 failures were so widespread that most communities had suffered from at least one bank suspension. The widespread banking panic led to local, then to state, and finally to a national banking moratorium. About 11,000 banks failed between 1920 and 1933, and over 4,000 more were suspended during 1933.[5]

National Banking Holiday.—In 1932 bankers begged depositors not to demand their deposits. Then local, state, and, finally, national banking holidays were declared in order to relieve banks temporarily from their legal obligations to pay on demand. Although labelled "bank holidays," no one was fooled by these proclamations, all appreciating that they were banking moratoria. In preceding chapters references have been made to the emergency legislation of 1932, which included provisions for the Reconstruction Finance Corporation (January), the Glass-Steagall Act (February), and the national bank note currency rider attached to the Home Loan Bank Bill (July); but on March 4, 1933, all banks had been closed by orders issued by the governors of the forty-eight states in co-operation with the Comptroller of the Currency.[6] Since many of the state moratoria were declared for but one day, the President had to act before Monday morning, March 6. On that morning he declared a national banking moratorium for three days, pending the convening of Congress. While Congress was assembling, the administration drafted the Emergency Banking Bill, and, when Congress met, the bill was passed in record-breaking time.

Emergency Banking Act.—The Emergency Banking Act (March 9, 1933) contained provisions which confirmed all emergency acts of the President and a plan for managing and reorganizing unsound banks which were either kept closed or placed under the administration of conservators. The act allowed banks to issue preferred stock to depositors in reorganizations if this was acceptable to 75 per cent of the depositors or two-thirds of the stockholders, or both. The Reconstruction Finance Corporation was permitted to help in reorganization by purchases of preferred stock or capital notes. The Federal Reserve banks were given permission to issue Federal Reserve bank notes to be backed by government bonds or commercial

[5] *Annual Report of the Federal Reserve Board,* 1933, pp. 206-23.

[6] *Ibid.,* pp. 8-14.

paper. Individuals were permitted to borrow directly from the twelve Federal Reserve banks; and, by paying a penalty rate, member banks were permitted to use noneligible collateral to obtain advances.[7]

CHART VIII

NUMBER OF BANK SUSPENSIONS, 1922-39*

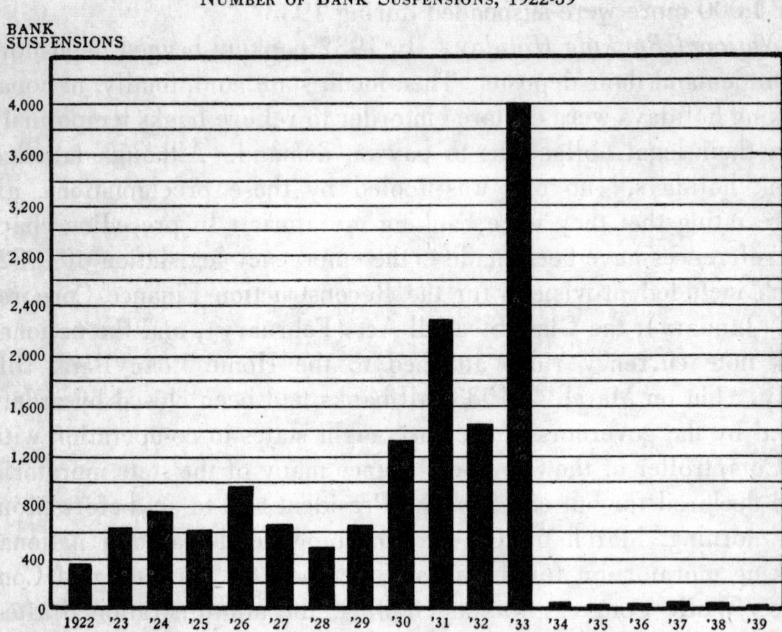

* The number of bank failures since 1939 by years have been 1940, 22; 1941, 8; 1942, 9; 1943, 4; 1944, 1; and 1945, 0.

Source: Board of Governors of the Federal Reserve System. Annual and monthly reports.

It was necessary to examine the banks in order to pass upon their credit standings and make effective certain provisions of the Bank Emergency Act; consequently, the banking holiday was extended for three days. On Saturday, March 11, just one week after the President took the oath of office, the Federal Reserve banks were reopened. The next Monday, all sound banks in Reserve cities reopened; on Tuesday, similar banks in clearinghouse cities; and on Wednesday, all the remaining sound banks.[8]

---

[7] *Federal Reserve Bulletin*, March, 1933, pp. 115-18.

[8] *Annual Report of the Federal Reserve Board*, 1933, p. 14.

The Government Helped to Refinance Banks

There were two classes of banks after the national banking moratorium—licensed and unlicensed. There were 13,500 of the former and 4,500 of the latter. Many banks in the second group were considered hopelessly insolvent, and, during 1933 and 1934, over 2,000 of them were placed in receivership, and practically all the remainder were reorganized with the financial assistance of the Reconstruction Finance Corporation.[9]

By the end of 1934 the Reconstruction Finance Corporation's investment in banks amounted to $850,000,000. Additional stock purchases and capital loans were made in 1935 and part of 1936, when the head of Reconstruction Finance Corporation announced that such investments would soon be discontinued. In 1935 the Corporation's peak investments in banks reached $900,000,000, which was reduced to $250,000,000 ten years later. Refinancing with funds provided by the Reconstruction Finance Corporation includes some transactions consented to by banks in order to remove the stigma that might have otherwise been associated with the sale of capital account items by financially weak banks. For this reason, some of the most conservative banks sold capital account items to the Corporation in 1933 and in 1934. In the city of New York, some of the largest banks were the ones "to break the ice," and in other communities, Syracuse, for example, the clearinghouse association members agreed that if one bank sold stock or capital notes to the Reconstruction Finance Corporation all members would do likewise. When the financially strong banks sold stock or capital notes to the Corporation, usually they were liquidated promptly.

During World War II there was only a moderate rise in the capital accounts of banks, because the increase of $200,000,000 in par value of common stock was largely offset by the retirement of about $130,000,000 of capital items owned by the Reconstruction Finance Corporation. Most of the $1,000,000,000 increase in capital account items was due to the retention of earnings. When the period since 1934 is considered, the total expansion of capital account items has been in excess of $2,000,000,000, but this is far out of line with the total expansion of deposit liabilities. This decline in capital-

[9] *Ibid.*, 1933, pp. 25-26; 1934, pp. 26-27. A similar refinancing of banks took place during and following the national banking moratorium in Germany during the summer of 1931.

deposit ratio is being brought to the attention of Congress in the annual reports of the Federal Deposit Insurance Corporation. (See Chapter XVIII.)

Banking Reform Acts of 1933 and 1935

In Canada, banks are chartered for but ten years, and, before a general rechartering act is passed, the banking codes and banking practices are reviewed. Outside experts are employed, hearings are held, and recommendations are made to Parliament. In the United States, most major banking reform legislation follows or takes place during some national emergency. Following the banking collapse of 1933, two major reform banking acts were passed—the Banking Act of 1933 and the Banking Act of 1935.

The Banking Act of 1933.—This act was passed by Congress in order (1) to correct specific abuses uncovered by the Senate investigating committee, (2) to increase the control of the supervisory authorities over the volume of bank credit, and (3) to provide for a federal deposit insurance plan. These provisions are explained more fully where the specific banking problem is discussed; but, for the convenience of the reader, it may be noted that the act: (1) provided for the separation of investment and deposit banking; (2) required holding companies, under certain conditions, to submit to examination and to follow certain financial practices; (3) placed limitations on and provided for regulation of banks' investments; (4) prohibited interest payments on demand deposits; (5) authorized the Federal Reserve Board to fix the maximum interest rates paid on time deposits; (6) permitted national banks to establish branches under the same territorial rules as those applying to state-chartered banks; (7) enlarged the membership provisions of the Federal Reserve System to include Morris Plan and mutual savings banks; (8) increased minimum capital requirements of national banks located in communities of 3,000 and less from $25,000 to $50,000; (9) permitted national banks to charge interest on loans and discounts at the legal rate, as provided by state law, or 1 per cent above the Federal Reserve banks' discount rate for 90-day commercial paper, or a different maximum rate if applicable to state banks, whichever is the higher (if there is no legal rate in a state it shall be deemed to be 7 per cent); (10) required directors to own stock in their banks and limited the number of directors to 25; (11) provided for removal of directors and officers under certain conditions; and (12) provided for federal insurance of deposits.

The Banking Act of 1933 provided for the temporary insurance of deposits up to $2,500 for six months. Before the six months had expired, the coverage was increased to $5,000, and the temporary plan was extended for a year. The permanent plan provided for in this act was modified by the Banking Act of 1935.

Banking Act of 1935.—The Banking Act of 1935 provided that the maximum coverage for deposits would be $5,000 per depositor per bank, that the insurance fee would be 1/12 of 1 per cent of the total deposits, and that insured banks would not be required to buy stock in the Federal Deposit Insurance Corporation.[10] The act provided for the reorganization of the Federal Reserve System. The Board was renamed Board of Governors of the Federal Reserve System, and its powers were greatly increased.[11] It amended the Banking Act of 1933 in order to make certain provisions more workable.

Failure to Correct Structural Defects.—The banking acts of 1933 and 1935 were of the "patching" and "propping" variety of legislation, not going far enough in the correction of certain structural defects in the banking system. There can be no quarrel with the two basic aims of the acts, even though they were antithetical. Congress sought to mend the banking system by correcting certain abuses by improving bank management through better governmental regulation and by setting up machinery in the form of deposit insurance to protect depositors in case the first did not work as planned. This desire to protect the public from the effects of poor bank management is recognition of the fact that the other provisions of the acts were inadequate. It does not mean that the provisions were unimportant but merely that the task of banking reform is incomplete.

Multiple Office Banking

Branch Banking.—Many Americans have looked with envy at the record of chartered banking in Canada and in Great Britain. In these, as in most foreign countries, banking is conducted by a few

[10] See Chap. XX.

[11] See Chap. XXVI.

large banks with many branches. They have no provisions for deposit insurance and relatively few regulatory laws and governmental supervisory authorities. Most of the work of supervision over banking consists of internal supervision of branches by the main or regional offices, with the government entering the field, if at all, at the main office level. The advantage of this system is apparent when it is noted that there are but 10 chartered commercial banks in Canada and 15 in Great Britain. In Canada four-fifths of the banking is done by the four largest commercial banks; and in Great Britain the Big Five handle about three-fourths of the banking business.

Branch banking consists of a system of branch banking offices emanating from a single bank or corporation. The territory served may be world-wide, state-wide, district-wide, or only within the city in which the bank is located. The branches have the name of the parent corporation, and they are all governed by one board of directors, which is sometimes assisted by local advisory boards in leading branch cities. Branch managers direct the local branch's affairs in accordance with regulations of the main office. The branches carry on the same kind of activities performed by a unit bank or a member of a group system similarly located. Large loans must be approved by the head office, where most of the credit work is done. Trust and other types of specialized banking are limited to the head offices and largest branches.

Under provisions of the Banking Act of 1933, national banks—in states allowing branch banking—are permitted to establish branches under conditions similar to those under which the state banks operate. This law leaves the control of the branch banking movement in the United States in the hands of forty-eight state governments. At the beginning of 1945 there were 1,230 banks in the United States operating 4,071 branches. Banks in all states, except Montana and West Virginia, participated in the branch banking movement.[12] Since about 48 per cent of the branches are located in the head office city, about 69 per cent within the head office county, and only about 31 per cent outside the head office county, the movement, considered from a state or national viewpoint, is still in the embryonic stage of development.

[12] *Annual Report of the Federal Deposit Insurance Corporation for the Year Ended December 31, 1944*, Table 102, pp. 112-20.

National banks, under certain conditions, were authorized to establish foreign branches in the original Federal Reserve Act (1913). With the permission of the Board of Governors of the Federal Reserve System, any national bank with a capital of $1,000,-000 may open foreign branches. In the 1944 report of the Board, 7 member banks were reported to be operating 67 branches or offices located in 16 foreign countries, exclusive of formerly occupied territory. Of the 7 member banks, 4 were national banks, and they operated 61 of the branches located abroad. Obviously, these reports, covering only member banks, are incomplete, because there are other American financial institutions interested in foreign branch banking. These include the great private banking houses, trust companies, and specialists dealing in foreign exchange business exclusively.[13]

Group Banking.—Group banking has been developed because of legal obstacles and local prejudices against branch banking. In group banking, a number of unit banks are held together and operated as a system. The Federal Reserve Board, in its annual report for 1930, recognized the following types, classified according to controlling agency:[14]

1. Instances where control is exercised by a holding corporation, which has usually been formed by interests connected with one or more of the principal banks belonging to the system.
2. Instances where control is exercised by the principal bank in the system, either through direct ownership of stock by the bank or through ownership by the stockholders or directors of the bank.
3. Instances of ownership of controlling or substantial interest in a number of banks by an individual, family, or group of individuals.

Recent developments have been conspicuously of the first and second types. Since the actual method and agency of control varies from time to time, these classifications by types of control are very general.

The group banking movement started about 1900, but nearly all the now known groups were organized during the last few months of the period of speculation preceding the stock market crash of October-November, 1929, and some did not complete their organization until

[13] Phelps, C. W., *Trends in American Banking Abroad.* Although not a bank, the American Express Company has been very active in opening foreign offices, which have aided in financing foreign travel and trade.

[14] See footnote, p. 20, in *Annual Report of Federal Reserve Board,* 1930.

after the panic. The movement has been most widely developed in those states where branch banking has been prohibited or restricted. Many groups cut across state lines and include units in several states. Since the holding company is not a bank, it does not come under the general banking laws of states or the national government. Numerous states have passed special laws providing for some control and regulation, and the Banking Act of 1933 made a number of provisions for federal regulation.

Since the holding corporation controls its subsidiary banks through voting privileges, this power, more than anything else, was brought under strict regulation. Before the holding company can vote the shares of a member bank, it must secure a voting permit from the Board of Governors of the Federal Reserve System. Before the permit is granted, the holding company must agree to submit to examination, to build up a surplus equal to 25 per cent of its holdings of bank stock, and to sever any connection that it has with investment affiliates or similar types of security selling organizations, except those dealing in government bonds.

Arguments in Favor of Branch Banking.—There are many arguments in favor of multiple office banking, the most important being the claims for (1) better management, (2) greater safety, (3) greater diversification of assets, (4) greater geographical mobility of funds, (5) greater uniformity in interest rates, (6) greater economy in reserves, (7) better clearing and collection services, and (8) better deposit and lending services for retail and other firms which have ceased being local in nature. The advocates of branch banking emphasize the fact that every major business served by commercial bankers has ceased being local in nature. True, some of the disadvantages of the local nature of banks in the United States have been offset in part by correspondent banking and the Federal Reserve System, but the fact remains that the United States is the only important country in the world that adheres to the old basically local unit banking system.

The chief argument against the multiple office banking system is the monopolistic nature of such a system.[15] This argument fails to recognize that there may be competition between branches of different banks in an area, as well as between unit banks, and that often

---

[15] See, for example, *The Annual Report of the Federal Insurance Corporation for the Year Ended December 31, 1944*, pp. 10-11.

the opening of a branch bank in a town has broken the monopoly formerly enjoyed by the local unit bank. The second argument is that the needs of small communities would be neglected by the main office. This argument is hard to substantiate in view of the experiences with branch banking in California and other western states. Any good banker desires to make profitable loans, irrespective of the domicile of the borrower, and this desire does not exclude those located in small communities. If a banker fails to make these loans, a rival branch office manager will; and when bankless communities are considered, their number was larger before branch banking was authorized in certain western states than it is today under state-wide branch banking laws.

It must not be concluded that the problem of bank failures would be eliminated by multiple banking offices, because branch banking systems may fail just as those dominated by single banks. While advocates of branch banking point to the records of chartered banking in England and Canada, those opposed point to the collapse of branch banking systems in Germany and Austria during the year 1931. There is no substitute for good management, nor is it guaranteed by any type of structural organization. If managers of single office banks are more efficient than those of multiple office banks, they have nothing to fear from a federal law permitting branch banking on a Federal Reserve district basis.

War Changes

During World War II, numerous regulatory and legislative changes were made which permitted an expansion of the means of payments, thereby making taxes easier to collect and bonds easier to sell. The Federal Reserve banks were permitted to buy $5,000,000,000 in government obligations directly from the government; all member bank reserve requirements for government deposits resulting directly from the subscription for United States government obligations were repealed; and all insured banks were exempt from assessment for deposit insurance on similar government balances. On June 12, 1945, the Federal Reserve banks minimum reserve requirements were reduced to 25 per cent against both note and deposit liabilities, and the provision that government obligations could be used as collateral for Federal Reserve notes was made permanent.

As shown in Table 14, the outstanding developments in banking during the war period were expansion in bank deposits and increase in investments. In 1945 bank deposits showed an increase of 247 per cent over 1939, while investments increased by 359 per cent during the same period.

TABLE 14

BANKING STATISTICS—JUNE, 1939, AND JUNE, 1945
(Dollar Accounts in Millions)

Class of Banks	Number	Deposits*	Loans	Investments	Total Loans and Investments
1939					
National	5,203	$24,534	$12,141	$19,462	$32,603
State member	1,127	13,493			
Mutual	553	10,521	4,931	5,411	10,342
Others	8,199	7,444	3,245	3,425	6,671
Total	15,082	$55,992	$21,318	$28,299	$49,616
1945					
National	5,015	$68,282	$12,369	$50,808	$63,177
State member	1,825	37,864	8,219	28,030	36,249
Mutual	542	14,426	4,307	10,827	15,134
Others	7,160	17,868	3,085	12,005	15,090
Total	14,542	$138,440	$27,980	$101,670	$129,650

* Exclusive of interbank deposits.
Source: Federal Reserve Bulletin, March, 1940, p. 223; and October, 1945, pp. 1032-33.

QUESTIONS AND PROBLEMS

1. What would have been the effect on the development of commercial banking if the National Banking Act as amended in 1864 had forbidden any bank other than a national bank to make a contract to pay money on demand?
2. What are the duties of the Comptroller of the Currency? What state official may be compared to him?
3. Monopoly of bank note issue was the chief reason for the success of the National Banking System. Explain.
4. Distinguish between note issue banking and deposit banking.
5. What significant changes took place in number, types, liabilities, and assets of banks from 1900 to 1910? Use Table 12.
6. The National Banking Act rejected the big bank idea and enthroned the local bank system. Explain.

7. Why did Secretary Chase expect "to defeat the South with the new National Banking System"?

8. Answer the same questions as stated in Question 5 for the period from 1915 to 1930. Use Table 13.

9. Make a list of all the facts you can find to support the following quotation: "No business in America has a finer record in educational effort than has banking." Quoted from the Inaugural Address of Mr. Robert Hanes, president (1940) of the American Bankers' Association.

10. Explain how correspondent banking was affected by the National Banking Act.

11. "I have tediously insisted that the natural system of banking is that of many banks keeping their own reserves, with the penalty of failure before them if they neglect it" (Bagehot, Walter, *Lombard Street*, p. 329). Is this view accepted today? Explain.

12. What was the bank holiday of March, 1933? Describe conditions under which banks were permitted to resume operations.

13. What are the advantages claimed for group banking over unit banking? Is it superior to branch banking? Why?

14. The 15,000 banks "seems to me a sufficient number of banks to provide ample banking facilities for the nation. The rest of the world manages to get along with less" (Viner, Jacob, "Recent Legislation and the Banking Situation," *American Economic Review*, Supplement, Vol. XXVI [March, 1936], p. 111). Does the United States have too many banks? If the number is reduced, must branch banking be extended? Why?

15. Professor J. H. Williams writes: "Our chief need is not reform of the Federal Reserve system but the much more fundamental reform of our commercial banking structure, organization, and practice" ("The Banking Act of 1935," *American Economic Review*, Supplement, Vol. XXVI [March, 1936], p. 104). Why? In what other way than by providing deposit insurance is the Federal Deposit Insurance Corporation fitting into the reform plan?

16. Compare the number of bank suspensions from 1922 to 1934 to the period since 1934. What factors have influenced this difference?

17. How would you answer the following questions on branch banking which were asked by the Society for Stability in Money and Banking? (*Source: American Banker*, December 24, 1936, p. 5). (*a*) Do you believe branch banks are more wisely conducted or are safer than the smaller unit banks, as a general rule? (*b*) Are branch bank managers likely to be better trained than the head officers of the smaller unit banks? (*c*) If the establishment of branches were restricted to an area not larger than the head bank's reserve district; and if branches could not be established in a locality already adequately served by one or more sound unit banks,

would you have any objection to branch banking? (*d*) Would the development of branch banking strengthen the banking structure and improve the practice of banking?

18. Answer the same questions as stated in Question 5 for the period from 1939 and 1945. Use Table 14.

REFERENCES

Agger, E. E. *Organized Banking*, chap. xii. New York: Henry Holt & Co., 1918.

American Institute of Banking. *Banking and the New Deal.* New York: American Institute of Banking, 1933.

American Monetary Reform Association. *Why 10,000 Banks Failed.* Flint, Mich.: The American Monetary Reform Association, 1936.

Collins, C. W. *Rural Banking Reform*, chaps. ix-xviii. New York: Macmillan Co., 1931.

Commission for Study of the Banking Structure. *Banking Developments in New York State, 1923-1934.* New York: New York State Bankers Association, 1935.

Dunbar, C. F. *Laws of the United States Relating to Currency, Finance, and Banking from 1789-1896.* Boston: Ginn & Co., 1897. (A source book.)

Gephart, W. F. "Our Commercial Banking System," *American Economic Review*, Supplement, Vol. XXV (1935), pp. 81-89.

Hammond, Bray. "The Banks, the States and Federal Government," *American Economic Review*, Vol. XXIII (1933), pp. 622-36.

Hilderman, L. C. *National and State Banks.* Boston: Houghton, Mifflin Co., 1931.

Kemmerer, E. W. "Banking Reform in the United States," *American Economic Review*, Supplement, Vol. III (1913), pp. 52-63; also discussion by thirteen economists, pp. 63-88.

Laughlin, J. L. *Banking Progress.* New York: Charles Scribners' Sons, 1920.

Members of the Staff, Board of Governors of the Federal Reserve System. *Banking Studies*, pp. 15-36; 43-62; 72-83; 113-40. Washington, D.C.: Board of Governors of the Federal Reserve System, 1941.

Nadler, M., and Bogen, J. I. *Banking Crises.* New York: Dodd, Mead & Co., 1933.

Schultz, W. J., and Caine, M. R. *Financial Development of the United States.* New York: Prentice-Hall, Inc., 1937.

Sumner, W. G. *History of Banking in the United States.* Revised. New York: Bradford Rhodes & Co., 1900.

Wallace, S. C. *The New Deal in Action*, chaps. iii and iv. New York: Harper & Bros., 1934.

White, Horace. *Money and Banking*, Book III, chaps xiv and xv. 5th ed. Boston: Ginn & Co., 1914.

Willis, H. P., and Chapman, J. M. *The Banking Situation*, chaps. viii and ix. New York: Columbia University Press, 1934.

Consult recent annual reports of the following government departments or agencies: Secretary of the Treasury, Federal Deposit Insurance Corporation, and Board of Governors of the Federal Reserve System.

Consult recent issues of the *Federal Reserve Bulletin* and other periodicals.

See the following volumes of the *Report of the National Monetary Commission*. Washington, D.C.: U.S. Government Printing Office.

a) Barnett, G. E. "State Banks and Trust Companies, since the Passage of the National Banking Act." 1911.

b) Davis, A. McF. "The Origin of the National Banking System," with supplement. 1910.

c) Kinley, David. "The Independent Treasury of the United States and Its Relations to the Banks of the Country." 1910.

d) Noyes, A. D. "History of National Bank Currency." 1910.

e) Sprague, O. M. "History of Crises under the National Banking System." 1910.

Chapter XVIII

THE BANK STATEMENT AND CHANGES IN EARNINGS

Importance of Bank Reports

Practically all incorporated banks are required to make reports on their conditions to federal or state officers. In 1832 Congress directed the Secretary of the Treasury to collect and compile annual statistics showing the condition of all banks in the United States. At that time, only one bank was operating under a federal charter, and there was no way in which complete and uniform reports from the remainder could be obtained.

The creation of the National Banking System was followed by standardization of reports from institutions belonging to this system, but satisfactory national figures were not obtainable. As a result of the establishment of the Federal Reserve System in 1914 and the creation of the Federal Deposit Insurance Corporation in 1934, greater uniformity was effected. Complete success has not been achieved because of the conflict of viewpoints and policies among the several supervisory agencies. Fortunately, these conflicts in ideas are gradually disappearing, and in 1938 the three federal agencies came to a general agreement upon principles.

The most complete current reports on conditions of banks are found in the *Federal Reserve Bulletins.*[1] They include semiannual reports, by classes, of all banks in the United States and all insured commercial banks, monthly reports of all member banks, and weekly reports of reporting member banks and of the 12 Federal Reserve banks. In addition, there are statistics on discount and other interest rates, prices, consumer credit, gold, reserves, money in circulation, international finance, industry, personnel of the Federal Reserve banks, and others. This material is of great value to students, regulatory officers, and government officials. These statistics reflect the growth of banks in different sections of the United States, changes

[1] *Banking and Monetary Statistics* by the Board of Governors of the Federal Reserve System is a helpful one-volume source of other statistics. It includes statistics for all banks by classes from 1914 to 1941; assets and liabilities of all member banks, branch, group, and chain banking, 1900-1941; currency, 1860-1941; money rates and security markets and foreign banking conditions.

in the nature of commercial banking, the story of the rise and fall in the business cycle, and the influence of war and war financing on the monetary and banking structure of the United States.

Bank Statements

Banks keep up-to-the-minute records of their assets and liabilities, and, with modern bookkeeping machinery and accounting practices, most banks can produce a statement of their condition within a short time. Statements for the use of the officers of the bank are prepared daily by the staff. The type of bank statement

TABLE 15

CONDENSED BANK STATEMENT OF LEE STATE BANK, LEE, NEW YORK

(Statement of Condition on September 29, 1945)

RESOURCES	
Cash and due from banks	$ 305,210.12
U.S. government securities	1,291,200.00
Local municipal investments	32,950.00
Investment bonds	5,800.00
Loans and mortgages	38,770.26
Furniture and fixtures	2,696.93
Other assets	53.43
	$1,676,680.74
LIABILITIES	
Capital	$ 30,000.00
Surplus	35,000.00
Undivided profits	14,026.24
Deposits	1,597,454.50
Other liabilities	200.00
	$1,676,680.74

prepared depends on the purpose for which it is to be used. Three types are illustrated in this chapter—the condensed, the nontechnical, and the uncondensed. The condensed and nontechnical types are the ones most widely distributed. They are published in local newspapers three or four times yearly, and copies are printed as booklets or folders and distributed over the counter or by mail to depositors, stockholders, and others. The uncondensed type is the most complete, and, therefore, of greatest value to students, officers, executive committee, and board of directors of the bank. It is the form used in making reports to government supervisory agencies and is the one on which consolidated banking statistics published in the *Federal Reserve Bulletin* are based.

Irrespective of type, a bank statement will always be divided into two parts: resources, or assets, and liabilities. Because of bookkeeping practices, total assets will always be equal to total liabilities.

TABLE 16

NONTECHNICAL BANK STATEMENT OF THE CORN EXCHANGE BANK AND TRUST COMPANY, NEW YORK CITY, NEW YORK

(January 1, 1946)

Our deposits and other liabilities (including $137,162,469.55 U.S. deposits)	$842,036,887.50
To meet this indebtedness:	
Cash in vaults and due from banks	$178,687,416.88
U.S. government securities ($161,093,824.37 pledged to secure deposits and for other purposes as required by law)	615,281,572.93
Federal Reserve bank stock	1,050,000.00
State, municipal, and other public securities	12,672,451.51
Other securities	1,309,321.94
Loans and discounts	55,445,680.79
First mortgages	5,974,354.87
Customers' liability on acceptances	137,401.83
49 banking houses	8,973,027.24
Other real estate	1.00
Accrued interest receivable	2,221,065.81
Other assets	295,608.91
Total to meet indebtedness	$882,047,903.71
This leaves	$ 40,011,016.21
Capital	15,000,000.00
Surplus and undivided profits	25,011,016.21

Courtesy: The Corn Exchange Bank and Trust Company, New York City, N.Y.

Changes in assets will be reflected on both sides or on one side of the bank statement. Thus, when an individual cashes a check drawn on a deposit in his bank, the bank's assets (cash) and liabilities (deposits) will be reduced by the amount of the withdrawal. But, when a government bond is sold, there will be a change only in asset items, investments will be reduced, and cash increased. Even in a small bank hundreds of such accounting changes will be necessary each day.

TABLE 17

UNCONDENSED BANK STATEMENT OF THE CHARLESTON NATIONAL BANK OF CHARLESTON, ILLINOIS*

(At the Close of Business on June 30, 1945)

	ASSETS		
1.	Loans and discounts (including $1,289.20 overdrafts)		$ 735,377.02
2.	United States government obligations, direct and guaranteed		3,703,785.00
3.	Obligations of states and political subdivisions		18,000.00
5.	Corporate stocks (including $6,750.00 stock of Federal Reserve bank)		6,750.00
6.	Cash, balances with other banks, including reserve balance, and cash items in process of collection		1,486,085.35
7.	Bank premises owned $1.00, furniture and fixtures $1.00		2.00
11.	Other assets		5,021.76
12.	Total assets		$5,955,021.13
	LIABILITIES		
13.	Demand deposits of individuals, partnerships, and corporations		$4,366,021.77
14.	Time deposits of individuals, partnerships, and corporations		330,314.50
15.	Deposits of United States government (including postal savings)		349,369.51
16.	Deposits of states and political subdivisions		611,317.40
17.	Deposits of banks		12,328.08
18.	Other deposits (certified and cashier's checks), etc.		7,996.45
19.	Total deposits	$5,677,347.71	
24.	Total liabilities		$5,677,347.71
	CAPITAL ACCOUNTS		
25.	Capital stock:		
	(*c*) Common stock, total par		$ 100,000.00
26.	Surplus		125,000.00
27.	Undivided profits		52,673.42
29.	Total Capital accounts		$ 277,673.42
30.	Total Liabilities and Capital accounts		5,955,021.13
	MEMORANDA		
31.	Pledged assets (and securities loaned) (book value)		
	(*a*) United States government obligations, direct and guaranteed, pledged to secure deposits and other liabilities		$ 571,000.00
	(*c*) Assets pledged to qualify for exercise of fiduciary or corporate powers and for purposes other than to secure liabilities		53,000.00
	(*e*) Total		$ 624,000.00
32.	Secured liabilities:		
	(*a*) Deposits secured by pledged assets pursuant to requirements of law		403,241.99
	(*d*) Total		$ 403,241.99

*Published in response to call made by Comptroller of the Currency, under Section 5211, U.S. Revised Statutes.

Courtesy: Charleston National Bank of Charleston, Illinois.

Capital Accounts

The first three items, and sometimes a fourth, appearing on the liabilities side of the condensed type of bank statement are the capital accounts of a bank. They represent the net worth or equity of the owners. These items appear as liabilities, because business enterprises such as banks are regarded as entities or artificial persons in themselves and are responsible or liable for the funds and property of the owners. It is the bank whose statement is being considered that is liable for the "capital," the "surplus," the "undivided profits," and "reserves for contingencies" or other types of special accounts created out of earnings. Considered from the viewpoint of the owners, these items represent proprietorship, or an asset, just as the deposit items represent assets to the bank's depositors owning them. So capital, surplus, and other capital account items are liabilities, that is, liabilities of the bank rendering the balance sheet or "statement of condition" as of a particular date.

The capital stock, surplus, undivided profits, and any other proprietary claim combined represent the equity of the stockholders. This figure, divided by the number of shares of stock, gives the book value of each share. The total of these proprietory items is but a small percentage of total liabilities, and this but emphasizes the importance of other sources of funds. However, proprietors' investments or capital funds are necessary to start a bank, to act as shock absorbers in case of losses, and to form a factor of safety for depositors. Each of the capital items has certain features that distinguish it from the others.

The "capital" item represents stockholders' money paid in at the time of the bank's organization. Federal and state laws require that banks must have a minimum amount of capital, and it may not be increased or decreased without permission of regulatory officers. The capital of a bank has been described as a trust fund for depositors that must be kept unimpaired at all times. Hence, depositors are assured that stockholders will always have a financial stake in their bank equal to the capital item. If, for any reason, this stake is impaired by losses, regulatory officers are responsible for such action as will protect the community, the depositors, and the bank. In cooperation with other governmental agencies, the directors and officers of the banks and others in the community may raise new capital funds to keep the bank functioning, or close it and later either reorganize it or liquidate it. Prior to the repeal of the double liability clause, it was a common practice to raise funds to offset the deficiency by an assessment levied on the stockholders. In case of insolvent banks, stockholders of national and most state-chartered banks were not permitted to charge off these assessments against claims or credits (deposits).

"Surplus" is an accounting item representing both an amount in excess of the par value of stock paid in at the time of organization and earnings of the banks which are being retained by the management. It differs from the capital stock in that it may be disbursed by management without making the bank subject to reorganization. When banks are formed it is customary to sell the capital stock for more than par value, thereby giving the banks funds with which to assume any possible loss without affecting the capital. Furthermore, some of the additional funds thus obtained are used to acquire bank premises, fixtures, equipment, and to make investments and loans so as to obtain income to help cover operating costs.

Most of the governments that repealed the double liability requirement replaced it with one that required banks to build up their surplus account to an amount equal to their capital, thus forcing some banks to do what the well-managed ones had already found it desirable to do. As a result, the proprietors were forced to make provisions out of earnings for double protection of depositors. Now there is a tendency to regard the surplus item in a bank's statement as a permanent part of the capital structure. This has had considerable influence on the management of the undivided profits account, which is now being handled in much the same way as the surplus item had been handled in the past.

The "undivided profits" account is an accounting item showing earnings that have not been paid out as dividends, placed in surplus, or placed in one of the reserve accounts that banks keep to offset losses. In rare cases it even includes funds paid into a bank in excess of capital and surplus at the time of organization. For example, in 1930 a bank was opened in Syracuse, New York, raising capital by selling its stock for $35.00 per share, with the amount received accounted for on a per share basis as follows: capital, $20.00, surplus, $10.00, and undivided profits, $5.00.

When earnings are placed in the undivided profit account, management has much greater freedom of action than when they are placed in the surplus account, and therefore this item is becoming more important on bank statements. The funds accounted for in the undivided profits account may be transferred to the surplus account, added to one of the reserve accounts for contingencies, or paid out to stockholders as dividends. Most banks prefer to have a stable dividend policy, which means that the undivided profit account will be built up during good years and paid out during lean years.

TABLE 18

CAPITAL ACCOUNTS OF INSURED COMMERCIAL BANKS, 1941 AND 1944
(Amounts in Millions of Dollars)

Capital Accounts	Dec. 31, 1941	Dec. 30, 1944	Change	Percentage Distribution	
				1941	1944
Total	$6,845	$7,990	$+1,145	100.0%	100.0%
Capital stock, notes, and debentures	$2,850	$2,912	$ +62	41.6%	36.4%
Common stock	2,470	2,660	+190	36.0	33.3
Preferred stock	306	202	—104	4.5	2.5
Capital notes and debentures	74	50	—24	1.1	0.6
Surplus	2,687	3,402	+715	39.3	42.6
Undivided profits	896	1,169	+273	13.1	14.7
Reserves	412	507	+95	6.0	6.3

Source: Annual Report of the Federal Deposit Insurance Corporation for the Year Ended December 31, 1944, p. 42.

The choice of location for earnings to be kept in the business may be influenced by the requirements that member banks must buy stock in their Federal Reserve bank equal to 3 per cent of their capital stock and surplus, and that lending to one name and investment in one issue are limited to 10 per cent of the banks' capital and surplus.[2] Federal Reserve stock pays 6 per cent cumulative dividends; and the higher a bank's capital and surplus, the larger is the amount that it may place in a single profitable loan or lucrative investment.

"Other capital accounts" represents earnings that have been placed in accounts to meet losses, need for unexpected outlays of

[2] The maximum loan to one name may be 25 per cent of capital and surplus if secured by government obligations.

funds as future developments may require, taxes, interest, and expenses that may not be provided for in any of the other liability items. The policies in regard to "reserves for contingencies" depend upon banks' managements, the financial positions of individual banks, the outlook for future profits, the attitude of regulatory officials, and sometimes the source of the profits. For example, if a bank has a large trading profit on investments, it probably should set aside a large "reserve for contingencies" to offset possible future trading losses.

In 1945 the distribution of total capital accounts (over $7,000,000,000 for all member banks) among the capital items discussed in the foregoing was as follows: capital, 34 per cent; surplus, 44 per cent; undivided profits, 16 per cent; and other capital accounts, 6 per cent. At the end of 1941 and 1944, the amount and percentage distribution for all insured commercial banks was reported by the Federal Deposit Insurance Corporation as shown in Table 18.

"Deposits" and "Other Liabilities"

The largest item on a bank statement is the one representing "total deposits" or simply "deposits." From the viewpoint of the depositors, these indicate money lent by them to the bank. Although these funds pass beyond the control of depositors and become the property of the bank, depositors retain the right to demand them at such time and under such conditions as were agreed upon when the deposits were made. Usually they may be withdrawn on demand, at the end of a specified number of days, or so many days after notice of intention to withdraw has been given. These agreements give rise to the popular classification of deposits as "demand," "time," and "savings," a subject which is discussed more fully in the chapter dealing with the deposit functions of commercial banks.

From the viewpoint of the bank, deposit items are promises to pay on demand or, if time and savings deposits, within a specified number of days or months. It is this situation more than any other which determines how the resources of a bank will be used. During a general banking crisis or during a "run" on an individual bank, there is usually no opportunity for second guessing, and when depositors demand their money it is either "putting up" the money or "shutting up" the bank.

From the viewpoint of society, deposits, and specifically demand deposits, are of major importance because of their use as a means of payment. In preceding chapters the influence of changes in the supply of the circulating media on general prices, a subject in which everyone has an interest, was discussed. So the study of deposits, their use, and measures to preserve and protect them is of interest to all members of our economic society and of special interest to those who are looking forward to a career in banking.

A glance at any of the bank statements reproduced in this chapter or practically any current bank statement will show that for each dollar provided by the owners of the bank, including all those earned and retained by it as part of its capital accounts, depositors provide from 10 to 20 dollars, the national average being 15. This situation verifies the statement that bankers are dealers in other people's money and hence in a position of trust never occupied en masse by those in any other business.

"Other liabilities," sometimes appearing on the condensed bank statement, includes such items as dividends declared but not yet payable, incomes collected but not earned (discounts), other suspense credits, expenses accrued and unpaid, borrowings from the Federal Reserve banks, correspondent banks, and others,[3] due to own foreign branches, securities borrowed, and other miscellaneous liability items. In case of national banks prior to March 4, 1935, it also included national banks' liabilities on note circulation.

Is Banks' Capital Large Enough?

Early in the nineteenth century failure to collect subscribed capital before or soon after opening a bank caused difficulties, and ever since lawmakers have given special consideration to this problem. Banking codes now contain specific instructions as to the time and the form in which the original subscriptions are to be paid. Underlying the laws and regulations pertaining to capital account items was a desire not only to strengthen banks but also to protect depositors from loss in case of bank failures. On a percentage basis

[3] Borrowings include the total amount borrowed on: (1) banks' own promissory notes, (2) certificates of deposits, (3) bills and notes rediscounted, and (4) any other instrument given for the purpose of borrowing money. It also includes loans and securities sold under repurchase agreements and "federal funds." See *Banking and Monetary Statistics*, p. 70.

the margin of protection to depositors is less than 7 per cent when the ratio of capital accounts to total deposits is 1 to 15. This margin provides even less of a "cushion," or "shock absorber," to a bank because its capital (on the average one-third of its capital accounts) must be maintained unimpaired.

During the 1930's, when many measures were taken to strengthen the banking system, one proposal was to require banks to maintain a ratio of capital accounts to deposits of 1 to 10. If this measure had been adopted, it would have checked a movement that has been going on for the last 100 years, that is, for the disparity between banks' capital and banks' deposits to increase. Any proposal to maintain a minimum capital account-deposit ratio has two aspects—its use as a device to limit the volume of bank credit expansion and its use as a device to protect depositors and Federal Deposit Insurance Corporation from losses in cases of bank failures.

One argument against the establishment of a uniform capital-deposit ratio is that it would decrease the elasticity of the deposit currency system. Since this subject has been discussed elsewhere, the only question that needs to be raised at this time is: May not our present deposit currency system have too much elasticity?

If the 1 to 10 ratio had been adopted previous to and maintained throughout World War II, there would have been less war financing with bank credit, and financing would have been more difficult. Interest rates would have been higher, and more taxation and more borrowing of savings would have been necessary. There would have been a smaller increase in the volume of deposit currency and less inflationary pressure on prices. There probably would have been fewer postwar readjustment problems.

Other arguments raised by bankers against the establishment of a minimum capital-deposit ratio are: (1) Banks have been passive rather than active factors in so far as the increase in deposits are concerned and therefore should not be penalized for their existence; (2) a law establishing a uniform capital-deposit ratio would force some banks to reduce their investments in government obligations to the possible detriment of this market; (3) without a sharp increase in interest rates there would be a decrease in bank earnings which would tend to weaken the banking structure; (4) those who sponsor this ratio plan fail to recognize that the chief protection of depositors is the quality of bank assets. A ratio even higher than 1 to 10 did not protect depositors from losses during the period from 1869 to 1938. The total dividends paid depositors in defunct national banks averaged only 67.4 per cent; that is, depositors lost over 30 per cent of their capital, plus the loss of their interest, during the liquidation period. In 1938 the average was slightly better (69.7 per cent), although the capital-deposit ratio was less favorable to the depositors. The experience of leading English banks tends to confirm the conclusion that management is the most important factor in sound banking. The ten leading English banks have been operating for many years on a capital-deposit ratio of about 1 to 15.5. (Since World War II, about 1 to 30.)

In place of the capital-deposit ratio, it has been suggested that a ratio be used which would recognize the risk factor in assets. This might be a ratio of "total capital accounts" to "total assets less U.S. government securities and cash assets." Without question, the present statutory provisions for minimum capital requirements, based primarily on the size of the community in which the bank is located, have little merit. The "total capital accounts" to "total deposits" ratio and the "total capital accounts" to "risk assets" ratio are the best substitutes proposed to date.[4]

"Cash and Due from Banks"

This item usually appears first on the condensed bank statement under resources or assets. It includes all the cash in the vaults of the bank, cash on deposit with other banks—including any with a Federal Reserve bank—and checks and other items in process of collection. Since banks must be in a position to meet demands of their depositors for cash, it is readily apparent why this item would appear first on a balance sheet designed primarily for a bank's own depositors to read.

In determining the amount of cash kept on deposit with other banks and in their own vaults, bankers have to face the dilemma of keeping too much and losing earnings or keeping too little and risk not having enough to care for needs of depositors. About 100

[4] Between 1941 and 1945 these ratios for all member banks changed as follows: total capital accounts to total deposits decreased from 1 to 10 to 1 to 15.6; total capital accounts to total assets less U.S. government securities and cash assets increased from 1 to 4.2 to 1 to 3.6. (Note: ratios are treated as fractions, and a change in ratio from 1 to 10 to 1 to 15 is a decrease of 1/10 to 1/15.)

years ago legislatures started to enact laws making it necessary for banks to hold a minimum of cash reserves against deposits, a practice that all good bankers had always followed. Since that time, the purpose of requiring legal cash reserves to protect depositors has been broadened to include, among other things, the control of the volume of bank credit.

Every member bank is required to keep a reserve, called "member banks-reserve account," with its Federal Reserve bank. State-chartered member banks may be permitted by state laws and regulatory agencies to meet Federal Reserve requirements in lieu of state requirements. Other state banks must meet legal requirements of the state in which they are located. Thus, banks located in North Carolina must keep a reserve of 15 per cent against demand deposits and 5 per cent against time deposits, either in their own vaults or in other banks.[5] In keeping deposits with other banks, bankers are guided by the same reasons as businessmen in leaving deposits with their banks. These deposits make it easy for a bank or a businessman to transfer funds from one community to another and to secure banking services such as borrowing facilities, collecting services, and purchasing and safekeeping of securities.

"Cash items in process of collection" includes all checks, drafts, interest-coupons, due bills, and notes that have been mailed for collection directly or indirectly to the banks on which they are drawn. These items are traced to one of the most important services performed by modern banks—the collection of credit items for their customers. Since most of the credits involved are collected the next day, they are "virtually cash" and hence are included in the total reserves of the banks.[6] These items may be regarded as deposits that have not been collected and so deducted from total deposits. They are so treated in computing net demand deposits in determining reserve requirements to be kept in Federal Reserve banks.

In banking, the word "reserve" is used in two ways: first, as an accounting device to denote reserves against contingencies which

---

[5] See Board of Governors of the Federal Reserve System, *Provisions of State Laws Relating to Bank Reserves as of December 31, 1944.* Practically all the state laws permit some of the required reserves to be kept in other depositories. This situation helps to explain the size of the item "interbank deposits" appearing on combined statements of condition of banks.

[6] For variations in methods of reporting these items, see *Banking and Monetary Statistics*, pp. 68-69.

are set up on the liabilities side of a balance sheet and appear as one of the items in the capital account; and, second, as an asset reserve which is accounted for as cash. In order to avoid confusion in this book, the accounting meaning will be used, when qualified as follows: "reserves for contingencies," etc., and at all other times the word "reserve" will mean "asset reserve."

Investments

Since good bank assets represent the chief protection of depositors, the second major class of items on the asset side of a condensed bank statement is usually United States government securities. They are now the most important earning assets of banks, both in quantity and in quality. These securities vary according to maturity and yield, with banks placing greater emphasis on short-term obligations than is true of ordinary institutional investors. Management of the investment account must be planned so that sufficient cash will be present or readily obtainable in order to satisfy depositors. At the same time, bankers must give thought to earnings, without which a bank cannot survive. Too much emphasis on liquidity and safety of assets may be harmful to a bank if it leads to too great a sacrifice of earnings. (See Chap. XXII.)

Second to investments in United States government obligations in point of safety are bank investments in (1) obligations guaranteed by the United States government, (2) obligations of government corporations not guaranteed by the United States government, (3) obligations of states, and (4) obligations of subdivisions of the state. Other investment bonds include banks' purchases of promises to pay of all types of corporations, including railroads, public utilities, communications, industrial, etc. This group tends to carry a higher yield than government securities because of the greater risks involved, less marketability, and other factors.

Total investments of banks represent over 80 per cent of the loans and investments of the average bank in the United States, and over 90 per cent of these investments are in United States government direct or guaranteed obligations. Therefore, banks are as sound as the credit of the United States government. Since there is no danger of the government's defaulting on its obligations, the chief risk assumed by a bank in buying government securities is that known as "capital market risk." Although it is often stated that banks lose from inflation, actually they are in a "hedged" position, because any fall in value of assets tends to carry with it an equal and offsetting fall in the value of their liabilities.

Loans

"Loans and discounts," "loans and mortgages," or simply "loans" on a bank statement represent funds lent to individuals, corporations, and others. Since most of them are made locally, a large total suggests the extent to which a bank is performing one of the primary functions of a bank. In pioneer days, it was the advancement of funds locally which made possible the purchase of rural and urban land, the construction of homes and farm buildings, the building of local factories, and the financing of other local projects on which community life is built.

While government obligations in all probability will continue to dominate banks' resources for years to come, bank lending is expected to increase. Emergency financing during the reconversion period is being financed in part by banks. Funds borrowed, pending settlements of terminated war contracts, are often guaranteed by the procurement services (War and Navy departments and Maritime Commission) under provisions of the Contract Settlement Act of 1944 and regulations of the Board of Governors of the Federal Reserve System. However, these termination or "T" loans are but a temporary phase of bank lending. Other types of guaranteed loans, including those for housing and those to veterans for a variety of purposes, will increase. Scarcity of homes will call for extensive construction and outlays of billions of dollars, and most of these funds will be obtained from local banks.

During the war the volume of consumer credit declined sharply, owing to (1) the restrictions placed on consumer credit, (2) the decline in the volume of production of semidurable consumers' goods, and (3) the abundance of cash in the hands of consumers. Changes from war to peacetime economy are rapidly changing this situation, and the volume of consumer credit has shown a substantial increase. Small loan departments are being expanded by banks in order to handle systematically the special problems peculiar to this type of lending. For example, under the Serviceman's Readjustment Act, the Veterans' Administration is guaranteeing loans made by banks for a variety of purposes, and these loans call for special handling. They are guaranteed up to 50 per cent, but in no case may the amount guaranteed exceed $2,000, except to finance the purchase of a home, in which case the amount may be $4,000.

Banks are grouping together to make loans which, because of their size or the risk involved, could not be made by an individual bank. The fact that a single loan is often in excess of 10 per cent of a bank's capital and surplus combined explains this need for banks to participate in group financing.

The conclusion to be drawn from this discussion is that the increase of loans and discounts on the commercial bank statement will herald in a new era of community and national well-being; more and better homes, more and better automobiles, and more and better things that mean a higher standard of living for all. Since 1937 government officials have requested banks to report their loans according to classes of borrowers or purposes for which the loans are made. These classes are: (1) commercial loans, including open market paper, (2) agricultural, (3) brokers', dealers', and other security loans for the purchase or carrying of securities, (4) real estate loans, (5) consumer loans, and (6) others.[7]

Real Estate and Other Assets

The items "bank premises owned" and "furniture and fixtures" represent the book value given to these physical assets. Since they are not earning assets (with the exception of a building which may have surplus space rented to other occupants) and usually have small liquidation value, the tendency is for bank managements to write down their book value considerably below their actual worth.

The "other real estate owned" item is usually the result of bad real estate loans and subsequent foreclosures which have become necessary in order to protect banks from greater losses. In other cases, "other real estate owned" may have resulted from purchases

[7] This class of loans includes overdrafts which represent extensions of bank credit to customers who have written checks in excess of their deposits, which the banks have honored, and other loans which have not fitted into the revised classification. Beginning December 31, 1942, consumer loans were divided into four categories, which had to be reported separately. Prior to World War II, they were the most important among the loans not reported separately, that is, included in "others."

of property by a bank planning to move to a new site, to open another branch, or to otherwise expand its operations. Sometimes banks' real estate investments take the form of holdings of securities of subsidiary companies which have been formed to hold the titles to the banks' premises and other real estate owned by the bank. All real estate holdings are carefully checked by bank examiners, because they are a nonliquid type of investment that should not bulk large in the statements of banks.

The item "customers' liability on acceptances" represents claims of the bank against customers for whom they have made grants of acceptance credit. Most of these claims arise out of the financing of foreign trade and are discussed in the chapter dealing with that subject.

TABLE 19

Distribution of Assets—All Member Banks, 1941-44

(In Percentage of Total Assets)

	1941	1942	1943	1944
U.S. government securities	27.3	35.0	51.1	55.4
Other securities	9.2	8.0	5.6	4.7
Loans	25.7	23.7	17.2	16.2
Cash assets	35.5	31.3	24.6	22.5
Real estate assets	1.9	1.6	1.1	.9
Other assets	.4	.4	.4	.3

Source: Federal Reserve Bulletin, May, 1945, p. 498.

The "income accrued but not yet collected" item is an accounting item showing income which has been earned during the accounting period but which has not come due and is not payable until sometime later. For example, banks have in their possession all types of promissory notes and bonds which have earned interest during the months or weeks preceding June 30 but which will not be collected until after that date.

"Other assets" is the catchall classification found on any balance sheet, and it includes all items which have not been covered in other classes of assets.

Table 19 gives the distribution of assets by classes of all member banks in terms of percentages of total assets. For the period considered, it shows the relative increase in United States government obligations and the relative decline in holdings of cash assets, loans, other securities, real estate, and other assets.

A Bank Statement Is Incomplete

There are many questions about the positions of banks which cannot be answered by studying their statements of assets and liabilities. These statements tell very little about the quality of loans and investments. These credit instruments may be overvalued or undervalued. Conservative accounting practice demands that their value shall be carried at cost price or market, whichever is lower. At present many government bonds are carried on the books below their market prices.

Many banks carry the value of their bank buildings at a nominal price, even though they may be worth thousands or even millions of dollars. Similar accounting practice is sometimes applied to other real estate. The value of many loans has been written down by orders of bank examiners, or voluntarily by bank officers. Later these loans may be collected in full or, at least, considerably in excess of the amount anticipated. As a result of understatement of the value of assets, many banks have hidden surpluses or hidden reserves. Such conditions exist during periods of good or improving business.

The quality of loans and investments held by banks may be the highest, but, in a market such as existed in 1931-33, they may have to be sold at a loss. In addition, bankers are required to decrease the book value of their assets to conform to the accounting rule of "cost or market, whichever is the lower." In brief, the bank statement must show "paper" as well as real losses. These adjustments on the asset side may be charged off against earnings, reserves for contingencies, undivided profits, and even the surplus; but the "capital" item must not be impaired, for, if it is, the bank is technically insolvent. If the balance sheet for the day shows a technically insolvent bank, the bank's own directors may voluntarily close the bank. Perhaps national or state examiners will bring on the crisis by forcing the bank's officials to write down or write off the value of certain assets.

The writing-down of the book value of bank assets magnified the serious banking situation in 1931 and 1932. In desperation, the state and national officials permitted banks to carry assets at what was called "normal value," which was above the market value. As a result, many banks that had been insolvent for months were not closed until the national banking holiday in March, 1933, when thousands of banks were closed and later reorganized or liquidated. Some of the liquidated banks would have been able to regain solvency in the rising markets following 1933, but, as noted earlier, in banking the opportunity for "second guessing" is limited.

The conclusion to be drawn from this discussion is that nonsolvency rather than nonliquidity is the chief cause of bank failures. Between the two world wars it was the reports of accountants rather than "runs" on banks by depositors that brought on the death knell of banks.

Earnings and Expenses of Commercial Banks

Over a period of years, a sound bank must earn enough to pay all its expenses, to cover its losses, and to provide a reasonable return on its capital accounts. Otherwise it is only a question of time until

TABLE 20
EARNINGS AND EXPENSES OF ALL MEMBER BANKS
(In Percentage of Total Earnings)

	1941	1942	1943	1944
Interest and dividends on securities	31.4	36.3	46.4	51.2
Earnings on loans	47.0	43.6	34.1	30.1
Service charges on deposit accounts	4.6	4.6	4.6	4.6
Other current earnings	17.0	15.5	14.9	14.1
Total earnings	100.0	100.0	100.0	100.0
Salaries and wages	30.0	31.0	29.5	28.0
Interest on time deposits	9.9	8.6	7.5	7.7
Other current expenses*†	29.8	27.8	25.9	24.4
Total expenses*†	69.7	67.4	63.0	60.1
Net current earnings*†	30.3	32.6	37.0	39.9
Net charge-offs, etc. (or recoveries +)	2.8	2.3	+3.8	+4.6
Taxes on net income	(1)	4.5	7.0	9.8
Net profit after taxes	27.5	25.8	33.8	34.7

* Beginning with 1942, taxes on net income are reported separately and shown just above net profits; previously they were included with other taxes in expenses.

† Recurring depreciation on banking house, furniture, and fixtures is included in expenses beginning with 1942 and in losses and charge-offs in prior years.

Source: Federal Reserve Bulletin, May, 1945, p. 498.

losses eliminate all capital account items that provide the cushion between claims of depositors and other creditors and the "capital" of the bank. This suggests the importance of profit and loss and earnings statements in appraising the financial positions of banks.

During 1931 banks were able to cover expenses, but during the next three years they suffered heavy losses. In 1935 banks as a whole showed net profits, the chief contributory factor having been the reduction in losses (real or paper). In 1936 member banks showed the greatest net profit on record up to that time, with the exception of the years 1928 and 1929. In that year recoveries were in excess

TABLE 21

CURRENT OPERATING EARNINGS REPORT OF THE CORN EXCHANGE BANK AND TRUST COMPANY, NEW YORK CITY

(Year Ending December 31, 1945)

Current operating earnings:	
Interest on loans	$ 1,393,856.83
Interest and dividends on securities	
Net after amortization of premiums	9,071,591.77
Other current operating earnings	1,707,669.86
	$12,173,118.46
Current operating expenses:	
Salaries and wages	$ 4,268,637.09
Interest paid	87,253.05
Other current operating expenses	3,746,503.48
	$ 8,102,392.62
Net current operating earnings	$ 4,070,725.84
Net current operating earnings applied as follows:	
Dividends	$ 1,800,000.00
Reduction of book values of banking houses	438,281.07
Added to undivided profits	1,832,444.77
	$ 4,070,725.84

Note: During this period all securities' profits and recoveries have been added to valuation reserves.

Courtesy: Corn Exchange Bank and Trust Company of New York City.

of losses, which meant that banks were still collecting frozen loans and assets at more than their current book value. However, it was not until the war years, 1943 and 1944, that banks showed spectacular increases in net profits. These profits were due to an increase in total earnings based largely on returns from government obligations.

As compared to 1929, interest payments on deposits and salaries and wages have been reduced, and these have contributed to the improvement in banks' positions. From 1927 to 1929, the average rate paid on time deposits was 3.5 per cent, and it declined thereafter until it reached a new low of less than 0.8 per cent in 1944. All payments of interest on demand deposits were practically eliminated by the Banking Act of 1933.

The chief expense of commercial banks is represented by total salaries and wages. In 1939 they were 25 per cent less than in 1929, and the increase during World War II was moderate. These changes have been due not to decreases in individual salaries and wages but to the introduction of many labor-saving devices, including machines that "do everything except talk." With the increase in the efficiency of personnel, banks' expenses have been reduced. Although most banks do not publish earning statements, there are exceptions, and one of these is reproduced in Table 21.

QUESTIONS AND PROBLEMS

1. How did each of the following contribute to bank reporting: (*a*) National Banking System, (*b*) Federal Reserve System, (*c*) Federal Deposit Insurance Corporation? What publication provides the most complete current information on banks and other business and financial statistics?
2. What changes will appear on a bank statement if (*a*) a deposit is withdrawn, (*b*) a government bond is sold, (*c*) stock dividend is paid that is not earned during the dividend period, (*d*) there is a loss not offset by current earnings, and (*e*) real estate and bond prices decline?
3. Which items on a bank statement make up the capital accounts? Why do they appear on the liabilities side of the statement?
4. "The fact that in the published statements the total of the assets is equal to the total of liabilities with unrelenting regularity shows beyond peradventure, in the opinion of many folks, that bankers must possess something of the dexterity of those of the juggling art" (Kaufman, C. L., quoted in *Banking*, Sec. 11 [October, 1936], p. 9). Discuss.
5. Compute the book value of one share of stock of the Lee Bank, assuming the par value to be $100. Making the same assumption, what is the book value of one share of the Corn Exchange Bank and Trust Company? The Charleston National Bank?
6. Is the book value the same as the market value? Why? What is the status of a bank when the book value of its stock is less than its par value?
7. Why does management have greater freedom of action in regard to the "undivided profits" item than with the other items in capital accounts?
8. "Bank statements have been used too exclusively as barometers of the conditions of banks and too little as barometers of changes in business conditions." How may a bank statement be used as a barometer of

changes in business in the community in which the bank is located? How may a combined statement of all banks be used as a barometer of changes in business conditions throughout the country?

9. What is the significance of "deposits" from the viewpoint of (*a*) the bank, (*b*) depositors, and (*c*) society?

10. How much can one tell about the position of a bank by studying its statements? Compare a current condensed bank statement to the one appearing as Table 10. See Index of Tables. Should banks be required to publish a profit and loss statement? Why?

11. What is meant by the "double liability" clause? Why was it repealed? What are the advantages of the substitute measure over the "double liability" provision?

12. How could a minimum capital-deposit ratio be used as a device for credit control? For protection of depositors? What are the arguments against it?

13. What is meant by "asset reserves"? Distinguish between "reserves for contingencies" and "asset reserves."

14. Why are minimum reserve requirements important to (*a*) depositors, (*b*) the owners of the banks?

15. List the classes of assets of banks in order of (*a*) safety, (*b*) liquidity, and (*c*) source of bank earnings.

16. Comment on "Banks are as sound as the credit of the United States government."

17. What is meant by the statement that "the chief risk assumed by a depositor is loss of purchasing power due to inflation"? Compare a depositor's position to that of a bank.

18. Obtain a printed bank statement of a local bank and that of other local business firms and compare them as to stockholders' equity or proprietorship interest, classes of assets, and classes of liabilities.

19. To what extent are a bank's expenses dependent upon the volume of its business and to what extent are these expenses relatively fixed in character? What is the significance of your answer in so far as service charges are concerned?

20. Describe the changes in earnings and expenses of all member banks from 1941 to 1944. What are the chief sources of earnings? How important are earnings from service and collection charges on deposit accounts? What are the chief expenses of banks? Would lower taxes be of any particular benefit? What was the situation during the decade preceding this period?

REFERENCES

American Bankers Association, Bank Management Commission. *Profit and Loan Operations.* Booklet No. 2. New York: American Bankers Association.

American Bankers Association, Bank Management Commission. *Survey of Bank Operating Ratios.*

American Bankers Association, Bank Management Commission. *Unprofitable Practices and the Remedies.* Booklet No. 4.

Beaty, J. Y. *How to Understand Banks,* chap. vi. Chicago: Business Publications, Inc., 1935.

Board of Governors of the Federal Reserve System. *Banking and Monetary Statistics,* pp. 5-15, 61-71, and 257-59. Washington, D. C.: Board of Governors of the Federal Reserve System, 1943.

Dunbar, C. F. *The Theory and History of Banking,* chap. iii. 4th ed. New York: G. P. Putnam's Sons, 1933.

Ebersole, J. F. *Bank Management: A Case Book,* Sec. 22. 2d ed. New York: McGraw-Hill Book Co., Inc., 1935.

Federal Reserve Bulletin. Washington, D. C.: Publication of the Board of Governors of the Federal Reserve System.

Garcia, F. L. *How to Analyze a Bank Statement.* New York: Bankers Publishing Co., 1935.

Harr, Luther, and Harris, W. C. *Banking Theory and Practice,* chap. vi. 2d ed. New York: McGraw-Hill Book Co., Inc., 1936.

Langum, J. K. "Earning Assets, Deposits, and Reserves of Member Banks, 1929-1938," *Financial and Investment Review,* Vol. VII, No. 7. School of Business Administration, University of Minnesota.

Members of the Staff, Board of Governors of the Federal Reserve System. *Banking Studies,* pp. 169-86. Washington, D. C.: Board of Governors of the Federal Reserve System, 1941.

Rodkey, R. G. *The Banking Process,* chap. xix and Appen. B. New York: Macmillan Co., 1928.

"War Finance and Banking," *Federal Reserve Bulletin,* August, 1944, pp. 743-52.

Whittlesey, C. R. *The Effect of War on Currency and Deposits.* New York: National Bureau of Economic Research, 1943.

Willis, H. P., and Edwards, G. W. *Banking and Business,* chap. xii. Revised. New York: Harper & Bros., 1925.

Woolley, E. S. *Bank Management Control.* New York: George S. May Co., 1940.

CHAPTER XIX

DEPOSIT FUNCTIONS OF COMMERCIAL BANKS

Distinctive Characteristics of Commercial Banks

Introduction.—In Chapter X the emphasis on deposits was from the viewpoint of their use as a means of payment. In this and the following chapters emphasis is placed on deposits as the chief source of a bank's lending power, types of deposits, service charges, and other problems as they are related to bank management. The functions which set the modern commercial bank apart from other financial institutions are the acceptance of demand deposits and the payment of these demand deposits to others or to owners on demand. Because of the dynamic nature of these demand deposits, commercial banks' lending has traditionally been limited to meeting the short-term needs of merchants, farmers, manufacturers, and others.

Primary Functions of Commercial Banks.—The primary functions of commercial banking still remain: to accept and safeguard demand deposits, to pay out these deposits by checks and thus provide the chief means of payment, and to lend funds at interest in order to meet the needs of commercial and other borrowers. Other financial institutions accept deposits and make short-term loans, but only commercial banks have developed the type of banking system that has given rise to deposit currency.

Noncommercial Functions of Commercial Banks.—That the commercial banks are losing their dominant commercial characteristics is evidenced by these facts: (1) They are accepting time and savings deposits which are not withdrawable on demand; (2) they are investing a larger percentage of their funds in noncommercial paper, a characteristic of investment banking; (3) they take orders from customers to buy securities, which is a function of brokers; (4) they are acting as dealers and are participating in the underwriting of domestic government securities, which are traditional functions of investment houses; (5) they are acting as trustees and fiscal agents for individuals and corporations, which are traditional legal functions of lawyers and trust companies.

Other Functions of Commercial Banks.—If banks accept deposit funds, it is only reasonable to expect them to make provisions for the safekeeping of other valuables, such as jewelry, securities, silverware, and personal documents of all types; and modern commercial banks do offer such services to their customers. In addition, commercial banks provide facilities for the rapid transfer of funds between communities in the same country (domestic exchange) and between different countries (foreign exchange). Finally, commercial bankers draw up model budgets for housewives, encourage thrift in various ways, and make personal loans to finance consumption. Although many of these functions are only remotely related to the primary banking functions, they reflect the many services which the general public expects of commercial banks.

Three Stages in the Development of Deposit Banking

Safekeeping.—The first type of deposit banking was the safekeeping of specie left with banks. Title did not pass to the bank, and a fee was charged for the service. When the depositor wanted his funds, he called for them in person. Later, depositors were allowed to draw orders on the bank, directing it to pay all or part of the money to a third party.

The banks were warehouses for the safekeeping of money, operating on the 100 per cent reserve principle. The Bank of Amsterdam, which was created by city ordinance, provides an illustration of this method of banking. The public understood that all deposits were supported 100 per cent by specie, but later it was discovered that the bank's officers were lending part of the specie in violation of the bank's charter. The public scandal which followed led to the failure of the bank in 1819, after it had been in existence for 182 years.

Lending of Money.—The illegal lending of part of the specie left with the Bank of Amsterdam illustrated the development of the second stage in the evolution of deposit banking. During the eighteenth century, goldsmiths, private bankers, and some chartered institutions were accepting deposits, but with the understanding that they could return an equivalent amount of funds. They received title to deposits left with them. Bankers realized that only a few depositors called for specie on a particular day and that most of the remainder could be lent or invested. A fractional reserve in specie was sufficient to satisfy the day-to-day demands of depositors for money.

Lending of Credit.—The third type of deposit banking appeared when banks began to lend their promises to pay in the form of book accounts or deposits. These accounts were transferable to others by written orders, that is, by checks. Very little specie was left at banks, new deposits being created by leaving credit instruments with the banks. Many of these instruments had their origin directly or indirectly in bank loans or investment operations, and so banks became, primarily, dealers in credit and credit instruments.

Summary.—The development of deposit banking represents a change of emphasis; it does not mean that a new type of banking entirely replaced the old. For example, the first type of deposit banking still exists in the form of special or safe deposits. When currency, securities, and other valuables are left in deposit boxes, title does not pass to the bank, and these deposits do not appear on the assets side of the bank's statement, nor do they appear on the liabilities side as deposits. The second type of deposit banking exists when coins are accepted by banks as deposits, specie is held as reserves against deposits, and coins and gold bullion are lent to borrowers. But these illustrations of the first and second types of deposit banking are of minor importance compared to the third type, which dominates modern commercial banking.

Importance of Deposits to Banks

Modern commercial banking is concerned chiefly with the handling of the temporary savings of the community. Banks attract depositors by investing a small amount of capital, renting or purchasing conveniently located buildings, buying banking equipment, and employing well-trained men. These things enable them to offer many services to their customers and to the general public.

If the organizers of the bank planned to use only their own capital resources, the proper procedure would be to lend and invest their own funds without going to any extra expense for buildings, equipment, and salaries. The capital and surplus of banks make up the foundation upon which they build their deposit structure. Other things being equal, the larger the deposits, relative to the capital account, the more profitable the bank will be to its shareholders. As noted in Chapter X, deposits are the result of three types of transactions—deposits of currency; deposits of checks, drafts, and other types of credit instruments; and lending and investment operations of banks. The first two are primary deposits, being the chief source of funds which are lent and invested by individual banks, and the last type is called derivative deposits. An increase in primary deposits will increase the "cash and due from banks" item on the assets side of the bank statement and will increase "deposits" on the liabilities side.

After computing legal and other reserve requirements, bankers feel free to lend or to invest any cash that remains. The total cash item tends to remain constant from day to day, representing a revolving fund, the content of which, from the viewpoint of the bank, is determined by passive as well as by active factors. The passive factors are the uses that are made of deposit accounts by depositors, and the active factors are the lending and investing policies of the bank.

If a check is drawn on a bank and deposited in it, the bank debits the drawer's account and credits the depositor's. The bank's total assets and liabilities are not changed, they are merely redistributed on the bank's books. If a check is presented for payment in currency, the bank will lose cash and will have less funds to lend or invest. Similarly, if a check is presented for payment by a second bank, the bank will lose cash unless this item is offset by a claim against the presenting bank. In the three cases it is apparent that it is to the advantage of a bank to have a large percentage of the liquid assets of the community left with it as deposits. As in the first case, the bank would avoid losses of cash if all checks drawn on it were presented for deposit by its own customers.

Certain facts should be recognized: (1) No individual bank will lend unless it has a surplus of funds on hand or available from other banks. (2) Deposits which are created by lending or investing will be checked out, and the surplus of funds in the lending bank will be redistributed among other banks. (3) Continued lending activities of an individual bank will depend upon the extent to which it attracts deposits. (4) Over a period of time a bank will close if depositors cease to patronize it.

While it is true that the banking system and individual banks create deposits by lending and investing, this remains true only as long as individuals and others prefer to keep claims to money in the form of deposits rather than in the form of money. If this preference were to be reversed, there would be no commercial banks as they exist today, and it is for this reason that banks advertise the advantages of checking accounts and the other services they offer to the general public. Deposits must be recognized as the chief source of funds with which individual banks operate. All important bank policies are based on this fact.

There Are Many Ways of Classifying Deposits

These include those classified according to (1) type of depositor —public and private; (2) origin—primary and derivative; (3) presence or lack of special protective features—secured and unsecured and insured and not insured; and (4) time, which includes demand, savings, and time.

Type of Depositors.—Classes of deposits according to depositors are public and private. The chief subdivisions under "public" are federal, state, county, municipal, and foreign governments. All others are called "private" depositors, and the chief subdivisions are individuals, partnerships, corporations, banks, and trusts. Most of the funds used by banks are normally provided by the first three classes of private depositors, but during the war years United States government deposits increased sharply.

Origin.—When deposits are classified according to origin, they are called "primary" and "derivative" deposits. "Primary deposits" are those which result from collections of cash items or deposits of currency. They are traced to the deposits of checks, notes which are due, drafts, interest coupons, and currency. The significant fact to recognize is that primary deposits give an individual bank new funds to invest or to lend. "Derivative deposits," sometimes called "secondary deposits," result from new bank loans and investments. They give the lending or investing bank no new funds to lend or invest, but as they are used they spread to other banks as primary deposits.

Presence or Lack of Special Protective Features.—When deposits are classified according to the presence or lack of special protective features, they may be referred to as insured or uninsured and as secured or unsecured. The Federal Deposit Insurance Corporation provides for insurance of deposits of individual accounts in an insured bank in amounts up to $5,000, but all individual deposits in excess of this amount are not insured. Although coverage is not complete, it must not be assumed that these deposits are unprotected. As already noted, the chief protection of depositors is the quality of the assets of banks. In addition, public deposits in banks may be protected by special pledges of government bonds or other securities. For example, all federal government deposits in banks in excess of the amount guaranteed by the Federal Deposit Insurance Corporation are secured by pledges of federal government securities. States, counties, cities, and other local governments usually require that similar collateral be given to protect their deposits with banks. The trust laws usually require that deposits of the trust department with other banking departments be similarly protected. All other deposits are classified as unsecured, but this term is misleading, because they are protected by reserves and other general assets of the banks.

Time.—This classification of deposits into demand and time deposits is the most important and the most widely used. "Demand deposits," as the name suggests, are those which usually may be withdrawn from a bank during banking hours. "Time deposits" are (1) those made for a definite period of time, as evidenced by certificates of deposits; (2) those known as savings or thrift accounts which are evidenced by passbooks that permit the bank to require notice before deposits are withdrawn; (3) those known as "time deposits, open accounts," which are evidenced by passbooks and include deposits for some particular thing, such as "Christmas savings," "vacation," "taxes," and others; and (4) those savings left with the United States Post Office, which have been redeposited with banks.

The proper classification of deposits is important to commercial banks, because the law does not permit them to pay interest on demand deposits, and the rules and regulations of supervisory officials require that a higher cash reserve be kept against demand than against time deposits. There has been a tendency for banks to make no distinction between demand and time deposits in so far as withdrawals are concerned. Congress has sought to check this practice in regard to deposits of corporations operating for gain, by requiring that such deposits must be evidenced by certificates of deposit and may not be withdrawn prior to maturity or without thirty days' prior notice. If such deposits are not withdrawn at the end of the notice period, or at maturity of the certificates, they must be reclassified as demand deposits. For other savings accounts, banks customarily honor requests for withdrawal without requiring advance notice.

The dividing line between what may be considered time and demand deposits is usually thirty days. Thus, if a bank receives $100 from a savings depositor and the bank book (or a signed agreement) stipulates that the bank has the right to request thirty days' notice, the deposit is classified as a time deposit. If a corporation brings $100,000 and asks for and receives a sixty-day certificate of deposit, this is also classified as a time deposit. On the other hand, if a private corporation or a government agrees not to remove part of its deposit for a ten-day period, such deposits are not classified as time deposits. In classifying deposits, the terms or conditions under which they may be withdrawn are the determining factors.[1]

One of the original purposes in providing for classification of commercial bank deposits as demand and time was to permit banks which were members of the Federal Reserve System to hold lower reserves against time than against demand deposits, thereby permitting them to compete with savings banks for savings or thrift deposits. The theoretical justification for requiring banks to keep a lower reserve for time deposits (on the average, this requirement is less than one-third of the reserve requirement for demand deposits) is the fact that their velocity of turnover is less than that of demand deposits, and the fact that time deposits are for small individual amounts representing savings which are not subject to regular withdrawals. Time deposits, furthermore, represent funds that may be invested in assets which are safe, but not necessarily liquid.

Demand deposits represent the temporary funds—subject to withdrawal on demand—left on deposit with banks by individuals, corporations, and others. The use of demand deposits as means of payment makes it necessary for the staffs of commercial banks to be much larger than those of savings banks, relative to the size of total deposits. After setting aside enough to care for current demand for cash and to meet the legal reserves as required by law or the rules of regulatory agencies, the banks find from experience that they may safely lend or invest the remainder if there is a demand for these funds. The earnings from funds invested or lent may not be sufficient to pay for the costs of handling them, and, if not, banks may make service charges against individual accounts. Handling and investing demand deposits is the most dynamic phase of banking, which helps to explain the higher reserve requirements for demand deposits and the stress placed on liquidity of commercial bank assets.

---

[1] See Regulation D, as amended, in *Federal Reserve Bulletin*, August, 1942, pp. 749-53.

The Growth of Deposits in Commercial Banks

The most significant recent development in banking has been the rapid growth of deposits in commercial banks. The relationship of this movement to war financing and government deficit financing has been considered. After bank credit lent to the government has been spent, it becomes the property of different economic groups. The members of these groups determine in what form the bank credit is

TABLE 22

DEPOSITS OF ALL INSURED COMMERCIAL BANKS
(In Millions of Dollars)

	1938	1941	1945*
Demand deposits:			
Interbank			
Domestic	6,595†	9,823†	11,217
Foreign	503	673	1,119
U.S. government	538	1,762	23,478
State and political subdivisions	2,942	3,677	4,698
Individuals, partnerships, and corporations	23,475	36,544	65,494
Total demand deposits	34,053	52,479	106,006
Time deposits:			
Interbank	157	158	66
U.S. government and postal savings	86	59	105
State and political subdivisions	575	492	482
Individuals, partnerships, and corporations	14,009	15,146	26,346
Total time deposits	14,827	15,855	26,999
Total deposits	48,880	68,334	133,005

* Year-end figures, except 1945, where June 30 figures were used.

† Includes reciprocal bank balances.

Source: Federal Reserve Bulletin, November, 1945, p. 1127.

to be kept. Although both demand and time deposits have increased, the expansion of demand deposits has been much greater, both absolutely and relatively. (See Table 22.)

Several surveys have been conducted by the Federal Reserve System[2] in recognition of the fact that uses made of these important accumulations of liquid assets will have an important bearing upon economic developments in the postwar period. Uses made of demand and time deposits, currency in circulation, and government securities

[2] See *ibid.*, August, 1943, pp. 713-16; October, 1943, pp. 917-22; May, 1944, pp. 433-35; November, 1944, pp. 1069-76; April, 1945, pp. 331-34; November, 1945, pp. 1100-1101; February, 1946, pp. 122-23.

held by individuals and nonfinancial institutions will have far-reaching effects on the position of commercial banks. For example, if any considerable quantity of the $100,000,000,000 of government securities held by individuals and nonfinancial investors is liquidated, commercial banks may be called upon to expand their volume of bank credit to an amount only equalled by the expansion during the war years.

One common fallacy in thinking about the spending of existing bank deposits should be avoided, that is, that this action destroys them. They are not destroyed, they merely change ownership. The only way in which the volume of bank deposits may be reduced is to reverse the process that created them, that is, to reduce the volume of government obligations, other investments, and loans held by commercial banks. The decisions made by businessmen and other individuals as to the use of their incomes and assets are reflected and will continue to be reflected in the volume and distribution of bank deposits. Changes in ownership of demand deposits are more suggestive of current financial and business changes than are changes in time deposits. Table 23 shows changes in ownership of deposits of individuals, partnerships, and corporations for selected deposit survey dates between 1941 and 1945. Demand deposits of manufacturing and mining firms, trade or mercantile depositors, and personal or individual including farmers and others show substantial increases.

Individual depositors who keep funds in banks for personal convenience are now more numerous than business depositors; but the deposits of the latter are more important and more difficult to manage. They may be subject to considerable fluctuation because of seasonal and cyclical business changes and because of financial policies of management. Department stores, manufacturers, and sales organizations tend to have considerable variation in deposits because of the seasonal nature of their business activities. Similarly, there will be major fluctuations in deposits because of changes in general business. Furthermore, changes in financial policies of corporations, as illustrated by their borrowing in the capital market, use of installment notes, and financing sales with or without trade acceptances, may have considerable effect on their dependence on local banks and, therefore, on the size of balances kept with them.

Commercial banks, foreign banks, insurance companies, and

TABLE 23

OWNERSHIP OF DEMAND DEPOSITS OF INDIVIDUALS, PARTNERSHIPS, AND CORPORATIONS

(In Billions of Dollars) *

	July, 1945†	Jan., 1945‡	July, 1944‡	Feb., 1944‡	July, 1943‡	Dec., 1941‡
Total domestic business....	42.4	40.5	37.6	35.9	36.3	24.8
Nonfinancial business:						
Manufacturing and mining	18.4	17.5	17.2	16.3	16.5	10.0
Public utilities..........	4.0	3.7	3.7	3.7	3.7	3.1
Trade..................	10.9	10.3	8.8	8.2	8.0	4.6
Other nonfinancial.......	3.8	3.7	3.3	3.4	3.4	2.7
Total..............	37.1	35.3	33.0	31.5	31.6	20.4
Financial business:						
Insurance companies.....	1.8	1.9	1.7	1.7	1.9	1.9
Other financial..........	3.5	3.3	3.0	2.6	2.8	2.5
Total..............	5.3	5.2	4.7	4.3	4.6	4.4
Personal:						
Farmers...............	5.2	4.7	4.0	4.2	3.3	n.a.‖
Others................	17.8	16.7	14.4	13.5	12.5	n.a.‖
Total..............	23.0	21.5	18.4	17.7	15.8	9.6
Trust funds...............	1.5	1.4	1.3	1.3	1.2	3.2
Nonprofit associations......	2.0	1.9	1.6	1.5	1.4	
Foreigners—business and individuals............	0.7	0.7	0.7	0.8	0.9	
Grand total.....	69.6	65.9	59.6	57.1	55.6	37.6

* Owing to rounding, details may not add to total.

† Preliminary.

‡ Revised.

‖ Not available.

Source: Federal Reserve Bulletin, April, 1945, p. 333, and November, 1945, p. 1100.

trustees appear as depositors. Similarly, foreign business firms and individuals keep deposits with American banks for business purposes, for safekeeping, and for other reasons, including personal expenditures. The demands made on foreign deposit accounts are less predictable than those of other classes.

Governments Limit or Prohibit Payment of Interest on Deposits

Demand Deposits.—The federal government and many state governments have taken steps to limit competition for funds which in the past often took the form of payment of excessive interest rates to depositors. Since 1933, member banks and others participating in the Federal Deposit Insurance System have not been allowed to pay interest on demand deposits. There have been a few temporary exceptions and one permanent exception, the latter permitting American banks to pay interest on demand deposits in branches located outside the United States.[3] This exception was made in order to permit them to compete with other banks located in the vicinity of the branches.

The justification for nonpayment of interest on demand deposits is twofold. First, the many services rendered by banks to their demand depositors adequately compensate the depositors for the use of their funds by banks. Depositors already have a sufficient incentive to keep their deposits subject to check, because they need them as means of payment. Second, if banks pay interest on demand deposits, they must increase earnings by investing in nonliquid and speculative long-term promises to pay. This latter policy is not in the best interest of the depositors or of the bank, because demand deposits should be invested only in liquid or highly marketable securities. An interest drain on the bank's earnings would prevent it from building up special reserves for losses, undivided profits accounts, and the surplus designed to help it through depressions. The movement to eliminate the payment of interest on demand deposits, particularly bankers' deposits, is not a new one. It has been an important issue since the panic of 1857, when a committee appointed by the New York Clearinghouse to study the causes of this panic recommended that the practice of paying interest upon bankers' deposits be stopped.

Under the National Banking System, bankers' balances continued to grow, with ever recurring disturbances during banking panics. The first constructive step taken on this issue was in 1913, when the Federal Reserve banks were forbidden to pay interest on interbank deposits. It was expected that the correspondent relationships between member banks would decline as a result of the free services and other privileges offered by the Federal Reserve banks. In addition, it was expected that there would be a decline in the call loan markets in New York and other cities which had made possible the payment of interest on bankers' balances. These developments did

[3] Some state laws require commercial banking departments of state banks accepting trust deposits to pay interest on them, whether time or demand.

not follow, and banks' funds (usually classified as demand deposits) continued to flow to New York and other cities, drawing interest at the rate then paid on bankers' balances.

Time Deposits.—The following reasons are advanced justifying the payment of interest on time deposits: They are not subject to check (therefore the amount of clerical work is small), they may be invested for a long period of time, and legal reserve requirements are small. Before 1929 interest payments of 5 per cent on savings accounts were not uncommon. The high rate necessitated investment in hazardous high-yielding securities, which led to heavy losses and a weakening of banks. The seriousness of the situation was appreciated by the Comptroller of the Currency in 1915, when he recommended in his annual report that limits be placed on the rate of interest paid for deposits. The New York Clearinghouse banks finally placed limitations on interest payments, and other associations adopted similar restrictions.

Following the collapse of banking in 1933, the banks were ready for elimination of interest payments on demand deposits and restrictions on interest rates for time deposits. Under the present law, the Board of Governors of the Federal Reserve System "shall from time to time limit by regulation the rate of interest which may be paid by member banks on time and savings deposits and shall prescribe different rates" for different types of deposits. The rates may vary according to maturities, conditions respecting withdrawals, or dissimilarities of conditions existing in different localities. Under deposit guarantee, where deposits are granted equal protection, the right to limit interest rates is a necessary weapon against unfair competition. Nonmember state banks participating in the Federal Deposit Insurance Plan are subject to similar regulations, and several state departments are limiting interest rates on deposits.

The Board of Governors of the Federal Reserve System and the directors of the Federal Deposit Insurance Corporation have fixed the following maximum rates for banks coming under their jurisdiction; savings deposits, 2½ per cent; postal savings deposits, 2½ per cent; time deposits payable in 6 months or more, 2½ per cent; time deposits for from 90 days to 6 months, 2 per cent; and time deposits less than 90 days, 1 per cent. These rates are but rarely the effective rates now being paid by banks, because (1) clearinghouse associations in the larger cities are providing for even lower maximum rates, (2) individual banks are paying lower rates or no interest on certain types of time deposits, and (3) certain states have provided for lower maximum rates than those provided by federal supervisory agencies. The legal rates have had their chief effects in rural sections, where time deposits represent a large percentage of country banks' deposits, and in individual cases, where banks have refused to co-operate with the program to eliminate an unsound banking practice.

What Is Interest?—Unfair competition may result from hidden interest payments in the form of free services given to depositors.[4] At various times during and since 1935, the Board of Governors has tried to define interest payments in terms broad enough to cover all direct and indirect payments. Failure to reach an agreement with the directors of the Federal Deposit Insurance Corporation on a definition of "interest payments" led to a decision to permit each agency to rule on specific practices of banks under its supervision. Finally, in 1937, the Board of Governors and the Federal Deposit Insurance Corporation agreed that the term "interest" shall mean for purposes of deposit-interest regulation "any payment to or for the account of any depositors as compensation for the use of funds constituting a deposit."[5]

The tenacity of the system of paying interest on deposits is to be explained on the basis of the competitive system of banking and the multiplicity of expansion of bank credit based on new reserves. Since a large percentage of bank costs are fixed, the management of an individual bank may strive to increase profits by increasing lending and investing. Such a policy is profitable only when new funds can be secured at costs sufficiently low to absorb new losses that might result, plus the small per unit cost in administration. If the total effect of this policy is a redistribution of funds among banks, then other banks will have to contract loans. This will tend to increase their per unit costs of administration. They may combat this situation by raising interest rates on deposits, thus giving rise to cutthroat competition so characteristic of commercial banking during periods when there is a demand for loans. Without co-operative or government control, this competition for funds usually goes to excess.

[4] See *Federal Reserve Bulletin*, February, 1944, pp. 126-32.

[5] *Annual Report of the Board of Governors of the Federal Reserve System*, 1936, p. 54; and *Federal Reserve Bulletin*, March, 1937, p. 187.

Effects of Deposit Interest-Rate Regulation

Liquidity and Safety.—The chief reason given for regulation of the rate of interest paid on deposits was that it would improve the liquidity and safety of banks. Freed from the necessity of earning large sums to pay interest on deposits, bankers were expected to invest the funds of their banks in safe, short-term, low-yielding securities. In addition, it was expected that banks' net earnings would increase, permitting them to build up greater reserves for contingencies, undivided profits, and surplus accounts.

The ratio of interest paid to total expenses of member banks has declined from about 47 per cent in 1928 to less than 8 per cent. This was achieved by the practical elimination of interest payments on demand deposits and a reduction in payments on time deposits from an average of 3.4 to about 0.8 per cent.

Because of the existence of the large volume of idle funds at the present time, owing to swollen war income, it is impossible to say how many of these changes would have been forthcoming without federal regulation. The prevalence of low interest rates on government securities and other earning assets of banks would have made the reduction of interest payments on deposits inevitable. Government regulation of interest payments on deposits has made the necessary downward adjustment easier. However, part of the gain due to lower interest payments has been offset by the reduction in yields on earning assets, and therefore banks' net earnings show no major improvement other than what may be explained by an increase in volume of assets and in efficiency of bank management.

Reclassification of Deposits.—Another result expected from deposit-interest rate regulation was the proper time classification of deposits. This problem dates from 1913, when Congress in the Federal Reserve Act specifically authorized national banks to accept time and savings deposits. True, many national banks had accepted them, but they were forced to keep the same fractional reserve against these deposits as against demand deposits, which meant that they could not compete extensively with state banks, mutual savings banks, and other agencies for savings accounts. So the Federal Reserve Act provided for a very low minimum reserve ratio (now 6 per cent). The first year-end report (1914) of the Federal Reserve Board showed that time and savings deposits of member banks were 20 per cent of their total deposits, which is approximately the same as the present percentage. But, in order to secure savings accounts, national banks had to meet interest payments being paid by savings institutions. This practice encouraged many commercial firms to reclassify their demand deposits in order to profit from interest payments on time deposits; consequently, much of the original distinction between demand and time deposits broke down. In brief, the many so-called time deposits were, in reality, short-term commercial deposits not subject to their proper legal reserves and receiving the interest rate paid on true savings accounts. Unsatisfactory loan and investment practices followed wherever bankers treated time deposits as being synonymous with savings deposits.

Since 1933 the temptation to classify demand deposits as time deposits has been increased by a provision in the Banking Act of 1933 making illegal the payment of interest on demand deposits. But further regulations of the classification of time deposits as authorized in the Banking Act of 1935 have discouraged this practice. Although time deposits in member banks doubled during World War II, their relative importance declined from 35 per cent of total deposits in 1940 to 20 per cent at the present time. Other factors may have been instrumental in this change; for example, low interest rates on time deposits make classification of deposits as "time" less important. However, the trend is unquestionably toward the reduction of the relative importance of time deposits in commercial banks, particularly in large banks.

Bankers' Balances.—Elimination of the interest payment on demand deposits was expected to reduce the practice of banks depositing idle funds with other banks. However, banks have other than investment reasons for keeping deposits with correspondent banks, and, during a period when idle funds aggregated billions of dollars, these reasons were sufficient to explain why old correspondent banking relationships were continued. Banks still want to keep correspondent services, credit information, contacts with the money and capital markets, and foreign and domestic exchange services. State banking laws permit nonmember banks to keep part of their legal reserves with city correspondents, and this also helps to explain the persistence of this practice.

Foreign Balances.—Many foreign commercial banks, central banks, and governments keep deposits with New York banks. At times, changes in location of foreign balances have been very disturbing, explaining in large part the strain on the gold standard during and following the international panic of 1931. As long as safety rather than investment is the chief reason for leaving these deposits in New York banks, the payment of little or no interest will have little or no effect on their volume. Not until more normal conditions exist at home and abroad will the effects of regulation of interest rates on these deposits be tested.

Summary.—Individuals who keep savings in commercial banks for safety and convenience alone have not been influenced by the lower interest payments on deposits, but those who regard savings deposits as investments for income have sought outlets for their funds elsewhere. These outlets include the purchase of savings bonds, stock in savings and loan associations, and deposits in savings banks. The location of savings in commercial banks has been influenced by factors other than a question of income, including the question of liquidity, local availability of other investments, the safety factor, inertia, and lack of information.

As long as the banking system has as its chief function the financing of the United States government, it is improbable that lower interest rates will have much influence on the composition of commercial bank assets. In the future, lower costs of bank funds may encourage banks to make loans to potential bank borrowers who now are not being financed at all or are being financed by other agencies at higher costs. Such a bank policy would contribute to the economic goal of full employment.

Service Charges

In the chapter dealing with the bank statement, it was noted that depositors provide most of the funds used by banks. On the other hand, the existence of demand deposits accounts for most of a bank's expenses. Even though interest payments on them have been practically eliminated, they still represent an important cost of banking. In addition, all insured banks must pay insurance premiums on deposits to the Federal Deposit Insurance Corporation at the rate of 1/12 of 1 per cent per year. Legal reserves must be kept to protect depositors; these average 18 per cent for demand deposits and 6 per cent for time deposits. Insurance must be carried to cover the hazards of burglary, robbery, and theft, losses due to mistakes of employees in paying funds to wrong parties, and losses due to dishonesty of employees.

After considering the costs of handling deposits, it is not surprising to find that banks have introduced a system of service charges. When given an opportunity, under the National Industrial Recovery Administration, to set up a code of fair competition, bankers took the position that every deposit account must pay its expenses. The law providing for the National Industrial Recovery Administration was declared unconstitutional by the Supreme Court, but the result of the movement then set in motion was the adoption, under local clearinghouse regulations, of minimum balances rules and service charges.

Service-charge plans vary from those which provide for careful analysis of costs and earnings of each account to those which provide for a flat price for each check written in excess of a number determined by the average or minimum balance. If the average balance is $500, then the number of free checks may be 10, that is, one for each $50 of the average balance. All drawn in excess of that number may be subject to a flat charge of 10 cents per check.

In analyzing a deposit prior to fixing the amount of service charge due for the month in question, both the costs to the bank and the earnings derived from the accounts are estimated. If the latter, called "earning credits," equal or exceed the estimated costs, no service charge is made for the month. If the estimated earning credits are less than the estimated costs, a charge is made. No surplus earning credits are carried over from the preceding month.

In estimating costs of an account, weight is given to such factors as overhead expenses, costs of insurance of the deposits, burglary and other types of insurance costs, and specific expenses in handling items in the account, including those of collecting local and out-of-town checks. In estimating earning credits for an account, loanable funds are estimated. These are found by taking the daily ledger balances and subtracting average float (checks and other items in process of collection) and idle funds kept as a reserve. Then the returns are estimated by multiplying by the annual rate of interest. One of the current criticisms of service charges suggests that too many banks are still figuring earning credit rates at an annual rate of 2 to 2½ per cent. This is much too high, judging from interest rates of less than 1 per cent paid on time deposits by member banks and their net current earning rate of 0.7 per cent on total assets.

Depositors have objected from the beginning to service charges. To the extent that bankers are able to support these charges on the basis of cost and earning credit figures, they have little to fear from any future legislative or congressional investigation. There is a growing feeling among the general public that too many banks are charging what the traffic will bear. Specific criticisms are: (1) the use of minimum rather than average balances in determining service charges; (2) loading depositors with overhead expenses for facilities which are not used in the same proportion by all depositors; (3) overestimating the per unit handling expenses, which have been reduced by modern bookkeeping machines; and (4) too high a per unit charge for each check drawn.

In addition to the application of service charges to checking accounts, many banks have been selling a "thrifty" check service plan. Customers are sold books containing from ten to fifteen checks, usually at a price of ten cents per check. No minimum balances are required, and no other charges are made against the account. This type of check service plan is particularly popular with professional and salaried groups.

Although service charges appear to be high from the point of view of the public, they represent about 5 per cent of total earnings of banks at the present time. However, their importance should not be underestimated. The returns are sufficiently large in the case of all member banks to pay two-thirds of the interest on time deposits, or all taxes other than that on net income, or 17 per cent of all salaries and wages. Furthermore, adoption of service charges has prevented much abuse of checking privileges, reducing their activity, and has thereby contributed materially to a reduction in the costs of banking.

QUESTIONS AND PROBLEMS

1. What are the distinctive characteristics of a commercial bank?
2. Identify the primary and secondary functions of commercial banks.
3. Identify the three stages in the development of deposits.
4. Assume that you are shown a deposit in your bank by one of the officers; what would you see? Explain.
5. "The other leading operations of banks, when analyzed, can also be

resolved into cases of the exchange of rights against rights, or of rights against money" (Dunbar, C. F., *The Theory and History of Banking*, pp. 15-16). Is this true of the deposit function? Explain.

6. How do deposits originate? Distinguish between primary and derivative deposits. Why are derivative deposits factors in bank credit expansion?
7. When a merchant sells goods, the public does not expect him to analyze the cost factors in the price he charges. Then why do bankers find it necessary to explain their service charges?
8. What relationship, if any, exists between an increase in service charges and an increase in currency in circulation? Explain.
9. Use Table 22 to answer these questions: (*a*) What is the relative importance of time and demand deposits among the various classes of depositors? (*b*) What percentage of total demand deposits were U.S. government deposits in 1938; in 1945? (*c*) What percentage of total demand deposits were deposits of individuals, partnerships, and corporations in 1938; in 1945? What explanation can you offer for these differences? (*d*) Answer (*b*) and (*c*) for time deposits.
10. Distinguish between demand and time deposits. Are all time deposits savings deposits? Distinguish between public and private deposits. Distinguish between secured and unsecured deposits. Are these differences important to depositors? To the banks? Why?
11. "Existing bank deposits may be destroyed by spending them." Comment.
12. Indicate changes in the ownership of demand deposits during the period from 1941 to 1945 for the following, using Table 23: (*a*) manufacturing and mining; (*b*) trade; (*c*) personal; and (*d*) farmers. What is the significance of these changes?
13. What is the present status of government regulation of interest payments on deposits? If such rules are good for banks, why did not bankers adopt them? Do bankers regulate the interest payments within limits fixed by laws and regulations of government officials?
14. How can deposit rate regulation be used as an instrument of credit control? What have been the effects of these regulations on deposits?
15. What relationship is there between deposit-interest rate regulation and the classification of deposits? How have these regulations affected savings deposits in commercial banks?
16. Why do banks appear as depositors of other banks?
17. Study and comment on the fairness of the following service-charge rules. All checking accounts are analyzed in accordance with the formula below, "except that, if more than 500 checks are presented against an account in any one month, the first 500 checks listed at 5 cents each, and the excess over 500 at 3½ cents each. When the average balance in an account for any month is less than $100, due to the existing investment

conditions, no earnings can be allowed. No charge is made for any month in which an account is entirely inactive; that is, when no checks are drawn, cashed, or deposited; unless the account remains inactive for six successive months."

Service performed:	
8 paid checks, 5c each	$0.40
2 items deposited (drawn on other banks), 3c each	.06
3 items deposited (drawn on this bank), no charge	.00
1 check cashed (drawn on another bank), 10c each	.10
Overhead:	
Maintenance per account per month	0.50
Total service performed	$1.06
Calculation of earnings:	
Average daily ledger balance	$144.00
Less: average uncollected funds	10.00
Available balance	$134.00
Less: cash reserves, 21%	28.14
Earning balance	$105.86
Earned for one month at 1.25% a year	0.11
Service charge	$0.95

Source: Your Checking Account, Costs and Earnings. Syracuse, New York: Lincoln National Bank and Trust Co.

REFERENCES

See end of Chapter XX

CHAPTER XX

BANK RESERVES AND DEPOSIT INSURANCE

Banks Must Be Safe

Bankers are merchants of credit, accepting funds from their depositors under various types of contracts and lending these funds to governments, to corporations, to depositors, and to others for a stated period of time or payable on demand. A bank's primary function may be thought of as the receipt, custody, and judicious use of depositors' funds while always maintaining the ability to meet depositors' demands. The ability to meet depositors' demands at all times is particularly important, because depositors use their demand deposits as means of payment.

From a social viewpoint, the existence of $20,000,000 in demand deposits in a community is much more important than this volume of the community's assets suggests. During a normal year it will enter into $400,000,000 of the community's business activities as a means of payment, and at the same time it will provide the bank with a $16,000,000 pool of funds for lending and investing.[1]

It is because of this dual function of demand deposits that the business of deposit banking cannot be placed in the same category with that of merchandising goods, manufacturing commodities, or investing savings. Demand deposits are the "things we live by," and no commercial bank should be regarded merely as another business venture. No community should be subjected to bank failures, with their resulting shock and blight, due to the temporary or permanent loss of its chief means of payment—demand deposits. In this chapter two means of protecting banks, their depositors, and their communities from bank failures are considered: (1) regulation of reserve requirements and (2) insurance of deposits.

Primary Reserves Are "Cash" and "Due from Banks" Items

Rapid turnover is one of the most significant characteristics of deposits in commercial banks. Unlike capital and surplus, a deposit

[1] These figures are secured by assuming that the normal velocity of demand deposits is 20 times a year and that 80 per cent of the funds of banks are lent and invested.

balance may be but a temporary part of the bank's funds. To meet the demands of depositors, banks are forced to have cash on hand or in other banks. These funds are called "reserves." The reserve ratio is found by dividing reserves by the amount of deposits and is always expressed as a percentage.

Legal Reserve Requirements.—In the United States banks are generally required by law to keep a minimum amount of reserves against deposits. Since the middle of the last century, governments have been legislating on this subject.[2] While different principles have been emphasized in justification of reserve requirements, the most common one has been that reserves are necessary to insure the liquidity of banks. Since 1935 changes in legal reserve requirements have been looked upon, to an increasing extent, as a device of credit control. The laws generally stipulate minimum reserve ratios, location of the reserves, and the form of currency or credit used as reserves. Detailed regulations covering computations of deposits and routine matters are handled by administrative agencies. Maximum and minimum legal reserves which must be kept by the three classes of member banks and two classes of deposits are fixed by law.[3] The actual percentages in effect within these limits are fixed by the Board of Governors of the Federal Reserve System. (See Table 24.)

Reserve Classification of Cities.—Central reserve city banks include almost all the member banks in Chicago and New York. By special permission from the Board of Governors small banks in the outlying sections of these cities may be classified as "reserve city banks." Reserve city banks include those located in about sixty of the leading cities in the United States, and country banks include those located in all other communities.

Banks are required to keep lower reserves against time deposits than against demand deposits, because of the greater activity of the latter. This same activity principle is used to justify the different legal ratios required for demand deposits in the three classes of member banks. The smallest legal ratio is required in rural sections, where demand deposit accounts are much less active than in reserve cities or

---

[2] See "History of the Reserve Requirements in the United States," *Federal Reserve Bulletin*, November, 1938, pp. 953-72.

[3] Section 207, Banking Act of 1935, reads in part: "But the amount of the reserves required to be maintained by any such member bank as a result of any such change shall not be less than the amount of the reserves required by law to be maintained by such bank on the date of enactment of the Banking Act of 1935 nor more than twice such amount."

central reserve cities.[4] During periods of banking disorders, large depositors, who are usually the customers of large banks, are more alarmed about their deposits and tend to withdraw them sooner than do small depositors, which is another reason for requiring banks located in central reserve and reserve cities to carry larger legal reserves.

TABLE 24

MEMBER BANK RESERVE REQUIREMENTS

(Per Cent of Deposits)

Period in Effect	Net Demand Deposits*			Time Deposits (All Member Banks)
	Central Reserve City Banks	Reserve City Banks	Country Banks	
June 21, 1917—Aug. 14, 1936	13	10	7	3
Aug. 16, 1936—Feb. 28, 1937	19½	15	10½	4½
Mar. 1, 1937—Apr. 30, 1937	22¾	17½	12¼	5¼
May 1, 1937—Apr. 15, 1938	26	20	14	6
Apr. 16, 1938—Oct. 31, 1941	22¾	17½	12	5
Nov. 1, 1941—Aug. 19, 1942	26	20	14	6
Aug. 20, 1942—Sept. 13, 1942	24	20	14	6
Sept. 14, 1942—Oct. 2, 1942	22	20	14	6
Oct. 3, 1942, and after	20	20	14	6

* Demand deposits subject to reserve requirements, i.e., demand deposits other than war loan deposits, minus cash items in process of collection and demand balances due from domestic banks.

Source: Federal Reserve Bulletin, November, 1945, p. 1115.

Bankers' balances are particularly volatile, and, since these balances are usually carried in central reserve city banks, there is an additional reason for the higher legal reserves required of the latter.[5]

Working Reserves.—In addition to the legal reserves, banks must keep other funds for banking purposes, which are called "working reserves." Cash in the vaults, or till money, is necessary for the

[4] For list of "reserve" and "central reserve cities" as they were classified in 1914 and subsequent changes in classification, see Board of Governors of the Federal Reserve System, *Banking and Monetary Statistics*, p. 401.

[5] Classification of cities and banks located in them as "central reserve," "reserve," and "country" has no necessary relationship to the location of the Federal Reserve banks or branches. However, all the cities in which Federal Reserve banks or branches are located are classified as "reserve" cities (New York and Chicago as "central reserve" cities), but there are many cities classified as "reserve" which do not have Federal Reserve banks or branches located therein.

over-the-counter transactions. In the past, this item was about 1½ per cent of the total time and demand deposits of member banks, but at present many banks are holding a much larger percentage of their cash in their own vaults.

The wide use of checks by the American public, the process of clearing checks, and the tendency for currency flowing out to be offset by currency flowing in, explain why banks need only a small percentage of their assets in currency. Another explanation is an increased dependence of the member banks upon the Federal Reserve banks and their branches for cash. The Federal Reserve banks pay the costs of shipping currency "in" and "out," and so the member banks have nothing to gain by holding it when the supply is excessive. Member banks located in the vicinity of the Reserve banks and their branches hold over 70 per cent of the total deposits of all member banks, but they are able to care for their currency needs by holding, relative to deposits, only one-half the amount of currency which banks less fortunately located have found it necessary to hold.

In addition to cash in vaults, banks keep demand deposits with their correspondent banks. The balances are used to pay out-of-town obligations and are sold to bank customers, who buy, for example, New York bank drafts to pay out-of-town bills, because they are more acceptable than personal checks. Many interior banks invest funds in the New York money market, and a bank balance in New York facilitates these operations. Other banking services are offered by New York banks, and interior banks find it to their advantage to obtain them by keeping deposit balances with these banks. All the cash reserve items (cash, deposits with other banks, including those with the Federal Reserve banks, and other cash items) are sometimes called primary reserves of banks in order to distinguish them from secondary reserves.

Secondary Reserves.—By secondary reserves is meant the highly liquid earning assets that may be converted into cash with little or no delay and at practically no loss. Included among the classes of assets most generally classified as secondary reserves are trade and bankers' acceptances, short-term government obligations, open-market commercial paper and brokers' loans, and similar types of call loans. "Secondary reserves" are earning assets and are discussed in more detail in Chapter XXII, entitled "Commercial Bank Portfolio Problems."

Many Factors Influence the Reserve Policies of Banks

The size and number of accounts are important. Because of the law of averages, a bank with a large number of small accounts needs a smaller reserve than a bank with a smaller number of large accounts. A large account may be withdrawn at any time, and the bank must be prepared for this contingency. As the number of depositors increases and the average size decreases, there is a tendency for withdrawals to be offset by new deposits. A study made covering deposit withdrawals of a selected group of banks suspended during the period 1930-33 suggests "that large demand deposits not only exhibited a greater instability than small ones, but also that the percentage reduction of balances in the period prior to suspension became progressively greater the greater the size of the account."[6] A breakdown in deposit withdrawals by classes of depositors suggests that (1) business account reductions are the largest single item in presuspension demand deposit reduction, (2) interbank withdrawals are second in importance in the total presuspension decline in demand deposits, and (3) large personal accounts are less stable than business accounts of the same size, but, because personal balances are predominantly small, they are as a whole more stable than business accounts. If it is true that deposit withdrawals are the chief cause of bank failures, then the major responsibility rests with large depositors or business firms. Deposit insurance in its present form will not prevent bank failures, because full coverage is limited to small deposits, and the reserve, lending, and investing policies for medium and large-size banks have not been changed by the existence of deposit insurance.

Before the reserve policies of individual banks can be decided upon, the nature and tendencies of all accounts, particularly the large ones, must be studied, because the nature of the business of a bank's customers is important. If customers are engaged in one particular field—for example, production of automobiles—the deposits will be subject to large seasonal fluctuations, and relatively large reserves will be needed.

---

[6] "Behavior of Deposits Prior to Suspension in a Selected Group of Banks," *Federal Reserve Bulletin*, April, 1939, p. 265.

American experience does not confirm that of England—the bigger the bank the smaller the reserve which it is required to keep (see Allen, A. M., and others, *Commercial Banking Legislation and Control*, p. 17). The American system of requiring progressively higher reserves originates in an effort to make allowance for the redepositing of reserves.

Another factor influencing reserve policies is the organization of the banking system. Under a branch banking system, seasonal, industrial, and geographical diversification may be obtained with widely scattered branches. By shifting funds from one branch to a second, according to demand, a smaller reserve ratio is necessary. Part of this advantage may be secured even in the United States, where unit banking still dominates, by depositing reserves in Federal

TABLE 25

ALLOCATION OF THE DECREASE IN DEMAND DEPOSITS BETWEEN BASE DATE AND DATE OF SUSPENSION IN ALL SAMPLE BANKS

Type of Holder	Percentage Composition of the Decrease in Demand Deposits	Percentage Composition of Total Demand Deposits on Base Date
Total demand deposits, inclusive of interbank	100.0	100.0
Public funds	4.3	10.5
Interbank deposits	25.9	19.1
Miscellaneous demand deposits*	14.9	18.7
Personal and business, total	54.9	51.7
Personal	12.9	13.3
Business	42.0	38.4
Less than $5,000:		
Personal	7.1	9.3
Business	5.0	9.3
$5,000 and over:		
Personal	5.8	4.0
Business	37.0	29.1

* Fraternal, charitable, other nonpersonal, inactive, unlisted, unidentified, and certificates of deposit.

Source: Federal Reserve Bulletin, April, 1939, p. 267.

Reserve banks under a centralized control. Finally, the amount of reserves kept depends in part upon the legal minimum reserve ratio requirements. Since very large reserves reduce earning power, banks do not normally carry excessive ones, except during times of stress or financial uncertainty, when they find it to their advantage to be fortified against unforeseen withdrawals.

An individual banker may increase the reserve ratio by increasing cash or decreasing liabilities. He may stop lending and investing, and the repayment of maturing loans and investments, if wisely arranged according to a carefully planned long-run maturity schedule, will build up his cash position. Since new loans create new deposit liabilities, a nonlending and noninvesting policy will cut them down. The banker may be able to persuade customers to leave cash deposits with his bank, but this is difficult at a time when banks are in greatest need of funds; or he may borrow from other banks, particularly his Federal Reserve bank; or he may sell some type of liquid earning asset which he holds for this purpose.

Legal Reserves, a Device for Credit Control

As previously noted, changes in loans and investments in the commercial banking system tend to cause similar changes in deposits. Theoretically, there is no limit to the extent to which deposits may be expanded if there is a demand for bank credit, and owners of the bank credit forego their privilege of demanding currency from their banks. Who could not increase his promises to pay without limit if he were not asked to pay in cash; and who would not gladly do so if individuals, corporations, and others would give him interest-bearing credit instruments in exchange? One device to limit the expansion of bank credit is the fixing of minimum legal reserve requirements. Such requirements are made in the United States, which is in sharp contrast to the situation in Great Britain. However, custom requires that reserves be maintained, and so English banks customarily keep cash in their vaults and deposits with the Bank of England.

By increasing minimum reserve requirements, the Board of Governors may force member banks to keep a larger percentage of their assets idle; and by decreasing minimum reserve requirements, the Board may permit member banks to lend or invest a larger percentage of their assets.

When the position of the Federal Reserve banks is considered, Congress may change their lending and investing position by increasing or decreasing their minimum reserve requirements. Before June, 1945, these requirements were 35 per cent against deposits to be kept in "lawful money" and 40 per cent against Federal Reserve notes to be kept in gold certificates.

On June 12, 1945, Congress reduced the minimum reserve requirements to 25 per cent for both classes of liabilities, specifying that it must be kept in gold certificates. This legal requirement may be suspended by the Board of Governors of the Federal Reserve System, under certain conditions as provided in subsection C of Section 11 of the Federal Reserve Act.[7] Thus, assuming a demand and no suspension of reserve requirements, the maximum increase in the volume of Federal Reserve liabilities subject to reserve requirements is four times the volume of gold certificates.

Member bank credit expansion may be greater than that of the Federal Reserve banks, because their minimum legal reserve requirement is less. In Table 24 there appear member bank reserve requirements as amended by The World War I Act of June 21, 1917, and subsequent changes by the Board of Governors under provisions of the Banking Act of 1935 as amended. During World War II, pressure on member banks' reserves, owing to expansion of deposits, was released by exempting government war loan accounts from reserve requirements, by reducing reserve requirements of banks classified as "central reserve city banks," and by use of more Federal Reserve bank credit as reserves. While it is apparent that the tendency has been to reduce reserve requirements during the war, the Board may reverse this policy if postwar inflationary developments warrant. Since an increase or decrease in reserve requirements is a device of credit control for which the Board of Governors is responsible, it is more appropriately discussed in Chapter XXVIII, entitled "Credit Policy of the Federal Reserve System."

Multiple Expansion on New Reserves

The effects of new reserves on the amount of new deposits in an individual bank and on the banking system are considered under two assumptions: (1) that there will be a demand for bank credit

[7] The Board may "suspend for a period not exceeding thirty days, and from time to time renew such suspension for periods not exceeding fifteen days, any reserve requirement specified in this Act: *Provided*, That it shall establish a graduated tax upon the amounts by which the reserve requirements of this Act may be permitted to fall below the level hereinafter specified: *And provided further*, That when the reserve held against Federal Reserve notes falls below 25 per centum, the Board . . . . . shall establish a tax of not more than 1 per centum per annum upon such deficiency until the reserves fall to 20 per centum, and when said reserve falls below 20 per centum, a tax at the rate increasingly of not less than 1½ per centum per annum upon each 2½ per centum or fraction thereof that such reserve falls below 20 per centum. The tax shall be paid by the Reserve bank, but the Reserve bank shall add an amount equal to said tax to the rates of interest and discount fixed by the Board of Governors of the Federal Reserve System."

and (2) that the total proportionate reserve will be 20 per cent. If an individual bank receives a new $20,000,000 deposit, it has new funds to lend. The original entries are: additional deposits, $20,-000,000; cash, $20,000,000. The usual practice is to set aside 20 per cent of the new deposit and to lend or invest the remainder. After lending, the entries will be as follows:

Deposits........$20,000,000 (primary)	Cash..........$20,000,000
Deposits........$16,000,000 (derivative)	Loans........$16,000,000

No borrower will keep the proceeds of a loan on deposit, and so it is assumed that all will be withdrawn by checks which will be deposited with a second bank. The latter now has new cash, and the entries appear in this second bank as follows: additional deposits, $16,000,000; cash $16,000,000. The second bank, like the first bank, will lend 80 per cent of the new deposit, and then the result will be as follows:

Deposits........$16,000,000 (primary)	Cash..........$16,000,000
Deposits........$12,800,000 (derivative)	Loans........$12,800,000

This bank will lose the proceeds of the loans, the assumption being that the new checks written by the borrower will be deposited with a third bank. The latter will likewise expand its loan operations, with the resulting loss of the new deposit to a fourth bank, and so on, for other banks in the banking system. At the end of the expansion period, the effects will be as they appear in Table 26.

The expansion procedure noted here results in a fivefold increase in the volume of deposits. If legal and other reserves were but 10 per cent, a tenfold expansion would be possible. Thus, the size of the reserve requirement is an important factor in determining the amount of deposits in the banking system. In practice, a member bank may lend more than 80 per cent of its new deposits, because many checks come back to the bank which made the new loan, some borrowers may be required to keep part of their funds idle as a "proportionate balance," and others may not use all their deposits immediately. On the other hand, if some depositors preferred currency to deposits, there would be a loss of reserves without an increase in deposits.

If the borrower from the first bank had taken the proceeds of his loan of $16,000,000 in currency, there would have been no new deposits in the second bank to be used as a basis for further deposit expansion. Furthermore, if a depositor demands cash after the multiple expansion takes place, his bank is forced to sell assets in order to obtain it. This would cause other banks to lose reserves, and, in order to make up their deficiency in reserves, they in turn would be forced to sell assets. Thus pressure would be brought on other banks, and so the multiple expansion of deposits also works in reverse.

The fear of deposit withdrawals is an important factor influencing commercial banks' lending and investment policies. This possibility of deposit withdrawal explains: (1) why any banking system must have a central bank that can provide commercial banks with an

TABLE 26

DEPOSITS EXPANSION ON NEW RESERVES

	Additional Deposits Received (100%)	Additional Loans Made (80%)	Additional Reserves Retained (20%)
1st bank	$ 20,000,000	$16,000,000	$ 4,000.000
2nd bank	16,000,000	12,800,000	3,200,000
3rd bank	12,800,000	10,240,000	2,560,000
4th bank	10,240,000	8,192,000	2,048,000
5th bank	8,192,000	6,553,600	1,638,400
6th bank	6,553,600	5,242,880	1,310,720
7th bank	5,242,880	4,194,304	1,048,576
8th bank	4,194,304	3,355,443	838,861
9th bank	3,355,443	2,684,355	671,088
10th bank	2,684,355	2,147,484	536,871
Total first 10 banks	$ 89,262,582	$71,410,066	$17,852,516
Other banks in turn	$ 10,737,418	$ 8,589,934	$ 2,147,484
Grand total	$100,000,000	$80,000,000	$20,000,000

Source: Board of Governors of the Federal Reserve System, *The Federal Reserve System—Its Purposes and Functions* (1939), p. 73.

almost unlimited supply of currency, unhampered by collateral and reserve requirements, as happened in the United States during the period 1930-33; (2) why a loss of confidence in banks and a preference for holding currency rather than deposits force banks to liquidate their assets during periods of financial disturbance, when an opposite policy is socially desirable; (3) why sudden withdrawals on a national scale create a condition justifying a national banking holiday; and (4) why almost 100 per cent confidence must be maintained in the safety of bank deposits and in the banks which hold them.

Guarantee of Bank Deposits Is a Type of Insurance

The federal and state governments merely create agencies or set up corporations that carry on this insurance business. These agencies collect funds from banks, sell securities, borrow money, approve claims of depositors, collect insurance fees, and perform the other functions specified in their charters.

History.—The first insurance or guarantee system was the Safety Fund System of New York State, which provided a bank pool of funds managed by the government to guarantee the payment of depositors and holders of note obligations of the participating banks. Interest in deposit insurance again appeared after a series of bank failures following the panic of 1893[8] and was one of the objectives of the Populist party. Following the panic of 1907, and in response to a popular demand in the West and South, deposit insurance was one of the planks in the platform of the Democratic party in 1908.

In 1907 Oklahoma adopted a state deposit insurance system. It was followed by Kansas, Texas, Nebraska, Mississippi, the two Dakotas, and Washington. All these systems failed because (1) distribution of risk was inadequate, since all the states involved were agricultural; (2) only state banks were members (these banks were the weakest and a handicap to any system); (3) administration was inadequate, involving political and personal favoritism; and (4) many bankers took advantage of the fact that their depositors were insured and made many speculative loans. These state experiments were not successful, but a knowledge of their history has been helpful in the organization and operation of the Federal Deposit Insurance Corporation and the Federal Savings and Loan Insurance Corporation.

The creation of the Federal Deposit Insurance Corporation was the most controversial, if not the most important, feature of the Banking Act of 1933. It was established to create confidence in the banking system and to protect depositors from losses due to bank failures. In March, 1933, the government accepted moral responsibility for all bank failures. President Roosevelt assured the American public that only sound banks would be allowed to reopen after the national banking holiday, but the federal government did not have full jurisdiction over all banks, and many were allowed to

[8] See Robb, T. B., *Guaranty of Bank Deposits.*

reopen even though they were not sound. The general public did not realize this situation, but bankers and large depositors did. As a result, there was a great deal of shifting of deposits from weak to strong banks, and there was danger of a large number of bank failures. For this reason administration leaders agreed to a plan, sponsored by Senator Vandenburg, to insure deposits.[9]

The Banking Act of 1933 provided for a temporary and a permanent plan of insurance.[10] The temporary plan went into effect on January 1, 1934, and was to remain in effect for but six months; however, it remained in force for nearly twenty months in modified form. Of the 14,219 banks in the temporary plan that joined the permanent plan on August 23, 1935, 14,163 were commercial banks and 56 were mutual savings banks.

Ownership.—The Federal Deposit Insurance Corporation was chartered by the federal government, and all its capital is owned by the government and the twelve Federal Reserve banks. The government's subscription of $150,000,000 is equal to the amount which the Federal Reserve banks had paid to it as a franchise tax. Each Federal Reserve bank's subscription was equal to one-half its surplus as of January 1, 1933. The stockholders have no vote and receive no dividends. The Federal Reserve banks have written off their subscription, and it no longer appears on their combined statement as an asset, but it does appear on the statement of the Federal Deposit Insurance Corporation as a liability under capital accounts.

Management.—The Federal Deposit Insurance Corporation is governed by a board consisting of three directors, appointed by the President, with the consent of the Senate. The Comptroller of the Currency is an ex officio director. One of the other two directors, designated as chairman of the board of directors, is the administrative head of the system. The term of office is six years and is so arranged that the appointment of one director is made every two years. For convenience in operations, the United States is divided into twelve districts, which differ from the Federal Reserve districts in that they do not cut across state boundaries.

[9] Professor J. H. Williams writes: "Having the kind of banking system that we do, it seems necessary also to have deposit insurance, though it would seem much more desirable to improve the banking system itself than merely to protect the depositors against its defects" ("The Banking Act of 1935," *The American Economic Review*, Supplement, Vol. XXVI [1936], p. 105).

[10] For original provisions for the insurance of deposits in commercial banks, see *Annual Report of Federal Deposit Insurance Corporation*, 1934, pp. 117-27.

Participating Banks.—All members of the Federal Reserve System must participate in the Federal Deposit Insurance System, and commercial banks, trust companies, Morris Plan banks, and mutual savings banks that are not members of the Federal Reserve System may participate if they meet the requirements for membership.[11] At the end of 1944, 13,460 of the 14,710 banks in the United States and its possessions were participating in the insurance plan. Of these, 13,268 were commercial banks and trust companies and 192 mutual savings banks. Of the total deposits in all banks of over $142,000,000,000, over $134,600,000,000 are in insured banks.[12] Thus over a period of ten years the volume of deposits in insured banks increased from over $40,000,000,000 to $134,600,000,000.

At the end of 1944 there were 1,250 noninsured banks, of which 816 were commercial banks and trust companies,[13] 83 were trust companies not accepting deposits, and 351 were mutual savings banks. These noninsured mutual savings banks have total deposits of $4,400,000,000. With the abandonment of the New York State Mutual Savings Plan (see Chap. XXXI, "Savings Banks") and the reinsurance of deposits in the Federal Deposit Insurance Corporation, the most important groups outside the plan became members. As a result, the volume of deposits in insured mutual savings banks amounted to $8,900,000,000, which is about two-thirds of the total deposits in all mutual savings banks.

Cost of Insurance.—Under the present law, member banks have been freed from all contingent liabilities for losses. They are required to purchase deposit insurance on a single premium basis, the yearly premium amounting to 1/12 of 1 per cent of their total deposits. Theoretically, participating banks are buying deposit insurance from the Federal Deposit Insurance Corporation in the same way that they would from a private company, but it should be emphasized that banks pay insurance premiums based on total deposits rather than on insured deposits. The effect of this system of requiring payments on total deposits is to place most of the burden of

[11] Under the temporary plan as amended, mutual savings banks were insured in a separate fund known as Fund for Mutuals. In 1935 it was merged with the commercial bank fund, when the modified permanent plan went into effect.

[12] *Annual Report of the Federal Deposit Insurance Corporation for the Year Ended December 31, 1944*, Table 103, p. 120.

[13] This group includes 35 of a total of 40 banks located in possessions of the United States.

the plan on the large banks; and, in a few cases, their costs of insurance are over 50 per cent of the total volume of their insured deposits.

Liquidation of Weak Banks.—The policy of the officers of the corporation is to make the system self-supporting, which can be done by preventing the failure of insured banks and by closing weak banks before their assets are dissipated. Such policies will eliminate or reduce the deficits to be made up out of the Federal Deposit Insurance Corporation funds. The corporation may assist in the liquidation of weak banks and in the merger of weak with strong ones by making loans, by buying nonliquid assets, and by guaranteeing liabilities assumed by a second bank. Within recent years the most common practice has been for the corporation to buy assets under an agreement that any excess recovery from their liquidation, minus deduction for costs and interest on funds used, will be returned to the bank from which they were purchased. The depositors in the insolvent or hazardous banks which are merged are fully protected, and the transfer is made without a break in banking services.

In effecting bank mergers, the Federal Deposit Insurance Corporation may suffer losses, owing to its guarantee of assets; however, the purpose of the corporation in financing bank mergers is to eliminate weak banks and thereby avert future losses of greater magnitude.[14] In his annual report for the year ended December 31, 1939, the chairman of the board of directors of the corporation stated that this program was nearly completed. "Disbursements during 1939 of some $72,000,000 to protect the 393,000 depositors of 60 insured banks brought the program for rehabilitation of known problem banks near completion."[15]

Supervisory Functions.—In order to improve the quality of bank management and to keep insured banks sound, the corporation was granted many technical or routine powers possessed by national and state regulatory officers. From the first, it was realized that a successful guarantee deposit system necessitates strict control over banks

[14] L. T. Crowley, chairman of Federal Deposit Insurance Corporation, was quoted as follows: "Our records indicate that a great many uneconomic banks were extended the benefits of deposit insurance because the original law compelled us to admit banks which were merely solvent. This fact, coupled with the low earning power of these institutions, convinces us that it will be far cheaper for the corporation in the long run to merge the unsound banks with the stronger and better ones" (*New York Herald-Tribune,* March 17, 1936).

[15] *Federal Reserve Bulletin,* April, 1940, p. 310.

participating in the system. Deposit insurance must in no way be permitted to encourage unsound or careless banking, as happened in some of the state guarantee banking systems over two decades earlier. Other proper subjects for regulation are loan and investment policies, payment of interest on depositors' funds, carrying of burglary insurance, and fixing the ratio of capital stock and surplus to deposits. Duplication of examination is avoided by limiting those of the Federal Deposit Insurance Corporation to insured nonmember state banks.

In general, nonmember state banks are subject to the same examinations, compulsory reports, and other supervisory requirements as are members of the Federal Reserve System. In the future their loan, investment, and other policies will meet standards set for member banks. This means that, for all practical purposes, participating state banks must meet higher banking standards than those required in many state banking codes and by many state examiners. The policy of the corporation is to make annual examinations of insured nonmember state banks and to review the reports made by national bank examiners of national banks and those made by the Federal Reserve System of state member banks. On rare occasions, with the approval of the above agencies, it will make an examination of an insured member bank. In order to guard against too many banking offices, the corporation must approve of the opening of branches by insured nonmember banks. If a nonmember insured bank desires to change its capital structure, approval must be obtained from the Federal Deposit Insurance Corporation.

Acts as Receiver.—Administration leaders expected the deposit insurance system to eliminate bank failures, but this view was too optimistic. Since the beginning of deposit insurance "the Corporation has been called upon to make disbursements totaling $260 millions to protect depositors in 397 banks . . . . ."[16] Most of the causes of suspensions have been traced to real estate and other loans and investments made before their admission into the system.[17] The

[16] *Annual Report of the Federal Deposit Insurance Corporation for the Year Ended December 31, 1944*, p. 7.

[17] During 1944, for example, proceedings were initiated against a bank for continued operation with its capital impaired, under management that had not taken steps to correct the unsound condition of the bank, with an excessive amount of substandard assets, with insufficiency of earnings, with failure to obtain financial statements and other information from borrowers, with permitting borrowers to renew their obligations, and with classifying real estate as loans.

original law forced the corporation to admit all banks that were solvent, and many unsound banks entered the system. This situation explains why the corporation has been active in protecting depositors in unsound banks by financing mergers and liquidation and by insisting that other banks increase their capital stock by selling preferred stock to the Reconstruction Finance Corporation.

When the corporation pays off a depositor, it receives an assignment of the depositor's claim against the suspended bank. When the receiver of the bank liquidates the failed bank's assets, the amount allocable to these assigned claims will be paid to the corporation. Not only do depositors receive protection on deposits, but the plan offers the additional advantage of making deposits almost immediately available. Payments of the insured deposits is started promptly after the respective receiverships become final. Payments are made in the office of the closed bank, and the procedure is similar to the closure of an account.[18] A new bank may be created to accept and pay the insured deposits, or a second bank or some other agency may be designated as the paying agent. During the first eleven years the corporation placed 245 insured banks in receivership and merged 152 with other banks. It made $260,000,000 of disbursements to protect 1,297,000 depositors from losses and from the inconvenience of having all or part of their deposits of $499,000,000 frozen in suspended banks. Only 5,000 depositors will suffer losses on their accounts (maximum coverage per account is $5,000), and the total of these losses are expected to be about $2,600,000, or approximately ½ of 1 per cent of total deposits involved. The corporation's losses are estimated to be less than $39,000,000. (See Table 27.)

The power to close a bank remains with the state or federal authorities and the bank's own board of directors. A decision to merge a bank with another is made by a bank's stockholders. The power of the corporation is limited to the termination of insurance of a bank that is found to be financially unsound or whose management persists in following unsound or illegal banking practices. The corporation is required to serve as receiver for national banks, and it may be appointed by state authorities to serve as receiver for state banks. The corporation expects to be compensated later for its pay-

[18] At the time accounts are closed, depositors subrogate their rights to dividends to the corporation to that part of their account paid by the corporation. Claims of the bank against an account are deducted before insurance is paid.

ments of insured deposits, out of "dividends" from the sale of the defunct bank's assets. It shares in the dividends after expenses are deducted, on the same basis as other uninsured creditors of the suspended bank. It is estimated that the corporation will recapture about 75 per cent of the claims it pays. To increase returns to depositors not insured and to the corporation, the cost of liquidation of the suspended banks should be kept low. The corporation is well

TABLE 27

INSURED BANKS SUSPENDED OR MERGED WITH AID OF FEDERAL DEPOSIT INSURANCE CORPORATION, 1934-44

Item	Total	Banks Placed in Receivership	Banks Merged with Financial Aid of F.D.I.C.
Number of banks	397	245	152
Depositors:			
Paid in full*	1,250,068	333,361	916,707
Partially paid	4,788	4,788	....
Filing no claims	42,361	42,361	....
Total	1,297,217	380,510	916,707
Deposits:			
Estimated recovery by depositors	$496,188,000	$106,545,000	$389,643,000
Estimated loss by depositors*	2,614,000	2,614,000	....
Unclaimed deposits	431,000	431,000	....
Total	$499,233,000	$109,590,000	$389,643,000
Disbursement by F.D.I.C.	$259,696,000	$ 86,979,000	$172,717,000
Estimated loss to F.D.I.C.	$ 38,810,000	$ 18,611,000	$ 20,199,000

* 1,635 depositors will lose an estimated $2,532,000 in accounts, which exceeded the limit of $5,000 insurance, and were not otherwise protected; and 3,153 depositors will lose about $82,000 in accounts which had been restricted or deferred prior to 1934 or were otherwise ineligible for insurance protection.

Source: Annual Report of the Federal Deposit Insurance Corporation for the Year Ended December 31, 1944, p. 15.

prepared to perform this function, and most states have authorized it to act as receiver for closed insured state banks. Even more important, the officials of the corporation are well informed about security markets and have wide banking contacts, which make it possible for them to liquidate the assets of the suspended banks at more favorable prices than those usually obtained by individual receivers.

Summary.—Federal deposit insurance has met with wide approval, and, as long as the management is permitted to operate along present lines to improve bank management and to strengthen the capital structure of the insured banks, there is little need to fear that the gloomy forecasts of 1933 will be fulfilled. Most of the insurance costs are paid by the large banks, but the burden is usually diffused, because most of the costs of insurance are passed along in the form of service charges to their large depositors—insurance companies, correspondent banks, railroads, public utility companies, and other corporations and large business units.

The operation of the Federal Deposit Insurance Corporation has greatly reduced the local shock which normally accompanies bank failures. In addition, it has helped to reduce overbanking in many communities by assisting in the mergers and liquidation of unprofitable banks. The corporation has kept the costs of all its activities (management, insurance payments, examinations, supervision, liquidation, and mergers) so far below income that it has been able to add a surplus of $462,985,000 to its original capital of $289,000,000.

The total income of the corporation was $99,500,000 for the year 1944, of which $80,900,000 came from insurance premium payments and the remainder from earnings on investments and other sources. Disbursement of $100,000 was made for deposit insurance, and $3,800,000 was for administrative expenses. The surplus of the corporation was increased by $103,300,000 during the year.

The Federal Deposit Insurance Corporation has had the good fortune to have operated throughout a period of increasing business, which has been characterized by a small number of bank and other business failures. Not only has this reduced the claims against the corporation, but it has permitted it to show a high percentage of recoveries when taking over financial responsibility for paying depositors of suspended banks. Although capital account items of the corporation have increased, the ratio of the corporation's assets to insured deposits has declined because of the more rapid expansion of the latter.

In formulation of policies, the corporation has been the champion of the small banks. It approved the bill before Congress in 1943 that would have prevented the interpretation of the absorption of exchange charges as interest payments on demand deposits. It has objected to the development of so-called monopolistic practices through extension of branch and group banking. It favors a policy of refinancing and continuing insolvent banks rather than liquidating or merging them with a second institution.

In addition, the corporation has favored an increase in the capital-deposit ratio of banks, drawing attention to the fact that, with the decline of proprietorship interests, there is less protection for depositors. It has also proposed an increase in coverage of insurance from $5,000 to $10,000 per deposit account per bank. At the same time it favors a reduction in the annual assessment or premium on total deposits of 1/12 of 1 per cent.

While deposit insurance has been successful in the United States, care must be taken to avoid the overconfidence that all good times tend to breed. Although the "shakeout" of weak banks was not complete prior to the insurance of deposits in 1934, the suspension of 15,000 banks prior to that date must have contributed considerably to the excellent record of the Federal Deposit Insurance Corporation. Instead of aiding in the development of a sound banking structure, the success of the Federal Deposit Insurance Corporation may hinder it, by blinding the public to the inherent defects of a system made up of a large number of small banks.

QUESTIONS AND PROBLEMS

1. "Demand deposits are the things we live by and no commercial bank should be regarded merely as another business venture." Discuss.
2. Identify: (*a*) primary reserves; (*b*) secondary reserves; (*c*) legal reserves; and (*d*) working reserves.
3. What member bank reserve requirements are now in effect? What important changes have been made since 1917? (See Table 24.)
4. What are the chief factors that influence reserve policies of banks?
5. Discuss the significance of the statement that "large demand deposits not only exhibit a greater instability than small ones, but also that the percentage reduction of balances in the period prior to [bank] suspension became progressively greater the greater the size of the account," on reserve policy, bank investments, and deposit insurance.
6. Explain why reserve requirements are a device of credit control. May changes in them have little effect on the volume of commercial bank credit? Why?
7. What World War II changes were made in reserve requirements? Why? Was there a parallel change during World War I?

8. What is meant by a clearinghouse run on a bank? Compare with the historic or popular concept of a run.

9. "The real basis for the charge of premiums on uninsured deposits is to be found in the fact that many of the small banks are not paying their way and cannot afford to pay their appropriate share of the insurance cost, . . . " (Viner, Jacob, "Recent Legislation and the Banking Situation," *American Economic Review,* Supplement, Vol. XXVI [March, 1936], p. 112). Is this a desirable situation? Criticize.

10. "Deposit insurance is good only as long as through careful supervision and efficient management the general banking structure is kept in a sound condition" (Wilde, A. E., *Banking,* Sec. 11 [September, 1936], p. 5). Then is deposit insurance necessary?

11. "Bank debt, which is almost entirely short-term, is the most important type of internal debt because to an important extent it performs the function of money in the community" (Clark, *The Internal Debts of the United States,* p. 326). Is this a sufficient reason for guarantee of deposits by the federal government?

12. Many economists and bankers fear that the success of the Federal Deposit Insurance Corporation will delay bank reform in the United States. Why?

13. A reserve city bank has $14,330,000 in net demand deposits subject to reserves and $6,541,000 in time deposits. How large a legal reserve must it keep against each class of deposits? Compare to reserve requirements for 1929 and 1912 for the same classes of deposits.

14. The Hillsdale Country Bank has $25,500,000 in demand deposits. The time deposits amount to $5,000,000. Calculate the amount that this bank must pay semiannually to Federal Deposit Insurance Corporation.

15. To what extent is there justification in the movement to have the deposit insurance fee reduced from 1/12 of 1 per cent to 1/15 of 1 per cent? Would it be wiser to increase the insurance coverage from $5,000 to $10,000 and keep the same insurance rate?

16. All cities within which Federal Reserve banks or branches are located are classified as reserve or central reserve cities, but all cities classified as reserve cities do not have a Federal Reserve bank or branch in their midst. Is this true? Explain.

17. Give as many reasons as you can to justify the higher fractional legal reserve requirements for central reserve and reserve city banks.

18. Which class of depositor is chiefly responsible for bank failures? Is this in agreement with popular opinion? Explain. Use Table 25 as a reference.

19. Explain significance of the following: "In strengthening their reserve positions, the strong banks weakened the other banks and unknowingly forced some banks to close their doors" (Tuttle, F. W., "Society's Stake

in Commercial Banks," *Social Science*, Vol. XV, No. 2 [April, 1940], p. 158).

20. "The purpose served by ultimate cash reserves in the banking system is a double one. First, there is the classical purpose of 'maintaining confidence' in bank credit. Secondly, may be mentioned the restrictive influence that underlying reserves exercise on the superstructure of credit erected upon them, i.e., credit control" (Agger, E. E., *Relationship of Banking to Money* [New York: The Monetary Standards Inquiry, 1943], p. 4). Discuss.

REFERENCES

Agger, E. E. *Organized Banking.* New York: Henry Holt & Co., 1918.

American Bankers Association, Bank Management Commission. *Service Charge Survey, 1938.* New York: American Bankers Association, January, 1939.

American Bankers Association, Bank Management Commission. *Does the Account Pay?* Booklet No. 5; *Manual for Determining per Item Charge,* Booklet No. 15; *Manual for Installing the Measured Service Charge,* Booklet No. 13; *Practical Bank Analysis of Measured Service Charges,* Booklet No. 9; and *Uniform Account Analysis,* Booklet No. 22.

Annual Report of the Federal Deposit Insurance Corporation (for the year ended December 31, 1934, to date). Washington, D.C.: Superintendent of Documents.

Bezier, R. A. "The Right Price for What Banks Sell," *Banking,* May, 1944, p. 31. New York: American Bankers Association.

Board of Governors of the Federal Reserve System. *Banking and Monetary Statistics,* Secs. 3 and 7. Washington, D.C.: Board of Governors of the Federal Reserve System, 1943.

Board of Governors of the Federal Reserve System. *Annual Reports* (1936 to date).

Comptroller of the Currency of the United States. *Annual Reports* (1934 to date).

Dunbar, C. F. *The Theory and History of Banking,* chaps. i and ii. 4th ed. New York: G. P. Putnam's Sons, 1922.

Harr, Luther, and Harris, W. C. *Banking Theory and Practice,* chaps. i, viii, ix, and x. 2d ed. New York: McGraw-Hill Book Co., Inc., 1936.

Hetzel, F. W. *Analyzing Checking Accounts Scientifically.* New York: Bankers Publishing Co., 1936.

"History of the Reserve Requirements in the United States," *Federal Reserve Bulletin,* November, 1938, pp. 953-72.

Kniffen, W. H. *The Practical Work of a Bank*, chaps. v and vi. 8th ed. New York: Bankers Publishing Co., 1934.

Morton, W. A. "Zero Deposit Rate," *American Economic Review*, Vol. XXX, No. 3 (September, 1940), pp. 536-53.

Ninety-fourth Annual Report of the Superintendent of Banks, State of New York. Legislative Document (1945), No. 21. Albany.

Ninety-fifth Annual Report of the Superintendent of Banks, State of New York. Legislative Document (1946), No. 21. Albany.

Phillips, C. A. *Bank Credit.* New York: Macmillan Co., 1920.

Report of the Research Committee, Indiana Bankers Association. *A Study in Recent Banking Trends*, Part I; and *Merchandising Your Bank's Services*, Part II. Indianapolis, Indiana.

Robb, T. B. *Guaranty of Bank Deposits.* Boston: Houghton Mifflin Co., 1921.

Rokahr, Theodore. "The Right Price for What Banks Sell," *Banking*, May, 1944, p. 30. New York: American Bankers Association.

"Sources of a Bank's Lending Power," *Federal Reserve Bulletin*, February, 1940, pp. 99-100.

Thirtieth Annual Report, Federal Reserve Bank of New York for the Year Ended December 31, 1944, pp. 5-35. New York: Federal Reserve Bank of New York.

University of Denver. *Service Charges of Commercial Banks in Colorado.* Business Study No. 91, Vol. XIV, No. 3 (September, 1938).

Watkins, L. L. *Commercial Banking Reform in the United States*, pp. 73-133. Ann Arbor: University of Michigan, 1938.

Whittlesey, C. R. "Problems of Our Domestic Money and Banking System," *American Economic Review*, Supplement, Vol. XXIV (March, 1944), pp. 245-59.

Whittlesey, C. R. *The Effects of War on Currency and Deposits.* New York: National Bureau of Economic Research, 1943.

Willis, H. P., Chapman, J. M., and Robey, R. W. *Contemporary Banking.* New York: Harper & Bros., 1933.

Chapter XXI

LENDING AND INVESTING FUNCTIONS OF COMMERCIAL BANKS

Supplying Credit Is a Primary Banking Function

Lending and Investing.—The concept of "lending" traditionally carries with it the idea of permitting the use of things, with the condition that they or their equivalent be returned; while the concept of "investing" traditionally carries with it the idea of committing or laying out money, with the view to obtaining an income or profit. In the financial field, both lending and investing include the use of funds, for which interest is paid.

In so far as bankers are concerned, lending includes those transactions in which the borrowers come to the banks for funds; while investing generally includes those transactions in which the bankers take the initiative. Thus, a bank lends to a customer on a real estate mortgage but invests in a government obligation or a real estate bond. Usually in a lending transaction, the bank is the only creditor in so far as this particular credit instrument is concerned, while in an investment transaction the bank may be one of many creditors. Bank lending involves a promise or order to pay, while investing may involve both promises to pay and shares of stock.

On pages 426 and 427 loans are classified in a general way as those made to regular customers and those placed in the open market. The latter include acceptances bought and loans to brokers and dealers in securities in the New York and other capital markets (so-called "street loans"). Open market loans have one characteristic in common with investments—they are acquired at the initiative of the bank, while the other loans are made in response to requests of customers.

There Are Many Ways of Classifying Loans

Bank loans and discounts may be classified in the following ways: (1) according to the presence or lack of security—secured and unsecured; (2) according to the technical procedure in collecting interest costs—loans and discounts; (3) according to the source of the loan—over the counter and open market; (4) according to maturity—short-term, intermediate, and long-term; and (5) according to borrowers, which suggests the purposes for which the loan is made—commercial, industrial, agricultural, purchasing and carrying of securities, real estate, consumer, and interbank. Each of these major classes of loans may have several subdivisions.

Secured and Unsecured.—A loan is "secured" when title to goods, real estate, collateral, or any other form of property or property right is left with the lender with a signed agreement that permits it to be sold if the borrower defaults on any part of his contract. The borrower is still liable for any debt that may remain if the thing pledged is sold; and he receives any surplus that may be left after all the loan obligations are paid. If secured loans are classified according to the thing pledged, the chief types are real estate mortgage loans, chattel mortgage loans, merchandise loans, insurance policy loans, loans on assigned accounts (notes and accounts receivable), and loans on stocks and bonds as collateral.

Unsecured or clean loans are made without deposit of collateral or of a specific lien on goods or property. Repayment of the loan depends primarily upon the integrity and financial ability of the borrower. The bank is not a preferred creditor, and, if the borrower fails, the bank shares in the assets of the bankrupt firm on the same basis as all the other general creditors. Often corporations secure lines of credit which involve both secured and unsecured loans. A line may authorize borrowing $100,000 without security and an additional $50,000 with security.

When unsecured loans are made to business borrowers of high standing, they bear the name of the maker only. If the paper is endorsed by a second party, it is known as "two-name paper" but is still unsecured. If the maker defaults, the endorser must assume responsibility for the paper. Many unsecured loans are granted for commercial purposes, and, if they are made to corporations, they are usually endorsed by the company's officers.

Certain factors must be recognized in accounting for unsecured loans: (1) business houses whose credit standings are good are able to arrange for loans without pledging collateral, because of the keen competition among bankers for their accounts; (2) many business firms do not possess collateral which could be pledged conveniently as security; and (3) the costs of handling unsecured loans are much less than for secured. Within recent years the banking trend has been to require borrowers to pledge specific assets as backing for loans, and this makes the banks preferred creditors.

Loans and Discounts.—A bank loan, in the narrow sense of the word, includes those contracts which call for repayment of the principal and payment of interest sometime in the future. If the loan is for a long period of time, or made subject to call with no maturity date, interest is collected at periodic intervals. If the loan is for a short period, interest is collected when the principal matures. A discount, on the other hand, means that the interest is deducted in advance. In other words, the bank gives the customer only the present value of the paper, and the customer pays to the bank the face amount of the obligation when it comes due. Broadly speaking, all discounts are loans, for the meaning of this word includes all acts of granting the temporary use of money, credit, or property.

When banks discount paper, they are receiving a higher rate than when they make a straight loan. For example, assume that a borrower gives a bank a note for $100.00, which is discounted at the rate of 6 per cent. He is paying $6.00 for the use of $94.00 for a year. In a loan transaction he receives $100.00 and repays $106.00. Here he pays $6.00 for use of $100.00 for a year, which is the same amount that he paid for the use of $94.00 in the discount transaction.

Call loans, real estate loans, and others which are made for a long period are necessarily on a loan basis; but most of the banks prefer to discount all short-term obligations. If the obligation is repaid before maturity, many banks will give a rebate on the money taken as a discount. All bills and commercial paper purchased in the open market and most short-term loans are now discounted. The chief reason for the continuance of the classification of paper as "loans" and "discounts" is because of accounting procedure which gives rise to such items as "income accrued but not yet collected" and "income collected but not yet earned."

Over the Counter and Open Market.—Most over-the-counter lending transactions of banks involve close personal relations between the bank and the borrowers. In the case of corporations and large enterprises, close contacts are kept with the officers and key personnel. Credit files are kept on each borrower, and a typical folder on a business name may contain a record of the bank's expenses with the account, size of the bank account, service charges, record of overdrafts and returned checks, bank officers' annual report on the name, balance sheet comparative statement for a number of years, memoranda on interviews, copies of correspondence with the borrower and with banks and others that have had experience with him, reports of investigations, clippings and circulars, and copies of reports of Dun and Bradstreet and other mercantile agencies. While the credit file on nonbusiness borrowers would not be so elaborate, the practice of accumulating and filing facts on each name is a general one.

Open market lending procedure is practically identical with that of investing. Commercial paper and bankers' acceptances are purchased from commercial paper houses and bill brokers or acceptance dealers, and the lending bank has little or no contact with the debtor. When these short-term credit instruments come due, they are rarely renewed.

Usually only short-term credit needs are financed in the open market. Two types of paper are involved: promissory notes, which are usually unsecured, and bankers' and trade acceptances (bills), which may or may not be secured. The first type is handled by note brokers, who are usually referred to as "commercial paper houses." They do not take title to the paper, which they sell to banks and others at a discount, and they are compensated by a small commission, paid to them by the borrowers. The second type of paper is handled by bill dealers who do take title to the bills which they handle, usually endorse them, and sell them at a lower discount or a higher net price to banks and other buyers. In the typical open market transaction, the investing bank has no personal relationship with the borrower, but, as noted later, this is not true when "accepting banks" purchase their own bills.

Maturity Classification.—Classification of loans as "short-term," "intermediate," and "long-term" needs no special comment other than that the first usually includes those with terms of a year or less; long-term, those with terms of five years or more; and intermediate, those for terms in between the short- and long-term loans.

Classification According to Borrowers.—Classification of loans according to borrowers has the advantage of suggesting the general purposes for which the loans are made. It is the one called for when banks' reports are made to federal supervisory officials and the one on which the statistics appearing in Table 28 are based. Commercial loans, including open market, are those made to finance borrowers in the fields of manufacturing and merchandising. They may be short-term, intermediate, or long-term and may be secured or unsecured. They may be used to finance the purchase of goods or some fixed capital need.

Agricultural loans are those made to finance borrowers in the agricultural field. The volume of these loans made by banks (see Table 28) is only part of the total volume, because most of these credit needs are cared for by specialized institutions operating in the field of agricultural credit. (See Chap. XXXV.)

Most loans for purchasing and carrying securities are made by New York banks to brokers and investment bankers in order to facilitate buying and selling in the security markets. When brokers borrow, they scatter their loans among a number of banks in order to avoid financial embarrassment in case one bank should call its loan; and usually the same impersonal relationship exists between the broker and the bank as noted for open market borrowers. During World War II, government officials approved of purchases of government securities by individuals with funds borrowed temporarily from banks, provided the loans were for a short term or on an amortization basis, repayable within a period not to exceed six months.

Real estate loans are made to help finance the purchase of urban and rural property by homeowners, farmers, businessmen, and others. Both state and national laws place limitations upon the real estate loans of commercial banks, for they are not easily liquidated or marketed. Real estate mortgage loans of member banks must be secured by first mortgages upon improved real estate, including improved farm land and improved business and residential properties. If secured by an amortized mortgage, real estate loans may be made up to 60 per cent of the appraised value of the property and may run for ten years, provided that the instalment payments are large enough to amortize 40 per cent of the loan in that time. Other mortgage loans may have a maturity up to five years and be for 50 per cent of the appraised value of the property. Since all loans may be renewed, the effect of these two time restrictions is to force a periodic reappraisal of property. The amortization loan plan places commercial banks in a better competitive position and gives them protection against a "sour loan" in the middle of the amortization period. However, these restrictions do not apply to loans which are guaranteed under the provisions of Title II of the

Federal Housing Act, and these loans now tend to dominate all banks' real estate lending.

Total mortgages held by banks are limited to 60 per cent of their time and savings deposits or 100 per cent of their unimpaired capital and surplus, whichever is the greater. This limitation does not apply to real estate bonds, other real estate obligations which represent only

TABLE 28

LOANS AND INVESTMENTS OF ALL INSURED BANKS

(In Millions of Dollars)

	Dec. 31, 1938	Dec. 31, 1941	June 30, 1945
Loans (total)	16,021	21,258	23,376
Commercial, including open market	5,636	9,214	7,501
Agricultural	1,060	1,450	1,632
Purchasing and carrying securities	1,887	1,276	6,714
Real estate	3,857	4,773	4,413
Consumer	3,583 (Consumer and Other, including interbank)	4,545 (Consumer and Other, including interbank)	2,105
Other, including interbank			1,008
Investments (total)	21,449	28,030	88,978
U.S. government obligations (total)	14,506	21,046	82,401
Direct:			
Bills	290	988	2,831
Certificates of indebtedness	......	......	17,204
Notes	3,648	3,159	16,454
Bonds	8,000	12,797	45,870
Guaranteed	2,568	4,102	43
States and political subdivisions	3,011	3,651	3,684
Other securities	3,932	3,333	2,892
Total loans and investments	37,470	49,288	112,353

Source: Federal Reserve Bulletin, December, 1945, p. 1220.

a part of the underlying obligation, and mortgages guaranteed by the Federal Housing Administration. The 10 per cent rule (a single loan cannot exceed 10 per cent of the bank's capital and unimpaired surplus) applies to real estate loans as well as to all others.

The former territorial limitations upon real estate loans were removed by the Banking Act of 1935, which makes possible much wider distribution of real estate investment funds. At the present time banks located in one Federal Reserve district which has a surplus of savings deposits may place them in districts less fortunate; and in the future many eastern banks will find a profitable market for their funds in guaranteed mortgages based upon urban property located in the poorly financed sections of the United States. Other aspects of urban mortgage financing, including facilities for making a national market for Federal Housing Administration mortgages, are considered in Chapter XXXIV.

Consumer loans to individuals have been required to be reported separately since December 31, 1942. Information was desired on this type of lending to aid in the regulation of consumer credit. (See Chap. XXX.) Other loans are residuals of total loans not reported separately. This classification includes loans made by one bank to a second, transactions which originated in the correspondent relationships that developed as a result of the unit banking system. It is usually agreed that in return for the use of bankers' balances kept with the larger bank, the latter shall provide the depositing bank with financial services of many types, including the lending of funds in case of need. The volume of bank loans to banks is now small, because member banks usually prefer to meet their short-term credit needs by selling securities or by discounting at their Federal Reserve banks. Most lending banks do not open a regular line of credit for bank borrowers but pass upon applications for funds when made. Invariably, such loans are secured by collateral.

Investments

Investments are classified according to the borrowers, as United States government obligations, obligations of states and political subdivisions, and other securities. There are two major subclasses of United States government obligations—direct and guaranteed. The latter first appeared in 1933 and continued to be of considerable importance until the government changed its policy of financing the Reconstruction Finance Corporation, Home Owners' Loan Corporation, and other government agencies. Now these agencies secure their funds directly from the United States Treasury. The outstanding guaranteed issues are being retired as soon as they become due or callable, and no new ones are being issued.

United States government direct obligations are divided into bills, certificates of indebtedness, notes, and bonds.[1] Bills are short-

[1] During World War II, for the first time, large quantities of bonds were issued that could be purchased by but one class of buyers. Nonnegotiable "savings bonds" were sold to individuals, certain obligations were sold to investors other than commercial banks, and other obligations were offered which could not be purchased by banks until the lapse of a number of years.

term obligations sold on a discount basis. During the two world wars certificates of indebtedness were used by the Treasury as a device for obtaining funds from banks pending the sale of bills, notes, and bonds. Notes are short-term and intermediate promises to pay, while bonds are long-term promises to pay.

Obligations of states and political subdivisions include all the promises to pay of state and local governments held by commercial banks. Other securities include both foreign and domestic types. The latter consist of bonds, notes, and debentures of government agencies not guaranteed by the United States government—railroads, utilities, and all others, both industrial and educational.

Member banks are required to buy Federal Reserve bank stock equal to 3 per cent of their capital and surplus (they must subscribe to another 3 per cent, which is subject to call by the Board of Governors) and may invest in the following types of corporate stocks: (1) foreign banking institutions (limited to 10 per cent of a bank's capital and surplus), (2) National Agricultural Credit Corporation (limited to 10 per cent of capital and surplus), (3) bank premises or stocks and bonds of a corporation owning premises of the bank (limited to the amount of the bank's capital stock), and (4) any corporation organized to conduct a safe-deposit business (limited to 15 per cent of the bank's capital and surplus).

Investing was considered a secondary activity of commercial banks until the middle thirties, when it came to be the most important of their portfolio problems. Investments had been considered an outlet for funds when local demands for loans were insufficient to absorb a bank's idle money. In the past investments were regarded by individual banks as secondary reserves, but the collapse of the bond market (1931-33) changed this situation. It has been only since the thirties that the investment portfolios of commercial banks have been scientifically managed.

Bankers Prefer Lending to Investing

When a banker is faced with a situation which permits him to choose between making a loan to a credit-worthy borrower and purchasing a bond, he prefers to make the loan. It is only logical that he should, because loans generally yield better returns and are generally more profitable to banks than are investments. When current earnings of member banks are considered, the average yield on loans is 3 per cent, whereas the average interest rate on investments is 1.5 per cent; and when the recoveries on past "paper" losses, less those on current transactions (directly applicable to both types of transactions), are considered, the net return on loans is over 3.1 per cent as compared to 1.8 per cent on investments.[2]

Any assumption on the part of the general public that bankers lend grudgingly shows ignorance of the fact that this type of asset is the most profitable that a bank may hold. It is only natural that bankers seem to hesitate if the applications for credit have not been preceded by credit analysis and the establishment of lines of credit. Even more important than lending is the need to avoid making uncollectable loans. Since "net profit" is only 0.6 per cent of total earning assets for member banks, it is readily apparent that it would take a large sum invested for a year to offset an added loss of but $100. Unlike other business enterprises with which customers have contact (retail stores, etc.), the margin of profit on which banks operate is very small. There is no comparison between the risks that a bank and a mercantile firm may take in granting credit.

A bond investment is a trading transaction which usually involves the immediate withdrawal of all the funds so invested; on the other hand, a lending operation increases balances that will be withdrawn over a period of time. Lending also builds up bank-customer relationships and the basis for future patronage, including such sources of income as service charges on demand accounts, rentals on safe-deposit boxes, and fees for trust business. It is not surprising then to find that bankers are reluctant in changing from lending to large-scale purchasing of government and other securities. In doing so they are in competition with insurance companies and investing institutions having many advantages, including the services of investment specialists, lower per unit cost of operation, and less need to keep their assets in liquid or marketable paper.

The ability of banks to get back funds invested in bonds depends on their salability and the presence of other buyers in the security markets. Since all banks tend to buy bonds at the same time, their prices tend to be high when purchases are made; and, since the financial and business factors causing one bank to sell its bonds to increase liquidity also operate in the case of other banks, the dis-

---

[2] See *Federal Reserve Bulletin*, November, 1945, p. 1161.

turbances created in the bond market when sales are made will lower prices and cause capital losses to the banks. Even though no sales are made, banks assume the risks of bookkeeping losses due to declines in the market value of securities because of a rise in the market rate of interest. In purchasing long-term securities, banks assume both "credit" and "interest" risks.

The seasonal loan is the bankers' ideal loan, because it gives to the bank true liquidity. It is based on economic transactions—the harvesting of a crop, the marketing of goods, or the production of goods—which at their fulfillment provide the funds with which to pay the loan. In addition to being a satisfactory outlet for bank funds, commercial loans meet the test required by adherents to the banking school of thought, that is, that changes in commercial bank credit should be made in response to increases or decreases in business activity.

Commercial Loans Are Declining

In spite of bankers' preference for lending over investing, the fact is that investments have largely replaced loans as the chief earning assets of commercial banks. Since this situation existed before World War II, it cannot be dismissed as being due to temporary conditions that will disappear with the return to peacetime economy. Certain fundamental changes in business which affect the volume of commercial bank credit are discussed below.

Cash Sales and Credit Terms.—The two chief purposes for which commercial credit is used are the purchasing of merchandise and the carrying of credit accounts. Credit needs for the first have been greatly reduced by improvements in transportation and communication facilities that permit merchants to carry smaller stocks of goods relative to total volume of sales. A merchant no longer needs to tie up credit in a six months' supply of goods, because prompt replacements can be secured.

The need for bank credit to carry accounts receivable is being reduced by an increase in cash sales and improvement in collections. The increase in chain-store merchandising with emphasis on low prices and cash sales has greatly reduced the demand for commercial credits. Better collection methods have resulted from a large number of factors, including better management, credit bureaus, collection agencies, and consumer education. The Board of Governors has been a factor in shortening the time that charge accounts are in use, by freezing them at the end of sixty days if they are not paid in whole or in part.

Financing without Bank Credit.—The use of instalment financing by more "lines" and its more extensive use by others gives merchants discountable paper which is sold to finance companies and small loan companies, thereby making borrowing from banks unnecessary. Bankers are meeting this competition by opening personal loan departments and discount divisions, which are designed to compete more actively with the personal loan and finance companies for this credit business. Another factor in the decline of commercial loans has been the increase in the size of manufacturing and merchandising units, many of which are incorporated and can obtain working capital funds directly in the investment and money markets through sales of securities.

Growth of Time Deposits.—Although the increase in time deposits in commercial banks does not explain the decline in short-term borrowing, the presence of these funds in commercial banks has been a factor in the increase in banks' long-term lending and investments in bonds and the relative decline in the importance of commercial loans. Such funds, in so far as they represent savings deposits, may be invested in bonds and mortgage loans on real estate with greater stress on yield and less on liquidity.

Investments and Noncommercial Loans.—Banks' investments represent over three-fourths of all the earning assets of commercial banks, but most of this increase is due to the increase in the holdings of United States government obligations. There is a possibility that the substantial increase in loans which has taken place since 1938 will be lost sight of. In the future, loans should become both absolutely and relatively more important in bank statements.

Perhaps no more than 5 per cent of the following types of earning assets are commercial loans in the traditional sense: mortgage loans on real estate; loans on securities, whether time or call; consumer loans; loans to farmers, industrialists, and manufacturers; and investments in all types of securities. This situation helps to confirm the conclusion that present-day commercial banks have as their chief credit function the financing of the investment needs of governments, business, and others. For this reason there is considerable justification for describing them as investment rather than as commercial banks.

Large Customers Establish Lines of Credit with Their Banks

In order to avoid costly delays, most large borrowers secure lines of credit from their banks at the beginning of their fiscal years. A line of credit is the maximum amount which a bank agrees to lend to one customer. Before fixing a line of credit, the bank analyzes the credit position of the customer. This analysis is made by the credit department[3] and includes (1) an examination of the customer's financial statements; (2) personal conferences with the officers; (3) a visit to the customer's place of business; (4) a check with other banks upon their experiences with the customer; (5) a review of the customer's rating as made by special and general mercantile and credit agencies, for example, Dun and Bradstreet, and local credit bureaus; and (6) the opinions and experiences of those with whom the customer trades.

The work of credit analysis, as practiced by banks, helps to explain the small losses incurred on this type of bank asset. During the past twenty years, after making allowances for recoveries, operating member banks' losses have been at the annual rate of less than ½ of 1 per cent on loans. Large banks have excellent bank credit departments with staffs skilled in the analysis of balance sheets, profit and loss statements, surplus accounts, business budgets, and trial balances.[4] Small banks, although lacking trained specialists, are in a position to depend upon close contact with an intimate knowledge of local borrowers.

The amount of the line of credit is subject to change without notice, and it may provide for the granting of credit with or without security. The customer may or may not use his line of credit, but in order to keep it open the bank usually requires the customer to keep a proportionate balance on deposit with the bank. Many banks keep a continuous check upon the financial standings of their customers,

---

[3] See the following publications of American Bankers Association, Bank Management Commission, *Credit Department Organization*, Booklet No. 7; *Loan Administration Policies*, Booklets No. 1 and No. 21; and *Duties and Qualifications of Executive Bank Officers*, Booklet No. 6.

[4] See Prochnow, H. V., and Foulke, R. A., *Practical Bank Credit*, pp. 3-28.

while others merely recheck the financial standing when loans are made.

Small borrowers have a choice of a number of lending agencies, but, to an increasing extent, commercial banks have established personal loan departments or special divisions to accommodate small borrowers.[5] These loans are based upon the instalment principle of repayment. The instalment payments either go into a savings account until the loans are cancelled or they are applied directly to the principal until the loan is repaid. Rarely are personal loans made upon grants of lines of credit.

In all cases where loans are made, the banker must secure satisfactory answers to the questions of how the funds are to be used and how the borrowers expect to repay them. While the young businessman may properly establish his credit with a bank by borrowing for some legitimate purpose and then repaying the loan, the practice of borrowing, keeping the funds hidden, and then bringing them out to repay the loan, merely to establish one's credit, is a serious reflection on Mr. Jones's or anyone else's banker who would permit such a transaction. It is a violation of the cardinal principle of bank administration—knowledge of how borrowers are using funds lent by a bank. Such a transaction in no way provides a test of how the borrower can handle funds, and it cannot be used as an index of his ability to repay a larger loan which he may request in the future. The correct way for a young man to establish his credit at a bank is to build up his deposit account, pay cash for purchases, increase his earning power, and establish a reputation for prompt payment of all obligations.

Governments Influence Investing and Lending

There is no quarrel with the statement that good banking is primarily a product of good bankers; but many banking laws originally opposed by bankers are now generally approved by them. Although the charge has been made that bankers have been opposed to every constructive banking legislative act in the United States, this is true only of a small number of bankers who think: "He who

[5] During 1945 13 additional state banks in New York State opened personal loan departments, which brought the percentage of the total of state banks operating such departments up to 52 per cent (*Ninety-fifth Annual Report of the Superintendent of Banks, State of New York*, Part I, p. 30).

governs least, governs best." The lending and investing functions of banks have been considerably influenced by legal limitations placed on the use of bank funds by its officers, the guarantee of loans by the government, and the regulation of loans and investments.

During the 1931-34 Senate investigation, it was disclosed that many of the "good bankers" of the twenties were borrowing heavily from their banks for speculative and other purposes.[6] Sound banking requires that every application for a loan should be reviewed by disinterested persons. When officers borrow from their own banks, they are judges of their own credit. Obviously, such a situation is dangerous, and in 1933 Congress prohibited all such loans. In 1935 this rather drastic provision was modified, and two exceptions to the general provisions that executive officers may not borrow money from their own banks were made, namely: (1) all officer loans made before June 16, 1933, could be extended for not more than five years (later this was extended for another five years); and (2) with the prior approval of a majority of the bank's entire board of directors, any executive may borrow from his bank an amount not exceeding $2,500.

If an executive officer borrows from any other bank, he must make a written report to his own bank's board of directors. His written report must contain all the information about the loan, including amount, date, security, if any, and the purpose for which the proceeds have been or are to be used. Officers who violate these provisions may be removed from office by the Board of Governors of the Federal Reserve System.

Government Guarantee of Loans.—The loan guarantee principle has been generally accepted by bankers. It was introduced in 1934 with the passage of the Industrial Loan Act and the National Housing Act. In the former, Congress provided for both direct lending and the guarantee of bank loans to business enterprises by adding Section 5*d* to the Reconstruction Finance Corporation Act and Section 13*b* to the Federal Reserve Act.[7] In the National Housing Act, Congress provided for government guarantee of real estate and home improvement loans. (See Chap. XXXIV.)

During World War II, the guarantee principle was used to insure

[6] See Pecora, Ferdinand, *Wall Street under Oath;* and Committee on Banking and Currency, *Stock Exchange Practices*, Senate Report No. 1455, 73d Cong., 2d sess.

[7] See "Regulation S" in *Federal Reserve Bulletin*, May, 1942, pp. 428-30.

loans made by banks and other financing institutions for the purpose of financing contractors, subcontractors, and others engaged in any business essential to the prosecution of the war.[8] The Federal Reserve banks were used as the agents in carrying out the guaranteeing provisions. On April 6, 1942, the Board of Governors issued Regulation V, which contained general rules and policies for guidance of the Federal Reserve banks.[9] During the war over $10,000,000,000 in bank credit was made available to borrowers under Regulation V. At the end of 1943, when banks' war loans were at their peak, 55 per cent were guaranteed. During the next six months, when the total declined, the percentage of those guaranteed increased to 66 per cent. This guarantee loan program ceases with the settlement of war contracts.[10] Regulation V has been broadened to simplify previous arrangements for termination, or "T," loans as authorized in the Contract Settlement Act.

Reference has already been made to the provisions for guaranteeing veterans' loans (by the Veterans' Administration) up to 50 per cent, with the amount guaranteed not to exceed $2,000 except for purchases of real estate, when it may be $4,000. Other examples of the use of government-guaranteed credit are in the field of foreign trade, with the Export-Import Bank assuming the dominant role.

Other Sources of War Loans.[11]—Any business enterprise engaged in operations connected with the war effort could have secured funds from (1) a bank by assignment of claims under a government contract or otherwise, (2) the Reconstruction Finance Corporation, (3) the Smaller War Plants Corporation, (4) the War Department, Navy Department, or Maritime Commission, (5) a Federal Reserve bank under the provision of Section 13(*b*) of the Federal Reserve Act, (6) or a combination of two or more of the foregoing. In addition, if a business enterprise held a prime contract, advances were obtainable from the War Department, the Navy Department, or the Maritime Commission.

[8] The legal basis for the insurance of war loans was Executive Order No. 9112, issued March 26, 1942, under the President's wartime powers. The order gave the War Department, Navy Department, and the Maritime Commission the power to guarantee war loans.

[9] See *Federal Reserve Bulletin*, May, 1942, pp. 424-27.

[10] Conkling, G. W., "Loans for War Purposes," *Federal Reserve Bulletin*, November, 1945, pp. 1102-05; American Bankers Association, Bank Management Commission, *War Loans*, Bank Management Publication No. 101.

[11] See American Bankers Association, Bank Management Commission, *ibid.*, p. 12.

Regulation of Banks' Investments.—Because of the increase in importance of investments in the portfolios of banks, more attention is now being given to them by state and federal supervisory agencies. National banks are limited to the purchases of investment securities which are defined by law as follows: "As used in this section the term 'investment securities' shall mean marketable obligations evidencing indebtedness of any person, copartnership, association, or corporation in the form of bonds, notes, and/or debentures, commonly known as investment securities, under such further definition of the term 'investment securities' as may by regulation be prescribed by the Comptroller of the Currency." But in "no event shall the total amount of the investment securities of any one obligor or maker, held by the association for its own account, exceed at any time 10 per centum of its capital stock actually paid in and unimpaired and 10 per centum of its unimpaired surplus fund, except that this limitation shall not require any association to dispose of any securities lawfully held by it on the date of the enactment of the Banking Act of 1935."[12]

Regulation made by the Comptroller of the Currency (February 15, 1936) defined the term "marketable securities" as those having "such a market as to render sales at intrinsic values readily available." Bonds may not be purchased that are convertible into stock at the option of the issuer, that are in default as to interest or principal, and that are rated as speculative. The issue must be large enough to make marketability possible and must be distributed under conditions that insure marketability. Where "there is doubt as to the eligibility of a security, such eligibility must be supported by no less than two rating manuals."[13] This has reference to the highest classes in Moody's, Standard Statistics, Poor's, and other manuals. The effect is to exclude those securities of local governments not rated by the investment manuals. For example, of the 185,000 local governments in the United States, less than 15,000 are rated in Moody's Manual. As a result of criticism of this rule,[14] the regulations were modified to permit purchases of local issues under certain circumstances[15] and later led to other changes, noted below.

[12] See *Federal Reserve Bulletin*, March, 1936, p. 194.

[13] *Ibid.*, pp. 194-95; and June, 1938, pp. 421-23.

[14] See Palyi, M., "Bank Portfolios and the Control of the Capital Market," *Journal of Business of the University of Chicago*, Vol. XI, No. 1 (January, 1938), pp. 70-111.

[15] *Federal Reserve Bulletin*, July, 1938, pp. 563-66.

Changes in Examiners' Classifications.—Further encouragement to capital lending has been given by a 1938 revision in bank examination procedure. The chief change has been to abandon "the 'slow' classification of assets and recognition of the principle that bank investments should be considered in the light of inherent soundness."[16] The Board of Governors of the Federal Reserve System states the position of the three federal supervisory agencies as follows:

In considering the question of bank examination and supervision recognition was given to the great changes which have occurred during the past 20 years in the composition and character of bank assets, the substantial decrease in the holdings of short-term, self-liquidating commercial paper, and the great increase in the holdings of investment securities, both in aggregate amount and as compared with total assets.

As a result of these developments, banks find it necessary to look, to a considerable extent at least, for other forms of loans to replace the lost volume of short-term commercial loans and to treat the security account more as a permanent investment account than as a means for the temporary investment of idle funds. Changes made by the Banking Act of 1935 in the law regarding advances by Federal Reserve banks and the revised regulation on this matter issued in 1937 by the Board of Governors were designed to assist banks to meet these changed conditions. The new policies with respect to bank examination and supervision were framed with the same end in view. The revised examination procedure does not represent a relaxation of standards. It was worked out as a measure which, with its emphasis on fundamental soundness of assets of every type, would further the maintenance of a sound banking system and enable banks better to serve their depositors and their communities.

The classification of loans as "slow," "doubtful," and "loss" was abolished, and in its place was introduced the system of classifying loans as Groups I, II, III, and IV. The meaning of these groups as applied to loans is as follows: Group I are loans, or parts thereof, which it appears certain that debtors will pay. Group II are loans or portions thereof which appear to involve a substantial and unreasonable degree of risk by reason of an unfavorable record of the debtor or other unsatisfactory characteristics of the loan. There exists a possibility of future loss unless the bank's management gives careful and continued attention to them. Examiners do not classify loans in this category if ultimate payment seems reasonably certain in view of net worth of maker or endorser, his character and earning capa-

[16] Board of Governors of the Federal Reserve System, "Problems of Banking and Bank Supervision," reprint from *Annual Report*, 1938, pp. 27-28.

city, or the presence of collateral or other security of sound value. Group III are loans or portions thereof, the ultimate collection of which is doubtful, in which a substantial loss is probable but not yet certain as to amount. Bank management should give vigorous attention to such loans, with the purpose of salvaging whatever value may remain. Group IV includes loans or portions thereof, the ultimate collection of which is so improbable that it is recommended that bank management charge them off as losses. This does not mean that nothing will be salvaged, because even in bankruptcy cases some loans may be repaid, even though the debtor may not be legally required to do so.

Securities are divided into groups as follows: Group I are those which are predominantly investment in character; Group II are those which are speculative in character; Group III are those in default; and Group IV include stocks. Group I securities are carried at book value, with provision that if purchased at a premium the premium will be amortized. This group makes up most of the investments of banks, including the four highest ratings in rating manuals as well as equivalent securities not rated. Group II includes general market obligations below the four highest ratings and unrated securities of equivalent values. They are appraised by examiners at the average market price for eighteen months preceding the examination. Securities in Groups III and IV are appraised at their current market price.[17]

QUESTIONS AND PROBLEMS

1. Distinguish between lending and investing from the viewpoint of a bank.
2. Distinguish between (*a*) secured and unsecured loans, (*b*) loans and discounts, (*c*) over-the-counter and open market loans.
3. Give the chief classes of loans according to purposes or borrowers.
4. What are the chief classes of commercial banks' investments? What important changes have taken place in the investment holdings of commercial banks in recent years? Why?
5. What justification is there for calling commercial banks "investment banks"? Explain.
6. Why do banks prefer lending to investing?

---

[17] Standard's and Poor's services, Moody's Investors' Service, and Fitch services give general information about important issues and give ratings such as "AAA" or "A 1+" for the highest and "AA" and "A 1" for the second.

7. Explain why commercial loans are declining.
8. Describe the procedure followed by banks in arranging to finance the needs of customers that borrow large amounts of funds.
9. Identify: (*a*) a bank's credit department, describing its work, and (*b*) a personal loan department.
10. Distinguish between (*a*) short-term and long-term loans, (*b*) bankers' and trade acceptances, (*c*) lines of credit and commercial loans, and (*d*) "one-name" and "two-name" paper.
11. "Few of you like real estate loans, yet you can have no better loan in your bank than a properly amortized real estate loan" (Jones, J. H., *Banking*, December, 1938, p. 86). Discuss.
12. Identify: (*a*) government bills, (*b*) government certificates of indebtedness, (*c*) government notes, and (*d*) government bonds.
13. What risk is inherent in banks' investments in bonds? Explain.
14. "While the ideal of automatic elasticity in the volume of a bank's deposits was always something of a mirage, the clear-cut displacement of private debt by government debt as the principal basis of demand deposits has dispelled even this mirage." Do you agree? (*Source:* Whittlesey, C. R., "Problems of Our Domestic Money and Banking System," *American Economic Review*, Supplement, Vol. XXXIV [March, 1944], p. 249).
15. "This very large increase in government security holdings is important to banks in several ways. Now the public's deposits . . . . are almost dollar for dollar covered by government securities. Their portfolios of government issues provide the banks with an almost inexhaustible capacity to supply credit to business and industry." What are some of the reasons why the situation described is important to banks, and to the public? (*Ninety-fifth Annual Report of the Superintendent of Banks State of New York*, Part I, p. 13).
16. "At a quick glance it would hardly seem there was a cloud in banking's sky. Yet the trends in the real estate market for more than a year have been cause for concern. . . . It has been said that booms do not take place in real estate except that lenders make it possible." Discuss and then compare to quotation in Question 11. (*Source: ibid.*, pp. 6-7.)
17. Since deposit insurance represents an attempt to protect the means of payment, may it be justified when the guarantee of an individual bank asset may not? (See *Annual Report of the Federal Deposit Insurance Corporation for the Year Ended December 31, 1944*, pp. 12-14.)
18. If banks are unable or unwilling to extend loans without government guarantee, is there justification for our banking system in its present form?

REFERENCES

See end of Chapter XXII

Chapter XXII

COMMERCIAL BANK PORTFOLIO PROBLEMS

Meaning of a Bank Portfolio

Definition.—The word "portfolio" usually refers to a portable case for holding papers and documents of all sorts. In governmental circles it refers literally to a case for documents of the state, but more generally to the office and government functions involved in connection with these documents. Thus an appointment to a cabinet position is refered to as receipt of the portfolio of state, navy, or war. Similarly, in banking, the word "portfolio" refers to the case containing the bank's documents, particularly the loans and investments, because they are the most important assets of the bank. A description of the "loan and investment portfolio" of a bank includes a description of the bank's holdings of the various types of credit instruments considered in the last chapter. There are usually many subdivisions, depending upon the departmental organization of the bank, management policies, and the size and nature of the bank. Real estate loans may be handled by a real estate department, personal loans by another, commercial loans by a third department, and investments by still another.

Emphasis on the Ends to Be Accomplished.—A bank's portfolio must be considered with reference to the types of deposits, the amount of cash reserves, and the specific things the management of the bank expects the total loans and investments and each subdivision therein to perform. Just as no good monetary system can be made up of but one type of money, so no good bank portfolio can be composed of but one type of security. The problem is one of determining just how each proposed loan and investment fits into the general loan and investment policies of the individual bank.

Banks are using funds of depositors, and the officers have the primary aim of always being in a position to return them upon request. Therefore, on maturity of some items in the loan and investment portfolio, the bank may decide to keep the funds uninvested in order to meet demands of depositors for cash. Such decisions are made daily by all commercial banks. In addition, bankers want to cover expenses, earn profits for their shareholders, and earn interest for time depositors, by investing as large a portion of the bank's funds as conditions seem to justify. The lending and investing of a bank's funds should not be thought of as a water faucet that is shut off when no new cash is coming into the bank and turned on only when new deposits or cash from repaid loans and investments are available. What actually happens is that the faucets are always open, with the rate of flow regulated so as to keep stable the level of funds in the cash reservoir. However, it must be emphasized that, in building up a portfolio, bankers may use their discretion only within the limits as provided by law and rules of supervisory officials, and then only in so far as local and general economic conditions permit.

Importance of Earnings.—Bank proprietors, like other owners of business firms, are interested in earnings. Although there may be disagreement as to their proper size and source, no one who believes in private ownership of banks would question the desire of bankers to secure earnings large enough to pay all expenses of their institutions and to provide a reasonable return on the capital that has been invested in them.

Banks obtain earnings to meet operating expenses from service charges on deposit accounts and from fees, commissions, and other charges made for special services performed by the banks for their customers. Important as these are, in the aggregate they represent only a small percentage of those earned as "interest and dividends on securities" and "interest and discounts on loans" (about 80 per cent of total earnings). It is readily apparent that the earning assets of banks are the most important source of earnings, without which our banking system, as we know it, could not exist.

Importance of Liquidity.—One of the conflicts in managing the funds of a bank is the question of earnings versus liquidity. One hundred per cent liquidity could be obtained by keeping all funds in the form of cash, a policy which the bankers and stockholders would not relish and which the borrowing public probably would not desire. The actual amount kept as reserves is influenced by law, regulations of government supervisory agencies or officials, business habits of customers of the bank, public psychology, which affects confidence in banks, the business cycle, and the investments of the bank. If banks are holding and buying credit instruments that are liquid or marketable, that is, easily and automatically convertible into cash without loss, the cash reserves may be low.

Liquidity is essential when plans are made for building up a secondary line of defense for meeting depositors' seasonal or extraordinary demands for funds. Distinction should be made among (1) liquidity of a single asset, such as a seasonal loan to a well-known commercial customer that will be repaid as soon as the commercial transaction for which the loan was made has been completed; (2) liquidity of an individual bank, which means its ability to pay depositors without delay; and (3) liquidity of the banking system as a whole, which means its ability to provide any required amount of hand-to-hand money to pay depositors. This means that if the banking system is liquid, even though there may be many types of nonliquid assets in bank portfolios and nonliquid banks, there will be some banking or monetary agency that can be called upon to provide any amount of currency that a panic or any other situation seems to demand. This agency is usually the central bank, which should always be in a position to provide any commercial bank with cash, provided the latter has government securities or other acceptable assets to give in exchange or to pledge as collateral for loans.

The risks assumed by banks are three: (1) a sudden or abnormal demand for cash by their depositors, which will make it necessary for banks to dispose of some of their earning assets in order to get currency; (2) the possibility of nonpayment of funds lent or invested; and (3) loss in market value of assets. If a bank is in a position where it does not have cash and cannot secure it easily and without great loss, it is nonliquid; if a bank is in a position where its assets are not equal in value to its liabilities and its capital is impaired, it is insolvent. Nonliquidity tends to follow when total assets of a bank become congealed or frozen; insolvency tends to follow when general or specific changes in business have a deflationary effect on the total market value of bank assets, but in individual cases it may result from inability of a few large borrowers to repay their bank loans in full.

Present Situation.—The primary reserves of member banks, of which three-fifths are in the form of reserve balances with Federal Reserve banks, are the largest in history. In 1940 "excess reserves" were at a peak, but, because of the growth of deposits since then, the situation has changed radically. Excess reserves have practically disappeared in so far as the central reserve and reserve city banks are concerned. Country banks are still maintaining large balances with correspondent banks, and their holdings of cash in vaults are in excess of those of all the central reserve and reserve city banks combined. Although the cash items of member banks have shown a relative decline compared to deposits, this loss in liquidity has been more than offset by their holdings of secondary reserves. At the present time banks have more to fear from a possible decline in asset values and subsequent insolvency than from nonliquidity.

Secondary Reserves—Key to Liquidity

By "secondary reserves" are meant highly liquid earning assets that may be converted into cash with little or no delay and at practically no loss. This definition, when considered from the viewpoint of the banking system, eliminates all long-term bonds and all short-term paper which may have to be sold at a loss. Factors which influence the amount of secondary reserves include the amount, size, nature, and seasonal and cyclical fluctuations of deposits, the percentage of primary reserves, the capital-deposit ratio, the condition of the loan and investment portfolio, and general economic conditions.[1]

Influence of Deposits.—Fewer secondary reserves will be required when deposits have great stability, and this depends upon their type, size, and location. Time deposits are more stable than demand; small deposits are more stable than large; and country bank deposits are more stable than those of city banks. Although commercial banks are to some extent savings institutions, experience shows that their time deposits are more volatile than those of savings banks. During panics the distinction between time and demand deposits in commercial banks is more artificial than real. Thus commercial bankers cannot regard the $40,000,000,000 of time deposits in the same way as mutual savings bankers regard their savings accounts.

Foreign Experiences.—The tendency abroad is to place less emphasis upon primary reserves and more upon secondary reserves, which is contrary to the general practice in the United States.

[1] American Bankers Association, *Secondary Reserves and Security Buying*, Booklet No. 3, pp. 3-4. (Issued by the Clearinghouse Section.)

European banks with an adequate supply of secondary reserves can build up primary reserves whenever conditions justify and, at the same time, have the advantage of having larger percentages of their assets employed in earning an income. The European policy resulted from their longer experience with bills and other forms of commercial paper, the dominant position of the central banks in the money markets, the absence throughout most of their history of minimum legal reserve requirements (except for central banks), the development of branch banking, and the smaller national area in which each operates.

Primary reserves have been important in America because of legal reserve regulations, the large number of small unit banks, and the recent development of the bill market. Under normal conditions, a wise long-run reserve program for American banks would be to place greater stress on secondary reserves and to diminish the present emphasis on primary reserves. In England the average reserve balance kept by the banks is about 11 per cent, of which about 3.5 per cent or less is kept with the Bank of England. English bankers rely to a great extent on their holdings of acceptance and exchequer or Treasury bills to give their banks liquidity.

Capital-Deposit Ratios.—The capital-deposit ratio is important in planning a secondary reserve program, because a bank that has a 1 to 16 ratio should have more secondary reserves than a bank with a capital-deposit ratio of 1 to 8. The same investment losses would be twice as serious to the first bank as to the second, and therefore this factor must be considered in the secondary reserve of an individual bank. A low percentage of capital to deposits must be accompanied by a high secondary reserve position. This is typical of the portfolio of English banks. The normal distribution of assets of an English commercial bank would be as follows: cash, 11 per cent; call money, 9 per cent; bills and investments, 30 per cent; and advances (loans), 50 per cent. At the present time, English banks, like American banks, find their portfolios dominated by government obligations.

Nature of Loans and Investments.—The nature of bank loans and investments is also important in determining the secondary reserve position; the less marketable the securities held, the higher must be the secondary reserves. A loan and investment account dominated by real estate holdings, real estate loans, capital loans, and long-term bonds demands that the bank keep a higher secondary reserve position than is necessary for a second bank whose loan and investment portfolio is dominated by short-term commercial loans and highly marketable investments.[2]

Business Cycle.—During boom periods, when business is approaching the cyclical peak, secondary reserves should be at their peak.[3] In so far as conditions permit, the bank investment accounts should have been gradually shifted in the direction of shorter maturities and higher qualities. Bankers must anticipate increases in demands for cash during periods of declining business; and they must foresee a tendency for "gilt-edged" bonds to shift from the classification where "money risk" will be replaced by "credit risk."

Security market conditions during boom periods permit improvement in banks' investment portfolio by increasing government bond holdings, the prices of which are the lowest near the peak of the business cycle. However, as tempting as the possibility of trading profits may be, the banker should not build up his bank's government bond portfolio at the expense of liquidity. While gradual shifts toward and away from gilt-edged bonds may be the leading investment policy during the business cycle, it should never be carried to excess. Most of the seasonal shifts in needs for cash are best cared for by purchases of short-term paper whose maturities are timed to care for these peak seasonal needs.

Sources of Secondary Reserves.—These income-producing assets are held to provide the banks with primary reserves whenever such reserves become depleted. Two situations are involved—seasonal and others. Banks are subject to seasonal losses of primary reserves because of seasonal lending and withdrawal of deposits. Since both of these movements tend to come during the last quarter of the year, secondary reserves must be arranged to meet these needs. In addition, banks must be in a position to meet cyclical and other withdrawals of deposits, some of which may not be predictable.

Secondary reserves of the seasonal type are usually selected from (1) the trade and bankers' acceptance or bill market, (2) the open market for commercial paper, (3) the call loan market, and (4) the short-term government security market. Interior banks are practically excluded from some of these divisions of the money mar-

---

[2] *Ibid.*, p. 8.

[3] Wilkinson, J. H., Jr., *Investment Policies for Commercial Banks*, p. 21, *passim*.

ket because of the prevailing low discount rates, the fees charged by correspondent banks for placing funds in the markets, and the ability of metropolitan banks to supply all the funds required by borrowers in the market. But the abundance of short-term government obligations makes it possible for the banks to hold all the secondary reserves desired in any scientifically planned portfolio.

Secondary reserves of the nonseasonal type may be selected from promises to pay of the federal, state, and local governments and the promises to pay of corporations. All items must have two requisites: prime quality and a maturity of less than four or five years. By careful spacing of these maturities, a bank may have a continuous return of funds to meet unexpected demands for primary reserves. If the secondary reserve account is regarded as a revolving fund to be invested in similar securities, banks are able to maintain the liquidity of their portfolios and still earn 1 per cent on their accounts.

Weakness of Bonds.—Because of money risks involved, long-term government securities should not be considered as secondary reserves. Obviously, all banks cannot sell their government bonds or even a small percentage of the total without destroying or seriously disturbing the market for them. True, a small bank may dispose of its bonds without much effect on the market, but if the large banks try to do so the result may be a sharp fall in bond prices. In September, 1939, with the outbreak of war in Europe, there developed a near panic in the bond market. Treasury bonds with maturities of twelve years or more declined more than 10 points in market value; without Federal Reserve banks' purchases of over $400,000,000 of securities, the liquidation might have assumed panic proportions.

Normally, bankers adjust the reserve positions of their banks by selling acceptances, discounting commercial paper, calling brokers' loans, or selling Treasury bills; but before the war they were showing a tendency to adjust their reserve positions by selling government bonds.[4] This policy if maintained would add to the instability of the price of bonds and further weaken their position as secondary reserves. There is a tendency now for banks to make reserve adjustments by selling their short-term obligations and holding their long-term investments. This trend has been strengthened by the government's policy of maintaining an orderly market for govern-

[4] Langum, J. K., "Federal Reserve Open-Market Policy, 1934-1939," *Financial and Investment Review,* Vol. VIII, No. 4 (December, 1939), p. 8.

ment securities. To what extent the Federal Reserve policy of buying and selling securities "with the view of preserving an orderly market" will be successful is impossible to forecast, but, because of the present size of the government debt, an orderly market will be difficult to maintain.

An estimate of ownership of United States government debt is shown in Table 29. Prospective shifts include any number of possibilities. Liquidation of holdings of nonmarketable savings bonds

TABLE 29

OWNERSHIP OF UNITED STATES GOVERNMENT DEBT
(Estimates, in Billions of Dollars)

	Outstanding		Increase
	Sept. 30, 1945	Dec. 31, 1941	
Federal Reserve banks	23.3	2.3	21.0
Commercial banks	83.5	21.8	61.7
Mutual savings banks	10.0	3.7	6.3
	2.8	1.3	1.5
Total banking system	119.6	29.0	90.6
Individuals*	58.5	13.5	45.0
Corporations and associations, excluding banks and insurance companies†	30.0	4.3	25.7
Insurance companies	23.2	8.2	15.0
State and local governments	5.0	0.5	4.5
U.S. government agencies and trust funds	23.8	8.2	15.6
Total nonbank investors	140.5	34.7	105.8
Total interest-bearing direct and guaranteed debt	260.2	63.8	196.4

* Includes unincorporated business.
† Includes brokers, dealers, and foreigners.
Source: Federal Reserve Bulletin, November, 1945, p. 1096.

by individuals may require the Treasury to borrow from commercial banks in order to obtain funds with which to redeem them. The inflationary effects of such a movement have been anticipated; and between Armistice and Pearl Harbor days, 1946, the Treasury revitalized the savings bond sales campaign. Funds obtained from these sales are being used to retire short-term debts held by banks. Business corporations other than banks and insurance companies may liquidate their government bonds to meet accrued tax liabilities or cash needs for reconversion and other purposes. Markets for these securities are insurance companies, private trusts administered largely by banking institutions, trust accounts administered by the federal government, savings banks, and commercial banks.

The banking system as a whole purchased more than two-thirds of the United States government securities offered during the war and continues to hold about the same proportion. With no increase in the total debt expected, normal shifts in holdings of government obligations from businesses to financial institutions should be absorbed by savings institutions without expansion of commercial bank credit.

The Capital Market and Credit Risks

When commercial banks buy long-term bonds, they are assuming two different types of risks: the first pertains to the quality of the bond and the second to the capital market. The price of any bond is determined by the credit of the obliger and the level of money rates in the market. Where there is practically no question of the credit standing of the debtor, the fluctuation in the price of the bonds is dominated by the money rates—the higher the money rates of interest the lower will be the price of bonds, and the lower the interest rates the higher will be the price of bonds. Where the credit risk is large, the value of the bond will be influenced more by changes in the economic condition of the debtor, the industry, and the country than by changes in the interest rate.

Money Risks.—Contrary to popular opinion, banks are assuming risks when they buy government securities, and these risks become greater as the volume of all investments increase relative to the size of a bank's capital account. This situation is apparent when one considers the hypothetical effect of but a 6 per cent decrease in the value of all assets upon the capital account of all member banks. Such a decrease in the value of assets would eliminate all capital items except "capital," and this would be seriously impaired for the average bank. The decrease in the value of assets by the above percentage is magnified in its effects upon the capital account because of the progressive decline in the ratio of capital account items to deposits. The present record-low interest rates have created a dilemma for bankers; their continuance means loss of earnings, while an increase would tend to mean capital losses. Banks' large investments make these institutions sensitive to changes in interest rates if the latter are permitted to affect adversely the prices of government bonds and if bank examiners follow the policy of forcing banks to take paper losses in making reports. Over a period of time, banks would profit from an increase in money rates by obtaining greater returns from earning assets.

Credit Risks.—Every business transaction, every credit transaction, in fact every application of wealth and labor, necessarily involves risk. Bankers desire to find outlets for banks' funds in which the element of risk is small, but they cannot find one in which it is not present. Every theory of lending and investing must recognize this ubiquitous risk element. The degree of risk assumed varies, and it is the function of bank management to appraise them accurately; but losses will continue as long as human judgment is fallible.

Arranging Maturities of Investments

Banks desiring to invest in securities need not depend upon control agencies to maintain stability in the money rates. In buying securities they may arrange maturities so as to remain in a safe and liquid position and still suffer no destructive capital losses. When interest rates are increasing, long-term bonds naturally decline more in value than short-term promises to pay. As short-term securities mature, they provide banks with funds which may be lent at higher interest rates. If a bank portfolio contains sufficient short-term promises to pay, a government bond that does not mature for ten years would not need to be sold to obtain funds for current demands. But, if the contrary is true, and if other banks are also trying to find purchasers for such bonds, bond prices will decline unless the Federal Reserve banks, the Treasury, and other buyers appear in the market in sufficient number. In order to be able to provide depositors or new borrowers with funds without disturbing their bond investments, banks are arranging the maturities of their loans and investments so that a percentage of their assets are maturing each year.

In accepting the policy of arranging maturities to provide funds automatically, it is assumed that banks have perpetual lives. If bonds decline in value, they will be at par at maturity and may be retained in the bank portfolio without loss. (Allowances must be made for effects on bank statements of writing down the value of assets as market prices decline.) If bonds are purchased in the market above par, a reserve fund must be set up to eliminate the premium out of earnings and in this way prevent capital losses.

Since 1938 member banks have been reporting their holdings of bonds as those maturing within 5 years and those maturing after 5 years. In case of government bonds, a more detailed maturity distribution is being reported, namely, within 5 years, 5 to 10 years, 10 to 20 years, and after 20 years. This more detailed information permits analysis of the liquidity and marketability of banks' assets as well as providing the Treasury with information as to potential markets for different types of securities it may desire to offer. In general, the government has used short-term obligations in securing funds from commercial banks; and, in specific cases, it has prevented banks from buying longer-term and higher-yielding obligations by providing that some of the latter could not be purchased by commercial banks and that others could be purchased by them only after the lapse of a given number of years.

The state and local government securities held by member banks are influenced by the more conservative borrowing policies of state and local governments, their use of serial bonds in financing, and their practice of borrowing from banks in anticipation of tax receipts and other income. The maturities of other securities held, which include chiefly corporate bonds, notes, and debentures, are longer than those of government securities. Part of this situation is traced to the fact that most corporations whose credit standings warrant bank purchases of their securities raise their long-term capital needs by selling bonds with callable features. This privilege permits refinancing during periods of low interest rates, and this type of private security selling has dominated the capital market during the last decade. Since the credit risks are greatest in this group of securities, they present a greater management problem to banks than do other types of investments.

Are Banks Poor Bond Buyers?

The problem of investment management is a major one for commercial bankers because of the shift in the nature of banking from commercial to investment. If holdings of securities continue to be a major part of the loan and investment portfolios of banks, better investment policies are in order for many banks.

Poor Timing of Bond Purchases and Sales.—One criticism of the banks' investment purchase program has been their poor timing of purchases and sales. When bond prices are high, bankers tend to purchase; and, when bond prices are low, bankers tend to sell. Banks are heavy buyers when money rates are low, business is dull, borrowing is small, and the banks have surplus funds to invest. When business improves, demands for loans increase, and high-grade bond prices decrease. In order to accommodate their customers, banks sell all or part of their bond holdings. This reasoning is based on the assumption that banks normally attempt to accommodate their loan customers first, which is logical, because of the closer personal relationship and the more profitable nature of a loan transaction. Instead of causing net loss to the bank, the shift in the portfolio from bonds to loans may be profitable. Thus actual losses to banks from the selling of bonds in order to accommodate customers' loan demands are small.

Since 1920 pressure on banks to sell bonds in an unfavorable market has come not from customers' demands for loans but from depositors' demands for money. Between April, 1929, and April, 1933, the average price of forty high-grade bonds declined by one-third. Under these circumstances, bankers found bonds to be unsatisfactory as secondary reserves. Whether because of depositors' demands for money, customers' demands for loans, the accounting risk due to bank examiners' "cost or market whichever is the lower" rule, or to a combination of these, an investment portfolio including only gilt-edged long-term bonds is inadequate.

Federal Reserve banks are permitted to lend up to 100 per cent of the par value of government bonds pledged as collateral by bank borrowers, but this does not relieve the debtor banks from loss if the value of the collateral declines. Selling bonds to secure funds, even though it may involve a small immediate loss, may be preferable to using them as collateral for loans at the Federal Reserve bank. The banking system should not be in a position of being forced to liquidate investments in large amounts at one time. Better planning by individual banks of maturities of loans and investments, greater emphasis upon income from investments, and less emphasis on trading profits would reduce the peak purchasing and peak selling periods for securities and would bring greater stability in their market values.

Poor Diversification Policy.—Bankers are limited in their investment transactions by law and by regulations of supervisory officials; but, within the limits permitted, they have considerable discretion as to the types of securities they may buy. The problem involved is not only diversification as to borrowers but also the arrangement of maturities so as to meet the ends sought. Provisions in the Banking Acts of 1933 and 1935 force banks to diversify their investments in private securities to a degree not legally necessary before these dates. The maturity problem is being met by better spacing of maturities, better arrangement of maturities, and a general recognition of the limitations of the use of long-term bonds as secondary reserves.

Poor Quality of Securities.—During 1931-33 one of the most common causes given for bank failures was the decline in the value of the bond investment accounts of banks. Without question, the decline in market value of bonds during this period was one of the most troublesome features in the loan and investment portfolios of banks, and, to a considerable extent, it was beyond the control of banks. Since bond prices were readily obtainable, these quotations were reflected immediately in the book value of assets of banks. Later, other features of banks' loan and investment accounts were recognized as being equally, if not more, troublesome. Foremost among these were real estate loans. Actually, losses taken on bonds have been less than the percentage of losses taken on loans.

One of the specific charges against certain banks' management of bond accounts has been the unwise selection of individual issues. These include real estate bonds, "industrials," railroad bonds, and others. Bankers may refuse to purchase credit bonds and avoid the risks attached to them, and this is probably the best policy for most country bankers. This statement is no reflection on the ability of country bankers but merely a recognition of the fact that errors made are seriously reflected in their capital accounts. Only a few minor mistakes are sufficient to place them in insolvent positions because of their normally small reserves for contingencies and other funds available to cushion their losses. But second-rate bonds were considered to be necessary evils, and numerous conferences were held throughout the nation to educate the bankers and make them better bond buyers. The principles covering individual selections involve the study of investment principles as treated in advanced courses in finance. Now, fortunately for banks, the prospects for earnings from government obligations and loans are such as to make it unnecessary for banks to purchase second-grade bonds.

Loan Portfolio Problems

The same problems of liquidity, marketability, safety, and earnings are present in the management of the loan portfolio as in the investment portfolio, but in different degrees. Throughout the history of commercial banking a great deal of emphasis has been placed on the importance of self-liquidating commercial paper. These loans were made to finance the needs of commerce, industry, and agriculture for short-term current working capital needs. As noted in the preceding chapter, owing to fundamental changes in inventory control, sales policies, growth in size of commercial and other units, improvements in transportation, and growth of financial specialists, the volume of self-liquidating loans in commercial banks is now small.

Since most of the loans in the banks' portfolios are no longer self-liquidating in the traditional sense, new principles have been applied to the management of loans. If funds are to be borrowed for fixed capital expenditures which may be liquidated over a period of 10 years, a logical procedure would be to require the amount to be repaid in instalments over the ten-year period. This practice is now being followed. Similarly, real estate loans are now being made that require periodic repayments of principal and interest. Personal or consumer loans have always been chiefly of the type that require liquidation in instalment payments. Because of their size, legal nature, and for other reasons, long-term loans possess less marketability than investments. The use of the instalment principle of repayment greatly reduces the risk factor.

Call and time loans made for the purchase and carrying of securities are traditionally of the type that depends on shiftability in case of need for cash, but even some of these loans, when made by bank customers to purchase securities in anticipation of income, are repaid on the instalment basis. However, most of the loans made to brokers and investment bankers are of the traditional type, depending on the ability of the borrower to secure funds elsewhere if the bank calls those made on demand or does not renew those made on time. If the borrower cannot secure a new loan elsewhere, he is forced to sell the collateral pledged as security. The bank's primary problem is to see that an adequate margin is maintained at all times so as to prevent bank losses. For all practical purposes such a loan is just as liquid as any investment that possesses marketability.

Loans made under lines of credit are usually subject to "annual liquidation," but often they are renewed, and in other cases they are liquidated with funds borrowed from other institutions. If this situation is normal, then the borrower is financing a permanent need for capital with bank loans. Such funds should be obtained by financing in the investment market or with a capital loan repayable in instalments over a period of years. Although the marketability of such loans is less than in the case of investments, the yield is much greater. When the remainder of a bank's portfolio permits, these loans may be made at a profit to the bank.

QUESTIONS AND PROBLEMS

1. Bank assets may be grouped into cash, secondary reserves, loans and investments, and others. What is the meaning of each? How would the distribution among commercial bank assets compare to those of a savings bank or insurance company?
2. Explain the meaning of (*a*) "bond portfolio" and (*b*) "loan and discount portfolio."
3. What is meant by secondary reserves? Distinguish them from primary reserves. Describe the factors that influence the size of the secondary reserves of commercial banks.
4. What types of investment risks are assumed by banks when they purchase long-term bonds? Explain.
5. Why is a large investment account more dangerous to a bank with a capital-deposit ratio of 1 to 20 than to a bank with a capital-deposit ratio of 1 to 5? Explain.
6. Give the arguments opposed to the adoption of a "trading policy" by a bank. In what way may such a policy lead to a markup in the inventory of a bank?
7. What is the price paid by banks for liquidity? For nonliquidity? Explain.
8. What justification is there, if any, for the assumption that banks have been poor bond buyers?
9. Are the Federal Reserve authorities, the Treasury, and the Federal Deposit Insurance Corporation interested in the investment holdings of member banks? Explain.

10. What are the principles that guide banks in the management of their loan portfolios? Are they similar to those used in managing bond portfolios? Explain.
11. In Germany commercial banks were required to keep secondary reserves equal to 30 per cent of their deposits. Should such a requirement be made of American banks? Is it a wise policy to follow? Why?
12. What is the purpose of the 10 per cent loan limitation rule? Why are restrictions placed by law upon the investments in one issue by national banks?
13. "Cheap money in the United Kingdom was the result of banking policy, while in the United States it was achieved at the cost of a heavy addition to the national debt" (League of Nations, *Money and Banking, 1935/36*, Vol. I, p. 38). Discuss.
14. "The primary objective of the Securities Act of 1933 is to protect investors by requiring full and fair disclosures of material facts concerning securities publicly offered for sale in interstate commerce or by use of the mails and by preventing misrepresentation and fraud in the sale of securities" (*Tenth Annual Report of the Securities and Exchange Commission Fiscal Year Ended June 30, 1944*, p. 2). Explain how banks have been beneficiaries of this policy.
15. "A decrease in the volume of Treasury obligations held by banks could chiefly come about through a net repayment of debt by the government or a transfer of federal obligations from the banks to investors. The probability of either of these possibilities taking place in the near future does not appear great" (Whittlesey, C. R., "Problems of Our Domestic Money and Banking System," *American Economic Review*, Supplement, Vol. XXXIV [March, 1944], p. 248). What is the significance of such a situation during a period of declining business?
16. "Due to the abolition of interest on demand deposits and reduction of interest on time deposits, the spread between the cost of money and the yield on prime investments is still as great for some banks as in predepression days, or perhaps greater" (Riddle, J. H., "Have a Long-Term Investment Policy," *Banking*, May, 1939, p. 91). Discuss.
17. "I wonder what poor banker convinced [him] that 'banking losses have not been so much the fault of management as of economic instability.' . . . . Those are the perennial excuses of the banker who has been a failure at bank management. Good bankers know that there is such a thing as economic instability and prepare for it" (Upham, C. B., "Discussion" at "Round Table on Banking Reform through Supervisory Standards," *American Economic Review*, Supplement, Vol. XXX, No. 1, Part 2 [March, 1940], p. 235).
18. To what extent do the rating agencies (Moody, Poor, Standard Statistics, etc.) influence the flow of bank investment funds? Are investments in railroads and public utility industries being affected? Explain.

REFERENCES

American Bankers Association. *Secondary Reserves and Security Buying.* New York: Issued by the Clearinghouse Section of the American Bankers Association.

American Bankers Association, Bank Management Commission. *War Loans.* New York: Bank Management Publication No. 101, American Bankers Association, 1943.

American Bankers Association, National Bank Division. *Comparative Ratio Figures on Earnings and Expenses of All National Banks, 1937, 1938.*

Beckhart, B. H. "Monetary Policy and Commercial Bank Portfolios," *American Economic Review*, Supplement, Vol. XXX, No. 1, Part 2 (March, 1940), pp. 17-26. Also "Discussion," *ibid.*, pp. 39-43.

Bond Investment Policies for Banks. Proceedings of the First Annual Michigan Bankers Association Study Conference. Ann Arbor: University of Michigan, 1938.

Dunbar, C. F. *Theory and History of Banking*, chaps. i and iii. 4th ed. New York: G. P. Putnam's Sons, 1922.

Goodbar, J. E. *Managing the People's Money*, chaps. iii and vi. New Haven: Yale University Press, 1935.

Greef, A. C. *The Commercial Paper House in the United States.* Cambridge: Harvard University Press, 1938.

Harr, Luther, and Harris, H. C. *Banking Theory and Practice*, chaps. xxi and xxii. 2d ed. New York: McGraw-Hill Book Co., Inc., 1936.

Kniffin, W. H. *Better Banking*, chaps. viii and ix. New York: McGraw-Hill Book Co., Inc., 1934.

Langum, J. K. "Earnings Assets, Deposits, and Reserves of Member Banks, 1929-1938," *Financial and Investment Review*, Vol. VII, No. 7, March, 1939. School of Business, University of Minnesota.

Langum, J. K. "Federal Reserve Open-Market Policy, 1934-1939," *Financial and Investment Review*, Vol. VIII, No. 4, December, 1939. School of Business, University of Minnesota.

Lockhart, O. C. "The Development of Interbank Borrowing in the National System, 1869-1914," *Journal of Political Economy*, Vol. XXIX, pp. 138-66; 222-40.

Miller, M. D. *Bank Loans on Statement and Character.* New York: Ronald Press Co., 1927.

Munn, G. G. *Bank Credit.* New York: McGraw-Hill Book Co., Inc., 1925.

Osterlenk, B., and Massie, A. M. *How Banks Buy Bonds.* New York: Harper & Bros., 1932.

Palyi, M. "Bank Portfolios and the Control of the Capital Market," *Journal of Business of the University of Chicago*, Vol. XI, No. 1 (1938), pp. 70-111.

Prochnow, H. V., and Foulke, R. A. *Practical Bank Credit*, Parts III and IV. New York: Prentice-Hall, Inc., 1940.

Rodkey, R. G. *The Banking Process*, chap. xviii. New York: Macmillan Co., 1928.

Stronck, H. N. *Bank Administration*, chaps. xi-xiv, and xix. Chicago: Rand McNally & Co., 1929.

Wilkinson, J. H., Jr. *Investment Policies for Commercial Banks.* New York: Harper & Bros., 1938.

Willis, H. P., and Chapman, J. M. *The Banking Situation*, chap. xxv. New York: Columbia University Press, 1934.

Wooster, J. W. *Bankers Handbook of Bond Investment.* New York: Harper & Bros. 1938.

See also references at the end of Chapter XX.

CHAPTER XXIII

FOREIGN EXCHANGE MARKETS

Sources of Demand for and Supply of Exchange

Nature of Foreign Exchange Business.—The International Monetary Fund would operate so as to maintain stability in the exchange rates and thereby permit banks and other exchange dealers to carry on their normal exchange functions. Since the Fund operates through central banks, treasuries, or some other government agencies such as the stabilization funds, it would not be in touch with individuals, firms, and banks that were in the market as buyers or sellers of foreign exchange.

When Americans sell goods abroad they may be paid in credit instruments denominated in foreign currencies, and when they buy things abroad they may be requested to pay in foreign currencies. As a result, there will be individuals in the United States who will be demanding bank drafts or other claims to foreign currencies, while there are other individuals who have foreign bank drafts they want to convert into dollars. It is the function of the exchange market to bring together the buyers and sellers of the rights to foreign currencies.

In most markets those who produce the things that are sold rarely come in contact with consumers, because it is more economical for them to deal through merchants and other middlemen. Similarly, commercial banks and other exchange dealers are the "merchants" of the rights or claims to foreign currencies.[1]

In domestic exchange, banks usually act as agents for their customers in collecting checks and other credit instruments payable in other cities; but, in foreign exchange transactions, the customary role of a bank is to buy the claims to foreign currencies, thus acting as principal rather than as agent. The reason banks buy these foreign exchange credit instruments is to increase their deposits in foreign banks. American banks are interested in increasing the amount of

[1] One English banker defines the foreign exchange business as follows: "It is simply purchase and sales of other countries' currency and our own" (Kindersley, Sir Robert M., before Committee on Finance and Industry, *Minutes of Evidence*, p. 98).

deposit currency abroad for the same reason that shoe merchants increase their stocks of goods, that is, in order to have merchandise to sell (foreign exchange in the case of banks). Thus, at the same time that banks are buying claims to foreign currencies they are selling their own foreign drafts to their customers. By keeping their "inventories" at a minimum, bankers, like all good merchants, are able to make a profit without speculating in foreign exchange.

As a foundation for foreign exchange business, American banks establish relationships with foreign banks, making arrangements for keeping deposits with them, for fees, commissions, and other charges for banking services, for borrowing, and for other privileges. Thus the same type of correspondent banking relationships are built up between banks in New York and London as between banks in New York and Chicago.

The extent to which certain banks are engaging in the foreign exchange business is suggested by certain items in their detailed bank statements. The item "balance with banks in foreign countries," which appears as an asset, gives the dollar value of deposits kept in foreign banks. These deposits are usually in terms of the monetary unit of the country in which they are kept, but for convenience their value is computed at the cable rate of exchange and reported as "dollars" in American bank statements. The item "deposits of banks in foreign countries" under liabilities shows the deposits kept by foreign banks in the United States.

Some American banks have found it more profitable to open their own branches abroad. On the balance sheet of the parent bank there will appear as an asset "due from own foreign branches" and as a liability the item "due to own foreign branches." Although these two items cover interoffice transactions, they are reported separately in order to portray the fundamental differences in transactions between offices located in different countries as compared to transactions between offices located in the United States. The parent bank, in dealing with the foreign branch, will still be buying and selling claims to the currency of the country in which the foreign branch is located.

Economic Roots of Foreign Exchange.—The reasons why Americans have claims to foreign currencies that they want to convert into dollars and the reasons why they want means of payment denominated in foreign currencies are almost as varied as their reasons for wanting domestic hand-to-hand money and deposit currency.[2] The largest of the general sources of demand for and supply of foreign exchange are traced to the import and export of merchandise. Because of their size, the movements of goods have been more widely emphasized than other transactions, being commonly referred to as the "visible" items of foreign trade. In the past, a nation was considered to be in a particularly favorable position when its exports exceeded its imports, because specie would have to be paid in settlement for the excess of exports over imports. This thought is related to the misconception that the well-being of a nation or individual depends on how much money is owned and not on the volume of goods and services produced. To those who think that if a nation has gold it can secure goods and services, the answer is that this is impossible if they have not been produced. That the strength of a country is dependent on its productive capacity and not on gold holdings was demonstrated by the position of the United States in 1944, as compared to 1940, when the production was twice as great, even though the gold stock had declined.

In addition to merchandise transactions, there are two other general classes that explain the demand for and supply of foreign exchange—those dealing with capital and those dealing with services. Since World War I, because of the shift in the international credit position of the United States from a debtor to a creditor nation, there has been an increase in the interest of Americans in this class of invisible items of foreign trade.

With the current postwar emphasis on reconstruction and development abroad, American foreign investments will increase. Many of these investments may be made without involving the foreign exchange market. Thus, if the Export-Import Bank lends $200,000,000 to the French government, the latter may spend it in the United States and none of the funds would leave here. In the balance of payments statement, the French government's promises to pay would appear as imports to offset the export of merchandise from the United States. Under normal circumstances, the imports of securities or short-term credit instruments increase the demand for bank drafts or bills of

[2] See U.S. Department of Commerce, Bureau of Foreign and Domestic Commerce, *The Balance of International Payment of the United States* (annual statements); Heilperin, M. A., *International Monetary Economics*, chap. v; and Edwards, G. W., *International Trade Finance*, chap. i.

exchange in the same way as imports of merchandise. Similarly, the purchases of securities in the New York capital market by foreign investors increase the supply of foreign bank drafts in the exchange market in the same way as exports of merchandise increase the supply of foreign exchange.

The third class of international transactions is service items, which include receipts and payments for foreign services, tourist expenditures, interest and dividend payments, government transactions, immigrant remittances, charitable contributions, motion-picture royalties, and other miscellaneous service and trade items. Between the world wars these service items increased greatly in importance, owing to many factors, including improvements in means of transportation and communication and growth in international investments.

Payment for shipping services provided by foreign ships increases the demand for foreign exchange. Americans traveling abroad purchase travelers' checks, travelers' letters of credit, and foreign money orders to finance expenditures abroad. Payments of interest and dividends by the governments and corporations to foreign owners of American securities constitute a demand for foreign exchange. The United States government must purchase foreign exchange in order to pay for goods bought abroad (as corned beef from Argentina for the United States Navy) and to settle its normal unfavorable balance due to the sale of foreign money orders. Likewise, immigrant remittances and charitable contributions to American-financed foreign missions, schools, hospitals, and other eleemosynary institutions are sources of demand for foreign exchange. Foreigners make similar service payments to the United States, and these constitute sources of supply of foreign exchange. The sources of demand for and supply of foreign exchange are summarized below.

Sources of Demand for Foreign Exchange

1. Merchandise or goods purchased from foreigners (imports)
2. Capital items
   a) Long-term investments in foreign securities and repurchase of foreign-owned American securities
   b) Short-term loans by Americans to foreign borrowers and repayments of American short-term borrowing from abroad
   c) Speculative purchases of foreign currencies (long transactions)

   d) Panic shifts of funds from the dollar to "safer" currencies abroad
3. Service items
   a) Services rendered Americans by foreigners (banking, communications, insurance, shipping, etc.)
   b) Expenditures of American tourists traveling abroad
   c) Interest and dividends on foreign-owned American securities
   d) All other items, including immigants' remittances, expenditures of Americans for charities abroad, etc.

SOURCES OF SUPPLY OF FOREIGN EXCHANGE

1. Merchandise or goods sold to foreigners (exports)
2. Capital items
   a) Long-term investments in American securities by foreigners and repurchase of American-owned foreign securities by foreigners
   b) Short-term loans by foreigners to American borrowers and repayments of American short-term loans to foreigners
   c) Speculative sales of foreign currencies (short transactions)
   d) Panic shifts of funds to the dollar from foreign centers
3. Service items
   a) Services rendered foreigners by Americans (banking, communication, insurance, shipping, etc.)
   b) Expenditures of foreign tourists traveling in the United States
   c) Interest and dividends on American-owned foreign securities
   d) All other items involving payments by foreigners to Americans

There Are Wholesale and Retail Exchange Markets

In order that a bank may perform properly its foreign exchange functions, it must have a personnel that is familiar with foreign banking methods, foreign commercial law, foreign languages, and foreign business conditions. Businessmen expect their banks to provide them with foreign credit information, translations of letters and documents, foreign funds, and foreign collection services. Only the large metropolitan banks are in a position to offer such services. They have established foreign credit departments, translation divisions, correspondent relationships with foreign banks, and foreign branches or foreign subsidiary corporations.

Small banks in the interior have arrangements with their correspondent banks that make it possible for them to take care of their customers' foreign exchange needs. They also act as agents for the

American Express Company and telegraph and cable companies. Most of the banks in the United States should be considered as retailers of foreign exchange, because most of the foreign exchange operations are performed by or through a few large banks in New York and other large cities. These banks are wholesalers as well as retailers of foreign exchange.

New York Exchange Market.—Normally the exchange market is open to all buyers and sellers. This statement must be qualified at the present time because of the many war and pre-war restrictions that are still being retained; but when the purposes for which the International Monetary Fund was created are achieved, this qualification will no longer be necessary. In every exchange market there are people who have drafts on foreign banks and people who want drafts on foreign banks. But it is only through intermediaries that the claims on foreign countries are made available to the buyers of such claims. Since World War I, the large incorporated banks have replaced the large private investment banks and brokerage houses in their former dominant role in the exchange market. These banks seldom deal directly with one another, preferring to buy and sell through brokers, who receive a small fixed commission for their services.

The distinction made between a broker and a dealer tends to break down when the activities of those operating in the market are considered. (This is also true of those operating in the stock market.) Instead of acting as agents for banks, brokers may purchase bills of exchange for their own accounts, thus taking title until they are sold to other exchange dealers. In such transactions they are acting as principals, being compensated for the risks assumed by the spread between the buying and selling prices. Some brokers may prefer to limit their activities to the handling of the business of clients, leaving the business of dealing in exchange to banks and such specialists as so-called "commercial bill brokers" and acceptance dealers.

The so-called "commercial bill broker" buys and sells bills of exchange that originate in exports of merchandise. He usually represents business firms that prefer to send their bills of exchange directly to New York instead of selling them to local banks. The commercial bill brokers buy and sell foreign exchange, arrange for future foreign exchange contracts, and sometimes maintain foreign accounts. Most of their business is done with New York and foreign banks.

Acceptance dealers, as the name suggests, buy and sell time bills which have been accepted by banks. The right to accept time bills was first granted to national banks by the Federal Reserve Act. Therefore, acceptance credit and acceptance dealers are fairly new developments in the United States. In 1917 the Discount Corporation of New York was organized by a group of accepting banks in order to deal in their own and other banks' accepted bills, and now there are eight well-recognized acceptance dealers. Many foreign banks have agencies, correspondents, or subsidiary corporations in New York.

Today the Treasury Department is taking a leading role in the exchange market. In 1934 the Stabilization Fund was created to be operated in secrecy by the Secretary of the Treasury. Its function is to stabilize the foreign value of the dollar.[3] In performing this function, the managers of the fund buy and sell foreign exchange whenever conditions seem to justify such purchases or sales. For example, in the fall of 1936 they purchased large quantities of sterling bills which were thrown upon the market by the central bank of Russia. In the spring of 1935, at the time the gold clause cases were before the Supreme Court, they purchased large quantities of French exchange. The latter money was being sold at low prices, because many speculators expected an unfavorable decision on the gold cases. Usually the managers of the fund are called upon to do the opposite of what private sellers are doing in the market. The risks involved are great because of the great instability in exchange rates. If and when the International Monetary Fund succeeds in stabilizing foreign exchange rates, the foreign exchange activities now being performed by this Stabilization Fund can be abolished or transferred to the Federal Reserve Bank of New York. Of the $2,000,000,000 allotted to the fund, $1,800,000,000 has been earmarked as part of the United States contribution to the International Monetary Fund.

Under the powers granted in the Federal Reserve Act, the twelve Federal Reserve banks may carry on most types of foreign exchange transactions. They may purchase and sell gold, gold coins, cable

[3] *Statement of Secretary Morgenthau before the Sub-Committee on Monetary Policy, Banking and Deposit Insurance of the Senate Committee on Banking and Currency, March 2, 1939.*

transfers, bankers' acceptances, and other bills of exchange. They may open and maintain accounts in foreign countries, appoint correspondents, and offer member banks ordinary foreign exchange facilities. The Reserve banks have made extensive use of their privilege of rediscounting accepted drafts. Most of their operations are carried on by the Open Market Committee, which buys most of the bills for the Federal Reserve banks in the New York market. These operations have strengthened the already dominant foreign exchange position of New York.

The specialists and other exchange traders are not organized into a central trading body, and they have no set rules or regulations under which they operate. There are many transactions between these middlemen. Their purchases and sales are made in the over-the-counter market, which could more accurately be called an over-the-telephone market. These bankers rarely carry on their business face to face, for most of their trading is done by mail, telephone, wire, or cable. Competition is keen, and, because of rapid means of communication, there is a surprising uniformity of prices at any moment in the market. The exchange manager must keep in touch with foreign markets as well as other exchange managers in New York; and all exchange managers in Chicago and other cities in the United States must keep in touch with those in New York.

Retail Markets.—The sources of supply of and demand for rights to foreign currencies originate in every city and town in the United States. When large and moderate sums are involved, interior banks, through their New York correspondents, care for most foreign exchange transactions, but other agencies are important when small sums are needed to care for such items as immigrant remittances, services, and traveling expenses. Among these agencies are the United States Post Office, the American Express Company, Western Union Telegraph Company, and other wire and cable companies.

The United States Post Office offers both a domestic and a foreign exchange instrument in the form of a post office money order. By agreements among members of the international postal union, the practice of one post office of selling drafts collectible at other offices has been made international in scope. Before wartime restrictions prevented, individuals in the United States could go to their post offices and buy money orders denominated in any important foreign currency. The regulation form consists of a stub, which is kept by the local postmaster; a receipt, which is kept by the sender; and the order, which is sent by mail to the payee. The payee must endorse the order before it is cashed at a post office, for example, at Thionville, France, or some other legally recognized agency. (In Germany this could be the local municipal bank.) When the payee cashes the order, the obligation which the United States Post Office has assumed to the payee is ended, but the foreign post office must be reimbursed for the funds it gives to the payee. During a year this postal order will be but one of thousands sold by the United States Post Office for transfers to foreign countries and but one of thousands that foreign post offices will sell for transfers to the United States. By balancing credits and debits among postal systems, settlement is made with but a small movement of funds. The United States Post Office usually sells more orders on foreign countries than it cashes against these countries, and, consequently, the United States government must go into the exchange market to purchase bills to offset the unfavorable balance.

The maximum amount for which a single money order may be issued is $100, but there is no restriction as to the number of foreign money orders which may be issued in one day to the same remitter. Local post offices are kept informed by post office authorities regarding the rates for converting American money into moneys of foreign countries. The system is very popular among those recent immigrants and others who want to send small sums abroad. The fee for foreign postal money orders is higher than that for domestic postal money orders.

In 1882 the American Express Company introduced a satisfactory method of making small payments at home and in foreign countries in the form of an express money order.[4] Express money orders are issued through the offices of the company, by banks, and other agents of the company. The form consists of an agent's stub, a receipt for the remitter, and the order. Orders are freely cashed at banks and hotels as well as at offices of the American Express Company. Before World War II, the company maintained thirty offices in

[4] In 1918 the American Express Company consolidated with three other express companies to form the American Railway Express Company. In 1929 the domestic express business was sold to the Railway Express Agency, Inc., which is owned by class 1 railroads. The American Express Company now operates (1) a financial business which includes the sale of travelers' checks, travelers' letters of credit, domestic money orders and drafts, and foreign remittances; (2) a travel business; and (3) a foreign shipping business.

principal cities in this country and Canada and sixty offices in foreign countries. The company also had representatives or correspondents in practically every city of importance throughout the world. Although the war interfered with its foreign business, the company is reopening its foreign offices and re-establishing its foreign exchange and other business as rapidly as conditions permit. Now many banks are selling a similar money order.

When immediate transfer of money is necessary, the fastest device available is by wire, cable, or wireless. The principle involved is simply that of sending an order to an agent, telling him to pay a certain sum of money to a designated party. Before the war, Western Union foreign cable money orders were available in every large city in the world. Remote places were reached by sending currency or local money orders by registered mail from the nearest large town. In the United States there are 6,000 cities and towns where money orders may be sent and received by the Western Union Telegraph Company, and, in addition, this company has arrangements for payment of telegraphic orders with banks located in 9,000 other places in the United States.

When large amounts are involved, foreign telegraphic transfers are made through foreign correspondents or branches of American banks. A bank, in order to avoid any possible mistake, usually sends an advice to its foreign office or to its correspondent bank informing it of the transaction. The advice, which is sent by wire or mail, contains information as to amount, the name of the account, and anything else that might assist in preventing fraud or in aiding recoveries. Before World War II, when exchange rates were subject to considerable fluctuation, cable transfers were more popular than during the period when the countries were on the gold standard. By making funds almost immediately available, cable transfers reduced the risk of exchange to a minimum.

There Are Several Classes of Foreign Exchange

Short-term credit instruments payable in moneys of foreign countries are classified by such monetary units as sterling exchange, mark exchange, franc exchange, etc. This means that the credit instruments are payable, respectively, in English, German, and French moneys. Sterling, mark, or franc exchanges are classified further according to time, parties, presence or lack of security, and the purposes for which credit is used.

Time.—There are three major divisions under the time classification; cable transfer, sight or demand exchange, and time bills. A cable transfer is an order sent by cable or wireless, directing a bank to pay a certain sum of money to a specified payee. Messages are sent in code and are later confirmed by mail. The chief advantage of cable exchange is speed, and, owing to difference in time, spot cable on London, which is purchased in New York today, will probably be paid in London tomorrow. In making a contract to transfer funds by cable, banks insert a disclaimer clause, which protects them from damage claims growing out of delays because of cable difficulties. Cable transfers are sold at the cable rate, plus the charge for sending the message, and they correspond to the telegraphic transfers in domestic exchange.

A sight or demand exchange is a written order, usually drawn by a bank in the United States on its branch or correspondent in a foreign country, directing that bank to pay to a specified individual a sum of money on demand. This order is the same as a domestic draft. As a precaution against loss, drafts are made out in duplicate and sent by different mail steamers; the first to arrive is presented by the payee for payment. The New York bank (drawer) sends a letter (advice) to the correspondent bank on which the draft is drawn, advising the foreign bank of the transaction. Bank drafts are usually in terms of foreign monetary units, but they may be drawn in terms of dollars. In case of dollar drafts, payment is usually made in the currency of the foreign country at the current sight rate of exchange on New York. For example, if the current rate in London on New York is $4.00, then the payee receives £250 for a $1,000 draft. But if the rate of exchange increases from $4.00 to $4.10, the payee receives approximately £244. When foreign drafts are drawn in terms of dollars, the risk of exchange is borne by foreigners.

Many foreign exchange bills are payable a specified number of days after the date of acceptance. They are called "time bills," and most commercial and trade bills are of this type. The time period varies according to custom, distance, and established trade practices. During periods of unusual fluctuations in exchange rates, there is a tendency to shorten the time period.

Parties.—There are three types of exchange in which the classification is according to parties, namely, bankers', commercial, and trade. Bankers' bills are drawn by a bank on a bank; commercial bills are drawn by an individual, firm, or corporation on a bank; and trade bills are drawn by an individual, firm, or corporation on a nonfinancial institution. Conditions under which bills of exchange are drawn are usually specified in a letter of credit. Commercial bills and bankers' bills are obligations of banks and are therefore more extensively used in foreign exchange transactions than are trade bills.

Presence or Lack of Security.—Foreign exchange credit instruments are classified as secured and unsecured; the secured bill is preferred, other things being equal. The thing pledged as security for a specific credit instrument is usually the merchandise or security which is being financed. Another classification of these instruments is one made according to the purpose for which they are used—to finance trade, travel, and short-term international loans.

Rates of Exchange Are Prices

The rate of exchange is the price of a particular kind of foreign bill of exchange. It is the price of a bill drawn in the money unit of one country quoted in terms of the second country. There are different rates for cable, for demand, and for time bills.

Methods of Quoting.—Before considering the different rates of exchange, it should be noted that there are three methods of quoting exchange rates: (1) the direct-price method, (2) the premium-discount method, and (3) the indirect-price method. The direct-price method is the one generally used by dealers in the United States. It is illustrated by the prices appearing in Table 30. Thus a £1,000 bankers' demand draft would have sold for $4,850 on December 29, 1928. The premium-discount method is sometimes used in quoting exchange between countries having the same monetary unit. For example, the Canadian dollar during the latter part of 1939 "showed a stronger tendency, and its discount against the United States dollar narrowed from 13⅜ to 11⅜ per cent."[5]

---

[5] Federal Reserve Bank of New York, *Monthly Review,* January, 1940, p. 5. The Federal Reserve banks are required to certify to exchange rates to the Treasury under the Tariff Act of 1930. The noon buying rates for cable transfer in New York, valued in United States money, are published in the *Federal Reserve Bulletin.*

The indirect-price method of quoting gives the number of units of foreign currency that can be bought with a unit of home currency. In England, the market uses the indirect method of quoting, which at first is puzzling to American businessmen, students, and others who are not familiar with this practice. For example, after the outbreak of World War II, the official English buying and selling rates for American dollars were fixed, respectively, at $4.03½ and $4.02½. This might lead one to conclude that the English government was paying more for American dollars than it was receiving. Actually

TABLE 30

RATES ON POUND STERLING BILLS*

	January 26, 1940	December 29, 1928
Cable	$3.98⅝	$4.85 7/16
Demand	3.98⅝	4.85
Commercial (60 days)	3.96¼	4.80 13/16
Commercial (90 days)	3.95¾	4.79

* Closing prices.

Source: Commercial and Financial Chronicle.

just the contrary was true; the authorities would receive in a £1,000 dollar-exchange purchasing transaction $4,035 and sell $4,025 in a £1,000 sterling-exchange transaction, leaving the dealer a gross profit of $10.

Rates Move Together.—Rates vary with different time classes of exchange, as illustrated by Table 30, showing actual rates quoted on various types of sterling bills. Over a period of time the rates for the various types of exchange rise or fall together, and these movements are explained in terms of general factors which affect international trade and finance. The changes which took place between 1929 and 1940 are accounted for in part by the changes in monetary standards of the United Kingdom in 1931 and the United States in 1934.

The Spread Varies.—Cable exchange usually sells at a higher rate than demand or sight exchange, owing to the fact that payment by cable may be completed sooner than by sight draft. The latter is sent by mail on fast steamers, but the former is sent by wireless or cable. There is no stated transmission time on cablegrams between

New York and foreign places; a great many cable transmissions have been delivered in less than one minute, but thirty minutes is perhaps the average time technically necessary. Because of the time differential, a cable order to Europe must be filed early in the day if it is to be delivered before closing time; actually, most cable transfers from New York to Europe are paid on the following business day.

The purchasers of cable exchange are given the benefit of the foreign funds sooner than the purchasers of demand drafts, the difference in time being the difference between mailing time and cabling time between the two exchange centers. The sellers of cable transfers lose interest on foreign funds, and, therefore, they ask and receive higher prices for their foreign funds when they are to be transferred by cable. This loss is much greater during periods of high interest rates than it is during periods of low interest rates. On the other hand, buyers of cable exchange have their funds tied up in transfers for a shorter period of time than when they purchase sight or time exchange; and they are willing to pay a higher price for cable exchange. Naturally this time preference is greater during periods of high interest rates than during periods of low interest rates. Therefore, we may conclude that (1) because the buyer of a cable saves interest and because the seller of it loses interest, cable exchange sells at a higher rate than demand or time drafts; and (2) the greater the savings of interest by the buyer or the loss of interest by the seller, the greater the spread among time, demand, and cable exchange rates.[6]

The rates of exchange for time bills decrease with the length of time the bills have to run, for the same reasons that demand bills sell for a lower price than cable exchange. Drafts for 90 days cost less than those for 60 days, and those for 60 days cost less than those for 30 days. The amount of spread depends upon interest rates; for example, the spread between the different types of exchange was much greater during 1928 than in 1940. In January, 1940, there was only a 2⅞ point spread between cables and 90-day commercial bills, as compared to 6 7/16 points in 1928. (See Table 30.) This difference in spread on the two dates under consideration was due primarily to the differences in interest rates. Other minor factors which cause part of the spread between long bills and demand exchange are stamp taxes, commissions, and profits.

[6] Whitaker, A. C., *Foreign Exchange* (2d ed.), p. 441.

Credit Risks.—Another factor which affects exchange rates is the credit risk. The rates on prime bank bills, which are the ones reported in Table 30, are usually higher than on trade bills of the same maturity. The market not only discriminates in favor of bank bills but shows a preference for those drawn upon the larger and sounder banks. Bills drawn upon branches by the head office, or vice versa (called "pigs on pork"), sometimes sell at a less favorable rate than those drawn upon a second bank, because they are the obligation of but one bank, while the second type of bill is, after acceptance, the obligation of two banks. Among commercial bills, grain and cotton bills sell at more favorable prices than those secured by general merchandise.

Rates Are Equivalent.—After allowance is made for interest and risk, the rates for all types of exchange classified according to time in one market are equivalent. If there is too much spread between sterling cable and sight, exchange dealers quickly take advantage of the situation. Cable will be sold and sight exchange purchased, and the effects will be to bring the prices of the two closer together. If time exchange is selling at a relatively low rate, exchange dealers will buy it in preference to cable or sight, and the effect will be to bring about an adjustment among them.

Dealers Buy and Sell Credit.—Exchange dealers are buyers and sellers of different types of exchange at the same time. They are in the position of any middleman who has prices at which he buys and higher prices at which he sells or desires to sell. Exchange dealers purchase large amounts of foreign credit instruments in order to build up or replenish their foreign balances, that is, deposits with their foreign banks. While the Guaranty Trust Company is buying bills of exchange aggregating £5,000,000 sterling from cotton exporters, it is selling other similar credit instruments to importers of pottery, textiles, and other British merchandise. When the cotton bills of exchange are collected, the deposit of the Guaranty Trust Company with its London correspondent bank will be increased; but when the British merchants cash the drafts which were sent to them by American buyers, the Guaranty Trust Company's foreign deposit will be decreased. The fundamental thing to keep in mind is that foreign exchange transactions are but transfers of bank credit, appearing on the bank's books as deposits. It is but an extension of the domestic exchange system to include foreign countries.

Arbitragers Help to Stabilize Rates

When free exchange markets are functioning, rates in two or more markets tend to be equivalent for each type of exchange, a situation which results from the arbitrage operations of traders and banks.[7] The word "arbitrage" means buying and selling the same thing in different markets at the same time in order to make a profit out of the differences in prices in the two or more markets.

After allowances for natural and artificial barriers, commodities, securities, and foreign exchange sold upon well-organized markets should have the same price. Thus, wheat, cotton, and federal government bonds should be selling at the same or equivalent prices in Liverpool, London, Chicago, and New York. If local conditions drive down the price of wheat in Chicago, and it is out of line with the price in Liverpool, arbitragers buy in Chicago and sell in Liverpool. These operations soon eliminate the former discrepancy in prices.

Exchange Arbitrage.—As organized before World War II, exchange arbitrage was a separate business within exchange departments of commercial banks which dealt in transfers of gold and silver and bills of exchange. A third type of financial arbitraging, which consists of the buying of bonds and stocks, was an adjunct to the brokerage business; but some firms were organized so as to carry on arbitraging in the "precious metals," exchange and securities. Arbitraging is different from speculation because it involves the making of a profit from differences in prices at a particular time, while speculation involves making profits out of changes in prices over a period of time. If the calculations of the arbitragers are correct and the orders to buy and sell go through as scheduled, no risks are involved; but in speculation there are always risks, which the speculators assume. In arbitraging in the exchange markets there may be two, three, or more exchange markets involved. A hypothetical illustration of three-point arbitrage appears here under the conditions as assumed:

Cable in New York on London—$4.00
Cable in New York on Paris—$0.01
Cable in London on Paris—401 francs per pound sterling

A cable transfer of 10,000,000 francs sent directly from New

[7] For a more complete discussion of arbitrage, see *ibid.*, pp. 297-314.

York to Paris will cost $100,000. A banker notices, however, that a profit may be made if the transaction is made through London. With $100,000 he purchases £25,000, which, in turn, is used to purchase 10,025,000 francs, or 25,000 more than was possible by direct purchase. The transaction is completed by a sale of a cable on Paris for 10,025,000 francs for $100,250, and there is a gross arbitrage profit of $250 from which to pay commissions, cable charges, taxes, and other expenses. These transactions may be illustrated as follows:

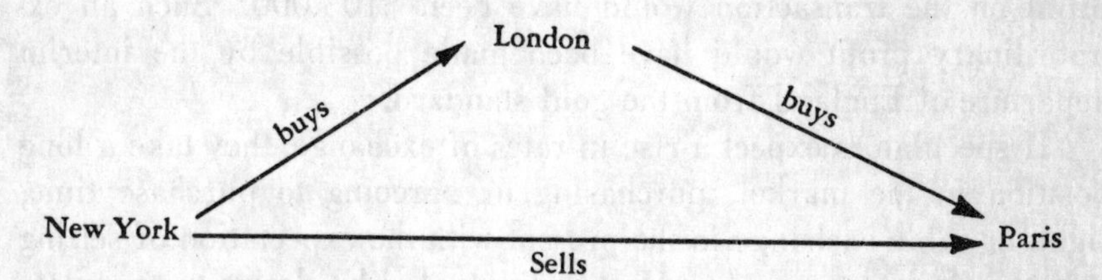

Although margin or profits are small in arbitraging, the amounts dealt in are large. The financial success of such operations depends upon the speed with which they are performed. The transactions are in the hands of skilled operators who are aided by parity sheets worked out to suit their own particular needs. They are on a constant lookout for profits to be made and are in continuous touch by telephone with developments in other markets. Since operators buy and sell related exchange in different markets at the same time, in order to profit from differences in prices, and since European financial markets are closed during most of the period when American banks are open, arbitraging is not so widely practiced in New York as in London.

Speculators Help to Stabilize Rates

Speculators buy and sell exchange in order to make a profit because of differences in prices at different times. The trend of the rates of exchange plays a part in all exchange transactions. In financing trade with future contracts, the conservative banker usually covers at once by purchases of time bills or a forward contract of some kind. He knows the market better than his customer and is able to secure a better future contract than he gave. He is satisfied with the profit made from the difference in prices.

Other less conservative exchange dealers may prefer to take a chance on the market and remain uncovered. If the exchange rate decreases, they make a speculative profit from the transaction. In addition, exchange dealers may sell time bills in order to take advantage of the expected fall in rates. In other words, they are short on the market and hope to cover later at a lower price. For example, if an exchange dealer had sold a £100,000 sterling 60-day bill on September 1, 1931, at $4.82, he would have been in a position to cover 60 days later by purchase of cable at $3.79. The total gross profit on the transaction would have been $103,000. Such an extraordinary profit would have been made possible by the interim departure of England from the gold standard.

If speculators expect a rise in rates of exchange, they take a long position in the market, purchasing or agreeing to purchase time, sight, or cable exchange in the present with the expectation of selling it in the future at a profit. Most individuals who desire to speculate buy sight drafts through their exchange dealers and hold them for a rise in price. Other individuals prefer to buy foreign currency, but this type of speculation is objected to because of the greater costs involved. At the present time many foreigners are holding American paper, not only because they think it is safer, but also because they expect to profit in the future from an expected increase in the value of the dollar in terms of their own currency.

Sight drafts and currency do not bear interest; therefore, many exchange speculators prefer to buy drafts on foreign banks and send them abroad to open savings accounts. During 1932 and 1933 large sums were transferred abroad and used in this way, and large profits resulted. But still greater profits were made by international bankers who opened gold accounts in France which they later brought back to the United States at a gross profit of 69 per cent, owing to exchange profits resulting from the devaluation of the gold dollar.

Other individuals prefer to invest in foreign government bonds and private securities. Large profits were made by purchasing English government and other foreign securities during the first part of 1933, when the sterling exchange rate was low, and later selling them when the sterling rate had increased. For example, when the sterling rate was $3.34, ten £100 sterling government bonds at par would have cost a speculator $3,340. Six months later, had the bonds still been at par, he could have sold them for £1,000, which, when converted into dollars at the new rate of exchange ($5.04), would have amounted to $5,040. The gross profit on the transaction would have been $1,700, or over 50 per cent.

Since 1934, most of the international investment transactions offering speculators an exchange profit as well as safety and earnings on their funds have involved purchases of American bonds and stocks. Foreigners who purchased federal government bonds before September, 1939, have a "paper" exchange profit on their investments equal to the reciprocal of the percentage decline of their currencies in terms of the dollar. The opposite picture is shown by the exchange losses (paper) which American investors in foreign securities have suffered since the appreciation of the American dollar in terms of the foreign currencies in which their investments are contracted.

Thus during periods of international financial disturbances there are opportunities for tremendous profits; they are so great, in fact, that international speculators and bankers have been charged with creating conditions which made it impossible for certain countries to remain on the gold standard and made it necessary for governments to inaugurate some type of foreign exchange control system.[8]

Forward Exchange[9]

As previously noted, one of the differences between domestic and foreign financing is the risk of exchange, which increases the hazards of financing foreign trade, investments, and travel. However, this risk may be avoided by individuals and banks by merely buying and selling forward or future exchange as a "hedge" against the exchange risk. Assume that Mr. White, a seller of goods, expects to receive a £5,000 draft, a month hence, which he must convert into American money at the rate of $4.00 in order to make a profit. Because of the fear that the rate of exchange may decline to less than $4.00, he may contract with an exchange banker to buy the sterling bill at or near that price, thereby shifting the risk of exchange to the exchange dealer.

[8] "As the foreign countries got on the gold standard, of course, the interest in the business [foreign exchange] and the profits in it gradually disappeared . . . . because the fluctuations are within narrow limits with the exception of a country like Spain that will not go on the gold standard, and, therefore, is the prey of everybody who wishes to speculate in foreign exchange" (Kindersley, *loc. cit.*).

[9] See Einzig, Paul, *The Theory of Forward Exchange.*

In the market at the same time there will be buyers of American goods who are contracting to pay pounds sterling for goods purchased. Faced with the possibility of a rise in the exchange rate, one of the buyers may contact the same exchange bank and ask for a future contract to deliver say £5,000 a month hence. Owing to the contract already made with Mr. White, the exchange dealer is in a position to make a contract to sell £5,000 future exchange as requested. The profits on the transaction will be the spread between the dealer's purchase price and the sale price.

If dealers are in a position in which they cannot secure forward exchange to offset sales calling for future deliveries, they may go into the market and buy sight or "spot" exchange to cover their future commitments. Since the price of future exchange is usually below that of sight exchange, their profits will arise from commissions charged and from the earnings (if any) on the deposit balances in foreign banks. Some dealers may choose to speculate on future exchange rates, expecting to cover their future commitments by buying cable exchange or sight exchange at a lower price when their future contracts to deliver exchange come due.

During periods of financial disturbances, when there is a lack of confidence in a foreign currency, those who wish to sell cable, sight, and forward exchanges will exceed those who wish to buy them. Foreign exchange dealers will want to withdraw all except already committed balances; dealers who have made forward contracts will wait for a more profitable time to cover; buyers of goods will wait as long as their contracts permit before arranging for payments; and speculators will offer forward contracts at "bargain prices." The increase in supply of cable, sight, and forward offerings and the decline in demand are reflected immediately in the prices of all classes of exchange. It is during such periods that equalization funds are most helpful to the market. By buying large quanties of foreign exchange the managers of the funds may increase the rates, forcing speculators to take heavy losses. These periodic "shakeouts" of the market may be helpful if conditions which cause the loss of confidence in the foreign currency are but temporary. Some of the problems discussed in this chapter will be among those faced by the managers of the International Monetary Fund, whose chief function is to stabilize exchange rates of participating countries in co-operation with central banks and other national agencies.

War Changes

During World War II, because of various credit arrangements such as Lend-Lease and foreign exchange control, foreign exchange trading was of minor importance. The Canadian dollar selling rates and buying rates were pegged at $0.9091 and at $0.9009, and the British sterling pound rates at $4.03½ and $4.02½. After liberation, new rates were established by a number of the countries in western Europe. A military rate of 10 cents for the German Reichsmark was established for troop pay and military procurement purposes. In the Philippines the pre-war rate of 2 pesos to the dollar was re-established. In 1946 the French franc was revalued at the present rate of 0.8 cents, after having been pegged at a rate of 2 cents from June 6, 1944, to the end of 1945.

QUESTIONS AND PROBLEMS

1. In what way will the International Monetary Fund aid the foreign exchange business? (See Chap. XIII.)
2. Enumerate and explain the items on bank statements that suggest that they are carrying on a foreign exchange business.
3. "Foreign exchange transactions are but transfers of book-credit that appear on banks' books as deposits, even though gold is used." Explain.
4. "What then is foreign exchange? Foreign exchange is direct barter of monies used in different countries. E.g.: Exchanging dollars directly for pounds, francs, marks, yens, etc." (Coughlin, Rev. Charles E., *Money: Questions and Answers*, p. 154). Is this a good definition of foreign exchange? Can you do better? Try it.
5. The general principle of foreign exchange is "that bills of exchange drawn on any particular place constitute a new kind of article, subject to the laws of supply and demand" (Jevons, *Money and the Mechanism of Exchange*, p. 296). Explain.
6. What is meant by the "economic roots of foreign exchange"?
7. Identify: (*a*) favorable balance of trade, (*b*) "invisible" items of foreign trade, and (*c*) "visible" items of foreign trade.
8. What financial middlemen are found in the foreign exchange markets? What is meant by saying that it is an open market? Should it be organized and conducted along lines similar to the New York Stock Exchange? Why?
9. Distinguish among: (*a*) foreign postal money order, (*b*) cable transfer, and (*c*) express money order.

10. Explain how the following tend to affect the rate of exchange in New York on London: (*a*) increase in sales of cotton to London, (*b*) buying of postal money orders to be sent to England, (*c*) an increase in interest rates in New York, (*d*) travel in England by Americans, (*e*) import of cloth from England, and (*f*) interest payments to Americans.
11. Identify the different ways of classifying foreign exchange.
12. Assume that the rate of dollar exchange in London is quoted by exchange dealers as $4.04 bid; $4.02 asked. Do the dealers lose on their purchases and sales? Explain.
13. Account for the spread among cable, sight, and time rates of exchange. Is it always the same? Explain.
14. How do foreign exchange dealers make their gross profits? Does this principle apply to all types of merchandising?
15. What difference is there between arbitrage and speculation in foreign exchange?
16. Is there any relationship between the New York price of the "Mexican dollar" and the silver purchase price of the United States Treasury?
17. Comment on the following: "The Canadian dollar also showed a stronger tendency, and its discount against the United States dollar narrowed from 13⅜ to 11⅜ per cent" (Federal Reserve Bank of New York, *Monthly Review*, January, 1940, p. 5).
18. Report on the recent developments in the foreign exchange market. Use Federal Reserve Bank of New York, *Monthly Review*.
19. Check with a local bank on (*a*) the amount of its foreign exchange transactions, (*b*) the names of its correspondents used for this purpose, and (*c*) the types of local interest served.
20. Make a table showing average noon buying rates for cable transfers in New York for Canadian, English, Brazilian, French, and Chinese currencies. For reference, see last issue of *Federal Reserve Bulletin*.
21. What is the significance of the following? "Continuing the steady, rapid rise of previous years, the total volume of funds (dollar balances, earmarked gold, and United States Government securities and other investments) held by the Federal Reserve Banks for account of foreign central banks and governments rose above 6 billion dollars in February 1944" (*Thirtieth Annual Report of the Federal Reserve Bank of New York for the Year Ended December 31, 1944*, p. 53).

REFERENCES

See end of Chapter XXIV

Chapter XXIV

FOREIGN TRADE FINANCE

Financing with the Use of Letters of Credit

Commercial banks extend credit through the issuance of letters of credit and similar documents, and, as a result, there appear as assets on detailed bank statements of certain banks the items "customers' liability on letters of credit" and "customers' liability on acceptances," and as liabilities the items "liability on letters of credit" and "liability on acceptances." These items represent "credits" and "obligations" which have arisen from financing trade, travel, or borrowing with the use of letters of credit. Since this form of credit is used primarily, but not entirely, to finance foreign trade, short-term foreign investments, and foreign travel, this subject is discussed in this chapter.

After the preliminary arrangements are made by the customer with his bank, the bank gives the customer a letter of credit.[1] The letter of credit is a special form of letter addressed by one party (the issuer), who is usually a bank, to another bank, individual, or business firm (the beneficiary), authorizing the latter to draw drafts directly upon the issuer in accordance with the terms specified in the letter of credit. This letter varies in content and form, depending on the time period and the transaction to be financed. Hence there are commercial, travelers', and financial letters of credit.

The bank is merely assuring the seller or beneficiary that when drafts are drawn under provisions of and according to the terms of the letter of credit they will be honored. It is the draft drawn under the letter of credit that is the negotiable instrument. In form, these drafts or bills of exchange are similar to those used in domestic exchange. Financing with letters of credit and drafts drawn under them has certain advantages for the bank, the borrower, and the beneficiary.

---

[1] Many small banks act as agents for larger metropolitan banks in issuing letters of credit. The latter will deal through the local bank in issuing the letter of credit and will charge the local bank but one-half the normal commission. The local bank will make the formal application for the letter of credit and will guarantee the repayment of the funds involved. The local bank will charge its customer a total commission of at least twice the charge it pays the issuer.

No immediate outlays of funds are made. Thus, a bank that has already committed all its loanable funds may, under certain circumstances, increase its earnings by issuing letters of credit, for which it will charge a small commission.

The commission varies, depending upon the credit standing of the borrower, the credit terms specified in the letter, and general market conditions. A minmum charge of $5.00 may be made, irrespective of whether or not the letter of credit is used. Typical charges on letters of credit, payable in dollars, on the face amount of the draft are: sight and 30 days' sight, 1/8 of 1 per cent; 60 days' sight, 1/4 of 1 per cent; 90 days' sight, 3/8 of 1 per cent. On a per annum basis these would be equivalent to a 1 1/2 per cent interest rate. In a letter of credit authorizing the drawing of drafts denominated in a foreign currency, the commission would be larger, in order to include charges made by the bank's foreign correspondent.[2]

The buyer, by paying a small fee to the bank, obtains a document assuring payment to the one from whom the purchase is made. By giving the seller the guarantee of a widely known bank in place of the buyer's promise to pay, business that might otherwise have been impossible, except on a cash basis, can be done. Therefore, the borrower has the advantage of not being required to pay for his merchandise until he receives documents indicating that the goods have been insured and properly shipped.

The seller of the goods benefits from the financing with the use of a letter of credit, because it enables him to expand his business to include sales to unknown and often distantly located businessmen. Since the credit standing of the issuer (bank) is well known among local bankers, he has no difficulty in cashing, at a small discount, the drafts drawn under the letter of credit. Thus the seller has the advantage of selling for cash, and the buyer has the advantage of buying on time.

When arrangements are made for letters of credit, the customers sign agreements whereby they promise to reimburse the bank for drafts drawn under the letters of credit. Thus there will appear on the bank statement the item showing customers' liability on letters of credit and an offsetting item, bank's liability on letters of credit. If,

[2] The fees charged by correspondents include those for making payments to the beneficiary, for "accepting" in case of time drafts, and for inspecting the documents to see that all the terms of the letter of credit are complied with.

in the aggregate, the latter exceed the former, it means that some of the bank's customers have in whole or in part paid cash for letters of credit. When drafts drawn are paid or, in the case of time bills, are accepted, these two items will be taken off the bank's statement unless they have been replaced by others. If bank drafts are accepted, these two items will be replaced by customers' liability on acceptances and bank's liability on acceptances outstanding.[3]

Financing with the Use of Acceptance Credit

In the preceding paragraph reference was made to the bank statement item "customers' liability on acceptances" and the offsetting item "bank's liability on acceptances outstanding." These two items result from the drawing of time drafts under letters of credit and their presentment to the bank on which they are drawn, first for acceptance and later, when they come due, for payment. The accepting process consists of stamping "accepted" on the face of the draft and then dating and signing it. This amounts to an endorsement of the draft, which adds to its marketability. During the period between acceptance and maturity, it may be sold at a slight discount in the open market.

Bank credit involved in the use of acceptances may be used to finance imports and exports, the domestic shipment of goods, the shipment of goods between foreign countries, the storage of goods abroad, and the creation of dollar exchange.

Financing of Imports.—To further clarify the use of letters of credit and bankers' acceptances, let us assume that a department store in New York is buying cloth from a manufacturer in London, England. The letter of credit is issued by a New York bank, and it contains the following terms: The tenor of the draft to be drawn is 30 days and is to be for approximately $10,000. The expiration date of the terms is June 10, 1946, and the documents to be provided by the seller of the goods must include a commercial invoice, an ocean bill of lading, an insurance certificate, and a consular invoice.

[3] Member banks report as "acceptances outstanding" amounts of outstanding drafts and bills of exchange accepted by the reporting banks, or accepted by other banks acting as their agents, less their own acceptances acquired through purchase. If own acceptances are held by the reporting banks, they are required to be reported as loans. Since December 31, 1938, the liability of national banks on acceptances of other banks and foreign bills of exchange sold with their endorsement are excluded from the balance sheet and reported merely as contingent liabilities.

A copy of the letter of credit[4] will be mailed to the seller in London, or, under certain circumstances, the terms may be cabled by the bank to its correspondent in London, and this correspondent will notify the seller in writing.[5] On receipt, the letter of credit is examined by the seller, and, finding the terms in agreement with the sales contract, he proceeds to prepare the goods for shipment. He makes out a commercial invoice, secures a consular's invoice from the American Consul in London, insures the shipment with a marine insurance company, and obtains a bill of lading from the steamship company when he delivers the merchandise. These and any other minor documents that may be necessary are then taken to the seller's bank, where a draft equal to the selling price of the goods is drawn, that is, for example, $10,000.

The dollar credit may be and usually is sold to the seller's bank, and so the draft will be drawn in favor of the exporter's bank. Since the draft will have a term of 30 days after acceptance and it will take the draft a week to be received in New York by mail, the amount paid the seller may be $9,975 (assuming a 1/4 of 1 per cent discount on the face amount for five weeks). The drafts with documents attached will be sent by mail to a New York bank acting as correspondent for the London bank. When the draft and accompanying documents reach New York, they will be sent to the bank that issued the original letter of credit.

The bank issuing the letter of credit will check the documents to ascertain if the terms have been complied with. If the documents are correct, the bank will stamp the draft "accepted" and then date and sign it. (In case of a sight draft, the bank will pay it and immediately charge the account of the customer.) The accepting bank will retain the documentary set and then give it to the New York department store against a trust receipt. The department store will use the bill of lading to obtain possession of the goods as soon as they arrive. On or before the maturity of the bankers' acceptance, the department store will pay the bank.

[4] One copy of the letter of credit is retained in the files of the issuing bank, and a nonnegotiable copy is furnished the customer for his own record. In addition to the regular letter of credit, there is a revolving form that may permit drafts to be drawn in amounts up to $10,000 per month for a period of 5 months. It may be cumulative or noncumulative, that is, if drafts are not drawn for the full $10,000 in one month they may or may not be drawn in excess of the amount at a later period.

[5] Other documents that may be required are a certificate or statement of origin, a certificate of quality, and a weight certificate.

The disposal of the acceptance depends upon instructions. It may be held by the accepting bank for crediting the $10,000 to the account of the presenting bank at maturity, it may be discounted or sold in the bankers' acceptance market with the funds disposed of according to instructions, or it may be returned to the presenting bank. If discounted in the acceptance market or returned to the presenting bank, the acceptance will be presented to the accepting bank at maturity.

Financing of Exports.—The financing of exports with the use of letters of credit may be identical with the procedure outlined above, with the foreign buyer arranging through banking channels for a letter of credit issued by an American bank.

If the buyer insists on financing the transaction by having a draft drawn on him or his bank in terms of his own currency, the American exporter will be subject to the so-called "risk of exchange." After he makes a commitment to sell goods for so many francs, or whatever the buyer's currency may be, he may hedge against a possible loss by arranging for the future sale of the draft to an exchange dealer. Since the latter is selling forward or future exchange, a favorable contract may be made. When the goods are ready for shipment, the draft denominated in the foreign currency will be drawn by the American exporter and sold as provided for in the forward contract. The exporter may wait until the goods are shipped and then try to find a market for his foreign bill of exchange. If the discount is too high, he may send the bill to the drawee (the buyer or his bank) through banking channels for collection.[6]

Since the time period necessary for collecting and securing the remittance in dollar exchange may be months, an exporter may arrange with an American bank for acceptance credit secured by the assignment of the funds represented by the foreign draft. The exporter will draw under this second acceptance agreement, present it immediately to the bank for acceptance, and then sell it in the acceptance market for cash. This gives him funds to meet pay rolls, to purchase materials, and to meet other expenses. The second bill is

[6] In the Orient, prior to the opening of branches of European and American banks, banking services were inadequate, and the difficulties were sometimes met by the Chinese buyer by arranging through banking channels for an "Authority to Purchase." The draft would be drawn on the Chinese merchant by the exporter and then sent to the American bank that had agreed to buy it. Thus, by securing a guarantee from a bank that there would be a market for the draft, business that otherwise might have been impossible was carried on. Such transactions are rare except in the Far East.

ILLUSTRATION VII

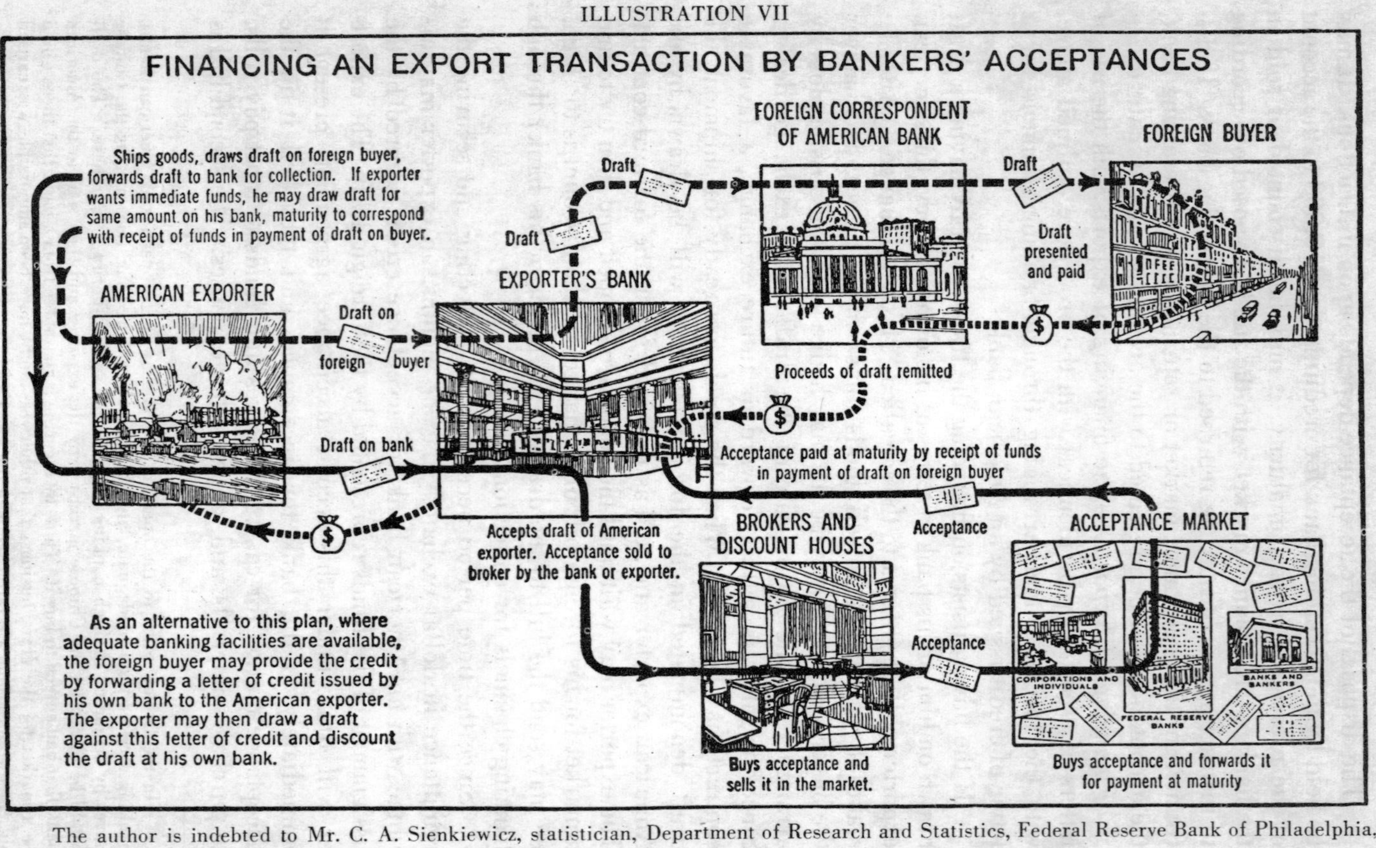

The author is indebted to Mr. C. A. Sienkiewicz, statistician, Department of Research and Statistics, Federal Reserve Bank of Philadelphia, for a copy of the above chart.

liquidated when the first draft is collected. Any balance left after fees and commissions are subtracted is paid to the American exporter.

The transaction just described is graphically portrayed by Illustration VII. It should be noted that the original transaction pictured in the upper right half of the illustration shows the use of a trade bill, that is, one drawn on a buyer and not on his bank. In the lower right-hand corner is a picture representing the acceptance market, which will be described after a discussion of other uses of bankers' acceptances.

Other Trade Uses of Bankers' Acceptances

Domestic Shipments.—American banks may be requested to finance domestic shipments of goods with the use of acceptance credit. Financing procedure involves the same general steps already noted. The bill of exchange is drawn by the seller or his bank under terms stated in the letter of credit, secured by shipping and other documents, and then sent to the accepting bank for its acceptance. The drawer of the accepted drafts obtains funds immediately and economically by selling the accepted draft in the acceptance market. When the draft matures, the accepting bank pays the draft with funds provided by the purchaser of the goods. In the United States the use of the trade acceptance, wherein bills are drawn by sellers on buyers, as in the case of automobile manufacturers on dealers, has been considerably more important than bankers' acceptance in financing domestic shipments.

Shipments between Foreign Countries.—An American accepting bank may receive a request to finance a shipment of goods between a European seller and a South American buyer. The former is willing to sell goods to the latter, provided he arranges through his bank for the issuance of a letter of credit by a New York bank. If this is done, the financing proceeds as follows: The European exporter ships the goods to the buyer, draws a draft on the New York bank, and discounts it with his bank. The European bank forwards the draft to its New York correspondent bank, to be presented to the drawee bank for acceptance. At maturity, the American bank meets the draft with funds provided by the importer located in South America.

Storage of Goods Abroad.—Similar problems arise in financing the storage of goods which may or may not be of American origin.

Accepting banks should ask for and see satisfactory evidence of storage warehouse receipts and should obtain letters of guarantee from actual takers of the credit. Although the practice of financing shipments of goods between foreign countries and the storage of goods abroad by American banks has been criticized, English bankers have successfully financed such transactions for many years. Experienced American bankers should be able to judge the risks accurately and should be able to expand these two types of foreign trade financing profitably.

Domestic Storage of Goods.—In order to promote orderly marketing of goods, particularly agricultural staples, it is necessary to hold them from season to season. Owners may secure financial help from local banks under ordinary lines of credit, but it is usually more economical to borrow in the acceptance market. The owners may arrange for a line of acceptance credit, permitting them to draw drafts on the accepting banks. After acceptance, the drafts are sold in the bill market, and the beneficiaries will have funds with which to purchase more staples or to finance other needs. The acceptance credit is secured by warehouse receipts, and, when the goods are removed from the warehouse, these receipts are exchanged for trust receipts. The bills of exchange are liquidated with funds received when the goods are sold.

Risk due to market fluctuations may be removed by requiring the owners of the staples to sell a future contract when the acceptance credit is given. If the price of the commodity falls, the loss is offset by the profit on the future contract. When transactions are protected by hedging operations, many banks will give acceptance credit to finance storage of staples for as much as 90 per cent of their market value.

Creating Dollar Exchange.—Acceptance credit may be used in special ways to aid foreign trade. One important special use is to make dollar exchange available to those buyers of American goods who are in poorly developed financial centers. By dollar exchange is meant New York drafts or other drafts drawn on banks in the United States. Normally, buyers of goods in most foreign financial centers are able to secure adequate dollar exchange from their local banks. But assume that steamships stop but once per month at some Central American port and the one bank in the community keeps a balance of only $25,000 with its New York correspondent bank. During the seasonal buying period, the steamship unloads $100,000 worth of goods sold by exporters in New York to the local merchants. There is an immediate need for $100,000 in New York drafts, which the local banker is unable to provide with his $25,000 balance in New York. There is no other local bank or exchange dealer in the community to which he may go for help.

Assume that the Central American banker had previously opened a line of acceptance credit with a New York bank. Under this credit agreement he is authorized to draw time drafts, which he now proceeds to do. He draws a 30-day time draft for $80,000, which he sends to New York to be accepted and then sold in the acceptance market. The proceeds from the sale will be credited to his deposit account in New York. In the meantime, the Central American banker will have sold sight bills (New York drafts) to his customers for $100,000. He knows that the time draft will have been sold and that funds are available in New York to take up his sight drafts when presented. During the next 30 days he can build up his deposit in New York so as to take up the time bill at maturity.

The American accepting bank must make good on the time draft when it matures, even though the Central American banker may be unable to cover his obligation. Unlike other grants of acceptance credit that are used to finance foreign trade, this type is not secured by the goods being financed. The accepting bank may require the bank to which they are granting acceptance credit to keep securities on deposit with it. Special restrictions are placed upon this type of accepting business by the Board of Governors of the Federal Reserve System. American banks must secure special permission from the Board before they can grant acceptance credit on which this type of dollar exchange is drawn. They may offer services to banks located in only a limited number of countries, as specified by the Board. The total amount of acceptance credit of this nature cannot exceed 50 per cent of the accepting bank's capital stock and surplus. Finally, the amount of such credit extended to one name cannot exceed 10 per cent of the accepting bank's capital stock and surplus.

Acceptance Credit Aids International Short-Time Borrowing and Lending

The same financial machinery noted in the foregoing may be used to finance transactions other than trade. Bankers' long bills or bankers' time bills are used to borrow funds abroad for a short period. In some cases they are renewed with such regularity that they constitute almost a continuing obligation.[7]

Suppose that an American bank desires to borrow in London in order to finance a large bond deal in New York, to build up its funds to help a customer, or for other reasons. It cables the Midland Bank for permission to draw bills upon it. The Midland Bank may or may not request a deposit of collateral as security with a New York trust company. However, let us assume that the request is granted. Time bills of exchange are drawn by the American bank and sold to a local exchange dealer, which gives the American bank funds to finance its customers. The exchange dealer sends the drafts to its London correspondent bank, which presents them to the Midland Bank for acceptance and then sells them in the London acceptance market. Before the bills come due, the American banker calls his loans, or liquidates his bond holdings, takes the proceeds, and buys sight or cable exchange on London. This is sent to the Midland Bank, which collects it and uses the funds to meet the bankers' time bills of exchange drawn under the terms of the acceptance credit.

The bankers' long bill may be used to take advantage of an expected rise or fall in the exchange rates. If sterling is expected to decline, bankers will not only sell drafts on their deposits in England but will also make arrangements whereby London bankers will accept drafts drawn upon them. Three or four months later, when the time comes to cover their short sales, the American bankers go into the exchange markets and buy sight or cable exchange.

A Well-developed Acceptance Market Is Essential

Since 1929 there has been a world-wide decline in the volume of time bills of exchange because of the decrease in international trade and the increase in the use of cable and sight exchange. As noted in the preceding chapter, the "merchants" or intermediaries in the acceptance markets are acceptance or bill dealers who operate as individuals, firms, or corporations. In addition to buying and selling acceptances, they are also brokers or dealers in commercial paper,

---

[7] Under the famous stillhalting (stand still) agreement of 1931, foreign bankers, particularly American, English, and French, agreed to postpone dates of payment of short-term acceptance credits of several hundred million dollars granted to German institutions.

short-term government obligations, bonds and sometimes stocks; and, consequently, they have wide contacts with houses in the money and capital markets.

Since the beginning of the acceptance market in the United States, the Federal Reserve banks have adopted a policy of taking all eligible bankers' bills offered to them. Their buying rates are reviewed weekly but may not be changed for long periods of time. Since the Reserve banks purchase all eligible bills offered, their discount is usually the highest in the market (the lowest price). The Federal Reserve System, in supporting the acceptance market, is following the same rate policy as that of the Bank of England, that is, keeping the bank rate above the market rate. The Reserve banks also help the acceptance market by purchasing bills under resale agreements, and the privilege of selling acceptances under such terms is very important to dealers because they operate extensively with borrowed funds. Under certain circumstances, the Reserve banks may even lower their buying rate to prevent the dealers from losing. In addition to supporting the domestic market, the Federal Reserve banks also act as correspondents for foreign central banks by buying and holding bills for them. Their holdings are divided into two classes: those held for their own accounts and those held for foreign correspondents.

Over one-half of the fifty leading accepting institutions, and eight of the first ten, are found in New York. All types of financial institutions participate. National banks, state banks, Edge corporations,[8] subsidiaries of foreign banking houses, private banks, and investment houses are represented in the list of leading acceptance bankers in

[8] On December 24, 1919, "Section 25*a*" was added to the Federal Reserve Act. This is popularly known as the Edge Act (41 Stat. 378, chap. 18). It authorized the organization of corporations for the purpose of engaging in international or foreign banking. Subject to regulation by the Board, the banking powers include the right to purchase, sell, discount, and negotiate or guarantee promissory notes, bills of exchange, cable transfers, and other evidences of indebtedness; to purchase and sell securities with or without endorsement or guarantee; to accept bills or drafts; to issue letters of credit; to purchase and sell coin, bullion, and exchange; to borrow and lend money; to issue debentures and to receive deposits outside the United States and such deposits in the United States as are incidental to the carrying on of its business.

The minimum capital specified was $2,000,000. National banks are permitted to hold stock in such corporations in amounts in the aggregate that are not to exceed 10 per cent of an individual national bank's capital and surplus. Two types of corporations have been organized—one to deal in short-term credit instruments and the second to deal in long-term credit, that is, investment trusts.

this country. The accepting banks not only give acceptance credit and make possible the supply of bills but also are the chief buyers of the accepted drafts. Their holdings are divided into two classes—own bills and bills bought. "Own bills" represent the bills which the holding bank has accepted and, as previously noted, must be reported as loans. When a bank holds its own bills, the fundamental difference between acceptance credit and loan credit breaks down. Under acceptance credit a bank lends only its credit standing and executes the credit by accepting drafts. The drafts are sold in the acceptance market, and the buyers of the drafts finance the transaction. When the bank buys its own acceptances, it is lending the money to the customer, which is the same situation which exists when it lends directly to a borrower. In spite of protests of acceptance dealers, the practice of holding one's own accepted drafts has increased since 1930, which is another factor in the decline in the volume of acceptances as reported by member banks.

Although accepting banks do not lend their funds, they do assume liabilities and should use the same care in this type of financing as in lending on a straight loan basis. Since acceptance credit presents greater opportunity for abuse than straight lending, the Federal Reserve Act provided for more careful limitations and regulations of acceptance credit than for other credit activities of commercial banks.

The regulations of the Board of Governors of the Federal Reserve System, under powers granted in the Federal Reserve Act as amended, cover the important questions of volume, maturity, purpose, and security of acceptance credit. The volume of general acceptance liability which may be assumed at one time by one bank is 50 per cent of its capital and surplus. This rule applies to all member banks, including state member banks, if the latter are authorized by law or charter to deal in acceptance credit. If conditions seem to justify, the Board may permit certain member banks with surpluses of at least 20 per cent to accept for an additional 50 per cent of their capital and surplus, that is, an amount at one time equal to the individual bank's capital and surplus. However, the aggregate of acceptances growing out of the financing of domestic shipments and storage of goods may not exceed 50 per cent of the member bank's capital and surplus. Furthermore, the Board may authorize certain banks to accept bills equal to another 50 per cent of capital and surplus (a total of 150 per cent) when they are drawn by foreign banks for the purpose of furnishing dollar exchange. Drafts or bills drawn for the last purpose are limited to those of maturities of not more than 90 days' sight, exclusive of days of grace, while drafts drawn under the other provisions may have maturities of six months' sight, exclusive of days of grace.[9]

Reference has already been made to the purpose for which member bank acceptance credit may be granted. These include import and export of goods, domestic shipment of goods, shipment of goods between foreign countries, domestic and foreign storage of goods, and creation of dollar exchange.

The rules pertaining to security include the following: If the amount a bank accepts for one name is in excess of 10 per cent of its capital and surplus, the excess credit must be secured by bills of lading, warehouse receipts, or some other form of title document or collateral giving adequate security. If the acceptances result from domestic financing of goods, they must be accompanied by shipping documents or warehouse receipts at the time of acceptance. Bills of exchange resulting from foreign trade need have no specific collateral, but they are usually accompanied by title documents at the time of acceptance.

Banks and Other Agencies Finance Foreign Travel

One function of banks and exchange dealers is to provide travelers with acceptable means of payment for services, hotel accommodations, and goods when traveling abroad. Since it is unwise to carry large sums of currency, two credit instruments have been created to finance travelers, namely, travelers' checks and travelers' letters of credit.

Travelers' checks are printed blanks which may be purchased from banks, express companies, leading hotels, and other agencies, both here and abroad. The purchaser signs his name in the upper left-hand corner on each blank. The blanks, put up in book form, may be in denominations varying from $10 to $200. When issued, the agent collects the full value of the checks, plus a small commission. When they are cashed at banks, hotels, express companies, or at other places, the traveler signs his name in the lower left-hand corner in order to make them negotiable. Travelers' checks may be

[9] See "Regulation C," *Federal Reserve Bulletin*, September, 1946, pp. 996-98.

secured in terms of dollars, sterling, francs, and other currencies. If they are in terms of dollars, they will be paid in foreign countries at the prevailing rate of exchange for sight drafts on New York. To avoid this risk of exchange, travelers' checks may be made up in the terms of the currencies of the countries in which traveling is planned.

The principle involved in the use of travelers' letters of credit is similar to the commercial letter of credit. The issuer (bank) makes it possible for the beneficiary (traveler) to purchase things in the foreign countries in which he is temporarily residing. The letter of credit is a printed form of letter addressed by a bank to its correspondents in foreign countries. It authorizes the beneficiary named in the letter to draw drafts on the issuer, which the correspondent banks are requested to honor. Since this letter of credit establishes the credit of the holder, it is similar to a commercial letter of credit. Because it is addressed to more than one bank, it is sometimes called a circular letter of credit.[10] The drafts drawn under a travelers' letter of credit are negotiated in the presence of the correspondent bank that is asked to cash it. The drafts are unsecured (clean bills), and extra care is taken to see that fraud is not committed.

In order to clarify the use of the travelers' letter of credit, let us assume that Mr. White is planning to travel throughout western Europe, and, in addition to a small quantity of cash and travelers' checks, he wants to use a travelers' letter of credit. He goes to his local bank and arranges for one for $2,000 by depositing and/or assigning his account for $2,000, or depositing and assigning $2,000 worth of marketable securities, or simply signing a paper guaranteeing to pay the drafts as presented. In addition, the bank gives him a special form of letter of introduction on which he writes his signature. This is known as a letter of identification and is used in connection with the letter of credit. This, as well as the letter of credit, will be officially signed by his bank. Since all correspondents have received copies of the official signature, they will be able to determine if the documents are authentic. Finally, Mr. White receives a list of the banks where he may negotiate drafts.

On arriving in London, and desiring pound sterling for shopping and other needs, Mr. White checks the list of correspondents and notes the name of the Chase National Bank. He checks the address

[10] Letters of credit addressed to one bank are known as "special letters of credit."

and then goes to the West End Branch of the bank, which is located at 51 Berkeley Square. In order to obtain a draft for £50, he presents his letter of identification and letter of credit. On a blank provided by the bank, he draws a dollar draft for the equivalent of £50 (assume $200). The bank checks the documents to make certain that the time has not expired, that the letter has not been exhausted by previous withdrawals, and that the signatures are correct. If no further identification is necessary, the bank cashes the draft, provided it shows the number given in the letter of credit and the signature of Mr. White is authentic. Before returning the letter of credit to Mr. White, the bank indicates in the space provided on the reverse side the amount of the draft, the date of negotiation, and the bank's own name. The bank charges a small fee for its services.

The Chase Bank then presents the draft through banking channels to the bank that issued the letter of credit and receives dollar credit in payment, probably at the head office in New York. The New York office collects as it would for a personal check through the local clearinghouse or, if drawn on an out-of-town bank, through the Federal Reserve System. The bank that issued the letter of credit charges Mr. White's account for the amount of the draft, plus a small commission (usually ½ of 1 per cent). This procedure is repeated in Paris, Brussels, Luxembourg, Rome, and other cities, until the total amount of credit is exhausted. The correspondent bank negotiating the draft which exhausts the credit takes up the letter and returns it to the issuing bank. In the meantime, the issuing bank has been called upon to pay the drafts drawn at various places.

Both travelers' checks and travelers' letter of credit may be used to finance travel in the United States. Emphasis has been placed on the use of the travelers' letter of credit to finance travel, but this same document is also used to finance trade when buyers make their purchases in person. Thus, a buyer from a New York department store may contact a seller of china in England and pay for a consignment of goods by drawing a draft under a travelers' letter of credit.

QUESTIONS AND PROBLEMS

1. Identify the following items that sometimes appear on bank statements: (*a*) "Customers liability on letters of credit," (*b*) "Customers liability on acceptances." What are the offsetting items on the liabilities side of the bank statement?

2. Explain how banks are compensated for issuing letters of credit. What risks do they assume?
3. Explain how buyers and sellers of merchandise benefit from the use of commercial letters of credit.
4. What is the fundamental difference between a grant of acceptance credit and an ordinary bank loan? Does this difference break down when the acceptance bank buys its own bills? Explain.
5. What factors in foreign trade explain the wide use of acceptance credits and bills of exchange? Do the merits of trade acceptances and bankers' acceptances justify their use in domestic trade? Why?
6. Show how acceptance credit is used in financing an import of goods. Outline steps taken and give reasons for them. Illustrate by drawing a chart similar to that appearing as Illustration VII.
7. Show how acceptance of credit is used in financing an export of goods when there is no market for the foreign bill of exchange. Outline steps taken and give reasons for them. Use Illustration VII.
8. What are the documents attached to a commercial bill of exchange? Describe them.
9. Assume that a bank has lent and invested all its funds. May it finance its customers by grants of acceptance credits? Would it be justified in doing so? Why?
10. Explain how the storage of cotton may be financed with a grant of acceptance credit.
11. What is meant by the use of acceptance credit to create dollar exchange? Why does the government place geopraphical limitations on the use of this type of acceptance credit?
12. How may acceptance credit be used by an American bank to secure financial help from London? What is the name given to bills drawn under this type of acceptance credit? Are they clean or secured?
13. What institutions are necessary to the existence of a well-developed acceptance market? Why?
14. Explain how banks and other agencies finance foreign travel.
15. The Export-Import Bank of Washington furnishes credit accommodations to exporters and importers, guarantees credit with and without recourse, and makes direct advances. Explain.
16. How have the Federal Reserve banks assisted in the development of the American acceptance market? Explain.
17. American banks have lost funds because of their accepting business, but there is no record of loss suffered by any investor in a bankers' acceptance. Why?

18. Federal Reserve banks' minimum buying rates on bankers' acceptances as established on October 20, 1933, and still in effect on January 31, 1946, were as follows: 1–90 days, ½ of 1 per cent; 91–120 days, ¾ of 1 per cent; and 121-180 days, 1 per cent. Justify the higher rate for the last type of bills. What justification is there for keeping the same rates in effect for such a long period of time? What are the present rates? See current issue of the *Federal Reserve Bulletin.*

19. Check on the current exchange rates for the following in a metropolitan newspaper and past rates in the *Federal Reserve Bulletin:* (*a*) Canadian dollar, (*b*) English pound sterling, (*c*) French franc, (*d*) Netherlands guilder, and (*e*) other rates in which you are interested.

REFERENCES

"Bank Money Orders," *Banking*, May, 1944, pp. 74 and 76.

Baster, A. S. J. "The International Acceptance Market," *American Economic Review,* Vol. XXVII, No. 2 (June, 1937).

Cross, I. B. *Domestic and Foreign Exchange,* chaps. v and vi. New York: Macmillan Co., 1924.

Edwards, G. W. *International Trade Finance,* chaps. i, ii, and iii. New York: Henry Holt & Co., 1924.

Einzig, Paul. *The Theory of Forward Exchange.* London: MacMillan & Co., Ltd., 1937.

Ellsworth, P. T. *International Economics,* Part I and chap. xi in Part II. New York: Macmillan Co., 1938.

Escher, Franklin. *Modern Foreign Exchange,* chaps. i and ii. New York: Macmillan Co., 1935.

Evitt, H. E. *Exchange and Trade Control.* London: Sir Isaac Pitman & Sons, Ltd., 1945.

Feis, H. *The Investment of American Capital Abroad.* New York: Institute on Postwar Reconstruction, New York University, 1945.

Fox, A. M. "Quantitative and Qualitative Changes in International Trade during the Depression," *American Economic Review,* Supplement, Vol. XXVII, No. 1 (March, 1937).

Graham, F. D. "Recent Movements in International Price Level and the Doctrine of Purchasing Power Parity," *American Statistical Association Journal,* Supplement, Vol. XXX (March, 1935).

Heilperin, M. A. *International Monetary Economics,* chap. iv-x. New York: Longmans, Green, & Co., 1939.

Heuser, H. *Control of International Trade.* Philadelphia: P. Blakiston's Sons & Co., Ltd., 1939.

Nadler, M., and White, H. D. *Financing America's Foreign Trade.* New York: Institute of Postwar Reconstruction, New York University, 1945.

Phelps, C. W. "War's Impact on U.S. Banking Abroad," *Banking*, September, 1944, pp. 41 and 118-20.

Prochnow, H. V., and Foulke, R. A. *Practical Bank Credit*, pp. 480-514. New York: Prentice-Hall, Inc., 1940.

Steward, M. S. *What Foreign Trade Means to You.* New York: Public Affairs Committee, 1945.

United States Department of Commerce, Bureau of Foreign and Domestic Commerce. *The Balance of International Payments of the United States.*

Ward, Wilbert. *Bank Credit and Acceptances.* Revised ed. New York: Ronald Press Co., 1931.

Chapter XXV

GOVERNMENT SUPERVISION AND OWNERSHIP OF BANKS

A Swing to the "Left" in Bank Regulation

Since the development of the practice of making loans of bank credit for interest, there have been two schools of thought on banking. One school has felt that banking should be left in the hands of individual bankers, unrestricted by governmental interference. A second group has felt that the government should own and operate the banks. Prior to 1945, Great Britain provided the best illustration of the teachings of the first school. With the exception of note issue, the English banks were subject to no special banking legislation.[1] Russia, where the banks are owned and operated by the government, provides the best illustration of the teachings of the second school.

The status of banking in the United States is somewhere between these two extremes: self-regulation, on the one hand, and nationalization, on the other. For over 100 years commercial banks in the United States have been subject to periodic examinations by government officials, to statutory and regulatory limitations on activities, and to compulsory filing of reports on conditions. From the beginning of chartered banking in the United States, the federal and state governments have, at various times, owned and operated banks.

Within recent years the governments' relations to banks, both in the United States and in many foreign countries, have been much closer.[2] There are many reasons for this current trend to either nationalize banks or regulate their activities more thoroughly. First, it should be recognized that such legislation here and abroad is but a part of the more socialistic character of modern legislation. Second, there is a more general appreciation of the quasi-public nature of the banking business. Third, banks have been recognized as instruments to be used in obtaining the objectives of monetary management.

[1] During 1945 the Bank of England and several of the large banks of deposit in France were nationalized by their respective governments.

[2] See Allen, A. M., and others, *Commercial Bank Regulation and Control*, pp. 3-52.

Who Should Supervise Banks?

For many years governments have regulated and supervised banking in the United States. Today there is controversy over the extent to which regulation should go and as to whether all commercial banks should be placed under federal supervision. There also remains unanswered the question of which of the numerous federal agencies should be dominant in supervision and regulation of commercial banks. Supervision of banks and other financial agencies is now a major government activity, with forty-eight state departments and many federal agencies engaged in this work. There has been a tendency to regulate banks more intensively and to extend supervisory activities to include new agencies as they develop. Thus, after "nearly a century of chartering and supervising banking organizations, the Banking Department [New York State] was directed by legislative enactment in 1944 to broaden its activities to include the licensing and supervising of a relatively new type of business —the business of cashing checks."[3]

Bank supervision covers many activities that have already been considered, including: (1) the organization and liquidation of banks, (2) opening and closing of branches, (3) changes in capitalization, (4) examinations and classification of loans and investments, (5) submission of reports, and (6) issuing of regulations covering detailed administrative procedures such as the computation of reserves, the volume of deposits subject to reserves, the preparation of cash and noncash items for collection, and many others.

National Problem.—To conclude that governments should supervise banks leaves unanswered the questions as to which government and which agency should perform this function. One reformer group asserts that at least those banks which handle checking accounts should be supervised and regulated by the federal government.[4] The power to coin money and regulate its value is vested by the Constitution in Congress; and, since commercial banks now handle the most important means of payment—checking accounts—they

---

[3] *Ninety-fourth Annual Report of the Superintendent of Banks, State of New York,* Part I, Legislative Document (1945), No. 21, p. 5.

[4] The constitutionality of such change cannot be seriously disputed. See Federal Reserve Board, "Constitutionality of Legislation Providing a Unified Commercial Banking System for the United States," *Annual Report,* 1932, pp. 229-59. The chief reason for not passing such legislation is "practical politics."

should likewise be supervised by the national government. In addition, the banking business is national in scope and should be subject to federal control and supervision. Finally, banking disturbances are of national importance and, as illustrated in 1933, can best be eliminated by national action. This group of reformers claims that the ineffectiveness of government control has been due to the dual banking system and the resulting division of responsibility.

The opponents of nationalization of control have argued that many of the advantages of our present dual banking system would be destroyed if all banks were forced to adhere to practices fixed by federal agencies. Among the contentions of this group is the belief that correct banking standards for institutions in one section of the country may not necessarily be the best banking standards for institutions in a second section of the country.

Complexity of the Present Situation.—At present the banks are subject to regulation by various state and federal agencies, with little or no regard for the country's needs as a whole. The complexity of the present structure is suggested by Chart IX. Forty-eight state banking departments are responsible for chartering, closing, regulating, and examining state banks. In 1863 the office of Comptroller of the Currency was created to charter and regulate banks operating under provisions of the National Banking Act. In 1913 the Federal Reserve Act was passed, and it gave to the twelve Federal Reserve banks and the Federal Reserve Board (now Board of Governors of the Federal Reserve System) certain regulatory powers. Originally these powers pertained chiefly to state member banks, but since 1933 they have been enlarged and now deal with such special problems as use of credit for speculation and for consumption.

Since 1931 further confusion has been caused by creation of the Reconstruction Finance Corporation (1932) and the Federal Deposit Insurance Corporation (1934). The Reconstruction Finance Corporation has made loans and purchased preferred stock and capital notes from many banks, and, as a result, it has "proprietory and contractual powers of supervision" over banks that have secured funds from it. The Federal Deposit Insurance Corporation has received many supervisory powers over insured banks which are not members of the Federal Reserve System. In addition, several laws have increased the ability of the Secretary of the Treasury to influence banking practices. The United States Treasury has many

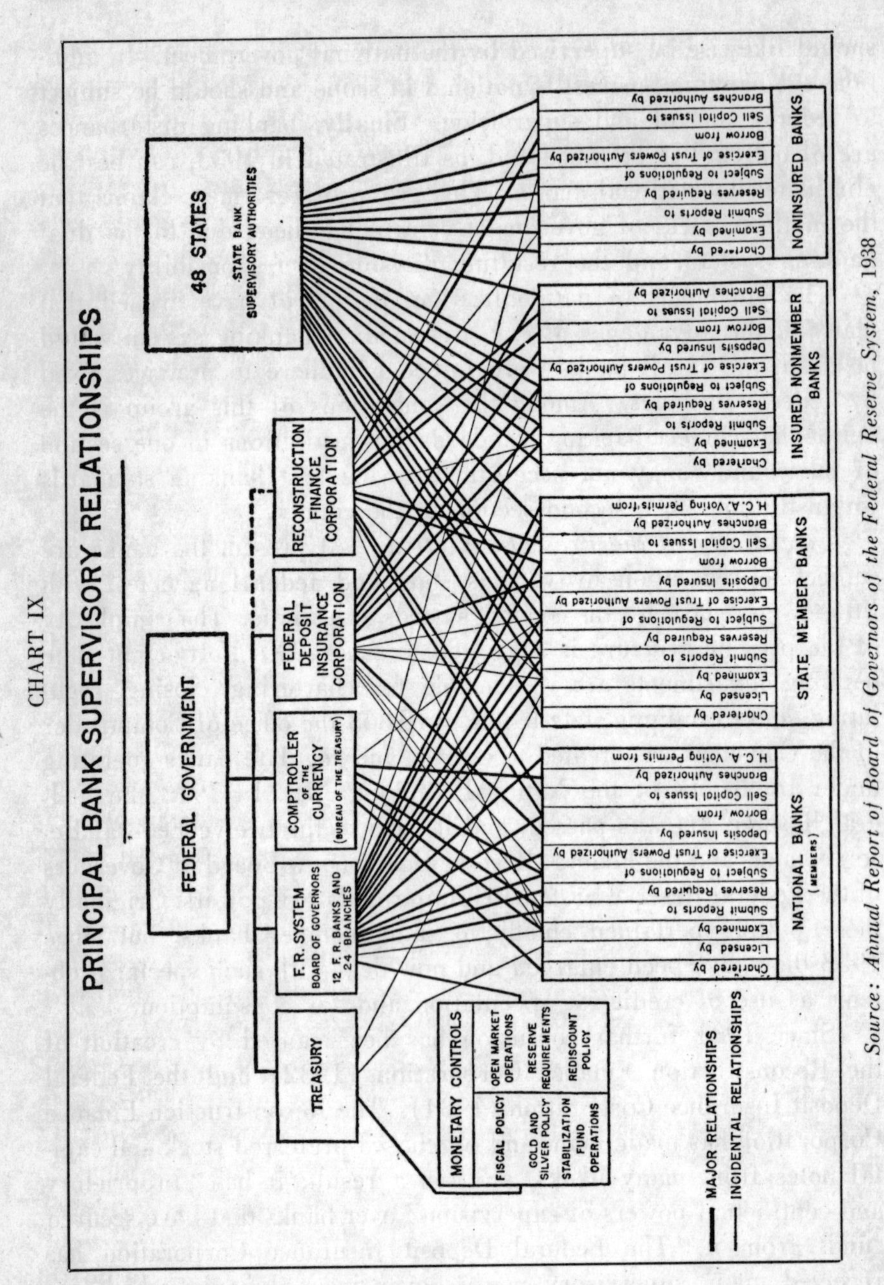

Source: Annual Report of Board of Governors of the Federal Reserve System, 1938

powers over the monetary standard, is responsible for licensing of banks under the 1933 Bank Emergency Act, and must approve purchases of bank stock by the Reconstruction Finance Corporation.

Finally, other federal agencies, such as the Federal Housing Administration, have had considerable influence on special phases of banking.

The present complexity of governmental regulation is confusing even to bankers, because the control of various features of banking is sometimes delegated to two or more agencies. For example, confusion has resulted from the lack of agreement among control agencies as to classification of deposits, definition of interest, and the fixing of maximum interest rates to be paid on time and savings deposits. Movements to charter new banks and license branches have found the federal agencies working in opposition to one another. There is no agreement on policy to be followed in remitting checks at par. Only after many years of delay was a plan worked out to provide for uniformity of examinations and of reporting procedures. Since these arrangements are the result of voluntary agreements, they may be of only temporary importance unless a national act is passed to centralize authority and responsibility.

Office of Comptroller of the Currency Should Be Eliminated.—If the greatest amount of uniformity is to be achieved, the Federal Deposit Insurance Corporation should be made responsible for the regulation and supervision of banks. This corporation, through its insurance of deposits, now contacts about 94 per cent of the commercial banks. With the assistance of an advisory council representing the state superintendents of banking, the Federal Deposit Insurance Corporation is securing increased uniformity in accounting procedure, reporting, examinations, and classification of assets of nonmember banks.

The office of Comptroller of the Currency should be abolished, and all its functions should be transferred to the Federal Deposit Insurance Corporation. The holder of this office should be permitted to continue as one of the three directors of the Federal Deposit Insurance Corporation. However, it must be recognized that an increase in the regulatory powers of this corporation would tend to decrease the credit control authority of the Federal Reserve System. For example, the adoption of strict examination policies by the corporation would tend to nullify an "easy money" policy of the Board, or vice versa.[5] So a final step in the centralization of responsibility

[5] See "Round Table on Banking Reform through Supervisory Standards," *American Economic Review*, Supplement, Vol. XXX, No. 1 (March, 1940), pp. 237-39.

would be to make the directors of the Federal Deposit Insurance Corporation responsible to the Board of Governors of the Federal Reserve System. The resulting centralization of powers would be preferable to the present situation and is perhaps the only politically practical solution to the problem of overlapping supervision.

Creation of State Banking Boards.—Many states have taken steps to improve the regulation and supervision of state-chartered banks and financial institutions. Since the beginning of state regulation of banks, most states have created an office of Superintendent of Banks, which has been responsible for the granting of bank charters, bank examinations, and general supervision of banks. In recent years states have provided for advisory banking boards;[6] and most states have one or more boards concerned with the administration of banking laws.[7] There are three types of banking boards: (1) designated state officials (ex officio); (2) bankers, businessmen, or both; and (3) state officials and others. The functions vary: some are administrative in nature, others purely advisory, and others have certain limited and specific functions. While the powers differ, there are some common to all, including disciplinary powers (to close banks, revoke charters, remove officers and directors), definition of unsafe and unsound banking practices, enlargement upon the list of legal investments for trust funds and savings accounts, study of existing banking practices, and recommendation of legislation.[8]

The Purposes of Bank Examinations

Supervisory officials are interested in enforcing "the common law codification of the standards which good banks have recognized and imposed upon themselves down through the years."[9] Their rules pertain to (1) the requirement of a reasonable capital ratio, (2) liquidity requirements of assets other than reserves, (3) the require-

---

[6] American Bankers Association, Research Council, *Banking Boards, Statutory and Factual Study* (January, 1938).

[7] Connecticut, Delaware, Iowa, New Hampshire, Ohio, and Wisconsin have more than one banking board.

[8] See "Report of the Banking Board for the Year 1945," *Ninety-fifth Annual Report of the Superintendent of Banks, State of New York,* Part I, pp. 58-62.

[9] Upham, C. B., "Round Table on Banking Reform through Supervisory Standards," *American Economic Review,* Supplement, Vol. XXX, No. 1, Part II (March, 1940); "Discussion," p. 235.

ments to hold relatively riskless assets, (4) the control over number of operating banks, and (5) the "requirement for recapitalization, reorganization, or closing of any bank whose assets are found to have a value less than the amount of the liabilities (one definition of insolvency), or less than the amount of liabilities plus the par capital (capital impairment)."[10]

Who Examines Banks?—A bank in the United States may be examined by the following: its own officers or board of directors (some laws require annual examination by directors); by the clearinghouse association of the community in which the bank is located; by the state banking department, in the case of a state-chartered bank; by the Federal Reserve banks, in case of a member bank; by the Comptroller of the Currency, in case of a national bank; by the Federal Deposit Insurance Corporation, in case the bank is not already examined by some other federal agency; and by the Reconstruction Finance Corporation, if the latter has a loan or investment interest in the bank. Some trust departments are examined by local courts having jurisdiction over fiduciary activities.

Specific Purposes of Examinations.—The primary interests of examiners in banks are (1) the finding of evidence of the existence of assets and their legal ownership by the bank and (2) the appraisal of the assets and liabilities of the bank. The examiners try to discover in the least possible time and without disturbing the routine of the bank the financial condition of the institution being examined. The most convenient time for banks to be examined is after the close of business for the day, but the examination of smaller banks usually starts in the morning. Some of the specific purposes of examination are (1) to disclose malpractices of officers and other employees, (2) to uncover inefficiency and carelessness in bank operations, (3) to expose operations which are illegal or unsound, (4) to provide bank officers and directors with a statement of the bank's condition, and (5) to suggest improvements in operating practices and in investment and lending policies. In performing their functions, examiners contribute to better banking by stimulating better bank management.

"The bank examiner has been described as the eyes and ears of

[10] Jones, H., "Round Table on Banking Reform through Supervisory Standards," *American Economic Review,* Supplement, Vol. XXX, No. 1, Part II (March, 1940), p. 230; and *Annual Report of the Federal Deposit Insurance Corporation for the Year Ended December 31, 1938,* pp. 23-25 and 61.

the supervisory agency."[11] After presenting their credentials to the officers of the bank they are going to examine, examiners establish control over the assets and records of the bank. They seal all the vaults or vault compartments containing cash, securities, or notes; take possession of the general ledgers; and take physical possession of cash and other assets at the counters. The latter are verified promptly and then released so that the employees may continue with the routine business of the bank. Next the assets are verified and then released.[12] After physical inspection and a check to insure correct entries, the examiners begin the appraisal of the assets, and this is one of the most important parts of the examiner's duties.

Agreement on Principles.—In 1938 an agreement was reached among the various examining agencies on questions of general principles of examinations. Special attention was given to the most disturbing and controversial problems arising from the loans and investments of banks. If a bank fails, it is usually due to losses, "paper" or real, originating in sour loans and/or investments. If examiners adopt a rule that investments must be carried at "cost or market whichever is the lower," many downward adjustments must be made during periods of declining business, falling security prices, etc. The effects of this practice were clearly demonstrated in 1930, 1931, and 1932, when much unnecessary liquidation of bank credit, and even bank failures, was traceable to examiners' reports on conditions of banks. The psychological effects resulting from having assets classified as "slow," "doubtful," and "loss" (replaced in 1938-39 by Groups II, III, and IV), which later may be paid in full, are disturbing.

During business recovery bank loans and investments may show hidden profits, owing to increases in market values of securities. The examiner's "pat on the back" during such periods encourages bankers to make more loans and investments, thereby contributing to the inflationary developments in process during the upswing in the business cycle. In the past, bank examinations and reports contributed to the inflationary and deflationary factors at work during the business cycle.

---

[11] See Members of the Staff, Board of Governors of the Federal Reserve System, *Banking Studies*, p. 219.

[12] Verification includes any necessary correspondence with correspondent banks to check on securities held by them as custodians for the bank being examined.

In 1938 the revision in bank examination procedure agreed to by federal agencies and accepted in principle by representatives of the National Association of Supervisors of State Banks abandoned the slow classification of assets and stressed the principle of safety rather than those of liquidity, quick maturity, or marketability, as measured by day-to-day market fluctuations. Other changes were made, including the recommendation that larger accounting reserves should be kept in order to offset loan and investment losses. If the new rules are enforced and if responsibility for the supervision of banks is centralized, the future record of bank supervision should be an improvement over its past record.

Why Not Nationalize Banks?

The proposal to nationalize banks has received warm support from many students who feel that under private ownership there can be no solution for chronic banking troubles. There are many arguments to support their position, particularly in regard to commercial banks, which handle our most important means of payment. The arguments are similar to those already referred to in justification of bank supervision. In addition, those favoring nationalization are critical of the record of government supervision, without recognizing that the latter has never been given a trial on a national scale.

The chief objection to government operation of banks is the type of management that would probably result. The major dangers in governmental banking are the inability of the government bankers to say "no" for fear of making political enemies and the inability to collect loans after they have been made, for the same reason. These dangers are particularly great in a democracy, where everyone has an equal vote in elections.

In the foregoing pages reference has been made to the changing nature of commercial bank assets as reflected in their statements. Now all but a small percentage of their assets are in the form of government obligations or assets guaranteed by some governmental agency. When the liabilities of banks were considered, it was noted how the government found it desirable, if not imperative, to create a system of deposit insurance. In making provisions for intensive and extensive regulation and supervision of banks, reference was made to the tendency to include more types of credit, more credit agencies, and more detailed items that might more properly be handled by bank management.

Emphasis has been placed on the importance of bank management. Now the question may properly be asked, management of what? If the primary function of a bank, or a financing agency, is to appraise and assume risks, then what risks? If the primary function of banks is to handle checking accounts of a community, then is there justification for the present type of bank management, which presupposes the existence of many of the traditional risk-taking functions of banks? If banks are not directly facilitating the production of goods and services by making commercial loans to local industry without guarantee by the government, may not the public be paying too much for bank management? Finally, if banking is to be a business that involves the administration of only routine activities, may it not be more efficiently carried on by the government? For years political scientists and economists have recognized that this type of activity is suited to government operation.

Another argument in favor of nationalization of commercial banks is that banks have been permitted to increase their income by using a government prerogative of creating means of payment. In "monetizing" the national debt, the commercial banks are receiving compensation in the form of interest payments for performing a government function. May not this function be performed more economically by governmental agencies?

To raise these questions is not to advocate nationalization of commercial banks but to direct attention to the current reasoning on this subject. Abroad, there has been an increase in the number of banks of deposit that have been nationalized for the reasons suggested. For those who are in favor of the continuance of the present private banking system, the line of action is obvious, that is, a return to the traditional type of banking, which involves less dependence on government credit either in the form of guaranteed loans or in the form of direct government obligations.

At every session of Congress numerous bills are introduced that would extend the guarantee principle to include additional lending. Usually such bills are sponsored, or at least approved, by the agency responsible for the guarantee of credit. Some of the legislation providing for guarantee of credit has had the sponsorship of bankers, as illustrated by the Export-Import Act of 1945. Other more far-seeing bankers have protested against this development, and the Federal Deposit Insurance Corporation has called attention to the "serious long-run implications to the free enterprise system."

At the present time banks have regained public esteem, which was at such a low ebb during the 1930's. They have protested against multiplication of governmental agencies in the lending field; but they have not extended the credit that made the creation of these agencies necessary. This may not be the fault of the individual banks but of the unit banking system. However, many banks are increasing the types of services offered to their customers. This suggests that the existing financing devices are adequate in number, flexibility, and variety to satisfy all the legitimate needs of business.

Government Corporations and Credit Agencies

To dismiss the "nationalization" movement of banks by calling it "socialistic" is to ignore the extent to which government ownership and operation of financing institutions has already appeared in the specialized fields of finance. Every issue of the *Federal Reserve Bulletin* contains statements showing the assets and liabilities of government corporations and credit agencies. Most of these institutions have been considered elsewhere in this book, and they are noted here merely to emphasize the extent to which the federal government has gone into the banking field.

Most of the government corporations and credit agencies were provided for by Congress during the depression of 1931 to 1934; but the federal land banks were authorized in 1916, the intermediate credit banks in 1922, and others during World War II. When the lending activities of the government corporations and credit agencies are considered, agriculturalists and homeowners are the chief beneficiaries. Among the other beneficiaries are railroads, banks, and industry. Over one-half of the total assets, other than interagency, are in the form of investments in buildings and equipment. During World War II the volume of credit extended by government corporations and credit agencies in financing the war effort expanded rapidly, but liquidation of farm and home mortgage loans that had been in process since 1936 continued. Although the assets of some agencies declined, the total increased from $14,600,000,000 in 1941 to over $34,000,000,000 before the end of hostilities. (See Table 31.)

TABLE 31

GOVERNMENT CORPORATIONS AND CREDIT AGENCIES
(In Millions of Dollars)

Corporation or Agency (Sept. 30, 1945)	Total Assets*	U.S. Government Interest‖	Privately Owned Interest‖
Department of Agriculture:			
Farm Credit Administration			
Banks for co-operatives	234	227	7
Federal intermediate credit banks	346	75	....
Federal land banks	1,279	176	227
Production credit corporation	123	123	....
Regional Agricultural Credit Corp.	15	14	....
Others†	21	19	....
Federal Farm Mortgage Corp.	244	232	....
Rural Electrification Administration	398	398	....
War Food Administration			
Commodity Credit Corp.	1,545	505	....
Farm Security Administration	469	465	....
Federal Crop Insurance Corp.	36	31	....
Federal Surplus Commodities Corp.	3	3	....
National Housing Agency:			
Federal Home Loan Bank Administration			
Federal home loan banks	300	125	92
Federal Savings and Loan Insurance Corp.	162	100	....
Home Owners' Loan Corp.	985	945	....
Federal Public Housing Authority and affiliate			
Federal Public Housing Authority	550	540	....
Defense Homes Corp.	58	67	....
Federal Housing Administration	163	122	....
Federal National Mortgage Association	9	9	....
R.F.C. Mortgage Company	59	55	....
Reconstruction Finance Corp.‡	9,980	8,475	....
Office of Emergency Management:			
Smaller War Plants Corp.	176	175	....
War Shipping Administration	8,844	7,827	....
Others§	489	219	....
Export-Import Bank	230	141	....
Federal Deposit Insurance Corp.	923	150	139
Federal Works Agency	254	254	....
Tennessee Valley Authority	750	742	....
U.S. Maritime Commission	3,586	3,454	....
All others	2,005	1,942	....
All agencies	34,247	27,610	465

* Other than interagency items.

† Includes Agricultural Marketing Act Revolving Fund and Emergency Crop and Feed Loans.

‡ Includes 5 former affiliates now merged with R.F.C.; also includes War Damage Corp., an affiliate.

§ Includes 4 affiliates.

‖ Differences between totals of U.S. government interest plus private interests and total assets are due to use of borrowed funds and retention of earnings.

Source: Federal Reserve Bulletin, January, 1946, p. 67.

Permanent Banks Are Financed with or without Government Credit

Many of the permanent governmental institutions are, or will be, financed without the use of government credit. The present plan, under which several operate, calls for the sale of government-owned shares to private interests. The most important so-called government banks are the twelve federal land banks, the twelve federal home loan banks, the thirteen banks for co-operatives, and over a thousand federal savings and loan associations.

Many governmental institutions classified as permanent will be financed permanently in whole or in part with federal government funds. This group includes the twelve intermediate credit banks, the twelve production credit corporations, the Federal Deposit Insurance Corporation, the Federal Savings and Loan Insurance Corporation, and the Export-Import Bank of Washington. Although the billion dollar Postal Savings System has no capital, it should also be included in this second group.

Will the Government Collect?—Many individuals question the ability of the government to collect these loans amounting to billions of dollars. The book value of assets justifies the assumption that the government will be able to collect them. The spread between the cost of funds used by the agencies and the amount received by them from private and other borrowers is large enough to cover all costs of operations and a normal amount of bad loans. The major test will come when government banks are forced to take steps to collect from those who are able but unwilling to pay. To date the collections by all government banks have been good, and the percentage of delinquencies has been below expectations. Many debts have been entirely liquidated, and the volume of individual mortgages held by government banks is at the lowest level since 1936.

Economic Significance of Government Financing Is Far-Reaching in Possibilites

Just how the experiment in government banking will affect the future of American banking is impossible to say. At present there is a tendency for legislatures to expand governmental banking facilities whenever the need appears to be great enough to justify this move. The present plan is a compromise calling for greater supervision, regulation, and restriction, with emphasis on national control. The government has succeeded in making the nation "interest conscious," and practically all interest rates have been reduced, and much of this gain to borrowers is expected to be permanent. The government banks have made wise use of the amortization or installment plan of repaying loans, and this practice is being followed to an increasing extent by private lenders.

In urban mortgage lending, agricultural banking, and household or personal financing, emphasis is placed upon co-operative financing with government assistance. If cheaper credit results, it means better homes and higher standards of living for farmers, wage earners, and the middle classes. As long as the government keeps a financial institution responsible for all loans between the government financing agency and the borrower, the dangers of political favoritism will be held in check. The chief danger in the present situation is that all types of lenders and borrowers will, in the future, place too much reliance upon the government in emergencies.

Sooner or later the government must answer questions of the proper sphere of activity of government-owned banks, on the one hand, and privately owned banks, on the other. Many commercial bankers claim that they do not want the types of loans made by government agencies, others claim that the government is driving them out of business, but a majority of the bankers probably stand in between these two extremes. When bankers come into competition with the permanent government financing agencies, they feel that they have a just cause for complaint. They say that they are forced to compete with interest rates that are unfair to them as private lenders. In most cases the government banks are tax free, in whole or in part, and, in addition, they are sometimes given the free use of government funds (invested in the capital stock). Owing to these and to other types of government subsidies, they are able to offer lower rates than the banks can meet. The probability is that (1) many of the existing institutions will be a permanent part of our financial structure, (2) many of the temporary institutions or similar ones will be revived during the next major depression, and (3) banking will henceforth be looked upon as a permanent aspect of the federal government's activities "with indefinitely great possibilities of expansion and multiplication."[13]

[13] Cleveland Trust Company, *Business Bulletin*, Vol. XVII, No. 12 (December 15, 1936).

In the words of Chairman Eccles of the Board of Governors of the Federal Reserve System, "the Government must be looked upon as a compensatory agency in this economy to do just the opposite to what private business and individuals do." Thus when the period of deflation arrives, the government's policy must be such as to maintain "a more uniform availability of money and to encourage a more uniform flow or velocity than we had in the past."[14]

QUESTIONS AND PROBLEMS

1. Explain carefully the reasons why governments regulate commercial banks.
2. Who should supervise banks? Explain.
3. What future changes should be made in the centralization of supervisory activities of the federal agencies over banking? (Hood, G. P., "Future of Bank Supervision, *Banking*, November, 1939, p. 107).
4. What are the purposes of bank supervision and bank examination? Explain.
5. Surveying legislation on credit, rates of interest, investments, and other phases of bank management, "their chief emphasis has been on the minor aspects of banking and has not produced results of which this country can be proud. Other countries which have had a more successful banking history than ours—notably England—have a minimum of such minor laws" (Gephart, W. F., "Our Commercial Banking System," *American Economic Review*, Supplement, Vol. XXV [March, 1935], p. 85). What should be the future bank legislative program of the United States?
6. "Undoubtedly banking is the most important single public utility in our economy. If in private hands it cannot operate to serve the public, its nationalization seems imperative" (Clark, *The Internal Debts of the United States*, p. 404). Do you agree? Why?
7. Congressman J. B. Hollister proposed that a commission modeled after the National Monetary Commission should be created to study the banking problems of the country. Make a list of the topics which you think should be studied.
8. Is one justified in assuming that the American public places too much importance in government supervision of banks?
9. In 1938 what changes were made in the classification of bank assets? Why were these changes significant? Explain.
10. What specific things do examiners do in making bank examinations? Why?

[14] *Commercial and Financial Chronicle*, December 26, 1936, p. 4091.

11. "The Corollary of the proposition that men are not competent to manage the details of their private affairs is that they are not competent to manage public affairs" (Pound, Roscoe, *Banking*, December, 1938, p. 78). Do you think the quotation above has any bearing on governmental supervision and regulation of commercial banking?
12. What is the long-run danger to the private banking system in the guarantee by government of specific bank assets?
13. Why should not the government nationalize the commercial banks? What is the present tendency here and abroad? What other alternative is there?
14. Explain: "The wartime boom in bank earnings differs from that in many other industries in that the supporting conditions will not disappear with the end of the war—the earning assets of the banks will continue at substantially their present level or will increase" (*Source:* Seltzer, L. H., "Is a Rise in Interest Rates Desirable or Inevitable?" *American Economic Review*, Vol. XXXV [December, 1945], pp. 845-46).
15. Does the federal government assume risks through the Reconstruction Finance Corporation which it will not allow banks and, indirectly, the Federal Deposit Insurance Corporation to assume? Explain.
16. "For commercial banks the ultimate end of ever expanding governmental investing and lending would be conversion into mere safety deposit boxes for government securities." Long before this goal is reached what would probably happen to commercial banks? *Source:* Jacoby, N. H., "The Government Loan Agencies and Commercial Banking," *American Economic Review*, Supplement, Vol. XXXII [March, 1942], p. 258).

REFERENCES

Allen, A. M., and Others. *Commercial Banking Legislation and Control*, pp. 3-52; 377-475. London: MacMillan & Co., Ltd.

Altman, I. B. "Proposal for Complete Government Ownership of Currency and Credit," *Annals of American Academy of Political and Social Sciences*, Vol. CLXXXIII (January, 1936), pp. 157-62.

Anderson, G. E. "Government Lending Agencies," *Banking*, November, 1938, pp. 97-109.

Dowrie, G. W. *American Monetary and Banking Policies*, chap. iv. New York: Longmans, Green & Co., 1930.

Economic Intelligence Service of the League of Nations. *Money and Banking*, Vol. I, "Monetary Review"; Vol. II, "Commercial and Central Banks." New York: Agent, Columbia University Press, 1939.

Gayer, A. D. (ed.). *The Lessons of Monetary Experience*, pp. 3-22. New York: Farrar & Rinehart, Inc., 1937.

Harr, Luther, and Harris, W. C. *Banking Theory and Practice*, chap. xxvii. 2d ed. New York: McGraw-Hill Book Co., Inc., 1936.

Jacoby, N. H. "Government Loan Agencies and Commercial Banking," *American Economic Review*, Supplement, Vol. XXXII (March, 1942), pp. 250-60.

Members of the Staff, Board of Governors of the Federal Reserve System. *Banking Studies*, pp. 189-227. Washington: Board of Governors of the Federal Reserve System, 1941.

Morton, W. A. "Liquidity and Solvency," *American Economic Review*, Vol. XXIX, No. 2 (June, 1939), pp. 272-85.

O'Connor, J. F. T. *Banking Crisis and Recovery under the Roosevelt Administration*. Chicago: Callaghan & Co., Inc., 1938.

"Round Table on Banking Reform through Supervisory Standards," *American Economic Review*, Supplement, Vol. XXX, No. 1, Part II (March, 1940), pp. 230-40.

Seltzer, L. H. "Is a Rise in Interest Rates Desirable or Inevitable?" *American Economic Review*, Vol. XXXV (December, 1945), pp. 831-50.

Watkins, L. L. *Commercial Banking Reform in the United States*, chap. iv. Ann Arbor: University of Michigan, School of Business Administration, Bureau of Business Research, 1938.

See also: Annual reports of Board of Governors of the Federal Reserve System, Comptroller of the Currency, Federal Deposit Insurance Corporation, Federal Home Loan Bank Board, Reconstruction Finance Corporation, and the Secretary of the Treasury. Also see references at the end of Chaps. XX and XXII.

CHAPTER XXVI

THE ORGANIZATION OF THE FEDERAL RESERVE SYSTEM

Central Banks Are Responsible for the Smooth Working of the Credit System

Central banks are defined as banks of issue which act as fiscal agents for their governments and which hold all or a large part of the banking reserves of their commercial banking systems. The formulation of central banking principles are of fairly recent origin, even though the organization of central banks dates from the second half of the seventeenth century. Fairly early in the history of banking, theorists recognized that the "code of behavior" suitable for a commercial bank was not appropriate for a central bank. However, for almost two hundred years it was customary for the directors of the Bank of England to answer criticisms of the bank's policies by saying that "after all, their bank was just a bank like any other." In 1873 this position of the directors of the Bank of England was attacked in an unanswerable way by Walter Bagehot.[1] Now it is generally accepted that central banks must follow credit and currency policies that may be just the opposite of those followed by noncentral banks.

Fiscal Agents for Governments.—From the beginning of their history, central banks had one function that distinguished them from other commercial banks—they were the bankers of their respective governments. In this capacity they accepted government deposits, managed the public debt, and paid out funds on the orders of the Treasury. Many of them, including the Bank of England, the Bank of France, and the two defunct banks of the United States, trace their origin directly to the fiscal needs of the state.

Never before in history have the fiscal problems of the state been of such magnitude as they are at the present time. Although governmental control is not necessary in order to obtain the assistance of central banks, it is not surprising to find that modern governments are demanding and securing greater voice in the management of their respective central banks. Perhaps the most significant among

[1] Bagehot, Walter, *Lombard Street*, chaps. vii and viii.

these recent developments was the nationalization of the Bank of England in 1946.

Banks of Issue.—In return for assuming the responsibility of acting as fiscal agents for their governments, central banks receive the privilege of bank note issue. Because of this right, central banks are in a position to obtain those assets which are so necessary for the proper performance of their functions. For many years the privilege was shared with noncentral banks, but now central banks have acquired or are in the process of acquiring a monopoly of the right of bank note issue. In most countries, the United States being the chief exception, the governments have delegated the entire function of issuing paper money to their respective central banks. In addition to securing many "free services," governments usually share in the profits of central banks.

Custodians of Reserves.—It is chiefly because of the central banks' right to issue new paper money that there developed the last and most important function of central banks—the control over and responsibility for the maintenance of a sound system of credit. Early in the history of central banking, noncentral banks found it desirable to keep reserve deposits with their respective central banks. The exigencies of commercial banking demand that commercial banks be in a position to secure new cash in times of need. By keeping reserve deposits with their bank of issue, they are able to tap the one important source of new domestic funds. This practice, which is now required by law or custom, places great responsibility on the central banks. It means that central banks cannot be operated for "profit" as ordinary financial institutions. In order to be in a position to aid business when there is an unusual demand for currency and credit, central banks must keep idle a large part of their lending and investing powers. Therefore, the reserve ratios of central banks are usually very high in comparison to those of other banks. Since the central banks are responsible for most of the reserves of their respective countries, their investments must be in low-yielding, liquid, and safe investments; as a result, their investment earnings per dollar of assets are far less than those of other financial institutions.

The public is no longer satisfied with passive central banking functions such as acting as government bankers, banks of issue, and custodians of reserves. It holds that central banks are responsible for the smooth workings of its credit system. During periods of business booms, central banks are expected to adopt policies that will prevent overexpansion of business and excessive speculation. During periods of business recessions and depressions, central banks are expected to adopt policies that will check these developments and bring about business recovery. Central banks are expected to adopt active programs that will keep the volume of business, employment, and prices on an even keel in so far as monetary and credit action permit.

The Activities of Central Banks

All important countries now possess some type of central bank. The oldest, the Bank of Sweden, was established in 1668, twenty-eight years before the organization of the most famous, the Bank of England. Among the newest central banks are those of Ireland (1943), Nicaragua (1940), and Paraguay (1941). The wealthiest and most powerful, the Federal Reserve System of the United States, began operations in November, 1914.

The chief activities of central banks are those which come under the classification of policy decisions and those which are of a routine or semi-mechanical nature. In the first class are included all policies affecting the supply of money and credit (quantity control) and the general use of money and credit (quality control). The routine functions of central banks include (1) handling of money and checks, (2) sale and redemption of government securities, and (3) paying of funds on order of the government. Most of the 25,000 officers and employees of the twelve Federal Reserve banks and their twenty-four branches are performing routine or mechanical functions not involving any important policy decisions.

Defects of the Old National Banking System

The chief weaknesses of the National Banking System before the existence of the Federal Reserve System were: (1) lack of a central bank, (2) inelasticity of credit and currency, (3) pyramiding of reserves, (4) faulty domestic and foreign exchange systems, (5) an inadequate bill market, (6) lack of an independent government fiscal agent, and (7) discriminatory laws.

No Central Bank.—No single bank or group of banks was responsible for the general credit policy of the country, and gold reserves were scattered. Even though the banks in the United States held more gold than those in any other one country, the gold supply could not be effectively used in a national or international emergency.

Inelastic Credit and Currency.—Credit and currency systems were inelastic, because the rigid reserve requirements prevented an expansion of credit during an emergency, and national bank notes did not expand and contract readily with changes in the demand for currency. The inelasticity of credit was far more serious than the inelasticity of currency, although the latter has been emphasized more than the former.

Banks were often in the ironical position of being unable to lend, even though they possessed millions of dollars in gold, gold certificates, and other forms of currency. The 25 per cent minimum reserve requirement of the old National Banking System made it illegal for banks in New York to lend, no matter how great the needs of their customers when the reserve ratio was less than the legal requirement. Bank customers with excellent credit were refused loans on the plea that "we have no funds," even though they may have been in a position to see hundreds of thousands, or even millions, of dollars lying in the bank. Private bankers, operating both in the investment and in the commercial banking fields, were not subject to minimum reserve requirements; they were in a position to be dictators of the capital and money markets, a position which they were not loath to assume to their advantage.[2]

Pyramiding of Reserves.—Owing to the faulty reserve system of permitting small banks to keep part of their reserves with large banks, and also because of the practice of counting "items in process of collection" as reserves, a local panic often grew into a national calamity. Banks located in "country districts" were permitted to keep two-fifths of their legal reserves (15 per cent of deposits) in currency in their own vaults and three-fifths with larger banks; banks located in reserve cities were permitted to keep one-half of their legal reserves in their own vaults and one-half with larger banks; and banks located in central reserve cities were required to keep all their legal reserves in currency in their own vaults. Since 2 per cent

[2] See Morey, Lewis, *The House of Morgan;* and Larson, H. M., *Jay Cooke, Private Banker.*

interest was paid on bankers' balances, there was a tendency to keep in a bank's own vaults the minimum percentage of its required cash reserves. As a result, there was considerable "pyramiding" of reserves in New York, Chicago, and St. Louis (central reserve bank cities).

As a result of this system of redepositing reserves, a local run on banks located in Auburn, New York, might have led to a demand for currency on banks located in Buffalo, Rochester, and Syracuse. Banks in these communities would have drawn on banks located in Chicago and New York, where almost all unusual monetary demands were ultimately felt. During ordinary times it was easy for banks to withdraw their funds, for there was a tendency for new reserve deposits to offset the withdrawals; but, during emergencies, banks throughout the nation were demanding currency from their correspondent banks in the large cities. It was usually difficult for city banks to get additional currency, for there was no central bank on which to draw and no type of elastic currency which could be expanded readily in order to meet the unusual need for hand-to-hand currency. Furthermore, there was a natural tendency on the part of the banks to keep what currency they had in order to maintain their own legal reserve ratios. The refusals to make new loans and to renew old ones caused forced selling of commodities and securities, high interest rates, and general conditions which are usually described as a "money panic." It is little wonder that the old National Banking System was called the "panic-breeder."

Faulty Domestic and Foreign Exchange Systems.—The domestic exchange system contained many defects and was very expensive. Many checks were not collected at par, others were sent in roundabout journeys to avoid exchange charges, and the "float" (volume of items in process of collection) was large. Items in process of collection were counted as reserves, and domestic exchange rates fluctuated above and below par in a manner similar to foreign exchange.

Inadequate Bill Market.—There was no bill or acceptance market in the United States, and foreign banks financed most of the foreign trade of this country. Secondary reserves of American banks were primarily in the form of call loans, because surplus funds of banks flowed to the call loan market. The result was a close alliance between speculation and commercial banking. There was a need for a broader market for commercial, industrial, and agricultural paper and a reduction in spread between interest rates in different sections of the country.

No Independent Government Fiscal Agent.—There was no central bank to serve as fiscal agent for the government, which operated its own independent Treasury system. Under this system, the government operated banking offices in eleven cities in the United States. Originally, attempts were made to collect revenues and pay bills in specie, but this system of specie banking broke down during the Civil War, when banks were forced to suspend specie payments.[3] After the passage of the National Banking Act and the chartering of new national banks, the practice developed of keeping deposits with these banks and of using their capacities in a limited way as fiscal agents of the government.

After 1865 the division of government cash between commercial banks and the United States Treasury offices was subject to the whim of the Secretary of the Treasury. A policy of collecting specie and placing it in the Treasury offices was very disturbing during periods of heavy tax collections and governmental payments. The cycle was one of low bank reserves and high interest rates, followed by high bank reserves and low interest rates. These disturbing effects on credit could be avoided only by a policy of keeping all the government funds on deposit with banks, a policy which most secretaries of the Treasury followed only in part. Additional problems arose concerning the selections of banks to use as depositories and decisions as to how much was to be kept on deposit with each one. This situation brought about many charges of political favoritism.

Discriminatory Federal Laws.—The national bankers claimed that they were in an unfair competitive position because they could not carry on trust activities, conduct an investment banking business, make real estate loans, and carry on a savings bank business on the same legal basis as state-chartered institutions. The growth of these types of banking during the period following the Civil War and the decline in the relative importance of national banks seemingly justified their demands for more liberal general banking laws.

Following the panic of 1907, Congress passed the Aldrich-Vreeland Act, which provided for the issuance of emergency currency

---

[3] Kinley, David, "The Independent Treasury of the United States and Its Relations to the Banks of the Country," *Publications of the National Monetary Commission*, Vol. VII.

and the creation of the National Monetary Commission. The commission consisted of nine members of the Senate and nine members of the House of Representatives. It employed college professors to make studies of banking and currency both at home and abroad. Twenty-three volumes were published as a result of this investigation, and this collection of studies is the greatest single contribution to banking literature. The studies served as a basis for a proposed bill (called the Aldrich bill, after the chairman of the commission) to remedy the defects in the banking structure. Owing to a change in political control in Washington, the bill was not enacted, but the studies had considerable influence on the members of Congress and the administration responsible for the Federal Reserve Act.

There Are Five Divisions of the Federal Reserve System

The Federal Reserve System was created under provisions of an act signed by President Wilson on December 23, 1913. The Federal

CHART X

ORGANIZATION OF THE FEDERAL RESERVE SYSTEM

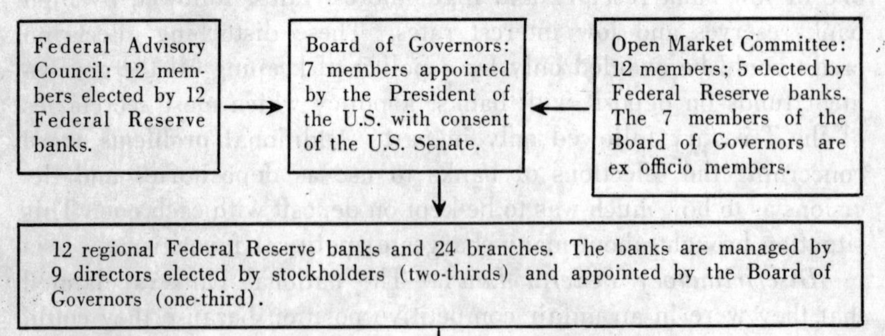

Reserve Act, with many supplementary amendments, provided for one of the most unusual banking systems in history. The preamble, or long title, of it is: "An act to provide for the establishment of Federal Reserve banks, to furnish an elastic currency, to afford means

of rediscounting commercial paper, to establish a more effective supervision of banking in the United States, and for other purposes."

The framers had as their purpose the strengthening of the existing banking structure without changing fundamentally the existing unit banking system. The chief elements of the Federal Reserve System are: (1) the Board of Governors of the Federal Reserve System; (2) the Open Market Committee; (3) the Federal Advisory Council; (4) the twelve Federal Reserve banks and their twenty-four branches; and (5) over six thousand member banks. The organization of the Federal Reserve System is shown in Chart X.

The Regional Plan Was Adopted

The framers of our central banking system believed that the economic interests of the United States could be cared for more rationally by twelve regional banks than by one central bank. The one central bank plan, which is customary abroad, was opposed on economic, geographical, and political grounds. The United States had had experience with one central bank plan, 1791-1811 and 1816-36, and did not favor it, because the American people are traditionally opposed to a great concentration of financial power. Wall Street, and what it stands for, is and was mistrusted by the majority of the American people.

The Federal Reserve System was created and developed under the jurisdiction of the Democratic party, which is traditionally in favor of state rights and in opposition to concentration of powers. In banking reform it favored the regional central banking system over the one central banking system. As a result of the Federal Reserve Act, the United States was divided into twelve districts, and a central bank was placed in each. This resulting decentralization is a peculiar but important characteristic of central banking in the United States. It permits the treatment of many local banking problems by regional Reserve banks and their branches, which are managed by directors and officers who are residents of their respective districts. A Federal Reserve Board (now Board of Governors), with adequate powers to make the system a national one in everything except name, was created to serve as the central controlling and directing agency for the Federal Reserve System.

The members of the Federal Reserve Board did not take office until August 10, 1914, and the difficult task of dividing the continental United States into districts and selecting cities as sites for Federal Reserve banks was given to an Organization Committee of three men—the Secretary of the Treasury, the Comptroller of the Currency, and the Secretary of Agriculture. The committee was permitted by law to form not less than eight nor more than twelve districts, with a Federal Reserve bank in each.

The Organization Committee held public hearings in eighteen cities; gave each national bank an opportunity to state by card ballot

ILLUSTRATION VIII

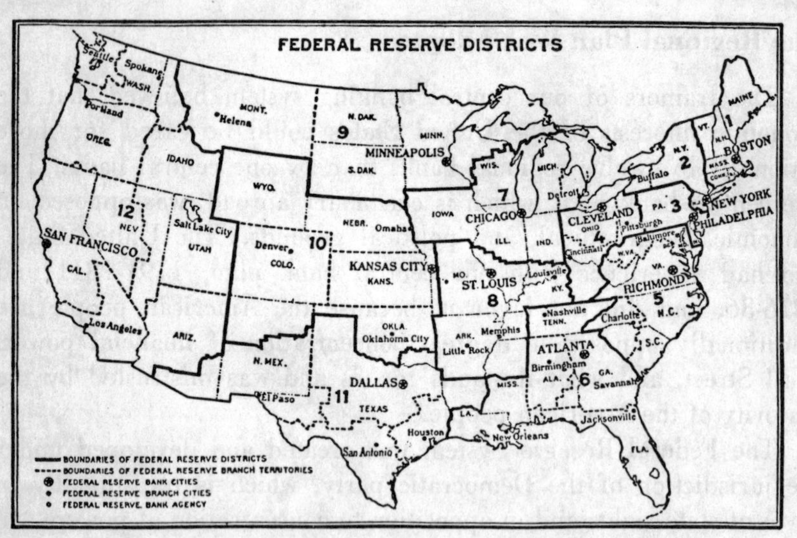

its choice of location for the Federal Reserve bank with which it desired to be connected; received petitions from clearinghouse associations, chambers of commerce, or other representatives of two hundred cities; and received requests from thirty-seven cities to be designated as the site of a Federal Reserve bank.

After three months of investigation, the Organization Committee announced its decision to create the maximum number of banks and districts, with Reserve banks in each of the following cities: Boston, New York, Philadelphia, Cleveland, Richmond, Atlanta, Chicago, St. Louis, Minneapolis, Kansas City, Dallas, and San Francisco. (See Illustration VIII.)[4] The economic factors which guided the

[4] For a criticism of the location of the districts and banks, see Willis, H. P., *The Federal Reserve System*, pp. 587-89.

Organization Committee in its work were: (1) existing financial, mercantile, and industrial relations between areas and cities within the proposed Federal Reserve districts; (2) normal transportation and communication facilities; (3) prevailing business activities within a region; (4) probable ability of the Reserve bank to serve its district; and (5) equitable distribution of member banks among the districts, with particular care taken to see that the future member banks in the district would be able to subscribe the required capital ($4,000,000) for each Reserve bank.

Although the Federal Reserve Board was authorized to adjust, after careful review, the organization map of the Federal Reserve System, no changes were made in location of regional banks, and only minor changes were made in district boundaries. Disappointed financial and commercial groups in cities desiring Federal Reserve banks were later appeased in part, with branch banks. Subsequently, branches were located in such important cities as New Orleans, Baltimore, Pittsburgh, Denver, Detroit, Omaha, Buffalo, and Cincinnati.

The Federal Reserve Bank of New York Is the Most Important

One of the chief arguments in favor of the decentralized central banking system, as adopted, was the mistrust of big business. However, it was inevitable that one or more of the Federal Reserve banks would be of greater importance than the others. Since the Federal Reserve Bank of New York was located in the wealthiest city in the world, where the clearinghouse banks alone own more banking resources than all the banks in the United Kingdom, it is not surprising to find that, during the history of the Federal Reserve System, the assets of this bank have represented between 20 and 45 per cent of the total assets of the System.

During the war years, many changes in the domestic economy were reflected in the Federal Reserve statistics. Notable among these was an increase in the relative improvement in financial position of the South and the West and of communities in which steel and other heavy industries are important. While the changes in the relative importance of districts, as measured by changes in Federal Reserve bank assets alone, may be objected to, the fact remains that other statistics support the conclusion that the relative importance of the Federal Reserve Bank of New York has declined. However, this bank is still the wealthiest central bank in the world. It is located in District 2 (see Illustration VIII), which consists of New York State and parts of New Jersey and Connecticut. It has one branch located in Buffalo. The activities of the Federal Reserve Bank of New York are more truly those of a central bank than of a regional bank, because of its location in one of the world's chief exchange, money, and capital markets.

TABLE 32

THE FEDERAL RESERVE SYSTEM

Bank	Total Assets (000 Omitted)	District	Branches
New York	$11,508,780	2	Buffalo
Chicago	7,423,946	7	Detroit
San Francisco	5,609,064	12	Los Angeles, Portland, Salt Lake City, Seattle
Cleveland	3,951,271	4	Cincinnati, Pittsburgh
Richmond	2,736,812	5	Baltimore, Charlotte
Philadelphia	2,712,516	3	None
Boston	2,546,506	1	None
Atlanta	2,430,136	6	Birmingham, Jacksonville, New Orleans, Nashville
Kansas City	1,854,478	10	Denver, Oklahoma City, Omaha
St. Louis	1,803,891	8	Little Rock, Louisville, Memphis
Dallas	1,522,472	11	El Paso, Houston, San Antonio
Minneapolis	1,050,779	9	Helena
	$44,850,651		

Source: Federal Reserve Bulletin, January, 1946, p. 44.

The Federal Reserve Bank of Chicago is the second most important in the Federal Reserve System. It serves District 7, operates one branch located in Detroit, and on questions of policy its authorities are often the spokesmen for the views of the "interior" Federal Reserve banks. On the basis of assets, the San Francisco, Cleveland, Philadelphia, or any other Federal Reserve bank rivals any other central bank in the world. The San Francisco Federal Reserve Bank is located in District 12, which is one of the largest geographical areas served by any central bank. The area involved is about the same as the combined area of Germany, France, Italy, the United Kingdom, and the Netherlands. The Federal Reserve Bank of Minneapolis is the smallest in volume of assets, being located in the least industrialized of the twelve districts. Table 32 gives the total assets of each bank, the district number, and the location of branches.

Federal Reserve Board Now Board of Governors of the Federal Reserve System[5]

The general supervision and control of the Federal Reserve System was placed under the jurisdiction of a board. The most important changes in the makeup and powers of the Board were provided for in the Banking Act of 1935. The law authorized the President, with the consent of the Senate, to appoint seven members to the Board. The term of office is fourteen years, unless removed sooner, for cause, by the President. The terms are so arranged as to have but one appointment every two years. This system insures continuity of policies, for a majority of the Board will always be experienced members. Under provisions of the Banking Act of 1935, a member who has served a full term of fourteen years is not eligible for reappointment, with the exception that those members who had served a partial term prior to the Board's reorganization in 1936 may be reappointed.

Supreme Court of Finance.—For many years the charge had been made that the policies of the Board had been dictated by the Secretary of the Treasury. This assertion may or may not have been true, but in 1935 Congress provided for the discontinuance of the Secretary of the Treasury and the Comptroller of the Currency as ex officio members of the Board. The ideal is to have an intelligent, courageous, and nonpolitical board. The new salary scale ($15,000 plus necessary traveling expenses, as compared to the original $10,000) is expected to be high enough to attract capable men. Although the Board and its staff are often thought of as government employees, they are paid from funds secured from levies upon the twelve Federal Reserve banks. Geographical and economic representation on the Board is insured by provisions which prevent the President from

[5] The new board members took office February 1, 1936. They included M. S. Eccles (chairman), J. A. Broderick, M. S. Szymczak, J. K. McKee, Ronald Ransom, and R. W. Morrison. The seventh member was not appointed (see *Federal Reserve Bulletin*, Vol. XXII [February, 1936], pp. 71-72). For names of members of the boards from 1913 to 1936, see *ibid.*, p. 84; and for names of the current board's members and members of the Open Market Committee, Federal Advisory Council, and chief officers of the banks and branches, see "Federal Reserve Directory" in the last issue of the *Federal Reserve Bulletin*.

appointing more than one member from a Reserve district and which force him in his appointments to have "due regard to fair representation of the financial, agricultural, industrial and commercial interest, and geographical divisions of the country."

In 1935 the name of the Board was changed from Federal Reserve Board to Board of Governors of the Federal Reserve System. Each member is now called "Governor." The President appoints one member as the chairman and another as vice-chairman. The term of office as chairman and vice-chairman is four years, but both may continue to be members of the Board after the expiration of their chairmanships. The chairman is the chief executive officer and spokesman of the Board, but he is subject to its supervision.

Is Responsible for the National Credit Policy.—The recent legislative trend has been to add to the powers and duties of the Board of Governors of the Federal Reserve System. The Board now has general supervision over all international banking activities of Reserve banks. These activities include the correspondent relationship of the Federal Reserve Bank of New York and other Federal Reserve banks with foreign central banks, international loan agreements, and formal or informal international agreements as to credit policies.

Responsibility for national and international credit policies now rests with the Board and the United States Treasury, as modified by the Bretton Woods Act of 1945. Since 1933 the Treasury has had an important role as the result of the federal government's borrowing policies, the existence of the Stabilization Fund, and the administration of recent acts of Congress, particularly the Gold Reserve Act of 1934. The board has control over the major instruments of credit policy, namely, changes in discount rates, member banks' reserve requirements, and margins to be prescribed for loans on securities. The Board of Governors, together with the five representatives of the twelve Reserve banks, is responsible for the open market operations of the Federal Reserve System.

The discount rates which Reserve banks wish to establish must be submitted to the Board for its approval every fourteen days, or more frequently if the Board desires. These provisions bring the discount rate policies of individual Reserve banks and the system as a whole under the control of the Board. The statutory provision for periodic submission of rates will eliminate any excuse for a lackadaisical discount policy.

The Board has the power of permitting or requiring one Reserve bank to rediscount for a second Reserve bank. The result of this power is to pool the resources of the system, thereby making possible the shifting of funds from one district to another as the need arises. This power has been used on two different occasions: during the panic of 1933 and from 1919 to 1921. The Board has the power to define the character of paper eligible for rediscount at the twelve Federal Reserve banks and to prescribe the rules and regulations as to rediscounting. In recent years the Board has shown a tendency to enlarge the group of "eligible" credit instruments; this is in keeping with the system's easy money policy.

The Board has the power to change reserve requirements, within limits provided by the Banking Act of 1935, of all member banks or of any class of bank or for time or demand deposits, without changes in the reserve requirements of any other class of deposits or member bank.[6] In addition, the Board by regulation prescribes the conditions under which member banks' reserves may be deficient.[7] It also has the power to suspend reserve requirements of the twelve Reserve banks for thirty days and to renew such suspensions for fifteen-day periods. Only on one occasion, March 3, 1933, was this power used. The Board suspended the reserve requirements for thirty days and established a tax on the amounts by which reserves were deficient. Because of the return flow of currency and gold to banks after the banking holidays, no further use was made of this suspension. At the end of the thirty-day period, the suspension was not renewed. The Thomas Inflation law gave the Board the power to increase all member banks' reserve requirements, with the approval of the President, but only as an emergency measure. The Banking Act of 1935 permits the Board to change the reserve requirements, without the approval of the President, "in order to prevent injurious credit expansion or contraction." However, the maximum reserve requirements of member banks cannot be more than twice the percentage in force when the act was passed; namely, 3 per cent for time deposits and 7, 10, and 13 per cent, respectively, for demand deposits in country, reserve city, and central reserve city banks.

[6] *Public Law 656*, 77th Cong., Sec. 2, approved July 7, 1942.

[7] *Ibid.*, Sec. 3. This law amended paragraph 9 of Section 19 of the Federal Reserve Act, which prohibits member banks from making new loans or paying dividends while reserves are deficient.

The keeping of required reserves with central banks is justified, because it gives central banks funds with which to operate, and it provides a means through which the central banking authorities may influence the credit policies of banks. During the formative period of the Federal Reserve System, the first motive may have dominated; but in recent years the second has been in the foreground.

The Board of Governors has been given certain powers for the purpose of preventing the excessive use of credit for the purchasing or carrying of securities, commodities, and real estate. Among other things, the Board is authorized to raise or lower loan values of securities used to obtain funds by brokers or other individuals. Since the most harmful speculation is done with borrowed funds, the Board may reduce this evil by simply raising margin requirements.

The Board of Governors and five Federal Reserve representatives constitute the Open Market Committee, which gives the Board a majority in voting upon questions of open market policy. This situation permits the Board to dominate all the Federal Reserve System's major instruments of credit policy.

Supervision, Examination, Removal, and Appointive Powers.—Since 1933 Congress has increased the powers of the Board in keeping with the tendency to make the Federal Reserve System a more effective central banking system. The most striking aspect of the new development has been the new provisions of the law, which apply directly to activities of member banks and their affiliate organizations. Now credit and other policies of member banks may be effected directly by rules and regulations of the Board rather than indirectly through Federal Reserve banks, as had been the usual central banking practice.

In supervising member banks, the Board is authorized, among other things, to pass upon admission of voluntary membership; to limit by regulation the rate of interest which may be paid on time and savings deposits; to expel a bank from membership; to reduce or suspend a bank's discount privilege; to regulate interlocking directorates; to pass on requests of a state member bank to establish an out-of-town branch; to pass on application of national banks for authority to exercise trust powers; to grant authority to a national bank to establish a foreign branch; and to regulate the granting of acceptance credit.

In supervising Federal Reserve banks the Board is authorized, among other things, to suspend the operations of any Federal Reserve bank for violations of the law, to administer it during suspension, and to reorganize or liquidate it if conditions seem to justify doing so. It permits or requires Federal Reserve banks to establish branches or agencies in their districts or to liquidate them if unprofitable. It has supervision over all international banking arrangements, including the formation of foreign branches, agencies, and correspondent agreements.

The Board of Governors is authorized to make examinations of Federal Reserve banks, Edge Act Corporations, bank holding companies, and state member banks. The Board has the power to require statements and reports from these institutions and now receives and publishes weekly reports from the twelve Federal Reserve banks and member banks located in 101 leading cities. The Board also has powers to examine affiliates of member banks[8] and to issue voting permits to bank holding companies which include in their groups one or more member banks. They may require Federal Reserve banks to write off doubtful or worthless assets.

The Board has the power to remove for cause any officers or directors of any Federal Reserve bank; it also may remove any officer or director of any member bank "for continued violation of the law or unsound practices in conducting the business" of their banks.

The Board's appointive power includes the duty of naming one-third of each of the twelve Federal Reserve banks' nine directors and approving the appointment of the chief officers of the Reserve banks. One of the three appointive directors is designated as the chairman of the Board of Directors and Federal Reserve agent. A second of the appointive directors is designated as vice-chairman and assistant Federal Reserve agent.

Note Issue and Collection of Checks.—The Board supervises and regulates the issue and retirement of Federal Reserve notes, which includes rules and regulations for safeguarding all securities held as collateral and all Federal Reserve notes not in circulation. The Board may act as a clearinghouse for Federal Reserve banks and may require the Reserve banks to act as clearinghouses for member banks. It has the authority to determine charges that may be made for the collection and payment of checks and drafts.

[8] Bank affiliates are incorporated or unincorporated enterprises owned by a member bank. These enterprises may be real estate companies, trust companies, or safe deposit companies.

Organization and Staff.—The chief divisions of the Board's staff are: (1) Office of the Secretary, (2) Legal Division, (3) Division of Research and Statistics, (4) Division of Examinations, (5) Division of Bank Operations, (6) Division of Security Loans, (7) Division of Personnel Administration, and (8) Division of Administrative Services.

Open Market Committee

An open market is one in which buyers and sellers of a given thing are brought together. The discount operations of Reserve banks are primarily for member banks. But, in purchasing government bonds, bankers' acceptances, and a limited group of other credit instruments, the Reserve banks may deal with any bank, dealer, or individual. This device of credit control is one of the most important weapons possessed by central banks.

Before 1922 there were few attempts to co-ordinate the open market operations of the twelve Reserve banks. Government bonds and bankers' acceptances were bought and sold by each Reserve bank in accordance with the decision of its own officers and directors. As a result, Reserve banks were competing with one another for government securities and were otherwise working at cross-purposes in open market operations. In the spring of 1922 the governors, now the presidents, of the Reserve banks, appointed a committee of the governors to supervise the purchases and sales of government securities. In 1923 the Federal Reserve Board reorganized the committee's procedure and appointed its own Open Market Committee, which consisted of the same governors as were on the first committee. Finally, the committee was enlarged so as to contain a representative from each Reserve bank.

In 1933 Congress made statutory provisions for this committee. Its operations were subject to the general regulations of the Board; but a Reserve bank could refuse to participate in an open market policy established by the committee. Those in favor of a strong central banking system objected to bankers' control over open market policies and the power to veto which remained with each Reserve bank. The Banking Act of 1935 provided that once a policy has been established it must be accepted by all Reserve banks. No individual Reserve bank may decline to participate; it is the policy of the System.

The new Open Market Committee consists of the seven governors of the Board of Governors and five representatives of the Federal Reserve banks (effective since March 1, 1936). On July 7, 1942, the President approved an act of Congress providing that only presidents or vice-presidents would be representatives or alternates and that the Federal Reserve Bank of New York would have one representative. The others are elected one each by the boards of directors of respective Federal Reserve banks, grouped as follows: Boston, Philadelphia, and Richmond; Chicago and Cleveland; Atlanta, Dallas, and St. Louis; and Minneapolis, Kansas City, and San Francisco.[9]

This arrangement gives the Reserve banks a voice in the open market policy but places the Board in a position to determine the System's policy. The reorganization of the Open Market Committee is in keeping with the movement to place responsibility for national credit policy in the hands of the Board of Governors of the Federal Reserve System. The chairman of the Board is also chairman of the Open Market Committee. The committee must keep a complete record of its actions, and all decisions must be made with reference to general credit conditions. In carrying out its policies, the Federal Reserve Bank of New York acts as agent for the Open Market Committee.

Federal Advisory Council and Conferences

The Federal Advisory Council.—The council is composed of one member from each district. Each member is selected annually by the board of directors of his Reserve bank. The function of the council is purely advisory. It makes recommendations concerning matters of banking and credit policies, confers with the Board on general business conditions, and has usually displayed a helpful and co-operative spirit. The council's approach to the problems of central banking is that of the private banker, with the interests of the member banks in the foreground. The council must meet in Washington at least four times a year, and more frequently if called by the Board. It was devised in order to meet in part the objections of those who were in favor of a banking system entirely governed by

---

[9] *Public Law 656,* 77th Cong.

bankers. It gives the bankers direct contact with the Board through a permanent committee created for that purpose.

The powers of the council are to confer with the Board, to call for information, and to make written or oral statements concerning matters of special or general nature. These statements may take the form of protests, warnings, or recommendations. They may pertain to district, national, or international banking; or to credit, monetary, or business affairs.

Conference of Chairmen.—The chairmen of the board of directors of the Federal Reserve banks, who are also the Federal Reserve agents, are organized into a Conference of Chairmen. The conference selects a chairman and an executive committee to perform such functions for the conference as are necessary. They meet from time to time to discuss matters of common interest and to advise and consult the Board of Governors.

Conference of Presidents.—Another nonstatutory organization is the Conference of Presidents of the Federal Reserve banks. Officers of this organization include members who act as president, vice-president, and secretary. This group meets from time to time to discuss matters of common interest and to advise and consult with the Board of Governors.

Federal Reserve Banks Are Bankers' Banks

The twelve Reserve banks have indeterminate charters issued by the federal government.[10] All their capital stock is owned by member banks. All member banks must subscribe for capital stock equal to 6 per cent of their capital and surplus, of which one-half must be paid in cash and the other one-half subject to call. The stock carries a provision for 6 per cent cumulative dividend, which has been paid every year since 1916. Attractive as this rate is, it is still considerably below that paid by foreign central banks to their stockholders.

Board of Directors.—Provisions for management of the Reserve banks is similar to that of other large banking institutions. Each of these banks has a board of directors of nine members. Six of the directors are selected by member banks (stockholders), and three are appointed by the Board of Governors of the Federal Reserve System (Class C directors). Three of the six directors selected by the

[10] Formerly 20 years, but made perpetual or indeterminate by the McFadden-Pepper Act.

member banks must be bankers (Class A directors), and three must represent industry (Class B directors). "Looking at the make-up of Reserve bank board of directors in another way, Class A directors represent lenders of funds, Class B directors represent borrowers, and Class C represent the interest of the general public."[11] In order to assure small as well as large banks a voice in management of Reserve banks, stockholders are divided into three groups: large banks, middle-sized banks, and small banks. Each group selects one Class A and one Class B director. Class A directors, as a matter of practice, are active officers of member banks. Under the law, Class B and C directors may not be officers, directors, or employees of banks, and Class C directors may not be stockholders of banks. At the time of selection, Class B directors must be actively engaged in commerce, agriculture, or some industrial pursuit located in their districts. Directors hold office for three years, the terms being arranged so that only two directors are selected each year. The selection of six of the nine directors gives member banks control over Reserve banks.

The President.—The regional autonomy of the Reserve banks is maintained by permitting the local boards of directors to select their own chief executive officers. The original Federal Reserve Act made no provision for administrative heads of the Reserve banks. Many authorities assumed that the chairman of the board of directors would occupy this position, while others assumed that one of the Class A directors would be elected by each board of directors to be the chief executive officer. After considerable deliberation, the Federal Reserve Board authorized each Reserve bank to select a chief executive, to be known as governor. The governor was employed by and responsible to his board of directors. He was not a member of the Board and had no vote, but he participated in the Board's meetings and was a member of the executive committee. He was usually the dominating personality in the affairs of his Reserve bank, and in some cases in the whole Federal Reserve System. The average salary paid him was more than twice that paid to the members of the old Federal Reserve Board. Some of the most outstanding men in Federal Reserve history have held the position of governor or president of a Federal Reserve bank.

The Banking Act of 1935 settled the question of who was the

[11] Federal Reserve Bank of New York, *The Federal Reserve System Today*, p. 12.

chief executive officer by providing for positions of president and vice-president (effective since March 1, 1936). These officers are appointed for a term of five years by the board of directors of Reserve banks, subject to the approval of the Board of Governors of the Federal Reserve System.[12] While this change leaves the appointive power in the hands of the local board of directors, it gives the Board of Governors the opportunity to pass upon the qualifications of candidates. The duties and powers of the president and vice-president correspond to those of the chief officers in any bank. All the banks have a first vice-president, and from three to nine vice-presidents. Usually one of the latter is cashier of his bank.

Federal Reserve Agent.—One of the Class C directors is at the same time the chairman of the board of directors and the Federal Reserve agent. He is required to maintain a local office of the Federal Reserve Board on the premises of the Federal Reserve bank, under regulations established by the Board of Governors of the Federal Reserve System. His salary is fixed by the Board but paid by the Federal Reserve bank to which he is designated. He must administer, with the help of assistants, the powers given to him by Congress, and such other powers as may be specified by the Board and by the board of directors of his bank.

The development of the Federal Reserve System placed the Federal Reserve agents in a secondary position, even though they were, before the passage of the Banking Act of 1935, the statutory titular chiefs of their banks. From 1914 to 1936 the governor (now president) of each Federal Reserve bank was the administrative head of his bank. The Federal Reserve agent was the chairman of the board of directors, and his duties were (1) to make reports to the Federal Reserve Board; (2) to issue Federal Reserve notes to his Federal Reserve bank and to hold the required collateral; (3) to manage a public relations department; (4) to examine member banks; and (5) to audit the accounts of his Federal Reserve bank. By 1935 many congressmen and others favored the elimination of the office of Federal Reserve agent and the transfer of its functions to the banking department of each Federal Reserve bank. Although this move was blocked in the United States Senate, the Board of Governors, under powers conferred by the Federal Reserve Act,

[12] The Board made active use of its "confirming power" in 1936. The first appointments of three presidents were not confirmed by the Board.

stripped the office of all its nonstatutory duties, placed the incumbents on a part-time basis, and eliminated their salaries. This was done in order to reduce the expenses of the Federal Reserve banks (over $250,000 in salaries) and to avoid a "dual executive responsibility at the Federal Reserve banks. . . ."[13]

Now all the statutory duties of the Federal Reserve agents which have to do with issuance and retirement of Federal Reserve notes are being performed by assistant Federal Reserve agents, who are employees rather than officers. The nonstatutory powers were placed under the general supervision of the presidents of the Federal Reserve banks; they include the bank examination and bank relations work, the research and statistical work, and the press and circular division work.

Branches Aid Member Banks

The Board of Governors of the Federal Reserve System has the authority to permit or to require the establishment of branches and agencies by a Reserve bank. It also has the authority to force any Reserve bank to close its branches. Twenty-five branches and two agencies have been established, but the Spokane branch of the San Francisco bank and the Havana, Cuba, agency of the Atlanta bank were discontinued in October, 1938,[14] and the Savannah agency of the Atlanta bank in 1945.

A branch is governed by a board of directors consisting of not less than three or more than seven directors. A majority is appointed by the Federal Reserve bank of the district and the remainder by the Board. A branch is in charge of a manager, who is also a director. All the affairs of branches are under the control of the head office, and all its property belongs to the parent bank. The deciding factors in placing branches are geographical and economic. When districts are large and it takes considerable time to reach outlying parts, branches are necessary. Compact districts within easy reach of the district Reserve city, such as district 1 (Boston) and 3 (Philadelphia), have no branches, and others have only one. But in the South and West, where the districts are large and transportation facilities are not so extensively developed, some Reserve banks have four and

[13] *Federal Reserve Bulletin*, March, 1936, p. 145.

[14] *Annual Report of the Board of Governors of the Federal Reserve System*, 1938, p. 32.

five branches. Each branch is assigned a territory, which includes banks that normally transact business with the city in which the branch is located. (See Illustration VIII.)

The specific activities of the branches depend upon general rules and regulations of the Board and grants of power by the parent bank. Some of the branches carry on independently the same activities as those performed by the parent banks. They are assigned a territory in which to operate, hold deposits, discount paper, and collect checks. During World War II the Federal Reserve banks increased the functions and powers of branches in order that they might give better service to the banks and the government. Now most of the branches have fiscal and certain other central banking functions comparable to those of the head office.

By creating branches, the Federal Reserve authorities have appeased local jealousies aroused when the Federal Reserve cities were selected, have given the Federal Reserve banks' relationship departments additional arguments for selling membership to state institutions, and, most important of all, have given to member banks in branch cities many of the advantages enjoyed by member banks located in Federal Reserve cities. These advantages include: (1) faster clearing and collection of checks and other claims; (2) reduction in vault cash because new currency can be obtained quickly, which permits investment of more funds and gives member banks greater protection against runs; and (3) closer personal touch between member bank officers and Federal Reserve officers, which enables the former to secure valuable information.[15]

Member Banks

Central banking before 1913 was a combination of ordinary commercial, government, and bankers' banking. In most European countries central banks compete for business with other banks, lending to and holding deposits of individuals, partnerships, and corporations, as well as lending to and holding deposits of financial institutions and the state. The creation of a central banking system which did not hold deposits and make loans to nonfinancial institutions was a new development in central banking. The principle of keeping a local financial institution between the central bank and

[15] Clark, L. E., *Central Banking under the Federal Reserve System*, pp. 294-95.

borrowers has been widely copied in creating new central banking systems abroad and noncommercial central banking systems at home.

In order to insure the success of the Federal Reserve System, it was thought necessary to require that member banks subscribe to the stock of the Federal Reserve banks, to keep deposits with them, and to otherwise participate in the activities of the Reserve banks. Therefore, all national banks in continental United States were required to be members, and all state banks and trust companies were permitted to be members. The national banks are the bulwark of the system, owning about two-thirds of the capital stock, one-half of their deposits, and comprising 80 per cent of membership.

All incorporated banks in the United States are eligible for membership, if they can meet the technical requirements, except federal land banks and federal home loan banks. Unfortunately, only a small percentage of the institutions which are eligible for membership have joined the system. In 1945, when there were 5,015 national bank members and 1,825 voluntary members, there were 8,700 nonmember banks. When only commercial banks are considered, the deposits of state member banks represent over 75 per cent of the total deposits in state commercial banks. While the wisdom of the policy of including many small banks in the system has been questioned, the fact remains that no truly national credit policy may be made effective when it does not apply to all banks, particularly commercial banks, for they create the chief substitute for money.

In 1933 the need for expanding membership in the system was recognized by Congress by permitting mutual savings and Morris Plan banks to join and by requiring all banks participating in the Federal Deposit Insurance System to join the Federal Reserve System; but later this last requirement was amended so as to apply only to state banks with deposits of $1,000,000 or over. Before this amendment went into effect, it was repealed (June, 1939).

Membership in the Federal Reserve System has not been desired by most of the state-chartered institutions. During the first six weeks of the existence of the system, only eight state-chartered institutions joined. Growth in voluntary membership proceeded slowly until World War I, when considerable expansion took place because of war financing, patriotic appeals, and further appreciation of the advantages of membership. During World War II the number of state banks to join the system increased considerably, and now the deposits of member banks, relatively as well as absolutely, are the highest on record. As the result of bank failures and bank mergers, there has been a decline in the total number of banks, including the number of member institutions.

Before admitting a state institution to membership, the Board gives consideration to (1) its history and the character and condition of its management; (2) its capital structure and earning prospects; (3) needs of the community served or to be served by the bank; and (4) whether its corporate powers are consistent with the purposes of the Federal Reserve Act.[16]

The general legal requirements for membership are: (1) Paid-up and unimpaired capital must be the same as for national banks similarly located. (2) The bank must subscribe for Federal Reserve bank stock in an amount equal to 6 per cent of its paid-up capital and surplus. Mutual savings banks have no stock, but their subscriptions must be equal to 6/10 of 1 per cent of their total deposits. One-half of the subscribed capital must be paid in, and the remainder is subject to call. (3) All member banks must keep a legal reserve deposit with their Reserve banks and must arrange for deposit insurance with Federal Deposit Insurance Corporation if not insured, or continue insurance if already insured. (4) They must supply their Federal Reserve banks with semiannual reports of earnings and dividends and make at least three reports on conditions each year. These reports also cover conditions of their affiliates.

In explaining the existence of a large number of nonmember banks, the first thing to note is that most of them do not meet the statutory requirements of membership. On December 31, 1939, there were 2,818 banks that had insufficient capital for membership, of which 429 were disqualified because they were operating branches and did not meet the higher statutory requirements made of multiple office banks. While these banks are in a position to increase their capital, there are reasons for not desiring to qualify for membership, the chief one being that more profitable banking may be carried on outside of the Federal Reserve System. Among these reasons are the following: (1) They secure considerable revenue from exchange charges on checks forwarded to them for collection, while member banks are required to remit at par. (2) Their legal reserve require-

[16] See "Regulation H, as amended" (effective November 20, 1939), *Federal Reserve Bulletin*, December, 1939, pp. 1055-64.

ments against deposits are smaller, and part of them may be kept as bankers' balances or deposits with their correspondent banks. (3) Laws affecting officers and directors are less rigid than those for member banks, there being fewer and less rigid laws against interlocking directorates, often no limitations on loans to officers, and no rules as to the minimum and maximum number of directors. (4) There are fewer restrictive laws pertaining to "multiple banking," that is, branch and group banking. (5) Finally, nonmember banks have fewer restrictions on loans and investment policies, less rigid examinations, and, in general, lower banking standards to meet than do members of the Federal Reserve System.

Advantages of Membership.—The chief justification for membership is the social responsibility of the banks to support the Federal Reserve System. All banks share directly and indirectly in the national economic advantages which result from the activities of the Federal Reserve System. The privileges of membership have been listed as follows:[17]

1. Facilities for rediscounting eligible paper and obtaining advances on promissory notes
2. Obtaining currency and coin promptly when needed
3. Direct use of Federal Reserve check collection facilities
4. Direct use of Federal Reserve noncash collection service
5. Transferring funds by telegraph
6. Drawing drafts on the Federal Reserve bank
7. Safekeeping of securities by the Federal Reserve banks for member banks located outside of Federal Reserve bank and branch cities
8. Use of the emblem, "Member of the Federal Reserve System"
9. Member bank deposits are automatically insured by the Federal Deposit Insurance Corporation up to $5,000 for any one depositor

While most nonmember state bankers recognize the advantages of membership, they argue that most of these advantages can be obtained without joining the Federal Reserve System. Many of them make direct use of the clearing and collection services of the system, and many secure central banking services through correspondent banks. Trust companies and mutual savings banks have little need for

[17] Federal Reserve Bank of New York, *The Federal Reserve System Today*, p. 35. See also Section 13, paragraphs 3 and 13 of the Federal Reserve Act and Sections 13*b* and 19, paragraph 8.

the rediscounting, check collection, and other services offered by the Federal Reserve banks.

QUESTIONS AND PROBLEMS

1. Identify the weaknesses of the old National Banking System.
2. What economic functions are performed by central banks? Why was not one central bank organized in the United States? Are there too many? Why?
3. Do you agree with the statement "public service rather than profit is the chief reason for the existence of the Federal Reserve banks"?
4. Who owns the Federal Reserve banks? Who manages them?
5. Should the Reserve banks' capital be increased by requiring member banks to purchase the full amount of their subscriptions? Why?
6. Should the Board of Governors be a more efficient body than the old Federal Reserve Board? Why?
7. Who selects the members of the Federal Advisory Council and the members of the Open Market Committee? What are the functions of each group?
8. "The public nature of the Reserve Banks is indicated by the character of their directorates" (Burgess, W. R., *The Reserve Banks and the Money Market* [rev. ed], p. 13). Is this true? Why?
9. What constitutes membership in the Federal Reserve System? What institutions must be members? What institutions may be members?
10. Who appoints the Federal Reserve agents and the presidents of the Reserve banks? What are their duties? How long are their terms of office?
11. What are Federal Reserve branch banks? Who owns and controls them?
12. "Few pieces of important legislation have been approached by the American Congress in a more realistic spirit than the banking legislation of 1935. . . . It concerned itself with conditions—not with theories" (Miller, A. C. [member of Federal Reserve Board, 1914-36], Address May 30, 1935, before District of Columbia Bankers' Association). Do the results justify this statement? Explain.
13. "There appears to be a good deal of confusion in the public mind as to the principles which should govern the relations of central banks to governments. Perhaps much of the confusion turns upon the failure to distinguish between 'governmental' and 'political' in a narrower sense" (Williams, J. H., "The Banking Act of 1935," *American Economic Review*, Supplement, Vol. XXVI [March, 1936], p. 99). Discuss.

14. Make a list of reasons why over 8,000 banks have not joined the Federal Reserve System.

15. As an economy measure, assume that all but five of the Federal Reserve banks are closed. On a map of the United States draw the five districts to be served by the five remaining Reserve banks. Which Reserve banks would you liquidate? Why?

16. What justification was there for the law which required the banks insured with the Federal Deposit Insurance Corporation to become members of the Federal Reserve System? Why was this requirement later modified to apply only to nonmember insured banks with deposits of $1,000,000 or more? Why was this provision repealed before it became effective?

17. Explain the changes which have been made in the positions of the chairmen of the board of directors of Federal Reserve agents by the rulings of the Board of Governors of the Federal Reserve System in 1936.

18. Use the *Federal Reserve Bulletin* and *Who's Who*, or a similar reference, to identify men who are (*a*) members of the Board of Governors of the Federal Reserve System, (*b*) members of the Federal Advisory Council, (*c*) presidents of the twelve Federal Reserve banks, and (*d*) Federal Reserve agents. Report on your findings.

19. Many nonmember banks are insuring their deposits in the Federal Deposit Insurance Corporation. Should the laws deterring them from membership in the Federal Reserve System be repealed? Use as reference, Members of the Staff, Board of Governors of the Federal Reserve System, *Banking Studies*, pp. 273-87.

20. "Of the matter of the System's interest in the smaller banks, I point to the fact that of a total membership of approximately 6,700 banks over 5,000 had deposits, as of December 1943, of less than 5 million dollars each. Over 3,200 of these had deposits of less than 2 million dollars each." Statement of M. S. Eccles, chairman of the Board of Governors of the Federal Reserve System, on bill, S. 1642. What is the significance of these statistics?

REFERENCES

See end of Chapter XXVIII

Chapter XXVII

OPERATIONS OF THE FEDERAL RESERVE BANKS

Federal Reserve Banks Are Central Banks

In the United States the twelve Federal Reserve banks are the central banks for the commercial banking system. Central banks are not usually the oldest or the largest banks in their banking systems. The importance of the twelve Federal Reserve banks is due not to age or size but to the services they perform for the government, their relationships to member banks, and their assistance in carrying out the monetary and credit functions of the government and the Federal Reserve authorities. As commercial banks, they perform the traditional primary functions of note issue, deposit, and discount. In addition, like any ordinary bank, they perform many secondary functions of banking for their customers.

The Statement of Condition of the Federal Reserve Banks

The interest and purposes of these statements (they appear weekly and cover the conditions of the Federal Reserve banks at the close of business on Wednesday night) are similar to those of the member banks which were considered in Chapter XVIII. The Federal Reserve banks are performing public as well as private functions, and it has been the policy of the system to disclose full information on all essential phases of its activities. The statement of condition is published weekly by metropolitan newspapers and financial magazines and monthly in the *Federal Reserve Bulletin.* (See Table 33.)

Bankers for the Government

The United States government has been by far the largest and most important customer of the Federal Reserve banks. Since their existence, the Reserve banks have acted as both the commercial and the investment bankers for the government. The statement of condition does not present a complete picture of the services performed for the federal government, but it does show the extent to which the Federal Reserve banks hold government deposits and the extent to which the Reserve banks have invested in government obligations.

Deposits.—The United States Treasury has been keeping its chief checking accounts with the Federal Reserve banks. The receipts from taxpayers, from sales of government securities, and from other minor sources are deposited with the Reserve banks, their branches, or selected member banks designated as general or limited depositories.

TABLE 33

STATEMENT OF CONDITION OF FEDERAL RESERVE BANKS
(December 26, 1945; in Thousands of Dollars)

Assets		Liabilities	
Gold certificates	17,062,565	Federal Reserve notes	24,736,391
Redemption fund	800,371	Deposits	
Total reserves	17,862,936	Member bank reserve accounts	15,657,678
Other cash	206,774	U.S. Treasury general account	1,198,710
Discounts and advances		Foreign	863,436
Member banks	445,027	Other	418,880
Nonmember banks, etc.	47,000	Total deposits	18,138,704
Total	492,027	Deferred availability items	1,378,553
Industrial loans	2,038	Other liabilities	12,781
U.S. government securities		Total liabilities	44,266,429
Bills under repurchase option	4,845,110	Capital accounts	
Other bills	7,957,459	Capital paid in	175,836
Certificates	8,167,461	Surplus (Sec. 7)	228,153
Notes	2,119,650	Surplus (Sec. 13)	27,165
Bonds	946,892	Other capital accounts	153,068
Total	24,036,572	Total liabilities and capital accounts	44,850,651
Due from foreign banks	110		
Federal Reserve notes of other banks	133,595	Commitments to make industrial loans	2,850
Uncollected items	2,019,476		
Bank premises	33,615		
Other assets	63,508		
Total assets	44,850,651		

Source: *Federal Reserve Bulletin*, January, 1946, pp. 43-45.

While the government finds it desirable to use the Federal Reserve banks as the chief medium through which to make disbursements, it has found it convenient to use other financial institutions to handle routine business not handled by the Treasury and to use member banks temporarily as special depositories to hold the proceeds from the sale of government securities. In case of need, the telegraphic transfer system of the Federal Reserve System permits easy transfers of government deposits from the member banks to the Federal Reserve banks; the reserve deposit of the member bank is debited, and the United States Treasurer's general account is credited on the books of the Federal Reserve bank.

Treasury Agents.—When the dollar value of items appearing in the Treasurer's account at the Federal Reserve bank is considered, the most important items have to do with management of the public debt. The financing of World War II and other Treasury transactions reached unprecedented proportions. The Reserve banks made allotments of securities in accordance with general instructions from the Treasury, delivered the securities, received payments, and credited the amounts received to the United States Treasurer's general account.

The Federal Reserve banks also handle most of the routine and detailed work involved in retiring outstanding federal securities, receiving the securities, and making exchanges in refinancing. During 1944 the Reserve banks' issues, redemptions, and exchanges of United States obligations numbered over 350,000,000 and had a value of more than $264,000,000,000. United States government coupons paid numbered over 1,482,000,000 and had a value of over $1,840,000,000. The volume of work in administrating the issuance and redemption of savings bonds became so burdensome, that, beginning in October, 1944, the Treasury empowered commercial banks to cash savings bonds, Series A to E. The Reserve banks not only handled the issuance and redemption of savings bonds but could, on request of the owners, hold these securities for safekeeping.

The Federal Reserve banks handled the allotment and allowance checks, in card form, issued by government disbursing officers to dependents of those in the armed forces. In addition, the Reserve banks continued to handle government currency, coins, and checks. Thus, during 1944, the Federal Reserve banks received and counted 3,000,000,000 pieces of paper currency that had a value of over $17,000,000,000. Coins received and counted exceeded 4,000,000,000, with a value of over $400,000,000. The volume of government checks handled was over 400,000,000, with a value of almost $128,000,000,000.

Agents of Others.—The creation of many new government agencies has greatly increased the complexity and volume of the fiscal work of the Reserve banks because most of the new financial institutions use these banks as depositories. Their deposit accounts appear as "other deposits" in the Federal Reserve bank statement. Most of the lending institutions make secured loans; and the Reserve banks lend their assistance by acting as custodians of the securities, the warehouse receipts, and other types of paper pledged as backing for the loans. Most important of the government agencies receiving these services are the Home Owners' Loan Corporation, the Reconstruction Finance Corporation, and the Commodity Credit Corporation. Finally, the Federal Reserve Bank of New York acts as the fiscal agent for the Treasury in handling the account of the Stabilization Fund, which involves transactions at home and abroad in the foreign exchange markets; handles the earmarking and release of gold for export; and holds deposits and acts as agent for certain foreign banks and governments.

Because of its location in one of the world's most important financial markets, much of the fiscal work of the government and of government agencies and corporations is done by the Federal Reserve Bank of New York. Not only does the government depend upon this bank for routine assistance, but it looks to the officials for advice and guidance in planning and completing financial transactions.

Most of the Deposits Are Reserves of Member Banks

Insurance Principle.—Since an amendment to the Federal Reserve Act in 1917, only the deposits with Reserve banks have counted as the legal reserves of member banks. Previous to the organization of the Federal Reserve System, legal reserves were kept in the banks' own vaults or with correspondents.[1] The required pooling of reserves in Federal Reserve banks is merely an application to the commercial banking field of the insurance principle of distribution of risk. No single bank could profitably set aside sufficient cash reserves to care for its needs in an emergency, but the combined reserves of all banks are large enough to care for all needs during any ordinary emergency.

How Reserves Are Built Up.—The procedure by which member banks build up their deposits is the same as that used by a businessman when he builds up his deposit account with his bank. The

[1] For history of reserve requirements, see "The History of Reserve Requirements for Banks in the United States," *Federal Reserve Bulletin*, November, 1938, pp. 953-72.

member banks may deposit currency or checks, borrow from the Reserve banks, transfer deposits from correspondent banks to the Reserve banks, sell acceptable paper to the Reserve banks, or sell government securities in the open market, transferring the proceeds from the sale to the Reserve banks. Reserves may also result from gold and silver imports which the importing bank sells to the government, receiving in payment a Treasury draft which it deposits in a Reserve bank. Sales of domestically produced gold or silver to the government would have similar effects, because the mining companies customarily deposit their Treasury checks with banks.

Figures of actual reserves with the Federal Reserve banks are shown on the financial statement of the condition of Reserve banks (see Table 33), but "estimated required reserves" and "estimated excess reserves" are not shown until after reports on deposits and required reserves are obtained from member banks. Under the present regulations of the Board, reserves are not required to equal the legal minimum requirements at all times but must at least average enough to cover the average requirements over designated periods of time. These periods vary from semimonthly for country banks to weekly for banks in cities.[2]

Reserve Accounts Are Used.—The reserve accounts of member banks are very active, being similar in this respect to any business firm's checking account. The Reserve banks are continuously receiving, sorting, collecting, and clearing checks and other credit instruments for their bank customers. They are taking in and paying out currency. As a result, the deposit reserve account of the average member bank is in a continuous state of flux, being built up by credit items and being torn down by debit items. The situation is similar to that of an individual who is required to keep an average minimum checking account balance with his bank in order to avoid service charges.

Excess Reserves.—Until recent years, changes in the volume of reserve balances carried with the Reserve banks were considered to be an important indicator or barometer of credit conditions. This theory was based on the assumption that member banks would not

[2] Prior to February 28, 1942, deficiencies in reserves of member banks located in cities where Reserve banks and branches were located were computed on the basis of average daily net deposit balances covering semiweekly periods, while other member banks in reserve cities were made on a weekly basis. Country banks compute reserves on a semimonthly basis (*Federal Reserve Bulletin*, March, 1942, p. 202).

keep idle funds with the Reserve banks and that any change in the volume of Reserve balances would necessarily indicate a change in the volume of member banks' credit; and that if the latter increased by 10 per cent there would be a proportionate increase in legal reserves.

Prior to World War II, member banks permitted their reserve balances with Federal Reserve banks to be greatly in excess of legal requirements. This situation was contrary to all banking principles—that banks organized for profit would not keep idle balances. It was due to the influx of gold and the volume of Federal Reserve credit outstanding, on the one hand, and the lack of demand for bank credit sufficiently large to use up the excess reserves, on the other. During the war, war borrowing changed the latter, and, as a result, "excess reserves" declined to but a fraction of their pre-war volume.

Other Deposits.—"Other deposits" include clearing balances for nonmember banks, special deposits to cover officers' checks, deposits to cover Reserve banks' transfers and exchange drafts, special deposits of the Treasurer of the United States, and deposits of the Reconstruction Finance Corporation, Commodity Credit Corporation, Home Owners' Loan Corporation, and other government agencies. The chief reason for the increase in the item "other deposits" has been the creation and growth of the new federal financing corporations and agencies. Although deposits of these institutions and that of the general account of the United States Treasury have increased, the reserve deposits of member banks represent over 80 per cent of the total deposits in the twelve Federal Reserve banks.

Correspondents for Foreign Central Banks

Two items in the Statement of Condition of Federal Reserve Banks appear as the result of the power given in Section 14 of the Federal Reserve Act to establish certain banking relationships with foreign banks. These items are: "Due from foreign banks" and "Deposits—foreign banks." At the end of 1944 the Federal Reserve Bank of New York held accounts for governments and central banks of sixty foreign countries. When the International Monetary Fund and the International Bank for Reconstruction and Development begin operations, it will be the chief depository of these two institutions. The correspondent relationships among central banks are similar to those among noncentral banks: maintenance of interbank deposit accounts; acting as agents in investing funds in bankers' acceptances and government securities; interbank lending, including opening of lines of acceptance credit under certain circumstances (the Bank of England was authorized to draw upon the Federal Reserve banks for $200,000,000 in 1925, when England returned to the gold standard); and performance of certain other functions.

During World War II the Federal Reserve Bank of New York assumed many of the fiscal activities of foreign governments which were performed by J. P. Morgan and Company, the National City Bank of New York, and other bankers during World War I. This was in keeping with the federal government's policy of preventing private interests from making profits out of World War II.

Lending to Banks

Most of the central banks in existence in 1914 were institutions that carried on ordinary commercial banking activities, such as accepting deposits from and lending to individuals, partnerships, and nonfinancial corporations, as well as performing central banking functions for their governments and for other commercial banks. The sponsors of the Federal Reserve System planned to create a central banking system whose activities would be limited to the central banking field and would not compete with the existing commercial banks. This represented a new principle in central banking and is one which has been accepted by all governments which have created central banks since 1914.

The Federal Reserve banks were authorized to rediscount agricultural, commercial, and industrial paper previously discounted by member banks. In order to be eligible for rediscount, the credit instruments had to meet certain time and other requirements. The proceeds from the original credit transactions must be used, or have been used, for producing, purchasing, carrying, or marketing of goods in one of the steps of production or trade. Paper resulting from industrial or commercial transactions must mature within ninety days from the time it is rediscounted, exclusive of days of grace. Agricultural paper based upon livestock may have a maturity not exceeding nine months. A member bank, desiring rediscount accommodations, submits an application to its Federal Reserve bank on an appropriate form and accompanied by the eligible paper it wishes to rediscount. If the paper is satisfactory, it is customary for the rediscount to be made and the resulting credit to be added to the member bank's deposit or reserve account.

Until 1916 the commercial, industrial, and agricultural paper rediscounted had to be accompanied by financial statements of the original borrower and endorsers and by other information furnished by member banks. There were many objections to this method of securing funds from Reserve banks. Many borrowers disliked having member banks rediscount their promises to pay, and many banks could not provide the financial statements and other information requested. On occasion, member banks desired to borrow for only a few days, in order to build up their reserves and enable them to meet unfavorable clearinghouse balances, or for other reasons. Rediscountable paper of the right maturity (five, ten, or fifteen days) and the right amount was not always available. In 1916 an amendment to Section 13 of the Federal Reserve Act became effective; it allowed the Reserve banks to make advances to their member banks based upon their promissory notes secured by eligible paper.

To help finance World War I, member banks were permitted to rediscount promissory notes of their customers secured by government obligations (called "war paper"). Member banks were permitted to use government securities as collateral for their own promissory notes, and thereafter reserve funds could be obtained by a member bank by discounting its promissory note secured by eligible paper or government bonds. Finally, during the depression of the 1930's, member banks were authorized to discount their notes collateralized by paper acceptable to the Federal Reserve banks. Now, when a bank cannot offer eligible paper or United States government securities as collateral for a bank's own promises to pay, a Reserve bank may accept other types of paper as collateral, but it must charge a rate of at least ½ of 1 per cent per annum higher than its discount rate. The new provision means that any type of paper, including highly speculative securities, may be used to secure Federal Reserve funds.

The liberalizing of the conditions under which member banks may borrow from their Federal Reserve banks is due to panic experiences of 1930-32, together with the decline in the volume of industrial and commercial borrowing, and the increase in savings accounts in member banks. Now any Federal Reserve bank may supply a member bank with any amount of additional reserves needed, provided the member bank can offer acceptable collateral. In other words, the liquidity (but not the solvency) of any member bank is assured.

Since 1933, paper which is acceptable to Reserve banks may be refused, when offered for discount or rediscount, if business conditions justify no increase in the volume of member banks' credit. The Banking Act of 1933 states that Reserve banks "may" discount acceptable paper, thus settling the argument as to whether discounting by member banks is a right or a privilege. Furthermore, the Board of Governors may forbid Reserve banks, and even member banks, to make additional loans under certain conditions.

Loans to Institutions Other than Member Banks Is a New Development

Making loans to nonbanking institutions has always been an important part of the activities of foreign central banks, but lending of this type is a recent development in the United States. In 1913 Congress had no desire to create institutions that would be competitors of the existing commercial banks, but the collapse of banking in many sections during the period 1931-34 made it difficult for many borrowers to secure funds for business purposes. In order to help them, the Federal Reserve Act was amended on July 21, 1932, March 9, 1933, and June 19, 1934, so as to permit such loans.

Emergency Loans.—The first amendment permitted Reserve banks to discount for nonfinancial institutions secured and properly "indorsed notes, drafts, and bills of exchange of all kinds and maturities made eligible for discount for member banks under other provisions of this Act . . . ." There was no intention on the part of Congress to permit Reserve banks to make copious use of this new power, for it was specified that they were to discount "in unusual and exigent circumstances," and then only after evidence had been obtained showing that the applicant was "unable to secure adequate credit accommodations from other banking institutions."

The Emergency Banking Act of March 9, 1933, contains paragraphs which authorize Reserve banks to make advances directly to individuals, partnerships, and corporations if the notes are secured by United States government obligations. Such advances may be made for periods up to ninety days. Since commercial and industrial borrowers with such collateral can readily obtain credit accommodations from ordinary commercial banking sources, this amendment is of minor importance to them; but it is of importance to nonmember banks, because it permits them to secure advances from the Reserve banks at the same rate of discount applicable to member bank advances.[3]

Industrial Advances.—The amendments of 1932 and 1933 which authorized Federal Reserve banks to make individual loans did not go to the heart of the commercial and industrial credit problem, because, while intermediate credit was needed, only short-term loans were authorized. The Industrial Loan Act of June, 1934, authorized the Reconstruction Finance Corporation and the Federal Reserve banks to supply business firms with credit, provided the obligations did not have maturities exceeding five years. The act was passed in order to aid small, well-established enterprises which could not borrow in the capital market or from commercial banks.

Industrial lending by the Federal Reserve banks is financed by the federal government. Funds obtained from the Treasury are accounted for under "Surplus, Section 13*b*." The total amount of funds made available by Congress was equal to the amount of stock of the Federal Deposit Insurance Corporation purchased by the Federal Reserve banks, namely, about $139,000,000. Funds are transferred to and from the Treasury to individual Reserve banks as needed, but only a small part of the amount authorized has been used at any one time. As shown by the statement of condition of the Federal Reserve banks for December 26, 1945, industrial loans were slightly over $2,000,000, commitments to make industrial loans were $2,850,000, and funds made available by the Treasury to finance the transactions were $27,165,000 (Surplus, Sec. 13*b*).

[3] Discount rates effective January 31, 1946, which were the same for all Federal Reserve banks except otherwise noted, were as follows: (1) advances to member banks secured by government obligations maturing or callable in one year or less, ½ of 1 per cent; (2) advances to member banks secured by government obligations maturing or callable beyond one year and discounts of and advances secured by eligible paper, 1 per cent; (3) other secured advances to member banks, 1½ per cent; (4) advances to nonmember banks secured by direct obligations of the United States, 1 per cent; and (5) advances to individuals, partnerships, or corporations other than banks secured by direct obligations of the United States government, 2 per cent at all Federal Reserve banks except New York, Richmond, Minneapolis, and San Francisco, which have a rate of 2½ per cent (*Federal Reserve Bulletin*, February, 1946, p. 148). In May the ½ of 1 per cent rate was dropped.

The Industrial Loan Act authorized the Federal Reserve banks to make capital loans for terms not in excess of five years: (1) directly, if the borrower is unable to obtain financial assistance on a reasonable basis from usual sources; and (2) through the medium of or in co-operation with banks, trust companies, and other financial institutions. In making loans or commitments, each Federal Reserve bank has the assistance of an advisory committee of from three to five industrial leaders in each Federal Reserve district.

Three types of loans have been made under the Industrial Loan Act. In the first group are those made directly to commercial and industrial borrowers. On the whole, these loans have not been numerous, and most of them have been made in the South and West. A second type of loan is made by a Federal Reserve bank with a financial institution co-operating. The third and most important type of loan is made by a financial institution, but only after securing a commitment from a Federal Reserve bank to purchase the paper on request. If the Reserve bank agrees, after careful investigation, the lending bank need not fear having frozen assets on its hands. If losses develop, the financing institution assumes at least 20 per cent of them. The financing institution pays the Federal Reserve bank a commission for the commitment, which varies according to the risks assumed.[4]

Because commercial and industrial firms were permitted to borrow under more liberal terms from the Reconstruction Finance Corporation, the volume of industrial lending by Federal Reserve banks has been small. The aid given by Reserve banks cannot be measured alone by the volume of loans extended, because the financial advice given has often permitted reorganization involving no Federal Reserve funds.

Simplification of the country's financial structure calls for a liquidation of the Reconstruction Finance Corporation, which was set up as an emergency corporation to aid financial institutions, railroads, and others during the 1932 emergency. In order to assure small businesses an adequate supply of capital funds, it is recommended that the Federal Reserve banks be permitted to use the funds appropriated by Congress to finance lending under the Industrial

[4] For rates on loans and commitments, see table entitled "Federal Reserve Bank Rates on Industrial Loans and Commitments under Section 13*b* of the Federal Reserve Act" in current issue of the *Federal Reserve Bulletin*.

Loan Act in order to guarantee capital loans made by financial institutions. During World War II, the Federal Reserve banks had considerable experience with this type of lending as agents for the War and Navy departments and the United States Maritime Commission. These involve the war production, or "V" loans, and war contract termination, or "T" loans.[5]

Investments of Reserve Banks Are Primarily in Government Securities

Reserve banks are not limited in their operations to making advances and rediscounts as described in the preceding pages. They have broad powers which permit them to buy and sell certain types of securities in the open market. In these transactions they may deal with bond houses, trust companies, commercial banks, individual dealers, and brokers of all types. Open market operations are considered to be an activity best administered by the system as a whole. An Open Market Committee was created for this purpose, and most of its transactions are in the New York market. The law requires that "the time, character, and volume of all purchases and sales of paper . . . . eligible for open-market operations shall be governed with a view to accommodating commerce and business and with regard to their bearing upon the general credit situation of the country."[6] In order to keep the assets of the Reserve banks in liquid and safe forms, these open market operations are limited to the following classes of securities:

a) Cable transfers, bankers' acceptances, and bills of exchange arising out of commercial transactions and the financing of the storage of staples

b) Bonds, notes, Treasury bills, and certificates of indebtedness of the United States government and all securities guaranteed by it

c) Warrants with maturity of six months or less, issued in anticipation of taxes or assumed revenues by the state, county, municipality, or other political subdivisions with the United States

d) Acceptances or debentures of federal intermediate credit banks, national agricultural credit corporations, and other agricultural institutions.

---

[5] *Federal Reserve Bulletin*, June, 1944, pp. 534-36.

[6] See Section 12A of the Federal Reserve Act, as amended.

Bankers' Acceptances.—All types of the foregoing classes of securities have been purchased, but in practice most of the open market operations are confined to bankers' acceptances and United States government securities. From the beginning, the Federal Reserve banks have supported the bill or acceptance market by purchasing all eligible paper offered to them at their buying prices. The basic reason for this policy was to help the credit system by establishing a market for acceptances, an indispensable part of the financing of foreign trade. The buying rate for acceptances is given little publicity and "does not ordinarily reflect judgment as to the general credit situation."[7] All sales transactions are initiated by the seller; the only way that the Reserve banks encourage or discourage such sales is by lowering or raising the discount rate. In practice, the open market purchases of bankers' acceptances are in the nature of discounts, being a passive rather than an active policy. As previously noted, the volume of bankers' acceptances held by the Federal Reserve banks is at a very low level, owing to the decline in foreign trade and the practice of accepting banks and others to hold them until maturity. For the first time since 1933 the buying rates were changed in June, 1946, now being: 1 to 90 days, 3/4 of 1 per cent; 91 to 120 days, 7/8 of 1 per cent; and 121 to 180 days, 1 per cent.[8]

Treasury Bills.—The present Federal Reserve policy is the same for Treasury bills as for bankers' acceptances. The Federal Reserve banks established rates at which they stand ready to buy all Treasury bills offered. Effective August 3, 1942, purchases of such bills by the Federal Reserve banks were made on condition that the seller could, if desired, before maturity, buy back a like amount and like maturity at the same rate of discount. Since May, 1943, all purchases have been made subject to this repurchase option. The Federal Reserve buying rate in effect is 3/8 of 1 per cent.[9]

Other Government Securities.—The open market policy, used in a narrower sense, signifies only those transactions in which the Reserve banks ordinarily take the initiative. Normally these transactions involve government obligations already in the market. During World War II, in order to facilitate war financing, the Reserve banks were permitted to buy government obligations directly

[7] Burgess, W. R., *The Reserve Banks and the Money Market* (1st ed.), p. 208.

[8] *Federal Reserve Bulletin,* August, 1946, p. 882.

[9] *Ibid.*

from the Treasury in amounts not to exceed $5,000,000,000. The purchases and sales of government obligations are guided by principles determined by the system and not by individual banks, and so open market policies are discussed in the next chapter. However, earnings from these securities are prorated among the Reserve banks according to needs and are the chief source of income of each of the Federal Reserve banks.

Reserve Banks Put Currency into Circulation

Bank Currency Item on Statement of Condition.—There are three items on the "Statement of Condition of Federal Reserve Banks" which result from the issuance of Federal Reserve notes: (1) redemption fund—Federal Reserve notes; (2) Federal Reserve notes of other Federal Reserve banks; and (3) Federal Reserve notes in actual circulation.

In order to provide for redemption of Federal Reserve notes in Washington as well as at the Federal Reserve banks, each Reserve bank is required to keep an amount on deposit in Washington equal to 5 per cent of the amount of its Federal Reserve notes in circulation not secured by gold certificates in the hands of the Federal Reserve agents. Federal Reserve notes held by other Reserve banks are those, for example, of the Federal Reserve Bank of Cleveland, which have been received through banking channels by the Federal Reserve Bank of New York. Since a Federal Reserve bank must pay a tax of 10 per cent on the notes of other banks that they pay out in circulation, these notes will be returned to the issuing bank or will be sent to Washington. Federal Reserve notes in actual circulation are those outside the Reserve banks and the United States Treasury in the hands of individuals, banks, and others.

Federal Reserve Note.—Since the characteristics of the Federal Reserve note were considered in Chapter IX, only slight consideration is given to them in this chapter. Federal Reserve notes—promises to pay of the United States government—are placed in the hands of the Federal Reserve agents by the Board of Governors, which secures them from the Bureau of Engraving and Printing. The agents are responsible to the Board for all Federal Reserve notes, or 100 per cent collateral, which Reserve banks give them in exchange for the notes. The agents issue weekly Reserve note statements which show the pertinent facts about collateral, volume, etc. The condensed statements for selected years appear in Table 34.

Federal Reserve Bank Notes.—In 1918 Federal Reserve bank notes were issued in small denominations to replace silver certificates which had been withdrawn from circulation when the silver dollars that served as their backing were melted down and sold abroad, as provided for in the Pittman Act. No Federal Reserve bank notes were issued from 1923 to March, 1933. In 1924 the obligation of the Federal Reserve banks for the outstanding small quantity was cancelled by depositing currency with the United States Treasurer. In 1933 these notes were reissued under provisions of the Bank

TABLE 34

FEDERAL RESERVE NOTES STATEMENT
(In Thousands of Dollars)

	June 30, 1928*	January 2, 1946†
Issued to Federal Reserve banks by agents.....	$2,002,811	$25,617,619
Collateral held by agents as security:		
Gold, gold coin, and gold certificates.........	1,143,205	10,523,000
Eligible paper..............................	1,263,985	155,032
U.S. government securities..................	....	15,388,221
Total collateral............................	$2,407,187	$26,066,253

Source: * Federal Reserve Board, *Fifteenth Annual Report* (1928), p. 81.

Source: † *Federal Reserve Bulletin*, February, 1946. p. 152.

Emergency Act, and at the beginning of 1940 the amount in circulation was a little over $25,000,000. In December, 1942, $660,000,000 of these notes were issued under provisions of the Bank Emergency Act of 1933. The Reserve banks immediately cancelled their obligations for them by depositing funds with the Treasury, and now they are classified as Treasury obligations and so do not appear on the Statement of Condition of Federal Reserve Banks.

All Types of Currency Are Elastic.—The Reserve banks' operations have given elasticity to all types of money in the United States. When member banks request currency, their needs may be met by shipments of silver certificates or any other type of money. When the need for emergency or seasonal currency is past, all types of currency are returned to the Reserve banks, which are the principal currency reservoirs for the nation.

The currency transactions between a member bank and a Reserve bank are similar to those between an individual and his bank. When an individual needs currency, he cashes a check or borrows from his bank. When a member bank needs currency, it, in effect, cashes a check or borrows from its Reserve bank. If an individual has more currency than he can use, he deposits it in his bank. When a member bank has more currency than it can use, it deposits the currency in its Reserve bank. The banks are encouraged to return unneeded currency, since all Reserve banks bear the costs of shipping currency to and from them; otherwise many banks would keep currency in their own vaults in order to avoid the insurance, packing, and shipping costs. Since currency is a nonearning asset, and since there is no member bank cost involved in returning it to Reserve banks, there is no reason why a bank should keep more than its day-to-day needs in its vaults.

The Reserve Requirements of Reserve Banks Are High

Since the Federal Reserve banks hold legal reserves of all the important commercial banks in the nation, safety demands that their assets be in the form of cash and liquid and marketable paper. Each Reserve bank is required to keep a reserve of 25 per cent in gold certificates against deposits and Federal Reserve notes. "Other cash" includes American coins and paper money of all kinds.

The relationship between cash reserves and demand liabilities, called the "reserve ratio," is one of the traditional guides to central bank policy. It is found by dividing the total reserves by the sum of the two items, total notes in circulation and total deposits. For example, if total reserves equal $14,000,000,000 and Federal Reserve notes plus deposits equal $16,500,000,000, the reserve ratio is over 84 per cent. The reserve ratio may be decreased (moved toward 80 per cent) by a decrease in the amount of reserves, an increase in the amount of demand liabilities, or both. The reserve ratio may be increased by an increase in the amount of reserves, a decrease in the amount of demand liabilities, or both. Throughout the history of the Federal Reserve System deposits have gradually increased, but the volume of Federal Reserve notes has fluctuated widely. The only periods of reserve stringency—1919-20, 1932-33, and 1943-45—were due to an increase in this type of liability.

During World War II the reserve ratio fell from over 90 per cent to 40 per cent; and, as a result, Congress changed the reserve requirement on June 12, 1945, from 35 per cent in lawful money against deposits and 40 per cent in gold certificates against Federal Reserve notes to 25 per cent against both types of liabilities. If Congress were to accept the banking principle of note issue, it would abolish the gold certificate and collateral requirements for Federal Reserve notes. This would permit elimination of the Federal Reserve agents and the Federal Reserve agent account. (See Table 34.)

Uncollected Items and Deferred Availability Items

These two items, which appear, respectively, as assets and liabilities, result from the clearing and collection services of the Federal Reserve banks for member banks, nonmember clearing banks, and other Federal Reserve banks. (See Chapter XI.) When checks and other items are received by the Federal Reserve banks, they are listed as deferred assets until they are collected. After collection they appear either as cash with the Federal Reserve banks or as deposits with the interdistrict settlement fund. But, because the work of collecting is a continuous one, there are always some items flowing through the Federal Reserve banks which are still uncollected when the books are closed at the end of the banking day.

On the liability side of the statement of condition, there appears the deferred availability item to offset the uncollected items which appear on the asset side. Technically, the amount involved should equal the amount of uncollected items; but, owing to the Federal Reserve banks' policy of giving reserve deposit credit to member banks for all checks within three days or less after receipt, the deferred availability total is less than that of the total for uncollected items. The extent to which Federal Reserve banks are giving member banks reserve credit for checks still uncollected (called the "float") is the difference between these two items.

Earnings and Expenses of Reserve Banks

In the foregoing pages emphasis was placed on the operation of Federal Reserve banks as reflected in their statement of condition. Additional information on the relative importance of certain phases of their work is suggested by the statement of earnings and expenses and distribution of net earnings. (See Table 35.)

TABLE 35

Earnings and Expenses of Federal Reserve Banks for Selected Years

Item	1939	1945
Current earnings:		
Discounted bills	$ 60,898	$ 1,977,081
Purchased bills	2,323	110
Industrial loans	615,169	100,755
Commitments to make industrial loans	128,577	12,533
U.S. government securities	36,903,367	139,552,881
All others	790,331	566,186
Total	$38,500,665	$142,209,546
Operating expenses:		
Salaries (incl. retirement contributions)	$20,662,528	$53,472,102
Directors' fees and expenses	134,268	128,363
Fed. Advisory Council, fees and expenses	16,102	15,480
Other traveling expenses	282,815	453,611
Postage and expressage	3,356,450	7,611,246
Telephone and telegraph	459,716	533,766
Printing, stationery, and supplies	782,704	3,241,708
Insurance (currency and security shipments)	236,389	28,292
Other insurance	232,087	220,365
Taxes on real estate, repairs, dep., etc.*	3,745,458	5,209,776
All others†	699,472	2,136,476
Total	$30,607,989	$73,051,185
Less reimbursements for certain agency and other expenses	$ 4,939,082	$31,384,732
Net operating expenses	$25,668,907	$41,666,453
Assessment for expenses of Board of Governors	$ 1,621,464	$ 2,340,509
Federal Reserve currency:		
Original cost	1,196,535	4,194,119
Cost of redemption	159,949	516,190
Total current expenses	$28,646,855	$48,717,271
Current net earnings	$ 9,853,810	$93,492,275

* Includes all expenses pertaining to buildings and equipment.

† Includes legal expenses.

Source: Federal Reserve Bulletin, February, 1940, p. 114; February, 1946, p. 194.

The distribution of net earnings of Federal Reserve banks reflects the public nature of these institutions. Dividend payments to stockholders (member banks) is limited to 6 per cent cumulative, and the remainder is transferred to the surplus or some other capital account of the Federal Reserve banks. Originally the government shared in the net earnings under certain conditions. The amount received prior to 1934, called a "franchise tax," was about $150,-000,000. In addition, the Federal Reserve banks were required to buy stock of the Federal Deposit Insurance Corporation in amounts equal to one-half their surplus as of January 1, 1933, or about $139,000,000. Since all the assets remaining after the liquidation of a Federal Reserve bank go to the government, the latter has not surrendered its rights to the excess earnings of the Reserve banks even though none of them are now being transferred to the government as a franchise tax.

While the expenses of the Reserve banks have increased steadily throughout the history of the Federal Reserve System, earnings have fluctuated widely. They were at peak figures during the years 1918-20 and during and since World War II. Since the allocation of net earnings on December 31, 1945, the amount in surplus (Sec. 7) is $358,355,000, or $206,635,000 in excess of the December 31, 1939, figure. Thus, throughout the history of the Federal Reserve banks these financial institutions have had net earnings of over $877,000,-000, about $230,000,000 of which has been paid to stockholders, the remainder being used to build up the banking structure of the United States.

In explaining these earnings it should be noted that the chief lending power of the Federal Reserve banks is dependent not on their capital and deposits, as is true of individual banks, but on their power to create money. Individual Reserve banks possess the right to create money, limited only by the demand for currency and the member banks' need to keep reserve balances, and the Reserve banks' gold certificate reserve requirements, which may be suspended. Their power to create deposits differs from that of a commercial bank in that it may make an investment or loan without being forced to meet withdrawals by using its reserves, except when there is a foreign demand for funds. Since it is in a position to issue Federal Reserve notes, requests for money may be met by its own promises to pay printed for this purpose. Since Federal Reserve credit is used as reserves by member banks, changes in its volume are particularly significant, because it is the basis for the multiple expansion of member bank credit.

Miscellaneous Operations of Federal Reserve Banks

Collection of Checks, Drafts, and Noncash Items.—The operation of a nation-wide clearing and collection system which includes about 90 per cent of all out-of-town checks has already been discussed. It is one of the most important services rendered the nation by Federal Reserve banks, with the assistance of the Board of Governors, which operates the Interdistrict Settlement Fund in Washington. In addition, Federal Reserve banks collect many noncash items (maturing notes, bills, securities, coupons, etc.) for member and nonmember clearing banks and make telegraphic transfers of funds for member banks.

Examinations.—The Federal Reserve banks are responsible for making examinations of state member banks in their respective districts and for examining state banks that have applied for membership. Each Federal Reserve bank has a bank examination department which co-operates with other national supervisory agencies and with the state banking departments in its Federal Reserve district. In carrying out examinations the Federal Reserve banks are guided by regulations issued by the Board of Governors of the Federal Reserve System.

Reporting.—Federal Reserve banks are responsible for keeping posted on the general character and amount of loans and investments of member banks so as to inform the Board of unsound credit conditions. They gather information and publish monthly reviews of business conditions in their districts. The senior officers travel extensively throughout their districts, keeping in contact through bankers' conferences and conventions with the banks' personnel of their district.

Administration of Board Regulations.—The Federal Reserve banks are responsible for carrying out most of the regulations of the Board, which now include all letters of the alphabet from A through W. Among those that do not pertain specifically to banks are: Regulation P, which pertains to voting permits of holding company affiliates; Regulation R, which concerns dealers in securities; Regulation T, which covers extension of credit by brokers, dealers, and members of the national securities exchanges; Regulation V, which pertains to loans guaranteed by the War and Navy departments and the Maritime Commission; and Regulation W, which is related to consumer credit.

Other regulations, some of which have already been considered, include: A, discount for and advances to member banks; B, open market purchases of bills and bankers' acceptances; C, accepting for member banks; D, reserves of member banks; E, purchase of warrants; F, trust powers of national banks; G, collection of noncash items; H, membership of state banks; I, increase or decrease in stock of Federal Reserve banks; J, check clearing and collection; K, banking corporations authorized to do a foreign banking business; L, interlocking directorates; M, foreign branches of national banks; N, relations with foreign banks and bankers; O, loans to executive officers of member banks; Q, payment of interest on deposits; S, discount purchases, loans, and commitments by Federal Reserve banks to provide working capital to commercial or industrial businesses; and V, loans by banks for the purpose of purchasing or carrying stocks registered on a national securities exchange.

QUESTIONS AND PROBLEMS

1. Why are the Reserve banks sometimes called bankers' banks? Why are they sometimes called government banks? Are they commercial banks?
2. How may the Treasury influence the volume of member bank reserves by increasing or decreasing its deposits with the Reserve banks?
3. Describe the "fiscal agency" activities of the Federal Reserve banks.
4. A first "principle which gives greater effectiveness to reserve under the Federal Reserve System is the insurance principle of distributing the risks" (Burgess, W. R., *The Reserve Banks and the Money Market* [rev. ed.], p. 26). Explain.
5. Distinguish among (*a*) "member bank reserve accounts," (*b*) "legal reserves," (*c*) "excess reserves."
6. Identify (*a*) "other deposits" and (*b*) "foreign deposits."
7. Explain the difference between eligible paper and acceptable paper. May ineligible paper be used to secure funds from Reserve banks? Explain.
8. Under what circumstances may the promissory note of the firm from which you purchase your clothes find its way into the portfolio of the Federal Reserve bank of your district? Explain.
9. Describe and account for the legal modifications made in the condition under which funds could be obtained by member banks from their Reserve banks.
10. Explain "loans to institutions other than member banks."

11. The following questions are based on the Statement of Assets and Liabilities of the Federal Reserve Banks (Table 33).
    a) What is the ratio of capital and surplus to deposits and notes? Is it too high? How does it compare to a similar ratio for all member banks?
    b) What is the reserve ratio? How much surplus reserves do the Reserve banks have?
    c) How much money is there in the 5 per cent redemption fund held against Federal Reserve notes? Is it enough? Why?
    d) What item or items show the amount of Federal Reserve credit in use?
    e) Identify "bills discounted."
    f) Are the types of government securities held significant? Why?
    g) Explain the existence of two surplus items.
    h) Identify "uncollected items" and "deferred availability items." Why are they not equal in amounts?
12. How will changes in the following factors tend to affect member bank reserves: (*a*) monetary gold stock, (*b*) currency in circulation, (*c*) volume of silver dollars and silver certificates, and (*d*) Reserve bank credit?
13. "Checks are cleared against reserves, but if reserves fall below the minimum requirements, they must be restored promptly" (Turner, R. C., *Member Bank Borrowing*, p. 13). Explain.
14. What is meant by "the discount rate"? May an individual Federal Reserve bank have more than one discount rate? (*Reference: Federal Reserve Bulletin.*)
15. Use Table 35 to identify (*a*) chief source of income of Reserve banks, (*b*) total expenditures of the Board of Governors, (*c*) chief expenses, (*d*) cost of postage and expressage, and (*e*) current net earnings.
16. How does the distribution of net earnings reflect the public nature of Federal Reserve banks?
17. What are the chief miscellaneous functions of the Reserve banks?

REFERENCES

See end of Chapter XXVIII

Chapter XXVIII

CREDIT POLICY OF THE FEDERAL RESERVE SYSTEM

A Credit Policy Involves Control over the Quality and Quantity of Credit in Use

Central banks affect the volume and types of credit used through their influence upon the credit practices of commercial banks. The Federal Reserve banks do not deal directly with the users of credit,[1] but indirectly through member banks and the money market. Their credit policy has been to influence the total amount of credit in use.

During depressions, when it is especially desirable in the public interest for banks to lend, the Reserve banks contribute to an easy credit policy by preventing depletion of reserves and by supplying new currency. During depressions the orthodox policy for central banks to follow is to contribute to recovery by making currency and commercial bank reserves abundant and to make the price of credit (interest rates) cheap. In the United States the Federal Reserve System has more influence on the amount of deposits than upon the amount of currency; therefore, much of the discussion of central bank credit control deals with control over member bank reserves. Although the system may provide the banks with enough reserves to make deposit currency available to agriculture, commerce, and industry at low rates, it cannot force the banks to use these reserves, it cannot force the businessmen to borrow, and it cannot force the public to spend the deposits when banks do make investments and loans.[2]

Commercial banking is very competitive; and, in a commercial banking system composed of thousands of banks, there are times when the financing of business transactions reaches undesirable proportions. Since periods of overexpansion are accompanied by overfinancing, the Federal Reserve authorities are expected to contribute to the attainment of stability by limiting the volume of currency and member bank reserves.

---

[1] Since 1931 direct loans have been authorized, but they are of minor importance (see Chap. xxvii).

[2] Board of Governors of the Federal Reserve System, *Monetary Measures and Objectives* (reprint from *Federal Reserve Bulletin*), p. 5.

A secondary factor that must be considered under the heading of "credit policy" is the types of business enterprises which are being financed, that is, the quality of credit in use. At all times the Federal Reserve authorities desire to provide ample credit for the legitimate needs of agriculture, commerce, and industry; but they are charged with the additional difficult task of preventing the excessive use of commercial banking resources for financing speculation in commodities, real estate, and securities.[3] How much is "excessive" and how to prevent the diversion of funds from legitimate to speculative financing are two difficult questions for Federal Reserve authorities to answer.

Although credit policy involves control over the quality and quantity of credit in use, a more accurate statement, when applied to Federal Reserve policy, calls for the use of the word "influence" in place of the word "control." The term "credit control" suggests the ability to shut off or turn on a credit machine whenever policies call for such action; but the loans and investments of thousands of banks and others cannot be controlled in this way. There are four major devices of control, namely, (1) changing the rediscount rate, (2) open market operations, (3) changing legal reserve requirements, and (4) control over credit used for speculative purposes, which includes the power to fix margin requirements.

Rediscount Policy Involves Changes in the Discount Rate

The traditional method whereby central banks influence the volume of commercial bank credit is to raise or lower the discount rate. Member banks customarily borrow at the Federal Reserve banks only to avoid deficiencies in their reserves, and changes in the discount rate make such indebtedness more or less expensive. The theory regarding the functioning of the discount rate is: if it is raised member banks will raise their discount rates to their customers, thus tending to check credit expansion; and if it is lowered member banks will lower their rates to their customers, thus tending to stimulate credit expansion.[4] In brief, the policy is to reduce the cost of credit

---

[3] See statement of the first Federal Reserve Board, *Annual Report,* 1914, pp. 17-18.

[4] The original Federal Reserve Act required that discount rates should be fixed "with a view of accommodating commerce and business" (*Federal Reserve Act, as amended,* Sec. 14, par. 5).

to stimulate borrowing or to increase the cost of credit to discourage borrowing. A change in discount rate is also important because of its psychological effects. The change in rate may be a minor factor in the cost of credit, but it is recognized the world over as a public announcement of a change in the credit situation.

Effects of Rate Changes Are Uncertain.—The success of the discount policy depends upon a definite relationship between the discount policy of the Reserve banks and the discount policy of commercial banks. Because of the large number of banks in the United States, the development of such co-operation is much more difficult than in England or France, where a few large commercial banks dominate the money market. The problem is not only one of controlling the volume of credit but also one of timing the credit control action.

Effectiveness of any policy of credit restriction or expansion depends upon the phase of the business cycle in which such action is taken. If the deflation psychology of businessmen becomes excessive, decreases in the money rates will not stimulate borrowing. Similarly, increases in discount rates, if delayed until inflation psychology is excessive, will not decrease borrowing by speculators and businessmen. In addition, many new speculative and other transactions may be financed with little change in the demand for new Federal Reserve credit.

An increase in the tempo of business may be financed entirely with an increase in velocity of member bank deposits, with no change in their volume and no change in the volume of member bank reserves. An increase in the velocity of deposit currency would increase the turnover of member banks' reserve accounts without necessarily affecting the average balances held at Federal Reserve banks. A decrease in business may be accompanied by a decrease in velocity of deposit currency, with no change in the amount of deposit currency and no change in the volume of member banks' reserves. The effects of an expansion or a contraction of member banks' reserve accounts on the total volume of deposit currency may be more than offset by a decrease in the velocity of deposit currency.

In the Banking Act of 1935, Congress made provisions for increasing the Board's control over the discount policy of the twelve Federal Reserve banks. Every two weeks, or more often if required, the twelve Federal Reserve banks must act upon their discount rates.

Before their action becomes effective, it must be approved by the Board of Governors. These changes in administration mean that now the Federal Reserve System may have a national discount policy rather than twelve regional discount policies. Although a change in the discount rates constitutes the traditional instrument of central bank credit control, it is now used in conjunction with other, and at times more important, devices of credit control.

Tradition against Borrowing.—While following a restrictive credit policy, the Reserve banks are aided by a tradition against member bank borrowing. Before the existence of the Federal Reserve System, most commercial bankers considered it to be a sign of weakness to have the item "rediscounts and bills payable" appear upon their bank statements. This tradition has continued, but the situation is complicated by the fact that sensitiveness to indebtedness is not the same among different banks and is not the same among all banks during different phases of the business cycle.

The aversion toward borrowing is greatest among New York banks, which, because of their contacts with the money market, are in the best position to avoid all except very short-term indebtedness at the Reserve banks. Other city banks are second in their avoidance of borrowing, while country banks are least reluctant to borrow. As a result, the effects of the use of Federal Reserve instruments of credit policy (expansion and contraction) are felt first in New York, then in Chicago, later in other more important Reserve cities such as San Francisco and Cleveland, and finally in country bank communities.

During the upswing in business, the need for liquidity is less pressing, borrowing becomes profitable, and banks are less sensitive to indebtedness. During the downswing in business, the need for liquidity is greater, borrowing is less profitable, and banks are more sensitive to indebtedness.[5] Although Reserve officials have encouraged seasonal and emergency borrowing, they have discouraged continuous borrowing by individual members.

History of Discount Policy.—When the Reserve banks were first opened, on November 16, 1914, seven of them announced a rediscount rate of 6 per cent on 30- and 60-day paper. The Atlanta and four western banks set the rate at 6½ per cent. The member banks hesitated to borrow because of the tradition against such

[5] Currie, L. B., *The Supply and Control of Money*, p. 97.

transactions and because of the slight business depression which existed at that time. Rediscount rates were soon reduced, but there was little demand for reserve credit until 1917. Thus the volume of rediscounting during the period preceding 1917 was small.

The heavy burden of financing the Allies during World War I fell upon the United States. Funds were raised by taxes and the sale of bonds. The demand for credit, from abroad and at home, was so great that it exceeded the savings of the American people. In order to buy bonds, Americans were forced to borrow at banks, and the banks were forced to borrow from the Federal Reserve banks. The Federal Reserve Board, acting under orders from the Treasury Department, encouraged such transactions by persuading Reserve banks to establish preferential rates on war paper. Government war financing was completed in the fall of 1919, and the Reserve officials were again free to establish their own credit policy.

In November, 1919, the Reserve banks raised their rates in order to check the rapid inflation which was taking place. The Board took the position that speculation in all fields, which was responsible for the price situation, must stop. Discount rates were further increased, and by May, 1920, several Reserve banks were rediscounting paper of 90 days' maturity at 7 per cent. In the United States, in May, a decline of prices began and proceeded so rapidly that a serious depression followed. The reserve ratio remained at a dangerously low level during 1920, and, if one accepts this traditional guide for credit policy, there was justification for the continuance of the high discount rates until 1921, when the rediscount rates were finally lowered.

Between the wars the discount policy of the system was guided primarily by business changes. During 1924, 1927, and 1930–40, the rediscount rates were kept at low levels in order to encourage business.[6] During periods of speculation, for example, 1919–20 and 1928–29, rates were at very high figures. The highest rates were in effect in 1920, when they ranged from 3 to 7 per cent. During World War II, Federal Reserve discount operations were directed toward the objective of making money cheap and abundant. For the first time since 1933, banks borrowed substantial amounts from the Reserve banks in order to maintain their Reserve positions. The rates in effect varied according to the type of transaction, from 1/2 of 1

[6] A factor influencing the discount policy for a short time in 1931 and 1933 was the fear of a continued loss of gold.

per cent to $1\frac{1}{2}$ per cent. Most of these rates had been in effect since 1942. The maintenance of the same rates for years at a time suggests the extent to which the Reserve authorities are willing to let this type of credit control remain dormant.

As long as the federal government and the Federal Reserve authorities are committed to a policy of easy money (low interest rates), it appears unlikely that changes in the discount rates will be an important instrument of credit policy. In 1946, the Reserve Board reaffirmed this cheap money policy and rejected the traditional device of raising interest rates to check inflationary developments. In support of its position the Reserve Board referred to the effects of higher interest rates on the federal budget, the levels of taxation, refunding operations, and the values of government securities. A sharp decline in the value of government securities, in the words of the Reserve Board, "could have highly unfavorable repercussions on the functioning of financial institutions and if carried far enough might even weaken public confidence in such institutions."

Open Market Policy Is a Federal Reserve Contribution to Central Bank Policy

A second way of influencing the volume of member bank reserve funds is through open market purchase or sale of federal government obligations. As already noted, the Federal Reserve authorities follow a "passive policy" in buying Treasury bills and bankers' acceptances; but they assume the initative in buying or selling other obligations, particularly government securities other than Treasury bills. The objectives of the Federal Reserve authorities' open market policy vary from time to time. In general, the policy as stated in the Federal Reserve Act is that "the time, character, and volume of all purchases and sales of paper . . . . eligible for open-market operations shall be governed with a view to their bearing upon the general credit situation of the country."[7]

Effects of Buying and Selling of Government Obligations by Reserve Banks.—If other things remain the same, purchases of government obligations by the Federal Reserve banks will increase the aggregate reserves of the banking system. If the sale is made in the open market through a broker, the seller will receive a draft on

[7] *Federal Reserve Act, as amended,* Sec. 12*A*.

a Federal Reserve bank, which he will deposit in his bank. When collected by the depository bank, the latter will have its reserve account credited with the proceeds. As a result, the amount of deposits and the amount of reserves in the banking system have increased by the amount of the transaction. The member bank, after setting aside the required reserve against its new deposit, will have new reserves available for lending and investing. If the seller of the obligation is a bank, there will be no increase in deposits; but the bank will have an increase in its reserve account equal to the dollar amount of the sale. It has merely exchanged an earning asset for a reserve account with its Federal Reserve bank.

If other things remain the same, sales of government securities by the Federal Reserve banks will decrease the volume of member bank reserves. If the purchase is made in the open market through a broker, the buyer will pay for his purchase with a check or draft on his bank. When the purchase is completed, the buyer will have lost part of his checking account, his bank will have lost part of its reserve account, and the volume of Federal Reserve credit will have declined by the amount of the transaction. If the government obligation is purchased by a member bank, the volume of the bank's deposits would not be changed, but the volume of the member bank's reserve account would have been decreased.

Perhaps it is needless to say that other things do not remain the same in the money market when the Federal Reserve authorities purchase or sell government securities. Among the things that may happen is the use of new Federal Reserve funds to liquidate loans at the Federal Reserve banks or to repurchase Treasury bills that have been sold to the Federal Reserve banks under a repurchase option—if so, there may be no increase in the volume of member bank reserves. Depositors may be hoarding currency, and foreign bankers may be withdrawing funds by requesting that gold be shipped—if so, these developments would tend to reduce the volume of member bank reserve accounts. Similarly, borrowing from the Reserve banks, sales of bills to the Reserve banks, and dehoarding of currency or imports of gold would tend to offset any open market policy that had as its purpose the reduction of member bank reserve accounts.

How Credit Policy Is Served.—Even though the effects of changes in the volume of member bank reserves may be offset by other developments in the money market, it does not follow that credit policy may not be served by the open market operations of the Federal Reserve authorities. An easy credit policy is aided by the purchases of government securities because of the effect upon prices in the capital market and the effect upon member banks' credit policy.

The purchases of government obligations tend to increase the price of government bonds, to reduce their yield as figured on market price, and to make it profitable for banks to sell them. If the bonds come out of the portfolios of member banks, the banks' reserves are increased, and these additional reserves may be used as a basis for new loans and investments. If, on the other hand, the bonds come out of the portfolios of individuals and corporations, the banks receive new deposits and new reserves, which may be loaned and invested. Banks may tend to shift their funds from government securities to other types of paper, and this will tend to stimulate the industrial bond market, the financing of heavy industries, foreign lending, and lending for commercial purposes.

If there are no surplus reserves and member banks are in debt at the Federal Reserve banks, the purchase of government securities by the Federal Reserve authorities will permit them to liquidate their debts. When member banks are out of debt they will tend to adopt a more liberal lending policy when customers apply to them for loans. Finally, there are banks which will not go into debt to the Federal Reserve or to correspondent banks; instead they will adjust their lending and investing policies and their loan and investment portfolios so as to maintain adequate reserves at all times. The Federal Reserve System's open market purchases will give them more Reserve funds, and they will tend to adopt more liberal lending and investing policies.

Similarly a "tight money" policy will be aided by the sale of government securities by the Federal Reserve banks because of the reduction in government bond prices and the effect on the credit policy of commercial banks. Lower bond prices make their sale by member banks unprofitable and also make bonds a desirable investment. Funds invested in these securities are not available for speculative or commercial purposes. Member banks may be forced to borrow from their Reserve banks in order to replace reserves lost when funds are used by individuals or others to buy government securities formerly owned by the Reserve banks. A member bank in debt or losing reserves tends to follow a more conservative credit policy. Those banks refusing to borrow from Federal Reserve banks will curtail loans and investments. The result is that banks tend to follow a "tight money" policy.

A Brief Summary of Open Market Policy.—Purchase and sale of government bonds in the open market did not become an instrument of national credit policy until 1922. Individual Reserve banks were buying government securities in order to build up their earnings, which were declining because of the liquidation of discounts and bills. Each Federal Reserve bank was buying independently in the New York bond market, and this resulted in bidding up prices and disorganizing the market. Since these purchases gave member banks more funds with which to liquidate their discounts, the purchases did not increase the earning assets of the Federal Reserve banks as expected. In order to eliminate or limit the competitive bidding and to co-ordinate the open market policy with the discount policy, the Open Market Committee, made up of five of the heads of the Federal Reserve banks, was appointed in 1922. In 1923 the committee was reorganized, and the following two guiding principles were recognized: (1) disorganization of the government security market was to be avoided and (2) purchases and sales were to be conducted with a view to "accommodating commerce and business."

In 1933 statutory provisions were made for the Open Market Committee, and in 1935 the committee was reorganized so as to give the Board of Governors a dominant voice in formation of policies. The law also made the committee's open market policy the policy of each Federal Reserve bank. Previously, individual Federal Reserve banks were hesitant about accepting the recommendations of the committee, because sales of government bonds might be desired when their price was low and purchases might be desired when their price was high.[8] Furthermore, practical bankers were interested in securing sufficient earnings to meet expenses. (Now the earnings from the system's open market account are distributed among the twelve Federal Reserve banks according to need.)

From 1922 to1940 changes in holdings of government obligations of the Federal Reserve banks were gradually co-ordinated, with changes in the discount rate. When the discount rate was increased, the

---

[8] In a free market the cycle of gilt-edge bonds tends to be just the opposite of the business cycle.

Reserve banks reduced their holdings of government securities; and when the discount rate was decreased, the Reserve banks increased their holdings of government securities. These changes were synchronized with business changes and gold movements. Thus, during 1922 the Reserve banks purchased $400,000,000 of government securities and lowered discount rates to combat the depression. Between June, 1922, and August, 1923, the system sold $515,000,000 of government securities because of a desire to offset the inflationary effects of gold imports. From November, 1923, to October, 1924, the Reserve banks purchased $500,000,000 in government securities to offset a decline in business, a policy which was reversed between November, 1924, and March, 1925, when the Reserve banks sold $230,000,000 in government securities. Between December, 1928, and September, 1929, the Reserve banks sold $450,000,000 in order to check the inflationary developments. Between September, 1929, and December 1933, the Reserve banks purchased $2,000,000,000 in order to check deflation. Further purchases would have been desirable, but the Reserve banks were handicapped by obsolete high reserve requirements and collateral requirements for Federal Reserve notes. The open market policy, "together with the concurrent reduction in discount rates, was an important factor in the general decline of money rates. . . . "

From 1934 to 1937 the Open Market Committee simply replaced securities that had matured with new purchases, with greater emphasis on long-term promises to pay. In February and March of 1937, many large banks sold their government obligations—particularly long-term bonds—in order to meet the increase in reserve requirements and to take accrued profits on their bonds. The result was a sharp decline in prices of government and other bonds. The Federal Reserve authorities increased their holdings of government bonds by over $400,000,000 in order to stabilize the market. An even greater break in bond prices accompanied the September, 1939, outbreak of World War II, which was checked by the buying program of the Federal Reserve authorities; and, as a result, at the beginning of February, 1940, the Federal Reserve banks were holding no Treasury bills, $1,100,000,000 of Treasury notes, and $1,300,000,000 of government bonds.[9] From 1934 to 1940 the open

[9] Langum, J. K., "Federal Reserve Open-Market Policy, 1934-1939," *Financial and Investment Review*, Vol. VIII, No. 4 (December, 1939).

market "operations have been used chiefly to help maintain orderly conditions in the market for high-grade bonds."[10]

During World War II the open market operations were directed to the maintenance of easy money conditions in order to facilitate the financing of the war. In the words of the Board of Governors, the operations "were directed toward the objectives of supplying banks with reserves sufficient to purchase such government securities as were not bought and held by other investors and of maintaining stable prices and yields on marketable government securities."[11]

Changes in Reserve Reqirements May Affect Volume of Credit

Primarily because of the gold situation, Federal Reserve authorities were given the power to increase or decrease the amount of excess reserves by raising or lowering, within limits, the legal reserve requirements of member banks. The Thomas Inflation Amendment (May, 1933) gave the Board of Governors the power to raise or lower reserve requirements in an emergency with the approval of the Secretary of the Treasury. The Banking Act of 1935 placed full responsibility for reserve requirement changes on the Board and prescribed that maximum rates could not be in excess of twice the amounts then prescribed by law.

Raising and lowering of reserve requirements aim to affect the availability of existing reserve funds for credit expansion. An increase may lead to an increase in discounting and a decrease in bank credit. If reserve requirements are increased, an individual bank may be forced to borrow, to sell some of its assets, to liquidate some maturing obligation, or to meet its reserve deficiency in some other way. If the bank already has excess reserves, less of them will be available as a basis for bank credit expansion. If reserve requirements are decreased, an individual bank will have free reserves that it may use to reduce any indebtedness or to lend or invest.

In August, 1936, the legal reserve requirements were increased

---

[10] Hersey, A, "Historical Review of Federal Reserve Policy," *Federal Reserve Bulletin*, April, 1940, p. 289.

[11] *Thirty-first Annual Report of the Board of Governors of the Federal Reserve System*, p. 3.

during the upswing in business; they were decreased in the spring of 1938, following the sharp decrease in business during 1937. In doubling legal reserve requirements from 1936 to 1937, the Reserve authorities sought to reduce excess reserves so as to bring them within the scope of possible Federal Reserve open market operations —a vain hope because of the further increase in reserves due to gold imports. In 1941 reserve requirements were increased to the maximum permitted under the law, with appreciable effects on excess reserves. Gold stock in the United States was now reaching its peak, and the influx was building up member bank reserves with greater rapidity than the demand for new bank credit. The outbreak of the second World War, the reversal of gold movements, the expansion of bank credit, and the increase in the volume of currency in circulation—all combined to change the reserve situation radically. Excess reserves in central reserve and reserve city banks declined, and banks adjusted their reserves by purchasing excess reserves of other banks (called federal funds), by selling Treasury bills in large quantities to Federal Reserve banks, and by borrowing from Reserve banks.

On three dates in September and October, 1942, the minimum reserve requirements against net demand deposits of central reserve city banks were reduced from 26 to 24 to 22 and then to 20 per cent, which brings them into line with the requirements for reserve city banks.[12] Reserves now in effect are 20 per cent against demand deposits of all reserve and central reserve city banks, and 14 per cent for country banks. The reserve requirements for time deposits are uniform for all member banks—6 per cent. Considerable relief was given all member banks when Congress provided that no reserves need be kept against Treasury balances resulting from member bank subscriptions to government securities for six months after the end of hostilities (called War Loan Deposit Accounts).[13]

Although the war has taken care of the excess reserve situation in the United States, the present conditions may be only temporary. When a bank has excess reserves, it is under pressure from stock-

---

[12] *Federal Reserve Bulletin*, August, 1942, pp. 748-53; September, 1942, p. 878; and October, 1942, p. 989.

[13] *Public Law 37*, 78th Cong., Sec. 2, April 13, 1943. Section 1 of this act exempted banks from payment of Federal Deposit Insurance Corporation assessments on these accounts.

holders, from potential borrowers, and from others to make loans and investments. Naturally, any individual bank is tempted to make use of its excess reserves because its profits depend in part upon the amount of its credit in use. It has been proposed that Congress permit the Board of Governors of the Federal Reserve System to raise reserve requirements beyond the limits now authorized by law, in order to be in a position at any time to reduce excess reserves to "manageable proportions."[14]

Although the present legal reserve requirements are almost twice those in effect from 1917 to 1935, they are comparable to those in existence before the creation of the Federal Reserve System. Under the old National Banking System, required reserves for central reserve cities, reserve cities, and country banks were, respectively, as follows: 25 per cent, 25 per cent, and 15 per cent. The present Federal Reserve System is superior to that of the National Banking System for the following three reasons: (1) the reserves are centralized in the vaults of the twelve Federal Reserve banks; (2) new reserves may be borrowed when the need arises; and (3) the reserve requirements may be increased for central reserve city banks or reduced for all or any group of banks or type of deposit by rulings of the Board if conditions justify such a change.

Quality of Credit Is an Important Aspect of Credit Policy

The Federal Reserve authorities' credit control devices considered so far have been those used chiefly to affect the volume of credit rather than the quality of credit. The original technical requirement for discounting favored short-term commercial, industrial, and agricultural paper. Paper arising out of speculation and investment transactions, with the exception of purchases of government bonds, were ineligible as security for advances or rediscounts. The Banking Act of 1935 permits Reserve banks to make advances upon any type of sound paper, but at a penalty rate of at least 1/2 of 1 per cent per annum. Although the basis for obtaining Federal Reserve credit has been broadened, the basic emphasis upon liquid short-term commercial, industrial, and agricultural paper has been

[14] Among its (1946) recommendations to Congress the Board suggested: "A further possibility would be to grant additional power to the Board to raise reserve requirements, within some specified limit, against net demand deposits." *Thirty-second Ann. Rept.*, p. 8.

maintained in the law. The current policy of the Federal Reserve authorities is to stabilize the market for government securities with emphasis on Treasury bills. As long as the Board guarantees the Treasury that the bill rate of 7/8 of 1 per cent will be maintained, it cannot use the traditional devices of credit control.

Reserve Credit Should Not Be Used for Speculation.—Following 1929, Congress had the greatest aversion to the use of credit for speculative purposes. During and since World War I, speculation has been the most harmful in real estate, commodities, and securities. In order to prevent undue use of credit in financing transactions in these fields, the Board of Governors was given the following direct powers over member banks and member bank officers:

1. The Board is given power to fix, from time to time, for member banks in each Reserve district, the maximum percentage of its capital and surplus which any member bank may lend, collateralized by stock and bonds. This percentage may be changed upon ten days' notice.
2. The Board may direct any member bank to refrain from an increase of its security loans for any period up to one year, under penalty of suspension of all rediscount privileges at the Reserve bank.
3. The Board may cancel the privilege that member banks have of borrowing on fifteen-day promissory notes supported by government securities and may declare existing notes due if member banks do not heed notice to decrease loans on collateral security.
4. The Board may, after due warning and a hearing, remove a bank officer or director for violation of a banking law or the following of unsafe or unsound banking practices. In order to avoid injury to the officer or to his bank, every opportunity is to be given for him to cease and desist from his offense. A copy of the order to the offender is sent to every director of the bank, and the local board of directors may take action. All proceedings are kept secret, except those which may be unavoidable with legal action.
5. The Board is given the power and responsibility of fixing from time to time the amount which holders of securities may borrow for the purpose of purchasing or carrying securities from either brokers, security dealers, or banks.

The Federal Reserve banks are required to keep the Board of Governors informed concerning individual cases where illegal, unsafe, and unsound practices exist. They are required by law to keep themselves informed concerning the general character and amount of loans and investments of member banks. They must ascertain if undue use is being made of member bank credit for the carrying of or the trading in securities, commodities, or real estate. Not only must the directors of Federal Reserve banks have this information, but they must use it to determine whether to grant or refuse member banks' requests for discounts or advances. If a member bank is permitting too much of its credit to be used for speculation, the Reserve bank authorities must so report to the Board of Governors, with their recommendations.

Moral Suasion.—In the past, reserve banks have had some influence on the loan and investment policies of banks. This influence has been called "moral suasion." It is best illustrated by the policy adopted during and following World War I. Banks were encouraged to borrow from their Reserve banks in order to finance the "borrow and buy government bonds" campaigns but they were urged to discriminate against speculative and nonessential loans.

Following the period of war financing, the Reserve banks adopted and carried on a successful campaign to drive war paper from the portfolios of Reserve and member banks. Individuals who had borrowed to buy government bonds were forced to liquidate their loans, and member banks were forced to liquidate their obligations to the Federal Reserve banks. In carrying through this campaign, reserve officials used one or more of the following banking practices:

1. Member banks were advised by mail and in person to reduce loans.
2. Several Reserve banks refused to accommodate certain individual member banks. Others did so at progressively higher rates of rediscount.
3. Banks stated their needs at the beginning of the year, and Reserve banks refused to accommodate in excess of the lines of credit established at that time.
4. Certain banks were notified periodically that their conditions were unsatisfactory.

The use of direct pressure was greatest in the agricultural districts. It was successful in part but was followed by a vigorous discount policy late in 1919 and during 1920. Political criticism of "direct action" was widespread, and numerous charges of favoritism were made by bankers, politicians, and the general public.

Reserve Credit Should Not Be Used for Profit.—Rediscount rates at Reserve banks are below the discount or interest rates of member banks. Member banks may be tempted to borrow funds in order to make a profit by relending them. The attitude of the Board is disclosed by the following statement:[15]

It is a generally recognized principle that reserve bank credit should not be used for profit, and that continuous indebtedness at the reserve banks, except under unusual circumstances, is an abuse of the reserve bank facilities. In cases where individual banks have been guilty of such abuse, the Federal Reserve authorities have taken up the matter with officers of the offending banks and have made clear to them that their reserve position should be adjusted by liquidating a part of their loan or investment account rather than through borrowing. Abuses of the privileges of the Federal Reserve System, however, have not been general among the member banks. The tradition against continuous borrowing is well established, and it is the policy of the Federal Reserve banks to maintain it.

The Board Controls Margin Requirements.—A large amount of speculation in securities in the United States is financed by grants of credit from bankers and brokers. The Securities Exchange Act of 1934 gave the Board of Governors of the Federal Reserve System the power to fix the maximum amount of credit that could be extended by banks or by brokerage houses on stocks registered on a national securities exchange. By lowering the loan value of securities, the Board may check speculation when it appears to be excessive. By increasing the loan value of securities, the Board may encourage speculation when it is at a low ebb.

The primary purpose of giving the Board the power to change margin requirements was to prevent too great a flow of credit into speculative channels, such as occurred during the period 1927–29, with resulting inflation of security prices. Since 1934 the loan value of securities "for the purpose of purchasing, carrying or trading in securities" has been fixed from as low as having no loan value to as high as 60 per cent of the market price of the security at the time of purchase. This means, in the first case, that speculators must pay cash for their securities, and, in the second case, that a person buying $1,000 of securities may borrow $600 from his bank, broker, or dealer, the margin requirement of the purchase being $400, or 40 per cent. Securities bought on an exchange must be paid for soon after purchasing, which means that the amount over the margin requirement ($600 in the foregoing case) must be provided by the bank or broker, whichever takes the speculator's order. If a broker

[15] *Annual Report of the Federal Reserve Board,* 1928, p. 8.

is financing the margin transaction, he borrows from his bank, and so in both cases bank credit is involved.

On January 21, 1946, when the Board specified that in "general accounts" no stock has a loan value and that the margin required for short sales shall be 100 per cent of the current market value of each such security, the regulations applied only to future transactions in securities. The regulations specified that the margin requirements for specialists accounts (brokers) shall be 50 per cent for long and short sales.[16]

Although control over margin requirements cannot prevent speculation in securities, as long as individuals have an abundance of cash, it can and has forced speculators to use a larger percentage of their own capital in carrying on their operations. Furthermore, those speculators who can and do borrow to the extent that their assets permit are forced to curtail their activities. The reduced volume of margin trading has increased the emphasis upon the investment phase of the brokerage business. This power over margin requirements affects brokers and dealers in securities, non-member banks, and member banks.[17] The inclusion of institutions other than member banks under this regulatory power means a broadening of the activities of the Federal Reserve authorities. If only the regulatory aspects of the problem were to be considered, there would seem to be justification for turning over this function to the Securities and Exchange Commission; but the purchasing and carrying of securities involves the use of bank credit, which has a very important bearing upon business in general, and thus the problem is properly placed in the hands of the central banking authority.

International Banking Relations.—Before 1933, officers of the Federal Reserve banks were leaders in arranging for international central banking relations which involved the Federal Reserve System. Former Governor Strong, of the Federal Reserve Bank of New York, took the lead in establishing correspondent relationships with foreign central banks of issue. The most extensive participation of the Reserve system in the field of international banking took place in 1931, the year of the international panic. During 1931 the Federal

[16] *Federal Reserve Bulletin,* August, 1945, pp. 769-74; February, 1946, pp. 126-27.

[17] Regulation T specifies conditions for "extension and maintenance of credit by brokers, dealers, and members of national securities exchanges." Regulation U specifies conditions for "loans by banks for the purpose of purchasing or carrying stocks registered on a national exchange."

Reserve Bank of New York, in association with the other Federal Reserve banks, entered into agreements with foreign central banks to purchase specified amounts of prime commercial bills bearing their guarantee of repayment in gold. The foreign banks in question were the Austrian National Bank (May 20), the Reichsbank of Germany (June 26), and the Bank of England (August 1). The Bank for International Settlements, the Bank of France, and other foreign central banks participated in all or part of these agreements, along with the twelve Federal Reserve banks.

In 1933 the Board of Governors was authorized to regulate all relations and transactions between Federal Reserve banks and foreign banks or bankers. Now the Board requires the Reserve banks to obtain prior permission before they enter into negotiations, agreements, contracts, or understandings (other than those covering routine matters) with any foreign bank, banker or government. The Board reserves the right to modify such agreements before they become effective and also reserves the right to be represented at any meeting that may be held with foreign bankers. It requires written reports of meetings, copies of agreements, and full information concerning all relationships and transactions with foreign banks, foreign bankers, and foreign governments.[18]

Responsibility for Gold Policy Is in the Hands of the Government

One of the functions of a central banking system is to insure the country a sufficient gold supply to back its credit and currency. In 1914 the United States owned over 25 per cent of the world's monetary gold supply, but it was scattered among thousands of banks. The first banking task undertaken by the Federal Reserve banks and the Board was to accumulate as much of this gold as possible. Following the entrance of the United States into World War I, this movement was intensified, with excellent results. Gold in the system increased from 25.7 per cent of the total domestic stock on January 1, 1917, to 62.2 per cent on January 1, 1919.

In 1922 the Federal Reserve System stopped its impounding of gold, and much of the new stock which the country gained during the next three years was placed in circulation in the form of gold cer-

[18] "Regulation N," *Federal Reserve Bulletin*, January, 1944, pp. 11-12.

tificates. The effect of this policy was to establish a secondary reserve which, in theory, could be mobilized by the simple process of paying out Federal Reserve notes when new currency was demanded and withdrawing the gold certificates from circulation. The Reserve banks used this method from 1930 to 1933. The accumulation of gold certificates was a slow process, and, as a result, the system had reason to regret its policy of paying them out.

At the end of January, 1933, over $1,100,000,000 in gold certificates were outside the system. During the next five weeks the amount outstanding increased, but this was due in part to the technical fact that the Reserve banks did not have on hand a sufficient supply of Federal Reserve notes and so met the demand for currency by issuing gold certificates. Federal Reserve notes could not be printed fast enough to care for the panic demands for currency.

Under provisions of the Gold Reserve Act of 1934 the responsibility for the gold stock of the country was given to the Secretary of the Treasury. As previously noted, there is little justification for continuance of this situation. The Federal Reserve Bank of New York is handling most of the routine work in connection with the export and import of gold and the operation of the Stabilization Fund. The logical procedure would be to return title to gold held by the Treasury to the Federal Reserve banks and to eliminate the present farcical setup, wherein the latter hold gold certificates. As advisors on international monetary policy, the Federal Reserve authorities would properly consult the National Advisory Council on International Monetary and Financial Problems as provided for in the Bretton Woods Agreements Act of 1945. The present situation, wherein the Board is primarily responsible for domestic credit and the Treasury for foreign credit transactions, through its control over gold, foreign exchange transactions, and foreign funds, should be eliminated.[19]

Member Bank Reserves and the Money Market

Chart XI summarizes much of the discussion which appears in this chapter. It is published in modified form in the *Federal Reserve Bulletin.* There are five lines showing (1) gold stock, (2) total mem-

[19] Under the Trading with the Enemy Act, as amended by the First War Powers Act of October, 1941, the Treasury rigidly controlled all foreign transactions in foreign exchange, securities, gold, coin, and currency during the war years.

ber bank reserves, (3) money in circulation, (4) reserve bank credit, and (5) Treasury cash and deposits.

Since changes in member bank reserves are regarded as the "key to the money market," changes in other factors will be considered as they affect member bank reserves. Thus an increase in gold stock during 1939 and 1940 tended to increase member bank reserves, and its subsequent decline tended to reduce them. The gradual in-

CHART XI

MEMBER BANK RESERVES AND RELATED ITEMS*

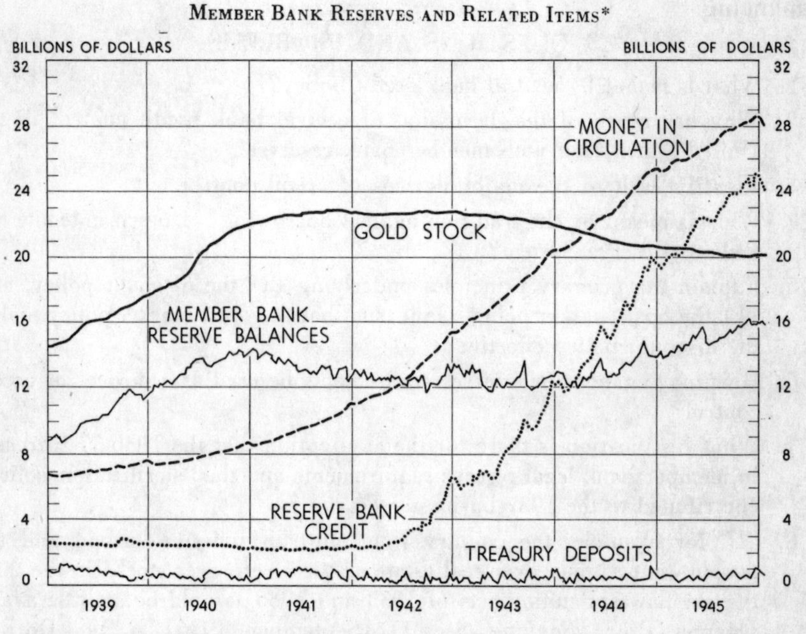

*Source: *Federal Reserve Bulletin*, February, 1946, p. 143.

crease in currency in circulation tended to reduce the volume of member bank reserves, which was offset by the sharp increase in Federal Reserve credit in use. Not only did the expansion of Federal Reserve credit meet the needs for new currency, it also offset the loss of gold exports and provided the member banks with new reserves during part of 1944 and 1945. Increases in Treasury cash and deposits tended to reduce member bank reserves, while decreases in Treasury cash and deposits tended to increase them, thus causing minor fluctuations in the volume of member bank reserves. A decrease in nonmember bank deposits will tend to increase member bank reserves, and an increase in nonmember bank deposits will decrease member bank reserves.

From the foregoing summary, the dominant role of the Federal Reserve authorities in the money market is apparent. Through purchases of Treasury bills, through open market operations, and by freely discounting at low rates all paper offered, they have offset the deflationary effects of gold exports and of the increase in money in circulation. They have provided the member banks with adequate reserves on which bank credit was expanded as needed for war financing.

QUESTIONS AND PROBLEMS

1. What is meant by central bank credit policy?
2. Why has much of the discussion of central bank credit control in the United States dealt with member bank reserves?
3. Identify each of the major devices of credit control.
4. What is meant by the tradition against borrowing? Does it antedate the Federal Reserve System?
5. Explain the primary principles underlying (*a*) the discount policy, and (*b*) the open market policy. Is it true that the open market policy makes the discount policy effective?
6. How may changes in reserve requirements be used as a device for credit control?
7. What justification is there for the assumption that the 1936-37 increases in member bank legal reserve requirements and the "sterilization policy" contributed to the 1937 business recession?
8. "If, for example, the country went into an inflation period and the people went as mad over real estate as they were over stocks in the 20's, the new laws [Banking acts of 1933 and 1935] would be of little avail" (Hanna, P. S., *Banking*, Sec. 11 [September, 1936], p. 1). Do you agree? Explain.
9. "The Federal Reserve System was founded on the belief that the working capital of the country (the deposit currency) must be protected against absorption in speculation" (Robinson, G. B., *Monetary Mischief*, p. 40). Was this accomplished? Are the Reserve authorities better equipped legally to achieve this goal today than before 1933? Why?
10. "Can a local banker refuse to follow the dictates of the Federal Reserve bankers? No. He must expand his loans, or call them in, as he is forced to do, regardless of what his own honest judgment may be" (Coughlin, Chas. E., *Money: Questions and Answers*, p. 46). Is this true?
11. "A policy of cheap and abundant money is the orthodox contribution of a banking system towards recovery from a depression" (Towers, G. F.

[Governor of the Bank of Canada], Address before First Annual Meeting of the Shareholders, February 25, 1936). Was this policy used in the United States?

12. Explain "Quality of credit is an important aspect of credit policy."
13. What is the attitude of the Federal Reserve authorities toward the use of Federal Reserve credit for speculation? For profit?
14. Explain how the Board of Governors may influence speculation.
15. What is meant by the "Twilight of the Federal Reserve System"? (See Westerfield, R. B., *The Annalist*, September, 14, 1939.)
16. "Today there is an over-lapping of functions between the Treasury and Federal Reserve authorities which means both inefficiency and administrative friction." Explain.
17. Explain why the government bond market has become such an important segment of the money market.
18. What was the World War II credit policy of the Federal Reserve authorities? Explain how each of the major credit control devices was used.
19. Explain the chart entitled "Member Bank Reserves and Related Items."

REFERENCES

Beckhart, B. H. *The Discount Policy of the Federal Reserve System.* New York: Henry Holt & Co., 1924.

Blaser, A. F., Jr. *The Federal Reserve Bank of Cleveland.* New York: Columbia University Press, 1942.

Board of Governors of the Federal Reserve System. *The Federal Reserve System: Its Purposes and Functions.* Washington, D.C.: Board of Governors of the Federal Reserve System, 1938.

Bopp, K. R. "Central Banking at the Crossroads," *American Economic Review*, Supplement, Vol. XXXIV (March, 1944), pp. 260-77.

Burgess, W. R. *The Reserve Banks and the Money Market*, chaps. ii-vi, and x. Revised ed. New York: Harper & Bros., 1936.

Chapman, J. M. *Fiscal Functions of the Federal Reserve Banks.* New York: Ronald Press Co., 1923.

Goldenweiser, E. A. *Federal Reserve System in Operation.* New York: McGraw-Hill Book Co., Inc., 1925.

Gregory, T. E. "What Can Central Banks Really Do?" *American Economic Review*, Vol. XV (1925), pp. 53-59.

Harding, W. P. G. *The Formative Period of the Federal Reserve System.* Select. Boston: Houghton Mifflin Co., 1925.

Hardy, C. O. *Credit Policies of the Federal Reserve System*, chaps. i and ii. Washington, D. C.: Brookings Institution, 1932.

Harris, S. E. *Twenty Years of Federal Reserve Policy*, chaps. i, vii, and x. Cambridge: Harvard University Press, 1933.

Hersey, A. "Historical Review of Objectives of Federal Reserve Policy," *Federal Reserve Bulletin*, April, 1940, pp. 279-89.

Langum, J. K. "Earning Assets, Deposits, and Reserves of Member Banks, 1929-1938," *Financial and Investment Review*, School of Business, University of Minnesota, Vol. VII, No. 7 (August, 1939).

Langum, J. K. "Federal Reserve Open-Market Policy, 1934-1939," *Financial and Investment Review*, Vol. VIII, No. 4 (December, 1939).

Langum, J. K. "The Statement of Supply and Use of Member Bank Reserve Funds," *Review of Economic Statistics*, Vol. XXI, No. 3 (August, 1939), pp. 110-15.

Laughlin, J. L. *The Federal Reserve System: Its Origin and Problems*. Select. New York: Macmillan Co., 1933.

Members of the Staff, Board of Governors of the Federal Reserve System. *Banking Studies*, pp. 249-414. Washington, D.C.: Board of Governors of the Federal Reserve System, 1941.

Reed, H. L. *Federal Reserve Policy, 1921-1930*. New York: McGraw-Hill Book Co., Inc., 1930.

The Federal Reserve Act as Amended to October 1, 1935. Washington, D.C.: U.S. Government Printing Office, 1935.

Thomas, R. G. *Our Modern Banking and Monetary System*. New York: Prentice-Hall, 1942.

Turner, R. C. *Member Bank Borrowing*. Columbus: Ohio State University Press, 1938.

Warburg, P. M. *The Federal Reserve System*. 2 vols. Select. New York: Macmillan Co., 1930.

Weissman, R. L. *The New Federal Reserve System*, chaps. iii-viii. New York: Harper & Bros., 1936.

Whittlesey, C. R. *The Effects of War on Currency and Deposits*. New York: National Bureau of Economic Research, 1943.

Williams, J. H. "The Banking Act of 1935," *American Economic Review*, Supplement, Vol. XXVI (March, 1936), pp. 95-105.

Willis, H. P. *The Federal Reserve System*, Books II and III. New York: Ronald Press Co., 1923.

Willis, H. P. *Theory and Practice of Central Banking*. New York: Harper & Bros., 1936.

Willis, H. P., and Chapman, J. M. *The Banking Situation*. Part V. New York: Columbia University Press, 1934.

Youngman, A. P. *The Federal Reserve System in Wartime*. New York: National Bureau of Economic Research, 1945.

See also annual reports of the Board of Governors of the Federal Reserve System (formerly Federal Reserve Board); and the monthly issues of the *Federal Reserve Bulletin*.

Chapter XXIX

MONETARY POLICY AND ECONOMIC STABILIZATION

Introduction

In the preceding chapter it was noted how the Federal Reserve authorities were able to achieve stability in the money market during the war. Now the question may be asked: "To what extent may monetary authorities aid in achieving the goal of maintaining full employment?" Throughout the history of the United States, wars and other periods of booms and full employment have been followed by depressions and mass unemployment. Many disturbing factors have been recognized as contributing to economic depressions, one of the most important being monetary instability. While advocates of the monetary theory of the business cycle have been accused of recommending a panacea which is too simple to solve the complicated problems involved, their answer is that they are only drawing attention to one important aspect of the problem.[1]

Reference has been made to the conditions under which means of payment are created in the United States. When production is increasing, producers obtain from their banks funds needed to meet pay rolls and other expenses. By lending, the banks increase the volume of deposit currency. Similarly, speculators desiring to make a profit from an increase in prices will borrow from banks, and these lending operations will further increase the volume of deposit currency. Bankers may take the initiative in putting new bank credit on the market by investing in securities which will further add to the already swollen quantity of bank credit.

With the inflationary swing under way, there is not much that an individual banker can do to check the development. If his bank refuses to lend and invest, there will be a tendency for cash reserves to flow into his bank. He will find it difficult to explain to members of his board of directors and other stockholders why his bank is keeping idle cash while other bankers in the community are finding profitable outlets for the funds of their banks. Under such circumstances, bankers must be businessmen first and philosophers second.

When production is declining, producers repay loans at their banks, and deposit currency is destroyed. When speculators' accounts

[1] Hawtrey, R. G., *Trade Depression and the Way Out* (2d ed.), pp. v-vi.

are closed, more deposit currency is lost. During the downswing in business, the most popular policy for bank management is one which stresses liquidity of assets, and this leads to sales of investment holdings and a further decline in bank credit.

With a deflationary swing under way, there is not much that an individual banker can do to check the movement. If his bank refuses to contract its volume of bank credit, there will be a tendency for the cash reserves of his bank to flow to other banks. While these reserves may be replaced by borrowing from his Federal Reserve bank, this policy may be difficult to explain to the satisfaction of his board of directors. While other bankers are following a conservative policy, he is putting their bank deeper and deeper into debt. Furthermore, the Federal Reserve authorities may be willing to carry such a bank for only a limited period of time, and bank examiners may object to such a practice if continued for any length of time.

Borrowers from commercial banks are both debtors and creditors. Although their debts are similar to those of other institutions, their credits are demand deposits which are means of payment. In an upswing in business, when deposit currency is expanding, investments are more than savings, because, among other reasons, the volume of bank credit is expanding. In a downswing in business, when deposit currency is contracting, investments tend to be less than savings, because, among other reasons, the volume of bank credit is contracting.

The 100 per Cent Reserve Plan

Volume of Means of Payment Stabilized.—The essence of the 100 per cent reserve plan is that commercial banks would be required to keep a 100 per cent reserve in cash against demand deposits in their own vaults or elsewhere. Commercial banks would be required to build up their present fractional reserves against demand deposits by selling assets or borrowing from their Federal Reserve banks or some newly created organization such as a Federal Monetary Authority, which would have the right of note issue. Bank notes would be placed in circulation through the demand deposit departments of the 14,500 commercial banks. The chief social advantage of the 100 per cent reserve plan would be the resulting stability in the volume of the means of payment available for spending or investing.

Under this system, checks would be cleared and collected as they are now under the fractional reserve system; but the banks gaining cash reserves would be required to keep them as reserves against their new deposits. If a depositor transferred part of his checking account to a savings account, the bank would shift the 100 per cent reserve to that department. If a depositor cashed a check, the volume of deposit currency would be decreased, but the volume of money outside the demand deposit department would be increased. If a bank customer deposited cash in his checking account, the volume of deposit currency would be increased, but the volume of currency outside the demand deposit department would be decreased. Thus the total volume of money and deposit currency would not be changed by these transactions. Loans from commercial banks would be made through the savings department, because the demand deposit department would have no excess reserves to lend. If the borrower wanted a checking account, the proceeds of the loans would be transferred to that department in the form of cash. Whether he takes a checking account, because of its convenience, or hand-to-hand money, the total volume of means of payment available for spending remains the same. The bank's customer would borrow existing funds and not newly created deposits.

Repayment of loans would have no effect on the total quantity of deposit currency and money. If a check were sent to the savings department in payment of a loan, cash would be transferred to the savings department from the demand deposit department. Thus, the decline in the volume of deposit currency would be offset by the increase in the amount of hand-to-hand money.

Monetary Expansion and Contraction.—The adoption of the 100 per cent reserve plan would mean that commercial banks would create no new means of payment in the form of deposit currency that could not immediately be covered by cash provided by the national monetary authority. In order to have an expansion or contraction of national currency, it would be necessary for the monetary authority to take action. While seasonal and cyclical fluctuations in the demand for currency would be cared for in part by a change in the velocity of money, there would be a long-run demand for new currency in order to care for the increase in population, the increase in the volume of production, and the increase in the volume of transactions. This demand for new currency would be satisfied through the open market operations of the monetary authority.

If an expansion of means of payment is desired, the monetary authority would buy government securities in the open market. The seller would receive a bank draft in payment, which he would deposit in his bank. The monetary authority would print hand-to-hand currency and make it available to the depository bank in order to cover the new deposit currency.

If a contraction in the volume of means of payment is desired, the monetary authority would sell government securities in the open market. The buyer would make payment with a bank draft or check, which, when collected, would be offset by a reduction in the volume of bank reserves. Thus the volume of the means of payment would be curtailed by the amount of the open market sales by the monetary authority.

The 100 per Cent Reserve Plan and the Federal Reserve System.—While certain advocates of the plan favor the creation of a new monetary authority, the chief advantages of the plan could be secured by permitting the Board of Governors of the Federal Reserve System to increase member bank reserve requirements against demand deposits to 100 per cent. Legal reserves could be kept, at the discretion of the commercial banks, in their own vaults or as reserve accounts with the Federal Reserve banks. Since the liabilities of the Reserve banks would have to be increased so as to match the present volume of demand deposits, it would be necessary to repeal the present minimum reserve requirements against Federal Reserve banks' liabilities. This would not weaken our banking system, because the transfer of the note issue privilege to central banks makes the currency principle of note issue obsolete.

The 100 per Cent Reserve Plan and Commercial Banks.—If the 100 per cent reserve plan were adopted within the present framework, all banks handling checking accounts would have to join the Federal Reserve System. They would receive credit on the books of the Federal Reserve banks or would receive Federal Reserve notes in exchange for government securities until their reserves were built up to equal 100 per cent of their demand deposits. The effects of the adoption of this plan upon the chief items in the commercial bank statement are suggested by Table 36. There would be no assumed change in liabilities, but there would be a decline in the loans and investments of commercial banks and a corresponding change in "cash or deposits with the Federal Reserve System."

One of the chief objections to the 100 per cent reserve plan is the loss of earnings commercial banks would tend to suffer. This loss might be offset by permitting banks to retain title to all or part of the government securities transferred to the Federal Reserve banks. This would be in keeping with the method used under the National Banking System, under which notes were secured by depositing government bonds with the Treasury, where they were held in trust for the depositing banks and the income from the bonds remitted to the banks. In case of bank failure, the securities were sold, and the proceeds of the sale were used to take up any notes in the hands of the public.

TABLE 36

EFFECTS OF ADOPTION OF 100 PER CENT RESERVE PLAN ON BANK ASSETS AND LIABILITIES

	Present System	100 per Cent System
Assets:		
Buildings, loans, investments, etc.	$10,000,000	$ 2,000,000
Cash or deposits with F.R.S.	2,000,000	10,000,000
Liabilities:		
Capital account	2,000,000	2,000,000
Demand deposits	10,000,000	10,000,000

Permitting banks to retain the earnings from the government securities, as suggested in the foregoing, would defeat one purpose of the plan, that is, a reduction in the debt service of the government. The Federal Reserve banks would be holding more than one-third of the national debt, and, since all surplus earnings would be recaptured by the government, the net cost of the debt would be reduced. Since most of the debt held by commercial banks was paid by usurpation of the monopoly power of the government to create money, the advocates of the plan argue that the transfer of the government securities would be morally justified.

It would be difficult to forecast with any degree of accuracy the effects of the plan on the operation of commercial banks. There would probably be a tendency to reclassify demand deposits as time deposits, because banks would be required to hold only fractional reserves against them. This type of "near money" might be used as a means of payment and thus defeat the purpose of the plan to stabilize the total quantity of means of payment. This possibility is so great that it might be necessary to require all savings institutions to enforce an "adequate notice" rule of thirty or more days before deposits may be withdrawn.

The adoption of the 100 per cent reserve plan would probably cause an increase in service charges against checking accounts, because demand deposits could not be invested in government bonds (or other securities), the earnings on which have partly offset the cost of handling these accounts under the present system. However, the issue is whether the general public should pay in part for these services under the present plan through interest payments on the government debt (with taxes) or whether the burden should fall upon those who use the banking services.

The loss of earnings of commercial banks may be offset in part by a reduction in costs of bank operation. There would be no need to insure demand deposits with the Federal Deposit Insurance Corporation, and this would involve a saving of 1/12 of 1 per cent. Investing and lending by banks would be decreased, and this would make possible a reduction in pay roll expenses.

The Effects on the Commercial Banking System.—The operation of the plan would probably reduce banking services to the general public and would tend to eliminate the present flexibility of the commercial banking system, which permits banks to iron out weekly, monthly, seasonal, and cyclical disturbances in the money market. It would encourage the development of instalment and other commercial financing companies. It might induce large industrial and other business enterprises to use their liquid balances to finance not only their own needs for short-term capital but also the credit needs of their customers. It might make it necessary for the government to provide for lending either through existing agencies or through newly created ones.[2]

The 100 per cent reserve plan would really mean no added security for deposit currency over and above that prevailing at the present time. During a crisis, additional paper money may be made available just as readily under a fractional reserve plan as under a 100 per cent

[2] See Brown, H. G., "Objections to the 100 Per Cent Reserve Plan," and Thomas, R. G., "100 Per Cent Money," *American Economic Review*, June, 1940, pp. 309-23; Higgins, B., "Comments on 100 Per Cent Money," *American Economic Review*, March, 1941, pp. 91-96; and Graham, F. D., "100 Per Cent Reserve: Comment," *American Economic Review*, June, 1941, pp. 338-40.

reserve plan. At the present time, the chief asset behind deposit currency is government securities. Under the plan, the statement that "banks are as safe as the credit of the United States government" would remain unchanged.

The Treasury and Credit Policy

Abolition of the Independent Treasury System.—One of the purposes of the Federal Reserve Act was to free the banking system from reliance on Treasury policy. During ordinary times the flow of money to and from the Treasury was disturbing to the banking system. The depressing effects of tax payments could be offset by leaving these funds on deposit with national banks, but the extent to which each administration used this device varied with the policy of the Secretary of the Treasury. Even when they used national banks freely as depositories, there were always charges of favoritism in their selections of banks to be used and criticisms of the arbitrary manner in which funds were withdrawn.

During panics, some secretaries of the Treasury went to great lengths to relieve banks. It was common practice to anticipate interest payments on the outstanding government debt; to purchase bonds, often at a premium, for sinking funds; and to increase the deposits of government funds in national banks. In addition, banks were sometimes permitted to accept federal deposits without keeping any reserve against them and to use municipal and state bonds as collateral for these deposits, provided the federal government bonds freed from this use were used as security for new issues of national bank notes.

In his report to the National Monetary Commission, Dr. Kinley criticized this situation, because it gave the Secretary of the Treasury too much power. In addition, such practices as payment of interest and other obligations before they were due were too trivial to be worthy of a great government. Furthermore, the practice of purchasing government bonds to provide banks with funds was expensive for the government.[3] As noted previously, Congress in the Federal Reserve Act authorized the Federal Reserve banks to act as the fiscal agents for the government. After these banks assumed their new functions, the independent Treasury system was abolished.

[3] Kinley, David, "The Independent Treasury of the United States and Its Relations to the Banks of the Country," *National Monetary Commission*, pp. 323-27.

Even though Congress may have desired to lessen the influence of the Treasury on banking policies, just the contrary has been true. Part of this situation has resulted from two world wars, but the chief reason has been the more socialistic approach toward banking and other problems.

Increasing Deposits with Federal Reserve Banks.—At times the Treasury has permitted its deposits with the Reserve banks to remain at a high level in order to reduce the volume of member bank reserves. When the Treasury sells bonds, it may leave funds with member banks, thereby increasing their deposits and therefore their reserve requirements. If these funds are transferred to the Reserve banks' "United States Treasurer—general account," the transfer is made by debiting the "member banks—reserve accounts" and crediting the account of the Treasurer. This transfer reduces the volume of member banks' reserve accounts, which remains true only so long as these funds remain unspent.

Treasury Cash in Own Vaults.—A modification of the policy of increasing Treasury deposits at the Reserve banks is for the Secretary of the Treasury to keep Treasury funds in its own vaults. Taxpayers will lose deposits, member banks will lose reserve accounts, and the Treasurer's deposits with the Reserve banks will be reduced. Before World War II, the total of these two funds fluctuated between $3,000,000,000 and $4,000,000,000, which seems to be a large amount to keep idle when the budget is unbalanced. However, the "Treasury cash" item included the unused $1,800,000,000 in the Stabilization Fund and other unused profits from devaluation of the gold dollar.

Sterilization of Gold Imports.—On December 21, 1936, the Secretary of the Treasury, with the approval of the President, announced a new government plan of sterilizing gold imports and neutralizing the effects of gold exports upon the domestic credit structure. This plan was simply one of buying gold, as had been the case since 1933, but with the supplementary new policy of borrowing and keeping unspent an equal amount of member bank reserve credit. Importers of gold continued to receive checks from the Treasury, which they deposited with their banks; these banks deposited the checks with their Federal Reserve banks, which gave them new reserve credit. Instead of depositing gold certificates with the Federal Reserve banks, as had been the practice in the past, the gold certificates were placed in the "inactive gold account" in the Treasury. The Treasury replenished its account with the Reserve banks by borrowing in the open market or by transferring existing Treasury balances in member banks to its account in the Federal Reserve banks. The effect in either case was to cancel the increase of member bank reserves created by gold imports.[4]

Desterilization of the Inactive Gold Accounts.—The sterilization of gold, inaugurated to keep member bank reserves within manageable proportions, was an expensive part of the Treasury's credit control policy. At the time the program was embarked upon, considerable attention was given to the danger of sudden withdrawals of foreign funds invested in marketable securities and short-term balances, with the resulting monetary disturbances. No such development materialized, and, during the 1937 business recession, provisions were made for desterilization of the "inactive gold account." The funds were transferred to the Treasurer's account with the Federal Reserve banks, and part of these credits were used to retire government obligations. The effect of these two steps was to increase the volume of total reserves of member banks. The chief result of this experiment has been to test a new mechanism of member bank reserve control which may be used in the future to prevent too great an increase in member banks' reserve balances.

Other Control Devices.—The devices of credit control already discussed do not complete the list of powers which the Treasury may use to check overexpansion of bank credit. A decrease in government borrowing from member banks and liquidation of government securities would tend to check the increase in deposit currency and to bring about a decrease in bank credit. Increasing taxes, hoarding social security funds instead of investing them in government securities, and decreasing government spending would be likely to be deflationary measures because of their effects upon private income. Decreasing the purchases of gold and silver would also have a tendency to check any increase in excess reserves.

Fiscal Policy and the Banking System

Deficit Financing.—Within recent years greater emphasis has been placed upon the role to be played by governments in preventing

[4] Langum, J. K., "Treasury Gold Policy and Member Bank Reserve Balances, 1934-1939," *Financial and Investment Review*, Vol. I, No. 12 (August, 1939).

booms and depressions. During the early 1930's, fiscal policy was designed to correct certain weaknesses and shortcomings in central bank policy. An easy money policy alone might not be sufficient to induce producers to borrow and invest. If potential borrowers refuse to borrow, then the deficiency in the volume of bank credit could be met by borrowing by the federal government. From 1933 to 1939 the government not only reflated the deposit currency structure by deficit financing through loans from commercial banks but also expanded the volume of deposit currency. By 1939 the volume of demand deposits was 50 per cent greater than at the peak in 1929.

The government borrowing policy not only contributed to an increase in the volume of deposit currency but also to a reduction in interest rates. Interest rates declined first in the short-term market for government obligations and then spread to other fields. During the thirties the reduction in rates was general, with those in the mortgage field having been least affected. Low interest rates have resulted in the following: (1) reduction in the costs of governmental borrowing, (2) stimulation of production, (3) encouragement of home building and home ownership, (4) reduction in the costs of farm ownership, and (5) stimulation of consumption by instalment buying, etc. However, "easy money" may prove a boomerang to borrowers, because interest payments are but a small charge compared to the costs of repayment of principal. The greatest disservice which a creditor may do a borrower is to lend him funds which he cannot repay. The stimulating effects of lower interest rates on building and production have been partly offset by increases in real property, corporate income, social security, and other types of taxes. Although private financing did not revive to the extent expected and excess reserves remained high before World War II, the central banking policy of making credit cheap and abundant was achieved largely through fiscal policy of the government.

Increasing Importance of Direct Monetary Control.—During World War II fiscal and monetary policies were determined by war needs. The expansion in the volume of money and credit made it easier for the government to raise taxes and to sell securities to the general public. The filling-up of the portfolios of commercial banks with government obligations has made the use of the traditional methods of credit control obsolete. The raising or lowering of interest rates is no longer a practical device of credit control. This means that in order to control inflation there must be less reliance on monetary control and greater reliance on fiscal policy and selective controls in the monetary field. The Board of Governors will have to make greater use of the newer devices of credit control than those which influence the price of credit.

The direct control devices that may be used include a supervisory policy directed to achieving greater economic stability, regulation of consumer credit, regulation of the maximum percentage of banks' capital and surplus that may be lent collateralized by stocks and bonds, fixing limits on the amount of mortgage loans that may be permitted, raising or lowering reserve requirements, influencing member bank policies directly by "moral suasion," raising or lowering interest rate payments on time deposits, placing a maximum on the amounts of long-term marketable securities that any commercial banks may hold against its net demand deposits, and by requiring all commercial banks to hold a specified percentage of short-term obligations as secondary reserves against net demand deposits.[5]

Fiscal Policy and Money Income

Governments may go beyond a policy of stabilizing the volume of currency and strive to achieve full employment by stabilizing money expenditures and money income at the high level reached during the war years. The use of national fiscal policy to control the levels of money income, employment, and productive activity is based upon the income-expenditure theory. The assumption is that there is a direct relationship between money income and real income, between an increase in investments and an increase in income, and between a decrease in investments and a decrease in income. In order to compensate an economy for loss of income due to hoarding and other increases in savings that are not invested, it is proposed that governments should intervene by borrowing and spending. To offset inflationary developments traced to an excess of investments over savings, the proposal is that the government should increase

[5] The Federal Reserve authorities have made technical modifications to facilitate the extending of Federal Reserve credit to the market. For example, in 1942 the Reserve banks, in conformity with instructions from the Open Market Committee, announced their readiness to buy Treasury bills at a rate of ⅜ of 1 per cent per annum. Later a repurchase option at the same rate was added (Bopp, K. R., "Central Banking at the Crossroads," *American Economic Review*, Supplement, Vol. XXXIV [March, 1944], pp. 268-69; and *Thirty-second Annual Report of the Board of Governors of the Federal Reserve System*, pp. 7-8).

taxation, reduce its debt, and limit the amount of private spending. To date, most of the attention has been given to how fiscal and monetary devices may be used to prevent deflation and not much to their possible use in preventing inflation.[6]

A fiscal policy to offset cyclical fluctuations would include a "cyclically adjusted public spending program" and "a cyclically administered tax policy." Public spending during the business cycle would include a consideration of public compensatory spending to offset fluctuations in private spending as well as "pump-priming," the multiplier principle, and other theoretical effects of government action.

Pump-priming.—During downswings in business, money incomes decline because of a decrease in spending. Most disturbances originate because savings are greater than investments. Funds are hoarded, debts at banks are paid, the volume of bank credit declines, and funds are withheld from the market by businessmen, by institutional investors, by banks, and by others. This decline in income tends to be cumulative, as illustrated by the decline in national income from $82,900,000,000 in 1929 to $40,100,000,000 in 1932, that is, more than 50 per cent. There were certain developments within the cycle which tended to check this movement. Accumulated savings are spent for consumption, and businessmen are forced to increase expenditures for merchandise, capital repairs, and new machinery. The increase in liquidity of banks, of other business firms, and of wealthy individuals tends to decrease the necessity for hoarding and for building up cash balances. The decline in the prices of real estate, securities, and commodities presents opportunities for profits, which are taken advantage of by those who are able to do so. As pessimism disappears, there is an increasing tendency for business and productive activity to be renewed.

The history of the business cycle suggests that there may be developments outside the cycle which will provide the impetus for

---

[6] Some attention has been given to possible ways in which government financing could be carried on without increasing inflation. According to the Board of Governors, "It has been the policy of the Government from the beginning of the war to sell the largest practicable amount of new securities to investors other than commercial banks in order to redirect into the war effort as large a part as possible of the income derived by the public from the Government's disbursements for the War. This policy was directed not only toward facilitating war finance but also toward diminishing the danger that income in excess of available civilian goods would bring inflationary pressure on prices" (*Thirty-first Annual Report of the Board of Governors of the Federal Reserve System,* p. 2).

recovery. Among these factors have been wars, threats of wars, new inventions, gold discoveries, and increases in exports due to crop failures abroad. Rather than wait for the business cycle to run its course, government spending has been advocated to check the deflation and to set the economy on its way toward full recovery. Thus, by pump-priming at the right moment, those natural forces which would bring about full recovery would be set in motion.

Compensatory Spending.—Another approach to the problem of stabilizing income is to have the government spend to offset a decline in private spending or private investment. This type of expenditure is considered to be successful, even though it does not increase national income by any more than the amount of government expenditure. Much more is expected of pump-priming.

If public expenditure is to be effective, it must be so financed as not to decrease private expenditure. If income which might otherwise be spent or invested is taken from consumers and others by taxation or borrowing, there is no net gain from fiscal spending. It is for this reason that deficit financing by borrowing from commercial banks with excess reserves has been so popular. A tax on corporations' undistributed profits was also used to encourage the distribution of these surpluses as dividends, so as to place more funds in the hands of consumers for spending.[7]

As a result of both fiscal and monetary policy, the national income increased from $40,100,000,000 in 1932 to $71,500,000,000 in 1937. The greatest effect of fiscal spending on national income occurred during the war years. From 1940 to 1945 the annual rate of government spending increased to $80,000,000,000. At the same time there was an increase in private spending for consumption, which was offset to some extent by a decline in capital outlays. As a result of these developments, the national income increased from $77,600,000,000 in 1940 to $160,700,000,000 in 1944.[8]

Multiplier and Acceleration Principles.—Whether the expenditures are designed to "prime the pump" or to compensate for the loss of private spending, the effects on income may be greater than the

[7] The effects of the undistributed profits tax on the net savings of corporations are suggested by the fact that they "dissaved" $700,000,000 more in 1937 than in 1938 when the tax was reduced to nominal levels (see Kuznets, Simon, *National Income and Its Composition, 1919-1938*, Table 22, p. 216).

[8] *Federal Reserve Bulletin*, February, 1946, p. 191.

amount spent. This is because of the effects on consumption and, as a result of increase in consumption, on investments.

If a million dollars is spent on public works, a part is paid to wage earners and others who will use it to buy consumer goods. The recipients of these funds will in turn spend them in part for consumption. Thus, during a year, the amount of new spending for consumption may be many times the original amount of the government expenditure. The stimulating effects on spending will gradually wear off, because some of the funds will be used to repay debts at banks, held as idle balances, or temporarily hoarded in the form of hand-to-hand money.

The new consumption which would result from governmental spending would also tend to stimulate investment. If an individual industrial plant is already in full production making consumer goods and the demand for the consumer goods increases, there will be an additional demand for capital goods. If this demand necessitates plant expansion as well as an increase in equipment, the amount of spending will be greatly accelerated.

Tax Policy.—The tax structure would be adjusted so as to encourage or discourage private spending. Sales taxes, social security taxes, and other taxes that weigh heavily on consumers would be reduced during depressions and increased during boom periods. Taxes that prevent a flow of new risk capital into industry would be reduced or eliminated during depressions and increased during business booms. Practically all taxes, with the possible exception of inheritance taxes, tend to discourage private spending, but, among the major ones, those on net income are the least depressing to business. They have the added advantage of being able to adjust themselves automatically to the business cycle, decreasing or increasing with similar changes in business.[9] The problem would be to reorganize the state and local tax structure so as to place greater reliance on this type of taxation and less on real property taxation.

---

[9] The attitude toward a balanced budget is suggested by the following: "There is nothing sacred in the budget in and of itself. In periods of depression it cannot be balanced; the choice then is between unbalancing it deliberately by doing what needs to be done to bring back prosperity and having it become unbalanced by a decline in revenue and by emergency outlays reluctantly made but unavoidable. In periods of prosperity, with a reasonable tax system, the budget would be in balance. In fact, a surplus of revenue for reduction of the public debt would be likely" (Goldenweiser, E. A., Hagen, E. E., and Garfield, F. R., *Jobs, Production, and Living Standards*, p. 16).

Economic Council.—At the present time it is recognized that banking, monetary, fiscal, and business cycle problems are inseparably intertwined. In February, 1946, the President signed the Employment Act of 1946. Congress in this act rejected the principle that booms and depressions were part of the inevitable course of things and accepted the principle that governments should do something to prevent them. The law provides for an Economic Council of three advisers to the President, at an annual salary of $15,000 each. Their duty will be to forecast economic disturbances and to recommend appropriate action. Reports and recommendations are to be made to a joint committee of seven men from each House of Congress, which is set up to study the periodic reports of the Economic Council and to devise appropriate legislation.

QUESTIONS AND PROBLEMS

1. May it be true that a country may have excellent banks and excellent bankers without having a good banking system? Explain.
2. "The 100 per cent reserve plan is reactionary in the sense that it involves a return to earlier, and in my judgment, sounder methods of banking." Explain. (*Source and reference:* Graham, "Partial Reserve Money and the 100 Per Cent Proposal," *American Economic Review*, Vol. XXVI, No. 3 [September, 1936], pp. 428-40.)
3. In what way, if any, is Professor Soddy justified in concluding that the public pays tribute to commercial bankers operating on the fractional reserve plan? (Soddy, Frederick, *The Role of Money*, pp. 69-73.)
4. Make a list of all the advantages of the 100 per cent reserve plan. Discuss them. (*Reference:* Fisher, Irving, *100% Money*, chap. i.)
5. "Issuing," says Mr. Nicholson, "is creating money; banking is managing money after it has been issued." (Quoted by Walker, *Money*, p. 445.) Do you agree? Why?
6. "Bank credit represents in the last analysis a hope, a prophecy of the future. It depends for its value on the value, or rather the prospective value, of the assets or enterprises on which the bank has loaned" (Berle, Dickson, and Others, *America's Recovery Program*, p. 31). Discuss.
7. What were the chief criticisms of the Independent Treasury System? What steps did Congress take to correct them?
8. Explain how increasing Treasury deposits with the Federal Reserve banks tends to reduce member bank reserve accounts.
9. What was the plan used by the Treasury in 1937 to "insulate the credit structure from the inflationary effects of gold imports"? How did it

differ from the practice of increasing Treasury deposits with the Reserve banks?

10. What is meant by the income-expenditure theory of the business cycle? Why do disturbances tend to originate in the relationship between savings and investments? Are all savings invested?
11. What is meant by fiscal policy?
12. Explain how "deficit financing" by borrowing from commercial banks reflated the volume of deposit currency from 1932 to 1937.
13. Identify "pump-priming" and distinguish between it and compensatory spending.
14. The results flowing from governmental spending from 1933 to 1937 were disappointing. Why?
15. "The deflationary effect of a reduction in war expenditures will be far greater this time than in 1918. War expenditures then absorbed about 25 per cent of the Nation's output; during 1944 and the first half of 1945, they absorbed almost 45 per cent." What are some of the favorable factors following World War II that were not present following World War I? (*Source and reference:* Goldenweiser, E. A., Hagen, E. E., and Garfield, F. R., *Jobs, Production, and Living Standards*, p. 19.)
16. What is the significance of the following: "The profits made in a competitive industry . . . . acts to increase the rate of savings, but they constitute an open invitation to investment. To put the matter categorically, a regime of monopoly means high profits which tend to be hoarded; a regime of competition means lower profits which tend to be employed"? (*source and reference:* Abramovitz, Moses, "Savings and Investments: Profits vs. Prosperity?" *American Economic Review*, Supplement, Vol. XXXII [June, 1942], pp. 52-88).
17. "To understand the economic impact of the government budget, the changes in public finances must be related to income and expenditures in the economy at large. The [President's] Message points up this relationship in a table containing both the Government's and the Nation's budgets" (*source and reference: Federal Reserve Bulletin*, February, 1946, pp. 109-18). Explain.
18. "Those who advocate vast governmental expenditures and deficit financing after the war as the only means of getting full employment, separate production and purchasing power sharply. Purchasing power must be kept above production if production is to expand in their view. If purchasing power falls off, production will fall off. The prevailing view among economists, on the other hand has been that purchasing power grows out of production" (*source:* Anderson, B. M., *Equilibrium Creates Purchasing Power;* reprinted from *The Commercial and Financial Chronical,* February 25, 1945, by the Economists National Committee on Monetary Policy, p. 1). What is the correct line of action suggested by the above quotation?

REFERENCES

Anderson, B. M. *Equilibrium Creates Purchasing Power.* Reprint from *The Commercial and Financial Chronicle,* January 25, 1945. New York: Economists' National Committee on Monetary Policy.

Angell, J. W. "The 100% Reserve Plan," *Quarterly Journal of Economics,* Vol. L, No. 1 (November, 1935), pp. 1-35.

Board of Governors of the Federal Reserve System. *The Federal Reserve System, Its Purposes and Functions.* Washington, D.C.: Board of Governors of the Federal Reserve System.

Bopp, K. R. "Central Banking at the Crossroads," *American Economic Review,* Supplement, Vol. XXXIV (March, 1944), pp. 260-77.

Chandler, L. V. *An Introduction to Monetary Theory,* pp. 115-83. New York: Harper & Bros., 1940.

Fisher, Irving. "100% Money and the Public Dept," *Economic Forum,* Vol. III, No. 4 (April–June, 1936), pp. 406-20.

Fisher, Irving. *100% Money.* New York: Adelphi Co., 1936.

Goldenweiser, E. A., Hagen, E. E., and Garfield, F. R. *Jobs, Production, and Living Standards.* Postwar Economic Studies, No. 1 (August, 1945). Board of Governors of the Federal Reserve System, 1945.

Graham, F. D. "Reserve Money and the 100 Per Cent Proposal," *American Economic Review,* Vol. XXVI, No. 3 (September, 1936), pp. 428-40.

Halm, G. N. *Monetary Theory,* pp. 247-334. Philadelphia: Blakiston Co., 1942.

Hansen, A. H. *Fiscal Policy and Business Cycles.* New York: W. W. Norton & Co., Inc., 1941.

Hart, A. G. " 'Model Building' and Fiscal Policy," *American Economic Review,* Vol. XXXV (September, 1945), pp. 531-58.

Hawtrey, R. G. *Trade Depression and the Way Out.* 2d ed. New York: Longmans, Green & Co., 1933.

Kuznets, Simon. *National Income and Its Composition, 1919-1938.* New York: National Bureau of Economic Research, 1941.

Simons, H. C. *A Positive Program of Laissez Faire.* Public Policy Pamphlet, No. 12. Chicago: University of Chicago Press, 1934.

Soddy, Frederick. *The Role of Money.* New York: Harcourt Brace & Co., 1935.

Spahr, W. E. *Fallacies of Professor Fisher's 100% Money Proposal.* New York: Farrar & Rinehart, 1938.

Villard, H. H. *Deficit Spending and the National Income.* New York: Farrar & Rinehart, 1941.

Williams, J. H. "The Implications of Fiscal Policy for the Monetary System," *American Economic Review,* Supplement, Vol. XXXII (March, 1942), pp. 234-49.

CHAPTER XXX

CONSUMER FINANCING INSTITUTIONS

Mass Production Involves Mass Consumption

Thirty years ago it was difficult to arrange for even an emergency personal loan on a business-like basis. Lending to finance purchases of automobiles and other consumer goods was shunned by banks on the assumption that it was in violation of the thrift principle on which banking was built. The need for borrowing or going into debt to finance consumption was regarded as a sign of shiftlessness. But, in spite of this attitude, consumers were going into debt to retailers and others for goods and services and were borrowing from pawnbrokers, unlicensed lenders, loan sharks, charitable societies, and friends to finance major and minor household needs.

The right to borrow in order to finance the operation of a business is old, but the right of the individual to borrow to finance the operation of a home is a very new concept. Operating a home calls for additional funds to finance births, sickness, deaths, and other emergencies. Until recent years, little was written about the correct procedure to use in financing the beautification and modernization of homes. This situation was changed in 1934, when Congress passed the National Housing Act. Under the provisions of Title I of the act, banks and other financial agencies financing alterations, repairs, and improvements to property and the purchase and installation of certain eligible equipment were insured against loss up to 20 per cent (10 per cent after April 1, 1936) of the totals of these loans. Although this act stimulated bankers' interest in instalment financing and other types of personal loans, there were already many banks and other financial agencies in the field.

Personal loans are usually for small amounts to individuals, payable in equal weekly, semimonthly, or monthly instalments. In general, three types of loans are made: (1) unsecured, or comakers', loans, which are endorsed by two names; (2) loans secured by chattel mortgages, wage assignments, insurance policies, and other acceptable collateral; and (3) discount of paper, which arises from the purchase of goods on the instalment plan. The chief requisites for credit, even though some loans are secured, are good character and a steady income.

The Russell Sage Foundation has been the pioneer research agency in the field of consumer credit. In principle, the program has been (1) to raise the buying power of the consumer by preventing too large a share of consumers' income from going to loan sharks and other unscrupulous lenders; and (2) to raise the standard of living by making credit available for financing purchases of automobiles, home equipment, and other durable or semidurable goods. By making possible the purchase of these goods, either with borrowed funds or in periodic payments, the use of consumer credit permits reduction in per unit costs. Thus the prices of automobiles, electric refrigerators, and other expensive goods are brought within the price range of things which may be purchased by a large number of consumers. Mass consumption permits mass production.

Regulation of Consumer Credit

During World War II the volume of consumer credit was greatly reduced by the government, the purpose being to check consumer spending so as to conserve strategic metals and other materials, to prevent inflation, to direct credit to the financing of the war, and to store up a backlog of buying power that would help to offset a postwar slump in business.

On August 9, 1941, the President issued Executive Order No. 8843 authorizing the Board of Governors of the Federal Reserve System to regulate the terms and conditions under which credit repayable in instalments and certain other types of consumer credit would be granted.[1] Under this order the Board issued Regulation W. At the time that Regulation W went into effect, the volume of consumer credit was expanding rapidly, the volume of instalment debt being $6,000,000,000 as compared to a little more than $3,000,000,000 at the beginning of 1939.[2]

---

[1] The Board issued Regulation W, which was amended 18 times up to 1946. The credit terms were first applicable to a list of goods found in the supplement to the regulation, which was later added to in order to further reduce consumer spending. See particularly *Federal Reserve Bulletin*, September, 1941, pp. 825-29 and 837-48; and May, 1942, pp. 399-424. The numerous amendments and interpretations are published in other issues of the *Bulletin*.

[2] *Federal Reserve Bulletin*, May, 1942, p. 404.

The Board of Governors in Regulation W, as amended, required all cash instalment lending (discounting and purchasing) banks and financial agencies and all vendors, such as stores, dealers, mail-order houses, and others, to conform to these regulations in granting credit.[3] All instalment financing agencies and vendors were required to register with the district Federal Reserve bank. All of them were authorized to do business under a general license. Failure on the part of a registrant to follow the rules as handed down by the Board resulted in suspension of its license to do business.[4] Several licenses were suspended, but in general Regulation W was strongly supported by most of the stores, financial agencies, banks, and others affected.

The Board's credit-term regulations increased the amount of down payments on purchases and shortened the time period for which consumer credit could be extended. The down payments for such goods as automobiles, refrigerators and other household appliances, and musical instruments were fixed at 33 1/3 per cent of the purchase price.[5] Maturities varied, the maximum being 18 months, and this was later reduced to 15 months or less for certain goods. By broadening the scope of the amendment to include more articles, charge accounts, single payments of $1,500 or less, as well as instalment loans, the control over the volume of consumer credit was fairly complete.[6] Although the volume of consumer credit declined, two factors other than credit control contributed to this decline. (1) Because of rationing and priorities, the volume of durable goods available for purchase declined. (2) The increase in cash in the hands of the general public permitted cash purchases without the use of credit. Because of the first, sales of durable consumer goods declined, and, because of the second, sales of nondurable consumer goods increased. The result was that the total volume of consumer spending during the war increased rather than decreased.

---

[3] Following the "hold the line" order of May 6, 1942, the original list of goods was expanded to include semidurable goods (*Federal Reserve Bulletin*, May, 1942, pp. 421-22). This amended regulation also provided, with reference to charge accounts, that unless payments were made by the tenth day of the second calendar month following the purchase, no further credit could be extended to purchase any listed article until the items in default were paid in full or placed on an instalment basis for payment within six months.

[4] See *Federal Reserve Bulletin*, December, 1942, pp. 1184-85; July, 1944, pp. 594-95; April, 1945, pp. 336-37; and March, 1946, pp. 249-51.

[5] *Federal Reserve Bulletin*, March, 1942, pp. 203-7.

[6] In September, 1946, Regulation W was made applicable to credits up to $2,000.

Sources of Consumer Credit

The sources of consumer credit are financing institutions (see Table 37), vendors (see Table 38), and sales finance companies. Although much progress has been made during the last thirty years

TABLE 37

CONSUMER INSTALMENT LOANS OUTSTANDING FOR SELECTED DATES
(In Millions of Dollars)

Financing institutions	Dec. 31 1933	Dec. 31 1941	Dec. 31 1945*
Commercial banks†	$ 29	$ 784	$ 469
Small loan companies	232	535	445
Industrial banking companies	121	298	200
Credit unions	27	217	125
Miscellaneous lenders	50	102	93
Repair and modernization loans insured by Federal Housing Adm.	....	301	182
Total	$459	$2,237	$1,514

* Preliminary.

† Includes only personal instalment cash loans and retail automobile direct loans and other retail direct loans not shown separately.

Source: Federal Reserve Bulletin, February, 1946, p. 188.

in financing the consumption and other needs of small borrowers, the bulk of our household credit needs are still being cared for by nonfinancial institutions. Some department, furniture, jewelry, and

TABLE 38

CONSUMER INSTALMENT SALE CREDIT OUTSTANDING FOR SELECTED DATES
(In Millions of Dollars)

	Dec. 31 1933	Dec. 31 1941	Dec. 31 1945*
Department stores and mail-order houses	$ 119	$ 466	$198
Furniture stores	299	619	283
Household appliance stores	199	313	14
Jewelry stores	29	120	74
Automobiles	459	1,942	227
All other retail stores	97	284	107
Total	$1,202	$3,744	$903

* Preliminary.

Source: Federal Reserve Bulletin, March, 1946, p. 334.

other stores finance their instalment sales with their own funds or with funds borrowed in the open market or from commercial banks. Merchants still supply more consumption credit than any one group of bankers, but there is a tendency for retailers of household appliances, clothing, automobiles, fuel, furniture, etc., to shift the financing burden to loan companies and banks by discounting their paper with them. During the 12 months ending September 30, 1941, registered vendors reported instalment sales of $6,761,000,000 and other credit sales of $4,665,000,000.

Cash Lending Agencies

The cash lending agencies in the field of consumer credit are: (1) individual lenders, (2) pawnbrokers, (3) Morris Plan and other industrial banks, (4) commercial banks, (5) licensed small-loan companies, (6) remedial loan associations, and (7) credit unions. Finance or discount companies are also active in financing sales of automobiles, household appliances, and other goods bought on the instalment plan.

Individual Lenders.—In spite of hostile public opinion, the amount of business done by unlicensed lenders remains at a high figure even though it has been reduced in recent years. Although many attempts have been made to eliminate illegal lending, the practice still persists. Before World War II, loan sharks in the United States were "reaping illegal profits of $100,000,000 a year" according to an estimate made by W. T. Foster in a study prepared for the Public Affairs Committee.[7] Illegal loans in the city of New York alone were estimated to have been in excess of $10,000,000, and the situation was much worse in the states which had no adequate provisions for small-loan companies.

The unlicensed lender made loans based upon whatever security he could obtain. It may have been a wage assignment, chattel mortgage on an automobile, or a pledged article left on deposit. In some cases he would accept a note signed by two comakers. In order to avoid usury charges, the loan was usually disguised in some way. When the borrower signed his contract, he may have agreed to pay a sum larger than that borrowed. For example, the borrower may have sold $60 of his next month's salary in exchange for $50 at the

---

[7] "Loan Sharks Profits Put at $100,000,000," *New York Times*, January 7, 1940, p. 50.

time of the contract. If but 15 days remained until pay day, the borrower would have paid $10 for the use of $50 for 15 days, that is, 480 per cent on an annual basis. If the entire amount could not be paid at the end of the loan period, a new contract was drawn to cover the balance.

Usual charges made by salary buyers were from 20 to 40 per cent per month (240 to 480 per cent per annum). In Dallas, Texas, borrowers had paid $85,000 interest on loans of $55,757, which averaged a little less than $22 per loan. Among 1,000 cases examined, the average interest rate was 271 per cent, the lowest 120 per cent, and the highest 1,131 per cent.[8] Although many of these small loans were illegal, lenders were able to collect for many reasons. Many corporations, in order to avoid the additional bookkeeping expense which would have been involved by extra salary disbursements, had a rule that salary attachments meant immediate dismissal. The rule was a help to loan sharks, because the mere threat of informing the employer of the salary attachment was usually sufficient to force payment. When other types of loans were made, threats of removing furniture and other nuisance practices led to repayment. Many states have unwittingly aided the loan sharks' and "salary snatchers'" business by passing stringent garnishee laws which permit creditors to take possession of all or a portion of a person's income with little legal difficulty. By securing a court order, a creditor may direct an employer to pay him a certain portion of an employee's salary. In New York State the percentage which may be attached on an income over $12 a week is 10 per cent, and only one attachment is effective at a time. Many other states have no limitations on the percentage which may be attached.

Salaried men and small wage earners were not the only ones to borrow from unlicensed lenders. Prosecution of usurious money lenders in New York revealed that small merchants were frequently paying more than 100 per cent per annum for their borrowed funds. Most of the illegal loan business was done by individuals operating in single offices, but a number of chain organizations had been created. Risks were large, but returns more than compensated for them. Probably 3,000,000 individuals borrowed from loan sharks annually. Former unlicensed lenders have been forced to register with the Board of Governors of the Federal Reserve System since September,

[8] *Ibid.*

1941. If Regulation W is continued indefinitely, many of the abuses associated with unlicensed lenders will be eliminated.

Pawnbrokers.—There are two types of pawnbrokers: those who make secured loans and those who purchase the property offered as security on agreement to resell to the borrower within a designated time. Pawnshops are patronized by two types of individuals: (1) those who are not poor but who are financially embarrassed because of accident, ill-health, scarcity of work, or requests from relatives; and (2) the traditionally poor. Before the war, about one-fourth of all pawnbrokers' loans were for business purposes, and the remainder were for household and personal use. The transactions required less red tape than loans from other institutions in this field. It was estimated that normally 85 per cent of the pledges are redeemed. Greatest profits were made on large loans and in selling unredeemed pledges. During 1931 and 1932 pawnbrokers' losses were high because of the shrinkage in value of articles pledged and an extraordinarily large number of unredeemed pledges.

Almost anything can be pawned, but jewelry is the most acceptable.[9] Most state laws prohibit the taking of goods from minors, intoxicated persons, servants, and apprentices. In order to check upon stolen goods, a register must be kept in which the property pledged is described. Some states require a description of the person who pledges the property. The pawn ticket is the pawner's only receipt; it shows the length of time allowed for redemption and usually the interest rate. It has been estimated that before 1930, 2,000 pawnbrokers made 20,000,000 loans annually, with an average value of $30 each to 7,000,000 individuals.[10] One-sixth of this business was done in New York. Since the average pawnbroker turns over his funds but 1.5 times per year, the amount of funds required to carry on the business is large. The bulk of these funds is supplied by banks.

The first legal regulation of pawnbrokers in the United States, in 1800, called for a license to carry on business, which was and is usually granted by city officials. If the applicant was of good character and could give a bond for surety, he was given a license. The majority of the states require state or local licensing, bonding, and

[9] The high-grade shops accept only gold, silver, and precious stones. They are called "jewelry shops." The shops that accept anything as collateral are called "bundle shops."

[10] Clark, Evans, *Financing the Consumer*, p. 41.

local supervision by police. The law specifies maximum charges, lenders' rights, and methods of sale of pledges. In spite of regulatory measures, sharp practices are common among pawnbrokers.

Industrial Banks.[11]—Arthur J. Morris, an attorney from Norfolk, Virginia, is given credit for the establishment of the first industrial bank in the United States and for the development of the Morris Plan system of banking. While legal advisor for a group of commercial banks, he was brought into contact with the credit problems of industrial workers. Many applicants for small loans were refused credit because the required loan was too small for the banks to bother with or because the applicant lacked collateral. This left the wage earner and professional man with small income at the mercy of the loan shark.

In 1910 the first industrial bank, the Fidelity Savings and Trust Company, was established in Morris' home town; now Morris Plan banks and other industrial banks are operating over 700 banks in the United States. These banks vary widely in relationship to the parent company (Morris Plan Corporation of America) in size, in corporate structure, and in type of business. They are influenced considerably by state laws, under which they operate. Most of the capital of individual industrial banks is locally owned and most of the funds are supplied by savings deposits, which usually receive the highest interest rate permitted by state or federal regulatory agencies.

Originally these industrial banks specialized in comaker loans, which were repayable on the instalment plan; but, within recent years, they have extended their operations to other fields. Collateral loans are made to merchants or individuals without the signatures of comakers and at a flat rate of 5 or 6 per cent. Morris Plan companies will lend as much as $5,000 on collateral or a comaker note, and many small merchants are now financed by these institutions. Since 1934 industrial banks have given active co-operation to the Federal Housing Administration in its campaign for remodeling and repairing homes. They have participated in instalment financing of automobiles, electrical equipment, and other merchandise.

A number of other companies operating along lines similar to the Morris Plan have been formed. The Wimsett System was created in 1921, and, within a few years, it had units in the United States,

[11] Herzog, P. W., *The Morris Plan of Industrial Banking.*

Canada, and Hawaii. Headquarters for the system are located in Chicago, and most of its offices are in Illinois and California. The Citizens Finance Company of St. Louis now heads the federated companies which make up the Citizens System. It is the third largest in the United States and contains units scattered throughout nine states in the Mississippi Valley.

TABLE 39

CASH INSTALMENT CREDIT, BY KINDS OF BUSINESS, SEPTEMBER 30, 1941
(Amount in Millions of Dollars)

Kind of Business	Number of Registrants*	Total Instalment Receivables	Retail Instalment Paper Purchased	Retail Instalment Credit Extended Directly	Personal Instalment Cash Loans
Sales finance companies...	3,237	2,074.0	1,976.0	60.1	37.9
Commercial banks and trust companies..............	12,586	1,699.1	776.7	475.9	436.5
Industrial loan companies or banks..............	756	229.7	68.7	33.2	127.8
State-licensed small loan companies..............	2,652	495.7	26.2	34.1	435.4
Credit unions..............	8,838	192.1	0.4	40.3	151.3
Other financial businesses†	8,662	352.2	45.2	174.8	132.2
Total lenders........	26,731	5,042.8	2,893.2	828.4	1,321.1
Total venders........	......	78.0	69.6	6.2	2.2
Grand total....	26,731	5,120.8	2,962.8	834.6	1,323.3

* Number reporting holdings of purchased paper or cash loans.

† Remedial and other small-loan companies, not state licensed; building and loan associations; mutual savings banks; agents, brokers, and dealers in real estate; holding and investment companies; mortgage companies; miscellaneous financial companies.

Source: Federal Reserve Bulletin, May, 1942, p. 435.

The industrial type of bank is less than forty years old, but it has won an important place in our banking system. In New York State these banks are permitted to accept deposits and carry on a commercial banking business. Their depression record was good, and, in the centers particularly hard hit by bank failures, they were among the first banks to reopen after the 1933 banking holiday. They have justified the system of periodic repayment of principal or the accumulation of a fund by periodic deposits for this purpose. The number of registrants, under Regulation W, with the Board of Governors in September, 1941, was 756. They reported their total volume of instalment credits or loans as being $299,700,000. (See Table 39.)

Many Commercial Banks Have Personal Loan Departments.—Before World War II, 1,600 commercial banks in the United States had formed personal loan departments to finance wage earners and salaried men, and by the end of the war over one-half of the banks in New York State had opened small-loan departments, and this is but an illustration of the nation-wide trend. In September, 1941, there were 12,586 commercial banks and trust companies registered with the Board of Governors of the Federal Reserve System that reported instalment and personal loans of $1,699,000,000. (See Table 39.) At the present time, practically all commercial banks have some special provisions for financing the purchases of goods on the instalment plan or lending to small borrowers.

Before 1934-35, the interest rates and other charges were the same as those made by industrial banks—6 per cent interest and 2 per cent service fee. Since then many of the banks have reduced their interest rate to 4 per cent without disturbing the 2 per cent service fee. Now certain banks are offering loans at 3½ per cent discount rate, plus a charge for life insurance to protect the bank during the loan period. In most states the interest rates charged by personal loan departments of commercial banks are subject to general bank statutes and not to special legislation, as in the case of small-loan companies and other "licensed lenders."

In 1936 a very significant step was taken by the state of New York when it authorized commercial banks to charge a gross 1 per cent per month rate on small loans. This law permits them to broaden the scope of their activities to compete with personal finance companies, remedial loan societies, and credit unions. The Federal Housing Administration home modernization and repair campaign did much to further the development of instalment loans by commercial banks and others. Title II of the Servicemen's Readjustment Act of 1944 as amended, which makes provisions for guaranteed loans to veterans, is giving an added impetus to personal financing by commercial banks.[12]

[12] "In order to permit small loan licensees to make loans to veterans under Title II of the Servicemen's Readjustment Act of 1944, the superintendent has authorized the granting of such loans in excess of $300, provided that the part of the loan above $300 is fully covered by the guaranty of the Administrator of Veteran's Affairs" (*Ninety-fourth Annual Report of the Superintendent of Banks, State of New York*, Part I, Legislative Document [1945], No. 21, p. 43).

When personal loans are made by personal loan departments of commercial banks, the regulations and conditions are similar to those under which industrial banks operate. Instead of borrowers repaying the funds borrowed on the instalment plan or by purchasing a deposit certificate, banks request them to open special accounts in which periodic deposits are made. The best accepted practice is to make this periodic deposit compulsory, and generally this practice is followed wherever the state law does not interfere. In some cases the borrower receives interest on these deposits. Not only are the bank customers benefited by the practice of accumulating funds to take up the loans, but often good savings habits are formed.

The personal loan business is a legitimate function of banking and is not only profitable in itself, but it also brings in new bank customers and new business for other departments of the bank. The plan is an excellent means of building good-will, a source of future profitable accounts, and a means of advertising the bank. The National City Bank of New York entered the field of personal loans through the creation of a special department in 1928. The chairman of the board of directors proudly referred to the work of this department in his annual report covering the year 1934 as follows:[13]

> Nowhere in the Bank are the human relationships so intimate as in the department which deals with Personal Loans. Here 99,353 people arranged loans during the year, at an average of $276, in the regular course of business; and 3,630 others were given loans totalling $2,184,290 in co-operation with the Government's program of loans for home modernization which went into effect in August. The department's loss on its loans during the year was at the rate of less than 15/100 of 1%.
>
> No man can know the operations of this department without a feeling of admiration for the integrity and character of the average American man and woman. Behind almost every loan is a story of good citizenship, and often of courage and faith. Homes are established, expenses incidental to the birth of children financed, lives are saved by timely surgical attention, the education of boys and girls, threatened by some unforeseen crisis, is continued.

The volume of such business done by commercial banks is suggested by Table 40, which gives the volume of their consumer instalment loans outstanding for selected dates.

Personal Finance Companies.—Over thirty states, the District of Columbia, and Hawaii have adopted the Uniform Small Loan law,

[13] Perkins, James H., *Report to Stockholders*, January 8, 1935.

which provides for regulation of the business of lending funds of $300 or less. A lender must secure a license, post a bond, and submit to inspection and regulation by the state banking department. The maximum interest rate is fixed at 3.5 per cent per month, or less in some states, on unpaid loan balances. The only fee that may be charged is one to cover actual filing charges. In order to protect borrowers, lenders are required to give a statement of the amount, security, rate of interest, maturity, etc., of the loan. The lender must permit borrowers to repay the loan in whole or in part at any time,

TABLE 40
CONSUMER INSTALMENT LOANS OUTSTANDING IN COMMERCIAL BANKS
(In Millions of Dollars)

Type of Credit	Dec. 31 1939	Dec. 31 1941	Dec. 31 1943	Dec. 31 1945*
Automobile (retail)				
Purchased	$ 218	$ 411	$ 55	$ 65
Direct	164	310	81	146
Other retail purchased and direct	155	288	68	97
Repair and modernization loans†	209	234	89	121
Personal instalment cash loans	347	451	221	300
Total	$1,093	$1,694	$514	$729

* Preliminary.

† Includes not only loans insured by Federal Housing Administration but also non-insured loans.

Source: Federal Reserve Bulletin, February, 1946, p. 189.

and the interest is computed to the exact date of repayment. The lender must give a receipt for all payments, and when the loan is paid all pledges and papers must be returned.

Loans are based upon chattel mortgages, wage assignments, and, to an increasing extent, upon the unsecured note of husband and wife, provided the borrower is a good credit risk and has been employed at one place for a number of years. The first type—a note secured by chattel mortgage, which usually covers household furniture or automobile—is the most common way in which loans are made. The chattel given as security would seldom cover the loss, therefore repossessions are few. The chief advantage of having this type of security is psychological; the borrower prefers to make every effort rather than go through the humiliating experience of giving up his furniture or his car.

Before the war, corporations operating under the Uniform Small Loan law, or its approximate equivalent, were doing an annual loan business of $350,000,000. On September 30, 1941, when all consumer credit was brought under the control of the Board of Governors, 2,652 state-licensed small-loan companies registered with the Board. Their cash loans and holdings of paper purchased totaled almost $500,000,000. (See Table 39.) About one-third of the companies are members of the American Association of Personal Finance Companies, and a large number are members of state associations. The large companies operate separate corporations in different states and branches within states, thus combining the principles of group and branch banking.

The personal finance companies have a decided advantage over institutions that require the signature of two comakers, because "Three out of every five applicant-borrowers cannot get any endorsers at all."[14] Even though signatures of comakers may be obtained, most borrowers prefer to pay more and give a chattel mortgage, which prompts the personal finance companies' policy of advertising "strictly confidential and private loans." In addition, the personal finance companies have found that their greatest collection difficulties and expenses have been in those accounts which depend upon the additional security offered by comakers. When all aspects of the problem are considered, it is apparent that the personal loan company can compete successfully with other agencies in the field.

Since the cost of making a loan of $200 is the same as for making one of $50, there has been a tendency for managers of loan offices to induce borrowers to make larger loans than they need. A compulsory graduated rate, which decreases as the size of the loan increases, would protect unwise borrowers from this danger. In New York State, the statute permits a maximum rate of 2.5 per cent per month on the first $100 of any loan, and 2 per cent per month on the remainder, which is computed on the unpaid principal balance.

Before World War II, loan companies were expanding their field of operations and were competing with discount companies and banks for the business of financing sales of goods on the instalment plan. They financed many sales not acceptable to their competitors because of size or lack of sufficient down payment.

---

[14] Fisher, C. O., Discussion on 'The Small Loan Business," *American Economic Review*, Supplement, Vol. XXI (March, 1931), p. 15.

The costs of credit investigation, collecting loans which had become delinquent, and absorbing the loss of bad debts made the total costs of this business higher than that of other types of licensed institutions. The success of companies operating under small-loan laws depends upon careful analysis of applicants and unremitting follow-up until accounts are paid. In comparing rates to those charged by other types of companies, the following facts should be recognized: (1) the rates charged are usually a percentage computed on unpaid balances of principal for the actual time the money is borrowed; (2) there are no fees, fines, or other charges;[15] and (3) the interest is figured on a loan rather than a discount basis. Like other lenders, there was a considerable decrease in their volume of financing during the war, but they had a smaller decline in business than other consumer financing agencies, "perhaps because they serve a type of clientele which has a continuing need for remedial loans."[16]

Remedial Loan Associations.—Some personal credit agencies have been established along philanthropic lines, but they are no longer of much importance, even though they were among the pioneers in the field. They do chattel mortgage or pawn-brokering, or both types of loan business. A unique type in this field is the Hebrew Free Loan Society, which makes no interest charges. In a few cases a nominal fee is collected to cover the cost of making the loan.

The remedial loan associations are now operating under the provisions of the small loan law. Capital funds are subscribed by public-minded citizens, and, in order to lessen the profit motive, dividends to be paid are limited to from 6 to 8 per cent by the charters of most of these associations. However, their losses have been small, and most of the companies have paid the maximum dividend.

Credit Unions.[17]—Today there are over 8,800 co-operative personal finance associations, called credit unions, which operate under a federal or state charter. On September 30, 1941, 8,838 registered with the Board of Governors and reported holding loans and instalment paper equal to $192,000,000. (See Table 39.) They are

[15] Monthly rates are based on the assumption that the instalment will be paid on or before the third day of the month. If the account is delinquent, a greater amount will be charged to interest, which is computed from the last date of payment.

[16] *Report of the Superintendent of Banks, State of New York*, Part II, Legislative Document (1944), No. 22, p. 11.

[17] Neifeld, M. R., *Cooperative Consumer Credit*, contains the best treatment on this subject.

nonprofit organizations operated for the benefit of members. Most credit unions are incorporated and accumulate funds by selling shares to members and accepting their savings deposits. From this pool of funds, loans are made to members, who pledge their shares. Most loans are based on unendorsed promises to pay, but some unions require the signature of two comakers.

The credit union movement started in 1919, but most of those in operations came into existence since 1930.[18] In 1934 a Federal Credit Union Act was passed, and this law makes it possible to organize these thrift and personal loan co-operatives in any state and in the District of Columbia. At the end of 1944, there were 4,048 federal credit unions, of which 233 were inactive. During the year, 285 charters were cancelled, and 69 new ones were granted.

The credit union movement has been sponsored and encouraged by Edward A. Filene, who in 1921 founded the Credit Union National Extension Bureau. This movement has had the greatest progress among employees of specific concerns or offices, railroads, municipal employees, and teachers' associations. Charters are granted to groups that have a common bond of association or occupation, usually factory, store, or office. In some cases the common bond may be religious, fraternal, social, or community.

Some of the aspects of credit union activities should be stressed. They appeal to persons who ordinarily have no bank accounts. Savings in amounts as small as 25 cents per month are encouraged. A member must own at least one share of stock, with a par value of $5.00 which may be purchased on the instalment plan. The credit union movement is co-operative, is mutually owned and managed, costs of funds are reasonable, interest rates are limited, and loans are made promptly. The cost of operation is low, because there are no large salaries to pay, since most of the work is done by the members without pay, and usually the overhead is nominal, because rent, heat, and light are donated by the organization or individual around which the credit union is formed.

By Executive Order Number 9,148, dated April 27, 1942, responsibility for examination and supervision of federal credit unions was transferred from the Federal Farm Credit Administration to the Federal Deposit Insurance Corporation. Statements of operations are

[18] In New York State the movement has been sponsored by the Russell Sage Foundation.

received annually, and a report summarizing the statement for the calendar year is published annually.[19]

Finance and Discount Companies

In addition to the lending specialists in the consumer finance field, there are many companies that aid in consumer buying by financing purchases or sales on the instalment plan. They are known by a variety of names, including finance companies, discount companies, credit companies, and investment companies. On September 30, 1941, 3,237 "sales finance companies" registered with the Board of Governors and reported holding over $2,000,000,000 of instalment paper and cash loans. (See Table 39.) In addition to financing consumer instalment purchases, many finance companies finance retailers, wholesalers, manufacturers, and others. Most of their loans are secured by receivables (accounts, notes, or bills), which explains why they are sometimes referred to as "receivable companies."

There is considerable overlapping in the statistics of financing of instalment sales, because commercial banks are financing companies, which in turn are financing instalment sales. But the annual prewar volume of retail merchant instalment sales was estimated to have been about $5,000,000,000, the bulk of which was financed by instalment sales finance companies. (See Table 39.) The chief business of finance companies is financing the sales of new and used automobiles. Other commodities which figure largely in the volume of their business are tractors, mechanical refrigerators, heating equipment, air conditioning equipment, furniture, electrical equipment, musical instruments, furs and clothing, jewelry, and farm machinery. The trend has been to sell new types of goods on the instalment plan and for a larger percentage of dealers in all fields of merchandising to sell on this basis.

Instalment Financing Principles.—An instalment sale is one which calls for a down payment of a part of the price of the article, plus a contract which calls for periodic payments of the balance. Before World War II, the National Association of Finance Companies had taken numerous steps to standardize business practices. During the war further standardization resulted from regulation of

[19] *Federal Credit Unions Annual Report of Operations* (Washington, D.C.: U.S. Government Printing Office).

consumer credit by the Board of Governors of the Federal Reserve System (Regulation W). The standard terms are based upon the following principles:

1. The buyer must have sufficient equity in the property to make him feel that he is a purchaser and not a renter.
2. The remaining salable value of the property, regarded as a used article, must be at all times greater than the unpaid portion of the price.
3. The unpaid portion of the price should at all times be small enough to encourage the buyer to complete the payments rather than lose his investment in tne goods.

Large Variety of Companies.—Sales finance companies vary in size from local unit companies to nation-wide organizations. They differ as to commodities financed, some financing almost any type of durable commodity sold on the instalment plan, while others limit themselves to one commodity or group of commodities. They vary also in the scope of their activities, some financing only extensions of credit by manufacturers; others finance merchants, and others finance manufacturers, wholesalers, and retailers. A few discount companies finance services, for example, hospital charges and doctors' and dentists' bills. Most of the funds used by finance companies are raised by borrowing from banks and by sales of stock, bonds, and collateral trust notes in the money market.

Interest Charges.—Finance companies, because of competition with other agencies in the consumer instalment financing field, have lowered financing charges, broadened their activities, and improved collection procedures. Financing charges vary according to the company, territory, amount of the contract, length of the time period, and the regulations of supervisory officials.

Finance companies have been criticized for concealing from their customers the actual costs of financing, which tend to conform to those charged by industrial banks and other institutions. In financing retail sales, the finance companies may require automobile and other dealers to endorse the customers' notes, making the dealers responsible for the paper (recourse companies). Dealers object to this extra risk, and so some finance companies take sole responsibility for the paper which they accept (nonrecourse companies). A third plan divides the risks, the dealer agreeing to repurchase the article being financed at a price to cover the remaining instalments if the finance company repossesses it, but, if repossession is impossible, the finance company assumes the loss. Owing to competition for business, the "repurchase" and "nonrecourse" types of financing have become more common.

Finance Companies Discount Receivables.—Many of the finance companies make loans to borrowers which are based upon accounts receivable and notes which may or may not have resulted from sales of goods on the instalment plan. Notes and accounts receivable represent a large percentage of the current assets of many business firms. Finance companies sometimes purchase these receivables or make loans upon them pledged as collateral. The chief borrowers of this type are new companies, rapidly growing companies, specialty houses, and dealers who have most of their current capital tied up in accounts receivable and merchandise. Because of the work involved, the charges made by finance companies on this type of loan are large, the usual charge being 1 per cent per month on the face value of the amount of the receivables or merchandise, plus certain additional fees which are agreed upon by the borrower and lender. Loans are usually made up to 60 to 80 per cent of the total amount of the receivables.

Many finance companies lend to dealers who are required to pay cash for goods purchased. The best illustration is provided by the automobile industry, whose manufacturers require dealers to pay cash for the cars, trucks, and tractors which they buy. At the time of shipment, the manufacturer draws a sight draft on the dealer and attaches the bill of lading; these documents are sent to the local office of a finance company, a bank, or other local agent, who presents this trade bill for payment. As in the case of foreign trade financing, when the dealer pays the draft, he gets the bill of lading and title to the cars. If he lacks funds, he may borrow from a finance company or bank.

The automobile dealers give the finance companies their promissory notes, which are secured by the cars being financed. If the cars remain in the possession of the dealer, the finance company accepts as security a trust receipt, chattel mortgage, or, more commonly, a conditional bill of sale. In a case where the credit of the dealer is seriously questioned, the cars may be placed in a public warehouse, and the finance company will hold the warehouse receipt. The note of the dealer is discounted at rates varying from 6 to 15 per cent.

This system of financing is sound, even though it places responsibility on the dealer and not on the manufacturers.

Trends in the Consumer Finance Field

Perhaps the most significant development in consumer financing is the rapid increase in the number of banks that have and are opening new personal loan departments. In seeking an outlet for loanable funds, banks are striving to capture the lending and discount fields formerly dominated by the personal loan companies, industrial banks, and discount or finance companies. The new aggressiveness of banks, their lower rates, and the prestige of dealing with banks will undoubtedly permit them to secure the cream of the small-loan and discount business. Their chief problem is to keep down the collection costs so as to show a profit on the smaller margin on which they are forced to operate.

The shifting of business away from finance companies is forcing the latter to finance many small discount transactions that were formerly handled by small-loan companies. In addition, some of the finance or discount companies have gone into the cash lending business. (See Table 39.) The personal and small-loan companies are extending their activities to include the financing of instalment purchases, in order to compensate for losses in volume of loans. For legal and competitive reasons, their activities are confined to smaller loans and discounts. Their future position may depend upon changes in the Uniform Small Loan Law, so as to permit them to make individual loans in excess of $300. In New York State they are permitted to lend in excess of $300 to veterans, if the amount in excess of $300 is fully guaranteed by the Administrator of Veterans Affairs.

Before World War II legislative attempts in certain states to force the small-loan companies to lower their interest charges caused the majority of them to liquidate or move to other states, leaving the field open to the return of the loan sharks.[20] Since from 40 to 52 per cent of all loans made by licensed lenders are in amounts not exceeding $100, it does not appear likely that the source of new business for small-loan companies will disappear.

[20] Following drastic experiences with lower maximum rates provided in 1929, New Jersey, Missouri, and West Virginia later increased their maximum interest rate laws.

Conclusions

There is no agreement among economists, bankers, and others as to the legitimate purposes for lending for consumption. What is a legitimate request by one individual may not be a legitimate request by a second. The purposes for which loans are made run the entire range of human desires. With certain exceptions, loans do not increase the ability of the borrower to repay; so repayments must be made from the borrower's normal income, and this is most conveniently done on the instalment plan. If a borrower returns repeatedly for loans it means that he is managing his personal affairs poorly;[21] he is not a good risk, and his application for a loan should be reduced or refused. For this reason agencies in this field are forced to make special efforts to secure new borrowers by advertising, one of the chief costs of carrying on a small-loan business. However, the average wage earner with a family finds it necessary to borrow money at least once every two years to meet some unforeseen emergency that cannot be financed from savings or from current income.

The costs of handling consumers' loans are high; the clerical work, the cost of credit analysis, and the costs of collection are practically the same for small as for large loans. The chief obstacle faced by the philanthropic research organizations interested in the subject is the difficulty of educating legislative bodies, borrowers, and others to the necessity of permitting lenders to charge more than 6 or 7 per cent per annum on small loans.

The methods used in analyzing credit risks vary, but, as a rule, the basic information is secured from the applicant. He fills in an application blank which calls for his name, age, marital status, number of dependents, residence (place and length of time), weekly earnings, other income, rent (amount and to whom paid), insurance (amount and beneficiary), real estate (value, title status, encumbrances, location, etc.), credit references, etc. When lenders require the signature of comakers, similar but less extensive information is demanded of them. The lending agency usually verifies the data on the information sheet. Special attention is given the answers to the place of employment, length of employment, amount of salary, rent,

[21] "The investigations made so far indicate that more than half these loans are made to repeaters. This is one of the most serious indictments against the operation of companies dedicated to the promotion of general welfare and the assistance of necessitous borrowers" (Fisher, "The Small Loan Business," *ibid.*, p. 14).

residence in one place, ownership of real estate and automobiles, and personal habits which have a bearing upon personal finance. All bankers weigh carefully the amount of annual income of the applicant, for this factor, along with spending habits, more than any other justifies the granting or refusal of the loan.[22]

Cost of consumer credit is very high, the legal rates varying from 6 to 42 per cent per annum, but illegal rates know no limits. Although the legal rates do not lend themselves to comparison because of the different types of loans involved and the misleading manner in which lending institutions quote the interest rate, the fact is that many borrowers are paying too dearly for the loans which they secure. Licensed agencies have suffered only small losses because of delinquent payments, justifying the faith of the sponsors of credit unions, industrial banks, and other small-loan institutions in the honesty and integrity of the working man, small householder, and professional man of limited income.

As noted earlier, the unscrupulous lender is just as much a menace to the credit system as the deadbeat and others who are able but not willing to pay their debts. The most important postwar problem is the need for regulation of the unlicensed lender in certain states where there are no small-loan laws. Regulation W was a defense and later a war measure, but it could readily be adopted permanently to cover a peacetime need for control of consumer credit. It could be used as a device to prevent inflation and thereby become a valuable device of credit control. It could also be used to prevent many of the sharp practices which have always been associated with the granting of consumer credit. The chief objection to the retention of Regulation W is that it is " bureaucratic," but the alternative is worse, particularly in those states having no adequate provisions for regulation.

QUESTIONS AND PROBLEMS

1. What has been the general attitude toward the business of consumer finance? How has this attitude affected the growth of legitimate types of consumer financing institutions?

---

[22] "The notion which we often hear naively expressed by theorists, to the effect that a business depression helps our business, is rank foolishness . . . . . Millions of men are out of work and cannot make their payments on time, which increases the number of our slow accounts and doubles the cost of collections" (Ryan, F. W., "Small Loan Business," *American Economic Review*, Supplement, Vol. XXI [March, 1931], p. 24).

2. Identify "Regulation W." To what extent did the Board achieve the purposes for which Regulation W was issued?

3. Identify (*a*) "instalment credit," and (*b*) "other credit sales." How important was each in 1941?

4. Identify the chief types of "cash lending" consumer financing institutions. (See Table 37.)

5. Compare the loan practices of the pawnbrokers to those of small-loan companies.

6. What advantages do commercial banks have over other lenders? What types of loans do they make? (See Table 40.) Is the guarantee principle involved?

7. "Those of us who have participated in consumer loans under Title I of the National Housing Act have discovered how safe and attractive this type of loan can be" (Griswold, H. H., *Banking*, December, 1938, p. 86). Describe these loans.

8. Compare the security required by an industrial or Morris Plan bank to that required by personal finance companies.

9. Why can credit unions make loans at lower rates than personal finance companies?

10. In his 1940 annual report to the stockholders of the National City Bank, Mr. Perkins reported that the average personal loan outstanding was $162. How does this compare to the average of those made by personal lending institutions in your community?

11. "Personal loans must be followed up even more rigorously than ordinary commercial loans" (Bonnell, R. O., *Banking*, January, 1939, p. 95). Why?

12. What types of institutions have been organized under the Federal Credit Union Law? Describe these institutions. Who supervises them? Why?

13. Rank the agencies extending cash instalment credit as follows: (*a*) number of registrants, (*b*) holdings of instalment receivables, (*c*) holdings of retail instalment paper purchased, (*d*) volume of retail instalment credit extended directly, and (*e*) personal instalment cash loans. (See Table 39.)

14. Explain the financing operations of finance companies in both the wholesale and the retail fields. Why are they sometimes called discount companies?

15. Compare the advertising needs of consumer credit financing agencies to those of a bank handling nonpersonal loans.

16. "There are sacrifice costs in connection with co-signer loans which in some cases make them more costly than chattel loans." What are these sacrifice costs? (*Source and reference:* Ryan, F. W., "The Small Loan

Business," *American Economic Review*, Supplement, Vol. XXI [March, 1931], p. 15).

17. "We found from a questionnaire study of two hundred persons in New Jersey, Massachusetts, and Iowa, that these persons [cosigners] were willing to give from $5.00 to $75 in cash rather than become co-signers on a note for $300. The average was $17." What is the economic significance of this situation? (*Ibid.*)
18. What were the chief pre-war trends in the field of consumer credit? What postwar changes may be expected?
19. In borrowing funds, what factors other than interest rates must be considered?
20. "Regulation W and a national program of educating banks appear to be two of the most important subjects which will affect the development of consumer credit in the post-war years" (*The Industrial Banker*, Vol. XI, [October, 1945], p. 7). Why? Should Regulation W be retained as a reform measure?
21. Part of Judge Gary's (founder of the U.S. Steel Corporation) will was the advice to his heirs not to sign or endorse other people's notes, checks, and other obligations. Do you approve? Why?

REFERENCES

Activities of Credit Unions in 1943. Bureau of Labor Statistics Bulletin, No. 797. Washington, D.C.: U.S. Government Printing Office, 1944.

American Bankers Association, Management and Savings Division. *Survey of Personal Loan Department Experiences and Practice*. Bulletin No. 74. 1938.

Bergengren, R. F. *Cooperative Banking*, chaps. i, ii, and iii. New York: Macmillan Co., 1923.

Clark, Evans. *Financing the Consumer*, chaps. i, ii, and iii. New York: Harper & Bros., 1930.

Cover, J. H. (Ed.) *Financing the Consumer*. Chicago: University of Chicago Press, 1937.

Federal Credit Unions Annual Report of Operations. Washington, D.C.: U.S. Government Printing Office.

Federal Reserve Bulletin. See particularly September, 1941, and May, 1942.

Griffin, B. W., and Greene, H. C. *Installment Credits and Collections and the Installment Market*. New York: Prentice-Hall, Inc., 1936.

Grobben, M. *Industrial Banking, A Phase of Consumer Credit*. New York: Consumer Credit Institute of America, 1940.

Hardy, C. O. (Ed.) *Consumer Credit and Its Uses.* New York: Prentice-Hall, Inc., 1938.

Herzog, P. W. *The Morris Plan of Industrial Banking,* chaps. i-iii and x. New York: McGraw-Hill Book Co., Inc., 1929.

Hubachek, F. B. *Annotations on Small Loan Laws.* (Legal.) New York: Russell Sage Foundation, 1938.

National Industrial Conference Board. *Savings Plans and Credit Unions in Industry.* New York: National Industrial Conference Board, 1936.

Neifeld, M. R. *Cooperative Consumer Credit.* New York: Harper & Bros., 1936.

Neifeld, M. R. *Personal Finance Comes of Age.* New York: Harper & Bros., 1936.

Nugent, Rolf. *Consumer Credit and Economic Stability.* New York: Russell Sage Foundation, 1939.

Nystrom, P. H. *Economic Principles of Consumption.* New York: Ronald Press Co., 1929.

Robinson, L. N., and Nugent, Rolf. *Regulation of the Small Loan Business,* chaps. i-iv, ix, and xii. New York: Russell Sage Foundation, 1935.

Robinson, L. N., and Stearns, M. E. *Ten Thousand Small Loans.* New York: Russell Sage Foundation, 1930.

Seligman, E. R. A. *Economics of Installment Selling,* Vol. I. 2 vols. New York: Harper & Bros., 1927.

Snider, J. L. *Credit Unions in Massachusetts.* Cambridge: Harvard University Press, 1939.

The Industrial Banker. Published monthly by the Industrial Bankers Association, Fort Wayne, Indiana.

CHAPTER XXXI

SAVINGS BANKS

Savings Banks Gather Funds and Make Investments

The savings bank is designed to collect the small and scattered savings of a community and to invest them safely and profitably for the benefit of the depositors. The savings bank movement owes its origin to humanitarians. The clergy led in the movement in England, Ireland, and Scotland. They desired to inculcate the habit of thrift among the people and thereby free the church of part of the load which poverty placed upon its finances. Numerous savings banks, which were operated on the donations of the wealthy, had been established before 1800; but the first modern one was started in 1810 by Henry Duncan, a Scottish minister, at Ruthwell, Scotland. The bank was operated on the earning power of the savings at work rather than upon donations from its friends.

The savings bank principle was introduced into the United States from Europe early in the nineteenth century. The citizens of three cities claim the honor of originating the savings bank movement. On November 20, 1816, at a meeting of prominent citizens in New York, plans were made for the first savings bank in the United States—the Bank for Savings in the City of New York. But there was some delay in putting the plan into operation, and the bank did not open until July 3, 1819. In the meantime, the Philadelphia Saving Fund Society had been organized, starting operations without a charter on December 2, 1816. The Provident Institution for Savings in the Town of Boston received its charter from the state legislature on December 13, 1816. The Savings Bank of Baltimore was founded soon after, commencing business on March 16, 1818. The movement spread rapidly, particularly during the last part of the nineteenth century, reaching its greatest development following the establishment of savings accounts in commercial banks during the twentieth century. Today practically every community in the United States is served by some type of savings institution.

Originally emphasis was placed on the need for savings for old age and unforeseen misfortunes, but now the more cheerful aspects of savings are stressed. Individuals are encouraged to save in order to satisfy some immediate want—in other words, to save to spend. Although the savings bank movement had its origin in poverty and charity, it has outgrown much of its humble beginnings. In form, many of the savings banks still have their original type of organization, but their present size and the wealth of many of their depositors have made nominal their charitable and benevolent purposes.

Total savings deposits represent about 25 per cent of all the deposits in banks in the United States, which is a relative decline since 1940, owing to the increase in the volume of demand deposits. This pool of $40,000,000,000 represents the most important single source of investment capital in the United States. Savings banks serve

TABLE 41

SAVINGS DEPOSITS
(In Millions of Dollars)

Class of Bank	June 30 1934	Dec. 31 1940	June 30 1945
Mutual savings	$ 9,691	$10,658	$14,426
National banks	6,772	8,329	14,585
State, commercial, trust companies, and others.	5,885	7,517	12,704
Total all banks	$22,348	$26,504	$41,702

Source: Federal Reserve Bulletin, July, 1944, pp. 690-91, and February, 1946, pp. 158-59.

as intermediaries between lenders or savers and borrowers. First safety and then yield have been the guides to their investment policies. Normally their funds are used in local real estate financing; but during World War II, investments in United States government obligations increased so sharply that by the end of the war they represented two-thirds of savings banks' total loans and investments. (See Table 41.)

The specialists in the savings bank field are mutual and stock savings banks. Within recent years stock savings banks have accepted deposits and have made short-term loans, and for all practical purposes they are commercial banks. No functional distinction is made between them and other commercial banks by the Federal Deposit Insurance Corporation and most other regulatory agencies. This leaves the mutual savings bank as the specialist in the field. Although certain savings banks have assumed some commercial bank functions, commercial banks have encroached upon the savings banks' business to such an extent that their savings accounts are almost double those of mutual savings banks. (See Table 41.)

Savings Banks' Rules Favor Small Depositors

When a person opens an account with a savings bank, his name, place of residence, and other information which will help to establish his identity are placed on an application card. After the applicant signs the card, or makes his mark if he cannot write, a passbook is issued to him. It contains his name, number, and the amount of his first deposit. The pages are conveniently ruled for additional notations. Entries indicate the amount of deposits with the bank, plus accumulated interest.

Interest is usually compounded semiannually, and generally interest is allowed on the amount remaining undisturbed during the interest period. The rate paid by savings banks varies with general economic conditions and regulations of federal, state, and clearinghouse associations. The maximum rate that may be paid by member banks is fixed by the Board of Governors, and the maximum rate for other insured banks is fixed by the Federal Deposit Insurance Corporation. The state officials in some states may specify even lower rates, it being 1 per cent in New Jersey and 2 per cent in New York State. Clearinghouse association members may agree on even lower maximum rates, and individual banks may actually pay even less.

The passbook generally contains a printed list of rules and regulations concerning the conditions of deposit and withdrawal. It "serves (*a*) as a contract between customer and bank, (*b*) as a miniature ledger of all deposits, withdrawals, and (*c*) as an instrument which is assignable."[1] Usually the depositor agrees to give the bank thirty or sixty days' notice before withdrawing his account. Under the terms of the Banking Act of 1935, a member bank cannot waive this requirement of notice unless it applies to all similar accounts. This change makes it impossible for banks to make special concessions in favor of large or favorite depositors. Although the notice of withdrawal requirement was designed to help the banks, in prac-

---

[1] Willis, H. P., and Edwards, G. W., *Banking and Business*, p. 313.

tice it has been beneficial to depositors, by preventing them from withdrawing their money hastily for some imagined need. Savings deposits are not subject to withdrawal by checks or drafts, although some savings banks have permitted a limited number of drafts to be drawn per month under rules laid down by the bank. The passbook must be submitted to the bank by the person legally qualified to have possession of it, or, in case of withdrawals as noted above, left with the bank so that proper entries may be made. When a person withdraws his whole deposit, the account is closed, and the passbook is surrendered to the issuing bank.

Most savings banks permit depositors to open accounts with $1.00 or more; and the state legislature usually provides for the maximum amount of an individual balance kept with one bank. The maximum deposit in one name in New York mutual savings banks is $7,500; other states place the maximum as low as $1,000. There is no rule against keeping deposits with more than one savings bank or of dividing an account among different members of a family in order to circumvent this rule. Most commercial banks do not limit the size of a balance kept in their savings departments. The maximum interest-bearing single deposit with the United States Postal System is fixed by law at $2,500.

The maximum deposit rule has been attacked on numerous occasions, but the primary reasons for its continuance are: (1) the savings banks are for small depositors; (2) the dangers of disturbances resulting from withdrawals of a few large depositors are eliminated; (3) smaller reserves are necessary when a given volume of deposits is divided among, say, 15,000 depositors than would be the case with 500 depositors.

A special form of savings or time deposit is one evidenced by a certificate of deposit. Its use is common among all banks other than mutual savings banks. Large depositors in commercial banks use this device to put temporarily idle commercial funds to work earning interest. Before 1933 these accounts were, in practice, withdrawable upon demand. Under provisions of the banking acts of 1933 and 1935, they cannot be paid before maturity, except under conditions specified by the Board of Governors of the Federal Reserve System and the Federal Deposit Insurance Corporation. The savings deposits in banks in the United States for selected dates are shown by Table 41.

Mutual Savings Banks

These banks are called "mutual" because they are owned by the depositors, they have no stock or stockholders, all the assets are the property of the depositors, and all earnings after expenses are paid belong to the depositors.[2] Depositors are paid dividends or interest at a fixed rate, and earnings above the amount necessary to pay interest charges are placed in the surplus. As a result of conservative management, most mutual associations have large surplus accounts. In order to prevent this amount from becoming too large, some states require that banks pay extra dividends to depositors after funds in the surplus accounts amount to a specified percentage of deposits. Since these banks are owned by depositors, they are considered to be co-operative institutions.

Management.—Mutual savings are not co-operative where management is concerned, because depositors have no share in management. They are managed by a board of trustees, each member holding office for life unless removed by his colleagues; and vacancies are filled by the board. Trustees usually serve without pay, but this does not mean that their stewardship is always nonmercenary. Many new savings banks are started by lawyers, and many old ones are controlled by representatives of that profession. Lawyers receive a great deal of business from savings banks. Titles of real estate which constitute security for mortgages purchased by the bank may be searched by lawyer trustees, and in New York State a fee may be charged for title searching if it is paid by the borrower and not by the bank.

Officers of commercial banks desire the savings banks' reserve deposits, which often amount to 10 per cent of savings banks' total deposits. If officers of commercial banks are trustees in savings banks, it would tend to help in securing these reserve deposits. Investment bankers find savings banks excellent customers for legal securities, and officials of title insurance companies find them to be a source of business. In some states savings banks may solicit life insurance, which makes trusteeship desirable to those in the insurance field.

[2] "Mutual savings banks are defined as banks without capital stock transacting a savings bank business, the net earnings of which inure wholly to the benefit of their depositors after payment of obligations or any advances by organizers" (*Annual Report of the Federal Deposit Insurance Corporation for the Year Ending December 31, 1935*, p. 48, n). These banks operate under special rather than general banking codes.

In theory, the individuals comprising the board of trustees presumably have no other motive in giving their services than devotion to the cause of thrift and community well-being.

The officers of mutual savings banks are selected by the board of trustees. Large savings banks have a president, one or more vice-presidents, a secretary, a treasurer, an auditor, a counsel, and many assistant or junior officers. In a small bank the major part of the work is performed by a secretary-treasurer; and the offices of president and vice-president are primarily honorary. The clerical work is carried on by tellers, bookkeepers, clerks, messengers, and assistants.

Location in the East.—Mutual savings banks have been organized in seventeen different states, but the movement is primarily an eastern one. Owing to mergers, suspensions, and reorganizations, the number of mutual savings banks in the United States declined from 634 in 1914 to 542 on June 30, 1945. The three great mutual savings bank states, with the number of banks are: Massachusetts, 191; New York, 131; and Connecticut, 72.[3] Total deposits in all mutual savings banks aggregate over $14,426,000,000, or over $26,600,000 per bank. These institutions contrast sharply with the humble benevolent institutions of a century ago. The two largest are the Bowery Savings Bank, with almost $500,000,000 deposits, and the Emigrant Industrial Savings Bank, with over $400,000,000 deposits, both located in the city of New York.

Investments.—The form in which mutual savings banks' funds may be invested is carefully regulated by law so as to insure safety of deposits. As long as the board of trustees keeps the bank's funds legally invested, it is not responsible for losses, unless negligence can be proved. The tendency is to limit investments to real estate mortgages and government, railroad, and utility bonds. Real estate mortgages normally make up about one-half of the assets of savings banks, but now, because of the wartime decline in building and amortization of mortgage debt, the bulk of savings banks' investments are in government securities. As a rule, savings banks are prohibited from discounting, buying, selling, or lending upon commercial paper, notes, and bills of exchange; but some states do permit these types of

[3] At the end of 1944 the distribution among other than the leading three states were as follows: Delaware, 2; Indiana, 4; Maine, 32; Maryland, 10; Minnesota, 1; New Hampshire, 42; New Jersey, 24; Ohio, 3; Oregon, 1; Pennsylvania, 7; Rhode Island, 9; Vermont, 8; Washington, 2; and Wisconsin, 4.

investments, because such paper gives the savings banks excellent secondary reserves.

Table 42 shows the assets of mutual savings banks for the years 1935, 1940, and 1945. The most striking investment change which has taken place is the emphasis on government securities. This development is due primarily to the increase in borrowing by the federal government, a drought of other legal investment securities, and a new stress on liquidity or marketability, as a result of depression experiences. Usually the classes of legal securities are subject to changes by legislative action, but in New York State the Banking Board, upon

TABLE 42

MUTUAL SAVINGS BANKS—LOANS AND INVESTMENTS

(In Millions of Dollars)

	Dec. 31, 1935	Dec. 31, 1940	June 30, 1945
	568 Banks	551 Banks	542 Banks
Loans	$5,183	$ 4,959	$ 4,307
Investments	4,532	5,289	10,827
U.S. government obligations	1,542	3,224	9,588
Other securities	2,913	2,065	1,240
Total loans and investments	$9,715	$10,248	$15,134

Source: Banking and Monetary Statistics, p. 23, and *Federal Reserve Bulletin*, February, 1946, p. 159.

application of twenty or more savings banks, may authorize these banks to invest in corporate interest-bearing obligations not otherwise eligible for investment and may revoke previous authorizations made by it.

The weakness of the old statutory provisions was their inflexibility, which kept public utility, telephone, and industrial obligations off the legal lists long after their investment status was unquestioned. Failure to change the "legal" list of investments is particularly serious when a large percentage of one type of securities—railroad bonds, for example—fails to meet the earnings, surplus, and other statutory requirements. Modification to keep abreast of investment changes, rather than abandonment of the principle of limitation, is the correct solution of the savings banks' investment regulatory problem. In New York State, since banks must make the request for expansion of the legal lists, the danger of outside pressure being brought to bear on the Banking Board to include some particular securities on the legal list is minimized. Other states in addition to New York are experimenting with the plan of permitting a state banking board or a state official to expand the list so as to lessen the evils of inflexibility not only as applied to investments of mutual savings banks but also as applied to trust funds.

Guaranty Savings Banks.—A peculiar modification of the mutual savings bank developed in New Hampshire. Known as "guaranty savings banks," these institutions have special deposits, which are virtually capital stock. After the customary interest is paid to general depositors, the surplus goes to the special depositors. The charters of the banks usually require that special deposits must equal 10 per cent of the total deposits. The special deposits constitute a guaranty fund to protect the earnings and assets of general depositors. There are only ten of these banks in New Hampshire, and they represent an insignificant part of the savings bank resources of the country. Most of the savings banks in New Hampshire are of the customary mutual type.

Growth of Mutual Savings Banks.—With an increase in the wealth of the average individual, there was an increase in the volume of direct investments in securities, which was paralleled by the introduction of more specialized investing institutions. With this development came a decrease in the need for the traditional type of benevolent savings institution, exemplified by the mutual savings bank. For these reasons the growth of mutual savings banks in recent years has not kept pace with the growth in time deposits in all banks in the United States or with the growth in investment funds in building and loan associations and in other investing institutions. Although the number of mutual savings banks has declined, as has been true of other types of banks in the United States, this change has been offset by an increase in number of branches. At the end of 1944 there were 85 mutual savings banks operating 140 branches.

Savings in Commercial Banks Exceed Those in Mutual Savings Banks

A most radical change in the development of the savings bank movement began in the latter part of the past century. As the newer sections of the country became wealthier and more densely populated, savings banks were not organized to handle the savings. Instead, the savings accounts were placed in the so-called "commercial banks" which were already in operation in the community. Many of the commercial banks which developed the savings bank business were located in communities which were not large enough to support more than one bank, and it was only logical for commercial banks to open savings divisions. However, commercial banks' participation in savings banking was not confined to the areas which lacked stock and mutual savings banks.

The commercial banks located in the eastern states now compete actively for savings, or so-called "time deposits." National banks, state banks, trust companies, and private banks participate in this movement. The percentage of national banks now receiving savings deposits has increased steadily since 1914, and 90 per cent of national banks now receive time or savings deposits. The aggregate of savings deposits in savings departments of all commercial banks is almost double those in mutual savings banks. (See Table 42.)

Problem of Segregation.—When savings deposits are accepted by commercial banks, the funds are mingled with other assets of the bank. Since the very nature of commercial banking requires that more risks be assumed than in the case of savings banking, time deposits are subject to more risks when left with commercial banks than with mutual savings banks. The savings depositors do not benefit from the risks associated with commercial banking, because they are not commercial borrowers and do not have the privilege of using their deposits as a means of payment.

During panics, savings depositors were required by some banks to give notice of withdrawal, while demand depositors were permitted to take away the cash and liquid assets of the banks. In case of suspension, this left the poorer assets, which were usually insufficient to cover the claims of the remaining depositors. During the seventy years from 1865 to 1934, 75 per cent of the total losses due to bank failures were taken by depositors with accounts of $5,000 or less.[4] Many bankers now regard the Federal Deposit Insurance Corporation as the solution to the problem of the need for protection of the small, time and demand, deposits; but a more equitable solution is the

---

[4] "Losses to Depositors in Suspended Commercial Banks, 1865-1934," *Annual Report of the Federal Deposit Insurance Corporation, 1934*, pp. 73-110.

proposal for the complete segregation of the two types of banking, even though they may be carried on by the same bank.[5]

Segregation of savings deposits requires (1) the complete legal separation of the savings department from the rest of the bank, (2) allocation of a proportionate share of the bank's capital and surplus to this department, and (3) investment of savings deposits in assets similar to those purchased by mutual savings banks.

Following the panic of 1907, several states adopted one or more of the above proposals, and now a dozen states provide for segregating savings deposits in commercial banks. Small banks vigorously opposed the plan to departmentalize the savings account business, because they considered the costs to be prohibitive. Without question the costs would be increased, but not so much as would be the case if two separate institutions conducted the commercial and savings bank business. Segregation of time deposits as proposed would still keep the advantages of combining several banking functions under the same management, in the same institution, and under the same roof. The added protection which would be given to savings depositors is of primary importance.

The United States Government Operates a Billion Dollar Savings Business

Government or public savings banks have existed in foreign countries for many years, being operated by local and central governments. The municipal savings banks are particularly prevalent in Germany and other countries in central Europe. The postal departments operate the central government savings banks in England, Canada, Italy, France, and elsewhere.

Owing chiefly to the opposition of bankers, the postal savings system was not adopted in the United States until 1911. It is managed by a board of trustees consisting of the Secretary of the Treasury, the Postmaster General, and the Attorney General. The demand for

[5] Prior to World War II, banks in Germany were required to segregate their savings business, that is, savings deposits and the investments designated to secure them, from the rest of their banking business. The savings business was shown separately in their annual balance and monthly statements and in the profit and loss accounts. The gross expenses of the savings bank operation was required to be clearly shown "at the annual closing of the books" (Secs. 24 and 25, German Credit Act of December 15, 1934). Exceptions could be made by the supervisory board.

the system was greatest among the foreign-born, who had had experience in Europe with the postal savings system and who were afraid to leave their funds in the care of bankers.

The chief arguments in favor of the establishment of the United States Postal Savings System were the following: (1) Adequate savings bank facilities were not provided by private enterprises and could not be provided by them because of the expenses of operating savings banks in many communities. (2) The thrifty needed greater protection against losses and inconveniences arising from bank failures. (3) Hoarded funds would be brought back into circulation. (4) Existing banks had nothing to fear from government competition, because they had the advantages of established clientele, higher interest rates, and higher maximum limits on individual deposits. (5) A postal savings system would aid the development of thrift, and postal savings deposits would be transferred to banks as soon as they reached the limit fixed by law.[6]

Anyone over ten years of age may open a savings account at any post office that is authorized to accept deposits. Instead of a passbook, certificates or vouchers are used to evidence deposits. They are issued in denominations of $1.00 up to and including $500. They are neither transferable nor negotiable. The maximum balance allowed one person is $2,500, exclusive of accumulated interest. An additional balance of $1,000 may be kept, but it draws no interest. Interest accumulates at the rate of 2 per cent for each full year, or ½ of 1 per cent for each quarter. Compound interest is not permitted; but a depositor may withdraw interest payable and include it in a new deposit, subject to the restriction that deposits will not be received for fractions of a dollar. Interest begins on the first day of the month following the day on which the deposit is made.

A number of proposals have been made to raise the interest rates, but they have been opposed on the grounds that the higher rate would intensify the competition with other savings institutions and would lead to the withdrawal of funds from them. Higher rates are not justified at the present time, because the reduction in rates of commercial and savings banks have made the Postal Savings System an active competitor of private banks.

Before World War I the amount of deposits in the Postal Savings

[6] See American Bankers Association, *Postal Savings System of the United States* (1937), chap. ii.

System was less than $100,000,000. Largely because aliens could not send funds home during the war, the quantity increased, until in 1919 it had reached over $167,000,000. Then there followed a decrease, which lasted until 1926. Thereafter there was a steady increase, and the movement became particularly rapid in 1930. Bank failures and loss of confidence in banks account for this movement. Just before the bank holidays, the total deposits in the Postal Savings System aggregated over $1,000,000,000 and represented 10 per cent of the sum of all deposits in mutual savings banks.

The number of depositors increased from 466,000 in 1930 to 2,342,000 in 1933. The number of depositories, that is, post offices permitted to accept deposits, increased from 6,800 to 7,500. This increase is the more notable when one recalls that about 5,000 banks failed during the same period. The average deposit increased from $375 to $500. In 1934 the assumption was that, with the return of confidence in banks plus the guarantee of deposits by the Federal Deposit Insurance Corporation, the postal savings deposits would return to normal. However, the trend has been upward, the total having been over $2,659,000,000 on June 30, 1945. (See Table 43.)

An analysis of new accounts suggests that alien depositors have been replaced or supplemented by a more purely American stock. Now a major portion of depositors comes from classes accustomed to banks. The continuance in popularity of postal savings is probably explained by the reduction of dividends and interest rates paid by savings and commercial banks. In some states, banking officials do not permit banks coming under their jurisdictions to pay any more, and sometimes they must pay less than the interest paid by postal savings (2 per cent); so the chief advantage which banks had over the government in competing for deposits has disappeared.

The opposition of the bankers to the original Postal Savings Act was modified when provisions were made to redeposit funds left with the post office depositories with local state and national banks. As the law required the banks to pay 2½ per cent for these deposits, this gave the Postal Savings System a gross profit of ½ of 1 per cent on which to operate. While banks had the use of the funds, individual depositors in the Postal Savings System were fully protected. The government was not taking risks, because each bank with whom the post office left funds furnished acceptable bonds as security for all deposits. Since 1933 no security is required for the small amount guaranteed by the Federal Deposit Insurance Corporation. Funds not asked for by local banks are invested by the board of trustees in government bonds. The statutory rate, 2½ per cent, is now too high for banks in many sections to pay; in New York, state banks are not permitted to pay more than 2 per cent to private or public depositors, and about one-half of the mutual savings banks are paying but 1½ per cent. The fact that funds are not being redeposited with banks is shown by the statement of assets of the Postal Savings System.

TABLE 43

Postal Savings System—Assets and Depositors' Balances for Selected Dates
(In Million of Dollars)

Year (June 30)	Depositors' Balances*	Assets			
		Total	Cash in Depository Banks	U.S. Government Securities (Total)	Cash Reserve, Funds, etc.†
1915	$ 66	$ 67	$ 69	$ 1	$ 6
1919	167	173	136	29	8
1925	132	138	98	33	8
1933	1,187	1,207	977	131	99
1940	1,293	1,337	43	1,224	69
1945	2,659	2,751	8	2,574	169

* Includes outstanding principal represented by certificates of deposit written off as unclaimed; excludes accrued interest and outstanding savings stamps.

† Includes working cash with postmasters, 15 per cent reserve fund and miscellaneous working funds with the Treasurer of the United States, accrued interest on bond investments, and accounts due from late postmasters.

Source: Banking and Monetary Statistics, p. 519, and *Federal Reserve Bulletin*, February, 1946, p. 157.

The justification for continuance of the Postal Savings System as based upon the arguments enumerated above no longer applies to the same extent (if at all) as it did in 1910. In other words, (1) most commercial banks have opened savings departments, which provide most communities with savings banking facilities; (2) since the organization of the Federal Deposit Insurance Corporation, savings deposits in insured banks have much greater protection than was true in 1910; (3) the system is in direct competition with banks for savings deposits; and (4) deposits in the Postal Savings System are not being redeposited with banks. Bank failures have deprived some communities of banking services, but most of the postal savings depositories are located in communities which have banking facilities.[7] Only 20 per cent of the postal saving depository offices are in bankless towns, and all of these are within 15 miles of communities which have banks. When the Postal Savings System is considered in terms of the original arguments for its creation, there is no justification for its continuance at the present time.

The Postal Savings System fully justified its existence during the 1930-33 depression period. It provided a safe refuge for money which would otherwise have been driven out of use into private hoards. If larger deposits had been permitted, much of the hoarded money of the country would have found its way to the Postal Savings System. Since money placed there is invested, it is not driven out of use. As early as the beginning of 1932, the hoarded money in this country was estimated to have been $1,300,000,000. Increasing the maximum deposit rule would have attracted a large percentage of this amount. The Post Office Department has recommended that the law be changed in order to raise maximum deposits from $2,500 to $5,000. All surplus earnings are given to the government as part of the postal revenue.

United States Government Savings Bonds

Before 1935 a postal savings depositor was permitted to exchange all or any part of his deposits for Postal Savings Bonds, which bore interest at the rate of 2½ per cent and were issued in denominations of $20, $100, and $500. Beginning in March, 1935, these bonds were replaced with United States Savings Bonds, which were offered to the public on a discount basis to yield 2.9 per cent. The features of the bonds which make them particularly attractive to small savers are their safety, relatively high yield, and convenience in purchasing or selling. The bonds may be purchased from or through post offices, banks, department stores, etc., and they are redeemable at their redemption value at any time after issue.

Many small savers use "the regular purchase plan" of savings, investing monthly, quarterly, semiannually, or annually, $18.75, $37.50, $75.00, $375, or $750 in "ten-year appreciation bonds," which have maturity values, respectively, of $25.00, $50.00, $100,

---

[7] *Ibid.*, pp. 67-68.

$500, and $1,000. The bonds are registered, nonnegotiable, and bear no current interest. The chief reasons for their purchase are for building up a retirement income, for emergencies, for cash estates, for future educational purposes, for home building, and for dependents.

School Savings Banks Secure New Depositors for Banks[8]

Banks have co-operated with the public schools in forming habits of thrift and saving among the younger groups. School banks have been established in a number of places to receive deposits from the school children, the older children in the school serving in various official capacities. These deposits are later placed with banks. Many systems are in use, but the stamp purchase system is the most common.

Some states have passed legislation correlating these school banks with local savings banks. In the peak year (1929-30) over 14,600 schools and 4,600,000 school children were participating in the school savings bank movement. Total deposits were over $29,000,-000, and the average individual deposit was $6.30. Since that time, the number of students and schools participating have continued to decrease. The twentieth annual report for 1938-39 contains the following figures. The volume of deposits for June 30, 1939, was over $12,800,000; deposits were made by 2,543,472 pupils in 8,448 schools located in 38 states and the District of Columbia.

In addition to encouraging school savings funds, savings banks have formed Christmas clubs, vacation clubs, tax or mortgage-interest payment clubs, "buy a new car clubs," and others. Savings banks encourage these clubs in order to create future business. School savings and, to a lesser degree, the other clubs are unprofitable because they require a great deal of clerical work, and the income received from the funds is very small. By advertising for small and short-term savings accounts, bankers are motivated by the desire to encourage the development of the thrift habit, to bring new customers into the bank, and to build accounts that will be profitable. Formerly, many banks automatically reclassified school savings deposits after they reached a certain amount. Before World War II, some banks

---

[8] See *School Savings Banking, School Year 1938-1939.* Compiled and published by American Bankers Association, Savings Bank Division, New York.

were showing reluctance to continue these unprofitable forms of business. During World War II, emphasis was placed on the purchase of "defense" or "war" stamps, which largely replaced the former school savings plans.

Savings Banks Have a Problem of Liquidity

During the depression of 1930-33 the chief problem facing mutual savings banks was that of liquidity, because depositors were asking for cash. Usually reserves are kept as deposits with commercial banks; but during this period, these institutions were in no position to help savings banks.

In 1932 the mutual savings banks in Massachusetts formed a Mutual Savings Central Fund to help one another. In 1933 the mutual savings banks in New York organized the Savings Bank Trust Company and the Institutional Securities Corporation. The Savings Bank Trust Company makes temporary loans to savings banks, for a maximum of six months, and otherwise assists them. The Institutional Securities Corporation purchases mortgages from mutual savings banks and, in turn, discounts them with the Reconstruction Finance Corporation or other financial institutions.

During 1932 and 1933 the United States government extended the privilege of membership in the Home Loan Bank System and in the Federal Reserve System to the mutual savings banks. In 1941, 3 mutual savings banks became members of the Federal Reserve System. The number of mutual savings banks joining the Home Loan Bank System has varied, there being 22 at the present time. In some states the necessary enabling acts have not been passed.

Mutual savings banks may become members of the Federal Reserve System on the same basis as commercial banks, excepting that mutual savings bank must subscribe for stock in the Federal Reserve bank of its district in an amount equal to 6/10 of 1 per cent of its total deposit liabilities. One-half of the subscription must be paid in, and the other half is subject to call. The surplus of a mutual savings bank must equal the amount of stock required by law for a national bank similarly located. Most savings banks have no commercial paper to discount at the Federal Reserve banks, but they may borrow from them on their own promises to pay, secured by government bonds and other assets acceptable to the Federal Reserve banks.

Safety Is the Primary Problem of Savings Banks[9]

The Federal Deposit Insurance Corporation was opened to all savings banks, but these institutions objected to it on the grounds that the costs were too high. They regarded themselves as preferred risks and entitled to lower rates than those paid by commercial banks. This argument was supported by statistics of mutual bank failures. Since the Civil War, their losses per $100 of deposits have been 1.7 cents. Fourteen banks were suspended during the years 1930-34. However, mergers, informal co-operation, and Reconstruction Finance Corporation loans have prevented other failures. Over one-third (214 out of a total of 577) of the mutual savings banks did join the temporary plan of the Federal Deposit Insurance Corporation; but before the permanent plan went into effect, most of them withdrew. In New York and Massachusetts the mutual savings banks set up their own insurance systems.

In New York a deposit insurance fund was created by 135 of the 138 savings banks of the state. The fund was left with the Savings Bank Trust Company, which is owned entirely by New York State mutual savings banks. The plan provided for full coverage of deposits, an original assessment equal to 1/5 of 1 per cent of deposit liabilities, additional assessment if needed, but not to exceed 1 per cent of total deposits, and annual insurance premiums of 1/10 of 1 per cent.

In Massachusetts the mutual savings banks created an insurance system called Mutual Savings Central Fund, Incorporated, and all mutual savings banks were required to join. The plan expired in 1942. Initial assessment was fixed at ¼ of 1 per cent of deposits, and maximum assessments were limited to 1 per cent. Full coverage of deposits was provided, but three years were allowed for payment of claims. The mutual savings banks of other states, which rank lower in number and importance, made no provisions for insurance. Their position was that the mutual savings banks did not need deposit insurance and that there is no justification for forcing their depositors to bear the costs of such insurance.

Acting on the recommendation of state officials, the New York State mutual savings banks voted to liquidate the mutual fund in

---

[9] "Losses to Depositors in Mutual Savings Banks, 1865-1934," *Annual Report of the Federal Deposit Insurance Corporation*, 1934, pp. 111-13.

1943. All the members obtained insurance from the Federal Insurance Corporation; as a result of this change, 192 of the 543 mutual savings banks in existence at the end of 1944 were participating in the Federal Deposit Insurance Corporation plan. The volume of insured deposits was $8,900,000,000, while $4,500,000,000 was uninsured.[10] At present all the mutual savings banks in New York, Vermont, and Pennsylvania, and most of those in New Jersey, have federal deposit insurance.

Savings Bank Life Insurance

Life insurance is designed to protect the family of the insured against economic loss due to death, old age, or loss of earning power of the insured. The states of Connecticut, Massachusetts, and New York authorize the mutual savings banks of their states to provide low-cost life insurance to their residents by establishing insurance departments under public supervision. The movement in Massachusetts dates from 1907, following exposure by Louis D. Brandeis of abuses of life insurance management. The pioneer bank in the field, the Whitman Savings Bank, opened its insurance department the next year.

An act passed in New York in 1938 authorized the mutual savings banks to open insurance departments, and now 53 per cent of the savings banks in New York are engaged directly or as agents in the savings bank life insurance business. The limitation to a $1,000 policy per person per bank, with a total limitation of $3,000 in New York State, has minimized the competition with ordinary life insurance companies. Although the $1,000 policy per bank rule applies in Massachusetts, the total amount of insurance written is limited to the number of banks with insurance departments times $1,000.[11] In 1941 Connecticut passed a law modeled after that of New York State, authorizing savings bank life insurance.

Relative to the total amount of life insurance written in the United States (over $100,000,000,000), the volume of business done by the savings banks is small. The amount of savings bank insurance

[10] See Tables 102 and 103 in *Annual Report of the Federal Deposit Insurance Corporation for the Year Ended December 31, 1944.*

[11] Berman, Edward, *The Massachusetts System of Savings Bank Life Insurance*, U.S. Department of Labor, Bulletin No. 615, p. 9.

in force in Massachusetts is over $100,000,000. In New York the total savings bank insurance outstanding as of October 31, 1945, was $57,000,000.[12] The mutual savings banks are in a position to reach many small depositors who carry no insurance. The banks are expected to supplement rather than compete with insurance companies for new business, with the general effect of expanding the volume of insurance in force. Most of the opposition to savings bank insurance originally came from life insurance agents, underwriters' associations, and publishers of life insurance periodicals.[13] However, the long-run effects should stimulate interest in all types of insurance, as has been true of veterans' insurance.

QUESTIONS AND PROBLEMS

1. What was the origin of the savings bank movement? When was it introduced in the United States? How important are "savings deposits"?
2. Explain how savings banks' rules favor small depositors.
3. Compare the growth of deposits in savings banks with the growth of similar deposits in commercial banks. See Table 41.
4. In what sense are mutual savings banks "mutual"? In what sense are they not "mutual"?
5. How do you account for the geographical distribution of mutual savings banks?
6. Often acts under which mutual savings banks operate require that all deposits except a limited percentage must be invested. Compare to minimum reserve requirements against time deposits in commercial banks.
7. What are certificates of deposit? How are they used? Why have deposits evidenced by this type of credit instrument declined since 1930?
8. What has been the trend in mutual savings banks' investments and loans since 1935? Give an explanation for each of these changes. Use Table 42.
9. What is meant by the "inflexibility" of legal lists? How has this been overcome in part in New York and other states?
10. What effect has the increase in the wealth of the average individual had on mutual savings banks? On other investing institutions?
11. What are the various reasons advanced for the proposed segregation of the savings departments from commercial departments of commercial banks?

---

[12] *Ninety-fifth Annual Report of the Superintendent of Banks, State of New York,* Part I, p. 45.

[13] New York Savings Banks Association, *Association News Bulletin,* June 23, 1939, p. 144.

12. Compare the organization and methods of operations of mutual savings banks and the Postal Savings System.

13. "The postal savings system is an anachronism." Explain. Do depositors agree? Why?

14. What has been the trend in number of depositors in the Postal Savings System? Since 1915, what changes have taken place in the system's use of banks as depositories? In investment of assets? Explain these changes. Use Table 43.

15. How may the purchase of United States Savings Bonds be used to provide retirement income, educational fund, etc.

16. What are the arguments for and against school savings banks?

17. Compare the investment problems of mutual savings banks to those of commercial banks?

18. To what extent are mutual savings banks taking advantage of their privileges of participating in (*a*) Federal Reserve System, (*b*) Federal Deposit Insurance Corporation, and (*c*) Home Loan Bank System?

19. Present the case for and against giving mutual savings banks the authority to write small life insurance policies.

20. How will the federal and state social security programs affect the primary function of savings banks?

21. "The local bank, to a great extent, invests its money locally. Through the Postal Savings System local money is 'syphoned' out of the district for use elsewhere" (from the Presidential Address of P. A. Benson before the Savings Division of American Bankers Association, September, 1936). Criticize.

REFERENCES

American Bankers Association, Savings Bank Division. *Savings Deposits and Depositors.* New York: American Bankers Association, 1939. (Pamphlet.)

American Bankers Association, Savings Bank Division. *School Savings Banks, School Year 1938-39.*

American Bankers Association, Committee on Banking Studies. *The Postal Savings System of the United States*, 1937.

Bennett, F. P. *The Story of Mutual Savings Banks.* Boston: F. P. Bennett & Co., Inc., 1924.

Berman, Edward. *The Massachusetts System of Savings-Bank Life Insurance.* U.S. Department of Labor, Bulletin No. 615.

Hamilton, J. H. *Savings and Savings Institutions*, chaps. i, ii, v, and vii. New York: Macmillan Co., 1902.

Kniffen, W. H. *The Savings Bank and Its Practical Work.* 4th ed. New York: Bankers Publishing Co., 1928.

"Losses to Depositors in Suspended Commercial Banks, 1865-1934," *Annual Report of the Federal Deposit Insurance Corporation* (1934), pp. 73-110.

Miller, C. A. *Savings Banks Trust Company and Institutional Securities Corporation.* Reprint from the *Bulletin of the Savings Banks Association of the State of New York*, 1935.

Orcutt, W. D. *The Miracle of Mutual Savings, 1834-1934.* New York: Bowery Savings Banks, 1934.

Sherman, F. J. *Modern Story of Mutual Savings Banks.* New York: J. J. Little & Ives Co., 1934.

Sutcliffe, W. G., and Bond, L. A. *Savings Banks and Savings Department Management.* New York: Harper & Bros., 1930.

Warburton, Clark. "The Trend of Savings, 1900-1929," *Journal of Political Economy*, Vol. XLIII (1935), pp. 84-101.

Willis, H. P., and Chapman, J. M. *The Banking Situation*, chap. xii. New York: Columbia University Press, 1934.

Also see annual reports of the Comptroller of the Currency, Federal Deposit Insurance Corporation, and Superintendent of Banks for the states of Massachusetts, New York, and others.

Chapter XXXII

TRUST BANKING

Trust Institutions Are Corporations Engaged in Trust Business

American Development.—Trust institutions include all trust departments of banks as well as fiduciary or trust companies engaged exclusively in the trust business. The word "fiduciary" is derived from the Latin word *fiducia*, which means "trust" or "confidence." It is practically synonymous in meaning with the Anglo-Saxon word "trust," which is more commonly used.

Lawyers and others have served as trustees and agents for individuals and associations for hundreds of years; but the incorporation of trust companies and the grants of trust powers to banks are recent and distinctly American developments.[1] Insurance companies were the first corporations permitted by law to perform trust functions; but, until after the Civil War, their trust business was a minor activity. The first company to do an exclusive trust business was not organized until 1853. Later, as the trust business developed, many insurance companies reorganized into trust companies, and new trust companies were formed with charters broad enough to permit them to carry on most types of banking.

Trust Banking.—Since 1900 the trust business has been closely allied to banking, and the modern trust company is one of the best illustrations of the results of the integration movement in banking. Because of the very nature of the trust business, trust companies are responsible for the investments and safety of large sums of money. In addition, they provide many agency services to corporations and others, and, as a result, they are in daily contact with many business institutions. It was but logical for them to accept commercial and savings deposits from their clients, to make loans, to clear and collect checks, and to perform all the other banking functions except that of bank note issue.

In its early stages trust banking was confined to New England

[1] To an increasing extent, English and other foreign banks are opening trust divisions to handle the trust business of their customers.

and the other more densely populated eastern states. From 1898 to 1930 the number of trust companies increased from 246 to 1,564, and the aggregate resources from less than $1,000,000,000 to $18,000,000,000. The Federal Deposit Insurance Corporation reports about 90 trust companies that do not accept deposits; but in many cities the trust company is the accepted and conventional type of commercial bank, whose number and assets are included in the statistics of state commercial banks.

The entrance of trust companies into the banking field under more liberal charters placed the national banks in an unfavorable competitive position; and many national banks gave up their national charters and reorganized either as trust companies or as state banks with trust banking privileges. In 1913, in order to check the movement of banks away from the national banking system, Congress authorized national banks to carry on trust business when it is "not in contravention of State or local laws."[2] Under this provision of the Federal Reserve Act, a national bank must secure special permission to carry on a trust business from the Board of Governors, and now over one-fourth of them have trust departments or trust divisions. Some national banks prefer to buy or establish a subsidiary corporation, with a state charter to operate their trust business, a situation not uncommon in the city of New York. After a state bank becomes a member of the Federal Reserve System, it must secure approval of the Board before it may exercise trust powers and must meet the standards as provided by law and by regulations of the Board of Governors for national banks.

Technically, a trust company cannot accept a trust that runs beyond its legal life. However, the McFadden-Pepper Act of 1927 gave indeterminate charters to national banks, thereby making it possible for them to accept perpetual trusts of the nonpersonal type, created to finance educational, religious, health, and other quasi-public activities; and to accept certain trust functions for business corporations which involve a long period of time. The McFadden-Pepper Act also provided that, in case of bank mergers, national banks could assume the trust commitments of state banks with whom they merged. At the present time about 1,800 national banks are permitted to carry on trust business.

[2] See Federal Reserve Act as amended, Sec. II (K). The act of September, 1918, broadened and strengthened the right of national banks to engage in the trust business.

Before giving a national bank permission to carry on a trust business, the Board of Governors of the Federal Reserve System considers such questions as: (1) Does the bank have sufficient capital and surplus? (2) Does the community need the kind of trust service applied for? (3) Is the applying bank sound? (4) Is its management satisfactory? (5) Are its officers qualified to supervise a trust business? (6) Are its trust officer or officers and legal counsel competent?

Trust Business Is Segregated from Other Activities of Banks[3]

All national banks and most state banks are required by law to separate their trust work from other departments in the bank. All the books and records are kept "distinct from other records of the bank." There is no mingling of assets of the trust department with those of the commercial, savings, or other departments of the bank. The only exception is when trust funds are held by a bank awaiting investment or distribution. In some states these funds may be used by the bank under authorization of its board of directors, provided that (1) adequate collateral is deposited as security, (2) the deposits are preferred claims on the assets of the banks, and (3) interest is paid on the deposits. In addition, many state laws require banks, acting in a fiduciary capacity, to deposit some of their own securities with state officers in order to protect trusts from fraud, negligence, etc.[4] Each individual trust must be segregated from others being handled by the department; and an institution having 1,000 trusts will have to keep 1,000 investment, earnings, disbursements, and other bookkeeping records. It is this requirement that explains the most noticeable equipment in a trust department, that is, filing cabinets.

The bank's board of directors is directly responsible for general supervision of the trust department—all investments, general policies, and disposition of trust investments. The board of directors or committee of the board must approve the acceptance of all fiduciary accounts and the closing-out or relinquishment of all old accounts.

[3] See revision of Regulation F, published in *Federal Reserve Bulletin*, May, 1936, pp. 327-32.

[4] If state officers refuse to accept securities deposited by national banks, the Federal Reserve bank of that district is authorized to accept them.

All trust funds are invested by a trust committee composed of three or more members who must be experienced officers or directors of the bank. The investment committee must review, at least annually, the assets held in, or for, each fiduciary account. It must "determine their safety and current value and the advisability of retaining or disposing of them; and a report of all such reviews, together with the action taken as a result thereof, shall be noted in the minutes of the trust investment committee."[5]

Ordinary bank statements do not contain reports of the assets in the trust departments, because the properties involved are held in trust for the beneficiaries as provided in the trust agreements and by law. The banking business of other departments may be suspended without seriously involving the work of the trust division of the bank. If an individual trustee dies or is incapacitated, the probate judge appoints a new trustee, and this principle applies to the "death" of a corporate trustee.

In case of liquidation of a bank, the trust work may be continued, with legal permission, by organizing the trust department into a trust company, by a reorganized bank, or by a transfer of the trusts to another trust company. Therefore, bank failures do not mean that the trusts must be liquidated or that the beneficiaries lose their rights to trust funds. Trustees are not insurers or guarantors of trusts left with them for management, but they are expected to act in "good faith" and in the sole interests of the beneficiaries, and to exercise ordinary care, prudence, and skill in making or "liquidating" investments of trust funds.

Banks Serve as Trustees and Agents

Used broadly, the word "trustee" means a person or corporation holding property in trust. It includes all types of trusteeships; but some types are known by special names, such as administrators or executors of estates, guardians of minors, and conservators of estates of incompetents. Sometimes the word "trustee" is used in a narrower sense to include all types of trusteeship except those having a special name, such as administrator, executor, and guardian.[6]

---

[5] See revision of Regulation F, published in *Federal Reserve Bulletin*, May, 1936, pp. 328-29; and December, 1939, p. 1054.

[6] Herrick, Clay, *Trust Departments in Banks and Trust Companies*, pp. 12-13.

A trust is the relationship which exists where legal title to property has been given to one person (the trustee) by a second person (the trustor) for the benefit of a third party (the beneficiary). The trustee may be an individual or a properly authorized trust institution. All types of property may be placed in a trust fund. The trust may be created to provide an income for the support of dependents, for the maintenance of educational institutions, for the equipment and supervision of public parks and playgrounds, or for the support of almost any project.

Considered from a broad economic viewpoint, the original and primary function of a trust company is to conserve wealth. The old adage, "three generations from shirt sleeves to shirt sleeves," has been dealt a severe blow by this new institution because, by using the services offered by a trust company, the spendthrift son or daughter may be prevented from wasting the principal of an estate. When a person has a large estate, he may desire to keep it intact; but, because of the rule against perpetuities, he can do this only to a limited extent.

At an early date English courts took the position that it would be harmful for society to hinder the alienation of property, because this would tend to (1) undermine commerce, (2) keep property in the hands of the wealthy after they had lost their ability to care for it, and (3) create the basis for the formation of a social caste, with a resulting curtailment of opportunities for individuals. The common law makes a personal trust void if the vesting of the title is postponed for a longer time than "a life or lives in being and twenty-one years." Under the New York State code, it may not extend beyond two lives in being and the minority of a third life.

Trust companies serve in various capacities as agencies for individuals and corporations. An "agency" is defined as the legal relationship which exists where one person, called an "agent," is employed and authorized by another, called the "principal," to represent and act for the latter in his business or contractual dealings with third persons. The main difference between an agency and a trust relationship is that the trustee holds legal title, whereas the agent does not.[7] Authority to act is derived from a simple request or agreement to perform certain definite acts. It may be in the form of

[7] Smith, J. G., *The Development of Trust Companies in the United States*, p. 120.

a letter or general or special power of attorney, which usually can be revoked at any time.[8]

The executive committee of the Trust Division of the American Bankers Association states that proper trust business consists of "settling estates, administering trust and performing agencies in all appropriate cases for individuals; partnerships; associations; business corporations; public, educational, social, recreational, and charitable institutions; and units of government."[9]

The special services of a fiduciary nature which a trust company may perform are covered by the laws of the state in which the trust company is located. This is true also of the trust work of national banks, even though these institutions are incorporated under federal banking laws. With the growth of the trust business, the powers granted by different states to trust banks have assumed greater uniformity. A state may authorize trust institutions to perform any fiduciary service which it would be lawful for a natural individual to perform. The fiduciary services usually authorized tend to conform to the trust powers recommended by the Trust Division of the American Bankers Association as outlined in the preceding paragraphs.

Trust Business Is Classified as Individual and Corporate, Court and Voluntary

Individual trust business includes all types of fiduciary and agency services performed for individuals. They result from court appointments or voluntary agreements. Corporate trust business includes all fiduciary and agency services performed for corporations, educational institutions, fraternal organizations, hospitals, and religious institutions.

Court trusts are defined as "those which are received by appointment of the courts having jurisdiction in such cases and for which accounting must be made to the courts." They include those in which trust institutions serve as executors, administrators, trustees, guardians, and conservators. Court trusts are the oldest and most important class of trusts.

[8] Kirkbridge, F. B., Sterrett, J. E., and Willis, H. P., *The Modern Trust Company*, pp. 300-301.

[9] Published in *Federal Reserve Bulletin*, May, 1936, p. 335.

Voluntary or living trusts result from private agreements between trust institutions and makers or creators of the trust. They include all types of fiduciary services and agency relationships. They may be revocable or irrevocable; they may go into effect during the life of the makers or sometime after their death.

Management of Individual Trust Is Personal

In many large trust institutions the fiduciary work is divided into two divisions—personal and corporate. This arrangement permits the trust institution to give more personal attention to the needs of individuals and allows greater specialization in handling corporate accounts. The executive committee of the Trust Division of the American Bankers Association drew up the following principles to serve as a guide to administration of personal trusts.[10]

SECTION 1. *Personal trusts.*—In the administration of its personal trust business, a trust institution should strive at all times to render unexceptionable business and financial service, but it should also be careful to render equally good personal service to beneficiaries. The first duty of a trust institution is to carry out the wishes of the creator of a trust as expressed in the trust instrument. Sympathetic, tactful, personal relationships with immediate beneficiaries are essential to the performance of this duty, keeping in mind also the interests of ultimate beneficiaries. It should be the policy of trust institutions that all personal trusts should be under the direct supervision of and that beneficiaries should be brought into direct contact with the administrative or senior officers of the trust department.

SEC. 2. *Confidential relationships.*—Personal trust service is of a confidential nature and the confidences reposed in a trust department by a customer should never be revealed except when required by law.

SEC. 3. *Fundamental duties of trustees.*—It is the duty of a trustee to administer a trust solely in the interest of the beneficiaries without permitting the intrusion of interests of the trustee or third parties that may in any way conflict with the interests of the trust; to keep and render accurate accounts with respect to the administration of the trust; to acquaint the beneficiaries with all material facts in connection with the trust; and, in administering the trust, to exercise the care a prudent man familiar with such matters would exercise as trustee of the property of others, adhering to the rule that the trustee is primarily a conserver.

The chief types of personal, fiduciary, and agency trusteeships

[10] See Regulation F. "A Statement of Principles of Trust Institutions," Article III, published in *Federal Reserve Bulletin*, May, 1936, p. 335.

are those which serve as (1) executors or administrators of estates; (2) trustees under wills of deceased persons or under agreements or deeds of trust; (3) guardians of property of minors and incompetent persons; and (4) fiscal agencies, attorneys in fact, and depositories in various capacities.

Executors and Administrators.—Individuals or trust companies may be appointed to take charge of the settlement of estates under wills (called "executors") or by orders of the court having probate jurisdiction (called "administrators"). In both cases the duties of a trust company or individual trustee are practically the same. They include the receipt of property, payments of all claims against the estate, and the division of the remainder among the heirs according to the law or the terms of the will. The authority of the executor is derived from the will, and the authority of the administrator is derived from the intestacy law. However, the administrators or executors cannot take possession of the property until authorized to do so by the court having probate jurisdiction. In the past, it was a common practice for the maker of a will to name an individual as executor, but, at present, there is a growing tendency to name a trust company or a trust department of a bank as executor. Because of the nature of the trust activity involved, the duties of executors and administrators are temporary in nature.

Trustees.—The maker of a will may want his heirs to enjoy the income of an estate but may not want them to take over its management. In that case he may select a trust institution to manage his estate after all the debts and other obligations are paid. A trustor may wish to place a part of his property beyond his own control in order to assure his family a certain income in the event of business losses. He may do this through a trust agreement in order to provide a separate income for his wife and children. Although the beneficiaries of trusts are usually third parties, the trustor may make himself the beneficiary until his death, specifying that after his death the benefits shall go to others, as indicated in the trust agreement or will. One of the most rapidly growing of all types of trust is the life insurance trust, which is made up of the proceeds from life insurance policies. This type of trust is of importance to residents and banks located in smaller communities.

Guardians and Conservators.—In the case of the death of parents (natural guardians), the protection of minors and their property is assumed by the state. A guardian may be appointed by will, by deed, or by the probate court. A trust company may serve as the guardian of a minor's property and, in some states, of his person. The guardianship ends when the ward reaches legal age. The principal duties of the guardian of an estate are (1) to accept the property of the ward, (2) to make investments according to law, (3) to keep accurate records of receipts and expenditures, (4) to render a final accounting when the guardianship terminates, and (5), upon the decree of the court, to deliver the property to the beneficiary.

Habitual drunkards, idiots, and insane persons are incompetent and, therefore, wards of the state. The courts, upon proper application, appoint guardians of their persons and property. The duties of the conservator (sometimes called "committee") of the estate are similar to those of a guardian. The life of the trust varies according to the needs of the case. If the habitual drunkard becomes cured or the insane person regains his reason, the trust may be terminated.

Fiscal Agents, Attorneys in Fact, and Depositories.—Trust companies act as brokers for clients in the purchase and sale of securities. They may be retained to rent, sell, repair, and manage real property. If one is to be absent for an extended period, a trust company may be employed to manage his personal business. In general, a trust company may serve an individual in the same fiscal capacities that one individual may serve a second. Escrow depository is one of the more complicated agency services offered by trust companies. They accept property on deposit which is to be delivered to another upon the fulfillment of specified conditions. It is a useful device in business transactions where the parties are separated by long distances; in real estate transfers where property is in dispute; in connection with alimony payments; and whenever the first party of a contract does not trust the second party, or vice versa.

Large Trust Institutions Supply Corporations with Trust and Agency Services

The need for corporate trust and agency services is confined to large centers of population, and for this reason many small banks limit their trust business to agency and fiduciary services to individuals. In administering corporate trusts and agency services, banks are expected to follow the same administrative principles considered under personal trusteeship. "Promptness, accuracy, and protection are fundamental requirements of efficient corporate trust service. The terms of the trust instrument should be carried out with scrupulous care and with particular attention to the duties imposed therein upon the trustee for the protection of the security-holders."[11]

Corporate trust business includes all fiduciary services given to corporations, educational institutions, fraternal organizations, hospitals, and religious institutions. The most important types of corporate fiduciary services rendered by banks are (1) to act as trustee under a corporate mortgage; (2) to act as trustee under reorganization plans, receiverships, etc.; (3) to serve as transfer agent, registrar, paying agent, etc.; (4) to serve as fiscal agent, attorney in fact, and depository in various capacities; and (5) to help in various ways societies and institutions.

Trustee under Corporate Mortgage.—When corporations borrow for long periods, they desire amounts too large to be provided by one lender. Through the medium of an investment banker, bonds are sold in convenient denominations, usually $500 or $1,000, to investors. A single mortgage or indenture agreement is usually drawn up and made payable to an "indenture trustee," that is, a bank or a trust company.[12] This mortgage or indenture agreement contains provisions to protect the bondholders. The corporation conveys title, under certain conditions, to all or part of its property to the trustee. This mortgage or indenture agreement is held in trust by the trustee for the benefit of the holders of the bonds which the corporation has issued thereunder. The trustee is usually not required to take action in case of default of mortgagor unless requested to do so by the holders of a certain percentage of outstanding bonds, generally 25 per cent. As a result, numerous abuses have developed, including a scramble among many self-appointed "protective committees" for the privilege (and fees and other rewards) of representing bondholders.[13]

---

[11] *Ibid.*

[12] An indenture trustee "shall mean a trustee under a mortgage, deed of trust, or indenture, pursuant to which there are securities outstanding, other than voting-trust certificates, constituting claims against a debtor or claims secured by a lien upon any of its property" (Art. II, Sec. 106, chap. x, of the National Bankruptcy Act).

[13] See Securities and Exchange Commission, *Report on the Study and Investigation of the Work, Activities, and Functions of Protective and Reorganization Committee,* Part I, "Strategy and Techniques of Protective and Reorganization Committee," 1937.

Prior to 1939, trust companies were not bond trustees in the true sense of the word but merely agents of the bondholders. They rarely took action on their own initiative, being guided by the traditional attitude, which was opposed to taking positive action. Even when trustees were given discretion to act, they rarely did so. As a result, bondholders did not have the protection which the word "trustee" denotes. However, trust companies were faithful in performing their routine functions in connection with their trust under corporate mortgages.[14]

One purpose of the Trust Indenture Act of 1939 was "to bring all indenture trustees up to a high level of diligence and loyalty and to place them in a better position to protect security holders. The means adopted is a requirement that bonds, notes, debentures and similar debt securities exceeding $1,000,000 in principal amount may not be offered for sale to the public unless they are issued under a trust indenture which conforms to specific statutory standards and has been duly qualified with the [Securities and Exchange] Commission."[15]

Trustees under Reorganization Plans, Receiverships, etc.—The work of trust institutions in reorganizations is usually passive. They accept the securities deposited with them by one or more of the reorganization committees. After the committees and the courts have worked out an acceptable plan for reorganization, the depository issues the reorganization certificates authorized by them.[16] Under requirements of the National Bankruptcy Act of 1938, the Securities and Exchange Commission must serve as advisor to the United States districts courts in connection with the proceedings for reorganization of debtor corporations in which there is "a substantial public interest."

Transfer Agents, Registrars, Paying Agents, etc.—Stockholders are the owners of a corporation's capital stock. The names of the owners and the number of shares held by each are shown on the books of the corporation. If title is transferred to a second party, transfer

[14] See "Trust Indenture Act of 1939," (*Public Law 253,* 76th Cong.). This act gave the Securities and Exchange Commission the power to approve or disapprove of trust indentures under which securities are issued.

[15] *Tenth Annual Report of the Securities and Exchange Commission Fiscal Year Ended June 30, 1944,* p. 5.

[16] Note new provisions for corporate reorganization in chap. x of the National Bankruptcy Act (*Public Law No. 696,* 75th Cong.).

of the certificate is not sufficient; the title must be passed on the books of the corporation. This transfer of title may be made by the corporation or by some trust institution appointed as the transfer agent. If a stock is actively traded in on a stock exchange, trust institutions commonly serve as transfer agents, since they are able to transfer titles to stock rapidly and skillfully.

In order to prevent fraud in the form of illegal issues of stock, the New York Stock Exchange now requires as a prerequisite for listing stocks the appointment of a transfer agent and a registrar, both to be be located in the Borough of Manhattan, city of New York. The registrar must be a trust institution. The registrar checks upon the transfer work of the transfer agent, receives the cancelled certificate of stock or a registered bond, and the new stock certificate or bond issued in its place. The cancelled certificate is examined to see if it is genuine and if the new certificate is drawn to represent the proper number of shares. Proper entries are made in the registration records, the registrar's certificate is signed, and it is then returned to the transfer agent.

Bonds may have interest coupons attached, or the bonds may be registered in the same way as stock certificates. Usually the bond coupons are payable semi-annually, the dates of payments being indicated on the coupons. For example, a bond of $1,000 denomination, dated January 1, 1937, and having a term of twenty years, will have forty coupons attached. The coupons will be dated alternately, July 1 and January 1, for twenty years, the first coupon being dated July 1, 1937. The holder of the bond clips the proper coupon on or immediately before the payment date and sends it to the paying agent. A trust institution may serve as payer, or this work may be done by the debtor. If a trust institution serves as paying agent, the debtor deposits funds with it prior to the interest, dividend, or maturing dates of the obligations. Trust institutions serve as paying agents for all types of corporations, public and private, and for other large borrowers.

Fiscal Agents, Attorneys in Fact, and Depositories.—Trust institutions also serve corporations in many of the special agency capacities in which they serve individuals. They act as liquidating agents for corporations which have decided to discontinue business, as escrow depositories, as managers of real property, as custodians of securities, and in other capacities.

Agents for Institutions.—Trust companies serve as trustees and agents for many types of foundations, educational institutions, hospitals, religious organizations, and other institutions. The community trust is a recent development in this field, the first having been created in 1914 in Cleveland, Ohio. Under a community trust, gifts and bequests are received by a trust company, which, with the help of an advisory board of citizens, expends the funds for public purposes. The community trust in New York is the largest in this country, being composed of thirty-six individual funds. There are about eighty such trusts and foundations in the United States.

Future of Trust Institutions Depends upon Wisdom in Management

Advantages of Trust Companies.—Although most trust functions may be performed by individuals, trust companies may be better equipped to perform certain specific services. The advantages of the trust companies over individuals may be summarized as follows:

1. They offer continuous administration, which the individual cannot do. Whereas the life of an individual is short, trust companies have perpetual charters. If an individual trustee dies or resigns, a successor must be appointed. This is usually costly, for it involves a complete accounting on the part of the former trustee or his estate, the cost of which is charged against the trust fund.
2. Trust companies offer continuous service at their place of business, but an individual trustee is not always at his home or office; moreover, his residence may be changed many times during the life of the trust. Many annoyances to beneficiaries and losses because of delay may result from these conditions.
3. Trust companies are more responsible than individual trustees. They are subject to periodic examinations by the government, and their capital resources are large. Trust companies are not, however, responsible for losses of trust funds unless fraud or negligence can be proved.
4. Trust companies have available expert services in the investment, accounting, taxation, and legal fields, circumstances which make the cost of administration less than is usually the case under management of an individual trustee.

Objections to Corporate Trustees.—The chief objection to corporate trustees is that they are impersonal in their treatment of beneficiaries and trust funds. Their primary consideration is to keep within the law and avoid future claims against them for illegal operations. Their activities are too passive and of too routine a nature. Even when they have been granted broad discretionary powers, they often hesitate to take seemingly necessary action, preferring the safer legal policy of doing nothing. Many individuals still serve as trustees, but trust institutions dominate the field. During the 1930–33 depression, trust companies, along with all other banking institutions, lost prestige. However, since 1933, the trust business of banks, especially national banks, has increased rapidly.

Problem of Investment.—The future of trust institutions depends to a considerable extent upon the success which they have in investing trust funds, it being a duty to keep all funds invested. While it is desirable for a trustee to secure a high rate of return, his primary consideration must be safety of principal. The creator of a trust may give definite instructions as to the character of investments, or he may leave it entirely to the discretion of the trustee. Unless otherwise specified in the trust agreement, the trustee must limit his investments to the so-called legal securities. These are determined by law and are, in general, the same as those that savings banks are permitted to purchase. In general, the legal lists include first mortgages on real property, government bonds, and the high-grade bonds of public utilities, railroads, and a few industrial corporations. Since 1933 the fear of inflation has led many trustees to seek permission to buy high-grade common and preferred stocks.

Since each trust fund must be managed separately, the advantages resulting from large-scale purchases are lacking for small trusts. For example, assume that Smith leaves $500 in trust with a trust company, the income to be used to buy current periodicals for his fraternity or school library. This sum must be invested separately, and, obviously, little diversification is possible. Some states, in an effort to correct this situation, have authorized banks to invest small accounts collectively, issuing participating certificates to each trust account. Since 1938, in New York State, the Banking Board may permit applicants to establish common trust funds. If common trust funds are to qualify for exemption from taxation as corporations, they must conform to Regulation F of the Board of Governors of the Federal Reserve System, which covers operations of common trust funds by national banks.[17] The amount that may be invested in a common trust by any one trust is $50,000. A trust institution is not required to accept trust accounts, and many are refused because they are too small.

Trust Institutions Are Compensated by Commissions and Fees

Large Banks Dominate.—The amount of clerical and other work in connection with trust banking is large. The overhead is so great that the small banks are in no position to handle any trust business except life insurance trusts, which require relatively little management. Therefore, trust banking is largely confined to the metropolitan centers and the wealthier states. Many of the trust departments of the smaller banks are being operated at a loss, pending an increase in volume to place them on a profitable basis, because contacts with the trust departments may bring new business to other divisions of the banks. But the ill-will created, as well as litigations resulting from losses suffered by beneficiaries of individual trusts, may more than offset the expected advantages from the trust business. Many banks in the United States prefer to leave the trust business to individual trustees or to a few large specialists in the field. Probably three-fourths of the trust business in this country is concentrated in the hands of the large institutions located in the metropolian centers.

Commissions.—The trust company is compensated for managing the trust by receiving a percentage of the income during the life of the trust and a percentage of the principal when the trust ends. The charges are fixed by law. For example, the table on page 668 shows the commission that a trust of $100,000 would pay to the trust company in New York State, assuming that the yield is $5,000.

The commissions on income are payable annually and on the principal when the trust terminates. The commission rates of an executor or administrator are the same as the principal charges noted in the foregoing. The commissions on voluntary trusts are fixed by trust agreements but are about the same as those allowed by law. Sometimes in voluntary trusts one-half of the commissions

[17] See amendments to Regulation F in *Federal Reserve Bulletin*, June, 1940, pp. 502-9; July, 1941, p. 618; January, 1942, p. 7; and August, 1945, pp. 772-74.

on the principal are paid when they are formed and the other one-half when they terminate. Agency fees are fixed by private agreements.

COMMISSION ON INCOME	
On the first $2,000, 5 per cent	$ 100
On the next $3,000, 2½ per cent	75
Annual commission on income	$ 175
COMMISSION ON PRINCIPAL	
On the first $2,000, 5 per cent	$ 100
On the next $20,000, 2½ per cent	500
On the next $28,000, 1½ per cent	420
On the remaining $50,000, 2 per cent	1,000
Total commission on principal	$2,020

Trust Institutions Are Now Subject to Better Regulation

The Banking Act of 1935 contains provisions which have as their purposes centralization of the regulation of trust work of banks. All books and accounts of member banks must be kept in forms approved by the Comptroller of the Currency or Board of Governors of the Federal Reserve System. Assets of each trust account must be examined by the bank's investment trust committee, and its work is audited yearly by a special committee of the bank's board of directors. When examiners, appointed by the Federal Reserve banks or by the Comptroller, examine trust institutions, they give special attention to the auditing, examining, and investment work of the trustees.

Before 1933 the policy of the national regulatory officers was to force national banks to conform to the regulatory and supervisory requirements of the state in which the bank was situated. The books and records were open to inspection of state examiners to the same extent as those of similarly located state-chartered trust institutions. This provision was amended by the Banking Act of 1935. Now the state banking authorities "may have access to reports of examinations made by the Comptroller of the Currency in so far as such reports relate to the trust department of such bank"; but it denies to state authorities the right to examine the trust department of a national bank without the bank's consent.[18] Under the leadership of the Trust Division of the American Bankers Association, standard rules and practices are being developed.

State Institutions May Carry on Title Search and Mortgage Insurance Business

Trust companies may operate a special department which insures the title of mortgages purchased by their clients. Their trust division buys large volumes of real estate mortgages, which constitute an important part of legal investments. As a result of title and real estate investigations, trust companies customarily have on hand a great deal of information on local real estate titles and real estate conditions. When investors want to buy real estate mortgages, trust companies aid them by bringing lenders and borrowers together, or by buying the mortgages and reselling them to investors.

Defects in title of property purchased, or upon which money is lent, affect the value of the property. Buyers of property and of mortgages based upon property sometimes employ lawyers to search records and prepare abstracts of titles. But lawyers do not guarantee the completeness or accuracy of their work. Trust companies not only offer to do this title search work but also, for an additional fee, agree to insure the title. When institutions make a specialty of this business, they are called title insurance companies.

From the work of title insurance, it is but a short step for financial institutions to guarantee the repayment of principal and payment of interest or real estate loans. Additional fees are charged, and reserves are accumulated to cover contingent liabilities. Normally the number of bad loans insured is small, and losses are nominal. These institutions are called "title and mortgage insurance companies." Because of the severity of the 1930–33 depression in real estate, most of these large companies were unable to meet their obligations and were liquidated or reorganized. This same type of work is now done by a division of the Federal Housing Administration.

National banks are not permitted to carry on title and mortgage insurance business. However, national banks located in communi-

[18] See Sec. II (K) Federal Reserve Act as revised by Banking Act of 1935.

ties with a population of 5,000 or less are permitted to act as mortgage brokers or agents for others. In addition, they may act as agents for fire, life, or other insurance companies. They may also sell insurance and collect premiums, for which work they receive fees and commissions. All national banks are specifically prohibited from guaranteeing or insuring titles, from paying premiums, and from vouching for accuracy of statements.

QUESTIONS AND PROBLEMS

1. Who handled individual trusts before the appearance of the trust company (corporate fiduciary)? How do you explain the late development of this type of banking?
2. Distinguish between (*a*) corporate and individual trusts, (*b*) corporate and individual trustee, and (*c*) trust and agency services.
3. Why is the trust business confined to the metropolitan centers and wealthier states? What type of trust is of most importance in less densely settled communities? Why?
4. In what respects is a trust company superior and inferior to an individual in the performance of fiduciary functions?
5. What are the principles laid down by the American Bankers Association to guide in the administration of personal trusts? Are they sound?
6. What are the most general functions performed by trust institutions for individuals? For corporations?
7. "In making investments of trust funds, the trustee is under a duty to the beneficiary, in the absence of provisions in the terms of the trust or of a statute otherwise providing, to make such investments as a prudent man would make of his own property having primarily in view the preservation of the trust estate and the amount and regularity of the income to be derived" (American Law Institute Restatement of the Law of Trusts, Tentative Draft No. 4, No. 219). Discuss.
8. Assume that a college graduate wants to endow a Chair of Finance in memory of his parents. How may this be done through the facilities offered by a trust company?
9. Compare the investment problems of a trust company to those of a bank. To what extent may funds be mingled? Is government supervision desirable? Why?
10. Was the change in length of time which national bank charters ran of aid to these banks in carrying on a trust business? Why?
11. Do you believe that national banks should be permitted to search titles, guarantee titles, and insure real estate mortgages? Why?

12. Are the trust departments of member banks an important source of earnings? Are these earnings the result of loans and investments? Explain.

13. "Prior to 1939 most of the average [trust] indenture was devoted to exculpating the trustee." Criticize this situation. What action has Congress taken on this matter? (*Source: Tenth Annual Report of the Securities and Exchange Commission, Fiscal Year Ended June 30, 1944*, p. 5; also see pp. 153-56).

14. All "property sooner or later must be transferred because of the deaths of successive owners. And remember that every transfer requires fiduciary service." Comment (Sinclaire, J. K., *Banking*, Sec. II [November, 1936], p. 9).

15. In answer to a question, "How would you invest an unrestricted trust fund of $100,000 cash, running probably 20 years with income to a widow who needed all the income possible?" Thirty-six trust executives answered with average results shown: government, 20 per cent; state and municipal, 14 per cent; corporate bonds, 38 per cent; stocks, 19 per cent; and other securities, 9 per cent (Malott, C., *Banking*, December, 1938, p. 75). Criticize.

REFERENCES

American Bankers Association, Trust Division. *Common Trust Funds: A Handbook on Their Purposes, Establishment, and Operation.* New York: American Bankers Association, 1939.

Conyngton, T., Knapp, H. C., and Pinkerton, P .W. *Wills, Estates and Trusts.* New York: Ronald Press Co., 1922.

Herrick, Clay. *Trust Departments in Banks and Trust Companies*, chaps. i-iv and xx. New York: McGraw-Hill Book Co., Inc., 1925.

Kirkbridge, F. B., Sterrett, J. E., and Willis, H. P. *The Modern Trust Company*, chaps. i and xiii-xiv. 6th ed. New York: Macmillan Co., 1925.

Lee, C. *Personal Trust Administration.* New York: Bankers Publishing Co., 1934.

Neilan, E. P. *Trust Examination.* New York: Research Council of the American Bankers Association, 1939.

Riddle, N. G. *Investment Policy of Trust Institutions.* Chicago: Business Publications, Inc., 1934.

Securities and Exchange Commission. *Tenth Annual Report, Fiscal Year Ended June 30, 1944.* Washington, D.C.: U.S. Government Printing Office, 1945.

Securities and Exchange Commission. *Report on the Study and Investigation of the Work, Activities, Personnel, and Functions of Protective and Reorganization Committees:*

Part I, "Strategy and Techniques of Protective and Reorganization Committees, 1937."

Part II, "Committees and Conflicts of Interest, 1937."

Part III, "Committees for the Holders of Real Estate Bonds, 1936."

Part IV, "Committees for Holders of Municipal and Quasi-municipal Obligations, 1936."

Part V, "Protective Committees and Agencies for Holders of Defaulted Foreign Governmental Bonds, 1937."

Part VI, "Trustees under Indentures, 1936."

Part VII, "Management Plans without Aid of Committees, 1938."

Part VIII, "A Summary of the Law Pertaining to Equity and Bankruptcy Reorganizations and of the Commission's Conclusions and Recommendations, 1940."

Smith, J. G. *The Development of Trust Companies in the United States*, Parts I and II. New York: Henry Holt & Co., 1928.

Stephenson, G. T. *Living Trusts*, chaps. i-v. 2d ed. New York: F. S. Crofts & Co., 1937.

Chapter XXXIII

INVESTMENT HOUSES AND ALLIED INSTITUTIONS

Meaning of Investment Banking

Used in a broad sense, the term "investment banking" includes the business of dealing primarily in long-term credit. The institutions now engaged in this business include practically all those considered in this book, even the so-called "commercial banks." However, there are distinctions among financial institutions, other than those based on the type of credit handled, which set the investment banking houses apart from other institutions. They are not "institutions of deposit," which differentiates them from commercial and savings banks; and they do not finance homeowners and farmers, which sets them apart from the institutions described in the two chapters which follow.

Used in a narrower sense, investment banking means the business of financing the long-term needs of government, railroads, public utilities, and other large industrial corporations. The term "investment banker" is not well defined, and one hears it applied to the small bond dealer as well as to the large underwriting and distributing house that usually has many branch offices and representatives covering the United States.

Investment bankers buy and sell new issues of bonds and stocks. Bonds are issued for long periods, and stocks have no maturity dates. Few individuals hold one particular stock or bond more than a few years, and it is for this reason that a secondary market for securities is necessary. So consideration is given in this chapter to both the work of the investment houses and that of the dealers and brokers who operate in the over-the-counter market and on organized securities exchanges.

Development of Investment Banking

Lenders of Own Funds.—During the early stages of the development of investment banking, there was no investing public; therefore, lenders used their own funds in making loans to borrowers, who were chiefly rulers and cities. Later, investment bankers helped to finance trading companies and other business ventures. During medieval times bankers were handicapped by the church's doctrine of usury, but by early modern times this had been modified so as to permit loans at interest. Interest rates were high because risks were large.

During the Middle Ages the property holding of rulers were extraordinarily large, and, where tax security was not sufficient, the rulers mortgaged parts of their estates. In general, the policy was to treat government finance as a private financial problem of the king. New lands were taken in the name of the king, and they continued to be his private property until granted to his subjects. These new lands were mortgaged to secure funds and, upon default, were seized by the bankers. Thus, the Welsers under Charles V obtained an entire province in Venezuela. Jacob Fugger built up one of the greatest fortunes the world has every known through loans to Maximilian (German Emperor, 1493-1519), Charles V, and Pope Julius II. "By 1524 the Fuggers had assumed control of a large part of the Spanish land taxes and mines; they had establishments in Poland, Antwerp, and Naples; and their operations and power extended from Belgium to India."[1]

Investment Bankers Are Middlemen.—The protection which democratic governments gave to property and property rights made savings popular and profitable. Thus the foundation was laid for the development of the modern type of investment banking. Investment bankers now act primarily as middlemen, merely bringing together the investing public and the borrowers of capital funds. In performing this function, investment houses sell stocks and bonds "without recourse."

Prior to World War I, the United States was a debtor nation. Securities were purchased by only a small number of American individual investors—fewer than 500,000. American securities were sold to institutional investors or sent abroad for redistribution through foreign banking channels. Since then, funds necessary for foreign as well as for domestic purposes have been raised in the United States.

Investment Bankers as Managers of Other People's Investments.

---

[1] Moulton, H. G., *The Financial Organization of Society*, p. 203.

—A third stage in the development of investment banking is one in which the investment banks assume responsibility for managing other people's savings. For example, there are investment companies, home and farm financing agencies, and savings and loan associations that sell their stock and/or obligations, using the proceeds to invest in other securities, and there are investment advisors who manage other people's investments. This stage in the development of investment banking is considerably above that wherein the investment banker acts primarily as a middleman in the merchandising of stocks and bonds.

Capital Issues in the United States, 1929-46

Federal Government Borrowing.—The statistics which appear in Table 44 show the amount of the United States government debt by

TABLE 44

UNITED STATES GOVERNMENT DEBT—VOLUME AND KIND OF SECURITIES*
(In Millions of Dollars)

	December 1933	December 1940	December 1945
Interest-bearing debt (total)	$23,450	$44,458	$277,456
Marketable public issues:†			
Treasury bills	$ 1,003	$ 1,310	$ 17,037
Certificates of indebtedness	1,828	....	38,155
Treasury notes	4,880	6,178	22,967
Treasury bonds	14,747	27,960	120,423
Total	$23,079	$35,645	$198,778
Nonmarketable public issues:‡			
U.S. savings bonds	....	$ 3,195	$ 48,183
Treasury tax and savings notes	....	....	8,235
Total	....	$ 3,444	$ 56,915
Special issues	$ 371	$ 5,370	$ 20,000
Noninterest-bearing debt	364	566	2,421
Fully guaranteed interest-bearing securities	....	....	553
Total gross direct debt	$23,814	$45,025	$278,115

* On basis of daily statements of United States Treasury.

† Includes amounts held by government agencies and trust funds, which aggregated $7,002,000,000 on Dec. 31, 1945. Also includes postal savings and pre-war bonds.

‡ Includes adjusted service and depositary bonds not shown separately.

Source: Banking and Monetary Statistics, pp. 509-10; and *Federal Reserve Bulletin*, February, 1946, p. 171.

volume and kind outstanding at the end of 1933, 1940, and 1945. Federal government financing has dominated both the money and the capital markets since 1931, a situation that most taxpayers hope will not be true in the future. Federal government issues are handled by the Federal Reserve banks, which act as the investment bankers for the government. But, after the original distribution, bond houses, dealers, and brokers, as well as commercial bankers, contribute to a

TABLE 45
NEW SECURITY ISSUES
(In Millions of Dollars)

	1929	1933	1940	1945
For new capital (total)	$10,093	$ 720	$1,951	$1,746
Domestic (total)	$ 9,420	$ 708	$1,948	$1,739
State and municipal	$ 1,418	$ 483	$ 751	$ 471
Federal agencies*	......	64	461	26
Corporate (total)	8,002	161	736	1,242
Bonds and notes	2,078	40	601	590
Stocks	5,924	120	135	651
Foreign‡	$ 673	$ 12	$ 2	$ 7
For refunding (total)	$ 1,420	$ 343	$2,852	$6,171
Domestic (total)	$ 1,387	$ 283	$2,852	$6,123
State and municipal	$ 13	$ 37	$ 482	$ 324
Federal agencies*	......	26	344	912
Corporate (total)	1,374	219	2,026	4,888
Bonds and notes	542	187	1,834	4,234
Stocks	833	32	193	654
Foreign†	$ 33	$ 60	......	$ 48
Total (new and refunding)	$11,513	$1,063	$4,803	$7,917

* Includes publicly offered issues of federal credit agencies but excludes direct obligations of U.S. Treasury.

† Includes issues of noncontiguous U.S. territories and possessions.

Source: Banking and Monetary Statistics, p. 487; and *Federal Reserve Bulletin*, February, 1946, p. 168.

secondary market for these securities. Usually new government obligations are priced below the market price, which makes it profitable for banks and others to request issues for secondary distribution at higher prices to investors.

New Security Issues.—In Table 45 there appear statistics of new nonfederal issues for selected years from 1929 to 1946. Usually these securities are sold to investment banks, who resell them to investors. In 1945 the volume of new securities was almost $8,000,000,000, of which over $6,000,000,000 was issued to refund old issues.

The increase in the relative and absolute importance of refunding issues is a direct result of the low interest rates prevailing in the capital market. Corporations with excellent credit standings are calling old issues of bonds when their debt contracts permit. Public

CHART XII
CAPITAL ISSUES*
(1927-45)

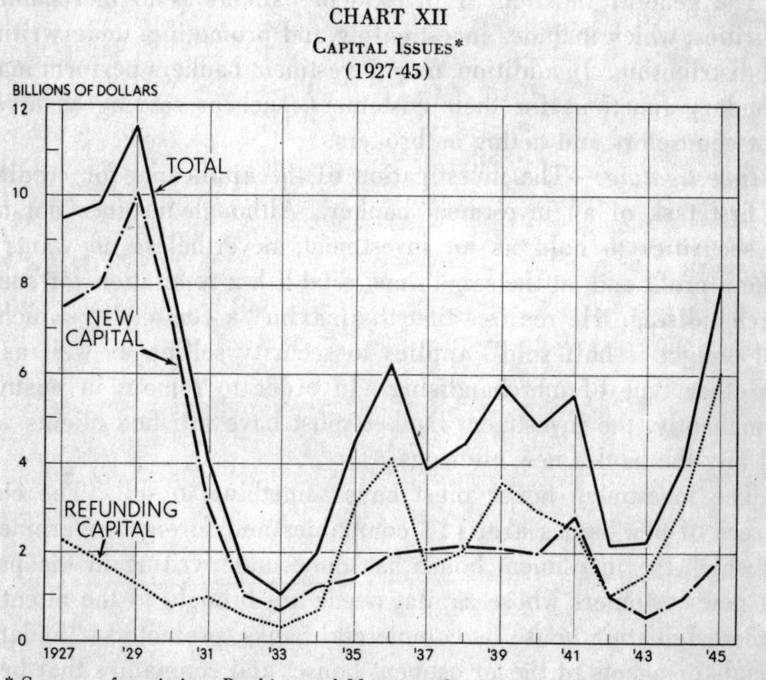

* Sources of statistics: *Banking and Monetary Statistics* and *Federal Reserve Bulletin.*

utilities and railroads usually regard their bonds outstanding as a part of their permanent capital and so are continuously refinancing in the market. State and municipal governments and federal agencies are also refinancing part of their debts as they come due or become callable.

The peak of total financing, other than "governments," was reached in 1929, when over $11,500,000,000 of securities were distributed. One-half of these securities were in the form of stock of old and new companies. The total of new and refunded issues was lowest for the calendar year 1933, when total issues were a little over $1,000,000,000. The most significant issues among the totals are those which show the amount of new capital being borrowed by corporations. "In order to provide a job for each worker in our mechanical industries, taken together as a whole, there has to be a capital investment of $8,000."[2]

Functions of Investment Bankers

The general function of investment bankers is to merchandise securities, which includes investigating and promoting, underwriting, and distributing. In addition, most investment bankers perform many secondary functions for their customers, such as serving as investment counselors and acting as brokers.

Investigating.—The investigation of the applicants for credit is the first task of an investment banker. Although he does not buy the securities to hold as an investment, nevertheless he wants to make a profit and, at the same time, establish a reputation for sound merchandising. He realizes that the maxim "a commodity which is well bought is half sold" applies to security selling as well as to any other type of merchandising. In order to remain in business permanently, the investment banker must have satisfied clients who will buy the bank's new offerings.

The investment house must have something to sell. The chief sources of new issues are: (1) companies and foreign governments for which the investment house has done underwriting in the past; (2) new customers whose capital needs are brought to the attention of the originating house by commercial banks, promoters, "finders," officials or agents of the investment house, and companies that bring their needs directly to the attention of the investment house; and (3) state and municipal governments, public utility companies, and railroad companies that sell all or part of their securities to the highest competitive bidder.

Most of the vendors of securities have established banking relations with the older banking houses, which the newer investment houses seldom interfere with, that is if they expect to continue in the investment banking business. Since many of the newer investment houses are permitted to participate in purchasing syndicates and sell-

[2] The Cleveland Trust Company, *Business Bulletin*, Vol. XX, No. 12 (December 15, 1939).

ing groups, they do not dare risk the loss of the good-will of the investment bankers who control most of the new investment issues. For years this established policy of investment bankers of not competing among themselves for established investment banking business gave to certain New York houses a near monopoly of the originating phase of the investment banking business.

Investment bankers finance only a small fraction of the projects which are brought to them. Many are rejected, some because they are too small and others because the risk involved is too great. Investment bankers show a preference for securities of large and highly reputed governments and of well-established companies whose names are well known to investors. The costs of investigating and selling are large; therefore, small companies are given practically no consideration by investment houses. In selecting companies to be financed, the originating house has the assistance of all types of experts, economists, lawyers, accountants, engineers, and statisticians.

Since the securities purchased are to be resold, attention must be given to the investment market as well as to the offering company. During certain stages of the business cycle it is easy to sell securities, but during other stages it is almost impossible to do so. There is the problem not only of when to finance but also of the type of security to offer the public. The corporation may be advised to sell a mortgage bond, a debenture, bonds with convertible features, or preferred or common stock. The kind of security recommended will vary, depending upon the existing financial structure of the company, the industry, the phase of the business cycle, the tax policy of the federal government, and the attitude taken by supervisory agencies.

Where conditions permit, certain securities are sold to the highest bidder. This method of merchandising is usually required by state law or regulatory action of one of the federal supervisory agencies in order to give the vendors a better price than could be obtained when the investment houses are contacted directly. Securities sold in this way include issues of (1) state and local governments, (2) registered public utility holding companies and their subsidiaries, (3) railroad companies (equipment trust certificates and certain others), and (4) all public utility companies in certain states.

Underwriting.—The word "underwriting" is often a misnomer when used to cover purchase contracts between the originating house and the vendors. Actually no more insurance is involved than among other wholesalers and vendors and considerably less than in the case of some produce dealers who guarantee the farmers a minimum price for their cabbage, potatoes, tomatoes, and other products. Because investment bankers assume certain risks in agreeing to pay a certain price for a security which is to be issued, and because the borrower is assured of his funds under certain conditions, the transaction should not necessarily be called "underwriting."

Underwriting does appear in the financing of established corporations selling their own stock. Old stockholders have a pre-emptive right to subscribe to new capital stock or to bonds which are convertible into stock. The reason for this requirement is to prevent dilution of stockholders' equity. The rights of a stockholder depend upon the number of shares he owns. If his holding represents one-thousandth of the capital stock of the company, he has that proportional right in the new issues, and his stock right is evidenced by a warrant which resembles a stock certificate. The owner may use this right or sell it, but the time period in which it may be used is limited.

Although well-established companies take charge of their own common stock and convertible bond financing, investment houses are invited to underwrite them. If all the stock or convertible bonds are not sold, the underwriters take up the unsold portion at a figure which may be several points below that at which the security was offered to the stockholders. The investment bankers then organize a selling group to sell the stock, and the procedure is similar to that already described for an original issue. Investment bankers receive an underwriting fee on the basis of the number of shares of the issue, plus the usual selling profits from securities which they may handle.

Distributing.—The last step in marketing securities is the public offering. Retailers of securities are invited to join a selling syndicate or selling group. The members sign an agreement covering selling price, selling dates, and other terms. These terms are fixed by the syndicate manager and agreed to by those participating in the selling syndicate or group. The selling syndicate buys the securities from the originating syndicate, which relieves the latter from further financial responsibility other than that arising as a result of the penalty clauses in the Securities Act of 1933 as amended. Members of the selling group do not assume title to the securities or risks for those which cannot be sold. Because of depression losses, transfer taxes, legal risks placed on underwriters by the Securities Act of 1933 as amended, and time hazards due to the legally required twenty-day waiting period following registration,[3] the selling group is the most important type of distributing organization at the present time. This is particularly true for new securities that must be registered with the Securities and Exchange Commission.

The advantages of the small risk assumed by the members of the selling group are offset by the lower commissions which they receive. Now the usual procedure is for the members of the purchasing syndicate to specify the number of bonds which they want for distribution and to invite other houses to participate in the distribution of the remainder of the issue. The large distributing houses have offices and salesmen scattered throughout the country. Just as soon as the terms of the syndicate agreement and the law (in case of securities that must be registered with the Securities and Exchange Commission) permit, the salesmen begin selling the securities to individuals and institutions.

Investment Bankers Participate in Four Systems of Merchandising

Public Offerings.—The most common method of financing, especially in the case of bond issues, is to purchase the security from the vendor and sell it to the public. The machinery for distribution is complex, but it is, fundamentally, only merchandising on a broad scale. Since the values involved in an issue may be many millions of dollars, special care is taken to secure as wide diversification of risks and as much selling pressure behind the issue as is possible. A new selling group or syndicate is formed for each issue. During an active market, a bond house may be participating in a dozen new distributions while planning at the same time to participate in other new ones. The ideal situation is to have a steady stream of securities flowing through the retail houses out into the hands of the investing public. In order to keep their "shelves clear," speed is essential.

[3] This clause originally applied to new securities registered with Securities and Exchange Commission, except foreign government securities, which are subject to a seven-day waiting period. In August, 1940, Section 8 (*a*) of the Securities Exchange Act of 1934 was amended to give the commission discretionary power to shorten this time period, depending upon the adequacy and ease of interpreting the information which had previously been made public, respecting the issuer.

As is true in all types of merchandising, the spread between buying and selling prices compensates the bankers for their time and risk. The spread varies, being only a fraction of 1 per cent for municipal and state government securities to as high as 3 per cent for some bond issues. The more speculative the issue, the greater the spread; and, if all costs of distribution exceed 20 per cent (including bonuses, stock buying rights, and other privileges), the investor had better call the Better Business Bureau or his banker before and not after he buys. Usually such securities border on the fraudulent type or are too speculative to be offered publicly. They generally originate with the smaller and more irresponsible houses, although the 1920's provided many exceptions.

Private Offerings.—Sometimes securities are purchased by investment bankers and then offered privately to a number of interested individuals. Common stocks of new companies may be disposed of by this method, because the stock is far too speculative for any conservative banker to offer to the general public. Only wealthy individuals who are in a position to assume risks should participate in such undertakings as buying stocks put out by new companies.

During 1928 and 1929 many bankers disposed of common stocks to individuals whose names appeared on their preferred lists. In some cases the price asked was several points below that in markets where the security was dealt in on a "when-as-and-if-issued" basis. When the purpose of private offerings is to build up good-will by granting valuable privileges to a small group of men, permitting them to buy, in the "when-issued" market, a security at $20 and then to sell it at $35, it is to be condemned for social, economic, and moral reasons. The primary purpose of private offerings is to place a new speculative issue in the hands of those who are financially able to bear the risk, and many of those on the preferred lists of 1928 and 1929 did hold their securities through the 1930–33 stock market debacle. Trading on a national exchange on the when-issued basis is forbidden now by the rules of the Securities and Exchange Commission.

Underwriting Offerings to Stockholders.—The stock of all well-established companies is placed upon the market by the issuing companies. Investment bankers participate by underwriting the issue, for which they receive an underwriting fee, usually a fraction of 1 per cent of the total issue. They agree to purchase all the securities which the company does not sell to its own stockholders. If the issue is successful, the underwriters merely collect their fees; but, if the issue is unsuccessful, the investment houses have to purchase the securities at the previously agreed upon price. Then they assume responsibility for the marketing of the issue and for the financing involved.

Marketing Bonds on a Straight Commission Basis.—Securities may be marketed by bankers without assumption of risks; the banker is merely a selling agent working for a commission. All the risks are assumed by the vendor, but this disadvantage is compensated for by lower selling costs. For example, Salomon Brothers and Hutzler sold $50,000,000 of 3½ per cent Socony-Vacuum Corporation bonds for a commission of 4/10 of 1 per cent, when a normal spread for underwriting such an issue would have been from 2 to 3 per cent. This type of distribution is not popular with the leading New York bond houses and has gained no standing in the market, although it does provide the vendor with low financing costs.

Financing without the Mediation Services of Investment Banks

The practice of direct or private placement of securities by corporations with institutional investors has increased since 1934. For example, a large public utility company may arrange for the direct sale of its bond issue to a few large insurance companies, savings banks, and commercial banks. For the ten-year period ended June 30, 1944, $22,300,000,000 of new corporate securities were offered for sale in the United States. Approximately two-thirds of these were registered with the Securities and Exchange Commission, and, of the exempt securities, about one-half were railroad and other transportation company securities issued under the authority of the Interstate Commerce Commission, and the other one-half were securities privately placed.

There are two primary reasons for the increase in the volume of private financing: the superabundance of funds in the hands of investing institutions, such as life insurance companies, and the desire on the part of the vendor to get as high a net price as possible for his bonds. By selling directly, vendors are able to avoid the middleman's profits, and, by offering the securities privately, they avoid the costs of registration with the Securities and Exchange Commission. After the 1941 ruling of the Securities and Exchange Commission that sales of securities by registered public utility holding companies and their subsidiaries had to be sold to the highest competitive bidder, private placement of these securities decreased. This suggests that the vendors were objecting to the low prices offered by the investment houses operating under the old monopolistic system rather than to the registration requirement of the Securities and Exchange Commission.

The Securities Act of 1933

This act deals chiefly with the distribution of securities which must be registered with the Securities and Exchange Commission (formerly with the Federal Trade Commission) before they are offered to the public.[4] Many new security issues are exempt, on the theory that they are already adequately regulated by other governmental agencies or that they do not involve interstate commerce. Included in the exempt classes are securities of domestic railroads, domestic governments, nonprofit corporations, those privately offered, and small issues (less than $300,000).

The registration requirements call for information from the vendor and investment bankers so sadly missing in the past. The commission does not pass upon the merits of the security, but it may issue a stop order suspending the effectiveness of the registration if omissions or untrue or misleading statements are suspected. The commission has all the powers of investigation necessary to the formation of judgment with respect to issuing such an order. Information that reaches the public about a security is published in the form of a prospectus, which must contain information as outlined by the law and regulations of the commission.

The Securities Act of 1933 embodies many of the principles of earlier state legislation; the purpose of the act is to supplement and not replace the regulatory machinery already in existence. Certain facts must be recognized. Buyers of securities are necessarily forced to rely largely on the statements of the original sellers, for a bond or

[4] Securities Act of 1933 (*Public Law 22,* 73d Cong., H.R. 5480). The long title is "An Act to provide full and fair disclosure of the character of securities sold in interstate and foreign commerce and through the mails, and to prevent frauds in the sale thereof, and for other purposes."

stock does not contain within itself information whereby one may judge its value. While general information is available, only a certain type of information about a particular company can be secured from the management or its investment banker.

Desiring to make sales, it is but human for salesmen to emphasize the strong features of an issue and to ignore the weak. Often the necessary facts for appraisal of securities are not available unless they are supplied by the vendors and investment bankers. For example, information is not always readily available on the cost of the financing of an issue of securities, which is an excellent guide to the speculative nature of a security. The public should have information about underwriting fees, markups in price, bonuses, and all direct costs of distribution; financial facts about the company and how the investors' money is to be used; and the identity of the chief officers, their salaries, and other facts about management. The primary purpose of the Securities Act is to force corporations to make public such information as every investor has a right to know before he invests his funds in the bonds or shares of a company.

Separation of Underwriting and Deposit Banking

The Banking Act of 1933 as amended by the Banking Act of 1935 contains provisions which forced commercial banks to give up their investment affiliate companies and to withdraw from the underwriting of all securities except domestic government issues.[5] In 1911 the National City Bank of New York organized the National City Company as a separate corporation to carry on an investment banking business which the bank could not legally engage in under the national banking law. This practice spread rapidly among banks, particularly after World War I.

In 1930 commercial bank affiliates retailed over one-half of all new securities distributed, and it seemed that they were destined to dominate the security business in the same way that foreign exchange departments of commercial banks had come to dominate the foreign exchange markets. The investment affiliates had several advantages

---

[5] Since 1931 this movement to separate commercial and investment banking has been world-wide, owing to the losses and dangers of nonliquidity inherent in investment banking. Belgium in 1934, Sweden in 1933, Germany in 1934, Argentina in 1935, and France in 1945 were among the countries placing limitations on "mixed banking."

over their competitors, the private banking houses. The commercial bank provided its affiliates with (1) the names of its deposit clientele to whom to sell securities; (2) the names of commercial borrowers who needed fixed capital; (3) abundant credit to care for operating capital needs; and (4) a name, prestige, and financial standing so necessary for successful operation in the investment banking field.

The investment affiliate evils disclosed by the Pecora Senate Investigation Committee were many. (1) Some investment affiliates speculated in and manipulated the stock of their own commercial banks, even though the ownership by a bank of its own stock was specifically prohibited by national law. (2) Others engaged in dangerous speculation and underwriting operations, which included the shifting of frozen bank loans from the bank to the public. (3) Some commercial bank officers advised depositors who were seeking disinterested advice to purchase securities from their affiliates. This situation made a mockery of the old maxim, "Consult your banker before you invest." (4) Speculation was encouraged when some officers and directors voted themselves interests in the net earnings of both the affiliates and the bank. (5) Inadequate reports were sometimes made by commercial banks of their own and affiliates' operations. (6) Large loans were made by some parent banks to their own investment affiliates, a practice which is subject to the same criticism made earlier of officers' borrowing from their own banks. (7) Some affiliates sold securities to their own banks, a practice which was dangerous, because the bank may buy securities at a price no other investor would pay. During the depression the dangers of the commercial investment banking tie were apparent. Loss of reputation not only hurt the affiliate but threatened the very life of the commercial bank. The failure of the large Bank of the United States in 1931 was traced directly to the affiliate situation.

The Banking Act of 1933 gave the member banks one year in which to dispose of their investment affiliates and forbade them to participate in the underwriting of securities. (This was later modified to permit them to underwrite domestic government securities.) Since restrictions were to be placed on the investment banking activities of commercial banks, their spokesmen asked Congress to place restrictions upon the deposit banking business of investment banking houses, which seemed reasonable enough; and so the Banking Act of 1933 contains provisions which forced the investment houses either to qualify as commercial banks and give up underwriting of securities or to give up their deposit banking business. Private bankers who carry on deposit banking must submit to supervision by either the national or the state regulatory agencies. When J. P. Morgan and Company gave up its underwriting banking activities in order to keep its deposit banking business, the world's foremost investment banker withdrew from the investment field.[6] Upon the liquidation of the National City Company, an affiliate of the National City Bank of New York, the world's leading distributor disappeared. Now commercial banks are permitted to underwrite government securities or government guaranteed securities (Banking Act of 1935) and to take orders to buy and sell stocks and bonds for their customers. Investment bankers are permitted to perform all their former functions except that of accepting deposits.

There Are Three Secondary Markets for Securities

As previously noted, investment involves a long-term commitment of funds, and, in order to make securities more attractive, it is necessary to have a secondary market for them. This secondary market is provided in part by investment bankers, dealers, and brokers who operate in the over-the-counter market or on stock exchanges. Investment bankers maintain a trading department to peg prices of their issues during the period of distribution, to dispose of bonds their clients have traded in for new issues, and to buy and sell securities formerly originated by them. Dealers buy and sell securities for their own account, brokers execute orders to buy and sell securities for principals, and stock exchanges are associations of brokers and dealers.

Over-the-Counter Market.—The expression "over the counter" is a loose term applied to the activities of dealers, brokers, bankers, and others in buying and selling unlisted securities. By provisions of the Securities Exchange Act of 1934, the over-the-counter market was modified to include all transactions in securities "which take place otherwise than upon a national exchange."[7] If it is desired to

[6] Morgan, Stanley and Co. was formed in 1935 by some of the former partners of J. P. Morgan & Co. and the grandson of J. P. Morgan. The firm was incorporated and assumed most of the investment business formerly held by the elder Morgan's firm.

[7] Statement of Commissioner George C. Mathews before the Senate Committee on Banking and Currency on S.3255, February 1, 1938.

buy or sell a stock or bond that is traded in on the over-the-counter market, it is necessary for the seller to communicate with prospective buyers through the medium of a broker or dealer. Those who specialize in this type of business often have private wire systems to other brokers' offices, which greatly facilitates the purchase and sale of unlisted securities.

The shares of most banks and insurance companies, and the stock of many public utility, railroad, and industrial companies are bought and sold in the over-the-counter market. There is also an enormous over-the-counter bond market, including the trading in federal, state, and local government securities. There are 100,000 securities not listed on stock exchanges as compared to 6,000 that are. Finally, the primary distribution of the underwriting houses usually takes place in the over-the-counter markets.

The Maloney Act of 1938 provides for organization of over-the-counter brokers, where national interests are involved, into self-regulatory associations under supervision of the Securities and Exchange Commission.[8] In August, 1939, the National Association of Securities Dealers, Incorporated, was registered with the Securities and Exchange Commission. It now has approximately 2,000 members and is the only national securities association registered with the commission. Its chief activity has been to raise business standards of all over-the-counter brokers and dealers and to devise uniform practice codes.

Public Auction.—Another section of the capital market not to be disregarded is the public auction. The principal one is the Auction Exchange at 14-15 Vesey Street, New York, where weekly auctions are held. Advertisements are published announcing the auctioneers, issues to be sold, and other information of general interest. The auctioneers act as agents for others who desire to sell securities, usually reserving the right to bid for the bonds and stocks themselves. Buyers vary from important banking groups interested in bankrupt sales of blocks of securities totaling millions (Allegany Corporation) to souvenir buyers and bargain hunters enticed by pieces of paper

---

[8] The long title of the Maloney Act (*Public Law 719*, 75th Cong., S.3255), "To provide for the establishment of a mechanism of regulation among over-the-counter brokers and dealers operating in interstate and foreign commerce or through the mails, to prevent acts and practices inconsistent with just and equitable principles of trade, and for other purposes."

having par values of hundreds of thousands of dollars that may be purchased for a few dollars.

Stock Exchanges.—Brokers and dealers who are members of stock exchanges provide the most important secondary market for securities. In a broad sense, a stock exchange is the meeting-place for buyers and sellers of securities. A more modern and correct definition is: "A stock exchange is an unincorporated association or incorporated company, the members of which trade in securities for others and themselves." Stock exchanges whose business is predominately interstate are, since 1934, under the general regulation of the Securities and Exchange Commission and are called national securities exchanges. At the present time there are 19 exchanges registered with the Securities and Exchange Commission, of which New York, Chicago, and San Francisco have two each.[9] All the leading cities of the nation have one or more organized exchanges, but most of them have such a limited volume of transactions as to make regulation impracticable. In 1944, when the market value of securities on all registered exchanges was $140,000,000,000, the value of stocks was $118,400,000,000; of bonds, $21,500,000,000; and of rights and warrants, $1,000,000,000. The largest, and by far the most important, exchange is the New York Stock Exchange, where stocks of national and international importance are bought and sold.

The smaller exchanges usually deal in local issues and a few issues of national importance. In the event of multiple listing, that is, listing stocks on more than one exchange, it is only natural that quotations on the New York Stock Exchange should dominate. Often local exchanges will deal in special classes of stocks; for illustration, the Boston Stock Exchange deals to a great extent in mining and textile shares; the Pittsburgh Stock Exchange handles a large volume of coal, oil, and glass shares; and the Cleveland Stock Exchange specializes in stocks of rubber companies.

The New York Stock Exchange

The New York Stock Exchange is a voluntary organization—an association—and as such is subject to internal regulation. It has a

[9] Other cities having "national securities exchanges" are Baltimore, Boston, Cincinnati, Cleveland, Detroit, Salt Lake City, Los Angeles, New Orleans, Philadelphia, Pittsburgh, St. Louis, Spokane, and Washington.

constitution and bylaws, no charter, and issues no property rights to its members. Admission to membership is dependent upon getting a member to retire in the applicant's favor,[10] a favorable (two-thirds) vote of the committee on admission, and the satisfaction of certain other requirements, including the payment of an initiation fee, which now is $4,000. Annual dues, which are payable quarterly, may not exceed $1,000. A person is not a member of the exchange until he has signed the constitution. Prior to February, 1929, there were 1,100 members. In that month each member received a right to one-quarter of one new membership, and the total number of seats was raised to 1,375. The word "seat" was first used literally, but now it refers merely to membership, which carries with it the privilege of buying and selling on the exchange.

Individuals or firms having seats on the New York Stock Exchange (corporations are barred by exchange rules) are classified according to their activities as follows: (1) inactive members, who rarely go near the exchange, but retain their membership as an investment or for social or noneconomic reasons; (2) commission brokers who buy and sell for outside customers; (3) floor brokers, who execute orders for other members, but particularly for commission brokers; (4) specialists in one or two stocks, who act as floor brokers for other brokers and as traders for themselves; (5) floor traders, who buy and sell for their own account; (6) odd-lot dealers and brokers, who buy and sell less than 100 share lots to commission brokers and others; and (7) bond dealers and brokers, who deal in bonds for their own account and for customers.

The general public makes purchases or sales on the stock exchange through commission brokers. A prospective buyer or seller merely goes to any broker's office or branch, of which there are several in every town of any size, and places his order to buy or sell. In the case of buying, if he has not already made credit arrangements with the broker, he must deposit cash or acceptable securities. The order will be executed and the securities delivered within a reasonable time. It is, of course, taken for granted that the brokerage house has a member on the floor of the exchange or a correspondent relationship with some member of the exchange on which the order is to be executed.

[10] New York Stock Exchange seats have sold for more than $600,000, but a more current representative figure would be $60,000.

If the customer desires, and the rules of the regulatory agencies do not forbid, a customer may buy on margin. This is a transaction whereby the customer puts up only a percentage of the selling price of the stock and the remainder is furnished by the broker. Margin trading is more dangerous than purchasing outright, but it enables the man with limited capital to buy more shares, thus affording him a greater chance for gain or loss, as the case may be. Although margin requirements are fixed by the Board of Governors of the Federal Reserve System (Regulation T), the routine inspections of books and records are made by the Securities and Exchange Commission. Since 1938, the inspection of the members of national securities exchanges has been left largely to the exchanges, and the commission has placed most of its emphasis on the inspection of nonmember firms. Numerous violations of regulations have been disclosed as a result of these examinations.

In 1938 the New York Stock Exchange adopted a new constitution which provided for better administration and greater public representation on its Board of Governors. The office of a full-time salaried president was created, and the number of standing committees was reduced from 17 to 7. The president must be a nonmember of the exchange and an executive of ability, whose job is to carry out functions formerly performed by committees made up of members. The membership on the board, which corresponds in power and duties to the board of directors of a corporation, was arranged so as to give the public, the commission broker, and nonmember partners or officers of commission brokerage houses at least an equal vote with other types of members of the New York Stock Exchange. On January 1, 1939, the new constitution was amended to include as "allied members" all general partners of member firms other than those holding seats on the exchange. This change made it possible for the exchange to discipline them for violation of the rules.

Securities and Exchange Commission Regulates Security Selling

The Securities and Exchange Act of 1934 has four purposes, namely (1) to insure fairness and honesty in buying and selling in all national securities markets, (2) to provide investors with more accurate information about the character of securities bought and sold, (3) to place control over margin requirements in the hands of the Board of Governors of the Federal Reserve System, and (4) to provide for regulatory machinery for all primary and secondary markets in securities.

On June 30, 1934, the President appointed the Securities and Exchange Commission, which consists of five members, not more than three of whom shall be members of the same political party. They hold office for five years and receive salaries of $10,000 per annum. The Securities and Exchange Commission now administers six laws, as amended: (1) Securities Act of 1933, (2) Securities Exchange Act of 1934, (3) Public Utility Holding Company Act of 1935, (4) Trust Indenture Act of 1939, (5) Investment Company Act of 1940, and (6) Investment Advisors Act of 1940. In addition, it performs various functions under Chapter X of the National Bankruptcy Act. The commission has set up ten administrative zones in the United States and maintains a regional office in each. It has shown a tendency to permit all investment bankers, brokers and dealers, associations, and security exchanges to police themselves.

Investment Companies

The Investment Company Act of 1940 requires investment companies to register with the Securities and Exchange Commission. The purposes of the act are to secure honest and unbiased management, greater participation in management by security holders, adequate and feasible capital structure, better accounting records and financial reporting, and lower selling costs, particularly in the case of open-end periodic payment, and face-amount certificate investment companies.

Congress, in the act, gives a quantitative definition of an investment company as one engaged primarily in the business of investing, reinvesting, or trading in securities, and owning "investment securities" that exceed 40 per cent of its total assets, exclusive of cash items and government securities. "Investment securities" were defined to exclude securities of majority-owned subsidiaries and of other investment companies.[11] In June, 1944, there were over 370 investment

[11] One of the chief administrative tasks of the Securities and Exchange Commission has been to determine what an investment company is. Holding companies and operating or managing companies' assets are primarily in the form of securities. These companies are most numerous in the public utility field and are supervised by the Securities and Exchange Commission under the Public Utility Holding Company Act of 1935.

companies registered with the Securities and Exchange Commission.

Investment companies are organized as voluntary trusts or as corporations, with the primary purpose of providing investors with an outlet for their savings which will pay greater dividends than the return offered by savings banks. The origin of the term "investment trust," which is often used to include all types of institutions in this field, is traced to the British and Scottish procedure in the last century of setting up pools of funds as a common venture, with trustees in control. The early movement in the United States (1921-31) was dominated by corporations, which are more accurately called "investment companies." Beginning in 1931, many voluntary trusts of the so-called "fixed" management type were formed in the United States, but the investment companies of the management type still represent the leaders in the field.

Since 1920 the assets of investment companies and investment trusts increased from an insignificant figure to an estimated value of over $7,000,000,000 at the peak in 1929. In contrast, the present value of their assets is in excess of only $2,000,000,000.[12] The investment companies are owned by 2,000,000 investors, and their proper functioning is of major importance to many small investors.

Sponsors of the general management type of investment company appeal to investors with the argument that the companies offer them the advantages of diversification of assets and continuing expert management. They claim that they can return a higher income from investments and give greater security to capital funds than investors would obtain by investing independently. Actually, the amount of diversification has been limited to common stocks for the most part.[13]

Some of the criticisms against management have been: (1) the absence of true professionalism in selecting securities, the inclination being "to follow the leader," with a tendency to overprice favored stocks; (2) purchases of securities offered by investment houses with which the management was allied, that is, "self-dealing"; (3) operation in secrecy and deficient accounting and financial reporting to stockholders; (4) charging excessive amounts for issuance (average

---

[12] *Tenth Annual Report of the Securities and Exchange Commission, Fiscal Year Ended June 30, 1944*, p. 158.

[13] Allen, E. D., "Study of a Group of American Management-Investment Companies, 1930-36," *Journal of Business of the University of Chicago*, Vol. XI, pp. 243-48.

about 10 per cent);[14] (6) a tendency in some cases to invest in companies in order to control them; (7) excessive speculation or trading in securities; and (8) failure to build up reserves out of trading profits to offset trading losses. Although the early investment trusts in the United States were modeled after the English and Scottish trusts, their four basic policies were ignored. These policies are: (1) diversification of investment, (2) conservative investments, (3) disinterested management, and (4) standardized low management charges. In spite of their 1929-33 record, the general management trust has had wide approval, and a few have had excellent records.

The unit investment trust is managed by a trustee acting in the interest of the beneficiary in much the same way that a trust institution serves the heirs of an estate. It is usually smaller than the general management companies and sponsored by some small investment house desiring something new to sell. The simplest of these trusts are usually set up for a twenty-year period, are administered by a trust institution, and give investors an interest in a common or commingled trust fund, which is divided among the holders of the trust certificates at the end of the trust period.

Unit investment and general management trusts have many variations. There are the periodic payment plans in which the investors agree to invest a given sum periodically, as they would if they were buying insurance. At the end of a period of years, the certificates have a guaranteed face value. Some trusts are of the open-end type, which permit the sponsors to offer their securities to the public, continuously, at a price equal to the costs of their investments, plus a "loading charge." Usually these open-end trusts make provisions for the redemption of their securities at approximately their asset value. The criticisms of these plans include excessive loading charges, usually collected from the early payments, and switching of assets and supplementary heavy loading charges.[15]

---

[14] At "the end of 1935, total expenses of British companies represented 41/100 of 1 per cent of net assets and less than 9 per cent of net income. As of the same date, comparable figures for American companies were 75/100 of 1 per cent and 20 per cent, respectively" (*ibid.*, pp. 242-43).

[15] *Tenth Annual Report of the Securities and Exchange Commission for the Fiscal Year Ended June 30, 1944*, p. 161.

Investment Advisors

On November 1, 1940, the Investment Advisors Act became effective, and 605 "investment advisors" were registered with the Securities and Exchange Commission. As the title suggests, investment advisors are engaged in giving advice (for compensation) to others with respect to securities. Of the registered investment advisors, 373 were engaged in other professions or enterprises, 170 were brokers and dealers, and among the remainder were accountants, engineers, lawyers, doctors, dentists, college professors, insurance brokers, and persons engaged in business and estate management. Among those registered (719 on June 30, 1944), 276 were engaged in giving continuous advice on the basis of individual needs of clients, 85 were giving advice solely through publications, and 118 others issued publications in one form or another.[16]

The compensation for services received by investment advisors varies, including one or more of the following: a fixed fee of $5.00 per bond bought or sold on the advice of the advisor, a fee equal perhaps to ½ of 1 per cent on the aggregate value of the assets managed, and a fixed fee of perhaps $5,000 per annum for managing an account. In the past some advisors would manage an account for a percentage of the trading profits or a percentage of the amount the account would appreciate during a period of time. The Investment Advisors Act of 1940 prohibited profit-sharing arrangements.

The act makes it unlawful for an investment advisor to engage in fraud or deceitful practices and requires them to disclose the nature of their interest in transactions executed for their clients. The Securities and Exchange Commission is granted authority to make investigations, and, by use of subpoena power, to obtain information; but it lacks the power to inspect books and records such as that granted in the Securities Exchange Act of 1934. It may revoke or deny registration.

QUESTIONS AND PROBLEMS

1. Identify: (*a*) investment houses, (*b*) securities dealers, (*c*) securities exchange, (*d*) over-the-counter market in securities.
2. Give the three stages in the development of investment banking. Explain the differences.

[16] *Ibid.*, pp. 180-81.

3. Distinguish between primary and secondary markets for securities. Which is more important? Why?
4. What is the relative importance of "new capital" and "refunding issues" in 1929 and 1945? Account for the differences. See Table 45.
5. What are the most important classes of new security issues (nonfederal)? See Table 45.
6. What are the three functions of investment houses? Explain each.
7. Give the distinguishing characteristics of the four different systems of merchandising new securities.
8. Do investment bankers guarantee the bonds which they sell? Why are certain bonds called "Morgan bonds," "Kuhn, Loeb and Company bonds," etc.?
9. Why has financing without the mediation services of investment houses increased?
10. "To that end this Bill [Rayburn-Fletcher Securities Bill, May, 1933] requires the publicity necessary for sound investment. It is, of course, no insurance against errors of judgment. That is the function of no government" (Roosevelt, Franklin D., *On Our Way*, p. 267). Is this a fair summary of the purpose of the act? Why?
11. What were bank investment affiliates? What is their present legal status? Were the changes provided for in the act of 1933 justified? Why?
12. What are the two basic types of investment trusts? What are the weaknesses of each type?
13. What provisions have been made for government regulation of security exchanges? Should the functions of brokers and dealers be separated? Why?
14. Describe the organization, management, and functions of the New York Stock Exchange.
15. Describe the activities of the Securities and Exchange Commission under Investment Companies and Investment Advisors acts.
16. The business cycle consists of four phases, which are revival, prosperity, liquidation or, at times, panic, and depression. What would be the relative public demand for stocks and bonds during each of these periods? Give reason for each answer.
17. Explain how security buyers and sellers are aided by Fitch, Moody, Poor, Standard Statistics, and other rating manuals. Check the ratings of one or more of your favorite stocks (actual or assumed) in these manuals. Report on your findings.
18. Look up the "International Capital Transactions of the United States," *Federal Reserve Bulletin*, and summarize your findings. Why is this information of value to students of money and banking?

REFERENCES

Allen, E. D. "Study of a Group of American Management-Investment Companies, 1930-36," *Journal of Business of the University of Chicago* Vol. XI.

Biddle, C. P., and Bates, G. E. *Investment Banking: A Case Book.* New York: McGraw-Hill Book Co., Inc., 1931.

Flynn, J. T. *Security Speculation, Its Economic Effects.* New York: Harcourt, Brace & Co., 1934.

Grayson, T. J. *Investment Trusts—Their Origin, Development, and Operation.* New York: J. Wiley & Sons, Inc., 1928.

Huebner, S. S. *The Stock Market.* Revised. New York: D. Appleton-Century Co., 1934.

Ketchum, M. D. *The Fixed Investment Trust.* Chicago: University of Chicago Press, 1937.

Lewis, E. A. *Laws Relating to Securities and Exchanges and Holding Companies.* Washington: Superintendent of Documents, 1938.

Livermore, S. *Investment, Principles and Analysis.* Chicago: Business Publications, Inc., 1938.

Meeker, J. E. *Short Selling.* New York: Harper & Bros., 1932.

Pecora, Ferdinand. *Wall Street under Oath.* New York: Simon & Schuster, 1939.

Proceedings of the Annual Conventions, Investment Bankers Association of America. Chicago: Investment Bankers Association of America.

Robinson, L. R. *Investment Trust, Organization and Management.* Revised. New York: Ronald Press Co., 1938.

Ross, James A. *Speculation, Stock Prices, and Industrial Fluctuation.* New York: Ronald Press Co., 1938.

Securities and Exchange Commission. *Annual Report,* No. 1–10 (1935–44), inclusive. Washington, D.C.: Superintendent of Documents.

Securities and Exchange Commission. *Report on the Study of Investment Trusts and Investment Companies,* Parts I–V. Washington, D.C.: Superintendent of Documents.

Senate Report No. 1455, 73d Cong., 2d sess., chaps. i, ii, and vi. Washington, D.C.: U.S. Government Printing Office, 1934.

Twentieth Century Fund, Inc. *The Security Markets.* New York: Twentieth Century Fund, Inc., 1935.

Weissman, R. L. *The New Wall Street.* New York: Harper & Bros., 1939.

Willis, H. P., and Bogen, J. I. *Investment Banking,* chaps. i-iv, viii, and Part III. Revised. New York: Harper & Bros., 1936.

Chapter XXXIV

FEDERAL URBAN MORTGAGE BANKING

Home Financing Is a Major Problem

The one most important class of wealth in the United States is real property, that is, land and buildings or other improvements attached to land. So it is not surprising that, when long-term private credit is considered, mortgages or liens on real property are important. In the preceding chapters reference was made to financing by the sale of bonds secured by mortgages (held by trustees) on office buildings, hotels, public utility plants, railroads, and other types of real property. In this chapter special attention is given to the financing of homes and dwellings.

TABLE 46

Urban Mortgages by Types of Investors for Selected Years*
(In Millions of Dollars)

Type of Lender	1931	1935	1939	1943
Savings and loan associations	$ 5,890	$ 3,293	$ 3,758	$ 4,554
Insurance companies	1,775	1,281	1,490	2,410
Mutual savings banks	3,375	2,850	2,680	2,660
Commercial banks	2,145	1,189	1,810	2,450
Home Owners' Loan Corporation	....	2,897	2,038	1,338
Individuals and others	7,500	6,000	6,440	6,100
Total	$20,685	$17,510	$18,216	$19,512

* Estimated balance of outstanding mortgage loans on nonfarm one- to four-family dwellings.

Source: *Twelfth Annual Report of the Federal Home Loan Bank Administration*, p. 42.

Many individuals as well as practically all types of lending institutions now make loans secured by liens on real estate. (See Table 46.) At the present time there are three federal systems in the financing fields—the Federal Home Loan Bank System, Federal Housing Administration, and the Federal Public Housing Authority. In 1942 all three agencies were placed in the National Housing Agency. (See Chart XIII.)

In 1933 the chief problem in the home financing field was a scarcity of home financing funds, which only the federal government was in a position to provide. In 1946 the chief problem in the home financing field is a scarcity of houses and an abundance of funds, which makes inflation not only possible but probable.

CHART XIII

FEDERAL URBAN GOVERNMENT HOUSING AGENCIES

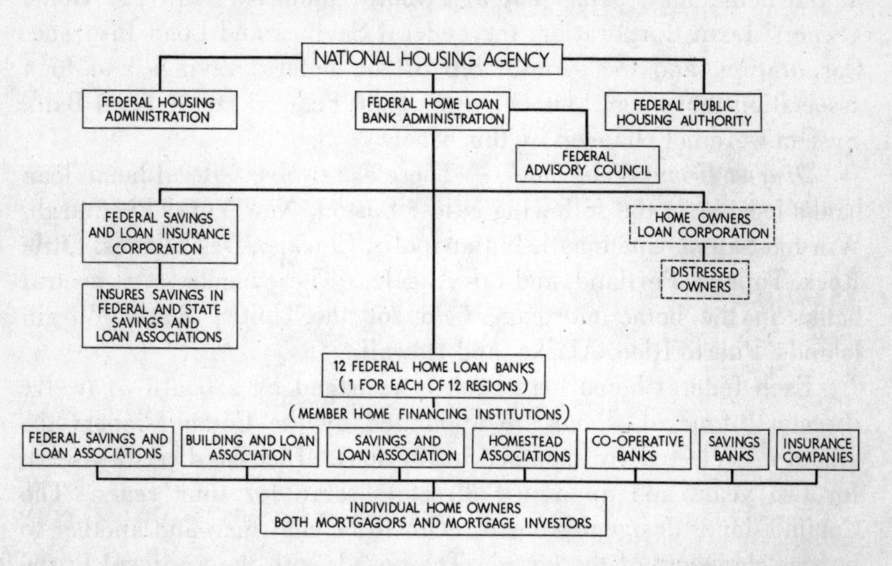

Urban Mortgage Central Banking System

Introduction.—In 1932, in order to strengthen the home mortgage banking institutions, Congress passed the Home Loan Bank Bill. This act provided for the same type of organization in the urban mortgage field as that found in the farm mortgage field (Federal Land Bank System) and in the commercial banking field (Federal Reserve System). Prior to February, 1942, there was a Home Loan Bank board of five members, whose functions were similar to those of the Board of Governors of the Federal Reserve System; an advisory council of 18 members, corresponding to the Advisory Council of the Federal Reserve System; 12 districts and 12 home loan banks similar to the 12 federal land banks and their 12 districts; compulsory members—the federal savings and loan associations, corresponding to national banks in the commercial banking system; and voluntary members, all of which were state-chartered institutions. These included savings banks, insurance companies, and various types of building or savings and loan associations. (See Chart XIII.)

Home Loan Bank Commissioner.—In February, 1942, by Executive Order No. 9070, the President made the Federal Home Loan Administration a unit in the new National Housing Agency. By the terms of the order, the duties of the former board were transferred to the Commissioner. These duties include not only those pertaining to the home loan banks but also those connected with the Home Owners' Loan Corporation, the Federal Savings and Loan Insurance Corporation, and the sponsorship of the federal savings and loan association movement. Other parts of the Federal Home Loan Bank System were not changed by this order.

District Home Loan Banks.—There are twelve federal home loan banks located in the following cities: Boston, New York, Pittsburgh, Winston-Salem, Cincinnati, Indianapolis, Chicago, Des Moines, Little Rock, Topeka, Portland, and Los Angeles. These banks act as central banks in the home mortgage field for the United States, Virgin Islands, Puerto Rico, Alaska, and Hawaii.

Each federal home loan bank is managed by a board of twelve directors, four of whom are appointed by the Commissioner; the others are elected by member institutions. Elected directors serve for two years and appointed directors serve for four years. The Commissioner designates one director to be chairman and another to be vice-chairman of the board. The board, with the approval of the Commissioner, may appoint any competent individual as president of the home loan bank. In addition to the board of directors and the president, the managerial staff of each bank includes an executive committee, a vice-president, a secretary, a treasurer, and a counsel.

The home loan banks are owned by the government and member institutions. Of the banks' total capital of $186,000,000, $61,000,000 is now provided by member institutions. As the interest of members in their home loan banks increases, the amount of stock held by the government is to be decreased.[1] Eventually the banks will be owned

[1] Members are required to buy stock in their home loan banks in amounts equal to 1 per cent of the aggregate of the unpaid principal of the subscribers' home mortgage loans. If, for instance, a building and loan association holds mortgages aggregating $1,000,000, on which debtors have made instalment payments of $300,000, leaving an unpaid balance of $700,000, it would have to subscribe to $7,000 of stock in its district central home loan bank. The minimum subscription is $500. Whenever one home loan bank accumulates capital provided by members equal to the government's subscription, one-half of all new member banks' subscriptions must be used to retire the government's stock. Thus gradual retirement of government ownership is made compulsory as soon as member institutions are able to finance their own home loan banks. Under certain conditions, government-owned stock may be retired voluntarily.

entirely by member institutions, which will mean that the system will be basically co-operative throughout, because the savings and loan associations, the most important members, are co-operative institutions.

The federal home loan banks may raise funds in the traditional mortgage banking fashion—by selling their promises to pay to investors, a privilege used for the first time in April, 1937. These issues may be short-term debentures or long-term bonds, and to date the first type has dominated in public financing. The securities were issued as the joint and several liabilities of the twelve federal home loan banks, carried a very low yield, and were well received in the market. With a continued increase in long-term lending by the federal home loan banks, bond financing is not only profitable but desirable. The banks may accept time deposits from the federal government and from member institutions, and the consolidated statement of the twelve federal home loan banks shows that over $20,000,000 is being carried as time or demand deposits by member institutions with their home loan banks. Interest of ½ of 1 per cent is paid on time deposits.

The federal home loan banks have a dual role in strengthening the existing home financing institutions, serving, first, as bankers' banks and, secondly, as a normal source of long-term credit to supplement local home mortgage funds. In 1944 outstanding advances of the federal home loan banks were over $128,000,000. Total advances made by the banks since 1932 have been in excess of $1,200,000,000, most of which has been repaid. The chief borrowers are savings and loan associations.

Members are examined by the Examining Division of the Federal Home Loan Bank Administration. Usually insured state-chartered banks are examined jointly by the Examining Division and their respective state banking departments. The average size of all member savings and loan associations is about $1,600,000, which is an increase of 71.4 per cent since June, 1938.

In addition to making advances to member institutions, the home loan banks and the Commissioner are striving to simplify the complex legal procedure involved in securing loans based upon real property. They are working for standardization of loan practices, elimination of costly financing fees, reduction of interest charges, and a general improvement in home mortgage financing machinery. In order to improve home construction, the Commissioner provides for technical assistance through its federal home building service plan.

Building or Savings and Loan Association Movement

Introduction.—There are many varieties of savings or building and loan associations in the United States and other English-speaking countries; this general classification includes federal savings and loan associations, state building and loan associations, co-operative banks, and homestead associations. These are the most important private groups among the nation's home mortgage financing institutions, originating about 37.2 per cent of the new residential loans in 1943 and holding about 23 per cent of the total home mortgage debt. Although savings and loan associations are among the most important financing institutions in the United States, they are among the least known, because (1) they deal chiefly with a "small man's business," (2) they are local in nature and until recently were of only local interest, (3) they are mutual and controlled by investors and borrowers, and (4) they are limited in activity to advancement of thrift and the financing of homes. In the United States the first building and loan association was founded in the suburbs of Philadelphia in 1831; in 1945 there were over 6,000 associations, with total assets of about $7,000,000,000.

Until 1933 all savings and loan associations were organized under state laws. One section of the Home Owners' Loan Corporation Act permitted them to be organized under national law. A promotion fund was given to the Home Loan Bank Board, which was made responsible for supervising the system, in order to expand the movement. The objective was to have at least one association in every county of the United States (over 3,000). This act as amended required all national chartered associations to have the word "federal" in their titles, permitted state-chartered associations to recharter under federal law, and required all federal savings and loan associations to be members of the Home Loan Bank System and to insure their accounts in the Federal Savings and Loan Insurance Corporation (maximum coverage $5,000). State members may or may not insure their accounts with the insurance corporation.

Home Builders' Club.—The early types of associations were merely home builders' clubs. Periodically each member paid enough money into a common fund to enable one member to build a house. If there were 200 members and each one paid in $20 a month, every month one member would be able to begin construction of a $4,000 house. All loans were secured by mortgages, and the borrower continued his periodic payment of $20 per month and, of course, the payment of interest on his loan. Such associations were continued until all members had built houses.

Interest payments gave the association more funds with which to work. Toward the end of the life of the association, the construction of several houses was being financed each month. The duration of the association was less than 200 months, depending upon the rates of interest paid by borrowers. The original practice was to auction off the use of the funds to the members. The one who was willing to pay the highest rate for them was to be the first to get funds with which to construct his house. When all shares matured, they were used to cancel the mortgage loans. The last member to build owned matured shares to finance his house without borrowing. By waiting, he avoided all interest charges.

Permanent Plan.—The first associations were temporary organizations, but later they were organized on a permanent basis. Serial plans of issuing shares were adopted, and additional members were permitted to join associations at stated intervals. New members came into the associations while others were maturing their shares and withdrawing. Whenever conditions warranted, new series of stock were offered to members.

Lending Practices.—Loans are based upon several fundamentally sound practices. Generally, associations are authorized to make loans up to 80 per cent of the value of the property being financed. This high percentage makes it unnecessary for the homeowners to enter the usurious second mortgage market for funds. The basic assumption in home financing is that the prospective owners are able to pay cash for at least 20 per cent of the cost of the property. A smaller percentage is inadvisable, considered from the viewpoint of both the owners and the lenders. Mortgage debts are repaid on the instalment plan, this requisite being an important contribution to the procedure in the field of long-term financing. When the instalment plan is used, debts are paid during good as well as bad times. Debtors are increasing their equity in their property and creditors are being given greater protection for their loans.

Savings Members.—Fairly early, association memberships were opened to investors or merely depositing members. With this development, greater emphasis was placed upon the savings feature of the association's work. More loans could be made to borrowing members, and funds were used to purchase homes as well as to build them. Investing members looked upon the associations as effective savings institutions. When the practice of permitting members to withdraw from the association before their shares matured developed, it became necessary to apportion the profits annually or semiannually among the members. Annual dividends now amount to about 4 per cent for many of these associations.

Accounts Are Insured.—In Title IV of the original National Housing Act, Congress made provisions for insurance of accounts in all federal savings and loan associations and participating state-chartered associations. The insuring agency is the Federal Savings and Loan Insurance Corporation, which is owned by the government and has a capital of $100,000,000. Over 2,400 associations, with combined assets of about $4,600,000,000, are now taking advantage of the insurance privileges offered by this corporation. Individual coverage is 100 per cent for accounts up to $5,000 in one association, and almost 4,000,000 accounts are protected. The premium is 1/8 of 1 per cent of all share accounts, and, in case of failure, the beneficiary receives either a new insured account in a solvent institution or 10 per cent in cash and the remainder in negotiable noninterest bearing debentures of the Corporation, one-half payable in one year and the remainder in three years from the date of the default. Before 1942 the Home Loan Bank Board acted as the board of trustees for the Federal Savings and Loan Insurance Corporation.

Home Owners' Loan Corporation

This institution was created by Congress in 1933 to refinance mortgage loans of homeowners who were in financial distress at that time. The lending period was limited to three years, during which the corporation received applications for over $6,200,000,000 in loans and made loans amounting to a little over $3,000,000,000. Since June, 1936, its activities have been confined to collecting and servicing loans and managing and selling property acquired. It has liquidated more than two-thirds of its loans, and more than one-third of the million borrowers have repaid their loans in full.

Homeowners have been the chief beneficiaries of the activities of the Home Owners' Loan Corporation, by having their mortgages refinanced on more liberal terms. The maturity dates of refinanced mortgages were extended from an average of from three to five years to from fifteen to eighteen years. Repayment of principal was made over the life of the loan on a sound amortization plan. Interest rates were reduced on the average about 1½ per cent, and in some cases there were reductions in the amount of principal, the benefit of which was passed along to homeowners. Homeowners were permitted to keep almost a million homes, which they were in danger of losing through foreclosure. Mortgagees (banks and others) gained by having over $2,000,000,000 in "sour" loans taken off their hands. Local and state governments received over $225,000,000 in delinquent taxes, which were sorely needed by them. Finally, all those directly or indirectly involved in real estate markets benefited from the appraisal activities of the corporation. The appraisal level of real property was placed so as to protect the real estate market, which, in 1933, was in a stage of rapid deterioration.

The Home Owners' Loan Corporation was the most widely known of all the federal mortgage relief agencies. Although its lending operations were for but a limited period of time and of the "salvaging" variety, it has had definite effects upon the home financing movement. It aided in the popularization of the long-term amortized mortgage, added a flexible feature to principal payment by permitting postponements not to exceed a total of those due in three years, reconditioned property before placing it on the market, acquired the bulk of dubious mortgages, and made the American public definitely government-finance-minded.

Federal Housing Administration

National Housing Act of 1934.—The act creating the Federal Housing Administration was a departure from the practice of strengthening old agencies or creating new ones to make loans to homeowners. The stated purposes of the act were "to encourage improvement in housing standards and conditions," "to provide a system of mutual mortgage insurance," to increase employment, and to deal with certain other aspects of the housing situation. Federal Housing Administration makes no loans, but it insures those made by private institutions. While the Home Loan Bank System has as its chief purpose the building of a strong specialized home mortgage system, the Federal Housing Administration has as its primary purpose the creation of a type of investment that would be attractive to all types of institutions.

Three of the titles in the act authorize insurance loans: Title I provides for insurance of instalment loans made to finance alterations, repairs, improvements, purchase and installation of certain eligible equipment, and construction of small homes; Title II provides for insurance of mortgage loans made on small homes and rental and group housing units; Title VI provides for mortgage insurance on new homes and multiple-dwelling units in war housing areas as designated by the President.

In order to perform its functions of insuring loans on a business-like basis, Federal Housing Administration must accumulate reserves out of insurance premiums and inspection and other fees in order to take care of future losses. Four funds were set up for this purpose: Title I Insurance Revolving Fund, Mutual Mortgage Insurance Fund, Housing Insurance Fund, and War Housing Insurance Fund.

Housing Renovation and Modernization.—Title I provides that the lending institution is insured against loss up to 10 per cent of all modernization loans (prior to 1936, 20 per cent) made under its provisions. Thus, if a bank makes $100,000 of such loans, losses up to $10,000 are fully covered by insurance. In practice this has meant complete coverage and helps to explain the popularity of such loans among banks.

Originally no insurance premiums were charged financial institutions for insuring loans under Title I, but the law was amended in 1939, and, since July 1, 1939, the lenders have been charged ¾ of 1 per cent on small loans and ½ of 1 per cent on those for home construction. (These charges cannot legally be passed along to the borrowers.) With these receipts the Title I Insurance Revolving Fund was set up.

Mutual Mortgage Insurance Fund.—Title II of the National Housing Act provides for insurance of mortgages on one- to four-family houses and for those on other structures designed for home rental purposes. F.H.A. loans for the first purpose are the most important. They may not exceed $16,000, or 80 per cent of the value of the property, whichever is the least. In the case of lower-priced property, loans may be made up to a higher percentage under certain conditions. Interest is fixed by statute at a 5 per cent maximum and by regulation at 4.5 per cent.

The total insurance outstanding under Title II is limited to $4,000,000,000, but may be increased to $5,000,000,000 by the President. At the end of 1944, estimated insurance in force was almost $3,000,000,000 on small loans, $95,000,000 on rental and group housing loans, and $63,000,000 on small home commitments. Insurance premiums charged mortgagors is 1/2 of 1 per cent, and lenders may not make a service charge in addition to interest. The Fund is a mutual with mortgages grouped according to risk characteristics. In 1944 a dividend amounting to $288,000 was paid to 13,000 mortgagors when they repaid their loans in full. Although the Federal Housing Administration was originally financed with $10,000,000 contributed by the government, it was expected that it would be self-sufficient, and this expectation has been more than justified.

Housing and War Housing Insurance Funds.—Originally the Mutual Mortgage Insurance Fund insured all mortgages made under Title II, but now there is a separate fund that insures rental property. Under Title VI, an additional fund was set up to insure war rental housing projects. These funds are not mutual in their operations, and any losses sustained by them will be absorbed by the government. The Housing Insurance Fund was set up to insure mortgages on rental property made under provisions of sections 207 and 210 of the National Housing Act. To date, relatively few properties have been insured under these sections of the act.

The War Housing Insurance Fund received an appropriation of $10,000,000 from Congress. The F.H.A. may insure institutional loans made to builders on a 90 per cent loan-to-value ratio, provided the amounts are limited, with maximum loans now ranging from $5,400 on single-family houses to $12,000 on four-family dwellings. In May, 1942, additional provisions were made to facilitate the construction of large-scale rental projects for war workers, by permitting F.H.A. to insure individual mortgages for as much as $5,000,000, which may represent 90 per cent of the value of the project. The insurance of mortgages under Title VI constituted most F.H.A. new insurance business during the war.

Volume of Insurance.—The yearly volume of Federal Housing

Administration insurance written from 1934 through 1944 is shown in Chart XIV. It has insured over $8,000,000,000 in home loans, of which $3,500,000,000 has been repaid. Because of the willingness of banks and other financial institutions to lend when loans are insured, Federal Housing Administration has been a major factor in contributing to the flow of private capital into home improvements and modernization and in the construction of new housing units. Its primary interest has been the financing of small homeowners.

CHART XIV

YEARLY VOLUME OF F.H.A. INSURANCE WRITTEN

(1934-44)

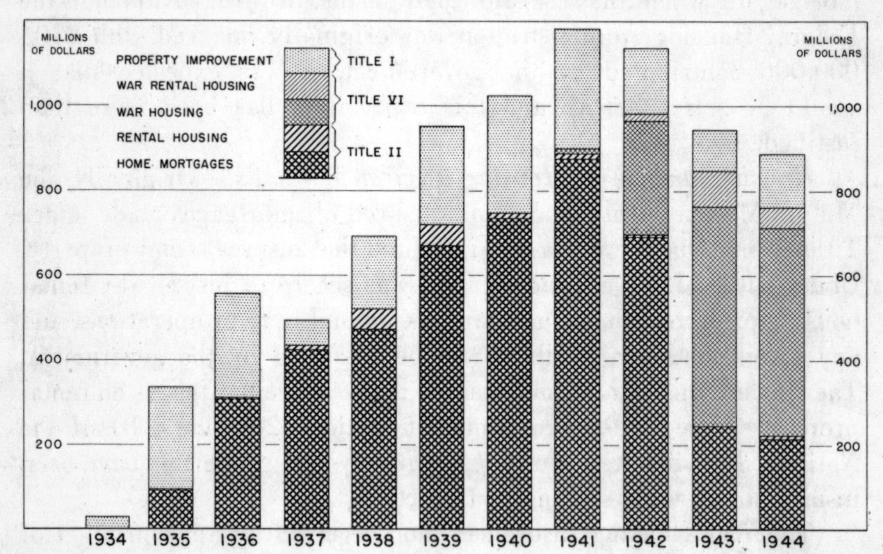

Source: Eleventh Annual Report of the Federal Housing Administration for the Year Ended December 31, 1944, Chart I.

Federal National Mortgage Association.—The National Housing Act, Title III, contains provisions which authorize private capital to organize national mortgage associations. These institutions are permitted to purchase and sell mortgages on new homes and rental housing projects constructed since January 1, 1936. In addition, the Federal National Mortgage Association may finance Federal Housing Administration mortgages on large-scale projects. Originally it was hoped that a chain of such associations would be formed and that this would result in a national market for standardized insured mortgages.

This part of the act was unattractive to private capital and bitterly opposed by the savings and loan associations. So the Home Loan Bank Act was modified in order to permit the federal home loan banks to lend to nonmembers on security of F.H.A. mortgages. Little use was made of this privilege, and so the Reconstruction Finance Corporation Mortgage Company agreed to purchase insured mortgages. Finally, in 1938, the Reconstruction Finance Corporation organized the Federal National Mortgage Association under Title III of the National Housing Act. Its success aroused the interest of private capitalists, but new amendments to the Federal Housing Administration Act gave the Federal Housing Administrator the

TABLE 47

INSURED F.H.A. HOME MORTGAGES (TITLE II) HELD IN PORTFOLIO, BY CLASS OF INSTITUTION
(In Millions of Dollars)

	December 1936	December 1940	June 1943	June 1945
Commercial banks	$228	$1,162	$1,700	$1,570
Mutual savings banks	8	130	252	265
Savings and loan associations	56	224	284	264
Insurance companies	41	542	1,071	1,047
Federal agencies*	5	201	235	43
Others†	27	150	158	134
Total	$365	$2,409	$3,700	$3,324

* The R.F.C. Mortgage Co., the Federal National Mortgage Association, and the F.D.I.C. and U.S. Housing Corporation.

† Includes mortgage companies, finance companies, industrial banks, endowed institutions, private and state benefit funds, etc.

Source: Federal Reserve Bulletin, February, 1946, p. 183.

discretionary power to refuse to charter associations, even though the applicants had met all the statutory requirements, and no charters have been granted. Present assets of the Federal National Mortgage Association total $50,000,000.

The goal of having a national market for insured mortgages has been handicapped by state laws requiring funds of savings banks and certain other state-chartered institutions to be invested locally. In 1943 the state legislature of New York authorized savings banks to invest in Federal Housing Administration mortgages on properties in adjoining states. By October 31, 1944, New York State savings banks held over $42,000,000 in mortgages on properties in New

Jersey, Connecticut, Pennsylvania, and Massachusetts.[2] To date the absence of a rediscount market for F.H.A. mortgages has not been serious. At present these mortgages are so popular with banks and insurance companies that no secondary market is necessary. (See Table 47.)

TABLE 48

TYPES OF INSTITUTION ORIGINATING, PURCHASING, SELLING, AND HOLDING MORTGAGES UNDER SECTION 203, 1944

Type of Institution	Mortgages Originated 1944	Mortgages Purchased 1944	Mortgages Sold 1944	Mortgages Held in Portfolio Dec. 31, 1944
	Per Cent	Per Cent	Per Cent	Per Cent
National banks	26.4	20.4	13.6	26.8
State banks	20.1	17.2	18.8	19.3
Mortgage companies	23.2	2.6	47.7	0.8
Insurance companies	15.5	41.9	6.6	31.6
Savings and loan ass'ns	7.5	3.3	4.2	7.9
Savings banks	5.4	11.9	0.1	8.3
Federal agencies*	....	1.1	1.8	2.0
All others†	1.9	1.6	7.2	3.3
Total	100.0	100.0	100.0	100.0

* Includes the R.F.C. Mortgage Company, Federal National Mortgage Association, and the Federal Deposit Insurance Corporation, only the first of which may originate.

† Includes industrial banks, finance companies, endowed institutions, private and state benefit funds, etc.

Source: Eleventh Annual Report of the Federal Housing Administration, Year Ending December 31, 1944, Table 8.

Federal Public Housing Authority

The third division of the National Housing Agency is the Federal Public Housing Authority. It includes the old United States Housing Authority and its affiliate, the Defense Homes Corporation. (See Table 31, Chap. XXIII.) The United States Housing Authority was organized in 1937, and the Defense Homes Corporation was created during the war in order to help finance housing needs in certain areas with government funds. Government funds invested in the

[2] *Ninety-fourth Annual Report of the Superintendent of Banks, State of New York,* Part I, Legislative Document (1945), No. 21, pp. 34-35.

latter now total $70,000,000, while those involved in Federal Public Housing Authority grants made to date are about $550,000,000.

Prior to 1942, United States Housing Authority was a part of the Federal Works Agency. It has assumed some of the activities formerly handled by the Public Works Administration. The purposes are "to aid the States and their subdivisions to remedy unsafe and unsanitary housing conditions and the shortage of decent dwellings for low-income families and to alleviate unemployment." All powers are vested in the United States Housing Administrator, appointed by the President with the advice and consent of the Senate, for a term of five years. The United States Housing Authority has a capital of $1,000,000 provided by the Treasury and $1,600,000,000 of governmental credits which may be lent for slum clearance and low-rent housing at an interest rate at least ½ per cent above the cost of money to the federal government. In addition to loans, the act authorizes the federal government through the United States Housing Authority to make annual contributions from federal taxes or other sources to help subsidize the low-income housing projects.[3]

The annual contributions will be reviewed at the end of 10 years and every fifth year thereafter for a total of sixty years. Before the war, the annual cost of United States Housing Authority subsidies to the federal taxpayer was $116 per family subsidized. The local and state governments must likewise make annual contributions equal to at least 20 per cent of those of the federal government. To date this contribution has been made in the form of tax exemption, one of the chief costs of owning real property. The exemptions are estimated to have a value equal to one-half that of the annual contribution of the federal government, which means that the total annual subsidy to every family living in the low-cost housing projects is $174 a year. Only families of low incomes may have the opportunity to live in these government-subsidized apartments and houses. Originally the income eligibility was as low as $450 in the South and as high as $1,149 in large cities in the North, but with averages ranging from $650 to $950 per year in a majority of the projects.[4]

---

[3] A substitute for the annual contribution plan, which has not been used by local housing agencies, is an outright U.S.H.A. grant limited to 25 per cent of the costs of the project, except that an additional 15 per cent may be granted for payment of labor by the President from unemployment relief funds.

[4] *Annual Report of the United States Housing Authority*, 1938, p. 6.

The local housing authorities are organized under state enabling acts as public corporations and are managed by a board appointed by the chief executive of the city in which the housing authority is located. The board is responsible for the construction and management of the buildings. Members serve without salaries, employing experts and others to administer the project. The management must keep uniform accounting records and make periodic reports to state and national housing authorities.

Under the present law, local and federal subsidies will continue for sixty years, and, at the end of that time, the local public housing authority may (1) continue the project without subsidies, (2) if the condition of the building justifies, secure a change in the law so as to obtain future subsidies, or (3) liquidate the project. While subsidies represent a considerable direct and indirect burden on the federal and local taxpayers, the costs may be offset by a decrease in social costs for crime, sickness, and other "intangibles" associated with slum sections of cities. Over 600 local housing authorities have been established, and advances have been made to cover 750 projects located in 550 cities.

During the war, Federal Public Housing Authority had responsibility for the bulk of the publicly financed war housing programs.[5] Largely through its subsidiary, the Defense Homes Corporation, it financed over 800,000 accommodations, including over 580,000 family dwellings, 166,000 dormitory units, and over 80,000 stopgap accommodations. Since the war, it has been instrumental in moving the latter to universities and colleges and other places of congestion in order to provide former members of the Armed Forces with temporary houses. Some of the more permanent projects have been sold to private investors.

Conclusions

In the home financing field there are commercial banks, mutual savings banks, savings and loan associations, insurance companies,

[5] Before 1942 the Federal Works Agency and the Army and Navy received funds appropriated by Congress for building dwellings for families of noncommissioned officers and civilian workers on military or naval establishments or near plants manufacturing articles for defense. In 1942 all off-post housing projects were transferred from the War and Navy departments to the Federal Public Housing Authority, along with certain agencies from the Federal Works Agency (Public Building Administration, the Division of Defense Housing, the Mutual Ownership Defense Housing Division) and the nonfarm and war housing projects of the Farm Security Administration.

mortgage companies, and individuals. In addition, there are numerous other investors in home mortgages, including endowed institutions, trust funds, credit unions (in some states), industrial banks, and finance companies.

Improvement in Lending Practices.—Since 1930, primarily because of the influence of federal home financing agencies, the practices of lending institutions have been standardized. Ratios of loan to valuation of property are higher, with a decline in the use of second and third mortgages. Interest rates throughout the nation are more uniform and are generally lower. The time period for loans is longer, and the practice of requiring periodic payments on principal is the current practice for new loans. In return for a reduction in interest payments, many old mortgagers have agreed to make periodic payments on principal. This adoption of the amortization method of repayment of loans, first popularized by savings and loan institutions, is one of the most significant developments in the home financing field. Unfortunately, it is too rigid, in that it does not permit increases in payments during good times and reduction in payments during depressions. It is this inflexibility in principal payments which constitutes the major weakness of the present mortgage payment plan.

Cost of Financing.—The average mortgage loan is small, and the cost of accounting for monthly payments is large. For example, the Federal Housing Administration mortgage requires the keeping of accounts for interest payments, amortization payments, fire insurance, taxes, and mortgage insurance. The Federal National Mortgage Association estimates the costs of servicing loans to be ¾ of 1 per cent of the outstanding principal. To the cost of servicing a loan must be added special commissions and the cost of originating the loan. Finally, the expenses involved in foreclosure must be recognized, and these vary widely from state to state, being over $300 in New York and Illinois and as low as $5.00 in Texas. In addition, there is a loss because of the time period involved in foreclosures, which is over two years in Alabama. State moratorium laws, which have as their purpose the protection of debtors, have further discouraged the flow of investment funds to the home financing field, thereby tending to increase the costs of home financing. In spite of legal obstacles to interest rate reduction, the actual savings in the costs of home financing have been substantial. Interest rates are from 1 to 2 per cent lower; however, because of the elimination of second and third mortgages, the savings to homeowners have been much greater than the figures above suggest. When payments for funds, risks, servicing of debts, and general costs of carrying on the business are considered, reduction of interest rates much below the present figure seems unlikely. Some improvement would tend to flow from the passage of a national foreclosure law, provided the courts would uphold the constitutionality of such a law, which would tend to make the home financing field more attractive to investment funds in certain states.

Co-ordination of Activities of Federal Agencies.—In the National Housing Agency there are three divisions: the Federal Home Loan Bank System, based primarily on private capital; the Federal Housing Administration, which insures loans made by private institutions; and the Federal Public Housing Authority, which uses public funds. The Home Loan Bank System has as its chief purpose the building of a strong specialized home mortgage system; the Federal Housing Administration has as its primary purpose the creation of a type of investment designed to be attractive to all types of investing institutions; and the Federal Public Housing Authority has as its chief function the financing of slum clearance and the subsidizing of community-owned housing projects.

In making home mortgages attractive to commercial banks, the Federal Housing Administration has promoted "mixed banking," which has weakened the development of the Home Loan Bank System, a type of specialized banking. Thus the commercial banks have been further diverted from their traditional commercial lending activities, and the Home Loan Bank System has not achieved the hopes of its sponsors. By sponsoring 750 tax-free public housing projects, the government has discouraged the flow of private capital into real property, the number of tenants for rental property has been reduced, and taxes have been increased on all taxable property in the communities having housing projects.

The Federal Housing Administration is a highly centralized agency exercising technical control over interest rates, appraisal procedures, instalment payments, and other aspects of mortgage lending. It has only secondary interest in the institutions that lend for the system. The Federal Home Loan Bank System has only limited authority as to interest rates and other technical matters pertaining to loans. Its primary interest is in the development of strong local home financing institutions. This basic conflict is best illustrated in the insurance principles, with the Federal Housing Administration assuming the risks for specific assets and the Federal Savings and Loan Insurance Corporation insuring accounts in institutions making loans directly.

The placing of the federal urban financing institutions under one agency will tend to reduce the amount of conflict among the different home financing systems. Faced with a house shortage of 10,000,000 homes, it seems improbable that any one system could meet the current need alone. The three systems may be made to operate so that each will supplement the others, with greater emphasis on the use of private capital when conditions permit. The activities of the federal home loan banks should be expanded so as to become the source of reserve funds for all home mortgage institutions.

QUESTIONS AND PROBLEMS

1. Explain the changes in the volume of home mortgages between 1931 and 1943. Use Table 46.
2. In what ways has the federal government contributed to home financing?
3. What justification has there been for the statement that the federal home loan banks were created to help institutions rather than homeowners?
4. Describe the organization of the Home Loan Bank System. Has this system achieved a place in the home financing field corresponding to that of the Federal Reserve System in the commercial banking field? Give reasons for your answer.
5. Describe savings and loan associations as to method of operation, management, and ownership.
6. Identify "Federal Savings and Loan Insurance Corporation."
7. What margin should be required on a loan secured by residential property? How does the margin required by savings and loan associations compare to that required by mutual savings banks? Justify this difference.
8. Which one of the various types of savings banks and savings institutions is best equipped to finance home purchasing? Why?
9. How do the following institutions secure funds: (*a*) Federal Home Loan Banks, (*b*) building and loan associations, and (*c*) United States Housing Authority?
10. Describe conditions prevailing in the home mortgage field when the Home Owners' Loan Corporation was created. What groups were benefitted by this corporation? What group may lose? Why?
11. Compare the federal savings and loan associations to mutual savings

banks as to (*a*) management, (*b*) dividend policies, (*c*) earnings, and (*d*) risk.

12. What relationship is there, if any, between home financing and each of the following: (*a*) the automobile trailer business and (*b*) rapid improvements in home construction and home conveniences?
13. Federal Housing Administration method of assisting homeowners "implies direct governmental control over home-mortgage interest rates; terms of financing, . . . down payments and length of loans; community development; types of material and construction to be used in private residential dwellings; and to some extent control over the types of lending institutions developed, by virtue of its encouragement of the brokerage concept of operation in contrast to the operation of community institutions [savings and loan associations] having a thrift and savings program along with their mortgage-lending activities" (Bodfish, H. M., "Toward an Understanding of the Federal Home Loan System," *Journal of Land and Public Utility Economics*, Vol. XV, No. 4 [November, 1939], p. 420). Analyze and discuss.
14. What is your reaction to the following: "I feel justified in making the challenging statement that no type of institution equals a bank in the three essentials required by depositors—namely safety, availability and interest return" (Benson, Philip A., *Banking*, December, 1938, p. 74)?
15. Distinguish between the activities of Federal Housing Administration under Title I and under Title II of the National Housing Act.
16. The passage of the United States Housing Act, although calling for but a small original appropriation by the federal government, has increased the federal government's budget each year by millions of dollars for at least 60 years to come. Explain.
17. Why are commercial banks opposed to the building and loan association movement? Why do they favor the Federal Housing Administration? Explain.
18. How do each of the following tend to affect the home building industries: (*a*) high real estate taxes, (*b*) volume of real estate in the hands of financial institutions, and (*c*) high costs of lending and foreclosure?
19. Two of the most important contributions to recent home financing are (*a*) elimination of the second mortgage market and (*b*) periodic repayment of principal. Explain.

REFERENCES

Bodfish, H. M. *Time Marches On in Thrift and Home-Financing*. Pamphlet. Chicago: U.S. Building and Loan League, 1936.

Bodfish, H. M. "Toward an Understanding of the Federal Home Loan Bank System," *Journal of Land and Public Utility Economics*, Vol. XV, No. 4 (November, 1939), pp. 416-37.

Bodfish, H. M., and Theobold, A. D. *Savings and Loan Principles*, chaps. i-xii. New York: Prentice-Hall, Inc., 1938.

Clark, H. F., and Chase, F. A. *Elements of the Modern Building and Loan Associations*, chaps. i-iv. New York: Macmillan Co., 1927.

Commissioner of Labor, *Building and Loan Associations*. Washington, D.C.: U.S. Government Printing Office, 1894.

Edmiston, H., and Anderson, G. "United States Government Corporations and Credit Agencies in 1939," *Federal Reserve Bulletin*, April, 1940, pp. 298-305.

Ely, R. T., and Morehouse, E. W. *Elements of Land Economies*, chap. vi. New York: Macmillan Co., 1924.

Federal Home Loan Bank Board (now Home Loan Bank Administration). *Annual Report*. Washington, D.C.: Superintendent of Documents.

Federal Housing Administration. *Insured Mortgage Portfolio*.

Federal Housing Administration. *Annual Report*. Washington, D.C.: Superintendent of Documents.

Fortune, Vol. XXXIII, No. 4 (April, 1946).

Killam, C. W. "Low-Cost Housing in the United States," *Harvard Business Review*, Vol. XIV (1936), pp. 299-311.

Lewis, E. A. *Home Owners' Loan Acts and Housing Act*. Washington, D.C.: U.S. Government Printing Office, 1934.

Piquet, H. S. *Building and Loan Associations in New Jersey*. Princeton: Princeton University Press, 1931.

Riegal, R.. and Doubman, J. R. *The Building and Loan Association*, New York: John Wiley & Sons, Inc., 1927.

Rowlands, D. T. *Two Decades of Building and Loan Associations in Pennsylvania*. (Reprint from *Pennsylvania Bulletin*, Vol. VII, Nos. 6-12; Vol. VIII, Nos. 1-4 [1940].) Philadelphia.

Sixth Annual Report, Federal Works Agency. Washington, D.C.: U.S. Government Printing Office, 1945.

The Twentieth Century Fund. *American Housing*. New York: The Twentieth Century Fund, 1944.

United States Housing Authority. *Annual Report*. Washington, D.C.: Superintendent of Documents.

Westerfield, R. B. *Commercial Banker Attitudes toward Federal Savings and Loan Associations*. Pamphlet. Chicago: U.S. Savings and Loan League, 1939.

CHAPTER XXXV

AGRICULTURAL CREDIT INSTITUTIONS

Agricultural Credit Differs from Other Types

Farmers require credit for long-term, intermediate, and short-term needs, corresponding in time to those of industry and commerce. The hazards of farming are great because of the uncertainty of weather, the inelastic demand for most farm products, and the large number of small producing units, which makes crop control difficult. Farmers are denied direct access to the money and capital markets, and formerly they were forced to pay high retail rates for funds as well as high financing and refinancing charges. The only way in which farmers may benefit from low rates in the money and capital markets is through large financial institutions which can borrow at low rates and pass funds along to them at a small increase in price. This has been made possible with government assistance.

In farming there is a close relationship between business and family affairs, because a farm is a home as well as a business. This situation complicates the problem of credit granting, because personal, as well as business, aspects must be considered. When a farm is foreclosed, the financial institution is not only taking the farmer's business plant but also his home. In some states, in times of distress, legislatures have passed acts to prevent foreclosures; in other states mobs have prevented them. Local or state disturbances are certain to have political effects in Washington, particularly in the Senate. The senators from rural states have been able to secure far-reaching financial benefits for their farmer constituents. As a result, a very complicated and complete federal farm financing system providing for every type of agricultural credit has been created.

Sources of Credit

Short-Term Credit.—The same sources of short-term credit which are available to businessmen and consumers are also available to farmers for the financing of their operations and for their consumption needs. They include, among others, "trade" or "store" credits, evidenced by book accounts or promissory notes, granted by merchants and others who have sold goods. In certain parts of the South, merchants have financed small landowners and tenants by lines of credit secured by liens on tobacco or cotton crops, plus chattel mortgages on property owned. This system was subjected to a great deal of abuse because of high discount rates charged and the practice of overpricing or overcharging for goods purchased. The debtors were at the mercy of the merchants, who, according to rural reformers, were creating a system of peonage.

Until recently, local commercial banks have supplied farmers with most of their short-term needs for cash. Such loans are usually protected by chattel mortgages on property such as livestock and produce. Smaller loans may be protected by chattel mortgages on automobiles, equipment, and household furnishings.

Produce dealers, canning factories, "cotton factors," and others have made many loans to farmers in the form of cash or seeds and other supplies. Later these credits are deducted from the price paid for the crops sold to the dealers, canning factories, and others. Automobile and other finance companies extend credit for the purchase of trucks, automobiles, and other things, on the same basis that they do for other buyers.

Since 1918 Congress has provided by special acts for many "emergency crop and feed loans." In 1943 the principal amount of these loans was $150,000,000, of which $42,000,000 was for drought relief loans of 1934-35, and almost $108,000,000 was for crop and feed loans made from 1918 to 1943. However, three-fourths of all loans made since 1918 have been repaid. Such loans have been administered by the Secretary of Agriculture, the Reconstruction Finance Corporation, and the Production Credit Commissioner. Administration of all such lending should be restricted to the last, which is the short-term lending specialist in the federal farm credit system. In recent years these loans have been limited to a maximum of $400; but, as a result of war conditions, the maximum was increased to $2,500 in Puerto Rico. During the fiscal year 1944, over 100,000 loans were made under the Emergency Crop and Feed Loan Program.

The Commodity Credit Corporation was organized in 1933 to make one-season loans to farmers. These loans were based upon corn and cotton crops, although later other commodities were added.

This corporation was organized to help carry out the provisions of the Agricultural Adjustment Act and the National Recovery Act. In addition to lending functions, it has the power to buy, hold, sell, and otherwise deal in commodities designated from time to time by the President. It was the use of this power which made it such an important war agency. In September, 1945, its total assets exceeded $1,500,000,000, of which $1,200,000,000 was in commodities.

Intermediate Credit.—The distinction between "short-term" and "intermediate" credit financing institutions cannot be sharply drawn; and many of those noted in the foregoing paragraphs are engaged in agricultural lending which involves credit periods longer than six months or a year. For example, sellers of farm machinery often make arrangements for payments on the installment plan involving as long as three years. Many bank loans are renewed in whole or in part at the end of a season and so become intermediate or even long-term. Special agencies operating in the field of intermediate farm credit are cattle loan companies, federal agricultural credit corporations, the Intermediate Credit System, and the Production Credit System. The last two are parts of the Federal Farm Credit Administration and are considered later.

Cattle loan companies are created to help finance the raising and fattening of cattle and sheep (hogs are too speculative) in communities where commercial banking facilities are lacking or inadequate because banking laws prevent more than 10 per cent of capital and surplus being lent to one name. Two types of loans are made: those to finance the raising of cattle and sheep on the ranges of the South and West (stocker loans) and those to finance the fattening of cattle and sheep in other sections (feeder loans). The procedure is for the cattle loan company to take a chattel mortgage on the livestock as security for the borrower's notes. The cattle loan companies endorse these notes and discount them at commercial banks, acting as intermediaries between the borrowing cattlemen and the lending institution in Chicago, St. Louis, and other financial centers. If there is a large loan (they vary from $1,000 to $500,000), parts are discounted with different banks. The "spread" between the borrower's rate of interest and the discount rate of the commercial bank is the margin of profit on which cattle loan companies operate.

Twelve regional agricultural credit corporations (one in each farm credit district) were provided for in 1932 as a part of President Hoover's farm relief program. They were created to meet the needs for short-term credit, particularly in the livestock industry. One year after the creation of the permanent production credit association (see below), these temporary credit corporations were placed in "orderly liquidation." They were organized, financed, and managed by the Reconstruction Finance Corporation; their original capital was $44,500,000, and they made loans, exclusive of renewals, aggregating over $322,000,000. Their administration was assumed by the Federal Farm Credit Administration in May, 1933. In 1937 a new corporation, known as the Regional Credit Corporation of Washington, D.C., was created, and now it is the only regional agricultural credit corporation in existence. Many of the old regional offices are being operated as branches, and new ones are being opened (or closed) as needed. During World War II, in order to assure the availability of adequate credit to finance the plans for increased food production, this corporation, under the direction of the Secretary of Agriculture, made two types of loans. "F 1" loans were secured by first lien on crops, livestock, or chattel, plus "unqualified personal liability" of the borrowers. "F 2" credits were advances on special war crops to meet cash needs.

Long-Term Credit.—The most serious and continuous credit problems faced by farmers are those resulting from long-term borrowing. There will always be farm mortgage problems as long as states in the United States keep their antiprimogeniture laws. In many European countries the first-born son has an exclusive right of inheritance in an estate, while in the United States the practice is for the intestacy laws to divide all property equally among the children. Thus a farm which is left as part of an estate is usually mortgaged following the death of the owner. If one of the sons remains on the farm, he mortgages it to pay the other heirs. If the farm is sold, the purchaser rarely has the cash to pay the full purchase price, which means that he must borrow the remainder. The process of paying off the mortgage begins anew, and it must be repeated each generation. In addition, long-term funds are borrowed to finance new farmhouses, barns, and other improvements. High mortgage debts are usually associated with highly productive farming. In certain sections mortgages also reflect a tendency for ambitious tenants and young farmers to go into debt to buy their own farms. Therefore, long-term farmer borrowing may be regarded as a natural product of our intestacy laws, a desire for better farms and farm life, and the democratic way of obtaining control over one's own farm.

The agencies or banks which are making farm mortgage loans are those in the Federal Farm Loan System, life insurance companies, all types of commercial banks, savings banks, and a few other financial institutions. Although individuals are not investing in farm mortgages as heavily as they were before the creation of federal long-term credit agencies, they are among the largest holders of farm mortgages. This is a natural result of sales of farms by retired farmers and the operation of the intestacy laws.

TABLE 49
FARM MORTGAGE LOANS—FOR SELECTED YEARS
(In Millions of Dollars)

Type of Lender	Dec. 31 1934	Dec. 31 1936	Dec. 31 1940	Fiscal Year Ended June 30 1944
Federal land banks*	$ 730.1	$108.6	$ 63.9	$ 64.2
Land bank commissioner*	553.0	76.9	36.4	31.2
Individuals†	219.6	255.3	225.6	381.7
Commercial banks†	110.9	186.1	219.9	250.8
Insurance companies†	45.7	115.1	145.5	167.4
Others†	80.8	60.4	81.2	74.1
Total	$1,740.1	$802.4	$772.5	$969.4

* Loans made.

† Estimated.

Source: The 11th Annual Report of the Farm Credit Administration (1943-44), p. 85.

About 40 per cent of the long-term farm lending is now done by the agencies which make up the Federal Farm Loan System. An even larger percentage would be done by them if federal land banks were not restricted to making loans up to 50 per cent of the appraised value of land and 20 per cent of the value of improvements. Farmers financing on less than a 50 per cent margin must go to lenders other than the permanent federal loan banks to secure long-term credit. Perhaps the most helpful long-term financing change that could be made by the federal government would be to lower this "margin," as has been done by federal and private agencies lending in the home financing field.

Private mortgage companies, insurance companies, and commercial banks are the chief private lenders in the long-term farm mortgage field. The private mortgage companies operate over a wide territory through local branches or agents. Applications for loans are received by local agents and then passed on by the head office. The credit period is short—three to five years—which makes renewals frequent and expenses high, because renewal charges are high.

Life insurance companies usually maintain their own agents in the field. In the past their lending policies were similar to those of mortgage companies, but in recent years many of them have adopted the long-term amortization plan popularized by the federal land banks. Services of the local mortgage brokers are sometimes used, although their role and that of other private agencies has decreased in importance. The function of the broker is to bring together the farmer borrower and the city lender. Mortgage lending by banks is considered in preceding chapters and is not discussed in this chapter.

There Are Four Permanent Farm Credit Divisions

In 1933 the Federal Farm Credit Administration was organized and placed in the Treasury Department, where it remained until July, 1939, when it was transferred to the Department of Agriculture. The chief executive, the governor of the Federal Farm Credit Administration, and four commissioners are appointed by the President, with the consent of the Senate. Before the Federal Farm Credit Administration was organized, federal agricultural credit agencies were supervised by the Federal Farm Loan Board, the Federal Farm Board, the Secretary of Agriculture, and the Reconstruction Finance Corporation. This situation resulted in duplication of services, unnecessary competition, high overhead costs, and general confusion to prospective borrowers. Since 1933, the Federal Farm Credit Administration has worked for simplification of operations, standardization of practice, co-ordination of systems, and elimination of waste and inefficiency.

Uniform Structural Pattern.—The Farm Credit Administration involves four central banking systems which are fairly uniform in structural outline. (See Chart XVI.) Each is under the supervision of a commissioner and has 12 regional banks. The latter serve the 12 farm credit districts and lend indirectly to farmer borrowers through some type of co-operative organization or financial institution. The only variation in this structural organization is in the co-operative system—it has a central bank in addition to the 12 regional banks.

Centralized Management in Farm Credit Cities.—From the beginning, steps have been taken to reduce the expenses of farm lending by combining under one management the regional activities of the farm credit system. Now all of the four banks located in each farm

CHART XV

ORGANIZATION OF THE FARM CREDIT ADMINISTRATION

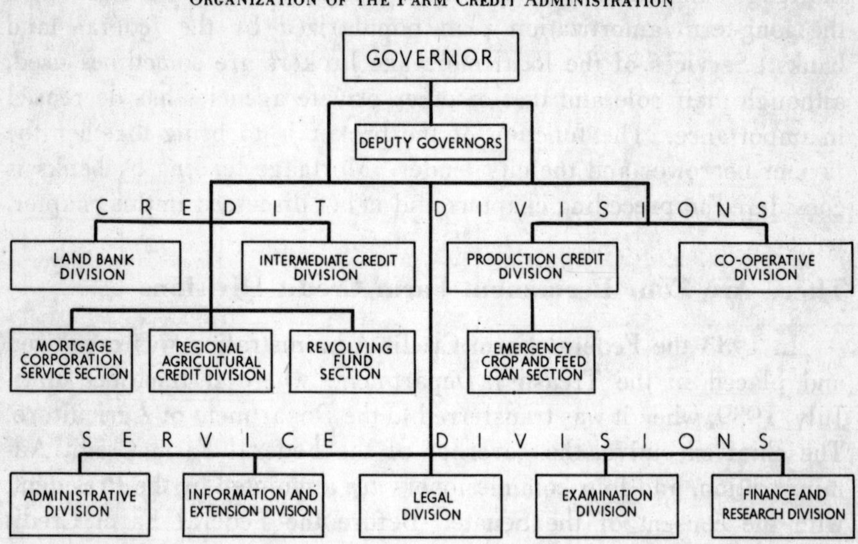

Source: Federal Farm Credit Administration.

credit city are managed by a farm credit board of seven directors appointed or elected to represent the different interests of the farmer borrowers and the government. Three directors are called local directors, three are called district directors, and the seventh is called the director-at-large. One local director is selected by the borrowers of long-term credit (federal land bank's credit), one by borrowers of short-term credit (production credit corporation's credit), and the third by borrowers of co-operative credit (co-operative bank's credit).

Since the government is an important investor in the forty-eight regional banks, the governor of the Federal Farm Credit Corporation appoints two district directors and the director-at-large to represent the public interest. The third district director is elected jointly by the chief borrowers in the Federal Farm Credit Administration (long-term borrowers) and the governor of Federal Farm Credit Administration; the borrowers nominate three names from which the governor selects one district director. Therefore, provisions are made for selection of thirty-six directors by borrowers, thirty-six by the government, and twelve jointly by the government and long-term borrowers.

CHART XVI
FEDERAL FARM CREDIT ADMINISTRATION
(Permanent Agencies)

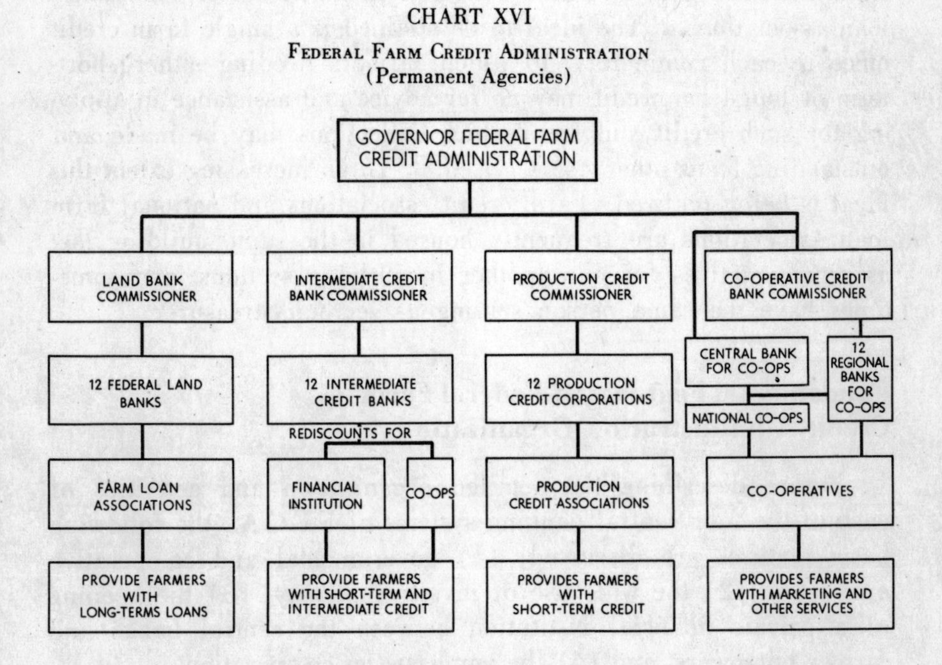

The Farm Credit Act of 1937 permits the appointment of a "uniform service staff" and combined accounting, bookkeeping, and other procedures to prevent duplication and waste in administration of the district affairs. The administrative work is supervised by a general agent, who along with the four presidents of the four district banks make up an advisory committee for all the regional agencies in each of the farm credit cities.

By way of summary, it may be noted that in the farm credit city located in District 1 there are (1) the Federal Land Bank of Springfield, Massachusetts, (2) the Federal Intermediate Credit Bank of Springfield, Massachusetts, (3) the Production Credit Corporation of Springfield, Massachusetts, and (4) the Bank for Co-operatives of Springfield, Massachusetts. All these banks are supervised by seven directors called a Farm Credit Board. This board selects a general agent, four presidents of the four banks, and a single staff, in so far as the business of the four banks permits.

After co-ordination of the central office and the offices of the four regional banks in each of the 12 federal land bank cities, the next logical step as recognized by the governor of Federal Farm Credit Administration is to co-ordinate the activities of local or community loan associations. "The ideal to be attained is a single farm credit office in each community, to which farmers needing either short-term or long-term credit may go for advice and assistance in applying for such credit and from which collections may be made and outstanding loans otherwise serviced."[1] To an increasing extent this ideal is being realized. Farm credit associations and national farm loan associations are frequently housed in the same building, act as representatives for one another in outlying sections, and sometimes have the same person serving as secretary-treasurer.

Fundamental Features of Federal Farm Credit Administration Organization

Before describing the detailed organization and activities of each of the four central banking systems of F.F.C.A., the following basic features are discussed; (1) governmental and co-operative ownership, (2) the wide use of investors' money, (3) the keeping of a private financial institution between the central banks and farmer borrowers, and (4) the emphasis on co-operation.

Governmental and Co-operative Ownership.—The government formerly owned most of the stock of the 12 federal land banks, and borrowers owned the remainder; but now the situation has been reversed, and most of the stock is owned by the farm loan associations. The legal ownership status of the 13 banks for co-operatives is similar to that of the federal land banks, but with a considerably larger percentage of the stock owned by the government. Present laws anticipate a gradual transfer of the government's stock to borrowers, that is, all types of farmers' co-operative marketing, buying,

[1] *Second Annual Report of the Farm Credit Administration* (1934), p. 8.

and business service organizations. The government owns all the stock of the 12 intermediate credit banks and the 12 production credit corporations. In addition, the government has contributed to the paid-up surplus of the federal intermediate credit banks and made arrangements to contribute more if necessary. No provisions have been made to shift the government's stock to borrowers.

Public Borrowing.—A distinction made in earlier chapters between a banker and a capitalist was that the banker uses "other people's money," making a profit from the difference between costs of use of funds borrowed and receipts from lending these funds. Owners' investments help to establish the credit of the bank and to provide funds with which to pay the costs of establishing and operating the bank. The banks in the two systems—land bank and intermediate credit—secure most of their funds by borrowing in the capital or money markets. Individuals, commercial banks, and institutional investors help to finance farmers by purchasing federal land bank bonds and intermediate credit bank debentures. The banks for co-operatives and the Production Credit Corporation do little or no public borrowing.

Indirect Lending to Farmers.—A third fundamental principle on which the Federal Farm Credit Administration is organized is the keeping of a private financial institution between the government-owned and -financed banks and the borrowing farmers. There are only emergency and temporary exceptions to this standard principle. This type of organization combines local responsibility with government help. It lessens the dangers of fraud and political influence and avoids the type of government administration usually classified as bureaucracy.

Co-operative Principle.—A fourth fundamental principle to note in the organization of the Federal Farm Credit Administration is the emphasis placed upon the co-operative principle. This is illustrated by the existence of farm loan associations in the farm mortgage banking field, production credit associations in the short-term credit field, and the many types of marketing and other associations in the intermediate credit fields. In final analysis, the future of farm credit rests upon the farmer members of these institutions. If farm loan associations, co-operative marketing associations, and production credit associations are wisely managed by the members, the future of farm credit machinery is assured.

The chief long-run threat to the proper development of the co-operative spirit is reliance upon the federal government for interest, principal, and other concessions. If left alone by Congress, the Farm Credit Administration and all allied agencies could be made to function so as to cover all expenses without aid other than the capital invested in the 49 central or regional banks. Farmers may well ask: "Why should we develop strong local co-operative associations to finance our needs when it is so easy to secure help through our congressmen?"

Two governors of the Federal Farm Credit Association resigned in protest against the trend to socialize the farm credit system. "After all the principal job of the farm credit administration is not the lending of government funds but the supervision of a group of self-sustaining co-operative credit institutions in which the farmers of the country have over $130,000,000 of their own hard-earned money invested."[2]

Federal Farm Loan System Was Established in 1917

The Federal Farm Loan Act (1916) made provisions for a dual system, a co-operative part composed of 12 federal land banks and national farm loan associations and a private part composed of joint-stock land banks. The act provided for a Federal Farm Loan Board, which had general charge over the system until the Federal Farm Credit Administration was formed and a single executive known as Federal Farm Land Bank Commissioner was appointed. (See Chart XVI.)

Joint-Stock Land Banks.—Any ten or more natural persons were permitted by the Federal Farm Loan Act to form a joint-stock land bank. The act gave existing mortgage banks an opportunity to recharter as national institutions, but few saw fit to do so. Almost all the federal joint-stock land banks were new institutions. The board issued charters to 88 joint-stock land banks, but careless loan practices and fraud hurt the system, and on May 12, 1933, the number had been reduced to 50, of which only 47 were under their own management and 3 were in receivership. In 1933 provisions were made for the liquidation of the remaining joint-stock land

[2] From press statement of F. F. Hill at the time of his resignation as governor of F.F.C.A., *Syracuse Post Standard,* December 21, 1939, p. 1.

banks; and, at the end of the fiscal year 1944, there were only 15, 5 of which were in voluntary liquidation and 3 in receivership. Gross assets of these banks are about $10,000,000.

Federal Land Banks.—These nonprofit banks are the central banks in the farm mortgage field, whose primary function is to borrow money in the capital market and make it available through co-operative financial agencies to farm owners. The capital of the federal land banks is divided into shares with a par value of $5.00, which are sold to farm loan associations, direct borrowers from the banks, and borrowers through agents. All borrowers are required at the time they secure funds from the land banks to purchase stock in quantities equal to 5 per cent of their loans. If the former has no money, the purchase price of the stock is withheld from the proceeds of the loans. Thus a farm mortgagor, after signing a first mortgage note for $10,000, would receive $9,500 in cash and $500 in stock. Thus as lending operations increased, the capital stock of the land banks also increased.

By 1932 most of the government-owned stock ($8,892,130 of the original $9,000,000) had been retired, but, because of the depression, Congress appropriated new funds for the land banks ($125,000,000 for purchase of stock and $189,000,000 for subscription to the paid-in surplus of the banks). Because of war prosperity, many borrowers have liquidated their accounts with the federal land banks, thereby permitting them to reduce their capital account items. Even before the war (1940) the Houston and Louisville banks had repaid all government funds, and by the end of 1946 most other banks except the St. Paul bank expect to complete the retirement of the government's financial interest.

Most of the funds lent by federal land banks are secured from those who buy their bonds, that is, insurance companies, banks, individuals, and others. These bonds are secured by farm mortgages and other collateral of the banks. The lending and borrowing procedure of mortgage banks is to use bank funds in securing farm mortgages which are to be used as collateral for a bond issue, in order to obtain funds to secure more mortgages which may be used as collateral for a second bond issue, etc. The law permits this borrowing and lending process to be repeated until the debt of the land bank is twenty times its capital stock and surplus.

The Federal Land Bank System makes it possible for farmers

to share in the benefits of the low rates prevailing in the investment market. The spread between the interest rate paid on bonds by the federal land banks and that charged by these banks on farm mortgages may not exceed 1 per cent. For example, if federal land banks borrow at a rate of 3 per cent, the most they may charge farmers who borrow through a farm loan association is 4 per cent. The maximum rate which banks may pay on their bonds is fixed by law at 5 per cent, which automatically fixes the maximum rate that farmers may be charged at 6 per cent.

The federal land banks' loans to one borrower may not exceed $50,000, and all applications in excess of $25,000 must be submitted to the Land Bank Commissioner for approval. All ordinary loans are based on the security of first mortgages on rural real property, which may not be in excess of 50 percent of the appraised normal value of the mortgaged land plus 20 per cent of the appraised insured permanent improvements. The purposes for which loans may be made are: (1) to "purchase land for agricultural uses; (2) to buy equipment, fertilizer, and livestock necessary for the proper and reasonable operation of the mortgaged farm; (3) to provide buildings and to improve farm land; (4) to liquidate any indebtedness of an eligible borrower if the debt was incurred prior to January 1, 1937, and to liquidate debts incurred for agricultural purposes without regard to the time when such a debt was incurred; and (5) to provide the owner of the mortgaged land with funds for general agricultural uses."[3] Most of the lending by the federal land banks has been to refinance existing debts.

National Farm Loan Associations.—In the United States there are over 3,400 co-operative farm credit associations entirely owned by members, all of whom are mortgage debtors to their district federal land banks. The national farm loan associations are not banks, but they carry on certain banking activities. There must be at least ten farmers in each association, and many of the associations have hundreds of members. Any natural person owning or about to own qualified real estate may become a member upon approval of two-thirds of the association's board of directors. Each member must subscribe to stock in the association equal to 5 per cent of the desired loan; and the association in turn subscribes for the same

[3] *Sixth Annual Report of the Farm Credit Administration* (1938), p. 17.

amount of stock in the district federal land bank. The association pledges its stock as security for the association's endorsement of the mortgage; and the farmer borrower pledges his stock with the association as collateral security for his loan.

The members of the association elect a board of directors of five or more members. The chief executive officer is a secretary-treasurer, who is not required to be a stockholder. A schoolteacher, a minister, or some retired businessman may take the office. Although the associations are co-operative in nature, some have perished from neglect, and others have failed for the same reasons that so many banks did during the twenties and early thirties. At the present time, perhaps 1,000 associations are hopelessly insolvent because of (1) claims arising out of the associations' endorsements of loans made by farmers through them and (2) inability to pay claims of former stockholders who have paid off their loans but have not been reimbursed for the par value of their stock.

In recent years steps have been taken to rebuild the national farm loan associations into sound self-supporting and self-servicing agencies. Associations have been consolidated, overlapping territories have been eliminated, more efficient local personnel has been employed, common boards of directors have been elected, and the same administrative officers often serve two associations. The Farm Credit Act of 1937 made other provisions for rehabilitation of associations whose capital was impaired. The number of associations has been reduced from 5,000 to 3,400, and these are operating out of 1,513 offices. The current policy of the federal land banks is to cut down on their staffs and pay the local associations to service the local business of the federal land banks.[4]

Federal Farm Mortgage Corporation.—In 1933 and 1934 Congress made provisions for emergency loans to financially distressed farmers who could not secure funds through normal channels. Congress, in the Emergency Farm Loan Mortgage Act of May, 1933, appropriated $200,000,000 of government funds to be lent by the Federal Land Bank Commissioner. In January, 1934, Congress provided that these funds should be handled by a newly created agency, the Federal Farm Mortgage Corporation, which is managed by an ex officio board of three directors, the governor of the Federal Farm

---

[4] See *The Eleventh Annual Report of the Farm Credit Administration* (1943-44), pp. 27-29.

Credit Administration, the Secretary of the Treasury, and the Federal Land Bank Commissioner.

The corporation assumed the $200,000,000 in "credits" granted in 1933 as its authorized capital, but most of its funds have been obtained from issuance of bonds unconditionally guaranteed both as to interest and as to principal by the United States government. The amount of bonds outstanding at one time was limited to

ILLUSTRATION IX

FARM CREDIT ADMINISTRATION

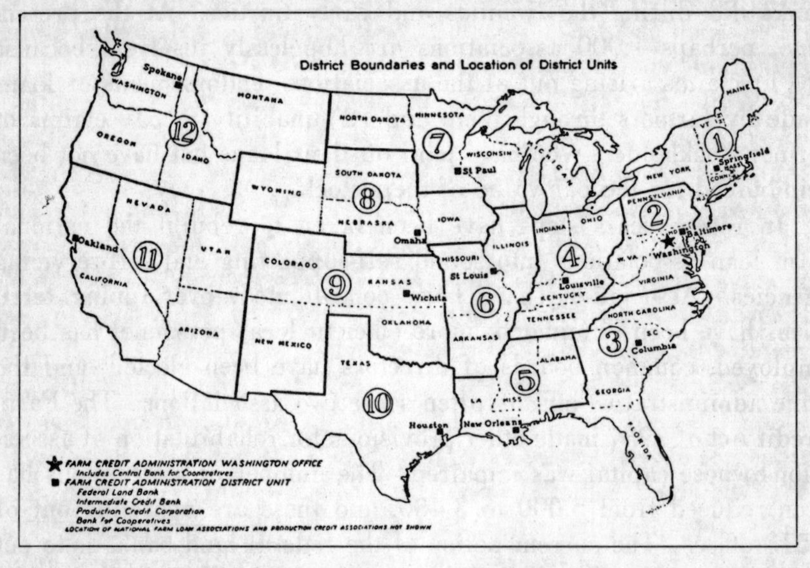

Source: Farm Credit Administration.

$2,000,000,000. Loans to farmers were made by the Land Bank Commissioner for the Federal Farm Mortgage Corporation. In addition, the corporation purchased bonds of the federal land banks during 1934 and 1935.

From May 12, 1933, to June 30, 1944, farmers obtained over 622,000 Land Bank Commissioner loans, amounting to $1,100,-000,000, of which 35.5 per cent represented first mortgages and 64.5 per cent second mortgages. By June 30, 1944, these loans had been reduced to less than $370,000,000.[5]

[5] *Ibid.*, p. 33.

Federal Intermediate Credit System Was Organized in 1923

The 12 federal intermediate credit banks are entirely owned by the government.[6] They were created to lend or to rediscount for commercial banks, co-operative associations, and others so as to assist in the orderly marketing and production of farm crops. Thus during the fiscal year 1944 the intermediate credit banks extended about $950,000,000 in credit for making advances to or rediscounting paper for production credit associations ($645,000,000), banks for co-operatives ($210,000,000), state and national banks and other privately owned financial institutions ($88,000,000), and to others such as farmers' co-operative marketing, production, storage, and other types of associations (about $7,000,000).

While the 12 intermediate credit banks have a capital of $60,000,000, accumulated earned surplus and reserves of $30,000,-000, and a revolving fund in the United States Treasury on which they may draw, most of their operations are with borrowed funds. Thus during 1944 they sold their collateral trust debentures in the money market and thereby raised $440,000,000 with which to operate. Most of the debentures run for terms of from three to twelve months, but they may be issued for a longer period. The intermediate credit banks are able to borrow at low rates, which they pass along to co-operatives, rural banks, and production credit associations. Their rediscount rates cannot be more than 1 per cent higher than the rate at which they borrow or for which they sell their debentures. The present discount rate is 1½ per cent per annum. Farmer borrowers benefit directly from these rates, because no note is eligible for discount or eligible as collateral for loans if the rate of interest is more than 3 per cent per annum above the intermediate credit banks' discount rate.

In summarizing the loan activities of the intermediate credit banks, one should recognize that they have problems not faced by the other systems. They are forced to deal with institutions over which they have little control. Many of the institutions to which they lend have nothing to pledge except assets, such as cotton, wheat, and tobacco. There is no capital backlog, because many of the co-operative associations have no general assets and often no stock issues.

---

[6] There is a statutory requirement that at the end of each fiscal year each bank must pay to the government 25 per cent of its net earnings after provisions for losses, expenses, and reserves. The amount in 1944 was $231,000.

Banks for Co-operatives Were Organized in 1933

The 13 banks for co-operatives (12 regional and one central bank) were created to lend to farmers' co-operatives. To be eligible for loans, co-operative associations must (1) operate for the mutual benefit of members, (2) do most of their business with members, (3) limit voting privileges so that no one has more than one vote, (4) limit dividends to 8 per cent a year, and (5) arrange so that 90 per cent of the voting rights are held by producers. Eligible borrowers must be associations engaged in one or more of the following activities: "(1) processing, preparing for market, handling, or marketing farm products; (2) purchasing, testing, grading, processing, distributing, or furnishing farm supplies; or (3) furnishing the farm business services."[7]

Three distinct types of loans are made for co-operatives: working capital loans, commodity loans, and facility loans. Working capital loans are made to supplement capital put up by members of co-operative associations. They are secured by liens on real estate, equipment, commodities, accounts receivable, inventories, notes, etc. These loans may be made for such time periods as conditions seem to justify, and most of them are retired at the end of the marketing season for which they were made.

Commodity loans are short term and secured by first liens on approved farm products or farm supplies. Facility loans are made to marketing associations to help finance purchase or lease of physical property required in the carrying on of their business of handling, storing, processing, and merchandising agricultural products. The loans are secured by mortgages on the property being financed. Most loans are made for ten years or less and are repaid in installments, and no loan is made for an amount in excess of 60 per cent of the appraised value of the facility.

Because of the war, there were great demands made upon farmers and their co-operative associations. The increase in foodstuffs and other inventories and their higher value made it necessary for the co-operative associations to borrow over $470,000,000 from the banks for co-operatives.

The 12 regional banks for co-operatives have a total capital

[7] *Sixth Annual Report of the Farm Credit Administration* (1938), p. 51.

of almost $105,000,000 and the central bank has a capital of over $77,000,000, most of which is provided by the government ($177,000,000). The remainder is owned by the co-operative associations, which must invest 5 per cent of their borrowed funds in the stock of the lending bank. Since many loans are for marketing purposes, and since the co-operatives can liquidate their stock when their loans are repaid, the nongovernment investment in the banks for co-operatives is small.

The co-operative banks may and do discount or rediscount their paper with the intermediate credit banks. In addition, the governor of the Federal Farm Credit Administration may make available additional government funds from the revolving fund established by the Agricultural Marketing Act of 1929, which was originally $500,000,000.

The co-operative bank system's primary function is to promote the co-operative farm marketing movement, which has a three-point program: (1) to increase farmers' profits, (2) to eliminate or reduce the middlemen's profit, and (3) to lower prices and increase the volume of sales to consumers. The commissioner's office is helping the movement in many ways other than financial. Its services include management suggestions, accounting and auditing services, legal advice on methods of organization, general advice on the co-operative organization movement, case studies on operating methods, and general field studies of commodity industries.

Production Credit System Was Organized in 1933

The function of this system is to provide farmers and stockmen with short-term credit usually supplied by commercial banks and cattle loan companies. It consists of the (1) production credit division of Federal Farm Credit Administration, under supervision of the Production Credit Commissioner, (2) 12 regional production credit corporations, and (3) 517 production credit associations with a membership of over 355,000.

The primary function of the 12 production credit corporations is to organize, supervise, and help finance production credit associations. All their funds are obtained from their earnings and the capital subscribed by the governor of the Farm Credit Administration in behalf of the government. It now aggregates $115,000,000, being invested in preferred stock (Class A) of the production credit associations and in approved securities to pay operating expenses.

The local production credit associations correspond to the farm loan associations in the Federal Land Bank System. They are formed by ten or more farmers, with territorial allotments providing enough business to permit sound operation and yet provide prompt and convenient services to farmer borrowers. The territory served may include several counties. Fifteen associations serve specialized producers, fruitgrowers, and livestock operators and have territories which cover entire states. Some associations which had insufficient business were merged or liquidated. Charters are granted by the district production credit corporation, but they must be approved by the governor of the Federal Farm Credit Administration.

Active borrowers from the association must buy stock (Class B) equal to 5 per cent of their loans. Inactive borrowers, production credit corporations, and investors purchase Class A stock. Only active borrowers have the right to vote, thereby keeping the control of associations in their hands. Each individual has one vote, irrespective of the number of Class B shares owned. Of the total number of members in 1944, 285,600 were Class B stockholders, and 69,500 were Class A stockholders.

Production credit associations make secured loans to their members to finance: (1) production, harvesting, and marketing of crops; (2) poultry raising, repairs of farm buildings, and liquidation of debts incurred for general agricultural purposes; (3) breeding, fattening, and marketing of livestock; and (4) purchase of feed, seed, farm machinery, and other items (including labor) required for general agricultural purposes. Acceptable security includes first mortgage liens on growing crops, livestock, and personal property. The loan period may be three years, but most loans run for less than one year. The minimum loan was fixed by law at $50. The maximum unsecured loan may be one-fifth and the maximum secured loan may be one-half of the association's capital and surplus. Interest rates charged on loans vary, depending somewhat on what the association must pay to the intermediate credit banks for loans. An inspection fee of at least $2.00 and other direct expenses incurred in making a loan must be paid by the borrower. Borrowers operate on a budget loan plan, repayment of loans may be made in instalments, and interest is charged upon the funds only for the time they are being used. Most of the associations are now charging farmers less for funds than would their local banks and are competing with them for short-term loans.

Associations may borrow from federal intermediate credit banks but not from other banks or agencies without specific approval of the governor of the Federal Farm Credit Administration. This forces the associations to meet not only the standards for loans made by their production credit corporations but also the rediscount requirements of the intermediate credit banks from which they normally secure most of their short-term and intermediate-term funds. The farmers' interest in the production credit associations increased during the war because of their greater need for credit. However, the government, through the production credit corporations, still has the dominant interest in the local associations. If reserves and unapplied earnings of the associations are added to farmer-owned stock, the government interest is still more than one-half of the capital used by the associations.

Other Farm Lending Agencies and Corporations

In this chapter emphasis has been placed on the operation of the larger and permanent agencies in the farm credit field, but there are others in the Department of Agriculture that should be noted in order to complete the picture of farm credit financing.

The Commodity Credit Corporation was organized in 1933 to make loans to farmers for the purpose of financing the carrying and orderly marketing of corn, wheat, and other farm products. Usually banks and other local lending agencies make the loans under an agreement with the corporation to purchase the "paper" from them under certain conditions. In communities where funds may not be obtained locally, the corporation may lend directly to farmers.

In order to "peg" the prices of certain farm products, the corporation places a loan value on the commodities pledged that may be higher than the current market price of the product. Later, if the product is sold for less than the value of the loan, the loss is absorbed by the corporation. Under the law, which provides for annual appraisal of the assets, the Treasury makes payments to the corporation in order to keep its capital unimpaired. Usually the products (chiefly cotton, corn, and wheat) are stored wherever produced (field warehousing), under conditions specified by the corporation. In effect, the producers are selling the products to the corporation under repurchase options upon payment of their notes. The commodities now held by the corporation (chiefly cotton) are valued at more than $1,000,000,000.

The Rural Electrification Administration was originally created by executive order in May, 1935, and was given statutory recognition in the Rural Electrification Act of 1936. It is primarily a lending agency to make loans "for rural electrification and the furnishing of electric energy to persons in rural areas." Loans are made permitting farm buildings to be served by power companies and to individuals for the purpose of financing the wiring of premises and the acquisition and installation of electrical plumbing appliances and equipment. Co-operatives are the chief borrowers from the Rural Electrification Administration. The influence of the agency has been greater than the amount of loans ($407,000,000 to date) indicates, because many private companies have taken an increasing interest in the movement. The demand for rural electrification is only a part of the movement to make farm life more attractive, and, incidentally, it has proven to be good business, because a study in New York State indicates that comparable farms are worth about $1,000 more if they have central electric service.[8]

Farm Security Administration was created in 1936 to replace the Resettlement Administration and the earlier Division of Subsistence Homesteads of the Department of the Interior. Among the projects financed by these agencies were Garden City communities, "Greenbelt" towns, and subsistence farms for industrial workers. Resettlement Administration secured most of its funds from the relief appropriations of Congress and made numerous relief loans to individuals and co-operatives that fitted into the general program of rural relief and rehabilitation.

The Bankhead-Jones Tenant Act (July, 1937) authorized the Secretary of Agriculture to make loans to American citizens who are farm laborers, tenants, and share croppers for acquiring land and making improvements thereon, at low interest rates (3 per cent)

---

[8] Department of Agricultural Economics and Farm Management, *Farm Economics* (published by Cornell University), No. 112 (April, 1939), p. 2752.

and for a long period of time (forty years). The fixed annual payments including principal and interest are but 5.326 per cent, which makes the capital costs of changing the borrower's status from tenant to owner very low. The chief activity of the division of Farm Security Administration, which is responsible for the administration of this act, has been in the South, where the farm-tenant problem has been most acute.[9]

In addition to the administration of the farm-tenant financing program, the Farm Security Administration is in charge of making loans to low-income farmers for rehabilitation, for temporary emergencies, and to facilitate farmers' community and co-operative enterprises. Most of the loans made to individuals are made to those who "cannot obtain credit from any other source and must agree to follow approved farming practices." These loans bear an interest rate of 5 per cent and must be repaid in from one to ten years.

Under terms of the Water Facilities Act, loans are made to farmers in arid and semiarid states for the purpose of supplying small water facilities, such as wells, pumps, stock pools, windmills, and minor irrigation facilities. In addition to the $500,000 approved by Congress, the Farm Security Administration has made $3,000,000 available to carry out this program.

Federal Crop Insurance Corporation was created by amendments to the Agricultural Adjustment Act (February, 1938) with a capital stock of $100,000,000 subscribed by the government. It is supervised by the Secretary of Agriculture, and all the directors are appointed by the secretary of that department.

With the increase in consumer income during World War II, the farm situation has changed from one seemingly calling for farm subsidies to one wherein the farmers are able to have a decent income without subsidization. With enough people having enough income to buy the foods they have always wanted, there is no longer a need for governmental assistance with farm production. Where the old type of policy has been followed (cotton production), the effect has been to create an artificial price and supply situation that is harmful to export trade and domestic consumption.

---

[9] Larsen, H. C., "Tenant-Purchase Plan," *Agricultural Finance Review*, United States Department of Agriculture, Bureau of Agricultural Economics, Vol. II, No. 2 (November, 1939), pp. 35-43.

QUESTIONS AND PROBLEMS

1. Explain why there will always be a farm debt problem in the United States. Compare to the mortgage debt situation in England.
2. Identify the farmers' chief sources of (*a*) short-term credit, (*b*) intermediate credit, and (*c*) long-term credit.
3. The government gives more attention to the credit problems of the farmers than to those of commerce and industry. Is this favoritism justified? Why? Is it necessary? Why?
4. What are the four farm credit divisions? How are they similar in organization? How are they co-ordinated? (See Charts XV and XVI.)
5. Discuss the trends in farm mortgage holdings from 1934 to 1944 of (*a*) federal land banks, (*b*) Land Bank Commissioner, (*c*) individuals, (*d*) commercial banks, and (*e*) insurance companies. Use Table 49.
6. How do the following institutions secure funds with which to operate: (*a*) federal land banks, (*b*) Land Bank Commissioner, (*c*) banks for co-operatives, and (*d*) production credit corporations?
7. What are the advantages of amortizing a farm mortgage loan to the farmer and to the investor in farm mortgage bonds? Are the latter repaid in driblets? Explain.
8. Compare production credit associations and national farm loan associations as to (*a*) ownership, (*b*) management, and (*c*) operations.
9. How may commercial banks participate in farm mortgage financing without entering the farm mortgage field directly? Are trust institutions of assistance? Explain.
10. What constructive steps have been taken to co-ordinate the different federal farm credit agencies at the national, regional, and local levels? What additional steps may be taken?
11. What are the principles on which the organization of Federal Farm Credit is based? Are they sound?
12. Which of the four types of regional banks in the farm credit system are most accurately described as government banks? Why?
13. To what extent does the success of the farm program depend upon the amount of farm income? How has the war affected the Federal Farm Credit Administration?
14. In the long run, which of the two chief approaches to the farm problem is the correct one: lower costs of farming or higher farm prices? Why? Is there a tendency to subsidize uneconomic farms? Explain.
15. Describe the public offering of bonds made by the federal land banks during the last two years. Reference: *Annual Reports of the Farm Credit Administration.*

16. "Institutional lenders have recognized the dangers of repeating the experiences of World War I and have thus far generally avoided making loans on an inflated basis." Is this still true? (*The 11th Annual Report of the Farm Credit Administration 1943-44*, p. 2.)

17. Every time a new emergency loan is placed in the Farm Credit Administration, the tendency is to build up the program for government lending and submerge the co-operative feature of this system. Do you agree? Who is at fault, Congress or the Federal Farm Credit Administration?

REFERENCES

American Institute of Banking. *Farm Credit Administration.* New York: American Institute of Banking, 1934.

Anderson, G. E. "Government Lending Agencies," *Banking*, November, 1938, pp. 97-110, 112-25.

Annual Reports of the Farm Credit Administration and Federal Farm Loan Board. Washington, D.C.: U.S. Government Printing Office.

Baird, F., and Benner, C. L. *Ten Years of the Federal Intermediate Credits.* Washington, D.C.: Brookings Institution, 1933.

Edmiston, H., and Anderson, G. "United States Government Corporations and Agencies in 1939," *Federal Reserve Bulletin*, April, 1940, pp. 298-305.

Horton, D. C., Larsen, H. C., and Wall, N. J. *Farm Mortgage Credit Facilities in United States.* Washington, D.C.: Department of Agriculture, No. 478, 1942.

Lee, V. P. *Principles of Agricultural Credit.* New York: McGraw-Hill Book Co., Inc., 1930.

Norton, W. A. "The Country Bank," *Harvard Business Review*, Vol. XVII, No. 4 (1939), pp. 402-13.

Palyi, Melchior. "Principles of Mortgage Banking Regulation in Europe," *Journal of Business of the University of Chicago*, Vol. VII, Part II, (October, 1934), pp. 1-38.

Production Credit Associations, A Case Study in Federal Credit Subsidies. Washington, D.C.: Citizens National Committee, Inc., 1944.

Schwartz, C. H. *Financial Study of Joint Stock Land Banks; A Chapter in Farm Mortgage Banking.* Washington, D.C.: Washington College Press, 1938.

Sparks, E. S. *History and Theory of Agricultural Credit in the United States.* New York: Thomas Y. Crowell Co., 1932.

Twentieth Century Fund. *Debts and Recovery, 1929-1937*, pp. 133-56. New York: Twentieth Century Fund, Inc.

United States Department of Agriculture, Bureau of Agricultural Economics. *Agricultural Finance Review,* Vols. I, II, and V (1938, 1939, and 1942).

Woodruff, A. M. *Farm Mortgage Loans of Life Insurance Companies.* New Haven: Yale University Press, 1937.

Wright, Ivan. *Bank Credit and Agriculture,* chaps. i and ii. New York: McGraw-Hill Book Co., Inc., 1922.

Wright, Ivan. *Farm Mortgage Financing,* chaps. i-vi. New York: McGraw-Hill Book Co., Inc., 1923.

Chapter XXXVI

FOREIGN BANKING SYSTEMS

American and Foreign Banking Systems Compared

Central Banks.—In the central banking field the United States has 12 central banks, and most foreign countries have but one. Today this difference is less significant than in 1932, because of the greater concentration of power in the hands of the Board of Governors of the Federal Reserve System. Now the United States may have a national credit policy, while recognizing certain basic differences in credit needs of different regions in the United States.

A second point of difference between central banking abroad as compared with the United States is the relationship between the central banks and institutions and individuals other than banks and bankers. Most of the older foreign central banks accept deposits, make loans, provide general clearing and collection facilities, and otherwise deal directly with individuals and nonbanking firms as well as with commercial banks and the government. This situation helps to explain the hundreds of branches of the central banks of both France and Germany.

For the most part, central banks which have been formed since 1913 have followed the model of the Federal Reserve System in that they serve as the banks of issue, bankers' banks, and bankers for their governments, but not as institutions to compete actively with existing banking institutions. As a result, the new central banks tend to have, relative to areas served, few or no branches.

When likenesses are considered, there is a marked similarity in the relationship of governments and central banks here and abroad. Central banks serve as fiscal agents for their governments, hold government deposits, and co-operate with government officials in stabilizing credit conditions. The central banks have acquired or are in the process of acquiring a monopoly of bank note issues. Irrespective of whether the central banks are owned by private investors, the government, or both, they are public institutions which place service ahead of profit-making

The central banks are bankers' banks. The functions performed by foreign central banks for their commercial banks are similar to those performed by the Federal Reserve banks in the United States for member banks. They hold the commercial banks' reserve deposits, discount their paper, supply them with currency, and serve as transfer agents. Central banks' activities are so similar, that one former Reserve official in the United States wrote: "These central banking organizations in different countries are extraordinarily alike. Even though their charters and special forms of organization may differ widely, they all perform in general the same sorts of functions. This is so true that an officer of the Federal Reserve System might walk through the doors of the Bank of England, the Bank of France, or the Bank of Japan, and feel himself immediately at home."[1]

Commercial Banking.—The greatest difference in banking and bank organization in foreign systems as compared to the United States is found in the noncentral bank field. The United States still retains the eighteenth and early nineteenth century small local unit banking system, which has been displaced abroad by a few large banks with hundreds of branches. Most of the commercial banking abroad is done in each country by a dozen or fewer banks.

The United States has more banks than all the remainder of the world combined, but this does not mean that it has better banking services. For example, England and Wales, with a combined population of less than one-third of that of the United States and an even smaller percentage of income, have 15 banks and over 10,000 banking offices. The United States has 14,500 commercial banks and 18,000 banking offices. On a per capita basis, there are twice as many banking offices in Great Britain scattered over one-fiftieth of the area. In so far as banking functions are concerned, those performed by commercial banks abroad are similar to those performed in the United States.

A second major difference in commercial banking abroad and in the United States is in the amount of government regulation. For the last one hundred years there has been more regulation in the United States than in any other country. There are a number of reasons for this situation, including forty-nine "free banking" laws, the large number of banks which were often managed by inexperi-

[1] Burgess, W. R., *The Reserve Banks and the Money Market* (rev. ed.), p. 1.

enced bankers, and the dynamic or speculative nature of American industry.

Before World War II, with the exception of Germany, relatively few regulatory requirements were placed upon bankers in foreign countries as compared to the large number in the United States. This does not mean that foreign banking systems were not subject to considerable regulation. Since World War I, and particularly since 1930, foreign countries adopted "a systematic control of banking operations."[2] During and since World War II, there has been a tendency abroad to increase control over banks in order to regiment all the productive resources behind the war effort; and, because of the postwar economic uncertainty, many countries are still retaining their wartime control over finance and banks. In some countries democratic governments have nationalized not only central banks but also some of the largest commercial banks in order to acquire ownership of the chief sources of the means of payment. The financial control over the economic life of France that rested with a few hundred families controlling the chief banks led to their being nationalized by the French government.

In the past, the difficulties of foreign banking systems have included bank failures, bank panics, bank holidays, and a general collapse of the commercial banking structure. In some countries the most recent of these panics occurred in the nineteenth century, while in others they coincided with the depression in the United States in the 1930's. The reactions abroad to these conditions were similar to those in the United States. In some countries government credit was widely used to bolster private credit structures, but as yet no foreign country has provided for insurance of deposits.

Noncommercial Banking.—No foreign country has achieved the complexity and completeness of banking institutions in the noncommercial banking fields as that found in the United States. In certain foreign countries there has been a tendency to strengthen and to expand existing sources of credit available to farmers, homeowners, and individuals rather than create new credit-granting institutions. The more complex development of noncommercial banking in the United States is due in part to the local nature of American commercial banks; the absence of regional or national branch banking, which

---

[2] Allen, A. M., and Others, *Commercial Banking Legislation and Control*, p. 6.

prevents the financially able banks from coming to the assistance of underbanked areas; and the complexity of American laws due to the existence of forty-nine legislative bodies. In the United States, local or state groups are continually experimenting with some new type of financial service arising out of some special need.

The commercial banks of the United States possess over one-half of the commercial banking resources of the world, and the noncommercial banking institutions possess an even larger percentage of the world's investment banking resources. In comparing the banking facilities of the United States with those of foreign countries, the dominant importance of the former must be kept in mind. For example, the New York banks alone possess far more assets than those of all the English banks, and the two largest banks in New York possess more assets than all the Canadian banks.

Banking Abroad

Prior to World War II, foreign banking problems were similar to those in the United States. Bankers were complaining about the prevailing low interest rates, the scarcity of commercial paper, the increasing dependence on government securities as an outlet for commercial banking funds, and the increase in governmental interference in banking. Bank managements were forced to operate on smaller margins of profit, to pay lower interest rates on deposits, and to install bookkeeping machinery and modern methods of accounting. As in the United States during the thirties, there was criticism of bankers and banking, both warranted and unwarranted.

Between the world wars, the structural changes in banking were: a decline in the relative importance of commercial banking in the great majority of countries; an increase in the relative importance of various types of savings institutions, building and loan associations, and other types of thrift agencies; and an increase in the importance of public or semipublic institutions in practically all countries.[3]

Commercial banks were holding more cash and other items of a cash nature. Their predominantly commercial nature had declined with a decrease in commercial loans and in discounts of commercial bills of exchange. In many foreign exchange markets the com-

[3] League of Nations, Economic Intelligence Service, *Money and Banking, 1938/39*, Vol. I, pp. 72-82.

mercial bill was of little or no importance because of the decline in foreign trade, the prevalence of exchange control, and the wider use of telegraphic or cable exchange. The commercial bill was of less importance in domestic trade because of the decline in the volume of trade financed on a credit basis and the increase in the use of overdraft as a means of financing in Great Britain and other western European countries.[4]

The loss in liquidity, because of the decline in commercial bills, was largely offset by the increase in Treasury bills. As in the United States, government securities held a dominant position in the loan and investment portfolios of most foreign banks. "By 1936, Government securities accounted for a particularly high proportion of total commercial bank assets in Canada (29.6%), the United States (33.1%), South Africa (26.2%), and the United Kingdom (23.8%). . . . ."[5] Treasury bills were estimated to have made up over one-half the total discounts of commercial banks in France and Italy, 38 per cent in Argentina, and 31 per cent in Germany. During World War II, government securities came to be an even more important part of the portfolios of banks, and in most warring countries they represented three-fourths or more of all the earning assets of the commercial banks.

During World War II, banking developments abroad were similar to those in the United States. There were no important structural changes in the organization of banking systems other than the creation of new central banks in certain countries (Ireland, 1942; Nicaragua, 1941; Paraguay, 1941). While underlying causes varied, there was, throughout the world, a manyfold increase in bank credit either in the form of bank notes or in the form of deposits, or both.

Canadian Banking System

Of all the foreign banking systems, the one of greatest interest to most students of banking in the United States is that of Canada. Depositors in the United States have looked with envy at the safety

[4] Banks' customers open lines of credit with banks which permit them to overdraw their accounts. Sellers receive cash payments for goods sold, which they prefer to the old system of drawing bills and then discounting them. See Committee on Finance and Industry, *Minutes of Evidence*, Vol. I, p. 36.

[5] League of Nations, *op. cit.*, p. 85.

record of the Canadian banking system, which has not had a single bank failure since 1924. The question often raised is: If Canadian bankers can prevent failure why cannot American bankers do as well? The answer is to be found, in part, in the organization of the Canadian banking system, with its inherent diversification of risks, the prohibition on real estate loans, and the elasticity of the currency system.

The Canadian banking system, in one sense, dates from the formation of the Confederation in 1867. In that year the federal government was given control of banking and currency. The first Dominion Bank Act was passed in 1871, although before that date many banks had been chartered by the provinces. The oldest of these banks are the Bank of Montreal (1817), Quebec Bank (1818), Bank of Canada (1818), Bank of Upper Canada (1818), and Bank of New Brunswick (1820); others soon followed. Their charters were very similar to that of the first Bank of the United States, containing in some cases the same essential clauses and even the same phraseology. The Dominion Bank Act of 1871 reflected this influence, and so it is "generally agreed that the Canadian banking system is a direct descendant of the first Bank of the United States. . . . ."[6]

The Bank Act of 1871 gave the commercial banks charters for but ten years, and ever since the unique policy of giving decennial charters and renewals has been followed. This policy forces the legislature to weigh its banking system every ten years and has brought about periodic improvements. This is in sharp contrast to the spasmodic type of legislation (after considerable damage has been done) that has characterized American and other countries' banking policies. Only on two occasions—from 1910 to 1913 and from 1933 to 1934—has the revision been postponed. The last decennial act of August 14, 1944, extended the charters of the 10 existing banks for another ten-year period.[7]

The Canadian Banking System consists of a Central Bank of Canada, established in 1935; an Industrial Development Bank established in 1945; 10 chartered banks with 3,000 branches; and government and other savings banks. In addition, there are a number

---

[6] *Report of the Royal Commission on Banking and Currency in Canada, 1933*, p. 15.

[7] *Journal of the Empire* (London, Empire Parliamentary Association), Vol. XXVI, No. 1 (February, 1945), pp. 130-39.

of specialized financial institutions which are in part a result of the restrictions placed upon the chartered banks. The most important of these noncommercial banks are trust companies, which are often affiliated with the commercial banks; mortgage banks; building and loan associations; about 100 bond or investment houses; co-operative credit unions; and other rural credit institutions.

The Bank of Canada.—This central bank began operations on March 11, 1935, and rapidly assumed an important place in Canadian banking. Although it began operation as a privately owned bank, it was completely nationalized in 1938. The chief function of the bank, as expressed in the preamble of the act creating it, is as follows:

Whereas it is desirable to establish a central bank in Canada to regulate credit and currency in the best interest of the economic life of the nation, to control and protect the external value of the national monetary unit and to mitigate by its influence fluctuations in the general level of production, trade, prices and employment, so far as may be possible within the scope of monetary action, and generally to promote the economic and financial welfare of the Dominion.

The Bank of Canada has its head office in Ottawa and may establish branches at home and abroad subject to governmental approval. In 1938 the capital was reduced from $10,100,000 to $5,000,000, all of which is owned by the Dominion government.[8] The bank is now under the control of a governor, a deputy-governor, and a board of eleven directors, all of whom are appointed by the Minister of Finance with the approval of the Governor in Council. The term of office for directors is three years, and that of the governor and deputy-governor is seven years. Directors may be reappointed, must be selected from diversified occupations, and may be removed, if incapacitated, by resolution of the board with the approval of the Governor in Council.[9] The Deputy Minister of Finance is an ex officio member of the board of directors but has no vote.

The Bank of Canada was given the note issue privilege, and provisions were made for the gradual retirement of the notes of the

---

[8] The privately held shares were redeemed at a premium of 18.4 per cent, and 2,000 shares ($100,000) owned by the government were cancelled.

[9] The amended act excludes from directorship (1) non-British subjects not ordinarily residents in Canada, (2) public employees, (3) directors, officers, and employees of chartered banks, and (4) individuals who are 75 years old or older (see "Amendment of the Bank of Canada Act," *Federal Reserve Bulletin*, August, 1938, p. 652).

chartered banks. After January 1, 1950, it will have a monopoly of note issue. A 25 per cent reserve is required to be kept against its notes and demand liabilities, either in the form of gold or in the form of foreign exchange. The notes, which are printed in English and French, are redeemable in gold bars weighing 400 ounces, but redemption may be suspended by the government and is suspended at the present time.[10]

Chartered banks must carry a 5 per cent legal reserve against deposits either as an account with the Bank of Canada or in their own vaults in the form of Bank of Canada notes, or as a combination of the two. (Deposits in about 150 foreign branches of Canadian banks are excluded.) Thus bank notes of the Bank of Canada may serve as the reserve for chartered banks, which is a more generous arrangement than in the United States, where Federal Reserve notes are not permitted to be counted as member bank reserves. The Dominion government, the provincial governments, and savings banks may keep deposits with the Bank of Canada, which has been designated as the fiscal agent of the Dominion government. The Bank of Canada is authorized to keep deposits with foreign central banks and the Bank for International Settlements, and to establish other correspondent relationships with foreign central banks. Canada was among the first to approve the Bretton Woods Agreements.

The authorized credit operations of the bank are similar to those of other central banks, including the rights to buy and sell (1) gold and silver; (2) foreign exchange and prime bank and commercial bills; (3) a limited amount of agricultural paper; (4) short-term government securities; (5) other government securities in limited amounts; and (6) securities issued by the United States of America or the United Kingdom maturing in six months or less, but not in excess of 25 per cent of the bank's paid-in capital. The bank may make advances to Canadian banks on any of the foregoing as collateral. During the war years the credit policy of the Bank of Canada was determined by war needs. It purchased government securities so as

[10] In April, 1940, an order in Council (Exchange Fund Order) provided for the sale of the bank's gold holdings to the Foreign Exchange Control Board and for continued suspension of the bank's minimum gold reserve requirement. Over $225,000,000 in gold was sold under this order. As a result of the passage of the United Kingdom Finance Act of March, 1942, the bank's holdings of sterling exchange were purchased by the Foreign Exchange Control Board and made available to the government. The proceeds of gold and sterling exchange sales were invested primarily in government securities.

to make central bank credit available (1) to offset loss of cash reserves of chartered banks, owing to the increase in money in circulation; (2) to replace the notes of chartered banks that had been retired; and (3) to expand the volume of cash reserves of banks.[11]

Chartered or Commercial Banking.—Contrary to the general opinion among American bankers, Canadian bankers are subject to considerable statutory and detailed regulation by the Dominion government, and the general trend has been to increase the amount of government supervision and regulation at each decennial revision of the banking legislation. Although nationalization is a current issue, the position of the government in 1944 was that it was not necessary to extend government ownership beyond the central bank at that time. The banking structure, made up of ten large chartered banks and their hundreds of branches, permits close internal supervision of branches by the head offices and adjustments to changes in economic conditions without epidemics of bank failures, so common in the United States. For example, Canada was "overbanked" in 1920, banking offices having increased from 2,962 in 1913 to 4,676 in 1920; but the subsequent adjustments reduced the number to 3,300. This adjustment was made with but one bank failure, and this failure was due to dishonesty and mismanagement.

The minimum subscribed capital for chartered banks is $500,000, one-half of which must be paid in before business may start. Shareholders are doubly liable, but provisions have been made to eliminate this clause when all their bank notes have been retired. Dividends are limited to 8 per cent per annum, unless the surplus is at least equal to 30 per cent of the paid-in capital. Actually most of the banks have a surplus equal to or in excess of the paid-in capital.

As in most banking systems, the right of note issue was originally granted to the Canadian banks, and, as in the case of the first Bank of the United States, the maximum issue was fixed at an amount equal to each bank's total paid-in capital.[12]

In 1890 provisions were made for a safety fund system for noteholders, called the Bank Circulation Redemption Fund. Each

[11] *Federal Reserve Bulletin*, April, 1945, pp. 334-39.

[12] By 1908 the elasticity of Canadian bank note circulation had just about reached its limit. The law was changed in 1908 to permit a bank to issue notes in excess of its paid-in capital during the crop harvesting season. This provision gave desirable elasticity to the note issue system (see Holladay, James, "The Currency of Canada," *American Economic Review*, Vol. XXIV [June, 1934], pp. 266-78).

bank contributed 5 per cent of its average yearly circulation to this fund; but, if necessary, banks were subject to further assessment. This fund was kept on deposit with the Minister of Finance (since 1944 with the Bank of Canada), and, when a bank failed, the fund was drawn upon to take up that percentage of the bank's notes not covered by other assets. The bank notes of a defunct bank bear interest from the date of failure until they are redeemed, and this provision prevents them from circulating at a discount during the liquidation period. The Bank Act of 1944 made the Bank of Canada the exclusive agency for redeeming notes of defunct banks and, after 1950, of existing banks.

The Bank Act of 1934 provided that the amount of bank notes be reduced at the rate of 5 per cent per annum for the first five years of the decennial period and 10 per cent per annum for the last five years. The Bank Act of 1944 took away the right of banks, other than the central bank, to issue or reissue notes in Canada (effective January 1, 1945) and provided for complete retirement of such notes after January 1, 1950. The law still permits the chartered banks of Canada to issue notes outside of Canada in amounts limited to 10 per cent of each bank's paid-in capital.

The chartered banks are permitted to engage in "such business generally as appertains to the business of banking." They receive both demand and time deposits, the latter being defined as those subject to fifteen days' notice of withdrawal. No charge for collection of checks and other items for services, or because of "activity," may be made against a checking account except upon expressed agreement between the customer and his bank. Collection and certain commission charges are regulated by law, and in this detail, as in many others, Canadian banks are subject to greater regulation than those in the United States.

Checks are cleared rapidly and efficiently through regional clearing centers which have been organized by the Canadian Bankers' Association. The results of these daily clearings are reported by telegraph to the Bank of Canada and are settled each day by crediting and debiting clearing balances kept there for this purpose by the chartered banks. Withdrawals of savings accounts are subject to notice, but this right of the banks is rarely used, and the savings accounts are often withdrawn by check.

As in the United States, reserves are classified into two categories

—cash and secondary reserves. The first includes all currency items, checks on other banks, and balances kept with foreign banks and those located elsewhere in Canada. Total cash reserves generally average a little more than 10 per cent. Secondary reserves are liquid earning assets, which include short-term promises to pay of governments, call and short-term collateral loans, and certain types of debentures and bonds of railways and other corporations.

Loans are made by local managers, but investments are usually made by the head office. The branch manager may make individual loans up to a maximum fixed for him by the head office. The amount depends upon the ability of individual managers, the collateral offered for the loans, and the size of the branch. Requests for loans above this maximum are passed upon by a district supervisor or the head office. Mobility of funds is obtained through the head office, which may withdraw funds from one branch and place them at the disposal of another. Loan policies are similar to those in the United States, large loans being made under lines of credit.

Part of the success of the Canadian Banking System is due to the restriction placed upon real estate mortgage lending. However, the banks may acquire real property in order to protect the banks from losses due to bad debts; but they must not hold real property, except that required in their own business, for more than seven years. While mortgages may be taken as additional security, loans are primarily protected in other ways. The restriction on this type of lending has eliminated from Canadian banks the most troublesome asset found in American banks' statements. In addition, there are general restrictions placed upon lending on the security of merchandise, goods, and wares, except as specified in the act. In order to facilitate the business of the borrowers, the banks receive merely an assignment of the merchandise or grain pledged as security for the loans. The legal result is that the banks become preferred general creditors.

The 1944 revision of the banking code permits banks to lend to farmers for longer terms, so that banks can finance their intermediate credit needs. The maximum interest rate was cut from 7 to 6 per cent for general loans. However, banks were authorized to discount at 5 per cent unsecured personal loans repayable in monthly instalments. This permits banks to compete more freely with small-loan companies for small loans ($500 maximum) that are not secured or secured only by insurance on the life of the borrower.

The almost universal tendency to restrict bank loans to officers is found in Canadian statutory laws as well as in those of the United States and other countries. Canadian banks are forbidden to make loans secured by their own stock, as is also true in the United States, and in addition are prohibited from making loans on any bank stock.[13] If the latter provision had been in force in the United States during the 1920's, many weird interofficer loans among banks based upon one another's bank stock would have been avoided, with a wholesome decrease in speculation in bank stock. Directors must be owners of shares of their banks, varying in amounts from $3,000 to $5,000, depending on the size of the bank.

Canadian chartered banks are not restricted in their investment operations, and many of them act as middlemen in the distribution of securities. In 1933 it was proposed that the banks be forbidden to engage in the underwriting of securities, but this suggestion was not adopted, even though a similar law was passed in the United States. The types of securities which may be underwritten are limited to governments, government guaranteed securities, and those of certain public utility companies. With the exception of the last group, the securities which may be underwritten are practically the same as those handled by American banks under the Banking Act of 1935.

Each bank must be audited at least once a year by two professional auditors elected by shareholders from a list selected by the Minister of Finance. The latter is authorized to require reports from the auditors (they must be from different auditing firms) upon the condition and management of the banks; and he may order a more complete or supplementary audit at any time. The information demanded may involve questions of insufficient security for large loans and other detailed matters.

Since 1924 an office known as Inspector-General of Banks has been located in the Department of Finance. This officer is required to examine the affairs of each bank at least annually. Since 1937 he has been required to check currently to see if banks are meeting the statutory requirement in regard to minimum reserves against deposits. The powers of the Inspector-General are as broad as those of

[13] Officers may not borrow more than $1,000 without the consent of the directors, and no more than $10,000 with their consent. Approval of two-thirds of the directors is necessary before loans of more than 5 per cent of paid-in capital may be made to any director or any company in which the director is an executive, partner, or shareholder (see Allen and Others, *op. cit.*, p. 112).

American examiners, including the right to suspend banks if they are insolvent.

The requirements in case of reporting are more extensive than those in the United States. In addition to the auditors' and the Inspector-General's reports, the banks must file (1) statements as to interest charges; (2) an appraisal of the market value of real estate held; (3) a monthly return of assets and liabilities on a schedule form provided by the Minister of Finance, which includes reports on subsidiary companies owned or controlled by the banks; (4) the names and addresses of directors and concerns with which they are affiliated; (5) a statement of dividends, interest, and deposits unclaimed for a five-year period; and (6) reports on many other items, some of which are made to the Central Bank of Canada.

The Canadian Bankers' Association performs many co-operative services for banks, and it sponsors the very important educational program conducted by Canadian banks. This educational program is similar to that of the American Institute of Banking. But most of the success in training the well-managed staffs for which Canadian banks are famous is due to the existence of the branch banking system and the opportunity it offers the management to shift personnel from position to position according to individual administrative records. The personnel of a branch may be small or large—may number two or three or several hundred. It is not the policy of Canadian banks to appoint a local man as branch manager, as is true in the United States. In Canada banking is a career, and bankers move up through the system rather than through one banking office.

Noncommercial Banks in Canada.—The chartered banks in Canada are permitted to perform investment banking functions. They participate in syndicates formed to sell securities to the public; they may purchase and sell securities on their own accounts; and they may accept orders to buy and sell securities for their clients, thereby serving them in the capacity of brokers. In addition to the chartered banks, there are over 100 investment banks that act both as brokers and as dealers. They have formed the Investment Bankers' Association of Canada. In the Dominion there are 7 different stock exchanges, the two oldest and most important being the Montreal Stock Exchange and the Toronto Stock Exchange.

Mortgage loan companies are chartered by both the Dominion government and the provincial governments. Ten of these companies have federal charters. The principal function of mortgage loan companies is to lend money secured by real estate. Building and loan associations, similar to those in the United States, have been formed chiefly to aid in home financing. Originally they were home builders' clubs similar to those first started in Pennsylvania. As in the United States, they are chartered by both national and provincial governments, and they secure funds from savings deposits and from the sale of stock. Rural credit institutions make loans to farmers to finance capital and short-term agricultural needs, and many of these institutions are financed by the provincial governments. In the six western provinces, amortization loans are made through the Canadian Farm Loan Board.

In Canada the trust business is separated from the commercial banking business, but many trust companies are closely allied to banks. The trust companies accept savings deposits and act as executors, trustees, and administrators, and serve in other fiduciary capacities. They also perform many agency and other trust services for corporations as well as for individuals. These functions are similar to those of trust institutions in the United States, and their loan activities are similar to those of the mortgage loan companies. Their funds are invested in first mortgages on real estate and other secured paper as provided by law. They are chartered by both the central and the provincial governments.

A system of People's Banks (Caisses Populaires) was introduced in the province of Quebec by Commander Desjardins. These institutions are similar to the People's Banks of Italy and France. Loans, made only to members, may be secured by first mortgages on real property, by bonds, or by tangible personal property. There are over 250 People's Banks located chiefly in Quebec, with total assets of about $10,000,000. They are the oldest co-operative credit banks in North America.

Canada has a post office savings bank, with over 1,300 offices; provincial savings banks operated by the governments of Ontario and Alberta; two institutions operated under the Quebec Savings Bank Act; and one Penny Bank. The postal savings banks, which began operations in 1868, are similar to those of the United States. Sums of $1.00 or multiples thereof may be deposited, and the maximum deposit account is fixed at $5,000, exclusive of interest.

The Ontario Savings Bank has been in operation since 1922, and most of its funds are used to finance farm loans. Seventeen branches are in operation, and total deposits are about $25,000,000. In Alberta, the provincial treasury receives savings deposits, issues demand savings certificates for terms of from one to three years, and issues time certificates which bear a higher interest rate. Total savings deposits in the provincial treasury of Alberta are approximately $10,000,000.

The two Quebec savings banks are similar to chartered institutions in that they are not permitted to invest in real estate. They carry on commercial banking as well as savings banking. The charters of these two banks are subject to decennial revision. Provisions for Penny Banks, which correspond to school savings banks in the United States, were made in 1927. The Penny Bank of Ontario has been the only one formed. Because of the savings facilities offered by the chartered commercial banks and because of the excellent records of these institutions, specialized savings banking has been less widely developed in Canada than in the United States, Japan, and other countries. Most of the specialized savings institutions are government owned. Small loan companies operate under special legislation that permits installment loans at an interest rate of 2 per cent per month for periods up to eighteen months.

In 1944 Parliament made provisions for the Industrial Development Bank, which is a subsidiary of the Bank of Canada. Its function is to assist small and new business enterprises. It may lend, may guarantee loans, and may enter into underwriting agreements with corporations. The bank's stock of $25,000,000 is owned by the Bank of Canada. It may sell bonds and debentures up to three times the amount of its capital and reserve funds.

Argentine Banking System

Among the most important banking systems in South America is that of the Argentine Republic. It was among the first of the South American countries to modernize its banking system. The present structural organization dates from March 28, 1935, when a series of six banking laws became effective. In Argentina, before 1935, as in the United States before 1914, the banking system suffered from the absence of a strong central bank and from divided responsibility for supervision of banks. Certain bank functions were divided among different government departments and the Banco de la Nación Argentina.

Since Argentina is a country subject to wide cyclical swings in trade and prices, the need for a central bank to stabilize currency and credit services was particularly urgent.[14] During the 1930-34 depression in Argentina, the banking system was severely affected by low commodity prices, frozen loans, and bank failures. Part of this situation was due to the overexpansion of bank credit, and this in turn was partly due to the wide variety of banks operating in Argentina. These included local banks dealing in agricultural paper, mortgages, and other types of nonliquid paper; national banks with branches scattered throughout the republic; and foreign banks chiefly interested in foreign trade financing. The country was overbanked, competition among banks was keen, and unsound practices were common; bank failures were the natural aftermath. Since 1939, the chief credit problem of Argentina and other Latin-American countries has been to prevent inflation based on the influx of gold and foreign credit arising out of the favorable trade balances of these countries.[15]

Central Bank of the Argentine Republic.—In 1935 a central bank was created in Argentina for the following purposes:

> (*a*) To concentrate sufficient reserves to moderate the consequences of fluctuations in exports and investments of foreign capital, on currency, credit and commercial activity, in order to maintain the value of the currency; (*b*) To regulate the volume of credit and the means of payment, adapting them to the real volume of trade; (c) To promote the liquidity and sound functioning of bank credit; and to apply the provisions of the banking law for the inspection, examination, and regulation of banks; (*d*) To act as financial agent and counsellor of the Government in foreign or internal credit operations and in the issue and service of public loans.[16]

The Central Bank is owned by the government. It is managed by a president and vice-president and a board of twelve directors. The bank was given the usual powers associated with a central bank—powers to issue notes, to buy and sell gold and foreign exchange, to accept deposits, to rediscount for shareholding (member) and nonshareholding banks, to make advances to member banks, to act as

---

[14] See "Fourth Annual Report of the Central Bank of the Argentine Republic," *Federal Reserve Bulletin*, 1939, pp. 1077-94.

[15] "Monetary Developments in Latin America," *Federal Reserve Bulletin*, June, 1945, pp. 519-30.

[16] Central Bank of Argentine Republic, Law 12, 155, Art. 3.

correspondent for foreign central banks and for the Bank for International Settlements, to act as fiscal agent and investment banker for the government, and to administer the clearinghouse system. It has a monopoly of paper money issues of 5 pesos (1 peso equals 30 cents) or higher denomination notes. The bank's total assets are over 4,250,000,000 pesos, as compared to about 6,500,000,000 in the other commercial banks. At the close of the war, about 80 per cent of the bank's assets were in gold and foreign exchange.[17] The chief liability of the bank is in the form of note issues, part of which are backed by noninterest bearing bonds. The Central Bank must keep a reserve in gold, foreign currency, or exchange equivalent to at least 25 per cent of its notes in circulation and its demand liabilities.[18]

Commercial Banking in Argentina.—In the General Banking Law of 1935, banking was defined as a business principally dependent on the acceptance of time and demand deposits. Each bank with a capital of 1,000,000 pesos (about $300,000) or more was required to subscribe to the capital of the new central bank. Fifty banks were involved, including the Banco de la Nación Argentina, 28 national banks, 12 foreign banks, and 9 provincial or mixed banks. In addition to buying stock, these banks had to keep at least two-thirds of their required reserves with the Central Bank, unless modified by regulatory decrees. Their position is similar to that of member banks of the Federal Reserve System in the United States. All other banks (nonmember) were required to apply to the government, through the Central Bank, for authority to continue their operations; and by the end of that year (1935) fifty-five applications had been received.[19]

The responsibility for regulation and supervision of the banks, under general provisions of the law, is in the hands of the officials of the Central Bank. This is superior to the type of divided control that now exists in the United States. Each bank, whether a member or not, must submit a monthly report to the Central Bank. The prescribed form includes a statement of the bank's condition, plus other information. A credit department examines the applications for advances and discounts, and a bank examination department inspects banks and also takes responsibility for liquidation of suspended banks.

[17] See League of Nations, *Money and Banking, 1942-44*, pp. 79-81.

[18] Art. 40, Law 12, 155.

[19] "First Annual Report of the Central Bank of the Argentine Republic," *Federal Reserve Bulletin*, July, 1936, p. 560.

Interest paid on demand and time deposits must be at least 3 and 1 per cent less, respectively, than the rediscount rate of the Central Bank, a principle taken from English banking. The definitions of the two classes of deposits are practically the same as those used in the United States. The purpose of deposit interest rate control is to eliminate cutthroat competition for funds, which has been one of the weakening factors in Argentine banking. The size of interest-bearing savings accounts are limited to not more than 20,000 pesos for individuals and not more than 50,000 pesos for co-operative or mutual savings banks. In case of bank failure, savings depositors with accounts up to 5,000 pesos are given a preferred claim to general assets. The banks are required to keep a minimum cash reserve of 16 per cent against demand and 8 per cent against time deposits. Member banks must keep two-thirds of their cash reserves with the Central Bank, and the balance may be held in notes or coins.

Under Article 4 of the Banking Law (12,156), all banks are forbidden: (1) to retain real estate not required for use of the bank and its branches, and this amount must be reduced to 20 per cent of the bank's capital and 50 per cent of its surplus; (2) to hold real estate acquired because of bad debts more than four years (may be extended under exceptional circumstances if the Central Bank approves); (3) to retain shares for more than two years after acquisition; (4) to retain debentures for more than two years if they represent more than 20 per cent of the capital of the issuing corporation or more than 10 per cent of the bank's capital and 25 per cent of its surplus; and (5) to participate directly in any commercial, industrial, agricultural, or other enterprises. The purposes of these restrictions were to secure the liquidity of assets and to prevent the banks from being involved in nonbanking enterprises. On the other hand, there were no legal minimum capital requirements, no restrictions on underwriting of securities, no limits on loans to one name, no prohibitions on loans to bank officers, no double liability provisions on the holding of bank stock, little regulation of security loans, and no system of licensing branches. In August, 1935, the government created an exchange equalization fund to maintain minimum prices for certain agricultural products and to reduce the cost of servicing the public debt.

Summary.—The experiences of Argentina in recent years have been typical of those of other Latin-American countries. An increase in exports, a shortage of consumer goods, an increase in gold reserves, and an increase in money and credit have brought about an inflationary development which has been due largely to foreign developments rather than to domestic expenditures for war purposes, as has been the case in the United States, European countries, and elsewhere.

Among the measures taken to prevent or to limit inflation were: repatriation of Argentine foreign indebtedness, particularly sterling bonds; increases in investments and bank balances abroad; sales of certificates by the central bank to "mop up" liquid funds in the market; and holding new foreign capital funds on deposit with the central bank until that institution approved of their investment as being noninflationary. The deflationary experiences of Argentina during the early 1930's and the inflationary experiences of the early 1940's illustrate the extent to which this country and the other Latin-American countries are dependent on foreign trade and therefore on economic developments beyond their control. However, the increases in their holdings of gold stock and foreign exchange during the war have improved their monetary and banking positions both at home and abroad. Because of the nature of their import and export trade, the Latin-American countries should benefit more than most nations from international economic stability resulting from the International Monetary Fund and the Bank for Reconstruction and Development.

QUESTIONS AND PROBLEMS

1. What are the advantages of a brief study of foreign banking systems to a student of money and banking?
2. Does the following quotation suggest the importance of studying the two foreign banking systems considered in this chapter? "The dollar area . . . . may be said to comprise most countries in the western hemisphere, which hold large balances in New York and settle their foreign payments mainly by transfers of U.S. dollars" ("Annual Report of the Bank for International Settlements," *Federal Reserve Bulletin* [September, 1945], p. 883).
3. Compare the activities of the central banks established before the organization of the Federal Reserve System to those formed since its organization. Explain.
4. "The greatest differences in banking and bank organization in foreign systems as compared to the United States is found in the non-central field." Discuss.
5. To what extent do banking trends abroad parallel those in the United States? Illustrate.

6. Justify this statement: "The Canadian banking system is a direct descendant of the first Bank of the United States. . . ." Why did not the American system develop along similar lines?
7. Explain and give advantages of the decennial chartering and renewal policy in Canada.
8. In what way does Canadian banking reflect the influence of British and American banking practices and organization?
9. Compare the ways in which "overbanking" is adjusted in Canada and the United States.
10. Is the assumption of many Americans that Canadian banks are unregulated justified? Explain.
11. Explain: "The Bank of Canada . . . . acts as a stabilizing influence upon the economy of the country . . . . " (*source:* The Royal Bank of Canada, *Monthly Letter*, December, 1944).
12. In what way may the Bank of Canada contribute to the following? "The Government desires and expects that low interest rates will continue after the war. It proposes to pursue a monetary policy which will encourage through low interest rates, the investment of funds in productive capital contributing to employment" ("Canadian White Paper on Employment and Income," *Federal Reserve Bulletin*, June, 1945, p. 542).
13. "The only reason advanced in favour of private, as against national, control is the fear of political influence. . . . I believe the selection of directors and executive officials by a Government would be as wise as that of a body of shareholders, the majority of whom vote by proxy" (*source:* Brownlee, J. E., "Memorandum," *Report of the Royal Commission on Banking and Currency in Canada*, p. 93). Do you agree?
14. One of the distinctive features of the banking system in Argentina is the simplicity of its organization. Discuss.
15. Compare the relationship between the central and noncentral banks in Argentina to those in the United States.
16. Compare the central banks of Canada and the Argentine as to (*a*) organization, (*b*) management, (*c*) functions, and (*d*) powers.
17. What are the advantages of the English and Argentine systems of deposit interest rate regulation? Compare to the American system.
18. What is the chief explanation for the increase in deposits in Canada as compared to Argentina and other Latin-American countries?
19. What is the significance of the following: "Latin America as a whole now has official gold and foreign exchange reserves of over 3.3 billion dollars —four times their 1939 level" ("Monetary Developments in Latin America," *Federal Reserve Bulletin*, June, 1945, p. 530)?

REFERENCES

See end of Chapter XXXVII

CHAPTER XXXVII

FOREIGN BANKING SYSTEMS *(Continued)*

The English Banking System

The English banking system consists of (1) a central bank, the Bank of England, which operates 9 branches; (2) 13 joint-stock or deposit banks with which the public in general deals and which operate 8,300 branches; (3) accepting houses or merchant bankers; (4) discount houses; (5) savings banks; and (6) a few specialized institutions operating in other fields as well as in banking.

The Bank of England.—The Bank of England (the official title is Governors and Company of the Bank of England) was chartered in 1694. It is generally considered to be the oldest central bank, but its charter was granted twenty-eight years after that of the Riksbank, or the central bank of Sweden. The Bank of England received its charter from the government in return for a loan of £1,200,000 at 8 per cent, which was equal to the amount of its capital. The original charter was for twelve years, and subsequent renewals have "coincided generally with the grants of additional loans to the State."[1]

The Bank Act of 1844 permits continuance of the bank's charter subject to termination by one year's notice. In return for the original loan, the bank was permitted to issue notes in an amount equal to its capital. Originally the bank carried on an extensive private banking business which included, in addition to note issue, the receipt of deposits and the making of loans on real estate and other collateral to individuals, banks, and other business units.

The present position of the Bank of England as head of the English banking system is due to its relations to the government and to its monopoly of the privilege of note issue, fully acquired in 1923. The relationship between the bank and the government, which has been particularly close in recent years, was publicly recognized in 1946, when the bank was "nationalized." In 1844, note circulation was brought under control by limiting note issues of all banks, except that of the Bank of England, to the then existing amounts. Provisions

[1] Committee on Finance and Industry, *Report*, p. 25.

were made for the retirement of non-Bank of England notes if issuing banks amalgamated with joint-stock companies not having the privilege of note issue or for other reasons. With the retirement of notes of other banks, the Bank of England was authorized to expand its fiduciary circulation by two-thirds of the amount of the contraction.

The present organization of the Bank of England is traced to the Bank Act of 1844 (also known as the Peel Act). Currency and banking reformers urged Parliament to separate the two functions: banking and note issue. They asked: Why give the jobs of creating money and of managing it to the same institutions? Reformers held that a union of the two was productive of evil, because bankers were too optimistic during booms and too pessimistic during depressions, creating too much money during the former period and overcontracting during the latter. When Parliament passed the Peel Act, it frankly recognized the fact that bank credit in the form of bank notes could be and had been a cause of economic disturbances, a principle which modern reformers have been applying to our modern system of deposit currency. Parliament was willing to allow elasticity of note issue to be sacrificed in order to prevent overissuance. During panics England suffered because of this situation, but not as much as one would expect, because the law has been suspended on several occasions (1847, 1857, 1866, and 1914).

The Peel Act provided for two departments—that of note issue and that of banking. The note issue department issues notes and holds the collateral given to it by the banking department. Notes must be secured by 100 per cent collateral in the form of securities or gold. Practically all the notes issued by this department are secured by government obligations ("fiduciary issue"), and others are secured by gold ("gold-covered issue"), although these have been unimportant since 1939. The status of the issue department is similar to that of the Federal Reserve agents in the Federal Reserve System; the officers in charge are trustees of the coins, gold, securities, and notes in their possession.

The Bank of England now has a monoply of note issue in England and Wales. Since 1928 the bank has been permitted to issue 10 shilling and 1 pound notes, but before that date the smallest bank notes were in denominations of 5 pounds. Before World War I England depended upon gold coins as hand-to-hand money in denominations between the 5 pound note and the largest silver coins. During

World War I the gold coins were impounded, and Treasury notes (Bradburys) took their place. The Amalgamation Act of 1928 provided for the withdrawal of Treasury notes and their replacement by small-denomination Bank of England notes.

The activities of the banking department of the Bank of England are similar to those of any central bank. It acts as a bankers' bank, serves as the fiscal agent for the government, and holds government deposits. Although banks are not required to do so, they usually keep part of their reserves with the Bank of England. Unlike the Federal Reserve bank, the Bank of England accepts deposits from and makes loans to the general public and carries on a general banking business. At the present time, the assets of the bank consist primarily of government securities. In this respect the portfolio of the Bank of England is similar to that of the Federal Reserve banks. The separation of the banking and issue departments is so complete that the banking department counts as an asset the Bank of England's own notes. All the profits from note issue go to the government.

The devices of credit control used by the Bank of England are similar to those which were used in the United States before 1935. They include raising and lowering the discount rate, open market operations, and moral suasion. The last is far more effective in England than in the United States, because the officers of the few large commercial banks feel a greater responsibility for credit conditions than the officers of the 14,500 banks in the United States could ever be made to feel. Before World War I the Bank of England borrowed funds it did not want in order to make the discount rate effective, but now greater reliance is being placed upon open market operations, which have been much more efficacious since the establishment of the equalization fund.

The Bank of England is managed by a board of 16 directors, a governor, and deputy governor (called the "court"), all of whom, under the terms of the Bank Bill of 1946, are appointed by the Crown (government). The 16 directors serve for terms of 4 years, so arranged that there will be 4 new directors appointed each year; the governor and deputy governor are appointed for 5 year terms. Prior to nationalization, the directors were elected annually, and, until World War I, a new governor was usually selected every 2 years. However, Mr. Montagu Norman, who came into office at that time, remained for 24 years as the head of the bank. Under the present law, a governor may be reappointed, as may a director. The Bank Act cut the number of directors from 24 to 16 but made no change in the organization of the staff of the bank, which is now being operated under the old governor and deputy governor. At the time of nationalization, each stock-holder received 3 per cent government bonds in amounts which were sufficient to provide him with the same annual income paid by the bank during the last 20 years (12 per cent).[2]

The bank issues a weekly statement which is printed in American as well as in English financial publications. In the past, no further information was revealed about the bank's affairs, and no reasons were given to the public or to Parliament for changes in rediscount rates or other credit policies. According to one officer, "The Bank of England is practically free to do whatever it likes with one exception . . . there is only one real prohibition that is imposed upon the Bank, and that is in the Tonnage Act of 1694 which says that in order not to oppress His Majesty's subjects the Bank is to be debarred for all time from using any of its funds in dealing in merchandise or wares of any description."[3] Now that the bank has been nationalized, it is expected that an annual report will be made of its operations.

There are two separate bank statements, one covering the circulation department and the other covering the banking department. (See Table 50.) Only a few items in the latter need explaining. "Proprietors' capital" and "rest" include the same items as represented by "capital" and "surplus" in American bank statements. "Public deposits" include the current accounts of the government's departments and funds and the accounts of the National Debt Commissioners. "Bankers' deposits" are chiefly those of the 11 members of the London Clearinghouse Association. "Other accounts" include the deposits of English banks whose principal activities are outside the United Kingdom and those of foreign central banks, colonial banks, discount houses, merchant banks, issue or investment houses, Indian and colonial governments, and private customers. Government securities" represent direct obligations of the British government (long-term, ways and means advances, and Treasury bills) and reflect the open market operations of the Bank of England. "Discounts and advances" consist of Treasury and commercial bills

[2] *The Economist*, Vol. CXLIX (October 13, 1945), pp. 513-14; 532-33.

[3] Committee on Finance and Industry, *Minutes of Evidence*, Vol. I, p. 6.

discounted and loans made to discount houses, bill brokers, and private customers. "Other securities" include commercial bills purchased by the bank on its own initiative, any balance held with foreign central banks, and other securities held except obligations of the British government. "Gold and silver coins" consist chiefly of silver coins; and "notes" are the promises to pay of the currency department, counted as assets by the banking department.

TABLE 50

BANK OF ENGLAND STATEMENT, 1936 AND 1946
(In Millions of Pounds Sterling)

Liabilities	1936	1946	Assets	1936	1946
Issue department:			Government debt...	£ 11.00	£ 11.00
Notes in circulation..........	£442.7	£1,331.4	Other government securities........	245.90	1,388.30
Notes in banking department....	65.9	68.8	Other securities....	3.00	0.70
			Silver coin.........	0.04	0.01
			Amount of fiduciary issue...........	£260.00	£1,400.00
			Gold coin and gold bullion..........	248.60*	0.20†
Total.....	£508.6	£1,400.2	Total.....	£508.60	£1,400.20
Banking departm't.:					
Proprietors' capital...........	£ 14.5	£ 14.5	Government securities............	£ 80.20	£ 230.00
Rest............	3.1	3.4			
Public deposits...	27.7	13.1	Discounts and advances..........	6.60	8.30
Other deposits...	127.9	287.6	Other securities....	19.50	14.30
Bankers.......	(86.5)	(232.8)	Notes.............	65.90	65.50
Other accounts.	(41.4)	(54.8)	Gold and silver coins	1.00	0.50
Total.....	£173.2	£ 318.6	Total.....	£173.20	£ 318.60

* Valued at 77s. 9d. per fine ounce.

† Valued at 172s. 3d. per fine ounce.

Dates: Week-ends of October 28, 1936 and January 30, 1946.

Joint-Stock Companies.—Early English banking was dependent on the note issue privilege. The Act of 1742 restricted note issues to the Bank of England and to partnerships of six or less.[4] The latter were the smallest and weakest banks, and, as a result banking con-

[4] The Act of 1742 confirmed and defined the monopoly of note issue first introduced in the Charter of 1709 (see Andréadès, A., *A History of the Bank of England,* p. 148).

ditions were unsatisfactory in the provinces. This situation was corrected in part after the panic of 1825 by giving the right of note issue to all banks outside a radius of sixty-five miles from London. This same act permitted the Bank of England to establish branches.[5] Note issue conditions were still unsatisfactory, and finally, as a result of the panic of 1837–40, the Peel Act was passed. It limited the privilege of note issue to existing banks and provided that, if any of these banks retired their note issues, the notes could be replaced up to two-thirds of their amount by an enlargement of the fiduciary issue of the Bank of England.

The restriction placed upon note issues naturally hastened the development of deposit banking, as was true also in the United States. After the passage of the Act of 1826, the question was raised—could a joint-stock bank with any number of partners be organized in London? This question was specifically answered in 1833, when an act was passed permitting chartered banks to exist in London territory but without the note issue privilege. Since that date the development of joint-stock companies has been rapid. The large London joint-stock companies dominate banking in the London territory and, by merging and opening branches, have extended their influence throughout Great Britain. Now 13 incorporated banks with 8,000 branches carry on most of the banking in England. At the end of 1945 the Big Five—namely, Midland, Barclays, Lloyds, Westminster, and National Provincial—had total assets of £4,420,000,000, or about 85 per cent of the resources of the English chartered banks.

The checking system is widely developed in England, giving the desirable quality of elasticity to her currency and credit system. There are a few local clearinghouses, but, for the most part, checks are cleared through London. The branch banks send their checks to their head offices in London, and the head offices clear through the London Clearing House. There are three divisions: city (financial district), metropolitan London, and country. Settlements of clearing balances are made by checks drawn on the Bank of England.

There are two classes of deposits—"current accounts" (demand) and "deposit accounts" (subject to seven days' notice). The Bank

[5] The branches of the Bank of England were first actively employed in the commercial business in the district in which they were situated; but now they are centers for the collection of balances and are used to hold government balances and to serve as currency centers for the receipt and distribution of coin and currency (Committee on Finance and Industry, *Minutes of Evidence,* Vol. I, p. 6).

of England pays no interest on deposits; other banks rarely pay interest on current accounts, and the rate paid on time deposits is tied by London Clearing House agreement to the Bank of England's discount rate (normally 2 per cent below, but when the bank rate was 2 per cent, it was fixed at 1/2 of 1 per cent). The discount houses, trustee (savings) banks, and other agencies normally pay a slightly higher rate than the London Clearing House members. The practice of tying the interest rate on deposits to the rediscount rate of the Central Bank makes the rate changes of the Bank of England far more significant than similar rate changes of the Federal Reserve banks in the United States.

The most interesting aspect of English banking, considered from the American viewpoint, is the absence of governmental regulation. With the exception of note issue, no specific restrictions are placed on English banking. There are no special or general banking laws, and the banks have the same legal status as any other joint-stock company. Each bank must file with the Registrar of Joint-Stock Companies a certified balance sheet, a list of shareholders, and a list of places where branches are located. There must be an annual meeting of stockholders.

Clause 4 of the Bank Bill of 1946 has come in for considerable speculation because of the effects it may have on policies of commercial banks. This clause empowers the Bank of England to "request information from or make recommendations to bankers" and, with the authorization of the Treasury, to "issue directions to any banker for the purpose of securing that effect is given to any such request or recommendation." This clause may be used to implement any policy that is now established by custom, or it may be used to direct banking resources into new channels. Since the initiative will come from the bank and not from the Treasury, it has been suggested that this clause will make no fundamental difference in bank policy, because in the past no individual bank was in a position to take lightly a suggestion of the Central Bank. On the other hand, it seems unlikely that a court (governors and directors) appointed by the government would not be willing to "initiate" action if suggested by the government.

In granting credit, emphasis is placed upon short-term commercial loans, and this emphasis is so great that English bankers have been criticized because they have neglected industry. Before the war, 44 per cent of the banks' earning resources were employed in advances to private borrowers, and 46 per cent represented direct and indirect advances to the government. In 1946 the corresponding percentages were 17 and 70.

Other war changes of importance are: (1) a shift in the chief sources of earnings, with those from advances and investments declining from 71 per cent to 42 per cent of the total; (2) decrease in gross profit margins as interest rates declined; (3) increase in expenses because of higher living costs and repairs to buildings; and (4) doubling of total resources with no change in capital.[6] Some of the solutions to the problems suggested by these changes are higher bank service charges to bolster earnings, sales of new capital so as to increase the capital-deposit ratio from about 1 to 30 to something approaching the pre-war 1 to 15 ratio.

English banks are not required by law to keep reserves against deposits, but they normally keep on hand, or on deposit with the Bank of England or a second bank, funds equal to from 10 to 15 per cent of deposits. This is considerably less than the legal and working reserves of American banks, but English bank reserves can be used more efficiently because of their branch banking system. Because of the size and geographical distribution of branches, multiple borrowing (borrowing from more than one bank) is unnecessary. Although English banks prefer to have advances cleared up yearly, many loans have been extended for long periods of time. There are no bank examiners to insist that loans be called, written down, or written off the books, and so the borrowers and bankers have all the freedom necessary to work out their debtor-creditor problems.

One system of extending credit which has been popular for years in England has been lending under lines of credit that permit customers to overdraw their checking accounts. This method of lending has the advantage of permitting customers to use credit only when it is needed. There is no need to secure funds in advance which will lie idle during part of the loan period, and part of them may not be used at all. The interest rate on overdrafts is slightly higher than on other types of loans, and fees may be charged.

Other English Financial Institutions.—The joint-stock banks have not only absorbed most of the incorporated banks but have also

---

[6] "The Banks in 1946," *The Economist*, Vol. CL (January 26, 1946), pp. 139-40.

taken over many of the activities of private bankers and accepting houses. Other institutions in the English banking system are discount houses, investment banks, colonial banks, branches of dominion banks and foreign banks, trustee (mutual) savings banks, and postal savings banks. Recently, many of the large joint-stock banks have formed trust departments and have gone into the fiduciary business. Investment banks are less numerous and far less important than in the United States, but discount houses, bill brokers, and accepting houses are more important, because of the wider use of trade and bankers' acceptances. The cash discount open-book system is rarely used in England or in other European countries; but the banks permit their customers to overdraw their accounts under credit agreements, which is an important factor in the decline in the volume of domestic trade and bankers' acceptances.

Merchant bankers, sometimes called "accepting houses," do a business similar to that of the accepting banks in New York. The merchant bankers compete with joint-stock banks for the accepting business, and, unlike the private banks in New York, they still retain a large percentage of the business. In addition to accepting bills, many of them act as investment bankers in placing long-term issues on the London capital market.[7]

Discount houses are specialists in the money market and handle domestic (inland) and foreign bills and short-term securities of the government (Treasury bills). They are similar to the acceptance dealers in the New York market and, like the latter, are now dealing more in Treasury bills than in commercial bills of exchange. There are 7 companies, 17 private firms, and 8 running brokers (who act only as intermediaries).

In addition to the savings accounts in the commercial banks, English depositors keep large sums in the Postal Savings banks, and the 370 Trustee Savings banks. In addition, national savings certificates are sold to those who prefer these instruments to savings accounts. During the war, over £1,500,000,000 were sold to investors. In addition almost £1,000,000,000 of 3 per cent defense bonds, £2,800,000,000 of 3 per cent savings bonds, and £3,400,000,000 of 2½ per cent war bonds were sold. The defense and

[7] Many of the merchant banking houses are of foreign origin; for example, Goschen, Hambro, Klienwort, and Lazard (see Committee on Finance and Industry, *Minutes of Evidence,* Vol. I, p. 70).

savings bonds remained on tap (that is, could be purchased at any time) until December 25, 1945.[8] The postal savings system is much older (1861) and relatively much more important in England than in the United States. The investment in national savings certificates and savings deposits increased primarily because the rates paid by the government and trustee savings banks are higher than those paid by commercial banks.

The problem of mortgage credit has been a minor one in England and Wales because of the inheritance system and the concentration in ownership of real property. As a result of this situation, real estate collateral is considered among the highest types that may be offered as security for a loan, and most of the agricultural and other mortgage needs have been cared for without specialized agricultural mortgage institutions.

English Equalization Fund.—England's departure from the gold standard in 1931 saved that country from much of the deflation to which the United States was subjected in 1932. Credit disturbances were less severe, industrial production less contracted, and banks were under less liquidation pressure than in the United States. Since 1931 the Bank of England and the equalization fund have been successful in giving England, and the countries whose currencies are allied to her currency unit, fairly stable domestic price levels.

The Scottish Banking System

This system has been called the "ideal banking system" and consequently warrants consideration. There are 8 Scottish banks, which operate 1,600 branches and subbranches. The oldest bank (Bank of Scotland) was established a year after the Bank of England. It was given a monopoly of note issue for twenty-one years, but this was not renewed. Now the 8 banks have the note issue privilege, and there are about £60,000,000 in circulation and competing with the legal tender notes of the Bank of England. There is no central bank in Scotland, but the banks are closely linked to the London money market either by ownership (4 banks) or through their London offices. However, the Scottish banks are usually lenders rather than borrowers in this market.[9]

---

[8] This is similar to the sale of savings bonds in the United States.

[9] See Committee on Finance and Industry, *Minutes of Evidence*, Vol. I, pp. 156-66.

The business of the banks includes the acceptance of current accounts (demand deposits) and time deposits on which interest is paid. Since 1928 most of them have dealt with savings depositors through savings departments, a fairly new practice in both England and Scotland when compared to the United States. Special features of the Scottish banking system are the cash credit system, uniformity of rates, and two types of bank directors. The cash credit system, which is two hundred years old, permits the borrower to repay from day to day with an interest charge only on the balance used by the customer. During an earlier period these loans were guaranteed by co-obligors or cosigners, the forerunner of a principle of lending that has played such an important part in Morris Plan and similar types of personal lending in the United States.

There is co-operation among Scottish banks similar to that found among members of local clearinghouse associations in the United States. A committee of the general managers meets regularly, and at these meetings general policies and uniform rules with regard to interest charges, commissions, and other matters of common interest are adopted. Loans of all types are made, but those of a short-term nature are favored. The banks are of moderate size, and emphasis is placed on personal relationships between clients and their banks. Overdraft lending is common, as it is in England, and is usually unsecured; but it is always arranged for under previously granted lines of credit. As is common in the United States, some large accounts are shared by two or more banks. Now most of the assets of the banks are invested in government securities, and loans and advances are of minor importance.[10]

The 8 banks of Scotland are managed by boards of directors of the ordinary type, which are responsible for their respective banks. In addition, each bank has a Board of Extraordinary Directors. This office is an honorary one, and the distinction is more nominal than real; but it is superior to the American system of adding inactive directors for "window-dressing" purposes.

The German Banking System

The German banking system is the largest on the Continent, tracing its origin to the organization of the Hamburg Giro Bank in

[10] See League of Nations, *Money and Banking, 1942/44*, p. 196.

1619, which was modelled after the Bank of Amsterdam. The banking system includes a central bank (Reichsbank) operating 455 branches[11] and several institutions associated with the Reichsbank;[12] the Big Six (Deutsche Bank, Dresdner Bank, Bank der Deutschen Arbeit, Commerzbank, Reichskreditgesellschaft, Berlin Handelsgesellschaft), with hundreds of branches; private banks; state banks; many small banks whose operations are confined to the communes, cities, and provinces within which they are located; 2,000 savings banks, with over 10,000 branches and agencies organized by municipalities and guaranteed by them; postal savings system with over 50,000 offices; mortgage banks; credit co-operatives; and a number of specialized institutions.

The chief characteristics of the pre-occupation German banking system were: (1) highly centralized control and supervision; (2) the dominant position of the Reichsbank, not only as a bank, but as an agency of the government in the control of foreign exchange and other totalitarian matters; (3) importance of savings banks, holding about 60 per cent of bank deposits; (4) heavy investments of the German banking system in government obligations (about 80 per cent of total bank deposits); (5) extensive use of the *Giroverkehr*, or "cashless transfer" system, which largely replaced the check system as known in the United States; and (6) the close relationship between banks, industry, and the government.

Although badly shattered by the war, most of the banks still function, in so far as any bank can function in an economic vacuum. During the Nazi regime and particularly during the war, German finance was subject to highly centralized control. It is this situation that has complicated military government in Germany, which is divided into four zones and, at this writing, is lacking a central government through which to administrate certain problems that can be handled only on a national basis. Considered from a financial viewpoint, the most important of these problems is the servicing of the national debt.

---

[11] There were 17 chief branches, or Hauptstellen, 83 branches, or Stellen, and 355 subbranches, or Nebenstellen. The head office in Berlin is called the Reichshauptbank. Each subbranch is subordinate to a branch or chief branch.

[12] The institutions affiliated with the Reichsbank include the German Gold Discount Bank, organized in 1924; the German Clearing Office; the Conversion Office for Foreign Debt, and the Reichs Credit Offices.

Most of the national debt is held by commercial banks and savings institutions and other institutional investors such as insurance companies. Since about 80 per cent of the banks' resources are invested in government obligations, it is readily apparent that a national government able to pay interest on these obligations is of prime importance to banks.

Reichsbank.—The Central Bank of Germany, created in 1875, soon after the formation of the German Empire, is called the Reichsbank. It took over the old Bank of Prussia. Throughout its history the Reichsbank has been closely linked to the government. During, and particularly after, World War I, it financed the government by the printing press method. At the end of 1923 the amount of its notes outstanding was a number represented by 15 followed by 20 zeros. The countries interested in reparations took a hand in reorganizing the Reichsbank (part of the Dawes Plan), and it was given a new charter in 1924 and placed under foreign control. In 1930 the General Council, created for this purpose, became inactive when all foreign members retired, and it was abolished in 1933. Many of the other provisions of the 1924 Reichsbank charter have been repealed, and the attempt of the Dawes Commission to separate the bank from governmental control has failed.

The Reichsbank discounts short-term commercial bills, provided they are three-named, although satisfactory collateral may be substituted for one name; makes Lombard loans, namely, loans secured by high-grade collateral such as public bonds, guaranteed railroad bonds, and trade and bankers' acceptances; and buys and sells all interest-bearing securities that are admitted to official trading on the stock exchange. It may serve as fiscal agent for the Reich, districts of the Reich, the states, the communities, and commercial associations.[13]

In addition to being a central bank for the government and other banks, the Reichsbank makes many loans to individuals. It reaches the general public through its 455 branch offices. The number of branch offices is in excess of needs for loans and investments and deposit purposes. The main reason for the establishment and continuance of certain offices is their usefulness as transfer centers.

In Germany the personal check is used primarily as a local means of payment. Germans use the *Giro* ("transfer") system to send funds

[13] See Sec. 19, *German Reichsbank Law of June 15, 1939.*

between communities. The transfer is made by arranging with an officer in one branch to have one's deposit account debited and the account of the second party, in another city with a second branch, credited with the amount of the transfer. Many businessmen as well as banks keep *Giro* accounts with the Reichsbank, while others depend upon the post office, private banks, and other private agencies. Among the recommendations of the Bank Inquiry Commission (1933) was one favoring expansion of the checking system because it was cheaper than the *Giro* system of transfer. The Reichsbank performs other services such as collection of bills and the purchase and sale of stock, etc., for individuals.

Commercial Banks in Germany.—Joint-stock banking of the modern type started in Germany in 1848 with the establishment of the Schaafthausen'scher Bankverein ("industrial banking company"), which did not have the right of note issue. This bank, and others chartered soon after, was established in order to promote industrial development by providing both long-term and short-term capital. Later other banks were formed, with greater emphasis on short-term finance; but mixed banking, one of the chief characteristics of the German banking system, persists. These banks financed companies by permitting overdrafts on demand deposits which were later repaid with funds raised by sales of long-term securities.

Some of the German banks own seats on the stock exchanges and do a regular brokerage business. They are, in large part, the promoters of industry in Germany, having taken the leadership in the formation of new industries, new companies, and the amalgamation and mergers of old ones. Many students give them considerable credit for the rapid strides in industry in Germany since 1870, and they have been referred to as the "masters of Germany's industries." They provide their customers with both types of capital—commercial and investment.

Commercial banking is so mixed with other types of banking that it is difficult to separate them. Depositors are divided into two main groups, with several subdivisions under each. "Creditors" (*Kreditoren*) include interbank depositors, demand depositors, notice depositors and time depositors. "Savings depositors" (*Spareinlagen*) include those who have accounts evidenced by passbooks.

Commercial bills have been more widely used in Germany than

in the United States, and they are eligible for rediscount if they carry three signatures. Promissory notes have not been in general use. Usually all borrowing transactions between the banks and their customers are entered in the current account. Lines of credit on which a bank charges a commission of 1/8 of 1 per cent are granted, and interest on the amount actually used is generally 1 per cent above the Reichsbank's discount rate. Banks may also honor overdrafts, on which a charge of 1/12 mill per day is made. The current account credit may or may not be secured. Balance sheets for unsecured credit of 5,000 or more reichsmarks are required.

Securities, which represent the chief assets of the German banks, are usually not kept in the vaults of the banks but at the Reichsbank in Berlin (*Wertpapiersammelbank*) or with its branches in the cities where stock exchanges are located. Transfers of ownership of securities and funds are made on the books of the Reichsbank. Many of the Reich issues of new securities were not printed at all, entries being made to the credit of the purchaser in the government's debt register (*Reichschuldbuch*) kept by the Reich Debt Administration in Berlin. These credits are negotiable.

Reserve requirements against liabilities other than savings deposits may be fixed by the Reich Minister of Finance, subject to the requirements that legal primary reserves shall not be higher than 10 per cent and that secondary reserves shall not be higher than 30 per cent of liabilities. In practice, the primary reserves were from 2.5 to 5 per cent, while the secondary reserves were in excess of 30 per cent. (There is no record to show that this power to fix reserves was ever used.) Primary reserves consist of cash in vaults and deposits with the Reichsbank and the *Giro* system, and secondary reserves consist of commercial bills of 90 days or less and government securities eligible for collateral for loans from the Reichsbank.

Savings deposits are held by commercial banks, postal savings banks, savings banks, and co-operative banks. Up to 1938 banking by the post office was limited to the postal check system, but, following the annexation of Austria, German post offices were authorized to accept savings deposits. The postal savings office in Vienna, which had operated the system in Austria, was made the central agency for the German postal savings system. At the end of 1943 there were 11,000,000 postal savings depositories, with average deposits of 450 reichsmarks.

The provisional government of Austria is now making arrangements to re-establish an independent banking and currency system,[14] but the question of adjusting postal savings claims must await the formation of a central German government.

Savings banks in Germany have been sponsored by local governments, and their primary functions have been similar to those of savings banks in the United States. Their traditional investments in mortgage loans and municipal securities have been largely replaced by direct and indirect investments in government securities. In addition to the usual functions of savings banks, these institutions operate a *Giro* system for settling obligations for customers and extend commercial credit. The savings banks are served by central and regional offices of the German Central Savings Bank.

There are two groups of co-operative banks: (1) about 1,500 urban or commercial banks and (2) over 17,600 rural banks. Most of these institutions are small, and they are assisted by the government-owned German Central Bank for Co-operatives in Berlin. Deposits in these banks increased sharply during the war. In addition to the credit co-operatives, there are three types of mortgage banks, one of which is organized on a co-operative basis.

Private bankers in Germany, like those in the United States, have declined in importance. Formerly they did most of the international banking and industrial finance banking of the country. Pawnshops are numerous, and some are owned by the municipalities, as in Berlin and Hamburg. Distinctly specialized financial institutions have been developed, and they include an industrial bank, labor bank, and bank for German airplane industry. Certain German firms have developed their own banks.

Military government aims in Germany have been (1) to denazify the personnel of German banks; (2) to utilize the banks, particularly the Reichsbank, in carrying out foreign exchange control, freezing and blocking of assets, and other policies of military government;[15] and (3) to maintain existing German economic controls and anti-inflation measures. No changes were made in the legal tender laws other than the addition of the allied military mark.[16] The exchange

[14] Following World War II the Central Bank of Austria was formed, and other financial institutions are being reorganized (see "Re-establishment of the Austrian National Bank," *Federal Reserve Bulletin*, January, 1946, pp. 33-35).

[15] See *Military Government Law No. 52* and *No. 53.*

[16] *Military Government Law No. 51.*

rate was not fixed, the rate of 10 reichsmarks to one dollar being for troop pay and procurement purposes only.

The French Banking System

With the collapse of Germany it is expected that the French banking system will play a much more important role in western Europe than it did before the war. The banking system of France consists of the Central Bank (Banque de France), the six large banks of deposit (Establissement de Credit), investment banks (*banques des affaires*), private banks, regional and local banks, colonial and foreign banks, savings banks, and public credit institutions. In all there were over 9,000 banking offices in France before World War II, not including the public and semipublic institutions.

The Bank of France.—The Bánque de France has a monopoly of note issue, is the fiscal agent for the government, and operates 660 branches and agencies in France. It combines the functions of a central bank with those of an ordinary commercial bank, competing actively with other banks for deposits, transfer (*Giro*) accounts, and loans.

The Bank of France was established by Napoleon in 1800, and three years later its organization and powers were specified by law. Throughout most of its history the bank has been jointly administrated by the government and the chief stockholders. The governor, two vice-governors, and three members of the General Council (board of directors) were appointed by the government. Only the 200 largest stockholders were represented at the annual meetings, each casting one vote, and they elected the remaining twelve regents of the General Council and three auditors. This alliance between the wealthy stockholders and the government was in effect until 1936. The Popular Front government increased the number of members of the General Council by five, reduced the number to be elected by shareholders to two, permitted all shareholders to attend the annual meeting, and gave each one one vote, irrespective of the number of shares held. The remainder of the members of the council are either ex officio, appointed by government officials, or selected to represent some special group. Further minor adjustments took place in the organization of the Bank of France in 1940 and 1945.

Commercial Banking.—Banking in France started at the beginning of the eighteenth century. In May, 1716, John Law secured a patent from the king of France permitting him to establish a private bank having the right of note issue. This bank acted as fiscal agent of the government and discounted commercial bills. The effects were to raise the nation "from the depths of misery to the heights of prosperity." If Law had limited his activities to the bank, "he would have been one of the greatest benefactors any nation ever had." Law proceeded to form the Company of the West, which was more commonly called Mississippi Company (August 28, 1717), to control the commerce of Louisiana, Canada, and the western coast of Africa. In December, 1718, the bank became a public institution, and the stockholders were reimbursed in specie for their subscriptions. These originally were made 25 per cent in specie and 75 per cent in bills of the state, which were at a discount of 75 per cent. The name of Law was magic, and, as a result, speculation in the shares of the Mississippi Company increased. Other trading rights were absorbed, the name was changed to the India Company, and new shares were issued. New bank bills were issued, hoarding of coins set in, prices increased, and attempts to maintain the value of paper money failed. After the bubble burst, all types of note issue banking were discredited until 1776, when the Bank of Commercial Discount was formed.

Before World War II, most of the commercial banking in France was carried on by the Big Six, which operated over 4,300 branches in France and over 30 in Algeria. These banks held about 70 per cent of the demand deposits in France.[17] In addition to the Big Six there are about 50 large regional and local banks operating in Paris and the provinces and over 700 small banks. Twelve of the regional banks are affiliated with the Industrial Credit and Commercial Bank (Crédit Industriel et Commerciel Banque), which is one of the Big Six.

Foreign and colonial banks have offices in Paris and some of the provincial cities. Included among the foreign banks are subsidiaries and branches of British and American banks. Some of the former are the branches of the Midland, Barclay, and Westminster banks. Among the latter are the Morgan et Cie, National Bank of New

[17] Because of the much wider use of paper money in place of checks and the use of *Giro* transfer system in settling intercommunity obligations, the volume of demand deposits is very small compared to those in the United States banks. Likewise demand deposits are small compared to the total of Bank of France notes.

York (France), and branches of the Chase National Bank and the Guaranty Trust Company of New York.

The commercial banks carry on a short-term lending business, including lending on overdrafts, discounting, dealing in Treasury bills and other government securities, and making ordinary loans. Four of the largest of the commercial banks were nationalized in 1945.

Investment and Private Banks.—Investment bankers specialize in underwriting of new issues of securities and as promoters of new firms. These banks (*banques des affaires*) have extensive foreign interests and have acquired an interest in some of the commercial banks. The most important of these banks, the Banque de Paris et Pays-Bas, has the French economist, Charles Rist, as a member of its board of directors. Its interests abroad are often handled by controlled banks and friendly corporations. The next largest among the industrial banks is the Banque de l'Union Parisienne.

Private bankers are more numerous in France than in the United States, there being over 1,200. "*La Haute Banque*" (higher bank), founded and controlled by a small number of families, has been the legislative target of recent liberal governments of France. Until 1936 it dominated the General Council of the Bank of France and before the war included the names of Rothschild, Lazard, Hottinguer, Demachy, Mallet, Vernes, and Mirabaud. Among the smaller firms were A. J. Stern, Worms, Dreyfus, and Seligman.

Savings Banks.—The savings institutions include 500 banks established by private groups and municipalities, the Postal Savings Bank, which operates 13,000 offices that accept deposits; and 17,000 post offices, where noninterest-bearing accounts against which checks may be written are kept. About 98 per cent of savings bank deposits are invested through a state institution (Caisse des Dépôts et Consignations) created for this purpose. Savings deposits are subject to 15 days' notice prior to withdrawal.

Other Financial Institutions.—In France there are over 50 mortgage banks that grant loans on real property; 100 agricultural credit banks with over 6,000 local offices; and 75 small people's banks, with 100 branches, that make small loans to merchants and tradesmen.

Nationalization of the French Banks.—In December, 1945, the French Assembly passed a law providing for reorganization of the French Banking System, the details of which have not all been carried out at this time. The first provision in the law arranged for the purchase of the stock of the Bank of France by the government. Although the bank had been completely dominated by the government since 1936, this step was in line with similar measures taken by the governments of Great Britain, Canada, and other countries which had nationalized their central banks in recent years.

The second step provided for in the act was the nationalization of the four largest banks of deposit,[18] which was a new departure in banking procedure for most nations in western Europe and other parts of the world, except Russia. Each of these banks will be managed by a board of 12 directors appointed by the government. Among the directors will be persons with banking experience and those representing (1) industry, commerce, and agriculture, (2) trade-unions and the banks' employees, and (3) the Bank of France and other credit institutions.

The third part of the French banking reform program is the elimination of mixed banking by the separation of deposit and investment banking. As was true in the United States in 1933, each bank is obliged to choose between retaining commercial or investment banking functions.[19] A deposit bank is one which takes sight and fixed deposits with terms shorter than two years and does not hold more than 10 per cent of the capital of any other concern except a bank or financial affiliate. Banks, other than deposit banks, may not hold deposits of shorter term than one year, except from subsidiaries.

The fourth part of the program is the provision for special control of the large investment banks. Each *banque d'affaires* that has assets exceeding 500,000,000 francs will have a government *commissaire* attached to it with the power to veto any decision contrary to national interest.

The fifth part of the banking reform program provides for a National Credit Council of 39 members, so selected as to represent varied interests such as trade unions, financial institutions, semi-

---

[18] The four banks are the Crédit Lyonnais, Société Générale, Comptoir d'Escompte, and Banque Nationale pour le Commerce et l'Industrie. They hold about 55 per cent of all bank deposits in France. The other two members of the Big Six were exempt because their business was not national in scope. The Crédit Industriel et Commerciel does have national coverage through its affiliates in the provinces. The Crédit Commerciel de France deposit business is more regional in nature.

[19] This choice must be made in three months, and the necessary adjustments must be completed within a year.

public bodies, and government departments. This council will be responsible along with the Bank of France, for the regulation and supervision of the French banks.

There are indications that the reform measures as listed above have not been completed. It is expected that new proposals to the Credit Council will lead to the nationalization of the two largest *banques des affaires* and also the two remaining members of the Big Six.

QUESTIONS AND PROBLEMS

1. "In this form the charter of the Bank [first charter of the Bank of England] gave little promise of its future importance." What were the chief provisions of this charter? Is this statement justified? (*Source:* Dunbar, C. F., *The Theory and History of Banking*, pp. 133-34; see also McLeod, *Theory and Practice of Banking.*)
2. What divisions in the Federal Reserve banks tend to correspond to those of the banking and issue departments of the Bank of England?
3. Distinguish between the "fiduciary" and the "covered" issues of the Bank of England. In what way is the English bank note issue system inferior to the provisions for the issuance of Federal Reserve notes? Explain.
4. What justification is there for the statement that the Peel Act of 1844 was chiefly a currency rather than a banking act? What debate is now going on among American economists which corresponds to the "note issue" debates preceding the passage of the Peel Act? Explain.
5. May tradition and custom be as instrumental as laws in determining banking policies? Give reasons for your answer.
6. Describe the "overdraft" system of lending. Compare to the type of bank lending common in the United States. What are the advantages of the first to the borrower? Are banks justified when they charge a higher rate for overdraft loans than other types, assuming that other things are the same? Explain.
7. What contribution has the Scottish banking system made to banking methods and practices?
8. Because of American participation in military occupation in Germany, is it more important to study the German banking system now than it was before the war? Why?
9. Why do the Reichsbank and the Bank of France operate more branches than other central banks?
10. The American commercial banks have been referred to as the "handmaidens of industry"; the German banks as "masters of Germany's industry." Are these terms justified? Explain.

11. "The Bank of France is the greatest and in many respects the strongest of the banks of the world, and its development exhibits many of the most interesting phases of banking history outside of Great Britain" (Conant, C. A., *A History of Modern Banks of Issue*, p. 38). Is the first part of the foregoing statement, made in 1902, still true?

12. Find the answers to the following problems in the "International Financial Statistics" section of the current issue of the *Federal Reserve Bulletin:*
    a) Total gold reserves of central banks and governments
    b) The percentage of the total gold reserves of central banks and governments held in Europe
    c) The dollar values of bills discounted by commercial banks in the United Kingdom, France, and Canada
    d) Discount rates of central banks of the United Kingdom, France, and Belgium
    e) Short-term money rates (open market rates) in the United Kingdom, France, the Netherlands, Sweden, and Switzerland.

13. Compare dollar values of the bank notes in circulation of the following central banks: (*a*) Bank of England, (*b*) Bank of France, and (*c*) Bank of Canada.

14. Many foreign countries, as well as the United States, have created equalization funds. Is this a desirable development? Should central banks take over their functions? Who performed the functions before their existence? What influence will the International Fund have upon the operations of exchange funds?

15. Comment on the quotation below, taken from the *Annual Report of the Chairman of the Board of Directors of the Midland Bank Limited*, dated December 31, 1945. ". . . . It is not, I think, always realized how highly responsive the banking system has been to the changing needs of the country's business. A hundred years ago it was in process of developing the mechanism of cheque payments to replace the more cumbersome and uncertain method of cash settlements. It devised overdraft lending as a more flexible and economical form of accommodation than the bill of exchange. It consolidated its structure to meet the needs and secure the economies of large-scale enterprise, while retaining through widespread branch systems its responsiveness to the requirements of local enterprise."

REFERENCES

Allen, A. M., Cope, S. R., Dark, L. J. H., and Witheridge, H. J. *Commercial Banking Legislation and Control.* London: MacMillan & Co., Ltd., 1938.

Andréadès, A. *History of the Bank of England*, 3d ed. London: P. S. King & Sons, Ltd., 1935.

Annual report of the Bank for International Settlements, and of the central banks of Argentina, Canada, Great Britain, France, and Germany in *Federal Reserve Bulletin.*

Bagehot, Walter. *Lombard Street.* New York: E. P. Dutton & Co., 1921.

Breckinridge, R. M. *The Canadian Banking System, 1817-1890.* New York: American Economics Association, 1895.

Clapham, John. *The Bank of England.* 2 vols. Cambridge: Cambridge University Press, 1944.

Committee on Finance and Industry (Macmillan Commission). *Minutes of Evidence.* London: His Majesty's Stationary Office, 1931.

Committee on Finance and Industry (Macmillan Commission). *Report.* London: His Majesty's Stationary Office, 1931.

Conant, C. A. *A History of Modern Banks of Issue.* New York: G. P. Putnam's Sons, 1902.

Crick, W. F., and Wadsworth, J. E. *A Hundred Years of Joint Stock Banking.* London: Hodder & Stoughton, Ltd., 1936.

Dixon, F. J. "Monetary and Banking Legislation in Canada, 1934," *American Economic Review,* Vol. XXV, No. 1 (March, 1935), pp. 73-84.

Dunbar, C. F. *The Theory and History of Banking,* chaps. viii and x. 4th ed. New York: G. P. Putnam's Sons, 1922.

Evitt, H. E. *Practical Banking; An Introductory Study of British Banking.* 4th ed. London: Sir Isaac Pitman & Sons, Ltd., 1937.

Holladay, James. *The Canadian Banking System.* New York: Bankers' Publishing Co., 1938.

Kisch, C. H., and Elkin, W. A. *Central Banks.* New York: Macmillan Co., 1928.

League of Nations, *Commercial Banks, 1913-1929; Commercial Banks, 1925-1933; Commercial Banks, 1929-1934; Money and Banking, 1935/36,* Vols. I and II; *Money and Banking, 1938/*39, Vols. I and II; *Money and Banking, 1940/42; Money and Banking, 1942/44.*

Mackenzie, Kenneth. *The Banking Systems of Great Britain, France, Germany, and the United States of America.* 3d ed. London: MacMillan & Co., Ltd., 1945.

McLeod, H. D. *The Theory and Practice of Banking.* Revised ed. Boston: Longmans, Green & Co., 1911.

Report of the Royal Commission on Banking and Currency in Canada. Ottawa: Printed by J. O. Patenaude, Printer to the King's Most Excellent Majesty, 1933.

Smith, V. C. *The Rationale of Central Banking.* London: P. S. King & Son, Ltd., 1936.

Stokes, M. L. *The Bank of Canada: The Development and Present Position of Central Banking in Canada.* Toronto: MacMillan & Co., Ltd., 1939.

Truptil, R. J. *British Banks and the London Money Market.* London: Jonathan Capt, Ltd., 1936.

Whole, P. B. *Joint Stock Banking in Germany.* London: MacMillan & Co., Ltd., 1930.

Willis, H. P., and Beckhart, B. H. *Foreign Banking Systems.* New York: Henry Holt & Co., 1929.

INDEX

D

F

T